88
July

NATIONAL POLICIES FOR EDUCATION, HEALTH AND SOCIAL SERVICES

COLUMBIA UNIVERSITY
BICENTENNIAL CONFERENCE SERIES

"Man's Right to Knowledge and the Free Use Thereof."

The Contributors

Gordon W. Allport

Harry Becker

Merle L. Borrowman

Lyman Bryson

Arvid J. Burke

Eveline M. Burns

Robert D. Calkins

William G. Carr

Hollis L. Caswell

Harold F. Clark

Nathan E. Cohen

Henry Steele Commager

George F. Davidson

Daniel R. Davies

Fedele F. Fauri

Hans F. Flexner

Marion B. Folsom

Julian H. Franklin

Howard V. Funk

Ralph H. Gabriel

A. Whitney Griswold

William Haber

Seymour E. Harris

Henry H. Hill

Oveta Culp Hobby

R. A. Hohaus

Grayson Kirk

Barbara Ward Jackson

F. Ernest Johnson

Kenneth D. Johnson

Pierre Laroque

Eugene S. Lawler

Richard A. Lester

Seymour Martin Lipset

Robert M. MacIver

James E. McCormack

Elizabeth G. Meier

Paul R. Mort

Mabel Newcomer

John K. Norton

Philip H. Phenix

Thomas J. Pullen, Jr.

Willard C. Rappleye

Mrs. Franklin D. Roosevelt

Beardsley Ruml

James E. Russell

Herman D. Stein

Adlai E. Stevenson

Arthur E. Sutherland

Henry Toy, Jr.

Henry P. Van Dusen

William S. Vincent

Barbara Wootton

Henry M. Wriston

Benjamin E. Youngdahl

NATIONAL POLICIES
FOR
EDUCATION, HEALTH
AND
SOCIAL SERVICES

Edited by

JAMES E. RUSSELL

DOUBLEDAY & COMPANY, INC.

GARDEN CITY, NEW YORK, 1955

Foreword

A great university may celebrate its birthday in many ways. Columbia University, faced with the opportunity to signalize two hundred years of continuous existence, has used the opportunity also to recall to attention the extent to which human freedom depends on free universities. A full year has been devoted to a series of events surrounding the Bicentennial Theme: "Man's Right to Knowledge and the Free Use Thereof."

One part of this series of events consisted of six major conferences: two on subjects of local or regional significance, two on themes of national significance, and two of international significance. Perhaps the principal intellectual contribution of the whole series of Bicentennial events lay in these conferences, of which the present volume reports one.

Any event as large and complex and as long-planned as one of these Bicentennial Conferences must be the product of the efforts of many persons. Literally hundreds of persons, in and out of the Columbia community, combined their efforts to make possible the Fourth Conference, reported here, on National Policies for Education, Health, and Social Services. The reader will note that the names of those who had major responsibilites for planning or administering parts of the conference are supplied in the appropriate context. He may wonder whether there were not others involved, behind the scenes, whose silent service made possible much of what was done. The generous service of these people ought to be recognized here.

The Office of the Bicentennial, its Director, Richard R. Powell, Dwight Professor of Law, its Assistant Director, James L. Malfetti, Assistant Professor of Health Education, and its entire staff, especially Mrs. Frances Bennett, deserve special recognition for their tireless and accurate handling of the vast mass of detail that such a conference entails and for their constant support of a sometimes harried conference chairman.

The Chairman of the Bicentennial Committee on Conferences, Louis M. Hacker, Dean of the School of General Studies, and his assistant, Miss Dorothy Streng, played a significant part in the over-all success of the conference, and particularly with reference to the opening banquet, the administration of which was largely in their hands.

The Director of University Libraries, Richard H. Logsdon, and his assistant, Miss Nancy Cedrone, took charge of adapting the Nicholas Murray Butler Library for the use of the Conference. This was the first time that great struc-

vii

ture had ever been put to such use. The ease with which the adjustment seemed to be made was due to their skill.

Preparation of the record of the Conference has required the efforts of many. The recorders of the various sections, whose names appear with their reports, fulfilled their responsibilities skillfully and promptly, which considerably eased the final preparation of the record. Final editing and preparation of the manuscript for publication has been largely the work of Mr. Charles H. Seaver, and I should like to express my personal indebtedness to him. I should like also to record a tribute to my secretary, Mr. Robert Paris, who kept full control of the administrative arrangements for the Conference, and has borne in addition the clerical responsibilities involved in preparing the record for publication.

Finally, it falls to me to express for the University gratitude to those many persons who came from far away to share with us their knowledge, wisdom, and experience in saluting our two-hundredth year, and the University's thanks to the great number of persons on its faculties and staffs who made similar contributions. To all these persons go the University's thanks, to which I should like to add my own.

JAMES E. RUSSELL, *Chairman*
Fourth Bicentennial Conference

Contents

PART TWO   Policies for Higher Education

PART SIX   Religion in Education

PART SEVEN Academic Freedom

PART EIGHT Finding a Reconciliation

Introduction

Conference IV, on National Policies for Education, Health, and Social Services, was, like the other Bicentennial Conferences, a product of a long development and the participation of a great many university persons. It had initially been planned, as one of a pair of conferences on national topics, to be preceded by conferences on local or regional topics and followed by conferences on topics of international significance. The thought of the earliest planners had been that one of the areas of interest to scholarly life and universities in general lay in the welfare activities of government, and they therefore planned a conference in this area. Once the general topic had been decided on early in 1952 an initial planning committee was formed, composed of Richard Hofstadter, Professor of History, Columbia University; Kenneth D. Johnson, Dean of the New York School of Social Work, Columbia University; John D. Millett, Professor of Public Administration, Columbia University; and James E. Russell, Associate Professor of Education, Teachers College, Columbia University, as chairman. Willard C. Rappleye, Vice-President of the University in Charge of Medical Affairs and Dean of the Faculty of Medicine, although not a member of the committee, conferred with the chairman on a number of occasions and provided detailed advice.

At a series of meetings in 1952 this committee reached agreement as to an over-all organization for the conference. It recommended to the central committee of the Bicentennial that the conference be organized in such a way as directly to mobilize the interests of the professional faculties of the University as well as its academic faculties, and that the focus of the conference be on such specific areas as education, health, social services, and like areas of social policy. We believed that the interests of all the professions concerned with welfare (in its widest sense) could be related to the general theme we agreed on, which is described below.

In September 1952 a final report of this committee was submitted to the Bicentennial Central Committee recommending that the conference be operated in the following fashion.

1. An opening general session at which two main speakers would present the underlying themes in the following light:

Social Responsibility for Individual Welfare, by which we meant to cover responsibilities of private groups and government to promote the growth and development of individuals, their opportunities to advance to the utmost of their capacities, and their security and health.

What Freedom Means to the Individual Today, by which we meant to cover social action from the point of view of the individual acted upon; that is, the issues of freedom of inquiry, of loyalty, of the right to be let alone, and of initiative and discipline, all of which have become issues because of the widened scope of social action; this address to pose the problem of the potential conflict between the individual values of human freedom and the social values of stability and planned meeting of human needs.

2. Seven principal section meetings (Parts), each of which was to meet simultaneously for two days. Subjects of the proposed sections, and those nominated to serve as chairmen, were as follows:

Section 1.—POLICIES FOR UNIVERSAL PUBLIC EDUCATION

> *Chairman:* John K. Norton, Professor of Education, Teachers College, Columbia University

Section 2—POLICIES FOR HIGHER EDUCATION

> *Chairman:* Lyman Bryson, Professor Emeritus of Education, Teachers College, Columbia University

Section 3—MEETING THE HEALTH NEEDS OF THE NATION

> *Chairman:* Willard C. Rappleye, Vice-President in Charge of Medical Affairs and Dean of the Faculty of Medicine, Columbia University

Section 4—SOCIAL SERVICES AND THE FREE ECONOMY

> *Chairman:* Kenneth D. Johnson, Dean of the New York School of Social Work, Columbia University

Section 5—INCOME SECURITY FOR A FREE PEOPLE

> *Chairman:* Eveline M. Burns, Professor of Social Work, New York School of Social Work, Columbia University

Section 6—RELIGION IN EDUCATION

> *Chairman:* Henry P. Van Dusen, President, Union Theological Seminary

Section 7—ACADEMIC FREEDOM

> *Chairman:* Henry S. Commager, Professor of American History, Columbia University

The subject matter of each section was spelled out in sufficient detail to enable the various chairmen to undertake further planning without risking duplication of the plans of other sections. Since the content of each section is described elsewhere in this volume there is no need to repeat the details here.

3. A closing session. The group specifically recommended that no formal attempt be made by the section chairmen to recapitulate the discussions of their sections, but that a strictly limited number of addresses be given, preferably only two; at least one, on the subject of the relation of national welfare to individual welfare, to cover both the problem of maintaining a stable and expanding economy in the face of demands for welfare services and the problem of reconciling individual and social values. This address was intended to find whatever reconciliation of social values would emerge in the conference.

These plans received the full endorsement of the Bicentennial Central

Committee on October 16, 1952, and James E. Russell was appointed to direct the conference, which was henceforth to be known as Bicentennial Conference IV, National Policies for Education, Health, and Social Services. The designated chairmen were asked to assume the indicated responsibilities and all agreed to do so.

Each of the chairmen then began planning the details of the section for which he accepted responsibility. In most cases special committees were formed to assist in making plans for the administration of their various sections.

The section chairmen, with the help of their subcommittees, decided who would be asked to participate. These invitations were then cleared with the conference chairman and the Office of the Bicentennial and went to individual participants officially as invitations from the President of the University and in the name of the University.

Detailed arrangements differed in each of the seven sections and are described in later pages.

The conference opened on the evening of June 2, 1954, with a dinner at the Men's Faculty Club of Columbia University. There were two addresses at this dinner, preceded by greetings from the University by its President and from the National Administration by Mrs. Oveta Culp Hobby, United States Secretary of Health, Education, and Welfare. A. Whitney Griswold, President of Yale University, spoke on "Freedom, Security, and the University Tradition." Mrs. Franklin D. Roosevelt spoke on "Social Responsibility for Individual Welfare."

Following the opening session the conference divided into seven simultaneous section meetings all of which met for the following two days in the Nicholas Murray Butler Library on the University campus.

The closing session occurred in the McMillin Academic Theater on the morning of Saturday, June 5, 1954. The speakers were Robert M. MacIver, Lieber Professor Emeritus of Political Philosophy and Sociology, who developed a reconciliation of individual and social values, speaking on the topic "Government and Social Welfare." An address by Adlai E. Stevenson then concluded the conference.

The Theme of the Conference

The underlying theme of the conference focused directly on one of the fundamental problems of our time—the relation of national policy to the needs and well-being of individuals. We had in mind that we might examine this problem in its philosophical and historical context, and that was to be done in the opening and closing sessions. We also had in mind that we could examine the problem in the manifold ways in which it presents itself in situations calling for policy decisions today. These situations are of direct interest not only to scholars in the academic disciplines but also to those in the professional faculties of the University. It therefore seemed that the theme pro-vided an unusually fruitful way of unifying the interests of so varied a uni-versity as Columbia, in which academic faculties combine with professional faculties in the pursuit of knowledge.

The question early arose as to whether or not the conference should attempt to provide guidance for governmental action, as might be suggested by its title. The decision of the committee planning the conference was that we could not exclude the opportunity to provide such guidance, but that it would not serve as the essential focus. We were thinking of national policy in the truly national sense of policy for all of us in our various collective activities, not just for government, and we hoped to cause a rethinking of our position and a reassessment of the social problems of an unsettled age.

A persistent and pressing problem of modern life has been to find the bal-ance between individual and social values. Too great a stress on the values of individualism is judged by many to have produced such dislocations as the great depression of 1929–1933, and too great a concentration on collective values is often judged to have produced the kind of suppression of individual rights that many think is associated with abuse of the congressional power of investigation. Individuals press for services from government, not only as in-dividuals, but also organized into pressure groups. Economic and business groups seek to raise or lower tariffs, depending on their various interests; veterans' organizations seek special and costly services; farm organizations seek subsidy; labor unions demand a protected free hand: altogether eco-nomic activity seems to be characterized by a constant search for special privilege from government.

To a major extent the entrance of government and other collective agencies into the field of direct action in support of individual welfare has resulted from pressures similar to those just described. And yet the same government which is called on increasingly to serve individual welfare may also take away in-dividual rights, injure individual welfare, and force upon the individual a variety of conformism which is at variance with long and dearly cherished tra-ditions of America. Freedom of inquiry and freedom of opinion are part of the American tradition. Yet those who exercise them may come to be viewed by government with substantial suspicion.

Thus government may at the same time be viewed as both a friend and an enemy of the individual. Where will we find a balance between these two aspects of government? How can we reconcile the apparent conflict? How do we assess the present position of this conflict? What have universities to offer in dealing with this problem? What stake have universities in its just solution?

All the above questions provided the starting point for the conference, underlay the opening session, and provided the ligaments that tied together the seven section meetings, for each of the areas we singled out for discussion could be developed in relation to the problem of reconciling individual and social values.

Here was a theme that justified the best efforts of a major university, a matter of interest to us all, in which wisdom, knowledge, thought, and research might make a significant contribution, and one directly related to the over-all theme of the University's Bicentennial: "Man's Right to Knowledge and the Free Use Thereof."

As the general theme was expanded and given specific professional application, the various sections devoted their discussions to the following topics.

Section 1—Policies for Universal Public Education

Section 1 divided itself into four group sessions, each of which met simultaneously during the first day. Then on the following day all Section 1 participants joined for general discussion of findings of the subgroups. The group sessions were on the following topics:

Group 1—*The Federal Government and National Interest in Universal Public Education.* This was an analysis of the degree to which the Federal government has been interested in public education and of present trends in this area. The leader of the group was William G. Carr, Executive Secretary of the National Education Association.

Group 2—*The Relations of the Various Levels of Government in Providing Universal Public Education.* This was an analysis of the major functions to be performed, the relations of education to other areas of government, and the responsibilities of the several levels of government. The leader of this group was Henry H. Hill, President of the George Peabody College for Teachers.

Group 3—*The Scope of Public Education in the United States.* This was an analysis of the size of the task of education as it has been in the past and as it now tends to be and of what organization and facilities are required to perform the task. The leader of this group was Harold F. Clark, Professor of Education, Teachers College, Columbia University.

Group 4—*The Quality of Public Education as Affected by the Levels and Distribution of Its Financial Support.* This was an analysis of the present levels of support, of the effectiveness of these levels, and of the effects of raising them. The leader of this group was Paul R. Mort, Professor of Education, Teachers College, Columbia University.

Full copies of the papers prepared in advance by the leaders and of the reports as submitted to the various sections are included in the appropriate places in the present volume. Here suffice it to say that the group was quite definite in its conclusion that the Federal government must assume a larger share of responsibility for the provision of universal public education, but must do it under circumstances that will remain consistent with the essence of American freedom found in the local control of local schools.

Section 2—Policies for Higher Education

Section 2 divided its discussion into two main parts, to each of which a single day of discussion was devoted. On the first day the discussion focused on "The Function and Opportunities of American Institutions of Learning." This was an analysis of the real functions of higher education in the United States today and of the question whether these functions can be performed effectively in the face of public and private attacks and demands for special services. The issues were laid before the group in the form of a statement by Henry M. Wriston, President of Brown University, which was then given general discussion. The following day the group shifted its attention to the economic aspect of higher education under the general title "The Resources for Maintaining American Institutions of Learning." This was an analysis of the problem of maintaining the strength of higher education in the United States, given our economic difficulties. What human and economic resources are properly devoted to higher education? The issues were introduced by Robert Calkins, President of the Brookings Institution, and a general discussion followed. These introductory statements and a report on the discussions are contained in the following pages.

The two days of discussions ranged over the unique functions of higher education in American life, touching on such aspects as who should receive graduate education, how it should be paid for, and the problem of relating professional to academic instruction, particularly in the area of training of teachers.

Section 3—Meeting the Health Needs of the Nation

Section 3 was conducted in a less formal fashion than any of the other sections. No special papers were prepared to introduce the discussion, and there was no effort to seek general agreement among the members of the group. The chairman and vice-chairman intended that the group was to establish its own agenda at its first session, selecting from among the following topics: What constitutes "adequacy" in health services? What facilities and personnel are required for an adequate service for the country? What are the relationships between physical health, mental health, and social well-being? What incentives are needed to improve recruitment and training of personnel for the health profession? Who should provide the facilities and financial support of an adequate health service? To what extent should provision of hospitals, clinics, laboratories, and other health facilities be the responsibility of the Federal government? To what extent should private agencies and other levels of government take the lead in the field? How should professional education for the health professions be financed? Discussion in this session ranged over the entire field of medical policy, but concentrated on certain aspects having to do not only with Federal relations to the provision of health services but also with the specific private arrangements that are in controversy within organized medicine today.

Section 4—Social Services and the Free Economy

Section 4 divided its discussions into four principal parts. The first of these, "Social Services—Need and Scope," provided the background and rationale of social services in terms of a philosophy of needs, rights, and responsibilities, as well as a description of the current range of public and voluntary social services. It was intended also to treat the political issue of the welfare state. The matter was introduced by a paper by Benjamin Youngdahl, Dean of the George Warren Brown School of Social Work, Washington University.

The second topic, "Responsibility to Meet Social-Service Needs," was handled by George Davidson, Deputy Minister of National Health and Welfare, of Canada, and William Haber, Professor of Economics, University of Michigan. The two papers covered the relative roles of public and private social services, problems of coordination of public and private endeavors and of the activities of various levels of government, the current status of the financing of social services, and a projection for the future. Mr. Davidson's paper emphasized the over-all question of public vs. private responsibilities and of coordinating their efforts. Professor Haber's paper was devoted to the problem of financing.

The third part of Section 4 was devoted to the "Limits of Social Service" under the leadership of Gordon Allport, Professor of Social Relations, Harvard University. This was a consideration of the limits of social service in a free economy from the point of view of ideological considerations, social attitudes, and available knowledge, including an appraisal of the knowledge available for the development and administration of social services, as well as a review of those aspects of social service and American community activity and attitude which suggest the potential of social services and the limit that should be set.

Section 4 concluded its deliberations with discussion of a paper by Nathan E. Cohen, Professor of Social Work, New York School of Social Work. His paper, which was prepared almost on the eve of the conference and was revised during the conference in the light of the discussions of the four preceding papers, served as a capstone for the section and attempted to find the consensus of the previous deliberations. Professor Cohen's paper summarized the discussions and indicated the degree of consensus among the participants. It served also to stress the many unsolved social-service problems, especially those whose solution is delayed by inadequate or insufficient knowledge.

Section 5—Income Security for a Free People

Section 5 also divided its sessions into four parts. This was the only section of the conference that not only had formal papers prepared but also assigned to specific discussants the responsibility of commenting on the papers to be discussed. The first session of Section 5 was devoted to major issues raised by contemporary trends in income-security policies as presented in a paper by Pierre Laroque, President of the Social Security Fund of France. It was an effort to survey the major trends in income-security laws and programs here and abroad to inquire how far the United States is likely to follow the currently observed trends and to explore the problems posed by these developments.

The second session dealt with the nature and levels of income security for a free society, as presented in a paper by Richard A. Lester, Professor of Economics, Princeton University. This session provided an opportunity to discuss such contemporary issues as the choice between an income-security system conditioned on a test of need and one conditioned on some other criterion, and the choice between uniform and differential income-security benefits; the appropriate relationship between socially insured income and income from participation in production; and the role of private pensions in relation to governmental guarantees.

Marion B. Folsom, Under Secretary of the Treasury, prepared the paper for the third session, "What Methods of Financing Income Security Are Best Calculated to Preserve the Values of Individualism?" This session dealt with some of the outstanding financial problems; provided an opportunity for an evaluation of the contributory system and of other sources of revenue for income-security programs; and gave consideration to the respective financial roles of various levels of government.

The fourth session discussed a paper prepared by Barbara Wootton, Nuffield Research Fellow, Bedford College, University of London, "The Impact of Income Security on Individual Freedom." Here was an effort to integrate the findings of the preceding session by presenting an overview of the area in which the problem of reconciling the two main objectives of income-security policy is especially acute and by drawing attention to the outstanding gaps in knowledge on which further research is needed if national policy is to be firmly grounded on social and economic reality.

In the treatment of the deliberations of this section below it will be noted that reports of the discussion are related to each paper as it was presented rather than to any effort to provide an over-all focus. The chairman of this session, Professor Eveline M. Burns, New York School of Social Work, provides a general summary.

Section 6—Religion in Education

The deliberations of Section 6, Religion in Education, began with an exploration of the significance of religion in American life. Two papers were presented—one on the historic role of religion in American life by Ralph Gabriel, Professor of History, Yale University; the other an examination of the issues involved in religion in education by F. Ernest Johnson, Professor Emeritus of Education, Teachers College, Columbia University. Here was an exploration of the significance of religion—an empirical fact in our society disclosed in institutions and observances—as a quest for truth and value and as a quality of the culture as a whole. The inquiry had a reciprocal character: how education serves or may serve the broad purposes of religion, and how religion performs or may perform its function through educational institutions.

Discussions then continued with special reference to religion in colleges and independent or private schools, and developed into a discussion of the place of religion at all levels of higher education both public and private, as well as in private and independent schools at the elementary and secondary levels.

The discussion of religion in public education came to a focus on the constitutional question with a paper "Constitutions, Churches, and Schools" by Arthur E. Sutherland, Professor of Law, Harvard University. This was an exploration of the present status of the religious issue in public education at the elementary and secondary levels. The matter was investigated from several different points of view, including those of the educator, the politician, the layman, the churches, and the constitutional lawyer.

These deliberations continued until the evening of the second day, at which time Barbara Ward Jackson concluded Section 6 with her own summary of the status of the issue as it appeared to her. This brilliant address was heard not only by the participants of Section 6, but also by participants of the other sessions of the conference, who convened in the Harkness Academic Theater of the Nicholas Murray Butler Library to hear her.

Section 7—Academic Freedom

Section 7 discussed four principal aspects of the problem. Each was under the chairmanship of a leader who accepted that specific assignment.

Erwin Griswold, Dean of the Harvard Law School, chaired the first session of the conference on the topic "How Can We Defend Academic Freedom against Pressure Groups?" The discussion centered around the associated problems of the various pressures exerted on institutions to limit the freedom of the individual and the defenses erected by the institutions to combat those pressures. The focus was on pressures emanating from "patriotic" societies, alumni or college groups, and public agencies.

The second session, "How Can We Educate the Public on the Values of Intellectual Freedom?" was chaired by Robert M. MacIver, Lieber Professor Emeritus of Political Philosophy and Sociology, Columbia University, and laid its stress on the intrinsic value of intellectual freedom, and how the public might be aided to appreciate better the values involved and the consequences of negative action.

The third session concerned the topic "How Should We Deal with the Alleged Communist Danger on the Campus and in the Public Schools?" and was chaired by Ernest Melby, Dean of the School of Education, New York University. In view of the vital importance of academic freedom to the whole society, the session dealt with the extent to which the allegation might be valid or might be irrelevant, unsound, or exaggerated, and then focused on how to counter this most effective weapon of the anti-intellectuals.

The concluding session of the Academic Freedom Section dealt with the question "Should There Be Any Limits to the Freedom of Investigation?" The leader was Richard Hofstadter, Professor of History, Columbia University. Since all rights carry with them associated responsibilities, some obligation was assumed to investigate the special responsibilities of those who exercise freedom of investigation, and to safeguard freedom of investigation and other freedoms by such restrictions as may be appropriate. The questions which this session sought to discuss are: What are these restrictions and who or what agencies have the right to fix them?

CONFERENCE RECORDS

Throughout Conference IV detailed records were kept of all plans, transactions, and proceedings. We did not know in advance whether or not we would make a significant contribution to national policies in the areas of our concern. But we were quite confident that the professional, academic, and governmental competence of the participants would justify their being listened to by an audience larger than that to be accommodated at the Conference. Study of the record, as it appears in the present volume, confirms our original view.

Each of the sections had a formally appointed recorder who accepted specific responsibility for preparing a brief of the proceedings of his section. This was done so that we could, in publishing the record, append to the various papers some indication of the tenor of the discussions they produced. A recorder's report is included for each section.

The present volume commences with transcriptions of the greetings and addresses which opened the conference. The following pages report in full the papers prepared for distribution to conference participants, together with an introduction by the section chairmen, the report of the section recorder, and a list of those who participated in the deliberations of the section. The volume closes with transcriptions of the addresses delivered by Robert M. MacIver and Adlai E. Stevenson, which concluded the Conference.

Because of their interest to friends of the University, the greetings brought to the conference by Grayson Kirk, President of the University, and Mrs. Oveta Culp Hobby, United States Secretary of Health, Education, and Welfare, are reproduced here.

A Greeting from the University

This is the beginning of the fourth conference in a series of six. It was planned a long time ago, to constitute not only an integral, but from an academic and intellectual point of view, perhaps the primary part of all our conference activities.

Thus far in our Bicentennial program we have had three splendid conferences, and I am confident, both from the arrangement of subject matter and from the quality of personnel, that this too will be enormously successful. Actually, you could not have a more important subject, or one which cuts across so many intellectual and academic disciplines. It is a subject of great urgency in terms of public policy; it is a subject of great importance to a university.

I am particularly pleased to see that you plan to devote a substantial amount of your attention to the problem of academic freedom about which some of us have done a great deal of speaking, whether futile or not, in the past few months and years. Also, in many of these other subject-matter areas, particularly with respect to health, social services, and education, we have problems that are urgent because there are vast differences of opinion concerning them throughout the country. This situation will go on, I am sure, for a long time as our society becomes increasingly urbanized and industrialized. We have made much headway in the sense of agreement upon the need for our public authorities to do many of these things. Now we need to discuss what and how, rather than if, and that is good.

It is right and proper that our universities concern themselves directly with these problems, because they can provide an unprejudiced approach to them, they can bring together groups of people such as this to help analyze them under conditions which ought to be most favorable.

And so I hope very much that during the next few days you will profit individually in your activities, and I am sure that we will profit from them after your deliberations have been concluded.

Grayson Kirk
President
Columbia University

A Greeting from the
National Administration

It is a very great privilege to be with you today and to join in celebrating the two hundredth year of Columbia University's tremendous contributions to the intellectual, spiritual, and moral growth of the Nation.

I have the honor to extend to you the very cordial greetings of President Eisenhower and to express to you his hope—indeed, his faith—that your conference will be a successful one, rewarding to each of you and to all Americans.

Your Bicentennial Theme, "Man's Right to Knowledge and the Free Use Thereof," is consistent with a very great and enduring American tradition—a tradition nurtured and cherished by American universities and colleges. The President in his address here in New York of a few nights ago eloquently summed up that close identity when he said:

"The pursuit of truth, its preservation and wide dissemination; the achievement of freedom, its defense and propagation: these purposes are woven into the American concept of education."

I agree wholeheartedly with his observation that "those who chose the theme of this Bicentennial could not have found a more American one."

It is pertinent, I think, to observe that better health, improved education, and the "general welfare" are among the very important purposes for which we cherish this American freedom. Both end result and objective, they represent that concern for the individual which is the very soul of our civilization.

In this connection you will recall, perhaps, Arnold Toynbee's comment on the material resources that are ours to command today.

"This sudden vast enhancement of man's ability to make non-human nature produce what man requires from her has for the first time in history made the ideal of welfare for all a practical objective instead of a mere utopian dream."

If this be true—and I think it is—your work here will be within the bounds of what may be realized—perhaps not tomorrow or the day after but within the finite future. Certainly we can agree that it is a consummation for which we can not only hope but toward which we can set our minds and hearts.

If I might choose a simple analogy to describe what I conceive of as our job in the Department of Health, Education, and Welfare in the effort to achieve better health, better education, and better security for the people of this Nation, I would liken it to a wheel: a wheel with the Department at the hub and the spokes running outward to the States and local communities; a wheel with spokes reaching, too, into such gatherings as these.

Both hub and spokes are necessary to the strength and the utility of the wheel.

It is both privilige and honor to be here for an additional reason, for it gives me the opportunity, if I may do so, to pay special tribute to one whose life and work in welfare has been truly distinguished. I know that you join with me in special salute to Mrs. Roosevelt.

And now may I wish you well in these important undertakings on which you are to embark.

> *Oveta Culp Hobby*
> *United States Secretary of*
> *Health, Education, and Welfare*

UNDERLYING THEMES

Freedom, Security, and the University Tradition

A. Whitney Griswold
President of Yale University

From the founding of Salerno to the two hundredth anniversary of Columbia University is a good thousand years; and from the founding of the two English universities from which both Columbia and Yale are directly descended, nearly eight hundred. These have not been years of contemplation. They have been years of mortal life, full of passions inimical to learning, innocent of its purposes, often hostile to its institutions. The university tradition has survived them all. That it has done so should give us courage who are entrusted with its welfare today; and for the part she has played in bringing that tradition to its present strength and prospects Yale salutes King's College and Columbia University.

It is fitting, too, that we should celebrate this occasion in the name of freedom. For what earth, air, fire, and water are to animate nature, freedom is to learning. A mind unfree, a mind possessed, dragooned, or indoctrinated, does not learn. It copies. Learning implies discovery. The unfree mind looks at maps but does not travel. It dares not. For at the edge of the maps is the jumping-off place, full of dragons and sea serpents. The unfree mind stays home, locks the door, bars the shutters. It is a hero in a crowd, a coward in solitude; it is a slave and a sloth. "High-day freedom" sings the boozy Caliban in Shakespeare's *Tempest* as he indentures himself to new-found masters, "I'll kiss thy foot!" And then, at the end of the play:

> I'll be wise hereafter
> And seek for grace. What a thrice-double ass
> Was I to take this drunkard for a god,
> And worship this dull fool!

Caliban recapitulates much human history. The unfree mind is perpetually gulled, systematically swindled, periodically disillusioned. At all stages of the process it is the stuff that tyranny is made of. The unfree mind founded no universities, wrote no Declaration of Independence. It built the pyramids. It went on sprees and suffered remorse. Its principal contribution to humanity has been to remind us, at times all too forcibly, of our simian past.

It is easy to say what freedom is not. But what is it? Only concrete realization can give it objective meaning or existence. Freedom as Utopia is a pipe dream. Freedom as the future reward for present enslavement is a calculated fraud. Freedom with its head under the covers or talking in whispers is a travesty. The only definition of freedom that is worth anything to mankind is a concrete one—one that finds direct expression both in principle and in practice; in laws and the way those laws are enforced; in institutions and the uses to which those institutions are put; in policies and the methods by which those policies are conducted. For this reason the process of defining freedom is never finished. It must continue endlessly or there will be no freedom.

This should give us cause for concern. Though we celebrate freedom here tonight, over a large part of the earth the concrete definition of it has utterly ceased and in our part it has slowed almost to a standstill. Why so? On the other side of the iron curtain the reason is obvious. But at home? Why should the life process of freedom falter among its creators? Partly because we fear and mistrust our enemies and must devote so much energy to protecting ourselves against them. Partly because we fear and mistrust ourselves and choose to devote so much energy to catechizing one another. We are disposed to regard our times and circumstances as unprecedented in history and to see compelling reasons for suspending the definition of freedom in face of the needs of security and national defense.

There are two fundamental errors in this judgment. The first is the notion that our times and circumstances are unique. The second is the belief that defining freedom is incompatible with national security and defense. History is full of examples of freedom struggling for and finding concrete expression in times like ours. Nor is the difference between those times and our own to be found in the awesome text of nuclear physics. The Black Death in 1347 killed three-quarters of the population of Europe. The Thirty Years War (1618–1648) reduced the population of Germany by more than a third, some historians say a half. Famine, with sudden and unexpected onset, malaria with endemic persistence, have reaped such a toll of human lives as it would take the worst of nuclear weapons to equal. Plague and pestilence, battle, murder, and sudden death have haunted the human race from time immemorial, in forms as cruel and terrifying as hydrogen or cobalt.

Fear seems to have been implanted in us, as it is in animals, for the self-preservation of the species. No sooner do we conquer it in one form than it is upon us in another: the forms change, but not the substance. If the definition of freedom had had to wait upon the perfection of security and defense measures in times gone by, the chances are there would be no freedom to talk about here tonight, and for that matter, no Yale and no Columbia.

Indeed, as we follow the history of modern democracy from its inception in the English revolutions of the seventeenth century to its culmination in the American Revolution and the Constitution of the United States, it would seem that the definers of freedom knew no times other than those of insecurity and war. In the seventeenth century, while Catholic power waxed and waned with the Thirty Years War, then grew steadily stronger and more menacing with the rising power of France, English political life was deranged by fears much like our fear of Communism today.

It became virtually impossible to carry on public discussion of any major question without evoking charges of subversion and treason on both sides. Pamphleteering plumbed the depths of diatribe. Accusations gained the force of convictions. Bills of attainder and star-chamber and impeachment proceedings filled the Tower of London. Differences of opinion ended in the pillory or on the scaffold. In 1634 Archbishop Laud condemned the Puritan lawyer and playwright Prynne to life imprisonment, a £5,000 fine, disbarment, and the loss of both his university degrees and his ears. Ten years later Prynne had his revenge, whipping up a hue and cry that sent Laud to the Tower and thence to the block. Milton's tutor at St. Paul's was sentenced to have his ears lopped off for drinking a sarcastic toast to the murderer of an incompetent general in royal favor. Both Protectorate and Monarchy sent Lilburne to jail, as one beheaded the king and the other the regicides. At length, in the 1670s, with both Charles II and his Whig adversaries taking money from the King of France, English political morality had sunk to its lowest depths and with it the security of the realm.

Yet it was out of these times and circumstances that came the classic definitions of freedom which form the basis of modern democracy; and it was these definitions that brought security as well as justice to England. The essays of Bacon and Milton, the Debates of the Army at Putney and Whitehall (a little-known colloquy on the meaning of free government that is as significant to the twentieth century as it was to the seventeenth), John Locke's *Of Civil Government,* and finally the Bill of Rights (1689) brought freedom down to earth and planted it firmly in a rule of law. This produced security and strength that no amount of hounding and hunting, of ear-lopping and head-chopping, had been able to produce.

The moral is plain. Cromwell perceived it, though imperfectly, in the midst of the wars, when he said he would

> rather have a plain russet-coated captain that knows what he fights for and loves what he knows, than what you call "a gentleman" and is nothing else.

Ireton sharpened Cromwell's perception when he declared in the Putney debates:

> I will tell you what the soldier of this realm hath fought for: . . . the danger that we stood in was that one man's will must be a law. . . . There is no other foundation of right I know . . . but this general justice, and this general ground of righteousness, that we should keep covenant with one another.

The perception was deepened a century and a half later by a graduate of King's College, Alexander Hamilton, whose words are preserved in the Records of the Federal Convention, under the date of June 6, 1787:

> A free government to be preferred to an absolute monarchy not because of the occasional violations of *liberty* or *property* but because of the tend-

ency of the Free Government to interest the passions of the community in its favour, beget public spirit and public confidence.

The moral is this: that the surest safeguard against treason is a polity so just and equitable that no one will wish to betray it. Such an inspiration of men's affection and men's confidence is a more dependable guarantee of national security than the most searching catechism or the most diligent secret police. As we depart from this principle we confess our weakness, to our enemies as well as to ourselves. As we are faithful to it we realize our strength and show it to the world.

Which is the greater risk, that in translating the principles of a free society into public policy some false idea of freedom may slip into the translation, or that by suspending the process we turn ourselves into a whited sepulcher surrounded by detectives and supernatural weapons? There was risk in Milton's time, and in Locke's and Alexander Hamilton's. All sorts of political philosophy competed for their attention from the communism and totalitarianism of Plato and Hobbes to the paper paradises and dream worlds of More and Rousseau, each touting its wares in the name of freedom. Yet the founders of democracy were not deceived. They were no Calibans nor overspecialized specialists nor inquisitors nor dialecticians. They were liberally educated men with both the wit and the learning to tell true freedom from false, undeceived by despotism because they knew at first hand the devious workings of one man's will, unterrified by it because they knew what they fought for and loved what they knew. Milton spoke for all of them when he said, "To sequester out of the world into Atlantic or Utopian polities, which never can be drawn into use, will not mend our conditions; but to ordain wisely in this world of evil, in the midst whereof God hath placed us unavoidably." And Benjamin Franklin summed up their achievement when he declared of the newly drafted Constitution of the United States, "It . . . astonishes me, sir, to find this system approaching so near to perfection as it does; and I think it will astonish our enemies, who are waiting with confidence to hear that our counsils are confounded like those of the builders of Babel." The spirit and standards of these men are ours by national inheritance.

Two things in particular enabled them to ordain wisely in this world of evil: liberal learning and due process of law. These too are ours by inheritance. Liberal learning is both a safeguard against false ideas of freedom and a source of true ones. Due process of law provides an orderly framework within which the definition of freedom may be carried on without fear of subversion by one man's will, by enemy agents, or by popular hue and cry. Liberal learning and due process of law are root and branch of the university tradition. By putting them to such practical use in their day the English and American founders of democracy greatly strengthened that tradition. By putting them to the same use in our day we shall give that tradition a new lease on life. In the name of this high purpose I welcome Columbia to the third of many centuries.

Social Responsibility for Individual Welfare

Mrs. Franklin D. Roosevelt

I am happy that in this remarkable conference that has been called to celebrate and to deepen the thinking and knowledge of our people throughout the country on these subjects, we should have the stress laid on this particular subject: "Social Responsibility for Individual Welfare."

Every woman is proud that the first woman to be in the Cabinet to head a Department of Social Welfare is Mrs. Oveta Culp Hobby, and we know that she will have the backing of the women of this country in every struggle to really bring to the people of the country a greater sense of welfare and opportunity and justice in the life of our land.

Now, it has come about that when you talk about the welfare state, as a rule people think that that is a rather derogatory term—that a welfare state is somehow not a good thing. But if we could just change it around a little and say that we believed that society had a responsibility for the welfare of the individual and that society included the government, the individuals themselves as individuals, and all other groups—universities, the people who form the policies, the industrialists, the people who guide commerce, industry, and agriculture—if we thought of them altogether as working together to increase the welfare of the individual, then we would cease, I think, to have a fear of just the mere words "a welfare state." We would have a truer conception of what the words really mean.

It is basic in a democracy that leadership for the welfare of the people as a whole must come from government. It is true that we pride ourselves on holding the reins of government, but we need leadership. We need a voice to define our aims, to put into words the things we want to achieve; and so we look to government to do just that—so that we do not stand still but move forward. Just as Alice in *Alice in Wonderland* had to run very fast to stay in the same place, we must run even faster to stay in the same place, and we have to do even more in order to go forward. We will go backward unless we go forward.

My husband used to say that we progressed by crises, that when the crisis was so bad that we wondered how we were going to meet it, then we were ready to try something new, to try something that perhaps we would otherwise have hesitated to undertake.

When sometimes I hear it said today that in my husband's time we started something dreadful, something which they called "creeping socialism," I wonder whether instead we didn't really face the fact that a democracy must meet the needs of its people, and whether what we did was not actually to save democracy, to save free enterprise, to keep for ourselves as much freedom as we possibly could. Had we not met the needs of the people, we might have waked up and found ourselves not just in a creeping socialism, but perhaps going actually to the far extremes of either fascism or communism, because we could not find a way to meet the needs of the people.

As I have been around the world it has seemed to me that we in this country, when we talk of capitalism or free enterprise, should explain what we mean, because there are many areas of the world in which it is not at all understood what we actually mean when we talk of our own capitalism, of our own development in the past thirty years or forty years, let us say.

We have had great changes, but they have been the changes which had to come if our people were to have a chance for full development. To be sure, some of the things were very new; now they seem very old. I can remember when we started old-age pensions. Now the idea is not very shocking to us—a mutual contribution towards this security in old age. We started care for the blind and the crippled. Many said that it was simply a humanitarian gesture, but it was more than that. It is real insurance so that they will not remain a burden on society. That is why we continue to develop the employment of the crippled and the blind. We continue to find useful ways of using people, even handicapped people.

Old-age pensions, as now accepted, are contributed to throughout the working life of every individual. Care for the blind and the crippled may sound completely humanitarian, but on the contrary it is really an insurance so that society will not have an obligation to carry handicapped people as a complete burden. In the underdeveloped areas of the world the only thing open to the handicapped individual is to beg. We not only try to extend the best medical care but we try to train these individuals to earn a living, and we are constantly working with industries to open occupations to trained handicapped people, while many industries also have undertaken training programs of their own. This whole program eliminates a burden from society, just the same as pensions do which are paid for during the working life of an individual.

We believe in unemployment insurance. We know that it is not perfect in operation. We know that a number of things that are done for general welfare are not perfect in the way they work out, but that it would be unwise to wipe out the whole of something because there needed to be certain reforms and changes. It was felt that as we went along we would realize that unemployment insurance was not just for the benefit of the individual; it was for the benefit of our economy. It was to try to keep us from having debacles, from actually having buying power so reduced as to hurt the economy of the nation as a whole. It is part of our economic insurance.

There are many things that, just like freedom, we must constantly be studying and watching when we do things for the welfare of people, because we do not want to remove from people their sense of responsibility and initiative. We want them to feel that they are partners in each thing that we do, that if they function in a democracy, then what their government does comes from them. They acquiesce, they work it out, and they must not lose initiative.

We have not completely solved the unemployment problem because it is still open to abuses. It is safeguarded to some extent by the fact that government offices try to find jobs for people within their range of employment, which they are expected to accept. But many people have had the experience of knowing individuals who took advantage of unemployment insurance when they really could have obtained work. The law was not written to encourage such people, and so ways should be sought to eliminate existing loopholes so that it would be impossible to get unemployment insurance unless one is unable to find work in a field where one is competent.

All these social measures were designed to protect society from sudden fluctuations in the economy and to protect the individual from situations beyond his control which he could not completely handle by himself. They were designed as cooperative measures between the individual and his government, which, I think, is a step forward. They should not tend to remove initiative from people nor keep them from feeling a sense of individual responsibility and ambition.

The advantage of a democracy over the socialist state would seem to be a greater freedom, which provides for the development of the individual for free choice of a way of life and for a sense on the part of the individual of participation in the decisions made which affect his life and his future. His government tries to remove from the individual a fear of want so that he may be freer to fully develop, but it does not countenance a stepping in of government to take over the major part of the responsibility for man's existence.

I was struck in France by the difference between our philosophy and theirs, which are still miles apart. They do not think that it is important that a man earn a living wage. We do. I think it is the basis of the welfare of the individual.

Under the social-security system of France nearly every employer pays his employees less than a living wage. He pays from 35 to 50 per cent of the wage, not to the employee, but into a *caisse* or fund managed by the government and distributed under government auspices to families according to their size. Under this system a man with five or six children receives a considerable sum more from the government than he earns. In a democracy like ours we think it important for industry to be so organized that a man receives wages commensurate with his work and on which he can support his family. In other words, what we hope to ensure to every individual is an ability to earn a living, and the benefits of a welfare state are simply auxiliary to meet emergencies and to help a human being to meet situations that may arise in his life which he ordinarily could not meet alone.

There I was told very calmly, "Oh, but you do not understand our system.

We know we don't insist upon a living wage, but the government gives to families, according to the number of children, an allowance. If you have five or six children you might almost as well not work because the government pays you so much more than you can possibly earn."

That is not my idea of what we really want to do for the basic welfare of the people of our country. We want to help the people to meet disaster; we want to prevent disaster, either the disasters that come from nature or the disasters that we might create for ourselves, from hurting our own country.

We have to recognize that our type of capitalism in this country is different from what the same word connotes in some other countries. From the time of the last depression we have taken great strides in the recognition of the responsibility of government and industry to cooperate to prevent any disasters to the normal economy of the country. We have to be prepared to meet disasters caused by nature. These we expect the government to cooperate in meeting, but we recognize the responsibility of industry today as well as of the individual. We believe that together we should strive to give every individual a chance for a decent and secure existence, and in evolving our social patterns we are trying to give both hope for better things in the future and security from want in the present. These aims should not affect either the initiative of the individual or his sense of responsibility, but should give him a feeling of partnership with his government and with the economy of his country as a whole, which we hope will be a pattern that far transcends the economic pattern of Communism.

Basically, all of us believe that where the people feel they have justice, opportunity, and freedom and can actually rely on the interest of their government and on the attitudes of society to help them achieve stabilization and as much security as one can ever count on in human life, there will be belief in the government and the security that no other isms will really undermine the faith in the ideas on which this country was founded.

We believe that together we should strive to give every individual a chance for a decent and secure existence; and in evolving our social patterns we are trying to give both hope for better things in the future and security from want as far as possible in the present.

These aims should not affect either the initiative of the individual or his sense of responsibility, but should give him a feeling of partnership in his government and with the economy of his country as a whole, which we hope will be a pattern that far transcends the economic pattern and the ideological promises that are made in parts of the world by Communism.

If we live and work for the basic ideals that our country was founded on and have justice and freedom, I think we need not have loyalty boards. We need not have inquisitions. We can trust that what we believe in and stand for will be strong enough so that we can trust each other and our people as a whole.

PART ONE
Policies for Universal Public Education

INTRODUCTION

Few other periods in American history have been characterized by so much conflict regarding our basic institutions as the present. And perhaps at no other time have these conflicts been more serious than today. Whether by choice or by force of circumstances, America has assumed a primary position among the free nations of the world at a time when freedom, both individual and collective, is meeting its most profound challenge.

To meet this challenge successfully, our fundamental values and premises need to be reaffirmed, and our basic institutions need to be reappraised so as to strengthen some and modify others. The way in which a free society pursues this momentous task is, of course, more than suggestive; for in this process, perhaps above all others, the means are quite as important as the ends sought.

The Fourth Bicentennial Conference has provided an opportunity for educational leaders throughout the country to exchange ideas concerning a problem of major importance to a free society—the achievement of a consistent national policy for universal public education. It is to be hoped that out of this conference, and similar ones, such a policy will be cooperatively formulated. To be effectual, however, it will have to eventuate in improved practices throughout the nation's school systems and in institutions of higher education preparing teachers and administrators. Moreover, such a policy must be formulated in cooperation with lay citizens and representatives of other disciplines, for only in this way will it be acceptable to those who will benefit from it and assure its success.

For purposes of convenience, the participants in Part One focused their attention upon four facets of the problem: (1) The Federal Government and National Interest in Universal Public Education, (2) The Relations of the Various Levels of Government in Providing Universal Public Education, (3) The Scope of Public Education in the United States, and (4) The Quality of Public Education as Affected by the Levels and Distribution of Its Financial Support. Each of these topics served as the subject of a paper prepared by designated group leaders and of discussions by participants.

John K. Norton
Professor of Education
Teachers College
Columbia University

The Federal Government and National Interest in Education

William G. Carr
Executive Secretary
National Education Association

From the earliest days of the United States, even prior to the adoption of the Constitution, national interest has been evident in the desire to make public education universally available. A glance at a variety of ordinances and statutes will reveal this fact.

ORDINANCES AND STATUTES, 1785–1900

Ordinances of 1785 and 1787

The Ordinance of 1785 set aside Lot 16 of each township in the western lands "for the maintenance of public schools within said township." Two years later the Northwest Ordinance proclaimed the concern of the national government for education. Repetition and the passage of time have eroded the sharp impact of its words. Yet there remains the thrill of rediscovery when one sees them carved in the stone over the doors of some school or a college building:

> Religion, morality, and knowledge, being necessary to good government and the happiness of mankind, schools and the means of education shall forever be encouraged.

"Forever be encouraged." Forever is a long time. But the American achievement in human freedom will indeed last as long as these words are remembered. And if the time should ever come when these words fail to command the assent and to spur the action of our citizens, then this nation will have lost something precious and irreplaceable.

The Constitution

The Constitution of the United States contains language which has, over the years, been construed to empower the Federal government to act so that education may promote the general welfare and the common defense. In Article I, Section 8, we read:

> The Congress shall have power to lay and collect taxes, duties, imposts and excises, to pay the debts and provide for the common defense and general welfare of the United States.

And at the end of that article Congress is endowed with power "to make all laws which shall be necessary and proper for carrying into execution the foregoing powers."

Furthermore, as the conservative Alexander Hamilton took pains to point out in another connection, the word *necessary* and the other expressions used in the article have "a peculiar comprehensiveness." The Constitution, he argued—and he won his point in the great debate with Jefferson on the National Bank—meant that the United States government could do those things which are "needful, requisite, incidental, useful, or conducive to" the general welfare and the common defense (letter to Washington).

In 1791 the Tenth Amendment to the Constitution was adopted:

> The powers not delegated to the United States by the Constitution, nor prohibited by it to the States, are reserved to the States respectively or to the people.

Since the conduct of education is not one of the delegated powers, does the Tenth Amendment shackle the arms of the Federal government in dealing with education—a social function which all agree is basic to the success of free institutions? By no means. Congress can still use the taxing powers of the Federal government to provide for the general welfare and the common defense.

In fact, beginning with Ohio, provision was always made that each new state set aside land for school purposes in each township. The subsequent history of this "endowment magnificent," as one historian has called it, is not particularly edifying. It is a story in many states of misused funds and lack of vision, of plunder and blunder. Nevertheless, many Western states still derive substantial school funds from the original grant made by the Federal government when they were admitted to the Union.

Founders

Beyond the legal texts a rich historical record shows that the men who wrote our first ordinances and our Constitution were keenly and continuously aware of the need for an educated citizenry. Washington referred to this matter in a famous passage in his Farewell Address. Let me repeat this quotation, in a slightly fuller context than that in which it usually appears:

> It is substantially true that virtue or morality is a necessary spring of popular government. The rule, indeed, extends with more or less force to every species of free government. Who, that is a sincere friend to it, can look with indifference upon attempts to shake the foundation of the fabric?

Promote, then, as an object of primary importance, institutions for the general diffusion of knowledge. In proportion as the structure of a government gives force to public opinion, it is essential that public opinion should be enlightened.

Clearly it is impossible to argue from this quotation that Washington denied the Federal government's interest in education. Washington used the word "essential." He identified indifference to this matter with a lack of sincere friendship for popular government.

One of the clearest expressions of opinion on this matter came from a distinguished alumnus of this institution whose Bicentennial we honor. Alexander Hamilton, in his Report on Manufactures made in 1791, said:

Whatever concerns the general interests of learning, of agriculture, of manufactures, and of commerce, are within the sphere of the national councils, as far as regards an application of money.

Note how unerringly and clearly Hamilton included learning, along with the great economic interests of agriculture, industry, and trade. Note, too, his explicit endorsement of Federal expenditures, the "application of money" for all these areas.

The Morrill Act

Unfortunately, the eloquent words and clear vision of such patriots as Washington and Hamilton were too little heeded. In 1859, President Buchanan sternly vetoed the first attempt to provide Federal assistance to the state colleges of agriculture and mechanic arts. The President asserted flatly that the proposal was unconstitutional. He said that the bill would encourage the states to rely on Federal aid instead of expending their own resources for education. He predicted a long series of other national catastrophes if such a law were to be approved.

Two years later another President, much better known to history, approved this same proposal. During all the years since Abraham Lincoln put his signature on the Morrill Act, the Federal government has given a modern program of assistance and encouragement to the state colleges. There is no evidence that this program has caused the states to relax their efforts. There is no evidence that it has resulted in Federal control of instruction in a single classroom in any of these colleges. Lincoln was a better prophet than Buchanan. Those who today prophesy the doom of the Republic if the Federal government pays one more penny to help the education of its least privileged citizens may well ask whether history has vindicated Lincoln or Buchanan on this issue.

Thus the first steps of our educational system, both schools and colleges, were facilitated by Federal grants. Of the land-grant colleges and universities the late Dixon Wecter has said: "The West built its collegiate and university structure, for cultural and vocational training, upon the base of state and Federal aid."

The Office of Education

In 1867, five years after the first Morrill Act, Congress established a Federal agency to deal with education. However, the new agency nearly died at birth owing to the attitude of some Congressmen who regarded it as an attack upon the prerogatives of the states. Nevertheless, thanks to the labors of such men as Henry Barnard and his successors in the Office of Education, the new agency gradually established itself in the confidence of the people. It has, however, remained chronically understaffed and its utility is not adequately recognized even today.

FEDERAL LEGISLATION FOR EDUCATION IN THIS CENTURY

Vocational Education

In 1917 a bill introduced by a senator and a congressman, both from Georgia, authorized Federal support of vocational education in public secondary schools. The Smith-Hughes Act became the first of a series of laws to promote the general welfare and the common defense by education in agriculture, industry, home economics, and, more recently, distributive trades.

Thus, prior to the 1930s the Federal government was already using several methods in partial fulfillment of its responsibilities toward education. It had made land grants for schools. It was making appropriations to certain public higher institutions. It was paying grants to the states for vocational education.

Relief in Education

During the depression years the Federal government became even more directly involved with public education. To counteract widespread unemployment, it sponsored the construction of school buildings. To give jobs to unemployed teachers, it operated schools. To teach citizenship, conservation, health, and useful occupations to young men, it established the Civilian Conservation Corps. Through the National Youth Administration, the Federal government operated schools and training centers, sometimes in competition with local public school systems. These programs were extensive. But their primary purpose was relief, not education. When better economic conditions returned, the programs disappeared. With them went many activities which, if more soundly organized, might have conferred more lasting benefits.

World War II and After

The entrance of the United States into World War II raised new problems. Colleges and universities, with enrollments reduced, were able to operate only by contracting with the Federal government for some sort of military program. In the postwar years enrollment in institutions of higher education was greatly stimulated by educational provisions of the G.I. Bill of Rights.

The effect on public elementary and secondary education was not so easily perceived at the time. We are only now beginning to reap the full consequence of teacher and building shortages traceable to the impact of World War II on our educational system. We have never caught up with these years of neglect in our educational structure.

HISTORICAL TRENDS

To summarize, from 1785 through World War II there have been several trends in Federal education policy.

From the General to the Particular

First, the Federal government has moved away from the general promotion of education to aid special purposes and areas of education. The early grants were intended to help lay the groundwork for a general system of education. Since the Morrill Act of 1862, however, the pattern has been fragmented. Federal subsidies have been given for agricultural experiment stations, agricultural extension, certain carefully enumerated phases of vocational education in secondary schools, vocational rehabilitation, school lunches, military educational programs, relief programs, civilian training related to the war effort, aid to impacted areas, and veterans' education.

Through World War II and several years following, millions of Federal dollars were spent for educational purposes, but only a small part was for general aid to the nation's schools. Although these Federal programs benefited education as a whole, such benefits were incidental and secondary.

By-passing the States

Second, there has been some tendency toward direct administration of Federal educational programs by Federal agencies. The by-passing of state educational agencies in favor of direct administration from Washington reached its height during the depression. Most of the educational relief programs were administered by employees and officers of the Federal government. In some instances during this period, Federal agencies went so far as to establish their own schools.

Dispersal of Responsibility

Third, it has been a growing practice—not to call it a policy—to scatter education among a wide range of Federal agencies. These agencies, however competent in their primary fields of operation, lack the ability to evaluate their own contribution to meeting the needs of education as a whole. The educational program of each special agency inevitably becomes a tool whereby its objectives can be furthered. As a result it has become increasingly difficult for the Congress and the people to retain control of many Federal educational policies. Confusion here has made its masterpiece. For the same Congress that has trembled in fear of general Federal control of education has in one law after another added at once to the diversity of Federal influence over education and to the difficulty of tracing responsibility. What Congress and the American people would never sanction by deliberate intent threatens to occur by indirection and indifference.

CHANGING CONDITIONS AND DEMANDS

Interdependence

To conclude this hasty review of the historical record, here are some recent changes in the American scene which have importance for educational policy. In the past four decades there have been two world wars, a major depression, and an international contest that is intermittently hot and cold. Since 1900 this country has increased in population from 76,000,000 to 160,000,000 people. The automobile has become almost indispensable to our mode of living. Even people of modest incomes think little or nothing of traveling several hundred miles to seek employment or recreation. In ways that are both too obvious and too numerous to summarize, our national life has become more closely unified. Each community and each region depends upon the whole nation.

This interdependence extends also to international life. We have played, especially in the past decade, a principal role of leadership of free and freedom-seeking peoples in international affairs.

Enrollments

Meanwhile the number of people to be educated has increased greatly. In the secondary schools and the colleges, enrollments have increased a *thousand per cent* over 1900. Nearly four out of five children aged fourteen to seventeen are enrolled in high schools, whereas in 1900 one in ten was similarly enrolled. The increase in elementary-school enrollments is less spectacular, but present (1953–54) enrollment in elementary schools is 23 million as compared with 15 million in 1900. By 1960, it will reach 28 million. These enrollments already strain to the utmost the physical capacity of the nation's school buildings.

Finance

The average cost of public elementary and secondary education meanwhile has increased from $17 per child for current operations in 1900 to about $250 today. Some of this increase is due to the fact that more students are staying in school longer. Some of it is due to inflation. Some of it is due to higher standard and quality of educational service—longer school terms, better teaching materials, better-trained teachers, for example. Perhaps the shift from rural to urban population has been a large factor.

More significant than the increase in what we pay for public education is the way in which the burden of supporting education has shifted from predominantly local revenue sources to a more nearly equal division of financial effort between state and local sources. In 1900, 75 per cent or more of the money spent on public schools was raised at the local level. Today state revenues account for almost 40 per cent of money spent on public schools.

Accomplishments and Limitations

In terms of improvements in both quantity and quality, we have reason to be proud of our American schools. Through their services, "the right to knowledge and the free use thereof" has become a day-to-day reality for American men, women, and children. Through our schools we have achieved and maintained national unity and strength. We have done so without an established national religion or peacetime conscription or state control of the press. We have done so through education open to all, with control vested mainly in the local community.

Along with these accomplishments there are also some significant and ominous limitations. We cannot claim a satisfactory minimum equality of educational opportunity in this country when one-fourth of our classrooms have less than $3,000 a year spent on them.

For inadequate education, of course, the nation pays later on in a more costly currency. In war, men are declared unfit for military service because they do not meet the minimum standard of literacy. If these men are trained to this standard while in military service, the cost per trainee is far greater than the cost per pupil of maintaining good public schools. In peace, educational deficiencies are a restraint on economic productivity and a handicap to effective citizenship. One need only consult the manpower studies prepared at this university to discover the high cost of an inadequate supply of skilled manpower.

What then are the roles of the Federal government as far as education is concerned? The first role is leadership, to focus public and professional inquiry on great national problems of education which transcend state and local boundaries. The second role is to assume some of the cost of public education, so that no American child will be denied a good minimum standard of education. Let us consider these roles in turn.

NATIONAL LEADERSHIP

The Importance of Education Restated

As we begin to consider the role of national leadership in education, none of us can be unaware of the decision on school segregation recently rendered by the Supreme Court of the United States. To consider the issues in this case is not directly germane to the subject assigned to me here. There is, however, one passage in the decision which serves as an excellent basis for our consideration of national leadership in education.

> Today, education is perhaps the most important function of state and local governments. Compulsory school attendance laws and the great ex-

penditures for education both demonstrate our recognition of the importance of our most basic public responsibilities, even service in the armed forces. It is the very foundation of good citizenship. Today it is a principal instrument in awakening the child to cultural values, in preparing him for later professional training, and in helping him to adjust normally to his environment. In these days it is doubtful that any child may reasonably be expected to succeed in life if he is denied the opportunity of an education.

These eloquent words, unanimously approved by our highest judicial body, are in a great American tradition. They reaffirm our reliance on education as an instrument for the preservation and extension of our national ideals and institutions.

The Federal Agency for Education

One Federal agency has been explicitly assigned responsibility for leadership in the crucial field of education. That agency is the U.S. Office of Education. Yet that agency deals with less than one per cent of the Federal funds appropriated for educational programs. The Office of Education was established for the purpose of "collecting such statistics and facts as shall show the condition and progress of education in the several States and Territories, and of diffusing such information respecting the organization and management of schools and school systems, and methods of teaching, as shall aid the people of the United States in the establishment and maintenance of efficient school systems, and otherwise promote the cause of education throughout the country." This remains an unrealized purpose. Many other agencies have under their jurisdiction Federal educational programs of far greater scope and impact than those lodged in the U.S. Office.

Why has this situation developed? The agency responsible for education within the government began as an independent agency. It was almost immediately shifted to the Department of Interior and then to the Federal Security Agency. Today the Office of Education is a small bureau in the Department of Health, Education, and Welfare. The unsuccessful effort to divest the educational agency of political stresses has merely succeeded in divesting it of prestige.

Proposed Improvements

What can be done to improve or to alter this situation? There was a movement in the 1920s to establish a cabinet department of education. During the 1930s various groups recommended for the Office of Education a more important status in governmental councils. In recent years, the education profession has clearly expressed itself in favor of a national board of education as an independent agency, reporting directly to the President, but without cabinet status. A Task Force, appointed by the Hoover Commission of 1949, recommended an independent educational agency in these words:

> The National Board of Education would fit well into this plan. The opportunity for partisan controls and abuse is reduced. It may be in a better

position to work with, integrate, and serve educational functions in other agencies of the government. It would be less likely to come under noneducational domination. There is no implication that its services are involved with charity and social service. It should be able to make its representations to the President and to Congress directly.

Unfortunately, the Hoover Commission did not accept this recommendation. It proposed instead that education be a part of a cabinet department of social security and education. A proposed advisory committee on education to the Secretary of Health, Education, and Welfare has yet to be authorized by Congress. Even if such a committee is established, its usefulness will depend wholly on the willingness of each successive Secretary to seek and to apply its advice.

Wherever the Federal educational agency is or may be placed, its problem is to exert a dynamic, noncoercive leadership for education. Today the Federal government is not well organized to carry out such educational activities. Citizen control over Federal educational activities is made extremely difficult because there is no focal point at which responsibility can be pinned. Furthermore, Federal educational programs under noneducational agencies are apt to involve direct or indirect Federal controls. The channels used by these agencies are not always those of the established state school systems. Without an independent Federal agency for education, Federal educational activities must continue to be a confused series of uncoordinated and piecemeal programs.

I can summarize this part of the discussion no better than by reading a portion of a statement issued in 1945 by the Educational Policies Commission of the NEA in conjunction with the Problems and Policies Committee of the American Council on Education.

> If education becomes federalized in the United States it will not be because the people want this to happen. At no one time will they clearly and decisively take action to make the national control.
>
> The federalization of education in the United States, if it occurs, will not be the fulfillment of a policy consciously adopted after mature deliberation by the majority of the American people. Rather, it will happen by default.

FINANCE

A second aspect of Federal responsibility for education is financial support. I have pointed out that the Federal government already spends Federal funds for education. It is time now for the Federal government to share in the financial responsibility for education. I am not proposing new special Federal educational programs; we have enough of such programs already. Instead of more Federal education, we should have state control of education with Federal financial partnership. There is all the difference in the world between shared support of state schools and a Federal school system.

General Federal support of education could take any one of several forms.

The Federal government might make funds available to the states for school construction. Since such expenditure is needed by all states, it would allow the states and the localities to use more of their tax resources for the actual operation of schools.

Again, the Federal government might assist the states with funds to be applied to current operations—for teachers' salaries, for instance.

Or the Federal government could combine both measures. It might well proceed at once to help relieve the school-building shortage. This could be a relatively short program designed to help the states and localities eliminate obsolete and unsafe school buildings, to anticipate classroom needs for, let us say, the next five years. This would help the schools over the hump created by years of neglect.

Once the backlog of construction, a legacy of the depression and World War II, was overcome and once housing was provided for the predictable enrollment increases up to 1960, the emphasis on Federal support could be shifted to operation. Meanwhile the proceeds of state and local taxation could be more readily spent on teachers' salaries and other current expenses, rather than to repay heavy local indebtedness.

For current operations the Federal government should assume, on a permanent basis, a portion of the expense of educating American school children. In effect the Federal government should permanently guarantee that some maximum amount to be agreed upon shall be available for the basic education of every American child.

Estimates of the Cost

How much would this cost? With regard to current school construction needs the Office of Education estimated that, as of September 1952, this nation needed to build 312,000 classrooms at a cost of $10.6 billion. The states and localities estimated that their applicable resources could provide $5.9 billion of this, leaving a nation-wide deficit of $4.7 billion. The states and localities could raise more money for construction—by more realistic property assessments, by removing outmoded restrictions on bonding, and by merging school districts into larger units. But this will not be enough, nor can we put our children into a deep freeze during the slow process of revising state and local tax structures. Our children have a right to knowledge and the free use thereof. They have a right to it *now*.

With regard to current operations, it has been estimated by the Office of Education that the cost of raising the level of classroom expenditure to the national median of $4,391 per classroom per year reported for 1949–50 would have been $633 million. A consideration of such a minimum program should be on the agenda of the state and national conferences on education proposed by President Eisenhower in his 1954 State of the Union Message.

In short, what is here proposed is that the Federal government become a partner with the states and localities in financing public education.

What are the alternatives to this proposal?

Some say that the Federal government should merely turn back to the states some of the taxing powers that it now exercises. The Federal government does not collect money from the states. It collects money from individuals and corporations. With the exception of a few special areas of taxation, such as the gasoline tax, there is no real prospect that the Federal government will relinquish any of its present sources of revenue.

Another alternative would be to let the present educational situation continue to get worse until the Federal government has to rush in to palliate the emergency situations which are sure to arise. The construction and operation of schools in defense-affected areas is one example of this approach. Another example is supplied by a news release from the Department of Defense announcing that 162,000 men in uniform were brought up to fourth-grade reading level by Armed Forces literacy education since 1950. The release did not give the cost, but it is a safe bet that such patchwork costs more than double the price of good basic education in public schools. If we do not wish to spend Federal money to help finance state-controlled schools, we shall sooner or later have to spend Federal money to pay the full bill for education completely controlled by Washington, and by the military arm of our national government at that. Meanwhile we lose valuable time and deny a basic American right. When we neglect the education of our children, we must not exhibit pained surprise if we have to spend far more heavily for the education of young men in uniform.

Thus neither of the alternatives to Federal partnership in the support of education is attractive. Basic modification of the assignment of sources of revenue is impractical and improbable. Continuance of the present neglect, with Federal palliative action on an emergency basis, is costly, inequitable, and dangerous to the principle of state and local control.

The Standard Objections

There are two familiar objections which are always raised against the proposal that the Federal government should accept some of its responsibility in the general financial support of education. To put them in the form of questions, these objections are:

1. Can we have Federal aid to education without Federal control?
2. Can we afford Federal aid to education?

Federal aid without control? We certainly *can* have Federal aid with Federal control. It would be possible, though not desirable, to write legislation which defines exactly how the states and localities should spend the Federal money allotted to them. But if we want to change educational policy in the public schools, we have other and better ways of doing so than through Federal statutes. If any issues of policy are to be resolved by Federal action, this should be accomplished through direct, open legislation which can be evaluated on its merits rather than by indirect financial pressures from Washington.

We can have as much or as little Federal control as the Congress may put into the law. Experience shows that no control ensues if Congress asserts that there is to be no Federal control over the shaping of policy or curriculum, or the selection of teachers. Contrariwise, when the Congress fails to make a clear declaration of policy on Federal control, or when it has placed the administration of an educational program in the hands of a noneducational agency, Federal control of education has developed.

The answer to Federal control, then, lies with our elected representatives in Congress. If we make our legislative objective clear, if we administer such a program through a Federal education agency, and if we enact only laws which respect the autonomy of the states and localities in educational matters, then we have no reason to fear Federal control. To deny this, it seems to me, is to deny the possibility of popular self-government itself.

Can we afford it? In May 1954 an important ceremony occurred at the White House. The President signed a bill which provides about one billion dollars per year in Federal aid to the states. A jovial crowd assembled in the President's study to witness his signature. So many souvenirs were requested that one pen had to be used just for making the period after the word Eisenhower.

The President expressed his gratification over the enactment of this legislation. He cited the great need for modernization and expansion to remove deficiencies and to meet the vastly increased demand. Primary responsibility, the President said, remained in the states but the law recognized that the Federal government had a responsible relationship in this problem.

I have not told you yet what the billion dollars is for, but I imagine most of you will have recognized by this time that it was the all-time record for Federal aid to highways.

Enthusiasm for this legislation ran high. When it was considered in the House, one congressman affirmed flatly that the greatest need of the nation today is better roads. Another legislator said that the great problem before the American people today is to provide adequate facilities on which to operate their automobiles. Other speakers expressed their regret that the fund was not at least four times larger. One enthusiastic member of the House called it "the most worthy, one of the most outstanding, one of the most necessary causes to which we can contribute our funds." Another representative called the existing condition of the highways inexcusable, and pointed out that the years of neglect caused by the war and defense expenditures made prompt help for highways imperative.

Through much of the discussion ran the theme of the nonpartisan nature of this bill. "We are all for better roads and improved highways," said one speaker. Yes, we are indeed. As a result of this beneficial legislation, many a man will be able to get to his work in fifteen minutes instead of twenty, and many a driver will be able to travel as safely at fifty miles an hour as he now does at forty.

An adequate system of highways is an important part of the national defense. But a nation that serves its people by building roads and which refuses, year after year, to face the question of help to its schools, is neglecting an aspect of national defense that is even more important than six-lane highways.

It is a strange business. Money can be found for every government activity until we come to education. Then the cry goes up that we have a staggering national debt, that our taxes are high (although we have sharply reduced them this year), and that it is impossible to support our schools. When it was proposed to earmark for education the resources under the outer continental shelf (not the resources formerly in dispute between the states and the Federal government, but the resources which all agree belong to the national government) the Director of the Budget replied that such resources should be used to retire the national debt.

As a people we do not reason this way about our immediate economic interests. Let some of the states go a few weeks without rain and their governors wing their way like homing pigeons to the national Capitol to demand and get Federal relief. Let a tornado strike or a dam break, and Federal aid literally flies to the stricken area. But the flood of children, the nation's hope and the nation's future, receives no such attention from either the chief executives of the states or from the Federal legislature. Congress seems to have more important matters . . . anyway, there isn't enough money . . . and if there were, the Federal government might control the schools . . . and besides there is a big national debt . . . and we ought to study the matter for another two or three years . . . and there are so many technical questions in drafting this legislation . . . and we might (perhaps) try to get to it at the next session of Congress—we hope.

Our government does what we, the people, want done. Thousands of children go to school day after day in unsuitable and dangerous buildings, are taught by underpaid and undertrained teachers on half-time shifts, or are otherwise unsuitably educated. The fault lies not in our government but in ourselves as citizens. We have not yet put first things first. When we do, we shall support education by the teamwork of all our governments—local, state, and national.

The Relations of the Various Levels of Government in Providing Education

Henry H. Hill
President
George Peabody College for Teachers

We run the risk of losing our visions and the thrill of our "victories for mankind" when we debate the specific workings and practical features of day-to-day operations. For this reason let us emulate the old-fashioned college chapel exercises and have what is in the nature of a devotional before starting out on the routine tasks of the day.

Our American system of universal public education, born and nurtured under difficulties, opposed and lambasted by all kinds of religious and political forces at one time or another, is no hothouse plant unable to stand the stretches of arid weather or the hot blasts of criticisms or even the impoverished civic soil where it has occasionally had to survive and grow. It is a hardy perennial, and deservedly so.

The American people have faith in public education. They send 88 per cent of their children to the public schools. It has been said that public schools are provided, not to see how much arithmetic can be learned by ten-year-olds, but to give all a chance to make something of themselves. It is this faith, almost blind and unreasoning at times, but stirring and honest, which will sustain public education as long as the United States shall remain a republic or democracy.

Public education has given most persons an unfettered chance in the race of life. It has kept us a fluid society, constantly freshened by the rise from the bottom social levels of springs of that natural aristocracy of virtue and creativeness. In totalitarian countries there is no rise save by the sword and rebellion as practiced by the Hitlers, Mussolinis, and Stalins, or by slavish conformity to arbitrary power.

A distinguished scholar of Columbia University states with conviction that the American public school system has kept us free. I would add that its doors swing open to all, regardless of color, creed, or circumstance.

With this educational devotional as an inspiration, let us examine together some of the choices in the intergovernmental relationships necessary to pro-

16

vide universal public education—first, horizontal relationships on the same level, and then the necessary vertical relationships extending through the three recognized levels. Such principles as will be enunciated are, by and large, based upon empiricism rather than theory. Until the turn of the century there was little theory applicable to the enormous business of education as we know it in these latter years. Universals, of course, are always true, but the techniques in school organization and administration are subject to change. Some of Horace Mann's views of over a century ago are sound today; but in his time only a relative handful attended school, and most of these for a short period of years. Numerically and financially, the *business* of education had not submerged the ideals and actual teaching of boys and girls, but today it takes both the science and art of good school administration to prevent overemphasis on machinery and mass effort.

LOCAL SCHOOL DISTRICTS

In many respects the core and substance of public education at its best, and occasionally at its worst, are found in the 66,000 local districts ranging in size from New York City, with over 900,000 enrolled, to hundreds of school districts in a few states with no enrollment at all. The number of districts, half that of 1932, continues to be reduced.

It has been my privilege to serve as a school administrator in four school districts in four different states. These have varied sharply in some respects. I propose to describe these four districts in the light of local autonomy, legislative and administrative machinery, and then to analyze both theory and practice as conceived and practiced in local districts generally.

Some Districts I Have Known

I was superintendent first in a small district with five hundred enrolled in the twelve grades. The school board of six members was elected by the people, and the tax rate within statutory limits was voted annually by the people. There was no town government to interfere or to help. The superintendent of schools did everything. The only threat of divided authority was an occasional careless but unintentional pocket veto by the secretary of the board. Into his hip pocket went the envelope with the minutes on the back. Sometimes the envelope minutes met the same fate as other memoranda when he absentmindedly dumped the contents of his pocket into the river when on a fishing expedition.

The board president headed the dominant bank faction, and he and his friends ran the community. We hear these latter days of elaborate studies of the power structure of a given community. A one-man power structure is easily identified and has some advantages along with its admitted faults.

In this small community I taught and superintended for nine years. There I learned most of what I know about human beings. I would like to pay tribute to the idealistic belief of these citizens in the value of a good high school. Although it was unconstitutional and illegal, it was my business as superintendent of schools to collect $45 annually from each student enrolled in the eighth, ninth, tenth, eleventh, and twelfth grades. The unrealistically low tax assessments and the comparatively slight revenue productivity, even if property had been assessed at full value, made it necessary for the parents to pay this amount of money in order to have a better high school than their tax base would support. There are few communities in the United States that would have been willing then or would be willing now to go to this nonlegal extreme in order to have a good school.

My second superintendency, in a city of 50,000, was or became nearly perfect, in both theory and practice. After operation of the schools under dual administrative control, the single executive type was substituted when the state statute was modified to permit this change. Fiscally independent of the city, the school board was free within statutory limits to levy taxes for current purposes, limited in bonding to a two-thirds favorable vote by the people. Board members were elected on a nonpartisan ballot at a separate school election. The board had no standing committees, no desire to get publicity, a real desire to have good public schools.

The civil city was run on an above-the-average level. Assessments were nearly 100 per cent of real value. The city collected the school taxes and turned over to the board of education the entire proceeds. There was no county machinery with jurisdiction, and the state exercised no arbitrary authority.

The relatively conservative, but not reactionary or stubborn, board served as good brakes to a young superintendent who might have taken too seriously something he read in a book or heard a young professor say. They would approve what was sound, and they did. It was possible to try out any meritorious reform in management or curriculum.

Next came St. Louis, with fiscal independence, a great tradition, and a tax vote by the people every four years. But alas! St. Louis had and still has a four-headed administration, never to my knowledge defended in print, but always retained by forces who like it that way. Another unfortunate feature is the twelve-member board which works little better in practice than in theory. The strong standing committees, each a little board in itself, and a system of election by the people from candidates for whom there must be several thousand petitioners, all fit together to make a breastworks of entrenchment which has withstood all attempts at change up to the present.

The continual passage of hundreds of erstwhile civic leaders out to the restricted dormitories beyond the city limits lowers the interest and concern of those who could change things. Despite these well-known handicaps, St. Louis has some wonderful teachers and professional workers and a superintendent who plays the well-obstacled course in as near par as is humanly possible. (There really ought to be a par worked out for the different kinds of school districts and city systems. "Doing fair" is par for many of them.)

Last came Pittsburgh. A certain vestige of duty and professional devotion prompted me to accept the position as superintendent. The professional honor and distinction which go with such a post are completely overbalanced by the necessity of fighting rearguard battles both within and without most big city systems. Apparently such an administration as that in a small city is next to impossible. Sometimes I think it is better in a big city to pick the best inside man than to bring in a theoretically abler outsider. A man reared over a saloon or over places of somewhat higher repute in the Lower East Side in New York will never especially mind noise nor contention nor rough-and-tumble debate. To him it may seem only normal. A man reared in a big city who does not know how much better the schools can and should be run will not worry over that, but get on with doing the best he can.

The Pittsburgh Board of Public Education, within low statutory limits, was free to fix the school tax rate. Fiscal and political independence was a privilege, albeit there came with it the hazard of being a political orphan when the Pennsylvania Legislature met biennially and the Pittsburgh school board sought money or favorable legislation.

The fifteen-member board was appointed by the sixteen judges of the Court of Common Pleas. Individually the members were distinctly above average. Fifteen is too large a board. The practice of having a committee of the whole, resolutely instituted and practiced by my predecessor, simply is not workable in actual practice. There cannot be the same sense of responsibility as would be felt by a smaller board.

The organization was four-headed, changed to two during my tenure. In both cases, the superintendent of schools in theory and in practice has been accorded first rank, but the time of a man runs out in the practice of consultation and winning over three other coordinate officers and fifteen board members. Here was the nub of the issue. Circumstances and the organization permitted unity of effort only through a personal leadership rather than through a program sound enough to stand on its own base.

Pittsburgh had a representative board: Protestants, Catholics, Jews, Whites, Negroes, Republicans, Democrats, labor leaders of AFL and CIO, management, men, and women. With three newspapers present in the persons of reporters eager to make news regardless of issues or no issues, it was a striking example of big-city democracy.

The city relationship was generally fair, although the city charged a fee for collecting school taxes. Only sophistry can justify this. The city has no more moral right to charge for the collection of school taxes than the school board has to charge the city government for running the schools. It is their job.

So much for four kinds of school districts, each with certain advantages and disadvantages, in which both theory and practice tend to identify certain administrative virtues and vices. Before discussing these, I would like to describe briefly the organizational setup in Nashville, Tennessee.

Nashville has a nine-member school board appointed by the mayor. While the appointments are staggered, yet in theory and in practice it is not too difficult for the mayor and his political faction to dominate the general school situation, for good or bad. Just recently the school board, after an executive session or two, voted to strip the superintendent of schools of his authority over the business and financial affairs and to appoint a business manager directly responsible to the board of education and apparently without regard to his experience or education. Impelled by press and teacher leadership and pressures, however, the board by a five-to-four decision reversed this action.

Since the Nashville school budget in total amount must be approved by the city council, we have what school administrators generally do not like, a fiscally dependent and politically appointed board of education.

Political Theory and Educational Experience

At this point I would like to insert in the record as fair a statement as I can make of the position of most of the political scientists and general government experts with regard to the status of the schools as part of a city or county government. They favor having public education in a subordinate position to the top management of the city. They favor having a single tax rate levied by a tax-levying body for the entire city. They look with disfavor on having any independent board, whether of education, parks and playgrounds, or what you will.

These experts advance two arguments which are entitled to consideration. They argue that all local government ought to be a unit. If one function is to be independent, then there is no logical reason why there should not be many other functions equally independent. This would result in chaos and take control too far away from the people. Since school systems have been kept freer of politics and for the most part have been better managed than have other city functions, they argue that the entire body politic should get the benefit of the good government practiced by schools.

There is a grain of reason in these arguments, but I do not accept either of them. All local government does not *have to be* encompassed in a single governing body. It is distressingly easy to make a logical, clear-cut argument for unity of any kind, especially when the argument is based chiefly on pure theory and not on practice. Could there be an unbiased, impartial inquiry to show that dependent fiscal school boards are accompanied by better total government, it would strengthen their argument. I doubt that such a thesis could be proved. I believe fiscally independent systems have worked better for the schools and have not adversely affected other local governmental functions.

There is no evidence that I know to show that freedom from politics in schools can be transferred to other branches of government. There is a reasonable chance that the schools will be pulled down to the level of other city divisions of government. We believe school government on the whole has been better.

Professional thinking in regard to the organization and administration of local school systems indicates certain desirable practices.

1. A local school system large enough to afford twelve grades should have a board of education elected by the people and responsible to them for the general organization and administration of the school system. Board members should be elected on a nonpartisan ticket, preferably at a separate election. The board is the policy-making body. Its most important task is to select a competent superintendent and to delegate to him, under proper rules and regulations, authority and responsibility for the welfare of the system. He should be appointed for a period of one, two, three, or four years, depending upon the wishes of the board.

2. The board of education should be small rather than large, preferably from five to nine members. It should be organized as a committee of the whole except for certain *ad hoc* or special committees. There should in all cases be a single administrative authority, directly responsible to the board of education. Such assistants as are needed in the fields of business, maintenance, or the other manifold tasks of the school system should be held by persons responsible to the superintendent of schools.

3. Ideally, the board of education should levy the tax necessary to operate the schools, subject to certain state regulations, and the taxes should be collected by another branch of the government which has that responsibility. The board of education should not be fiscally dependent upon the city council or any other politically elected branch of government. A normally cooperative relationship is possible, as the experiences of many cities have shown.

4. The direct election of school-board members through a nonpartisan ballot seems best in theory and in practice in school districts where the candidates are or may become well known to the voters. Whatever may be the theory, in actual practice in the larger cities of 500,000 and more, some method of appointment seems better. In Pittsburgh, for example, the average caliber of men and women appointed seemed superior to that of board members in St. Louis, a city of similar size but with direct election of school-board members. It seems difficult under the elective system to attract and then elect enough able men and women. They *will* accept appointment.

Appointment by judges, rather than by the mayor or city commissioners, seems on the basis of my limited experience and observation to offer hopes of better appointments. There is of course no way to secure good school-board members without an electorate which is interested and alert and willing to invest energy and work to secure the appointment or election of able persons.

5. When local communities have a board of education appointed by the mayor and fiscally dependent on the city government, there are safeguards that may prove helpful.

The National Citizens' Commission for the Public Schools over the past five years has encouraged the formation of local citizens' groups to support and encourage good public schools and to discover and reveal the facts in questions involving school problems and policies. Such a local committee may succeed in stabilizing the local schools. The parent-teacher associations on occasion provide this kind of help. The difficulty is that either group, dependent on lay leadership, may become involved politically or in personalities, but on balance both these groups have aided good schools decisively.

Cincinnati has enjoyed generally good results from a kind of informal but influential good-school-government group who pick good candidates for election to school-board membership. The effort there is to make a representative democracy work and to prevent some of the worst vagaries which happen when there is no able or dedicated group to provide stable counsel and broad knowledge for general school policies.

THE STATE SCHOOL AUTHORITY

Through proper constitutional and statutory authorization, the state board of education should be given general responsibility for the operation and administration of the public school systems of the state. Such authority should be general and should not be exercised, either through statutes or by rules and regulations, in such a way as to interfere unnecessarily with the responsibilities of the local school boards. The state board of education should have responsibility for the appointment of a state commissioner of education whose professional qualifications should be set forth in law. Such an appointment should be made for a period of years, with certain safeguards against political interference.

Under necessary rules and regulations there should be set up by law, with flexibility as to number and payment of staff members, provisions for the appointment and operation of a state department of education, all members of which will be responsible to the state commissioner of education.

Since we are here concerned primarily with the case of universal public education, we shall not devote our attention directly to the matter of teachers colleges, state universities, and other tax-supported institutions of higher learning. The best theory is that there should be some general guiding or controlling authority with respect to all of these institutions. It seems wise, however, that the state board of education have general jurisdiction over the state school system only through the high-school level, but that there should be a separate state board directly responsible for colleges and universities. Both practice and theory vary with respect to a single state board of education and its total responsibility for elementary, secondary, and higher education.

Courts have held that education is a state function rather than a local function; but for the most part they have safeguarded the natural and desirable initiative which has been left to the local school systems.

The authority of state boards of education or state departments of education varies widely among the forty-eight states. There are several distinct patterns of authority which we shall not develop in this paper. We would not if we could make each state education authority exactly like some one particular model. The same richness in variety which 66,000 school districts provide, even though there is more variety than necessary, should be permitted in the forty-eight state governments. The size and resources of each state, the density or sparsity of its population, and its traditions and history will modify the kind of school government to be set up.

In general, the state board of education should be directed to insure so far as possible a desirable minimum program for every school district in the state and to permit the well-to-do districts a maximum of freedom in going beyond this minimum program. Some politicians and political-minded educators have sought to use the idea of a foundation program of equal opportunity to hamstring unnecessarily the wealthier districts in the provision of richer opportunities for their own boys and girls. This is the antithesis of democracy, which provides a reasonable minimum but never enforces a uniform program which must be imposed if it is to work. The essence of democracy is to permit freedom of decision and a variety of opportunity. Out-of-bounds limits may be set forth specifically by the state board of education, but within these limits there should be a wide degree of freedom of choice left to the local districts.

In general, the supervision or regulation of all major educational enterprises supported by taxes should be lodged in the state board of education and not scattered all over the political lot. To a far greater degree than is true in the case of the Federal government, educational functions are concentrated in the state boards of education and the state departments of education.

In many states, the state superintendent of public instruction is elected on a partisan political ticket. The thinking of professional educators is against this; but there is evidence to show that the people, by and large, do not always support the opinion of the professional educators. In a county adjoining George Peabody College for Teachers, where considerable research and experimentation were carried on through the Cooperative Program of Educational Administration, it was found that 80 per cent of the people, according to a pretty well conducted sampling process, preferred the election of the county superintendent of schools to his appointment by the county board of education. How to educate citizens to see the advantages of appointment is a difficult question.

There is some evidence to show that states with an appointed state commissioner of education operate on the whole with better and more stable school programs.

Since World War I the state boards of education have had to assume more leadership in the matter of financing public education. Perhaps half the school systems in the United States could finance only with great difficulty, and some not at all, a substantial minimum foundation program. A better allocation of taxes between states and the Federal government would help the states tremendously in this great responsibility.

The state governments occupy an increasingly important position in the financing of public education. Most states today provide from one-third to over one-half the total support. States vary widely, of course, from almost complete state support in Delaware to negligible support in Kansas.

THE RELATIONS OF THE FEDERAL GOVERNMENT TO EDUCATION

On the Federal level there is no general support for elementary and secondary schools. Disagreement as to what the Federal government should do has produced a negative policy, notwithstanding the willingness of the Federal government to provide emergency and special-purpose grants.

The key agreement in the report *Federal-State Relations in Education,* made in 1945 by the Problems and Policies Committee of the American Council on Education and the Educational Policies Commission of the National Education Association, remains the clearest and best statement:

> In its relations to education in the states, the Federal government should limit its action to two broad functions: financial assistance and leadership of a stimulating, but non-coercive character.

There is ample precedent for bringing in the superior tax-gathering ability of the Federal government and for sharing with schools the Federal government's capacity to deal with emergency conditions. Emergency programs have dealt with adult schools and evening schools, with employment of unemployed teachers in emergency WPA schools, and with such legitimate pump-priming operations as the partial financing of necessary school buildings during the decade of the 1930s. The G.I. Bill has supplied funds with which many colleges have been able to improve their physical plants and their faculties by reason of the support of the Federal government provided for the tuition of the students eligible under this plan.

The fact that up to the present there has been no general Federal support of elementary and secondary education seems to provide evidence that it is possible to go so far and no farther with a certain program or in a certain direction. It is frequently argued that a certain kind of appropriation or a certain amount that is appropriated will be the beginning of a long-continued and finally abused prerogative. In the limitations surrounding past Federal programs, however, is some evidence to support the thesis that the entry of the camel's nose under the tent does not presage complete occupation.

Direct aid from the Federal government was used during the depression of the 1930s primarily to combat the economic effects of the depression and to provide needed school buildings. The general idea behind the Public Works Administration was that this kind of aid would be withdrawn when it was no longer needed. It was withdrawn.

There is already a well-established use of the taxing power of the Federal government to provide aid in dealing with emergency educational conditions which have been brought on by the Federal government, or with conditions which have been produced by disaster, or with conditions which have to do with the economic abilities of particular states at the lower economic level.

Partial Federal aid for the erection of school buildings could be obtained by appropriating a stipulated sum of money which would through proper state channels bring up to a certain minimum those school districts not able by themselves or through the resources of the state to attain decent housing for their children. Such a provision as this would be of untold aid to certain Southern states which have been long handicapped by the devastating results of the War between the States. It would be, it is true, a quite belated Marshall Plan, one which some might argue is no longer needed; but there would certainly seem to be as much equity in this kind of treatment as there is in the matter of spending billions of American dollars to do similar work for other nations. There are a few states outside the South which economically would qualify for preferred treatment.

We come back to the matter of Federal support for general elementary and secondary education; and to make this more specific let us say that this aid should go directly to increasing the salaries of teachers, either in every state or, more practicably, to certain depressed areas in the United States (which may include whole states) or to certain depressed areas within certain states, to be determined by accepted statistical indices of income or other like standards.

There is the argument that by general Federal aid to elementary and secondary education there would follow, sooner or later, undesirable Federal control over the curriculum and the teaching process itself. Proponents of general Federal aid are quick to disassociate themselves and what they advocate from Federal control. Apparently we are all agreed that there should not be *undesirable* Federal control, although we might disagree somewhat as to just what is undesirable. Neither proponents nor opponents of Federal aid want any kind of bureaucracy of men or any kind of laws which might involve arbitrary Federal control or interfere too much with what are the legitimate desires and aspirations—and responsibilities—of states and communities within those states.

There is considerable evidence to show that by and large there has not been any sustained undesirable Federal control of the curriculum or the teaching process in the case of Federal relationships with land-grant colleges and teaching enterprises, including the billions expended under the so-called G.I. legislation. That none would happen in the future because not any serious lapses have occurred in the past is, of course, a *non sequitur*. All in all, however, it seems to us that a pretty good case can be made that with Federal aid to meet some unmet school needs the evils of undesirable Federal control might at least in theory be in large measure avoided.

Speaking before the Fifth Annual Dinner of the National Citizens' Commission for the public schools in San Francisco, on March 12, 1954, Beardsley

Ruml estimated an increase in school-age children of 23 per cent by 1960 and an added cost annually of $3 billion, with another $1.5 billion annually to amortize school plant and equipment cost. Assuming an annual increase in productivity of 3 per cent, he arrives at an annual total income for the nation of $455 billion in 1960, an increase of around 25 per cent over present figures. His suggestion to use national income to provide an underpinning to schools' finances is worth quoting.

> The indications are therefore for Federal aid based on Federal access to national income and derived from the graduated Federal income tax. But we do not want Federal grants in aid at the price of Federal control or dominance of the public schools. Is there a solution for this problem? I believe that there is.
>
> Grants in aid, whether Federal or state, have usually been on some sort of an equalization basis. An equalization basis necessarily involves some criterion of need, and in the setting up and in the administration of any criterion, no matter how objective, the possibility of coercion by the higher authority of the lower authority exists, at least potentially.
>
> On the other hand, if Federal aid were given on a per-capita-child-in-school basis, subject only to a certificate of a proper state authority that the funds had been received and spent for education, under concepts and supervision legally specified by the state, then the dangers of intervention would no longer exist.

Ruml meets the obvious objection that the wealthy state may get more than it needs by pointing out how any excess may be used to reduce realty taxes or for other benefits.

His view is interesting because he approaches the problem from a fresh viewpoint, disregarding the prejudices and difficulties so well known to others who know only too well that nothing so far-reaching can be done. At the same meeting Walter Lippmann offered a contribution to needed basic thinking on the subject of the *educational effort* as measured by per capita expenditure in 1900 and *the task* as measured by the money consumed by Federal expenditure per capita. The ratio in 1900 was 1 to 2, is now 1 to 6! His rationale for more money for education is this:

> Our educational effort . . . has not yet been raised to the plateau of the age we live in. I am not saying, of course, that we should spend 40 billions on education because we spend about that much on defense. I am saying that we must make the same order of radical change in our attitude towards education as we have made in our attitude towards defense. We must measure our educational effort as we do our military effort. That is to say, we must measure it not by what it would be easy and convenient to do, but by what it is necessary to do in order that the nation may survive and flourish. We have learned that we are quite rich enough to defend ourselves, whatever the cost. We must now learn that we are quite rich enough to educate ourselves as we need to be educated.
>
> There is an enormous margin of luxury in this country against which we can draw for our vital needs. We take that for granted when we think of the national defense. From the tragedies and the bitter experience of being in-

volved in wars for which we were inadequately prepared, we have acquired the will to defend ourselves. And, having done that, having acquired the will, we have found the way. We know how to find the dollars that are needed to defend ourselves, even if we are to do without something else that is less vitally important.

There is the argument that general Federal aid to education would result in less money going to the schools because the Federal government "uses up" a sizable percentage of the moneys received from the states in administration and "politics." The implication is that the Federal government could reduce Federal taxes and that the states might thus be able to secure more revenue for the general support of elementary and secondary education. This overlooks too much the human beings who are concerned in such an enterprise. Could this too simple proposition be worked out, there would still be difficulties. If Federal aid is to strengthen the states less well-advantaged financially, resources from favored states must be made available to help the less able states.

Some other arguments seem to most reasonable men somewhat intemperate. There is the categorical statement that Federal aid is "socialistic" or even worse. Billions have been spent by the Federal government in encouraging the development of a Federal highway system. Surely, few would call this a commitment to socialism. It is a wise and beneficent use of the total ability of the entire nation to make things possible which all want to enjoy.

The practical politics of securing passage of a general Federal-aid law has an important bearing on the issues. In the past a well-disciplined and compact minority has been able to defeat the wishes of a less cohesive majority of Congress. All the necessary but sometimes not-to-be-bragged-of vagaries of practical politics would also affect the kind of bill which ultimately could be passed by Congress. For example, there has been raised at every hearing the controversial question whether Federal aid is to be given to parochial and private schools. The answer is always No, but there is a good deal of evidence that this kind of answer wins the solid opposition of a considerable bloc of votes.

If, then, to pass a general Federal-aid bill it is necessary to win over the votes of those who favor some distribution of Federal aid to parochial and private schools, then a considerable segment of opinion would agree that it is better for the schools to go along without it.

It may be stated fairly dogmatically that there is not now any national trend toward general Federal aid for elementary and secondary education.

Bearing on this short-term look is a passage from President Eisenhower's Budget Message, as given on January 21, 1954. The President said:

The citizen in a democracy has the opportunity and the obligation to participate constructively in the affairs of his community and his Nation. To the extent that the educational system provides our citizens with the opportunity for study and learning, the wiser will their decision be, the more they can contribute to our way of life.

I do not underestimate the difficulties facing the states and communities in attempting to solve the problems created by the great increase in the number of children of school age, the shortage of qualified teachers, and the over-crowding of classrooms. The effort to overcome these difficulties strains the taxable resources of many communities. At the same time I do not accept the simple remedy of Federal intervention.

It is my intention to call a national conference on education, composed of educators and interested citizens, to be held after preparatory conferences in the states. The conference will study the facts about the Nation's educational problems and recommend sensible solutions. We can then proceed with confidence on a constructive and effective long-range program. Pending the outcome of these conferences and the development of our educational program, the Federal Government is providing assistance to those communities where school needs have been greatly increased by the activities of the Federal Government.

It is always wise to take a long-term view on any matter which will be facing the United States for decades to come. The discussion of a far-reaching policy, covering Federal aid to elementary and secondary education, is timely. The responsible leaders of the United States do change their minds. They have done so in the past and for valid reasons. In the event of a severe economic decline or any chain of events which impairs the public schools, the great prestige of the Federal government and its money may be the one remedy.

It is well here to point out certain changes which have occurred in the economy of the United States since the publication of the reports of most of the studies which have come out rather emphatically for general Federal aid. Let us enumerate some of them.

Since the 1930s there has been a change in the relative economic position of the states, especially in the size of the economic gap between the Southern states and the wealthier Northern states. To use a single illustration, the average income per capita in New York State in the late 1930s was about five times that of the average income per capita in the state of Mississippi. But in 1952 the average of income payments to individuals in New York State was $2,038 and that in Mississippi, the lowest state by this particular measure, was $818. This is, of course, a tremendous disparity in ability to provide a good program of education; *but* it is a far cry from the day in the late 1930s when the disparity was 5 to 1. Though some of the glowing statements which have occurred in periodicals since the war covering the industrial development of the Gulf States may have given an exaggerated impression, it is true that this area of the country is enjoying an unusual and apparently a sustained economic upturn. This economic upturn does not invalidate the arguments which have been made over the last quarter of a century to the effect that states are not equal in their ability to support education; but it does to some degree take the urgency and emergency out of the situation.

A second changed factor has to do with the tremendous Federal government burden for defense purposes. During the 1930s the country was in a depression. The Federal government had a negligible budget devoted to defense as compared with that of today, in which an estimated 68 per cent or more goes directly for the expenses of past, present, and future wars.

Again, this changed status does not invalidate the argument for Federal support where Federal support is necessary in order to achieve the kind of schools needed in a broad and sustained defense program. It is, however, a factor which should be properly and critically appraised in trying to fashion a long-term policy with respect to the Federal government's participation in the financing of public education.

A third change has been the vastly improved schools in nearly every state in the Union, as measured in their quantitative aspects. In the late thirties, for example, Mississippi had thousands of children who had six months or seven months or eight months of schooling annually. Today every child in the state of Mississippi has the opportunity for nine months of schooling. This points to no perfect situation, of course, but it shows consistent and effective improvement. Somewhat similar statistics could be cited to show that in 1954, though the education and training of the average teacher in the United States still leaves something to be desired, yet in terms of years spent in college the teachers of almost every state in the Union, the poorest and the best, show a distinct advance. In other words, some of the necessity and pressure for spending Federal money in order to secure good schools has been alleviated for the time being. We do not think this is a permanent situation.

CLASSIFICATION OF FEDERAL AID

The attempt here is only to illustrate the different purposes and achievements in this field.

Contrary to the general notion that the Federal government ought to do nothing to influence the curriculum and teaching has been the idea that the land-grant colleges and vocational agricultural schools should with Federal aid improve farming practices. In other words, there has been and may continue to be a deliberate and enlightened and generally approved effort on the part of leaders in the Federal government to change farming practices in the country as a whole through stimulation and provision of money. Such an effort has had the general support of the country.

A second kind of Federal aid which has been generally approved is that which is extended to public agencies like the Tennessee Valley Authority or those engaged in the development of arid lands in the West, and where, through action of the Federal government, an unusual burden has been imposed upon a particular community or state.

There is another kind of Federal aid to schools, or to the children who are enrolled in the schools, which has been generally approved, at least so far as the continuation of the program by Congress session after session indicates approval. That is the provision for a Federally supported school-lunch program which provides, at a nominal cost and under certain circumstances at no cost at all, warm and nutritious lunches to children. Here the basic purpose was at least partly to support reasonable prices for certain agricultural products. In order to utilize for a good purpose the products purchased, turkeys, butter, fruits, potatoes, and other products were furnished for the use of school lunchrooms.

Federal aid has never yet been used to bring up each state in the United States from a very low level to an acceptable minimum of educational opportunity. In theory, a good case may be made for such use. The increased mobility of population, the penalizing of wealthy states by the entry of migrants who may become public charges because of poorer economic and educational opportunities, the need of improvement of health and education in underprivileged areas from which a proper percentage of eligible soldiers can not be obtained—these are a few of the arguments. These arguments have been rejected by Congress for one reason or another, apparently because of the apprehension of what might happen if the Federal government went into the business of supporting elementary and secondary education.

THE POSITION OF THE OFFICE OF EDUCATION

Education having to do with the Indians is not lodged under the U.S. Office of Education but under a different department of the Federal government. There are numerous similar examples. The Hoover Commission Task Force having to do with the place of education in the Federal government recommended that all educational activities of the Federal government be concentrated in the U.S. Office of Education, but this was overruled by the full Hoover Commission and has never been put into effect.

A more recent suggestion has offered the possibility of establishing what might be a national board of education, a quasi-independent agency, to which the U.S. Office of Education would be responsible and which would have an eminent lay group of public-spirited citizens serving as members.

Undoubtedly, however, the preponderating opinion of Americans is in favor of having a Federal office of education without extensive power and authority over the education that takes place in the states.

To make the U.S. Office of Education merely one division of the Department of Health, Education, and Welfare seems to overdo the subordination of education in the Federal government.

CONCLUSION

The late Senator Robert Taft once said, in an address to the American Council on Education, that the United States socialized education a hundred years ago. In response to a question he vigorously and convincingly defended his position, stating that anything which the Federal government or the forty-eight states severally require that everyone have has been socialized. If that term has been given a derogatory significance, perhaps we may say education has been democratized.

As agriculture and industry and business have made it easily possible to produce things to eat and wear and use without the employment of teen-agers, we have sent more and more persons to school and college. If we want to place the blame, *which we do not,* for the cost of having 37 millions enrolled in schools and colleges, then assuredly agriculture and industry and business must accept their share of responsibility.

Millions more will be added to our enrollments. Higher education will also be democratized. There is a trend toward what I have sometimes called *higher education unlimited.* This term is of course an exaggeration, but there is a considerable element of truth in it. It is a trend toward the democratization of higher education, paralleling to some degree the democratization of high schools which took place during the 1920s. It has some of the good and the bad involved in the whole process of democracy. Are bargain basements good? It seems to me they must be if the merchandise sold at a lower price is worth it and if the bargain basement is the means of extending to the majority some of the benefits hitherto reserved for a small minority. The extension of benefits to an increasing majority of our citizens is good.

Suppose we were to reverse that trend, as some would have us do, and cut the number enrolled down to 27 millions on the ground that there are 10 millions who have no business in school. An honest and responsible critic would have a pretty hard time telling me where to put the 10 millions you would take out of the schools, how you would employ them profitably, and what else you would have them do that would be less expensive to society than to let them attend the public schools.

Over the past thirty years the profession of teaching has developed more expertness, especially in public-school administration. We need more knowledge and more art in school administration, but the major problem today in a nation of big government, big business, big labor, and big schools is how to retain the lively interest and concern of the parents, especially the young parents with their fondness for large families. Let education become too professional and too far from the grasp of the average home and we may face tax rebellion, chaos, and the worst kind of mass education. Let teachers and administrators communicate with parents and children and listen in their turn, and the schools may retain their friendly concern for individuals.

It is this thought that points up once again the critical importance of the local school system. The state must help more to support it and the Federal government must lend noncoercive leadership and some financial support. But the battles of the future will be largely won or lost in the 66,000 school districts.

The Scope of Public Education in the United States

Harold F. Clark
Professor of Education
Teachers College, Columbia University

This section discusses the problem of the scope of public education in the United States with special reference to the personnel to be educated. It includes an analysis of the size of the task of education as it has been in the past and as it now tends to be, and of what organization and facilities are required to perform the task. This is a complicated way of saying who should go to school, how long they should go, and what will be some of the requirements if they go.

WHO SHOULD ATTEND ELEMENTARY SCHOOL?

In 1754, the year King's College was founded, possibly from 5 to 20 per cent of the population of the American colonies had received some elementary schooling. In 1854 the corresponding figure was possibly from 25 to 50 per cent. In 1954 close to 99 per cent of the appropriate age group had received some elementary schooling.

Possibly well over 90 per cent of the proper age group will ultimately finish the elementary school today. The problems of elementary education are still far from settled, but, at least on a quantity basis, essentially all of the population of the United States may be expected eventually to have had at least elementary schooling. Further great changes will have to take place in the elementary schools before the schools will be adequately adjusted to this great influx of population. Much more ingenious arrangements will have to be developed to see that the influx of all the students does not unduly handicap the extremely able students.

There are still many problems facing elementary education; however, this discussion will pay relatively little attention to them. Seemingly the public has decided that virtually all children shall have an elementary-school education. The compulsory attendance laws in all states are such that eventually practically all children will go through the elementary school. However, society will ultimately have to give very serious attention to the problems of the changes that should be made in elementary education growing out of this effort to educate virtually all the people.

WHO ARE IN SCHOOL NOW?

Let us look at the facts from another angle in order to see who are in school today.

In 1950, 99 per cent of the 7-to-13-year-olds were enrolled in school. About 94 per cent of the 14- and 15-year-olds were in school; 70 per cent of the 16- and 17-year-olds, and 25 per cent of the 18- and 19-year-olds. It is quite clear from the record that as far as school enrollment is concerned, the problem has been essentially solved for the 7-to-13-year age group. With 94 per cent enrollment, the problem has been practically solved for the 14- and 15-year-olds. Grounds for discussion begin to arise with the 16- and 17-year-olds, 70 per cent of whom are now enrolled in school. What is the desirable percentage? Of the 18- and 19-year-olds 25 per cent are in school. Is that too high, too low, or about right? In any case it is clear that the main discussion regarding possible expansion of schooling should center around the 16- and 17-, 18- and 19-year-olds.

Of 1,000 fifth-grade children in 1943, 505 graduated from high school in 1950; 225 entered institutions of higher learning in the fall of 1950; presumably as many as about 70 of them graduated from institutions of higher learning in June of 1954. This would indicate that a little over 50 per cent of the proper age group are graduating from high school, about 22 per cent are entering college or some equivalent institution, and about 7 per cent are graduating from college. Would the country be substantially better off if the numbers graduating from high school, entering college, and finishing college were greatly increased?

WHO SHOULD ATTEND HIGH SCHOOL?

The really serious discussion in this country concerning who should go to school begins with the age group from 14 to 17. This, in general, covers the four-year senior-high-school ages. Probably from 80 to 90 per cent of the children enter high school, and, as we have seen, somewhat over 50 per cent finish high school. An important decision the American public will have to reach is how high they want to push the percentage finishing high school. Present trends and forces might ultimately take it to 70 or 75 per cent.

To get the percentage much above this level will probably take either very drastic changes in the content of some of the courses offered or else it will take some major changes in the very conception of the school itself.

In general it may not be unfair to say that the secondary school is not too bad for the upper one-half of the population in general verbal ability. If one wanted to, he probably could make a pretty fair case for the fact that the secondary school as we know it was designed essentially for the top 10 or 20 per cent of the school-age population, but it is probably not satisfactory for the whole top half. To put another 25 per cent of the school-age population through this school in addition to the 50 per cent now going there will probably put great strain on the school itself and will almost certainly be highly unsatisfactory to the students.

Two problems have to be faced by society. First, whether it is wise to try to get another 25 per cent of the young people through high school. And second, what would be the devices that would have to be adopted in order to accomplish this end and what resources would have to be devoted to the effort.

What Would It Cost to Expand the Secondary School?

The annual expenditure for secondary education in the United States is something of the order of $1.8 billion. Slightly more than half of the enrolled students now graduate from secondary schools. One might be tempted to say that if it costs $1.8 billion to graduate half of the students, it would take twice that, or $3.6 billion, to graduate all of them. Fortunately, such is not the situation.

It is true that only about one-half of the 17-year-olds are in school. On the other hand, probably more than 90 per cent of the 14-year-olds are already in school. Consequently it would take very small additional expenditures to take care of the other 14-year-olds who are not now in school. An expenditure of $50,000,000 might very well take care of this. Much the same situation is true of the 15-year-olds. Over 90 per cent are already in school. An additional expenditure of $75,000,000 would take care of the 15-year-olds who are not now in school. The added expenditure for the 16- and 17-year-olds would be much heavier because a smaller percentage are in school. It would probably take $150,000,000 to take care of the 16-year-olds, and probably $200,000,000 to take care of the 17-year-olds who are not now in school.

It would probably take about $500,000,000 additional money spent on the secondary schools to operate the schools for all the additional secondary students. This assumes that the schools will be of the same general character as the present schools. It is more than doubtful if all the 16- and 17-year-olds could be forced to attend the present type of school without extreme difficulty. Substantial changes would probably have to be made in the operation of the schools, and many of the changes would be more expensive than the present type of schooling. It is probably reasonable to assume that expansion of the secondary schools to include essentially all the young people in the country would cost perhaps $750,000,000 a year. This would include some of the necessary changes that would have to be made in the schools. What are the advantages and disadvantages of recommending such a procedure?

What Facilities Are Needed for the Additional Students?

The number of children born each year is now about four million. The present school population is based upon a number of births well under three million per year. This means that over a period of years there will be ten or twelve million more children in school than there have been. This in turn will necessitate the building of at least 50,000 classrooms each year for a good many years. These 50,000 classrooms could well cost over a billion dollars at present prices. This amount of expansion of the school has to take place just to keep up with the growth of the population. Any extension of the amount of education will require further expansion of the school plant. The buildings can be provided if the American people want them.

It is going to be much more difficult to obtain the additional teachers than it is to build the extra classrooms. About 30,000 new teachers will be needed every year just to take care of the growth in population. This is in addition to the 125,000 new teachers that will be needed for normal replacements each year. It is already extremely difficult to get an adequate number of teachers. It will become much more so as far as greater numbers of teachers are needed. If the effort is made to add several million more students to the secondary school, the problem of obtaining an adequate number of teachers is going to be further complicated.

We now have about a million and a quarter teachers. By the time the schools have felt the full force of the expansion in population probably a million and three-quarters teachers will be needed. Possibly another 100,000 teachers would be needed if all the children who are now leaving secondary school without completing their courses were retained until the end of high school. The additional teachers can be obtained, but it will probably require very different approaches from any that have been used up to the present time.

Certainly there should be a fundamental series of investigations carried on to see if it is possible to organize education in such a way that fewer teachers can do the job more effectively.

How Much Education Should Be Provided?

We now have some idea of the size of the problem. What should we do about it?

There are many bases on which one could try to determine the extent to which elementary and secondary education should be provided. One of the simplest questions that might be asked is how much education will pay the community economically. This may not be the most important question to ask, but it is one that should have some effect on the answer any community gives to the question of how much schooling should be provided. There is little doubt that the general level of education desirable is partly a result and partly a cause of the level of economic welfare of the country.

It would be absurd for India or Egypt to attempt to provide twelve years of education for everybody. In fact it is extremely doubtful whether they should attempt to provide even one year of formal schooling for everybody at this stage in their economic development. They probably would be better off if they continued the education of a sizable number of persons far enough to be effective rather than spread their resources over the entire population. Some inexpensive mass education might be provided for everyone. Formal schools, with all children in classrooms—probably no. This is the situation at the extreme low end of the economic scale. Our country is at the upper end of the economic scale. There are strong reasons to believe that we shall be economically better off if we can devise a broad educational system that will provide nearly everybody with some rough equivalent of twelve years of schooling.

If one could determine on economic grounds the amount of education to provide, this would give only part of the answer. It so happens that the best evidence that we have indicates that an economic answer would indicate an amount of education substantially above the amount now provided in the United States. This amount of education is almost certainly a function of the complexity of the economy. If the economy becomes more complicated, the total amount of education provided will probably have to increase. Of course it does not follow that this has to be full-time formal schooling.

As a matter of fact, with the working week getting shorter and shorter, there are many reasons to think that much of education could go on easily after regular work experience has started. A great many adolescents are bothered about what to do with their leisure even after they have a full-time job. There probably would be no loss to society, and might be a very great gain, if additional education held a high priority in the minds of these individuals.

There is an additional basis, however, on which education can be purchased. A country where the national income is over three hundred billion dollars has an enormous amount of leeway in what goods and services it is going to purchase. The necessary minimum of food, clothing, and housing will take a relatively small amount of this total. Certainly a very large fraction of the total expenditure of the American people would have to be put under the heading of nonessential expenditures. At least they are not essential for the sheer physical existence of the people. This would indicate that the value system of the people would determine whether an additional billion or two billion or even a larger amount should go into education.

Clearly certain kinds and certain amounts of education could and should be bought the same way and for the same reason that the public buys grand opera or a symphony concert. There is no thought that either the opera or the symphony will affect the economic life of the country appreciably. It might even be doubtful whether they will have any profound effect upon the quantity of music the American people hear. They might have a very great effect upon the quality of music and possibly even the quality of life.

The American people can well afford to pay for a very great amount of opera and symphony music if they want it. The American people can well afford to buy very large amounts of education for exactly the same reason, simply because they want education and because they believe it will make for a better life. It could be bought as any other consumer item would be bought, simply because people want it. Obviously there is no very accurate way to estimate the amount of education of this kind that people should or will buy. Education up to about the end of junior college seems to be indicated on purely economic grounds for very large numbers. Millions of people would pay for education beyond this point simply because it is one of the things which they want and for which they are able to pay. The quantity of education that should be provided raises difficult questions, but the quality of education to be provided raises even more difficult questions.

WHAT QUALITY OF EDUCATION SHOULD BE PROVIDED?

Probably most teachers wish the human race were much smarter than it is. The chronic complaint of almost all teachers has always been that their students are not able enough. Probably even more strongly held is the wish that the variability of students were much less than it is. If all the students were as smart as the ablest ones, most educators would be much happier. At least this is what they say. First, then, the human race is much too stupid, and second, the human race has far too much variability to suit most teachers. For good or ill, however, the wishes of school teachers and administrators will not change either of these basic conditions. The schools are going to have to take the human race pretty much as it is and do what they can with it.

Historically, of course, the teacher has dealt with the problem by setting an arbitrary standard and simply failing the student who did not measure up to this. Many school systems in the world today are organized along this line. France is an outstanding example. A very large fraction of all the students in the French schools are failed at the end of the elementary school. Most of the remainder are failed at the end of the secondary school, and only a relatively small number move on to the university. There is no question but that this is a much more comfortable procedure for the teachers than any possible alternatives.

Europe historically has followed this policy of rigid selection and consequently high rates of failure. The United States and, to a somewhat lesser extent, Canada have adopted a policy of moving very large numbers of people on through the elementary and secondary schools. If almost all are to be moved to the secondary school, the failure rate obviously must be extremely low. Clearly the standard for the average student cannot be as high if 80 per cent of all students go through the secondary school as it can if only the ablest 5 per cent go on through secondary school.

In spite of the fact that most teachers today, as well as most of the past record of education, favor a policy of high failure, forces are at work to bring about changes in this situation in all countries. Explosive developments are taking place even in France. The man in the street is beginning to insist that his son or daughter be allowed to stay in school. The same movement seems to be at work over the entire world. The ordinary person is insisting on the right to education for his children. The educational authorities in all the countries of the world will probably have to make their peace within the present century with these new forces.

The first reaction to a great increase in numbers is almost always to force all the people to take the same work that was formerly required of the few. Although an effort is made to uphold the old standards, they slowly drop unless very great caution is used. There is little doubt that the top 5 per cent of the people today have had far better education than did the top 5 per cent of fifty or a hundred years ago. To expect 75 per cent of the people even to study the same material that 5 per cent would study is probably unreasonable. To expect them to approach the same standard of accomplishment is to expect the impossible.

What will be needed if 75 per cent of the people are going through the secondary school will be a great spread in the width of the material offered in the school. Definite steps will have to be taken to see that standards appropriate to the various abilities of individuals are set up. People who have extremely good verbal ability should be given the chance to demonstrate this ability. People with extraordinary mechanical ability should have just as much right to demonstrate their ability. There are many types of ability in the world, and the school that attempts to deal with the entire population will have to adjust its program to a great range of abilities in a great many different fields.

In the effort to accommodate all, standards for the able must not be lowered. Extraordinary efforts must be made to see that the top 5 per cent in ability are offered the opportunity to work to their capacity. To do less is to invite disaster to the nation.

IMPROVEMENTS IN PAYING FOR EDUCATION

Probably great improvements could be made in the process of buying and paying for more education and a higher quality of education. It is already easier in this country than in any other country in the world for a person to continue his education beyond the high school. But doubtless further great improvements could be made in the process of financing this education. Certainly most careful attention should be given to problems involved in enabling an individual to obtain education above the high school level and pay for it at a later time. There may be objections to installment selling of many commodities; education, however, would seem to be one thing that should be available on the installment basis if one wants to pay for it that way. It should be possible to get the education and then pay for it over a very extensive period of time.

In those fields and in those cases where it is a reasonable assumption that earning power will be increased, the period of payment might be extended over a very long period. If the education is purely a consumption expenditure, the period of repayment probably should be much shorter. Even in this case, however, the period of repayment could well be some years, rather than months. Experiments along this line would have to be developed to test the best procedures. But if installment buying has worked on everything from television sets to automobiles and houses, there is every reason to assume that valid methods can be worked out to help pay for certain advanced and specialized education.

There are two guiding principles to keep in mind. One is to make education more widely available to those who want it regardless of whether they happen to have the amount of money to pay for it at the time. The second thing would be to encourage society to keep as accurate estimates as are feasible on cost and benefits that would come from an expanded education. Society should undoubtedly pay much of the cost of higher education. On the other hand, there is everything to be gained by elaborate processes of making it possible for any individual to pay for his own education when he wants to do so. No artificial barrier should be raised against this, and every mechanical process and facility should be developed to encourage it.

NEED FOR GREATER FLEXIBILITY AND VARIETY

A century of experimenting has pretty well demonstrated the fact that a very broad and flexible program of education is necessary if a large fraction of the population is to be served. The type of school we inherited from Western Europe was probably designed for about 5 per cent of the population. It was recognized that more than this percentage probably could succeed in the program; but the occupational outlets of the school were so limited that only a very small fraction of the population was interested in attending school.

Up until about 1800, there was no very great demand for schooling except in an extremely limited number of occupations. The census of 1790 indicates that probably close to 90 per cent of the population were engaged in agriculture or closely related occupations. Most of the farmers probably cared very little whether they had much schooling or not. When one considers the way agriculture was organized, it probably made little difference whether one went to school or not. Most of what one needed to know on the farm could be learned from other members of the family and the neighbors. For a long time changes were sufficiently slow that this process of learning would work reasonably well. These conditions have changed and brought about changes in education, but more adequate adjustments to present reality are indicated.

A school program based largely upon foreign languages and mathematics probably would work reasonably well for 5 per cent of the population. Such a program probably will not work at all when you try to put 90 per cent of the population in school. One of the most difficult intellectual efforts of the last century has been the attempt to expand the curriculum of the elementary and secondary school. We are still far from any agreement as to how to do this or even what should be done. It is reasonably clear to most people that there must be a great variety of materials in the school, and these materials must be available at a great many different levels of difficulty if all the people are going to stay in school. We probably have a fairly passable curriculum for the top half of the population as measured by verbal ability. It is extremely doubtful if the typical high school program is very meaningful to a large fraction of the bottom half of the population as measured by verbal ability.

Some of the vocational schools were originally designed to deal in part with this issue. The teachers in the vocational schools wanted to be intellectually respectable, and many of them quickly raised their standards as high as those of the academic schools. Some trades and technical occupations need people of very high ability. However, somebody has to educate the bottom half and even the bottom quarter if they are going to stay in school at all. There probably needs to be a great deal more experimenting with all kinds of work programs particularly for the bottom part of the population.

Flexibility in Financial Support

If you have only a small school system for a small part of the population, its program probably could be fairly uniform in content. If only the top 5 per cent of the population in verbal ability is educated, a program built largely around language and mathematics could be used. A fairly uniform method of support of this small number of schools could also be used. However, if the schools are to approach universality, there will doubtless have to be very great flexibility even in the method of financial support of the schools. At this point a suggestion is bound to arise that may seem somewhat extreme to many people. Legally, education is a function of the states in this country. For this reason, why not have a good strong state minimum of education provided in large part from state tax sources?

In the United States the local school district is still the major source of support in most communities. Why not have a second level of support provided by the city or the school district? Both of these suggestions are customary and normal. But the third suggestion is unusual: to set up a local school district around every school building. This local school district would have a local board of education. This local board of education would have taxing power. The purpose of these one-school school boards would be to encourage the growth of a real community spirit around each school. The richer school communities could try all kinds of financial support for their schools. The lower-income communities would have a state minimum and a city minimum, and the people could do all kinds of additional things for the schools. The people around a school could provide all kinds of services for the school if they would organize to do so.

We need to get free of the idea that the only way to improve a school is to get more money from the state and Federal governments. We need flexibility in the methods that are tried. The taxes that can be raised at the state and city levels will be limited. I would have a very high limit or possibly no limit at all upon the taxes that the people in a local school district could levy upon themselves for school purposes. The purpose of this third level of support is to try to get back into each local area a great feeling of responsibility for its own school.

The results that should flow from this local responsibility should be good. There should be an enormous amount of experimentation. Schools would be trying to provide improvements of all kinds. They would have the power to make these improvements. Many of the school districts would have the financial resources to experiment in any way they wanted to. One of the great dangers of any large school system that tries to deal with all the people is that it will descend to a low average of mediocrity. If the responsibility and power were put back on each local school, great variation could develop, and as a result of experimentation rapid progress should take place. In addition communities should be able to make many adjustments to their needs that could not possibly be made by a state or even on a city-wide basis in large cities.

Flexibility in Attendance

The American public decided it was good for young people to attend school; so they passed laws compelling attendance until young people were twelve, then thirteen, then fourteen, then fifteen, and finally sixteen. In a few states compulsory attendance laws require young people to go on to school until they are seventeen, and in a very few states until they are eighteen. The intention here is undoubtedly good. On the average, it probably is wise for young people to be required to get a substantial amount of schooling. Serious questions could be raised, however, as to whether full time attendance until the eighteenth year of all young people in the present type of school is wise.

Again, here is a very specific suggestion for dealing with this matter. The present attendance laws seem to be simply the result of desperation plus good intention. They also represent in part a blind and uncritical faith in education, faith that just any kind of education is necessarily good for any person. In the early stages of the effort to develop compulsory education, this attitude may have been defensible. But surely at this late date it is no longer necessary to argue that school, though advantageous in general, is not as valuable as it might be for many people in many situations.

Its very lack of flexibility is one reason why education is no more profitable than it is to many people. The compulsory laws might very well be changed in one important respect. The educational authorities should be given a great deal of flexibility in determining when a student will be better off in school and when he would be better off working. Educational authorities should have the power to make this decision on educational grounds.

The attendance laws should be changed, then, in one important regard. Now the attendance law says that a young person shall attend school in a particular state until he is eighteen years of age. Under the new provision, the law would say he must attend school for, shall we say, 2400 days or the equivalent of 12 years of 200 days a year. But this attendance does not have to be completed by the time he is eighteen years of age. If the student is sixteen or seventeen and the educational authorities decide that he is not interested in school and wants to go to work, they may very well let him work for six months or even a year. The student may then decide to go back to school.

In any case, we will assume that the student has 400 to 600 days of uncompleted schooling that he must complete by the time he is twenty-five years of age. He could go back to full-time school, or the schooling could be worked out on a part-time or evening basis. The advantages of this procedure should be many and varied. Many students after a few months of work experience might very well see the great advantage of further education and really apply themselves to their studies when they return to school. Others might very well decide that working and going to school on a part-time basis meet their needs better than full-time school.

A realistic study of the situation in any typical large city today will show thousands of boys and girls forced to stay in school who do not want to be in any school that at all resembles the present ones. Many of these students, if they went to work, would find that further study would be a great advantage in their work. Many others would find out that there were problems involved in their own living with which the school could help. Some would want to know more about home and family life. Some would want to study the problems of buying a house. Some would want help on problems involved in the wise use of their leisure time.

The young person who goes to work for a forty-hour week has lots of time to do something else. Some additional schooling even on a compulsory basis might well be an advantage to many of these students. There would be nothing in the law to compel any student to stop his full-time schooling before he wanted to. On the other hand, the educational authorities would have the freedom to act if the student, the parents, and the educational authorities thought that some work experience would be advisable at an earlier age. The question involved is whether the school authorities should not be given much greater flexibility in trying to deal with the education of the entire population.

An attendance law that is not too bad when it tries to compel a small fraction of the population to attend school for a short period can create real problems when it tries to compel all people to attend school for a long time. This is particularly true if the conception of school has not expanded as much as the expansion in the numbers being forced to go to school.

Varieties of Education Needed

No country has really faced the implications of having all the people in school for ten or twelve years. There are some important changes that probably should be considered because of the effort to educate all the people. Undoubtedly, only a small fraction of the population likes to read. We know now that essentially everyone can be taught the mechanics of reading, but this is very different from saying they are going to use their reading skill to any appreciable degree after they leave school.

We have study after study that shows a relatively small amount of reading for most people after they pass the school age. With further improvements, probably some substantial expansion could be made in the number who will read after leaving school. In the light of the best information available today, however, it seems extremely unlikely that any changes could be made in education that would lead sizable numbers of those who are least able to learn to read to do much reading. In fact the evidence would indicate that large numbers in the more able half of the population are not going to do much reading. Seemingly, much of the reading that is done is pretty largely confined to newspapers, popular magazines, and comics.

According to recently released figures on consumer expenditures in the United States, the American public spends more on one little branch of toys than it does for all kinds of books. Wheeled toys account for a higher expenditure than all books put together—including detective stories, paper-bound books, the classics, research volumes, and all others. The expenditures on television are many, many times what the expenditures on books are. The number of hours spent by the average family looking at television is many times greater than the amount spent in reading. Schooling over a very long period might be able to affect those relations slightly and increase the amount of reading and probably even the amount of good reading.

On the other hand it is pretty clear that any school system that expects to be realistic for the entire population should deal not only with reading as a method of learning, but also with such things as television, radio, and the motion picture. For millions of people it is a perfectly safe guess to say that they will learn far more from television, for good or for ill, than they will from all the reading they will ever do. As long as education was confined to the top half of the population, it probably could be confined largely to reading and what was learned by reading.

If we are going to expand schooling to include the entire population, it is only the most elementary wisdom to begin work systematically to see what can be learned from these so-called mass media. Almost certainly at some place in the school systems considerable attention should be given to the problem of what can be learned from television, and how to learn from it, and particularly what can be done to improve it. Presumably a school for all the people should deal with the tools of learning that are going to be used by the entire population. Any answer we give regarding the number of people who go to school will inevitably be tied in part to the answer we give to such questions as those just raised above.

Learnings from Work Experience

Historically what has been called schooling in the Western world has pretty largely centered around learning something out of a book. That is a very important way for many people to learn some things. However, a fairly good case could be made for the fact that a very large fraction of what the human race knows has been learned from its combined experience with work. Much of our basic knowledge regarding housing, agriculture, pottery, weaving of cloth, and many other things has been developed quite largely out of working experience. Through very long periods of the world's history, and for a very large number of people, work has been one of the most educative of all experiences. A half century ago it became fashionable to speak of work as though most of it was highly repetitive industrial factory experience which had little possibility for education.

As a matter of fact, a rather small fraction of industry is repetitive factory experience. Only twelve or fifteen million people are engaged in manufacturing. A very large number of those are engaged in planning, supervision, and engineering work of all kinds. A fairly careful estimate would probably indicate that not more than five million people are engaged in repetitive occupations in manufacturing. Many of these jobs will succumb to the semiautomatic and automatic machine in the generation ahead of us. Much of the working life of America on the farms and in stores, offices, and factories could be made highly educative for many workers if proper attention were given to the task. American economic life will probably continue to become very much more efficient in the decades ahead. Some people raise the question what will be done with the time of the released workers. One of the things that should be done is to see that within practical limits working experience is made as educative as it can reasonably be made.

The evidence is overwhelming that normal people do not desire inactivity. Even extremely wealthy people prefer to do something rather than to remain idle. Professor L. P. Jacks, the principal of one of the famous colleges in Oxford University, stated a good many years ago: "The only reason a wise man can give for preferring leisure to work is that leisure provides the opportunity for better work." What Professor Jacks was saying was that the quality of the work was the important thing and that if this high quality was obtained in leisure time, that was fine. But if the high quality of work was obtained during what was called working time, then one would prefer his work to his leisure. There is little doubt that much of the work of the world can be made highly educative.

In all probability there are large numbers of young people in the United States who might well learn more from six months or a year of work experience properly planned than they would from equivalent time in what we historically have called the school. We need to explore very carefully the educational possibilities of work experience for millions of young people in the United States today. The educational authorities need to have freedom to decide when a student could probably learn more from a certain kind of work and when he would probably learn more from a certain variety of schooling. On the more general level, one of the greatest challenges to the American economy in the period ahead will be to improve the quality of work experience for as many people as possible.

CONCLUSION

In conclusion, it seems reasonable to assume that for most people "man's right to knowledge and the free use thereof" will depend in no small degree upon the wisdom with which the following questions we are discussing today are solved:

1. What would be the gains and losses in having a school board for each school building, with power to levy taxes? Would this provide flexibility in school support?

2. What are the advantages and disadvantages of abolishing the present compulsory attendance laws and substituting a law that will state the number of days a person must attend school by the time he is twenty-five? The law would give the educational authorities freedom to say when a young person may work. In other words the compulsory attendance law would be expressed in total number of days one must attend school and not in terms of sixteen, seventeen, or eighteen years of age. Would this give flexibility to the educational authorities for dealing with young people who might profit from some work experience fairly early in life?

3. It will cost close to a billion dollars and require drastic changes in the very conception of education in order to graduate from high school the forty per cent of the students who now leave school. How great an effort should society make to achieve the result of enabling essentially all of the appropriate age group to graduate from high school?

4. Are the advantages so large that society should be encouraged to expand greatly the quantity and quality of education as a consumption expenditure, on the ground that it would improve the quality of life?

Expenditure Level and the Quality of Public Education: A Symposium

INTRODUCTION

Paul R. Mort
Professor of Education
Teachers College, Columbia University

In the Institute of Administrative Research of Teachers College we have devoted more than a decade of study to many scores of factors that have been suggested as possible conditioners of educational quality. Originally, when this study got under way a number of years ago, there may have been high hopes of finding individual factors which would go a long way in explaining quality. In earlier studies the expenditure level had always proved to be that one of the known factors affecting school quality that was most closely related to the ability of communities to adapt to changing needs. But since in itself it would only explain little more than a third of the variation in quality among school systems, there was a hope that some more efficient factor could be found. However, after the extended search referred to above, the expenditure level still stands at the top of the list.

It seems now, as present researches mature, that an important theory emerges. This theory is that there is no single simple facet of the educational setting the manipulation of which alone will influence quality. Rather, in influencing school quality we must understand how groups of interlocking facets of the environment work together.

The plans for the development of the discussions reported here were in accordance with this theory. The problem was not to discuss back and forth the studies of the relationship of expenditure level to quality, but rather to search for new insights into the complex of factors in which the expenditure level is immersed, giving consideration to expenditure level both as an indicator of the priorities placed on education by a community and as a material means for purchasing education.

In preparation for the discussions on this subject, papers were submitted

46

by ten participants. These papers are reproduced below. Taken together, they constitute the basis for the following conclusions:

1. Education is moving into a new era in which the vast and various forces affecting it will become better coordinated. Education will cost more; and in spite of the increased cost the American people will be inclined to make the needed additional investment.

2. While the level of financial support is but one of a multitude of factors that interlock in a complex manner to determine the quality of education, the evidence supports the position that it can remain one of the three or four key centers of concern in shaping fiscal policy.

3. The community is expecting the school to assume responsibility for an ever-widening range of educational activities designed to develop capable, well-adjusted, and responsible citizens. While the schools should attempt to operate only in those areas in which they are technically competent, to meet even these responsibilities additional resources are required, i.e., resources which the community itself offers, personnel, and physical facilities.

4. Obviously not all schools meet the best modern educational standards. Weaknesses, wherever they exist, should be recognized and positive steps taken to eliminate them. In pursuing this objective teachers, administrators, and lay citizens must have a more thorough understanding of new techniques and insights—i.e., self-understanding, group dynamics, audiovisual aids, etc.

5. The modern school requires a new kind of leadership. Since the school program has been extended to involve lay participation, administrative leadership must recognize and work cooperatively with individuals and groups within the community.

6. In view of the nature of our national economy, public-school finance is not purely a local responsibility. However, fiscal policy should be based upon the assumption that local finance is basic and that necessary supplementing from state or Federal government will be done in such manner and will be accompanied by such ancillary provisions as will promote the vigorous use of local tax resources for the achievement of goals developed or wholeheartedly embraced by the communities.

7. State and Federal aid to assist communities and states now economically weak would seem to be inescapable.

Such aid should, however, be supplemented by major assistance to these weaker communities and states, looking toward the utilization of the schools and other agencies in the correction of these economic weaknesses. Sizable additional aid to all communities may be used as a potential means of helping each community to tap a wider tax base than the local system permits. Both of these types of central support have their origins in economic facts.

Beyond these two types of aid there is always the opportunity, one which perhaps should be given more sympathetic consideration, of using state moneys or Federal moneys in whatever amount is necessary to assure in every community the strengthening of the educational program in those aspects in which such strengthening is accepted as a national need. Examples might be a completely Federally supported adequate educational program in science and mathematics, and a complete adequate program for strengthening the American people in the communication arts. For such a purpose complete support might possibly be chosen as a means of making the program quickly available in all communities without risking the danger of warping the remainder of the educational program. An outstanding example of such use was associated with the program for the dissemination of agricultural knowledge projected throughout this country following the first decade of this century.

8. There is need for the schools to square up to the problem of evaluation. School systems should be able to provide tangible evidence of how and to what extent they are achieving concrete educational objectives, i.e., evidence regarding progress in the three Rs, etc.

9. However important it may be for us to maintain educational government as a unique form of government, this should not lead us to continue the practice of largely ignoring the need for assessing the effects of the over-all program of federal assistance to states and communities and the over-all program of state assistance to municipalities as well as school governments. We can be reasonably certain that in the immediate future those concerned with general governmental aid and with municipal aid will not appreciate fully the specialized problems of educational government. Under these circumstances it is necessary for the educational profession to broaden its view and achieve a sympathetic understanding of the trend in Federal aid to state governments and state aid to municipal governments.

10. There is a crying need for a far greater emphasis on basic and developmental research dealing with the content and results of public education and with the problems associated with its government and management.

EDUCATION AS A SOURCE OF NATIONAL WELL-BEING

Beardsley Ruml

Through growth and experience the human being becomes what he becomes. It is the task of education purposefully to see to it that this becoming yields a healthy, sane adult, able if he so wills to attain in large measure in actuality what he is capable of potentially. The means of education may be formal or informal, public or private, group or personal. More than one means and more than one method are generally suitable to the reaching of any particular objective.

For the individual to attain to even the least adequate degree the social, political, aesthetic, personal, and religious maturity in which he may actualize his potentialities, he must achieve minimum competence in certain *basics* which will be for him the tools and substance of his intuitions and of his will. These basics must be provided to a minimum degree for all, and opportunity for advancing well beyond the minimum must be easily available to all. Like other parts of education, the basics will be provided partly in the school, partly outside the school, partly formally, partly informally. But the supervision to make certain that the basics are provided is an essential duty of a democratic state.

Of the basics in education the most important are skill in communication and skill in computation. These skills underlie all else in a free society. We have taken them too much for granted. The interest of statesmen two centuries ago was to make sure that through education the voting citizen would have the ability to communicate and to compute. The deeper insights were left to religion and to the arts.

Have we today become so engrossed with the problems of our culture that we have not made sure that the citizen-about-to-be can read, can write, can listen, and can make the computations relevant to his personal and public interests?

DESIGNS EMERGING FROM A HALF CENTURY OF FERMENT

Howard V. Funk

Superintendent of Schools, Bronxville, New York

It is characteristic of our society to be constantly probing for more knowledge and understanding. This proclivity extends to education. Therefore, extensive research and experimentation have given better understanding of child growth and development and of the nature of the learning process. Consequently, education is in a state of flux which may be noted under a number of heads.

CHANGES IN SOCIAL AND ECONOMIC ENVIRONMENT

1. There is an increasing percentage of children in the population of the United States.

2. Greater numbers stay in school more years (more pupils thus completing both public school and college).

3. Society is able to sustain greater numbers in school.

4. The complexity of industrial society is constantly increasing.

5. Mobility of population has increased, making it essential that schools in every part of the country be up to at least minimum standards.

6. The rural population is decreasing and the suburban population increasing, particularly around metropolitan areas.

CHANGES DUE TO RESEARCH AND EXPERIMENTATION

1. More attention is being given to individual differences; there is an increased "appreciation of the whole child" and more tailoring of programs to fit individual needs.

2. Attempts are now made to provide for physical, intellectual, emotional, social, and spiritual growth for all children.

3. Strict adherence to a textbook is decreasing, and memorizing exercises purely for the sake of training memory are out.

4. There has been an enormous expansion of the curriculum growing out of understanding of individuals and their different potentials, in such subjects as art, music, shop, vocation, and languages.

5. Many special services have been provided to improve or foster individual well-being, such as health, physical education, mental health, and remedial reading.

6. Stress is now on learning by doing; on positivity versus directed activity.

7. Society now recognizes the public school as a potent factor in the solution of many of its problems: for example, mandated courses of various kinds, driver training, citizenship.

8. There is a new flexibility of program so far as both special fields and the daily time program are concerned.

9. There has been a tremendous growth in the kind of equipment and materials available. Contemplate, for example, educational materials shown at the A.A.S.A.

RECOGNITION THAT EDUCATION OCCURS IN ALL PHASES OF LIFE

It seems that we ought to try to assign commonly understood terms which will distinguish between total learning and that part which comes from the school—perhaps *education* and *schooling*. The recognition that education occurs in all phases of life gives rise to the following:

1. Concern with community factors and community betterment in order to induce better learnings for children.

2. Adult education courses and study groups of all kinds to help people understand their environment and adjust better to it.

3. Close liaison between home and school because it is recognized that each is contributing extensively to individual growth and learning.

RESULTS WITHIN THE SCHOOL

All of this has resulted in a need for school personnel trained in new ways.

1. There is need of teachers who are skilled in interpreting behavior, sensitive to individuals, willing to create specific programs for individuals, able to guide group processes, and knowledgeable in the ways by which children learn.

2. In administration, communities are calling upon the superintendents to be directors of education instead of simply directors of schools.

3. Administration is needed which exemplifies with the staff the best that is known about the learning situation with children. In other words, authori-

tarian administration cannot help teachers to produce the democratic understandings which are now expected to come out of all our class groups.

THE PLACE OF THE HUMANITIES IN PUBLIC EDUCATION

Thomas J. Pullen, Jr.

State Superintendent of Schools, Maryland

There is nothing wrong with the humanities that a little common sense would not cure. There is nothing wrong with the liberal arts; the trouble lies with some who think mistakenly that they are liberally educated.

Man just beginning to come out of the Dark Ages suddenly discovered man as an entity, as a single and separate integrity. About the same time he was startled with the written word; a little later, with the printed word. A whole treatise could be written upon the manner by which European man discovered himself after centuries of semipaganism; suffice it to say that he did. He did not understand this new concept; so naturally he looked for the answer in something else which he did not understand, but which, according to the half-literate esoterics of that day, offered a ready and plausible answer. And so the humanities were born or rather revived. They were simply the writings of the Greeks and the Romans, people whose culture exceeded that of the semibarbarians of Middle and Western Europe.

Supposedly the humanities are the "branches of learning concerned with man." It is easy to understand why man of medieval Europe would think that the answer to the riddle of mankind would be found with literature of the Greek and Roman writers. In the first place, it was about all the literature available, and of course only a limited few could read it. The child mind, regardless of the age in which it exists, is ever ready to worship the unknown and to look for and accept an authoritarian answer. Here was an authoritarian answer; it was supported by the half-literates of the day.

Medieval man accepted this intellectual dogma, and ever since servile minds by the millions have paid the same obeisance to something that they do not understand. It is futile for a free mind to say that the best study of man is man; the cult of the literate but not intelligent still say that the best study of man is the study of Aristotle and Plato, even if they do not quite understand them! Furthermore man, still being a vain creature even with the trappings upon him of an extensive literacy, gets an enormous satisfaction and even prestige among those of like mind who are able to repeat the dicta of those who are considered authorities in some discipline. In brief, instead of being truly educated individuals, they are but intellectual parrots, and would be scorned by the very authorities they quote so glibly.

The so-called humanities need rethinking. What are they? Are they, strictly speaking, only what the ancients have written or spoken? In the light of modern thinking these writings and sayings are only a part. Truly they are a part of the humanities because they are an expression of what the intelligent men of certain periods in history wrote or said; but they are not all. Thinking, observing, analyzing, and speculation did not stop with any period. For the dull and literal-minded, however, these writings and sayings fit into such a nice, easy pattern to learn and to mouth. Ergo, they are the epitome of intellectualism and education.

Then too the definition of what constitutes the truly educated man needs some rethinking. The educated man is not one who simply knows, but one who *is*. But what do we mean by *being* rather than knowing only?

In the first place, the educated man is humble. He has no pride in having "knowledge for knowledge's sake." Such an attitude is as immature intellectually as pride in the ownership of a trained flea! The truly educated knows that only the surface of knowledge has been scratched and all that he has is but an ephemeral and tentative thing; to think otherwise would be to admit tacitly that all thinking has been done and that all man has to do is to learn what others have thought. What sublime faith in the intellectual infallibility of our half-primitive ancestors; what little faith in man's improvability!

How often does the poet intuitively see and speak the truth!

> Knowledge is proud that he knows so much;
> Wisdom is humble that he knows no more.

Further, to what end does a man learn? First, to know and understand man better. Why? Because he lives in a world of man; the natural forces are quite secondary and their characteristics and controls can be understood easily by assiduous mediocrity. Parenthetically, it might be remarked that the greatest scientific discovery is the unexpected and not the planned, except of course in those cases in which enough unexpected discoveries have crystallized to the point of readiness for synthesis. Man, living in a world of men, must know and understand man. If the humanities are "the branches of learning concerned with man," the present concept of them and the truly educated man must be revised. No man is truly educated who does not understand man.

The humanities must be sufficiently comprehensive to include all the branches of learning that explain man as an animal, a being with a mentality, and a person with all sorts of forces playing upon him as an individual and as a member of a group. They must explain him and his actions in every period of history and in every habitat. Consequently anthropology, sociology, economics, psychology, political science and plain politics, biology, physiology, and possibly pathology, with some obeisance to psychosomatic influences, and other disciplines of comparatively modern origin are as essential in any modern program of the humanities as the opinions and plays of the ancients. The educative process lies not only in acquiring the knowledge of these and other branches of learning but also in perceiving and analyzing the elements that produce changes in man. This calls for speculative intelligence unrestricted by intellectual dogmas of the past; it is more difficult to perceive and understand a catalysis in human relationships than in a test tube.

To what end does man wish to know? Simply for what knowledge means and can do for him as an individual? Such a feeling is as base as the desire of the dumb animal for food and self-preservation. Man lives not only for himself but for others; his very intellectual life finds its being in the lives of others. Whether he wills it or not, his labors will benefit or injure others. The intelligent, educated man realizes this fact and he dedicates his talents to some worthy purpose. He realizes, too, that he is but the articulate exponent of ideas that simple but mute minds often perceive with clarity and endow with feeling. The truly educated man realizes that his education cannot separate him from his fellows; he "sees beyond the years."

On the contrary, the pseudoeducated man becomes a man apart; his so-called education becomes a barrier between him and his fellows. He has little or no interest in others, and he spends his time in his ivory tower thanking God that he is not as other men! How childish and how immature! Erasmus in his *Praise of Folly* treats such gentlemen with delicious satire. There is nothing more pathetic than a person educated beyond his intelligence (to quote Brander Matthews) and to no noble purpose. How immature it is for a so-called educated person in any profession to use subtle means for preferment and to prostitute himself and his profession for personal position. But the intellectually righteous are not so; they labor not for themselves alone, but for all those that seek learning.

> No man is an island;
> No man stands alone.

IDENTIFYING EFFECTIVE ADMINISTRATIVE PRACTICES
Paul R. Mort

Studies carried out in the Institute of Administrative Research of Teachers College over the past dozen years lead strongly to the conviction that achievement of an adequate educational program is an enterprise even more complex than most have supposed. It is a truism that the legal setting in which schools operate is of great importance. But since it is not the only element in the complex of factors, it tends, particularly in our time, to be subject to continued neglect. The economic and demographic character of the community appears to be of far greater importance than anyone has realized. There appears to be a general tendency to accept it as it is, rather than to analyze the influence of its various facets and look to the ways and means by which action today may influence the character of the setting for tomorrow. What is done in the day-to-day operation of the schools is of great importance, either in making the most of the potential of its setting or in interfering with it. In recent decades this area of day-to-day operation has received the lion's share of attention, as perhaps it should and must so long as it does not mean the exclusion of the other great groups of factors. But the evidence is strong that vastly important as the day-to-day operation is, it is by no means all-important, and that individual phases of such operations that we sometimes get greatly concerned with may be of relatively minor importance.

Accordingly there would seem to be a great need for sorting out the efficient operational elements from the inefficient ones and tagging each device with a power value. This problem of placing relative values holds, of course, for the elements of the social and economic setting and for the legal setting, so that the problem becomes one of broadening the realization of the scope of forces affecting the public schools, on the one hand, and of sorting out and evaluating these forces, on the other.

The work of the Institute of Administrative Research has developed a statistical mechanism that promises very considerable assistance both in the broadening of the field of consideration and in the sorting out of the elements according to their influence on education. Reference here is to the sequential simplex presented in my article in the January 1954 *Teachers College Record*.

This mechanism is built on a score or so of elements of the school and community environment which thus far have appeared to be the most effective of approximately three hundred factors in predicting school quality. The measures fall into four "families" of factors, each operating in a different degree of remoteness from the ongoing educational enterprise: (1) characteristics of the school, with emphasis on staff, (2) school-system policy, with emphasis on the budget, (3) community priorities for education as indicated by such measures as expenditure level for schools, and (4) the economic, social, and demographic character of the community. With such a group of status measures it is possible to identify the point of remoteness at which legal provisions, administrative policies, and operational acts get into the stream of influence. Once the "family" character of a provision, policy, or act is identified, it becomes possible to control a major part of the other factors which work along with it. The effect is to approximate a situation where other significant things are equal. The unique effect of the provision (policy, act) can thus be isolated. Also, it is theoretically possible to trace a force through its various manifestations as it moves from the community, step by step, to its effects in the school itself. For example, trace the unique effects of community wealth on school quality; of wealth on community school-support customs; of school-support customs on expenditure policy; of expenditure policy on staff quality; of staff quality on day-to-day school operation.

THE FISCAL STRUCTURE OF PUBLIC EDUCATION

Arvid J. Burke

Director of Studies, New York State Teachers Association

There is nothing magical about the level of school support at any particular time. All that money will do is enable schools, if they have competent management, to marshal personnel and materials. In a varying and fluctuating wage and price structure, the quantity and quality of services and goods that can be purchased for a given expenditure will differ in space and time.

Quality control in public education during the decade ahead will have to be achieved through operational audits, differentiating the quality of operations among teachers, schools, and school systems at a given time and within any particular classroom, school, or school system over a period of time. More attention will have to be directed to the quality of the results obtained and less to the quality of the means employed. This is most urgent since the pursuit of outcomes other than mastery of measurable skills and knowledge can prove to be extremely wasteful unless the results of such operations are known.

Starting from known qualitative differences in results, the search will then be directed to various factors, including money outlay, which can be manipulated to produce better results. Since the control of a single factor like money is not likely to bring about quality control in a complex operation like schooling, the search will be for combinations of factors which can be controlled to produce the results desired with the least outlay of services and materials. This is true economy.

The initial task in structuring is to make adequate provision for operational audits and research in quality control, to be undertaken cooperatively by the Federal and state educational agencies, private research agencies, and the operational units. The diversity of existing structural patterns and operational units found in the United States provides the best possible laboratory for discovering those combinations of structural elements which are conducive to obtaining given qualities in results, those which are detrimental to achieving given operational outcomes, and those which are neutral or not particularly crucial in operations. Through such research and experimentation should evolve the structural designs best suited to attain the outcomes for which the schools have assumed responsibility. It may also serve to define the kind of results for which the schools can assume responsibility with any chance of success at any given time.

In the meantime decisions will have to be made upon fiscal structure in terms of common sense, reason, intuition, and insight. First, perhaps, attention should be centered upon operations and the common-sense factors which affect their quality, such as carefully prepared and selected teachers. Next might come a performance budget for the operating unit representing the combined best judgment, sense of values, and insights of lay and professional leaders in the operating unit. Insofar as possible, provide a fiscal structure which will enable the operating unit to raise locally the money required to provide the kind of personnel and quantity and quality of materials required to perform the agreed-upon operations with the best possible results.

One of the reasons many operating units are not now performing up to their potentialities is the undue emphasis that has been placed upon relative local taxpaying ability in seeking aid from central governments. Too many localities get the idea that they are less able to support good schools than they really are. The true ability of most localities to support education is governed by willingness more than it is by economic resources. Even families with low incomes have a wide choice on how they will spend their money. The function of the budgetary process is to center attention upon the potentialities of education, the good that can come from the right kind of education, and the soundness of the budgetary program proposed, to the end that people will spend more of their money on better education and sacrifice somewhat of other satisfactions which are not so important to individual and community well-being. This process can be carried on best where operators of schools and payers of the bills are in close touch with each other, as they are in a community.

Performance of the kind here implied is not likely to take place in weak school districts. It is my hunch that more democracy, educational performance, and adaptability will come from enlarging school districts (not over-extending the area beyond what people regard as their community and not in excess of medium city size) and increasing their local taxing potential (property and nonproperty) than by allowing a weak local fiscal structure to persist, nursed along by central aids and hampered by limited property-taxing powers.

Central-government aid should be regarded as a necessary but not ideal part of the fiscal structure for education. Indeed the ideal fiscal policy of central governments would be one which, through increasing the productivity of people everywhere through the right kind of education, promoting fiscally strong local units, and encouraging improvements in the local budgetary process, school administration, and support of schools, would gradually eliminate the need for central assistance. All state policies and practices which run counter to this ideal should be re-examined. More important, the whole attitude of the education profession should be reconsidered. Too frequently the educational forces look upon central aid as the ideal and condone weak district structures, restrictive property-tax and debt limits, lack of nonproperty-taxing powers, central controls, and other restrictions on local operating units, because they force central governments to provide aid for schools.

This thesis presumes that states should gradually subordinate promotional aids, general aid, and corrupted equalization formulas to a policy of straight equalization aid tied to district reorganization, improvement in local management, and positive action to revive the local budgetary process, local taxation, and local initiative in educational affairs.

This will be a hard road to follow for those who want better education provided they can get someone else to pay the bill, or for those school officials who fear raising the educational standards of the community and telling the plain truth that those who want better education must be willing to pay for it.

THE MORE RAPID SPREAD OF AGREED-UPON IMPROVEMENTS

William S. Vincent

Executive Officer, Citizenship Education Project
Teachers College, Columbia University

Certainly one of the most disappointing features of education is the slowness with which new procedures spread throughout the various schools of the United States. I refer here of course to the well-documented thesis of the studies of the Institute for Administrative Research regarding the fifty-year lag between the development of an improved technique and its complete diffusion. This lag is by no means confined to education. We find it in other fields. Notable examples are the delay in the utilization of penicillin and in the use of the streamlining principle in the design of moving objects. However, though I know of no research on the matter, I would judge that the spread of new techniques in education is slower than that in most mature fields in our society today.

It would be my hypothesis that if diffusion in education is slower than present-day conditions would warrant, there are two primary factors underlying this circumstance. One is the fact that most school districts (up until the last ten or fifteen years at least) have tended to operate behind the walls of their own district lines—promotion from within, insufficient provision for planning with other school districts, lack of intervisitation among both teachers and administrators, and inadequate facilities for exchange of successful new practices.

The other factor relates to the fact that education, though one of our largest enterprises, is nevertheless a public enterprise in what is essentially a private-enterprise economy. Hence the motives which may keep an equally large number of small businesses on their toes do not operate in keeping individual school districts on their toes to make use of more efficient methods and more effective procedures.

About this latter factor, we can do nothing. About the former one, there are many possibilities. Already within the past ten or fifteen years newer types of cooperation promise improvement in the tempo of the spread of educational innovations. The Metropolitan School Study Council and the other councils throughout the country, the Associated Public School Systems, the National Citizens Commission for the Public Schools, the Cooperative Program in Educational Administration, and the Citizenship Education Project are all examples of wide-ranging cooperative undertakings whose primary purpose is to break down those unfortunate barriers that have more or less separated school systems and stimulate the interchange of information among school people. So great has been the success of the relatively few enterprises of this sort that the educational profession as a whole should now establish a policy of promoting and extending the growth of similar activities throughout the American school system.

Though the various cooperative undertakings mentioned above are similar in purpose, their methods of operation vary considerably. The method of the councils is policy conferences of administrative officers coupled with work and planning sessions by small groups of teachers and other school personnel chosen from a variety of school districts. The Associated Public School Systems relies more upon mass media coupled with stated meetings of school-system heads. The National Citizens Commission for the Public Schools relies upon stimulating lay cooperation on the well-justified grounds that public knowledge and interest in the schools will yield more adaptable schools. The emphasis of the Cooperative Program in Educational Administration is upon preservice and in-service preparation of professional personnel, coupled with interinstitutional and interschool policy, planning, and work sessions. The technique of the Citizenship Education Project relies upon well conceived and carefully developed planning tools for teachers and administrators, coupled with interschool planning sessions.

There may be a variety of other possible methods. They should be examined and tested. The methods that have been tested should be extended. The number of similar cooperative undertakings should be increased, so that no school system in the country should be unable to avail itself of the resources of one or more of these coordinating enterprises. Special financing may be required. But no other possibilities yet tried, so far as I am aware, show similar promise of reducing the fifty-year lag. On the basis of present experience, for example, it seems highly possible that the type of improvement in citizenship education spurred by the Citizenship Education Project will be fully diffused in twenty years rather than fifty.

Another facet of this problem of the more rapid spread of agreed-upon improvements relates to the slowness with which the results of research, both pure and applied, are funneled into the practical uses of schools. Though schools have made enormous strides in the past twenty-five years in the utilization in educational method of the results of psychological research, there is still an enormous gap between what the science of psychology has to tell us about the learning process and the practical use which schools have made of the scientific information provided. For example, one of the oldest subjects of investigation of modern psychology is individual differences, yet schools have not been able to design their procedures to take full account of such differences.

More research is needed. This is a truism that will remain with us until we know everything about human behavior and its causes. But even more than research right now, more pilot operations need to be developed in an attempt to implement the results of much scientific inquiry that have not yet been utilized. Compared with industry, the American public schools have developed nothing comparable to the pilot-plant operation that, coupled with emphasis upon applied research, has yielded such a high level of production in this country.

NEEDED CHANGES IN THE SELECTION AND DEVELOPMENT OF ADMINISTRATORS

Daniel R. Davies

Coordinator of the Cooperative Program in Educational Administration Teachers College, Columbia University

During the past century the administration of education and of educational institutions has been increasingly recognized as a differentiated function requiring special competencies and directed preparation. A little more than a hundred years ago the first local superintendency of schools was created; now that position is recognized and accepted widely in this country. A little more than fifty years ago the first serious attempt to provide professional preparation for school executives was made at Teachers College, Columbia University; now more than three hundred colleges and universities in this country offer such instruction. Few administrators at the public elementary and secondary levels enter their positions today without some kind of professional school preparation.

In this mid-century period, however, a wave of professional—or occupational—self-consciousness is sweeping over the ranks of school administrators in the United States. Spearheaded by a $3,500,000 grant from the W. K. Kellogg Foundation in 1950, current preparation programs have been under intense scrutiny for nearly four years. While the evidence is still accumulating, the following statements reflect much current opinion concerning future needs:

We need to develop and maintain an adequate supply of able persons wishing to become administrators

Present situation:

1. Almost no systematic recruiting efforts
2. Self-recruiting largely from ranks of education profession
3. Keen competition among all professions for top-quality manpower

Proposed:

1. A coordinated effort combining the resources of professional associations, professional schools, local school systems, school boards associations, and state education departments
2. Recognition of the important effect of high morale of teachers and administrators on recruitment

We need to know how to select candidates most likely to succeed in administration

Present situation:

1. Selection techniques which improve upon individual judgment are still experimental
2. Prevailing pattern for job placement is interview plus college and experience records

Proposed:

1. Selection should be the joint responsibility of the professional groups mentioned under the last heading.
2. Further experimentation to find tests useful in selection

We need to know how best to prepare candidates for entry into a given kind of administrative position for the first time

Present situation:

1. Wide variation in present practices ranging from no educational qualifications to two or more years of professional study
2. Wide variation in quality of professional schools
3. Recent job studies shedding light on needed basic professional preparation

Proposed:

1. *Two* postbaccalaureate years as minimum for certification, the *first year* to include subjects common to all administrative positions, and to terminate in a master's degree without certification; the *second year* to begin specialization, include internship, and to terminate in a degree or diploma
2. A *third year* optional but recommended for advanced specialization, to terminate in the Ed.D.

We need to learn how universities, state education departments, and the field can cooperate to use theory, research, and improved practice to enable both administrators and professors to improve their effectiveness

Present situation:

1. Rapidly changing conditions in society, in education, and in administration require the administrator and the professor to keep up to date
2. Most of the resources of professional schools have been concentrated on basic professional education
3. There is an oversupply of persons with a minimum preparation for administrative positions
4. Existing programs for continued professional development are spotty

Proposed:

1. State education departments should show effective leadership in promoting continued professional development

2. Support and resources should come from local school districts, professional associations, and school board associations

We need to strengthen and improve our professional schools

Present situation:

1. Wide variety in quality of existing schools
2. Little agreement on criteria for judging quality
3. Difficulty in building and maintaining high-quality service and personnel with low financial support
4. Inadequate support from professional associations
5. Inefficient utilization of professional schools

Proposed:

Strong professional schools as bulwark of a strong profession

NEEDED CHANGES IN THE RECRUITMENT AND TRAINING OF TEACHERS

Hollis L. Caswell

President
Teachers College, Columbia University

The problem of teacher recruitment in the years ahead has three main facets. First, there is the matter of quantity. Ways must be found to increase greatly the number of teachers available for American schools. Second, there is the matter of quality. Many able people now go into teaching; but in comparison with the number of leadership positions and the proportion of highly able people going into fields like medicine and law, teaching gets far too few of our top-level young people. Third, there is the matter of deliberate and early choice of teaching as a profession, so that sound, adequate preparation can be secured. At present all too many of those who enter teaching do so in a more or less offhand manner, often with the idea of remaining only a few years.

The outlook for solving the problem of teacher recruitment with any degree of success within the next five to ten years is not good. It will in fact require hard work to maintain a situation as good as at present, unsatisfactory as it is. The stakes for the nation are undoubtedly very great; for with sky-rocketing enrollments resulting in increased class size and double sessions, severe deterioration of the educational program is a very real possibility.

Strong action along two lines is needed to avert this outcome. First, teaching must be made sufficiently attractive, through increased social recognition and financial reward, to cause greatly increased numbers of young people to select it as a career. Second, educational institutions must formulate and put into action well-conceived, long-range programs of recruitment for teaching. Only through such positive steps can a real calamity for schools be averted in the near future and a course be laid that within the next quarter of a century may lead to real improvement in the teaching profession.

The program of teacher preparation in our country is widely diverse and complex. Institutions of many types share in the task. Not only the teachers colleges but the colleges of liberal arts and graduate schools now play an important role. The resources of all of these groups are needed in the sound preparation of a teacher. At the present time perhaps the greatest single barrier to fundamental improvement is lack of adequate cooperation among these groups. There are many aspects of the program in teacher preparation that can be improved. The promise of long-range improvement would be furthered more significantly by the establishment of stronger cooperation among those concerned with the general education of the teacher, those concerned with the professional preparation, and those concerned with subject specialization, than by any other single thing. Working in proper relationship, with sympathetic understanding and acceptance of a common goal, these groups could work out many of the problems of preparation erstwhile unsolved.

In brief, what is required for the years ahead is more teachers of higher ability who have chosen teaching as a profession deliberately and have received a course of preparation that draws the best from all groups that contribute to their preparation.

MOBILIZING THE PUBLIC TO ASSUME RESPONSIBILITY

Henry Toy, Jr.

Director
National Citizens Commission for the Public Schools

Our Commission has been deeply involved in this subject during the past five years, pushing toward its two goals: (1) to help Americans realize how important our public schools are to our expanding democracy, and (2) to arouse in each community the intelligence and will to improve our public schools.

To accomplish these objectives we have devoted much time to harnessing all the known means of mass communication to awaken the people of our country to the enormous problems facing public education, caused by years of neglect through periods of depression and war.

Because the present generation of parents and grandparents is so much better educated than were their predecessors in any other period in our history, not so much effort has had to be spent in selling the values of education. What the public did not know and has had to learn was the needs of our educational institutions.

It is significant that once aroused to the needs, the public has done its own mobilizing to assume responsibility. The Commission, believing this would be true, has further concentrated on informing an awakening public to their responsibilities. The statement by our chairman, Roy E. Larson, that "the problems of public education concern all of us, and it is time for all of us to do something about them," has been a watchword, and throughout thousands of communities citizens are mobilizing to assist the school authorities in helping to improve local school conditions.

Five years of studying and working with these citizens who have mobilized in behalf of public education have taught us that successful groups have these three common characteristics:

1. They are broadly representative of the entire community. They reflect as fully as possible all parts of it, all viewpoints, and all interests—economic, geographic, occupational, cultural, political, etc.—rather than any one.

2. They base all their recommendations upon a study of all available, relevant facts. They do not have an ax to grind.

3. They are independent in thought and action, but they always take steps to establish and maintain a cooperative working relationship with the legally established authorities.

One of the major defects of this mechanism is the defect of a great virtue—the virtue of a genuinely democratic institution requiring the active support and loyalty of a whole people. Let us on behalf of our schools and our country be thankful for a public that, spurred on by the inspiration of other successes, is mobilizing to work together for the public schools. By so doing, active citizens are raising the understanding and moral character of the adult level of our population as well as providing educational opportunity for our young people.

THE TASK AS MEASURED FROM THE CURRENT STATUS OF SCHOOL SUPPORT

Eugene S. Lawler

Professor of Education
Florida State University

There will be a continuing greater need of education in this country. Technology will require a rising level of literacy and competence. Civic problems to be faced will require all the competence and character than can be developed. One's personal life will require greater literacy and accomplishment. It will still be necessary to have a program to take care of young people until they are old enough to enter into productive pursuits, and the age for such entrance has been rising. If peace ever breaks out and our government ceases to spend such enormous sums for military purposes, it may be that the schools will be needed to take up part of the slack in demands for goods and services. It would be a wonderful thing if we could have even five per cent of what is being spent for defense. In a very short time beautiful school buildings would house the school children of the United States.

Another factor which will increase the size of the program we need is the fact that the birth rate has been increasing ever since 1940. The prospects for the State of Florida are that in a very short period we shall double the enrollment in our institutions of higher learning.

There is a great desire for educational opportunity. It is to be noted that in all the attacks that have recently been made on schools and educational methods there has been almost no intimation that there are too many schools or that too many children and youth attend schools. The youth of the country have been going in larger and larger numbers to institutions of higher education. In Florida, forty-seven per cent of the pupils who graduated from high school last year entered some school this year.

It appears that there will be no lack of ability to pay for schools. Recently a study, "Expenditures for Education at the Midcentury," has shed some light on how the people of the United States have recognized their need for an educational program. In 1939–40 the average expenditure per classroom unit was $1,875. By 1949–50 it was $4,475, an increase of 139 per cent. Since the cost of living had increased only 70 per cent during this period, it is evident that expenditures per classroom unit had increased approximately twice as fast as the cost of living. However, during this same period the income per capita, which appears to be the fairest measure of ability to support governmental services, increased from $539 to $1,325, or by 146 per cent. In other words the expenditure per classroom unit increased by 139 per cent while the per capita income increased by 146 per cent, which indicates that though the teacher is considerably better off, his welfare has not increased quite as much as that of the average citizen.

The per cent of income (after payment of Federal income taxes) devoted to current expenditure of public elementary and secondary schools was 2.62 per cent in 1939–40 and 2.28 per cent in 1949–50. This fact indicates a danger to the proper growth and functioning of the educational system to all those who see the great needs to be met. It is also a sign of hope, for it indicates that there is ability to meet increased demands if the proper desire can be aroused.

It is fortunate that so far this nation has had the ability to meet not only its vastly increased Federal and state expenditures for defense and other functions of government but also to provide all necessary revenues for education. Walter Lippmann states that in 1900 expenditures for education were $3.40 per capita, and Federal expenditures $6.85, a ratio of 1 to 2. In 1953 the expenditures for education were $76 per capita, and Federal expenditures were $467 per capita, a ratio of 1 to 6. Yet the standard of living of the average man, as well as the level of educational support, has continued to rise.

The support of schools has become more equitable. In 1939–40 there were in Florida 38,253 pupils in schools supported at less than $100 per classroom unit, and 19,497 pupils in schools supported at the rate of more than $6,000 per classroom unit, a cost ratio of 1 to 60. In 1949–50 there were 1,853 pupils in schools supported at a rate of less than $200 per classroom unit, and 15,326 pupils in schools supported at a level of more than $12,000 per year, still a ratio of 1 to 60, but both extremes have decreased, the lower one markedly.

A measure of how well a state system of finance provides for the maintenance of a reasonable level of support for all its schools is the per cent that the amount actually spent for the lower half of its classroom units is of the amount that would be required to support them as well as the median school is supported. This same measure can be applied to the schools of the nation.

In 1939–40 the half of the schools on the lower levels of support expended 61 per cent of what would have been required to support them as well as the median school. In 1949–50 the corresponding percentage was 69. This increase of 8 per cent indicates more improvement than at first appears, for the median increased from $1,649 to $4,391, an increase of 166 per cent.

Perhaps a more direct way to put it is that in 1939–40 the half of the schools least well supported accounted for 26.7 per cent of the total current expenditure for schools. In 1949–50 they accounted for 34.7 per cent, an increase of 8 per cent in the expenditures devoted to the lower half of the schools in addition to the general rise in the average level of school support. In many states the increase in support of schools in greatest need has been almost phenomenal. Instances are that the median support for Negro schools in the period from 1940 to 1950 increased from $300 to $1,675 in Alabama and from $268 to $1,334 in Arkansas. In Mississippi the improvement was from $154 to $562.

These increases in support of the neediest schools have for the most part been in states which are at the low end of the scale in ability to support education. Some idea of how much less able they are can be seen from the fact that in 1939 the extreme per capita incomes were $960 in Nevada and $195 in Mississippi, a ratio of almost 5 to 1. However, in 1949 New York had a per capita income of $1,584 while that of Mississippi was $581, a ratio of only 3 to 1. This indicates that the states with least wealth are gaining on the leaders.

In spite of all the progress there are many schools which are still supported below any reasonable standard applicable to the present day. There were 216,000 pupils in schools supported at less than $1,000 per classroom unit, 1,670,000 in schools supported at less than $2,000 per classroom unit, 5,144,624 in schools supported at less than $3,000 per classroom unit, and

11,135,566 in schools supported at less than $4,391 per classroom unit, the median rate of support per classroom unit.

Another striking fact is the relatively small additional outlay required to raise all the lower expenditure schools of the nation up to a somewhat reasonable level. The additional amount required to raise all the schools below the median up to the median expenditure of $4,391 was $633,000,000 in 1950, a rather small figure compared to those usually heard in discussing Federal finance.

The foregoing facts can be interpreted in either of two ways. A perfectly reasonable case can be made that industry is decentralizing and moving into low-income areas, that expenditures for education are increasing, and that the best and safest policy is to continue education as a strictly state and local affair.

On the other hand, it appears that education is of such vital importance that the nation should always be concerned with the education of its citizens. A minor outlay, as Federal expenditures go, can aid tremendously in raising expenditures and standards of education, and suitable safeguards in the appropriation of the funds can guarantee that education will remain under state and local control and primarily a state and local responsibility. It is this latter view that is supported here.

Report of the Recorder

Hans F. Flexner *

Associate, Cooperative Project in Educational Administration
Teachers College, Columbia University

An awareness of the values upon which the concept of universal public education is predicated is basic to the consideration of the concept itself. The founders of the American republic recognized that an informed citizenry is essential to a free society; history has shown that free public schools are a prerequisite of an informed citizenry.

A free society in which the franchise is universally held is dependent in large measure upon the judgment and intelligence of its citizenry. Policies affecting the national economy and security are determined and executed by its elected representatives. In such a society, moreover, personal accomplishments and achievements are highly regarded, as contributing both to the self-realization of the individual and, collectively, to the improvement of the whole. Education is consequently the concern of all of the people and its financial support the responsibility of all levels of government.

In view of the scope and complexity of the central topic, "Policies for Universal Public Education," a discussion of this topic, *in toto,* appeared to be a somewhat unrealistic undertaking for a two-day conference. It was decided, therefore, that a more manageable *modus operandi* would be to divide the central topic into four more or less discrete but obviously interrelated subtopics. This report presents an overview of the discussions of the various subtopics considered by Part I.

In presenting his conclusions Dr. William G. Carr, leader of the group dealing with the subtopic entitled "The Federal Government and National Interest in Universal Public Education" stated: "The responsibility of the Federal government to continue and to expand its program of aid to education should be kept constantly before the American people." Of special significance is the

* The following from Teachers College, Columbia University, assisted Mr. Flexner in the preparation of the record: Dr. T. C. Clark, Assistant to the Head of the Department of Educational Administration; Theodore Balcomb, Project Associate, Cooperative Program in Educational Administration; and John Stuart, Student Assistant.

word *continue,* for the Federal government has long been involved in supporting education. To cite a few examples: the Ordinances of 1785 and 1787, antedating the Constitution itself; Article I, Section 8 of the Constitution of the United States; the Tenth Amendment; the Morrill Act of 1862; the Smith-Hughes Act of 1917; the CCC, NYA, and other relief measures utilized by the Federal government during the depression years of the 1930s; the military and civilian training programs of World War II; educational programs for World War II veterans and Korean War veterans. Thus the Federal government has since its inception contributed to the support of education through both long-term legislation and temporary emergency measures.

What, then, should be its future role? The responsibilities of our educational system under present national and international conditions are not being met adequately without Federal participation. This participation could consist mainly of general financial support of education which, together with local and state revenues, should be sufficient to assure every American child an acceptable minimum educational opportunity. It should be emphasized that this does not imply a Federal school system, but to the contrary, it suggests shared support of state school systems.

The question of Federal control, then, is by no means insurmountable. If Federal aid for school construction or for current operations is accompanied by legislation guaranteeing state and local autonomy in the expenditure of such funds as they pertain to educational matters, the fear of Federal control need no longer constitute an obstacle to equal educational opportunities for all American children. Precedents for such fundamental provisions can be found in existing legislation; for example, the Morrill Act, the Smith-Hughes Act, and others. A free society must certainly have faith in the concept of popular self-government; and inherent in this concept is the assumption that the people, through their elected representatives, can and do establish legislation for the public good. Indeed, it is for this very reason that universal public education is basic to a free society.

Growing logically out of the foregoing discussion is the subtopic considered by the group headed by Dr. Henry H. Hill, "The Relations of the Various Levels of Government in Providing Universal Public Education." An underlying assumption of this group is that all levels of government must cooperate in providing universal public education, each level providing the kind of leadership and the resources which it best can.

Empirical evidence indicates that the management of local schools is more satisfactory when it is separate from that of other local governmental functions. This position—the fiscal independence of local school systems—can be defended in part by the unique character and function of public education. Partisan control of institutions whose purpose it is to teach the philosophy and method of self-government is at best inconsistent. History is replete with examples of schools that have fallen under political domination. A free, dynamic society seeks continuously to improve itself through examination of its institutions; the freedom of educational institutions safeguards the positive and constructive nature of this process.

The effectiveness of local school management is governed further by the size of administrative units. Thus while rural districts should be large enough to provide efficient and economical education, in large cities the problem of size requires considerable inventiveness to guarantee local neighborhoods a voice in the affairs of their schools.

The Constitution of the United States has reserved for the states the responsibility for the operation and administration of the state school systems. Since certain local districts within these states do not, and probably are not able to, meet acceptable minimum standards, the state governments are assuming an increasingly large amount and proportion of the total cost of financing education. It should be pointed out, however, that this provision should in no way prevent wealthier districts from going beyond minimum standards in providing richer educational opportunities for the children who reside in these fortunate localities.

In the discussion of Federal aid it was pointed out that the states control their respective educational programs. Hence relations between the Federal government and the states should be channeled through the chief state school officer. State departments of education should be strengthened by the addition of qualified and competent administrative personnel, to provide the necessary leadership and resources for local school systems.

Having considered, albeit in a cursory manner, policies for universal public education in terms of the interests and relations of the three levels of government, we turn next to a review of the conclusions of Dr. Harold F. Clark and his group regarding "The Scope of Public Education in the United States with Special Reference to the Personnel to Be Educated." Dr. Clark and his group raise a question of fundamental importance: Are the advantages so large that society should be encouraged to greatly expand the quantity and quality of education as a consumption expenditure on the grounds that it would improve the quality of life?

Obviously, the answer to this question is influenced by numerous factors; but two appear to be of primary importance: the meaning of "the quality of life" and that of "education." While an adequate discussion of the quality of life would, of course, demand a far more scholarly treatment than is possible in the limited space available, it may be well to attempt at least a brief explanation of the phrase. The quality of life is inextricably bound to the value system of the individual and the society in which he lives. The good life may be conceived quite differently in different places and under different circumstances. It is our purpose to outline those things which might be considered conducive to the improvement of the quality of American life. The following may be cited: the understanding, competencies, and attitudes requisite for citizenship in a free society; the knowledge and skills necessary for achieving the maximum degree of economic well-being; the cultivation of aesthetic sensitivity, appreciation, and creativity basic to profitable use of leisure time.

Education, in the context of this value system, suggests something more than the acquisition of the traditional verbal skills. This does not, of course, minimize the importance of verbal ability and the kind of education designed to increase that ability. It is realistic, however, to recognize that verbal skills comprise only one of the factors that contribute to the improvement of the quality of life. Even greater efforts should be exerted to provide such an education for those who can benefit most from it; however, proponents of universal public education recognize also the responsibility of a free society to the vast number of children who profit from a variety of educational experiences. It is apparent, consequently, that imagination and inventiveness must be applied to the problem of curriculum construction throughout all levels of education in meeting this responsibility. And it is certain that if education, properly conceived, is an effective instrument for the improvement of the quality of life, it is a commodity that the American people can well afford.

Since in the United States virtually all children of elementary-school age are actually attending school, and probably eighty to ninety per cent enter high school, the real problem involves the fifty per cent who do not graduate from high school. Whether or not this fifty per cent should graduate from high school may be determined, in part, by the appropriateness of the education offered. It has been suggested in the preceding paragraph that a reappraisal of educational programs is needed if universal public education is to be fully realized.

A second factor in determining who should graduate from high school is the level of economic welfare of the country. A technological society possessing vast resources will obviously require a different kind and amount of formal education for its citizenry than an economically backward society. It is quite reasonable to conclude that this country would benefit economically if everyone were to receive a broad education equivalent to approximately twelve years of schooling.

Considerable ingenuity is called for in providing such an education. A tentative and challenging suggestion for achieving greater flexibility in attendance laws was advanced by Dr. Clark. What, he asked, are the advantages and disadvantages of abolishing the present compulsory attendance laws and substituting one that will state the number of days a person must attend school by the time he is twenty-five? Such a plan might call for compulsory education for virtually all students up to a specified age, presumably between fourteen and sixteen years. Thereafter, the proper school authorities would determine the appropriate kind of educational program for each student on the basis of interest and ability. This plan is predicated upon the assumption that certain work experience, adequately supervised, is educative and may at various times contribute much to the total development of some students. It recognizes, also, the necessity of proper guidance and counseling throughout the program. Under this plan, a student may have a variety of educative experiences in the course of completing approximately 2,400 days of schooling.

A discussion of universal public education could hardly be considered adequate without some reference to the problem of personnel. The normal increase in population plus the expansion of the quantity and quality of education will most certainly require additional teaching personnel. Research may reveal new teaching methods and organizational patterns that will result in more effective teaching by fewer available teachers; for example, better utilization of the potential capabilities of students in the performance of routine tasks. Moreover, psychological research has shown the effectiveness of student teaching; that is, the ability of capable and interested advanced students to teach factual materials.

While these and other helpful measures will relieve the pressure somewhat, the shortage of competent, qualified teachers is becoming increasingly severe. The problem of teacher recruitment and selection demands immediate and thorough study. Minimum standards, based on greater understanding of what constitutes good teaching, must be established for all qualified teachers. To lower existing standards would be fatal both to the profession and to the students. A more constructive approach would be to increase the prestige of the teacher and to employ all feasible measures to attract intelligent and desirable persons to the teaching profession.

The fourth and final subtopic considered dealt with "The Quality of Public Education as Affected by the Level and Distribution of Its Financial Support." It may be well to preface this section of the discussion with a quotation from the paper prepared by Dr. Paul R. Mort, leader of the group which concerned itself with this subtopic. Dr. Mort writes: "The problem was . . . to search for new insights into the complex of factors in which the expenditure level is immersed, both as an indicator of the priorities placed on education by a community and as a material means for purchasing education."

While a multitude of complexly interlocking factors determine the quality of education, the level of financial support remains one of the three or four most important concerns. Some of the other factors of basic importance are the number of days of schooling offered each child, the size of the school district, and by whom and in what manner the budget is determined. In the final analysis, however, perhaps the single most important factor influencing the quality of education is the level of financial support.

It has been suggested earlier that public-school finance is not purely a local responsibility, but rather the responsibility of all levels of government. Since fiscal policy should be based on the assumption that local finance is basic, however, state and Federal aid should be accompanied by provisions designed to stimulate local communities to exert greater efforts in achieving their educational objectives.

Where communities and states are unable to achieve desirable minimum standards, state and Federal aid would seem to be inescapable. It is feasible, also, to supplement such aid with major assistance sufficient to enable weaker communities to utilize their schools and other agencies in the correction of economic weaknesses. All communities can be helped by sizable additional aid to tap wider tax bases than their local school system presently permit.

State and Federal aid can be used with considerable effectiveness to strengthen certain aspects of the educational program which fill a national need: for example, a completely Federally supported program in science and mathematics and the communication arts. Such aid would make the program quickly available in all communities without endangering the remainder of the educational program. Finally, while it is important to retain educational government as a unique form of government, it is necessary for the educational profession to achieve a more sympathetic understanding of the changes that have occurred in the financing of municipal governments generally.

Significant, too, are the changes in educational programs. Communities are expecting the schools to assume responsibility for an ever-widening range of educational activities to develop capable, well-adjusted, and responsible citizens. To meet these added responsibilities additional resources are required, resources which in many cases the community itself offers in the form of personnel and physical facilities. It is important, however, to recognize that the school is one of many community agencies which contribute to the total development of the individual and to the improvement of the community. It is therefore necessary for the schools to define clearly their reasons for assuming additional responsibilities before attempting to meet such responsibilities. Since it is true, however, that school programs have been extended to involve lay participation, administrative leadership must recognize and work cooperatively with individuals and groups within the community.

An extremely important part of the educational program, and one which greatly affects educational quality, is the process of evaluation. In order to evaluate educational progress, teachers and administrators must be able to supply tangible evidence of how and to what extent they are achieving concrete educational goals; that is, evidence regarding progress in the three Rs, etc. All schools obviously do not meet the best modern educational standards. Weaknesses, wherever they exist, should be recognized and positive steps taken to eliminate them. For this task teachers, administrators, and lay citizens must have a more thorough understanding of new techniques and insights, as, for example, those concerning self-understanding, group dynamics, and audiovisual aids.

Finally, in view of the complexity of the problems associated with public education—its objectives, content, methodology, government, and management—a vastly expanded, well-coordinated program of basic and developmental research is vitally needed.

PARTICIPANTS

Norton Beach, Professor of Education, Teachers College, Columbia University

ERNEST R. BRITTON, Superintendent of Schools, Midland, Michigan

ARVID J. BURKE, Director of Research, New York State Teachers Association

WILLIAM G. CARR, Executive Secretary, National Education Association

HOLLIS L. CASWELL, President of Teachers College, Columbia University

HAROLD F. CLARK, Professor of Education, Teachers College, Columbia University

ARTHUR F. COREY, Executive Secretary, California Teachers Association

LAWRENCE A. CREMIN, Associate Professor of Education, Teachers College, Columbia University

DANIEL R. DAVIES, Professor of Education, Teachers College, Columbia University

FINIS ENGLEMAN, Commissioner of Education, Connecticut

HANS F. FLEXNER, Associate, Cooperative Project in Educational Administration, Teachers College, Columbia University

WILL FRENCH, Professor of Education, Teachers College, Columbia University

HOWARD FUNK, Superintendent of Schools, Bronxville, New York

ARTHUR I. GATES, Professor of Education, Teachers College, Columbia University

ELI GINZBERG, Professor of Economics, Columbia University

HENRY H. HILL, President, George Peabody College for Teachers

WILLIAM JANSEN, Superintendent of Schools, New York City

JACOB K. JAVITS, former United States Congressman

FRANCIS KEPPEL, Dean, Graduate School of Education, Harvard University

EUGENE LAWLER, Professor of Education, Florida State University

JAMES L. MCCASKILL, Director, Division of Legislation and Federal Relations, National Education Association

WORTH MCCLURE, Executive Secretary, American Association of School Administrators

PAUL R. MORT, Professor of Education, Teachers College, Columbia University

JOHN K. NORTON, Professor of Education, Teachers College, Columbia University

RAYMOND H. OSTRANDER, Superintendent of Schools, Mineola, New York

FREDERICK RAUBINGER, Commissioner of Education, New Jersey

DOROTHY STRATTON, National Executive Director, Girl Scouts of America

CURTIS H. THRELKELD, Superintendent of Schools, South Orange, New Jersey

HENRY TOY, JR., National Citizens Commission for the Public Schools

WILLIAM S. VINCENT, Professor of Education, Teachers College, Columbia University

PART TWO
Policies for Higher Education

INTRODUCTION

Since the American people have such high confidence in education, and have been in the past so generous in providing for their youth, one might suppose that the only problems in the administration of American colleges and universities would be those essentially involved in their own subtle tasks. But this is not true; institutions of higher learning have to fight for the freedom to do their work and for the means, also. These two themes, how higher education was to be managed and how it was to be paid for, proved to be subjects of the greatest concern to a group of distinguished educators and leaders.

Higher education can be kept up to its great duties, and protected in its freedom, if its institutions are disciplined by each other, in emulation and the highest kind of competition. The intellectual and moral climate of the times may make this difficult but the colleges and universities themselves are chief factors in making the climate.

For this kind of work, material support will probably never be sufficient because it is the nature of higher education to outrun its resources in pursuit of its own constantly advancing goals. But there will be enough in money and in personnel to keep the ambition alive and this, perhaps, is as much as we should hope for.

These are not the conclusions of the group but the conclusions, briefly put, which were arrived at by one who listened to everything that was said and weighed the wisdom of others with his own experience.

Lyman Bryson
Professor Emeritus of Education
Teachers College, Columbia University

The Functions and Opportunities of Higher Education in the United States

Henry M. Wriston
President, Brown University

We live in an era of crises, but the speed and facility of communication and the dramatic quality it lends to news releases on radio and television have over-accentuated crisis. When one adds together all the threats to our liberty and our lives, it is clear that if they were taken at face value our situation would be hopeless. The National Safety Council does its best to take the joy out of every holiday by predictions of disaster and by keeping score on accidents and deaths, as if it were a grand game. Various medical agencies have so dramatized cancer, multiple sclerosis, and muscular dystrophy that one is reminded every moment of De Wolf Hopper's famous song of forty years ago: "Some little bug will find you."

If McCarthy isn't menacing our liberty, Executive Order 10450 regarding the loyalty check is. If neither of those is after us, something else is, such as congressional inquiries into Foundations. Meanwhile the Communists are pressing from without and boring from within and we have no adequate defenses! I suggest that disease is old, poverty is old, tyranny is old, hazards to liberty are perpetual, and we should not be so nervous or jumpy. We quote "eternal vigilance is the price of liberty" without realizing it applies to us, feeling the battle our fathers won should stay won.

The colleges and universities can perform their functions in a resisting medium as they always have. In some ways that resistance is an asset. L. P. Jacks, in his little book, *The Revolt against Mechanism,* reminds us that a resisting medium is necessary for the flight of an airplane, the progress of a ship—and for nearly every other mechanical operation.

He suggests that a resisting medium is necessary also for the triumph of an idea. The liberal ideal—that freedom of the mind and spirit from fear and all inhibiting emotions—is particularly valuable in a world enslaved to lesser objectives. If it could be easily achieved, it might be too little prized and would be lost. Now, whenever it is attained, it is something of a miracle. That gives its pursuit the aspect of adventure, and its achievement the quality of treasure trove. There is enrichment beyond that earned by the toil involved —a sort of unearned increment which is always unexpected, even though it is predicted by the guide.

If we quit feeling sorry for ourselves and speak with more courage and less defensiveness, we shall get along a lot better in the educational world. We should take as our motto Thomas Mann's remark: "Education is an optimistic and humane concept." The need at the moment is to accentuate the optimism.

The functions of a university are many, and they vary in intensity. All colleges and universities have some function in common; most have particular functions appropriate to their own structure, their own local responsibilities, and their means of support—independent, state, Federal, mixed.

The central problem of all universities is to achieve a paradox: they must cling to the past and open the way to the future; in that sense they must be simultaneously ultra-conservative and revolutionary.

They cannot follow the biblical injunction to cleave to that which is good; at least they cannot cleave only to the good. They must also cling to what is bad in the past and, for that matter, in the present. To fail to understand Russia, for example, would be fatal. If mankind is to learn from experience, the record of error, failure, and wrong is likely to be as illuminating as the record of triumph, achievement, and right. The university which does not study and restudy these lessons with persistence and penetration will fail in one of its primary responsibilities.

However, the university which puts its whole energy into the preservation and analysis of past data misses its complementary and compensating obligation to seek new truth in every field. This it must do despite the resistance of tradition and orthodoxy—scientific, religious, social, economic, or whatever. Universities must encourage and shield the pioneer. Historically the pioneer, whether a settler or a researcher, has had boldness of spirit combined with unorthodox methods and beliefs; he has often been intemperate and headstrong, whether attacking the untamed wilderness, or improving, as an entrepreneur, industry or commerce, or breaking new paths through the unknown in the world of knowledge.

The universities, therefore, must frankly accept the responsibility for tolerating error, lest in misevaluation, in ignorance, in prejudice, or in timidity they mistake truth for error and extinguish some new light in the darkness or overlook some new path into and through the wilderness.

There is a place for orthodoxy and there are institutions in which orthodoxy has its appropriate setting. It is the specific function of a university, however, to protect heterodoxy because it may develop the ideas and the structures of ideas which other institutions will later accept as the orthodoxy of the morrow. This is just another way of saying that every university must be dedicated to "the illimitable freedom of the human mind," as Jefferson dedicated the University of Virginia.

This poses a problem, for only in very special climates of opinion is heterodoxy popular. The history of mankind has long reaches where the flight from freedom was more conspicuous than the fight for freedom. Indeed we have been living in such an age. As fascism and Nazism spread Count Sforza said: "The significant symptoms of the mental disease which has seized upon European thought is this, that there should have been . . . intellectuals, sons of liberty, who failed to realize that in vindicating regimes destructive of freedom, they thereby disavowed their own fundamental principles." We know that the German universities accepted Hitler with little resistance; freedom was not worth an effort. Men will accept, in this materialist and deterministic age, a "saviour" who will lead them. Strength and the security it brings, not freedom and the hazards it entails, are too often prized. To fail to see the evidences of this drift in the United States is to be blind.

This current tendency to discount the values and virtues of freedom produces another paradox. Not only must the university be at once conservative and revolutionary; it must both cultivate public opinion and defy it. It must cultivate public opinion for, if the atmosphere in which it moves is too bitterly hostile, its privileges will be withdrawn; the church or the state will outlaw it; its properties will be confiscated, or the sources of new funds will dry up. It will be throttled or starved to death.

This dogma applies alike to public and private institutions. The tension between approval and hostility partially accounts for the fact that however great its resources, however imposing its buildings, the history of the university is always one of inadequate resources. Startling is the only way to describe the success of the effort to achieve its goals through the sacrifices of scholars, the unworldliness of their concern for physical and financial welfare. Their sense of dedication accounts for the progress that has been made.

The second common function of all universities, and of colleges as well, is instruction. They must transmit the knowledge accumulated in the past. It is not always done as formal "history"; sometimes it is compressed as the present state of knowledge. This is the usual method of scientists, who ordinarily feel that they must telescope most earlier scientific developments in order to get on with what seem, in a subject now in its most revolutionary phase, more urgent matters. Whether history is telescoped or not, it remains the foundation of instruction, for what we know is what the past has accumulated, just as what our successors will know is that plus what we add.

The ultimate compression of history is in theory, which is an effort to formulate the meaning of the past in such terms as to project our next steps along the path in the search for truth. On the basis of that formulation, theory might be called the extrapolation of experience.

We know, of course, that every extrapolation is an effort at prophecy. Where the premises have been soundly conceived and the variables taken adequately into account, the average success of extrapolations is high. Among the most conspicuous was the prediction of the elements not yet discovered and their definition before their isolation. But we know also that in social and political matters the variables are so many and so complex that in any given individual case the extrapolation is liable to error which may be serious.

In one sense every student is an extrapolation. His capacities can be determined almost statistically, but variables in the growth of his character and the direction of his interests are beyond calculation. The universities are handicapped very seriously in fulfilling their function by the crude character of predictions as to where interests will lie in individual cases, what motives will be dominant, and what degree of attainment is possible. This is why liberal learning has to lie at the root of higher education; its objective is to free the mind from prejudice, from trammels of preconceptions, from too early specialization, and to give time for a clearer perception of basic interests.

So far as barriers to the effective performance of education's basic function are concerned, not all the fault lies with public and private attacks and demands for special services. Education itself has been guilty of wild extravagances. In the days of President Morgan, the *New Republic* accepted Antioch at its own evaluation and hailed it as *the* answer to *the* problem. Antioch is still going, but it is not *the* answer to *the* problem. Stringfellow Barr and Scott Buchanan thought St. John's had *the* answer to *the* question. One had only to fix his eye upon the giants of the past and follow in their train. St. John's is still running; presumably it is still doing useful work; but it is not *the* answer. The University of Chicago promoted "the nature of the world and of man" as general education in science; later "timeless education" offered the answer. Still later a college out of step with everybody else was another "answer." These and many more have been messianic in their attitudes. Many programs have been promoted with a Madison Avenue fervor. But institutions would have made a greater contribution if each had been doing its own work, solving its own problems, and tending to its own business without pretending to set a pattern for everyone else. In other words, variety is the answer, local responsibility is the answer.

Institutions themselves have assaulted both these vital elements. They have been afraid of variety and have sought to limit and trespass upon local responsibility.

Variety, instead of being treated as an asset, has been called "chaos" and an effort has been made to set patterns. In the earliest days of the Carnegie Foundation the transfer of students from one institution to another was made difficult by lack of uniformity. Consequently there was developed what came to be known as the "Carnegie unit": an hour of sitting in one place was called a student-credit-hour and one hour was assumed to be as good as another hour. To this day this yardstick is fastened upon a good deal of the United States: a college degree is granted after 120 or 124 or 128 hours, depending upon the treatment of physical education. The analogy of interchangeable parts in industrial production has been applied where it has no relevance.

European universities also pressed 50 years ago to know from which American institutions to accept students. As a result the Association of American Universities set up a process of accreditation. It was a convenience; it gave quick answers, but time showed that the answer was as likely to be wrong as right. Careful studies revealed the fact that students admitted to graduate schools from nonaccredited institutions frequently did as well as those admitted from accredited institutions.

Then the regional associations went at it. They first called their process "standardization"; then, seeing the absurdity of that, they changed it to "accreditation." Later they set out to recognize some differences, but not enough. After 20 years of experience with a reformed type of accreditation, the most actively engaged association listed some of its assumptions. The first was "that quality can be engendered by requiring institutions to conform to a set of practices laid down by the accrediting association." The second was that it was possible to "evaluate a *particular* institution . . . in terms of practices found to be characteristic of quality institutions *in general.*" The third assumption was that outside examiners could make "an accurate appraisal of an institution . . . in a very brief period of time."

All these assumptions have proved wrong. In the first instance, the letter killeth but the spirit giveth life; aping the procedures of another and making an imitation are far from the real thing. On the second point, if you are looking for individual excellence you do not get it by conformity, and there is no question that the pressure is for conformity, which is a road to standardization. Finally, the assumption that strangers can come in and make a fair evaluation of a complex structure in a brief time makes no sense at all.

Moreover, historically the regions where accreditation has been weakest have produced the best institutions and those where accreditation has been strongest have not been freed of shoddy institutions. If, therefore, we are really interested in education being free, we should dismantle the vast apparatus of policing which has been set up by the institutions themselves.

Further to enmesh educational institutions, various pressure groups have embedded in the statutes and in state regulations all kinds of procedures. These are intended to determine how many "hours of education" a student must have before he can teach. Nearly every profession or occupation for which special training is appropriate now is controlled, to some extent, by such laws or regulations. It is embodied in law, for example, that one may not even take a bar examination unless he has fulfilled certain educational requirements which are expressed in terms with no relevance to what may have entered the mind of the candidate. John Marshall could not even take a bar examination. Across the nation there are laws and governmental regulations about engineers, chemists, nurses, doctors, pharmacists, veterinarians, and dozens of other professions. Few are designed solely for the purpose of protecting the public interest; often they are, as I have indicated, the work of pressure groups who, to some extent at least, have pretended to identify their own interest with the public interest. Many have done so without adequate evidence to justify any such pretension.

These are deliberate assaults not only upon variety but upon local responsibility. They have tended to take away from boards of trustees control of the management of their own institutions given to them by charter.

Educational functions can be performed efficiently in the face of public attack if we have courage and steadiness. But we have little right to complain too bitterly about public obstacles to individuality and responsibility while our own number promote and maintain vigilante groups pressing for conformity. At some point we must make our practice and our behavior accord with our philosophy and our preaching.

There is room in the United States for an almost infinite variety of patterns of institutions of higher education. We should bend our energies to clearing away the debris which serves as an obstacle to freedom.

Financing Higher Education

Robert D. Calkins
President, The Brookings Institution

The purpose of this paper is to clarify the problem of financing higher education, to explore some of the possible solutions, and to consider courses of action for the immediate future.

The financing of higher education is not an insoluble problem. It is not an issue subject only to that academic consideration which Bertrand Russell calls the "time-wasting occupation of inconclusive meditation on insoluble problems." The support of higher education is a very practical matter of great social import for which reasonable solutions can almost certainly be found if the academic world will interest the public in the extent of the problem.

It is no exaggeration to say that the problem of financing higher education has never yet been put squarely, frankly, and forcefully before the American people. That the issue remains unsolved is not, therefore, a matter of great surprise. Over a year ago the Commission on Financing Higher Education finished the latest, the most complete, and the most constructive set of studies yet made of college and university finances. Yet these volumes received very little public attention. They found their way so silently onto the shelves of libraries that many persons, even some greatly interested in the work of the Commission, were unaware months after the studies had been issued that the Commission had finished its work and published its reports. If we are to improve the financing of education we shall have to tell people, other than the librarians, about the matter.

Two questions have been suggested as the theme around which I might organize these remarks. They are: First, how are we to maintain the strength of higher education in the United States in view of the economic difficulties of our age? Second, what human and economic resources are properly devoted to higher education? The second question I shall dispose of briefly and then return to the basic issues of how to maintain the strength of higher education in these times.

HOW MUCH HIGHER EDUCATION?

There is no firm answer to the question of the amount of resources that ought to be devoted to higher education. The support that is appropriate depends on the type and amount of education the people of a free society want and are willing to pay for, and on what means they can provide for this education. To estimate the resources that ought to be devoted to higher education is a normative task that I, as a social scientist, am reluctant to undertake. I cannot speak for society, nor do I trust the estimates of others. The assumptions that underlie such estimates can rarely be validated. In these changing times, the estimates are soon outdated. Moreover they can be dangerous, for they offer guidance to public action long after they have become obsolete. If one considers the voluntary way we finance education, one is driven to conclude that, under existing conditions, the people are probably getting about the amount and type of higher education they want and are now willing to pay for. There is little convincing evidence to the contrary.

However, to suggest that the public is getting what it is now willing to pay for, is not to say that more and better education may not be desirable for society; nor does it suggest that the public could not be induced to pay for more and better education. It could. There are doubtless broad limits within which more or less education can be, and is, a matter of choice. At some unknown lower limit, representing too little devotion to higher education, youth could be inadequately prepared for their times, and this could impair the security of the nation, cripple the economy, slow down progress, and undermine the cultural life of the country. These results, we may be sure, society would not desire or knowingly elect. At the opposite extreme, so much of its resources might be devoted to higher education as to turn the nation into an effete society, dedicated to intellectual affairs to such a degree as to jeopardize its freedom and independence through want of precautions for self-protection and of the material things on which security rests in a world where might still rules. But between these wide limits there is a vast gap. This country is undoubtedly nearer to the lower limit than it is to the upper limit— it has too little rather than too much higher education.

This broad gap furnishes an open field for persuasion and free choice. In the contest for public attention and support educators, along with other competitors, are free to ply their trade—to exhort the public to place a higher value on education, to pay a higher price for it, and to buy more of it. The special virtues of education for personal self-development and enlightenment, however, confer upon the educator a duty to portray the values of education and to foster a higher respect for it. As representatives of truth and integrity, educators have an obligation to do this by reason and not by indoctrination; by persuasion and evidence and not by tricky emotional appeals. Thereby they perform a service to society—arousing a greater interest in education and a greater desire for it in open, dignified competition with other appeals. Such efforts have their effect on the amount of resources that are considered appropriate for the support of higher education.

The proper amount of education the public should desire may be said to be the quantity it can be fairly persuaded to want and to support in preference to other things. On the whole this country has done rather well over the years in convincing the public of the importance of education and in creating a desire for it. The percentage of youth of college age who are going to college, for example, has risen from about four per cent to about eighteen per cent over the last fifty years. Nevertheless the support of higher education has not kept abreast of this expanding interest. Although the nation has both the financial resources and the manpower required to maintain its institutions of higher learning, we have not induced society to direct these resources into higher education in sufficient amount to provide for the growing expectations of parents that their children should have better educational advantages than they themselves enjoyed. Higher education has a perennial problem of making ends meet. To that problem I now turn.

RISING COSTS AND EXPANDING REQUIREMENTS

The basic issue is correctly stated: How are we to maintain the strength of higher education in view of the economic difficulties of our age? The chief economic difficulties are on the one hand inflation and depression, and on the other the rising cost of war and defense.

Inflation over the past fifteen years has been a major complication. The Commission on Financing Higher Education has estimated that prices paid by colleges and universities increased approximately 76 per cent between 1940 and 1950. The official price index for consumers' goods rose 74 per cent in the same period. This is more than professors' salaries have increased and more than the revenues per student have expanded. Institutions have sought financial solvency by sacrificing the economic position of the academic profession, the upkeep and expansion of facilities, and the quality of education.

Depression has been another complication. The depression of the thirties created maladjustments and deficiencies which are still not wholly overcome. Although enrollments did not fall off as much as many institutions feared, budgets were strained. Institutions were hard put to reduce costs as much as their resources were cut. Plant expansion was drastically curtailed. Students sought less expensive institutions, and a rapid growth in public-supported institutions resulted.

But the basic problem in these times arises not so much from depression or inflation as from the rising cost of war and defense. Except for war and threats of war, the inflation of recent years would have been much milder or would not have occurred at all. In either event the financial affairs of education might have been considerably more favorable.

War and defense, however, continue to impose enormous burdens on society. In 1940 this cost was $24 per capita, and in 1950 (measured in 1940 dollars) it had risen to $198 per capita. War and defense represent the chief items of public expense that have increased markedly during the decade. The normal costs of government, Federal, state, and local—if we omit war and related expenditures and social security expenditures—have (in 1940 dollars) actually declined during 1940 to 1950 from $112 per capita to $104 per capita. Although the idea is widespread that government has spread all over the place enormously increasing its expenditures, the facts are that the increase on a per capita basis has occurred mainly in military and related expenditures and to a lesser degree in social security.

There is no prospect of marked reductions in the cost of these defense services in the immediate future. No prospect of peace is in sight for the next generation, and we must be prepared against the possibility of another major and devastating war within that time. Consideration of the dangers we face reveals clearly that these defense expenditures must have a high priority. Our independence and our freedom may depend upon them.

In spite of these heavy defense burdens the economy is sufficiently productive to support a more costly educational system if the public will sacrifice other things for education. If we could put the defense program on a pay-as-you-go basis and act promptly to counteract depression, we could maintain the economy with little danger of major inflation. Whether we will achieve such results or not depends heavily, of course, on political exigencies and courageous leadership. But, except for devastating war, there is no reason why we cannot support a strong educational system if the public can be convinced of its importance.

The problem of maintaining a strong system of higher education is not, however, merely a matter of more money for present activities. The comment so often heard, that institutions have no problems which more money will not remedy, generally indicates that money is really not the chief deficiency. Educational strength will not be attained until there is greater efficiency in educational effort, until the status of the academic profession is restored to a position appropriate to its importance, and until facilities and staff are kept abreast of the expanding requirements of the nation. Growth as well as improvement is necessary to the preservation of educational strength.

More efficient and more economical methods and facilities are required not only to strengthen higher education; they are essential if we are to avoid its degeneration in a world of growing needs. The system is dotted with weak institutions, obsolete facilities, ineffective professors, and outmoded customs. It is burdened with a reluctance to introduce more economical ways. Its advances too often are exacted under the compulsion of financial stringency, rather than through imagination and leadership. Many notable improvements have been made, of course, over the last few decades. It is doubtful whether we have suffered any serious deterioration in the quality of higher education during these years. Yet few who know higher education would contend that it is doing all it can to root out weakness and to improve its services. Of its inefficiencies more is said later.

The task of maintaining a strong educational system is aggravated by the deterioration in the economic and social position of the academic profession. The belief is widespread that too few brilliant, able scholars are entering the teaching profession. Our colleges and universities, it is feared, are falling too much into the hands of second-rate faculties made up of narrow, unimaginative specialists. Although one must often distrust these impressions, there is no doubt that academic careers have lost much of their appeal during a generation of depression, war, and inflation and of expanding opportunities in other fields. The strength of higher education cannot be maintained without scholars of the highest quality. Able scholars cannot be attracted in number unless we adjust their economic status and restore their social position in society. Even so we must expect serious shortages of academic personnel for some time. Although a rapid expansion of enrollment is assured over the next fifteen years, the next decade offers a declining number of youth in the age group (26 to 29) from which we normally draw graduate students for the profession. The upturn is not expected until after 1962. Because of these trends education must develop more effective ways to attract personnel during the next decade or longer.

The unexpectedly rapid growth of population requires that our sights be lifted to wholly new levels in providing educational facilities over the next two decades. The American Council on Education has recently issued figures on the growth in numbers of students of college age. These data indicate a 16 per cent increase by 1960, a 46 per cent increase by 1965, and a 70 per cent increase by 1970. If the proportion of youth attending college continues to grow, from 18 per cent to more than 20 per cent, as is expected, the increase in college enrollment will exceed 50 per cent in ten years and approximate 100 per cent by 1970. Such figures have substantial margins of error; yet they show that higher education will be called upon to provide for a doubling of its enrollment within relatively few years. Colleges and universities are only beginning to speculate on what this means in the way of staff, facilities, and funds.

No one can say how well the educational system will be able to meet these several requirements. On the one hand, vigorous leadership may succeed in so improving education and lifting it in public esteem that marked advances may result. On the other hand, a degeneration of higher education may occur unless institutions develop more efficient and economical methods, provide for expanding enrollments, improve the economic position of the professor, and obtain larger support for their activities.

A degeneration of higher education would be a national tragedy. It would jeopardize our social system because of our growing dependence on trained manpower—scientific, technological, and professional. It would impair our role of leadership in the world, for we urgently need the perspective, the knowledge, and the discrimination of an enlightened people—virtues to which the liberal arts contribute. It would weaken our cultural progress at a time when leisure is becoming more widely available and extending and deepening of cultural interests are possible. In brief, higher education is indispensable and we cannot risk a weakening of the system.

The future of the educational system rests mainly with the educators, for it is through their efforts and their leadership largely that improvement must be sought. Let us consider some of the things that may be done.

NEED OF MORE EFFICIENT METHODS

In the first place, there is the task of introducing more efficient methods. Anyone who compares academic affairs with those of other organizations will be impressed by the many loose, uneconomic, and inefficient practices that persist in institutions of higher learning. Education can do considerably more for the money it spends if it will improve its practices. Such improvements are important, for education will need increasingly to reassure the public that it is operating efficiently in order to command public respect and support. I shall refer specifically to a number of situations that deserve attention.

The first is the proliferation of courses. Few institutions have avoided the subdivision and multiplication of courses that leads to scattered enrollment and costly teaching. The efforts to check this trend are ceaseless, and efforts to reverse the trend are fraught with the utmost difficulty. Clumsy, ill-advised attempts to combine well-attended courses because of some similarity of subject matter are frequent, while on the other hand strict control over the introduction of new courses encounters faculty opposition. So the continuation year after year of costly instruction for few students regardless of its importance remains a sinkhole of scarce funds. Course offerings once introduced somehow persist and come to occupy their place years later with scarcely any appraisal of their importance.

That faculties, however conscientious, do not effectively police these offerings is illustrated in an experience at a state university. There the fragmentation of history courses had been carried to such a point that in order to complete the range of instruction thought necessary for the master's degree it was found that a student would need to enroll for approximately four years of graduate study. This is not an isolated instance. Numerous campuses have multiplied graduate offerings with little consideration of the time limitations under which students work.

With all due respect to the principle that courses should not necessarily pay their way, one may ask whether education can afford the continuation of courses drawing small enrollments without a periodical careful scrutiny of their justification. Ultimately this issue involves the question of how much freedom a faculty member shall have to introduce courses mainly of interest to himself. It is clear that greater control is required over the perpetuation of these costly forms of instruction. There is a limit to which any single institution should be expected to maintain such specialized courses, and there is no reason why a division of labor should not prevail among institutions respecting work in the less popular fields.

Such a division of effort among institutions has become both a necessity and a possibility in recent years. By collaboration or prudent refusal to duplicate the work of other institutions the offerings in some of the less popular subjects are being concentrated in a few institutions. The Board of Control for Southern Regional Education has worked out interstate collaboration by which the students of one state are sent to institutions in other states at public expense. The practice is now being copied in other areas. One of the serious obstacles to such arrangements is the "fadism" in education. In the 'thirties the fad was international relations; in the 'forties, labor relations and area studies. Programs in these fields were established all over the country, and after a few years the painful task of liquidation was necessary on numerous campuses. Such fads involve senseless waste.

Another such waste is to be found in teaching schedules. Teaching loads have been reduced from twelve to nine or six or even four hours, on the theory that the professors will devote their time to research. Administrative controls are slight and scandalous instances can be found on almost any campus of staff members who do no research, or who spend their time earning outside income. The whole practice calls for re-examination. Some institutions are finding a fairly heavy teaching load, with temporary relief for research or other duties, to be a more effective system. In this way administrative control can be exercised without constant supervision of the professor's activities. One may regret this departure from the combination of light loads and *laissez faire*, but to extend this combination uniformly to all professors is to incur an extravagance that institutions can no longer afford.

A third source of weakness is poor teaching and ineffective teachers. Substantial sums are being spent on educational routine that fails of its object. One is reminded of the comment of Wendell Phillips in which he speaks of "the second-rate men who rather occupy than fill our pulpits." To remedy defective teaching requires both the development of better teaching personnel and the positive encouragement of good teaching. Graduate schools fortunately are beginning to concern themselves with the preparation of better teaching personnel. But these efforts will yield small results unless the teaching atmosphere is changed. Until good teaching is more highly regarded, recognized, and rewarded, the hidden waste of ineffective effort will remain large. Much might be accomplished through more imaginative, more purposive, and more experimental methods. A vigorous quest for the appropriate use of lectures, discussion, tutoring, independent study, and other practices would be rewarding. A more scientific examination of teaching methods would help to overcome the paradoxical behavior of professors who insist on the most rigorous scientific standards for research, and yet accept the most off-hand opinions regarding the effectiveness of teaching and vigorously resist attempts to scrutinize the results of instructional methods.

If progress is to be made in the improvement of teaching, the presidents, deans, and department officials undoubtedly will have to foster it. Although faculty members often interest themselves in better teaching, a lively interest in good teaching seldom generates in a faculty without official encouragement. Here is an important respect in which presidents and administrators may exercise leadership and create the sort of atmosphere that will attract and stimulate able scholars.

Higher education has been slow to introduce economies partly because of inadequate records and ignorance of their costs. No large business today would endeavor to operate with such a paucity of reliable information as that on which university officials try to operate. Although fairly reliable cost methods can be devised, colleges and universities have been slow to adopt them. Calculations of the crudest sort are made for the allocation of costs between instruction and research, and most institutions make no such allocation of the professor's salary. The effect is to load research costs onto the instructional budget and expect student fees to cover the expense. At the same time the institution seeks outside research funds and characteristically underestimates the costs involved. Research has become a major university activity; teaching loads have been reduced to foster it; funds can be obtained for its support; and yet numerous institutions continue to operate as though research were a minor affair for which grants-in-aid were adequate. The practice inexcusably intensifies financial difficulties. But as long as universities are willing to offer first-rate research at cut-rate prices there will be buyers in a world that has become research-conscious. Here is one area in which more record-keeping is worth while.

In this connection one notes that Millett reports a reduction in costs per student (in 1940 dollars) from $289 to $277 between 1930 and 1950. This slight reduction is taken as an indication that instruction is not adequately financed. In view of the way costs are allocated, the inference is questionable. The figures may reflect economies, and one would suppose that a downward trend in costs per student is a thing to be sought. But until research is charged its proportionate cost we shall have no idea how misleading educational figures are in fact, or how seriously administrative decisions are distorted by relying upon them.

Once costs come to be considered, extravagance will be found in the use of the physical plant. Only a few institutions make any serious attempt to employ their plants fully. During summer, week ends, evenings, and even in regular hours on week days, facilities are often unnecessarily idle. This disuse of facilities presents an increasingly serious problem, which is aggravated by rising maintenance costs. Financial pressure may yet teach the importance of full utilization.

Some Special Adjustments

Improvements such as those suggested above would help to establish more economical operations. But there are other adjustments also that would contribute toward a more effective system.

As both publicly and privately supported institutions grow in size, more consideration needs to be given to two classes of students. One of the weaknesses of the large institutions is that the exceptionally able student proceeds at the pace of the less able and receives little special instruction to excite his interest or to develop his talents. Society needs the full powers of exceptional ability. Institutions must provide honor courses and special instruction for students of unusual powers if we are to develop the most precious talent the nation possesses.

The average student likewise needs more attention in most institutions. As we encounter shortages of trained personnel in one professional field after another, it becomes apparent that we must do more with the average talent available to us. We cannot hope to remedy the shortage of scientists, technologists, engineers, professors, doctors, and research men by buying only the best brains away from other fields. We must learn to use good average minds more effectively and the first step toward that goal is to train them more effectively. Here is a vast supply of under-utilized talent—already in college.

The system of tenure that has been erected in colleges and universities also needs to be examined. It has grown up mainly since 1900, and yet its effects have rarely been judiciously examined. There is much talk of instances in which tenure offered great protection to individual scholars, and of other instances in which it sheltered inefficiency for life; but there is no frank appraisal of the practice. Even if tenure should be maintained in certain positions, as I have no doubt it should, there may be real advantages in using more often term appointments of three, five, eight, or ten years. Such appointments offer an opportunity for review, and if the appointee is not productive, or effective, he is not allowed to coast for life. There is some danger that at the renewal period officials might use the occasion for the censure of unpopular views, but safeguards could be erected against this misuse. That full tenure is necessary for the protection of academic freedom under present conditions is doubtful. But in any case the matter needs an honest re-examination to make sure that the best arrangements for research and scholarship are being employed.

The foregoing issue is closely related to the difficult matter of professional responsibility. Not yet have we found a satisfactory solution of this problem. As a rule we try to defend a system in which the professor is assured complete freedom of expression in his own field in which he is presumably competent; and also his personal freedom to speak or publish anywhere on any subject with impunity for himself and such impunity as can be obtained for the institution with which he is connected. If we lived in a world where all subjects were academic, or where all persons were qualified judges of opinion, the matter would be simple. But, in fact, we live in a world where men respond vigorously to the action proposals of others. In a free society those who advocate action, whether as citizens or as office-seekers, must take the consequences of public reaction. The professor who enters the forum of opinion is entitled to no special privileges or protections that are not accorded others. It is questionable whether the guarantees of academic freedom can survive if they are regarded as offering a sheltered platform from which professors may advocate as laymen with impunity.

When the professor's nonprofessional expressions undermine his standing as a scholar and bring retaliations to his institution, deep issues are raised as to the scope of academic freedom that is to be protected. That the institution should protect the scholar against public pressures brought in response to his unpopular professional views there can be no doubt. But that it is similarly to provide safe shelter from the consequences of his public utterances outside his field is not clear; and the issue is not realistically resolved by a blanket defense or by abandoning the issue. As a matter of fact most professors exercise restraint and prudence in not taking a public stand on issues in which they are not experts, and they limit their public expressions to matters in which they have special competence. The social scientist often finds that he must restrict his expressions to matters on which he has special qualifications, if he is to command respect and influence as an expert. This practice is warranted. Scholars who insist on speaking as laymen with the protection of academic freedom often place themselves and their institutions in an indefensible position. There is little doubt that these practices are undermining the respect for the academic profession.

It is not so much the teaching of communism in classes, as it is the exhibition the professor puts on in public that arouses the citizenry. In these times it seems likely that the issue will be drawn more sharply. The scholar may find that he must make a choice between being a scholar and being an advocate. If he is to be a scholar, he may have to forgo the exercise of some of his freedom as a citizen in order to command respect as a scholar and consideration as an expert. But, whatever the outcome, one may be sure that society will not maintain special privilege and protection for the professor who wishes to pronounce as a layman on political and social issues.

A further aspect of professional conduct that is causing concern is the growing disposition of professional associations to behave like labor unions or pressure groups in fighting universities whose policies they disapprove. These actions jeopardize the prestige of the academic profession. If, instead of passing hostile resolutions of censure, these groups offered their good offices to find solutions for controversies between faculties and officials and between presidents and trustees, a constructive and statesmanlike service would be rendered. Such efforts might have resolved numerous difficulties without headlines and the impairment of institutions. But the present trend is to place the academic profession in a posture of hostility toward the institution's administration the moment a controversy arises. This is a dangerous trend. It is unfortunate that there is no organization or procedure through which those genuinely concerned with the welfare of scholarship and education may offer their assistance for the settlement of disputes that adversely affect educational institutions and the academic profession. Greater progress has been made in the amicable settlement of labor disputes where provision is made for the conciliator, mediator, and arbitrator who act in the public interest.

Finally there are several trouble spots in the structure of higher education that present special problems. They concern the small, weak institution, the liberal arts college, and the medical schools.

At a time when most institutions face serious financial and staffing difficulties, the small, weak college has generally lost ground. Some of the weakest education now offered is to be found in these institutions. Their future is uncertain, their tenacity remarkable, and the competition they face severe. The importance of these colleges to the educational system is a moot question. Unless the realignment of institutions proceeds rapidly, the expansion of enrollment in the 'sixties will doubtless save many of them from oblivion, whether they are economically justified or not.

The liberal arts college is caught in a transition and needs to find its place. It has been outdistanced by the rapid rise of professional schools. In the universities the arts college is being reduced almost to a service department for preprofessional training. The independent arts college is caught between a dedication to its small size and relentless financial pressures. The arts curriculum has become almost as specialized and narrow as professional instruction, and the student finds it difficult to obtain a liberal education in the true meaning of the term. As a result widespread efforts are afoot through general studies, integrated courses, and other devices to re-establish the elements of a broad liberal education. But these institutions need to rediscover liberal arts, to clarify their purpose, and to dedicate themselves to it in order to re-establish their influence in a society that is growing increasingly professional.

Medical education also presents a special problem. It is plagued with high costs and financial difficulties. Its faculties have offered their share of objections to the introduction of more economical forms of instruction. Government aid is suspect and private support is inadequate for the expanding needs of these institutions.

The plight of the medical schools is a deferred result of a notable achievement. That achievement was the reconstruction of medical teaching between 1912 and 1930 that in one generation carried this country from an obscure place to the leading position in medical education and research. This development was initiated as a result of Abraham Flexner's Report (*Medical Education in the United States and Canada,* 1910). It is so frequently suggested that what we need in the social sciences, the humanities, or some other field, is a Flexner report that will revolutionize the field, that I should like to refer to that experience briefly. Those who recommend this type of investigation rarely know the circumstances that led to Mr. Flexner's great success.

Mr. Flexner, himself not a doctor, reviewed conditions in 155 medical schools and noted with a devastating eye the "fatal difference between the best, the average, and the worst." He urged a variety of improvements, including full-time clinical teaching and a stronger scientific base for medical training.

Let me refer to relevant and not atypical passages of his report as it referred to medical education in Oregon. In a twenty-one-line statement on the University of Oregon Medical Department, Mr. Flexner noted that the entrance requirement was less than a high-school education and that the budget for 72 students and 41 members of the part-time teaching staff was $8,000 in fees and $1,000 from the University. He described the wretchedly kept building and the scanty equipment. After reviewing, in similar vein, the Willamette Medical Department, he concluded:

> Neither of these schools has either resources or ideals; there is no justification for their existence. The entire coast is oversupplied with doctors by immigration; unless something better can be made than can be thus readily obtained, the state will do well to let the field lie fallow.
>
> The Salem school is an utterly hopeless affair, for which no word can be said. Portland may conceivably some day maintain a distant department of the state university. Until, however, the financial strength of the state university permits it to develop there a school equal, for instance, to that which the University of Texas supports at Galveston, it has no right to allow a group of local doctors to exploit its name in the conduct of a low-grade proprietary institution. That out of its own slender revenues it should divert a thousand dollars annually into the coffers of this concern is well-nigh incredible. (p. 292)

In probably no field today could one find a situation warranting a report of this sort. Flexner was dealing with a situation incredibly bad, where good practices existed and could be used as a criterion for judgment. But it was not just the vigor and thoroughness of the report that produced the great medical revolution in this country.

Another aspect of this achievement, commonly overlooked, is that the Rockefeller and Carnegie philanthropies together contributed well over $100 million to carry out the reforms that Mr. Flexner proposed. To twenty-four medical schools the General Education Board alone contributed $78 million and at a time when the dollar brought much more than today. All told, several hundred million dollars were contributed from all sources for the renovation of medical schools between 1912 and 1928. If similar conditions were prevalent today, major educational reforms might be achieved; but today's problems seldom lend themselves to conclusions as definite as Mr. Flexner reached, nor can comparable funds today be mobilized for such a nation-wide reform. One of the persistent consequences of the medical achievement is that the excellent and expensive system of medical education that was erected now imposes a continuing financial drain on the other resources of the universities. Accordingly, the financial plight of the medical schools is of crucial importance both to this vital branch of education and to the universities that operate medical schools. If medical education could be properly financed, substantial income would be released for other university activities. Certainly for education of such great national importance some way can and must be found to support the 72 medical schools of the country.

The Alternatives

The foregoing remarks review some of the many problems of putting the educational house in order. When we consider the task of acquiring additional financial support two alternatives appear. Higher education may deal with the problem piecemeal and haphazardly, as it has in the past; or it can make a considered effort to formulate a sound rationale and policy by which the public may be induced to support education more adequately.

If the first course is followed, some of the results can be foreseen. An expansion and multiplication of publicly supported institutions will occur because funds will be available for their support. Their costs to the student are low, and public institutions have a democratic appeal. Simultaneously privately supported institutions seem likely to diminish in importance. Some will find it necessary to seek public funds; some will doubtless be forced to close. Some of the private institutions will no doubt elicit sufficient funds to continue to do an outstanding job. The organization of higher education is likely to change with the rise of the municipal college, the expansion of junior colleges, and the development of trade schools. The integration of liberal arts and professional instruction seems to be one of the likely developments in view of the rapid trend toward professional instruction and the need of professional students for liberal arts.

There are indications that a marked development of adult education may occur. Liberal arts need not be limited to students in their teens. There are great possibilities of organizing adult instruction—not of the sort typically represented by extension courses for those preparing for special occupations —but organized adult instruction for mature people with leisure and intellectual interests. Some institution with the courage to establish a campus for adults, thirty-five and over, could make a pioneering contribution by developing this new field. It would offer a new teaching experience for professors, some of whom could be recruited to this pursuit before or at their retirement. The experience would offer both students and faculty new incentives and a new stimulus for those who now look forward to a suspension of intellectual interests, or lack of opportunity to cultivate them, in their later years.

If higher education proceeds with no formal, more effective attempt to elicit the interest of the public, slow but substantial support may be forthcoming as educational crises are met one after another. There is no basis for expecting endowments to regain their former importance in university finance. Although yields have improved, great capital gifts are not in prospect unless new devices are invented to encourage them. Student fees will doubtless have to bear an increasing share of educational costs, while other income supports the students who cannot afford these fees. A better understanding of this problem would prevail if institutions set their fees at the actual costs of education and offered a partial or complete remission of fees for those who could not afford the charges. The publication of such figures would enlighten the public as to the costs of education and its dependence on donors or government.

But uncoordinated effort is not the only approach to educational finance. The resources exist, as I have suggested, and the public can be persuaded to support higher education more liberally. It can be persuaded to pay more liberally in fees for the instruction that its children receive. Students can be induced to pay back in later life the unpaid costs of their education. Donors can be encouraged to provide larger gifts during their lifetime and at death. Legislatures can be persuaded to give greater support to public institutions. Devices may be found whereby public funds may be made available to private institutions. In these and other ways the financial problem can be met if the public is sufficiently convinced that higher education deserves greater support.

The task of educators is to establish among the public a greater interest and confidence in higher education. This can be done successfully only if higher education through its performance deserves public respect and confidence. The measures I have suggested to improve the efficiency and economy of educational operations and to strengthen higher education are important steps in that direction. But it is essential also that the case for the support of higher education be more effectively presented to the public. While a respect for education is widespread in this country, an appreciation of the importance of a strong educational system is shared by too few people.

The enlightenment of the public must be based on valid analysis and not simply oratory. Last week in these Bicentennial meetings Professor Viner expressed the view that national defense was more important than opulence. It can be established that strong education is essential to our defense and to future opulence, but I have never seen the proposition convincingly developed. A persuasive analysis can be made of the value and place of higher education in modern life; but, instead of presenting such a statement to the public, educators are inclined to talk pleasing rhetoric to themselves. When one searches the literature for substantial enlightenment on these matters, one is reminded of Mark Twain's comment on the divergent estimates of the scientists respecting the length of the Mississippi River. He marvelled at "the fascination of a science where one gets such wholesome returns of conjecture out of such a trifling investment of fact."

If the public is to acquire a reliable idea of the needs of higher education, institutions will have to present more realistic estimates of plant requirements and operating budgets than are now generally employed. The public still has no impression of the magnitude of the financial problem.

In dealing with the public it is an illusion to suppose that many of the threadbare notions of educators will be accepted without question. For example, one continues to hear of the superiority of the liberal arts college over the professional school, of the private institution over the public institution, of the small college over the large university. The public no longer accepts these views at face value. There are humanists who consider that the most imaginative ideas on liberal education exist now in the engineering schools and not in the liberal arts colleges. Instruction in some of the public institutions is undoubtedly superior to that in many private institutions. Moreover, numerous large institutions offer better education than many of the small colleges. Old notions have by repetition become clichés that are no longer valid. The variety in higher education makes generalization difficult. While there are first-rate private institutions and liberal arts colleges, there are others ranking low on the list. The public thinks of the institution it knows and dismisses the sweeping statements of educators as special pleading.

If higher education is to present a sound statement of its position, a number of these old ideas will require re-examination. It is questionable, for example, whether the idea is still valid that the private institution enjoys and offers greater freedom and is a bulwark of freedom in the event of political strife. It is doubtful whether or not any institution—private or public—that appeals to the general public for support has retained its independence, except in so far as strong boards of trustees may have the courage to act as buffers for the institution. The power of public opinion and of the state can be opposed less successfully today than a half-century ago.

The public sees many of these issues very differently from the way educators see them. On the campus it is assumed that the liberal arts college must be saved, whereas the public asks whether it is worth saving. The small college stresses the importance of its small size, but the public sees it grow, sees that it must grow in an expanding society or lose its influence, and asks whether its claims are valid. The professor contests loudly over the issue of academic freedom, but the public sees a clannish defense of special privilege and questions the judgment or integrity of educators. These are but some of the issues which educators will encounter when they seek to interest the public in the affairs of higher education.

A great number of financial issues must be thought through before sweeping demands are made upon the public. Should institutions charge the student the cost of his instruction and make special provision for those who need financial help? Should it employ schemes for deferred payments of tuition, such as those suggested for medical schools, by which students may pay for their education during their productive years? To what extent can endowment be relied upon for the future support of higher education? Can measures be taken to encourage direct contributions to support institutions, as an alternative to the establishment of independent foundations? There is the problem of medical education. Will deferred tuition payments, public support of hospitals, private contributions, and the multiplication of research opportunities afford funds adequate to maintain these institutions? Can the medical schools safely accept public support? Can ways be found to permit business support without endangering the independence of education? How dependable is such support? Finally there is the matter of bequests and the question whether special tax provisions are required to encourage the support of higher education.

Reviewed here are some of the ways in which higher education can increase and maintain its strength notwithstanding the economic difficulties of these times. Some of the problems of financing educational institutions are touched upon. The tasks ahead are large and difficult. But, most of all, educators themselves need a better rationale of the value and position of higher education in order to enlist public interest and support.

The course of higher education in this country will depend heavily on the educational leadership of our colleges and universities. It will depend on the caliber and performance of the faculties. For this reason it is highly important that serious efforts be made over the next decade to attract scholars of the highest order into academic life. There are unique satisfactions in it. For, in the words of Lucretius,

> This is the greatest joy of all, to stand aloof in a quiet citadel, stoutly forti-
> fied by the teaching of the wise, and gaze down from that elevation on others
> wandering aimlessly in a vain search for the way of life, pitting wits one
> against another, disputing for precedence, struggling night and day with
> unstinted effort to scale the pinnacles of wealth and power.

In such service lies the hope of higher education and of posterity.

Report of the Recorder

Merle L. Borrowman
Assistant Professor of Education, University of Wisconsin

The heart of the meetings of the section chaired by Professor Lyman Bryson on Policies for Higher Education was the preceding statements by Presidents Wriston and Calkins. The members of the conference, distinguished and responsible leaders of higher education, discussed in a highly informal manner a number of ideas raised by these statements.

Some of these were very old ideas. Professor T. V. Smith, of Syracuse University, touched one such in describing a liberal education as a subjective experience which, once undergone, has intensive meaning and value in itself. Perhaps because the subjective aspect is so rich and startlingly clear to one who has undergone it, yet so easily lost when put in words for the uninitiated, men feel compelled to redefine it again and again. In any case, these conferees returned several times for anchorage to such an attempt.

Professor Smith's description was perhaps the most systematic and moving. Having described the liberal mind as one with the "capacity to entertain contrary-to-fact hypotheses," he considered the question of a philosophical base adequate to the development of such a mind. He rejected, as important but not sufficient, both the activism inherent in the John Dewey orientation and the cold rationalism of other philosophical schools. He suggested, as the best alternative, the "life of imagination," the emphasis on free fancy, which characterized much of the thought of Santayana and others.

There was, in all of the discussion, no inclination to underestimate the centrality of the liberal function in higher education. Apparently everyone, in this section at least, applauds the growing stress on this function regardless of the professional aspiration of students. The old argument of how to relate this emphasis to specialized professional education did come up at several points, but it was not pushed into the center of discussion.

It is interesting that no serious contention arose over this question which has been at issue on many American academic battlegrounds since early in the 19th century. The two contrary classical positions were mentioned (1) that professionalism must be postponed until the liberal arts training is finished, and (2) that, in the light of the interests of students and their parents in the occupational aspect of higher education, the best hope lies in carrying liberal arts education along simultaneously with the specialized or professional education. There was some dispute about what the public really wants in this respect, but the basic issue was not joined. Perhaps at long last the academic community is beginning to despair of settling such matters by argumentation. Indeed, with respect to this and several other problems, there seemed to be, in this conference, a rather general feeling that highly diversified experimentation is wholesome.

Three questions about how to encourage this experimentation came in for considerable discussion. In respect to the first, it will be noted that both Presidents Wriston and Calkins asked if present policies on tenure and academic freedom, and the resultant policing of the administration by the faculties, do not discourage the development of effective new programs.

This seems to be a crucial issue, especially on the undergraduate level. A balanced program of any kind demands a fairly high degree of coordination among offerings. Such coordination can scarcely result if instructors are given a great deal of freedom to organize their own subjects, and if they are inflexible in their interests. The task of bringing in profound change, which is resisted by a tenure-protected, individualistic faculty, without infringing on academic freedom is not easy. Even the significant new programs which have arisen in the past under the inspiration of a particularly gifted dean or president, have often solidified once the great innovators have departed.

A second source of inflexibility results from the pattern of preparing college teachers. The discussion of this factor revolved around two related questions, namely (1) how can the generalists suited to teaching at the undergraduate general education level best be developed in research-oriented graduate faculties, and (2) should prospective college teachers do some systematic studying of pedagogical subjects, such as the philosophy of higher education and the psychology of young adults, and be given some form of internship experience.

Here, too, some old arguments—those of the "academicians" versus the "educationists"—lurked beneath the surface. There appeared to be general support for some kind of professional internship and for occasional intensive in-service sessions on the problems of college teaching. There appeared to be a consensus against any preservice instruction in education.

At the heart of this teacher-preparation issue is the old dilemma posed by the marriage of an American liberal arts college to the German university, a wedding which brought together the complementary, but not always mutually compatible, emphases on specialized research and on breadth and wholeness. To the extent that the potential college teacher continues to conceive his professional role solely in terms of the graduate research ideal, he is apt to remain insensitive to the relationship of his offerings to the whole and to be uninterested in spending time on curriculum reform. The plan of bringing together young instructors in service for brief but intensive considerations of these problems in college education is one approach to this problem.

There is a deep-rooted suspicion that any earlier attention given to professional motivation and study will inevitably become "illiberal." This suspicion, no doubt grounded partly in historical fact, helps to explain the reluctance to encourage instruction in pedagogical subjects for potential liberal arts college teachers. The belief that the educationist will become a camel with his nose in the tent is combined with a feeling that studying how to do something too far in advance of the doing is ineffective. Moreover, the years of undergraduate and graduate school study are preciously short for providing the level of specialized knowledge needed to teach on the college level and also the liberal base for that knowledge.

Nevertheless, by the time they reach the last year of college, certainly after they enter the graduate school, the professional objective of most potential college teachers is sharply defined. It does seem that at this level, and while undergraduate experience is still fresh, a brief examination of the place of their own discipline in an over-all philosophy of liberal education and of the psychology of young adulthood would be useful. It may well serve to keep alive, in the graduate years which properly demand extensive specialization, some of the liberalizing aspect of the undergraduate years.

Such possibilities need the careful attention of the graduate faculties. It seems quite clear now that the theory of educationists, of whom the author is one, has been limited because it grew with only minor participation of people thoroughly sensitive to the demands of the graduate disciplines. If, however, as seemed apparent in this conference, the only real chance for improving programs of higher education lies in the development of more flexible and effective college teaching, every possibility should be explored. The stress which President Wriston and others placed on extensive experimentation and on the development of highly diverse patterns of higher education is important in this respect.

Such issues as these are not easily resolved; nor is the third problem which was cited as a barrier to experimentation. The third is, however, of a different order. It is the problem of accreditation. President Wriston argued vigorously that higher education has handcuffed itself intolerably in this respect. The well-known examples of accreditors who operate in an arbitrary and petty manner and of excessive paper work were cited. The underlying assumption seemed to be that all accreditation represents an arbitary effort to force undesirable standardization. This assumption was challenged by some members of the group.

That such a subject should have become a point at issue seems unfortunate. If it is true that accreditation proceedings have, in fact, come to destroy any real chance for flexibility and experimentation in higher education, this is a grave matter. Not only does it bode ill for the future of higher education, but it raises a question about the past judgment of educators or their former students. Is it true that they, failing to find more fundamental ways of improvement, have turned to short-sighted legalistic schemes—to the manipulation of petty administrative detail rather than to underlying reconstruction?

But perhaps the accreditation picture is not uniformly so dark as the examples cited would indicate. For example, Professor Edward S. Evenden pointed to the American Association of Colleges for Teacher Education as one agency which does not seek standardization. It strives, he argued, only to encourage and aid its member schools in their own efforts at reevaluation and improvement of practice.

In some cases, accreditation practice has been unduly restrictive. This is especially true when the accreditation agency is an outside one concerned with but part of the total program. But in other cases, these agencies have become scapegoats on which to unload the frustration engendered in unsuccessful attempts to improve institutional programs. In either event, the basic difficulty lies in the failure to discover adequate means of reforming and of relating effectively the general and the professional aspects of university education. This leads back to the question of the preparation of college teachers and to the amount of independence given to professors or departments in organizing their offerings.

The task of organizing effectively the program of a single institution of higher education is difficult enough. Yet each institution is, in turn, a member of a community of institutions and ought logically to organize its offerings in respect to the larger group. The conferees on Policies for Higher Education explored several ideas in this context. One of these had to do with defining the relative roles of the small private college, the large public university, and the great state university. A second involved the common attempt of individual universities to offer a complete program with specialization in every possible academic and professional area.

This role-defining process is further confounded by the need to enlist the public support in endowing and paying tuition to expensive private colleges and in sanctioning adequate appropriations for the public institutions. The fact seems to be that the public has no adequate concept of the functions of higher education in general, much less the unique functions of different types of institutions.

This is not surprising, since even such a distinguished assembly as this could not agree concerning the particular role of the private in respect to the public institution. The old claims that private institutions give greater individual attention and provide better teaching were explored and severely challenged by some members of the section. The argument that the private institution, being more free from the pressure to please the legislature, is therefore a basic force for freedom and of nonconformity, was urged with greater confidence. Even here, though, it was noted that as such colleges become less adequately supported by endowment and depend more on tuition and research grants, they become quasi-public agencies. The underlying dilemma for private higher education, and to some extent for public, is that cited by President Wriston, namely that the university must simultaneously be bitter critic of the public and at the same time command the public's loyalty and support.

Social roles of institutions as of individuals are not established by unilateral definition. A shared role concept presupposes that in the give and take of a social system people have come jointly to view each agent in a particular manner. People define the role of "liberal education" in terms of the actual results in their own experience of the activities of specific colleges. They will generally support or refuse to support higher education in terms of this experience. The difficulty of securing adequate public support was partly attributed to this fact, as was the success of some state colleges, which the public has accepted as particularly its own.

The clear implication of this aspect of the conference discussion is that the college must be actively involved in the work of the community if it hopes that the public will find it worthy of support. To demonstrate that advanced theoretical research in the pure sciences, the social sciences, and the humanities is of immediate value to the community is, of course, sometimes impossible. This suggests the need for the kind of faculty unity which will confront the public with the insistence that theoretical and practical disciplines are inseparable. It also suggests that faculty members, representing the theoretical and humanistic disciplines might, through effective social action, help the public to see the values of liberal education.

However, the conferees had to face, partly because President Calkins so sharply raised the issue, the fact that such participation can also bring down the wrath and disrespect of the community. What kind of protection the university owes the faculty member who makes pronouncements on public policy was an issue seriously debated. On the one hand it was argued that the protection of nonconformist and unorthodox opinion is one sacred trust of the university. On the other was the view that a scholar, when speaking outside of his area of scholarly competency, has no right to expect freedom from the same kind of consequences as would result if members of other professions so spoke. Should the institution try to protect a privileged status in this respect, it may well forfeit, and deservedly so according to this position, the confidence of the community.

Thus were raised a series of questions concerning the role of higher education in the present era. The discussion began with a recognition that diversity and creative experimentation throughout our colleges and universities are the best hope; it involved a recognition that certain practices within the university community constitute serious barriers to such experimentation; and it concluded with an examination of ways to achieve public understanding and support of the policies of higher education.

The part such conferences play in actually improving education bears some examination. The published versions of the more formal statements make some provocative questions and suggestions widely available. Beyond these statements, however, the discussion was inconclusive. Quite wisely, it seems, the conferees did not glibly proclaim generalized solutions for serious problems.

These were men whose judgment and inspiration would be of great value to a group of neophyte college professors who are facing such problems for the first time. One wonders, however, about their influence on each other. In most cases, the conferees were old acquaintances, their respective views are generally known to each other, and they have, in long experience, arrived at considered and rather stable opinions. That any of these opinions will change significantly from this discussion seems doubtful.

Moreover, there appears to be a growing tendency for such conferences to be given over to sweetness and light. In part a lack of sharp controversy is often indicative of the mature mind which refuses to indulge in childish argumentation over issues which are, in fact, settled outside any forum by the continuing practice of varying groups. One is relieved to find people who avoid the sort of contentious discussion which has little significant consequence in practice.

On the other hand, however, one wonders if certain grave issues which confront higher education might not more nearly be resolved if controversy were sharpened and opposing positions more searchingly criticized. Although such issues were suggested in the statements of Presidents Wriston and Calkins, there was little sharpened discussion of their controversial aspects. The only exception was in respect to the question how much protection ought to be given to the professor who makes nonscientific pronouncements on public policy. No doubt the sharp kind of exchange which occurred in the meetings of the National Education Association during the days of Presidents Gilman, Hall, Eliot, and Butler still takes place at some conferences. However, a reader of these old NEA debates, or the debates in the meetings of the New England Association of Colleges and Preparatory Schools or the Association of American Universities would have found this meeting by contrast a bit of a tea party.

A recorder has no responsibility to judge the responses of people whose ideas he reports or to criticize the conceptualization of the conference. However, in this particular case one of the primary issues was that of improving the program of instruction, while several other issues involved the relationship of institutions to each other and to the larger community. Outside of accreditation practices and of occasional books by college people the help which one institution receives from another is often through conferences such as this.

If the purpose of such a conference is to pronounce on public policy, then, besides having expert opinion present, the agenda needs to be rather explicitly outlined in advance and certain by-questions subjected to careful group judgment. If on the other hand the paramount concern is ritualistic—the opportunity to rethink, to be reassured that one's problems are not unique, and to be stimulated by one's colleagues—such a conference as this is of great value.

This particular conference section functioned as if the participants accepted easily the fact that the basic problems will not immediately be solved. There was deep respect for the underlying forces of shifting public opinion, of changing population and other economic factors, and of uncertain world and domestic political trends which are the real determinants of educational policy. While there was no tendency to minimize the threats inhering in these situations, there was, withal, a gratifying sense of optimism quite different from the aura of anxiety which colors too much current thought.

It is not of small moment that experienced and informed leaders have soberly, if briefly, examined the role of higher education in contemporary America without despair and without crying of impending calamity.

PARTICIPANTS

BRUCE BARTON, JR., Education Editor, *Time* Magazine

KARL W. BIGELOW, Professor of Education, Teachers College, Columbia University

MERLE L. BORROWMAN, Assistant Professor of Education, University of Wisconsin

LYMAN BRYSON, Professor Emeritus of Education, Teachers College, Columbia University

ROBERT D. CALKINS, President, The Brookings Institution

LAWRENCE CHAMBERLAIN, Dean of Columbia College, Columbia University

JOHN R. DUNNING, Dean of the Faculty of Engineering, Columbia University

EDWARD S. EVENDEN, Professor Emeritus of Education, Teachers College, Columbia University

FRANK D. FACKENTHAL, Trustee, Columbia University

CLARENCE FAUST, President, Fund for the Advancement of Education, Ford Foundation

FRANCIS R. B. GODOLPHIN, Dean of the College, Princeton University

ALAN W. HASTINGS, Rockefeller Center

THAD L. HUNGATE, Controller, Teachers College, Columbia University

ROBERT D. LEIGH, Professor of Library Service, Columbia University

M'LEDGE MOFFATT, Dean of Radford College, Virginia

JOHN M. RUSSELL, Executive Secretary, John and Mary R. Markle Foundation

WILLIAM F. RUSSELL, President Emeritus of Teachers College, Columbia University

AURA E. SEVERINGHAUS, Associate Dean, College of Physicians and Surgeons

T. V. SMITH, Professor of Philosophy and Citizenship, Syracuse University

GEORGE STODDARD, Chairman, Directing Committee, University Self Study, New York University

WILLIAM C. WARREN, Dean, School of Law, Columbia University

HOWARD WILSON, Executive Secretary, Educational Policies Commission

HENRY M. WRISTON, President, Brown University

PART THREE
Meeting the Health Needs of the Nation

INTRODUCTION

The discussions reported here were planned with emphasis upon the promotion of meaningful communication between several scientific disciplines. It was not the purpose to formulate resolutions, draw recommendations, or discuss in detail the numerous reports and studies that have been conducted on the health services of the nation. The emphasis was on opportunities for a multiprofessional approach to a wide variety of topics which have an impact upon the problems confronting our professions and the public. No prepared manuscripts were required of or used by the participants.

The maintenance and improvement of the physical and mental health of the people are primary responsibilities of any nation. Health ranks with other major features of the national economy, comparable in importance to food supply, education, housing, employment, industrial and agricultural production, and social security, with each of which it often has direct relationships. It is well known that knowledge regarding the diagnosis, treatment, and prevention of disease and disability and the maintenance of normal health is far in advance of its application to the needs of individuals, families, and the community. There is a great lag between what we know and what we apply. However, the American people are now convinced of the value of proper health services and are determined that in some way their benefits shall be made available to all.

Everyone today is aware of the broad public responsibility of medicine, which must be recognized as a social as well as a biological science, requiring technical knowledge and skills, facilities, organization, adequate financing, proper public relations, and all the implications of a broad community service.

Many of the factors influencing the provisions for adequate health care are recognized. Only a few illustrations need be given, such as the industrialization of our country; the high rate of urbanization; new methods of communication and transportation; the increasing age of the population; the conduct of government largely by pressure groups; the need of laboratory and therapeutic services for every population area; the recognition of specialization within the profession, and the importance of coordinating skills and talents of specialists into forms of group practice for those patients needing multilateral attention; the rapidly developing trends toward prepayment insurance for hospital, medical, and other health services; the essential contributions of preventive medicine by Federal, state, and voluntary agencies and the professional groups; and the financial problems of all these activities in an inflationary economy. Yet the needs in matters of health and disability are still individual and personal.

In view of the many factors arising from the growth of knowledge and skills within the professions and the numerous economic and social forces that have an impact on those services, changes in the forms of medical and health care in the future are inevitable. The evolution of sound plans of health services adapted to the needs of local communities would be helped immeasurably by thoughtful experimentation with different methods of accomplishing that end. Experimentation of that kind should be encouraged.

It is recognized that the level of any health service cannot rise above the competence of those individuals who participate in it. Hence, the recruitment and education of professional personnel are essential. Such education and preparation must be for the needs of the future, not those of the past or even the present.

Willard C. Rappleye
Vice-President in charge of Medical Affairs
and Dean of the Faculty of Medicine
Columbia University

Report of the Recorder

James E. McCormack
Associate Dean of Graduate Medicine
Columbia University

The discussions of Part Three touched on many aspects of national policy for health and social services. The many interrelated problems are treated here under two general headings—Health Professions, and The Consumers' Interest—thereby reflecting the points of view of professional practitioners and those outside the professions.

HEALTH PROFESSIONS

There is an obvious shortage of personnel in the dental and nursing professions; but evidence that there is a shortage of physicians is not convincing, though all are agreed that the distribution of physicians throughout the country is not optimal. It is difficult to evaluate statements concerning our resources of and requirements for medical personnel. Over a dozen different estimates for the future have been made. The estimates have varied from 6,000 more physicians than we shall need by 1960 to a shortage of 61,000 by that date. For nurses, estimates range from plus 47,000 to minus 163,000 by 1960. It is apparent that much of what is euphemistically described as evaluation is really only gathering of opinion. There is need for an accepted method of measurement and for more objectivity and less bias. The inadequate sampling techniques and the deceptive assumptions which underlie some estimates would make an honest statistician shudder.

The Dental Profession

One indication of the relative shortage of dentists is found in the fact that to satisfy the needs of the armed forces it has been necessary to draft civilian dentists to a degree that may cause some depletion of dental care available to civilians. Thus, in certain categories, physicians and dentists have been drafted by age, the youngest first. It has already been necessary to go to a

111

much higher age group among dentists than is even contemplated for physicians. It is probable that many Americans receive in the armed forces better dental care than they had as civilians. There are not quite half as many active dentists in the United States as there are physicians in active practice.

There is a real problem in recruiting qualified people for the dental profession. This is reflected in the experience of the scholarship fund of New York State. Each year there is a state-wide competition for the awarding of scholarships to medical or dental school for residents of New York State. There are 28 dental scholarships and 72 medical. Experience shows that, in contrast to those who win the medical scholarships, the students who win the dental scholarships are usually in the lower half of their class at college, many of them in the lower quarter. During the postwar period when, with the stimulus of privileges under the G.I. bill, there was a surplus of applicants for professional school, one dental school accepted 40 student applicants into its freshman class only to have 26 withdraw prior to registration because they had also applied to and been accepted in medical school and preferred the medical to the dental career.

There is no doubt that in order to fill their classes (which are usually smaller than medical school classes) it is necessary for some dental schools to accept second-rate students. Undoubtedly the financial rewards in the practice of medicine are on the average somewhat higher than in the practice of dentistry, and the expenses of equipping an office for the practice of dentistry are considerable. However, the most widely unappreciated fact is that the cost of dental education has reached a point where few can afford it. It is more expensive than medical education. Dental students pay the same tuition as medical students and at the beginning of their sophomore year they must pay out $1,030 for instruments. Opportunities for scholarship aid are pitifully limited and dental education is priced out of the market.

The Nursing Profession

In regard to the nursing profession, recruitment programs have had considerable success. About 7 per cent of the girls graduating from high school enroll in nurses' training schools. There is some increase in the total number of student nurses each year although the artificial high levels of the war years have not been maintained. It is probable that about as many girls in the upper half of their class in high school are now attracted to nursing as ever will be attracted. Actually the number of active graduate nurses in this country has increased steadily. Perhaps this is most strikingly considered in terms of the number of nurses per 100,000 population, which was 15 in 1900, 99 in 1920, 215 in 1940, and 237 in 1951. At the same time the ratio of physicians and of dentists to population has not changed significantly.

Recruitment of nurses is perhaps less important than the problem of keeping nurses in their profession and of using their services most effectively and most economically. There will continue to be a very large annual loss to marriage and the responsibilities of maintaining a home and raising a family. Only a little more than half of the active graduate nurses are engaged in hospital or other institutional practice. Higher salaries granted to other groups engaged in health service who are perhaps better organized, but who have not been in the health field as long as has the nursing profession, constitute one discouraging factor. Only in recent years has there been any effort made to raise the salary scale of nurses.

The introduction of nurses' aides and other groups points to an evolution in the functions of the professional nurse. Perhaps it is necessary to come to a clearer definition of the objectives for which nurses are trained.

On the one hand there are experiments in the training of nurses to be responsible for the complete care of uncomplicated obstetric cases. At the same time there are voices urging that the period of nurses' training now set at three years be reduced to two years. One woman who had been a chief nurse in a good hospital ten years ago withdrew to start raising a family. When she came back recently to the hospital practice of nursing, she listed more than fifty procedures which physicians had done in the earlier period and which are performed by nurses today.

At the same time it is clear that many unskilled or less skilled tasks formerly carried out by nurses have been delegated to others. Perhaps we should do more of what the British have referred to as "de-skilling the job." Sometimes by slight modification and other times by breaking up a task into segments, it is possible to recruit younger or less talented personnel for entirely adequate performance. It is helpful if such personnel can have some recognition. Thus the New York City Health Department in recent years has utilized high school graduates as "Public Health Assistants." With such status and title and a modicum of training they have become happy and useful employees. Indeed a certain courageous professor of pediatrics once announced that, because of the shortage of nurses, he would operate his premature nursery without nurses. The consternation of his colleagues is easy to imagine: "This is the one section of the hospital where you have to have the best trained nurses." He took one good professional nurse and a group of girls just out of high school, and even a few who lacked high school training. *Mirabile dictu,* his hospital service improved because there was no turnover, the girls did exactly as they were taught, loved their work, and felt very important doing the job.

The Medical Profession

The relationships of the physician in the relatively simple social order of the past were well understood and have been the basis of health services for generations. Health services have involved understanding of the impacts of unemployment, the economic and emotional life of the family, the anxieties and concern of the head of the family, and emphasis upon prevention as well as cure and treatment. The keystone in the arch of such a program of health services was, and still is, the family physician. He is the central figure in the constellation of professional talents and skills required in the light of present-day knowledge for the intelligent and adequate care of the family. It is this family physician whose judgment, understanding, humanity, and advice are essential in the evaluation and decisions that have to be made in regard to health matters.

One of the major considerations in the evolution of our concept of health services is the transition from the established methods of individual, solo private practice of medicine, on a fee-for-service basis, into a modernized plan consistent with the recent developments in specialization within the profession. Approximately one third of the active physicians in this country are certified specialists, and among recent graduates the proportion of specialists will be found much higher. It is provocative to raise the question whether there is a trend to overspecialization in response to the increasing complexity of medical care. Indeed medical schools have often been accused of thwarting the training of general practitioners and of exposing their students exclusively to the specialists' point of view.

There can be no doubt that when a patient drifts from one specialist to another there is a great increase in the cost of medical care. On the other hand, advances in medical science are so rapid that it is impossible for a physician to keep up with all of them, and the old-fashioned general practitioner who practiced general surgery and obstetrics and sundry other specialties as well as general medicine is on the way to becoming as obsolete as the horse and buggy with which he is associated in romantic nostalgia. When members of the family of a physician become ill, generally speaking, they consult specialists rather than a general practitioner.

Ideally everyone should have a personal physician, who should also be a specialist trained for the job of being a personal physician. His training is in the specialty of internal medicine. As an internist he is a diagnostician first of all. This diagnostic specialist should also be something of a psychiatrist or something of a psychosomatist. But he should be trained looking to the future, not to the past.

The position of the internist as personal physician is secure in the large centers and in organized group clinics. The area in which this admittedly ideal arrangement is possible is growing steadily, though there are still some areas so remote as not to attract specially trained physicians. There will continue to be general practitioners for many years to come, but the comforting ready availability of specialist consultation is getting closer all the time. The young physician trained in a modern medical center, with its battery of diagnostic laboratory facilities and array of various specialty talents, has been at times understandably reluctant to go far from the center when he establishes his own practice. He is anxious to maintain contact with other equally well-trained specialists and to have available modern diagnostic and therapeutic facilities.

Several recent socioeconomic developments, however, have modified this situation, so that each year specialist care including the services of the internist or personal physician specialist becomes available at greater and greater distances from the large metropolitan centers. Among these factors are the development of small but modern and well-equipped hospitals in smaller communities, largely stimulated by the Hill-Burton bill. There is also the ever-growing network of good highways which permit physicians and patients outside of urban areas to travel greater distances in reasonable time. Perhaps one might mention also the ubiquity of health insurance and the growth of group practice.

Obviously there is a transition going on in the present form of private and individual practice of medicine under the impact of pressures partly from within the profession and partly from more inclusive economic and social conditions. All concerned are quite conscious of the fact that this is an evolutionary process and cannot be soundly accomplished except by gradual steps. It is true not only of physical structures but also of human societies that outside pressure tending to change their form will meet opposing forces tending to resist these changes. Therefore it should be no surprise to learn that within the medical profession there is some resistance to change as manifested in pronouncements and activities which sometimes receive unpleasant publicity in the press. This publicity is unfortunate since the altruism of the medical profession at large, which surpasses that of most professions, is thus questioned. It should be emphasized that the evolution in form of practice has been going on, however slowly, within the profession; while it cannot be denied that outside groups have been exerting pressure to accelerate the change in modalities of practice.

There can be no doubt that uncontrolled, individual specialist practice has led to some increase in the cost of medical care. Whether or not the public is now thereby obtaining medical care of a better grade, it should be obvious that the solution of the problem lies not in reverting to the ancient general practitioner who did everything medical or surgical. More likely it lies in a coordinated teaming of specialists that keeps their activities under control and direction and gets the greatest degree of efficiency from them. One of the devices for doing this is group practice. When group practice has been established it has too often been in the face of rather firm professional opposition, whether the group practices on a fee-for-service basis or on a prepaid basis. When the group operates on a special prepayment plan controlled by non-medical people the opposition is especially vigorous. It may be worth while to reflect upon some of the reasons for this situation.

When an independent group of physicians, well trained in various specialties, decides to establish a group practice in an area which previously had available medical care only by independent general practitioners, it is natural for the general practitioners to fear the competition of the group; for the members of the group are apt to be better trained individually than the local practitioners, and collectively they bring complete expert medical coverage including the various specialties. In spite of the well-deserved attachment of the native population to their accustomed family doctors, experience shows that after a period of apathy or even resistance by the population, the group is soon accepted and recognized for what it is—a means of bringing better medical care to the area.

It has been repeatedly demonstrated that it is thus possible to attract well-trained physicians to a rural area. Furthermore, it has been well established that, through group practice, specialists working as a team can give complete medical coverage to relatively poor rural communities. Medical care of high quality can be offered at a fee schedule that the great majority of the people of the community can afford. In some situations families maintain a general practitioner as family physician and go to or are referred to the group clinic for special diagnostic or therapeutic problems. Eventually in most instances an internist within the group assumes the relationship of personal physician.

In most such groups the individual fee-for-service basis is employed, but in some of the larger groups there are arrangements whereby the group assumes responsibility for the care of families or employee groups or other aggregates of people on an annual per-capita-fee basis. The group has a business manager or staff which is, of course, more efficient than the usual office management of the average individual practitioner. The distribution of the annual income of the group is controlled in small groups directly by the physicians involved; in large groups, through the executive or governing body of the group. In any case there is no outside control to cause resentment among the professional staff.

In certain teaching institutions there have been established plans by which patients may pay for diagnostic study and frequently also for treatment, under the professional supervision of members of the teaching staff, in an arrangement that can only be described as group practice. The quality of medical care in such circumstances is, as may be expected, excellent; and additional benefits are derived from the fact that the patients may lend themselves for instructional purposes. However, the fees are often handled by the institution rather than by the individual physician or surgeon, the professional staff being on a fixed salary.

This practice too has met with criticism from time to time, even within the schools. The criticism has come from various sources, such as the so-called clinical teacher who, unsalaried and dependent on private practice, sees the group as immediate competition; or from the occasional member of the salaried staff who is convinced that the fees he draws to the group far exceed his own salary, forgetting that this may occur in any group and losing the lustre of his earlier inspiration. For at one time he must have been convinced that such a discrepancy between earning power and compensation would be rather less unpalatable in a teaching group, because it helped to support colleagues who might be too busy teaching and doing research to have time for many consultations.

The type of group practice which has encountered the most stubborn resistance is that supported by prepayment plans. Among such plans perhaps the best known are the Health Insurance Plan of Greater New York, commonly known as HIP, and the Kaiser-Permanente plan on the Pacific coast. It is alleged that because of opposition to the Kaiser-Permanente plan and to the physicians identified with it, it was necessary to build a Kaiser Foundation Hospital in an area which already had an excess of hospital beds beyond the community need. By way of retribution the new hospital is reported to be fully occupied while the other hospitals in the community have even more unfilled beds than they had earlier.

Among the reasons advanced in opposition to such plans would appear to be the fact that they are controlled by groups outside the medical profession and the allegation that the plans interfere with the patient's free choice of physician; for a patient who has prepaid for medical care through such a plan can go only to a physician working within the plan, unless he is willing to forfeit the benefits for which advance payment has been made by him or his employer or his union or other sponsor. If the argument that such plans interfere with the free choice of physician is examined carefully, one cannot fail to observe, on the other side of the coin, an admonition that one must not interfere with the right of a patient or a physician to join such a plan freely if he wishes. Indeed one might paraphrase the Bicentennial Theme and speak of man's right to medical knowledge and the unrestricted use thereof.

As a general principle there should be emphasis on the freedom to experiment for those properly qualified to experiment in forms of medical practice, in forms of remunerating physicians, in forms of training physicians for their various roles.

It is sometimes asserted that medical schools should become protagonists in the fight for prepayment plans for medical care; or, on the other hand, should indoctrinate more students toward general practice and less toward specialties. It is not the function of the medical schools to indoctrinate medical students toward one medical philosophy or another. If the medical students are exposed to specialists almost exclusively rather than to general practitioners during their years in medical school, this may reflect the fact that most of the best teachers are specialists but does not reflect any desire to discourage a student who may be interested in a career in general practice. The primary job of the medical school is to teach each of its students the best scientific medicine and the highest standards of ethics, no matter what form of career he may ultimately choose.

If freedom is our theme it must work both ways. The schools must be free not to indoctrinate. The medical schools of America have manifested great interest in the social aspects of medicine, but their main object is to maintain undiluted the highest possible quality in the training given their students. They should avoid indoctrination in terms of political aspects or economic aspects or even the specialties. The modern medical student is so intelligent and independent that, were his school to attempt indoctrination, he would very likely react with the suspicion that there must be something wrong with the thing for which indoctrination was attempted. Freedom of choice on the part of the students must be maintained.

The medical schools have participated in experiments in group practice and in other areas and have encountered many obstacles. Even today schools and teaching hospitals are criticized for employing on salary basis pathologists, radiologists, anesthetists, and other physicians engaged full time in the activities of the teaching center. The very profession that stands to gain the most by maintenance of quality is going to suffer if schools cannot be free. It is especially undignified when specialty groups snipe at the medical teaching centers upon which they rely for the training through hospital residency of the members of their own specialty, and upon which they depend for the advance through research of their own scientific disciplines. Many of the medical schools are poor as church mice and are having a difficult time keeping programs going, and fighting this rear-guard action slows their progress. The schools must be free to experiment and must maintain an educational program which will turn out physicians having the freedom and courage to choose the type of career they wish.

The Consumers' Interest

From the point of view of the consumers of medical care one might approach the theme of the health needs of the nation with a single, simple, and fundamental query. Are there unmet needs in the health picture of the nation, and if so, how serious are they? Or are the resources for supplying the health needs of the nation adequate, and, if they are not, what can be done?

Simple as this topic may seem, as it is launched, it immediately is washed against the rocky problems of trying to differentiate needs or indispensables on the one hand and demands or desires on the other. Need is a humble word, demand is arrogant. Furthermore, it is not always easy to distinguish in such discussion those elements which are primarily not medical but economic or political. Many a snowball thrown at the medical profession is built around a black coal of unqualified statistics which apply data that are solely economic and draw conclusions slanted against the medical profession rather than society at large. In any event, the discussion leads in many interesting paths, including the cost of medical care, the pervasive influence of health insurance, the good and sometimes disconcerting effects of recent developments in health care.

The Nation's Health Resources

Are the health needs of the nation adequate? In view of the emanations from certain quarters it may come as a surprise to some to learn that the health resources in this country are the best in the world. It may be true that the distribution of physicians is not optimal. The ratio of physicians to population is much higher in the heavily populated areas than in sparsely populated places; in the more backward states the ratio is lowest. In New York City and in the District of Columbia the ratio is undoubtedly too high. This, however, is a land of freedom, and a physician cannot be forced to practice in a community which he does not find sufficiently attractive any more than can a lawyer or an engineer, a teacher or an economist.

The solution is for the less fortunate areas to do something to enhance their attractiveness. There is probably maldistribution in most professions but the social scientists tend to focus attention on the medical profession. Not only of physicians is the ratio per unit of population higher in the urban communities than in the scantily populated and less progressive areas, but also of dentists, nurses, dietitians, physical therapists, clinical psychologists, X-ray technicians, optometrists, chiropodists, and social workers.

Even with distribution that is less than optimal, the health services generally available in this country probably surpass anything in the world. Very often, however, the population is not aware of the opportunities for health service. Many instances of people lacking medical care have been due not to their inability to get it, rather to their ignorance of how to get it. Many medical societies carry on health education activities for the general population. A county medical society in the West even advertised to the local populace that anyone could get medical care by just telephoning to ask for directions.

There are some extreme examples of ignorance of medical opportunities, such as was found by the Health Insurance Plan of Greater New York. Among the people enrolled in this plan, for example through certain labor union contracts, were various uneducated groups. During the early phase of the plan's existence the extent of this problem was not appreciated until certain union groups contemplated withdrawing from the plan because it did not bring sufficient benefit to the subscribing members. Then it was realized that many such subscribers could not understand English very well. Fruitful efforts were then expended to educate such people as to what services were available to them and instruct them in the simple matter of when they ought to call a doctor and how they should go about it.

In this country, almost anywhere, a person need have no money at all to obtain good medical care—if he is smart enough to know how to go about it. How much of this medical care, available for the asking, should be a free gift from the medical profession need not occupy our attention at this point. But if one were to assume that all economic barriers and all the barriers due to ignorance were removed so that everyone were to seek to avail himself of all the available health services, then indeed our system would break down and the demand could not be met. If every person were intelligent enough and economically able to have complete care of his teeth, there would not be enough dentists to satisfy the demands, even with the improvement in the problem of caries anticipated from the fluoridation of water supplies. If all the people who could profit from available facilities and techniques for rehabilitation were to seek to avail themselves of such opportunities, there would not be nearly enough facilities or trained personnel to take care of them.

It is a curious fact and perhaps not sufficiently appreciated how directly this situation has been produced by the accomplishments of the medical sciences and the healing arts. Successive conquests of water-borne diseases, communicable diseases of childhood, diabetes, pneumonia, venereal diseases, and presently tuberculosis, better knowledge of nutrition, improved anesthesia and better surgery have all contributed to the well-known increase in life expectancy so that more and more individuals live to a ripe age. Life expectancy at birth in 1900 was 47 and in 1949 was 68, and today is still higher. At the same time the development in the economic and social picture has been such that there are fewer opportunities for persons in the older age groups to be gainfully employed or even sufficiently occupied to prevent boredom.

There are a number of interesting and even amusing sidelights on this problem. The most oppressive concern of the aged is loneliness. When group social activities are encouraged for older persons, or old folks' homes are made sufficiently attractive, a number of interesting developments occur.

There is one interesting experience with four hundred old people who are the wards of a lodge and in a home, into which they have bought their way by a certain down payment, as is quite customary in old folks' homes. The medical care they formerly had was rather desultory. A well-known medical group made an arrangement affording comprehensive medical care for five dollars a month, per guest (as they call them), and gave them everything they might need as far as their medical services are concerned. As far as the medical services are concerned, the group did not make any money. It was a charitable gesture. But from the point of view of the board of trustees of this home, it had a rather unfortunate effect. Over the three years, it would now appear, with this type of care, the average length of life of these people is about six months longer than it used to be, and it has thrown their finances completely out of kilter. They are looking at the whole contract rather frankly at the moment, because they cannot turn it down on the evidence that better medical care has increased the length of life of these old people, but they cannot meet the costs that have been developed as a result of that; so it is a dilemma.

In another experience in a Western state there was started "The Little House" which was so called because it was a small house, the only one then available for an old folks' club. It has developed now into a club of about 600, and "The Little House" has grown into a big house which the community built with private subscriptions, and it is a rallying place for all the old people in the area, not only for social activities, but also for doing various things that are economically profitable but not seriously competitive with industry, such as making toys for children and a lot of things of that kind. They have an active social life. It has developed into something of a matrimonial agency as well, curiously enough. It filled a need for the community. It convinced all that old people like to be together in association with people of their own age, and they need a lot of retraining, at least to be retired. It seems that one actually needs a period of training for retirement now, if one is going to be happy at it. Some schools are considering this. In one university, for example, the psychology department, together with the education department, is trying to work out a curriculum for people to attend in preparation for retirement.

Related Community Problems

It is apparent that many of the problems touching upon the health of the nation are not primarily medical responsibilities and the medical profession cannot be blamed if the rest of society has not solved problems which touch upon the health of the nation. The health professions must continue the endeavor to do the best job they can, even if their success creates other problems for society. It is true in many fields that when one target or objective is reached the realization soon dawns that there are other objectives still more remote. Like Tantalus ever reaching for the fruit just out of reach, we are destined never to rest. In education society was content at one time to make the "three Rs" available to all. The persistence of illiteracy, as periodically we are reminded by such agencies as the Selective Service, indicates that this objective has not been fully accomplished; yet the objectives have been set higher, and now college and university education is the objective which many state and municipal governments make available to all, free or at a token payment.

Although education is not the primary responsibility of the medical profession, an important role in health education has been accepted. Similarly in other fields which are not exclusively medical the profession has offered assistance which has sometimes been accepted grudgingly or not at all.

For example, in the field of aviation it is particularly true that performance and safety are dependent on the tolerances of the human organism; the engineering of the plane cannot ignore these human health factors. Specialists in the field of aviation medicine have long since demonstrated that backward-facing seats are safer and have advocated the use of them in planes. Resistance to this proposal delayed any implementation for many, many years. Only recently has this resistance begun to yield.

Similarly in the field of automobile accidents. It is true that better highway design, improvements in automotive design, better policing, enlightened legislation, and public education are needed. Yet to the medical profession a condition that can kill 435 people in two days should be treated as vigorously as public health officials would treat an epidemic. The health professions would be castigated if an epidemic of preventable or controllable disease of this magnitude were permitted to go unchecked. Yet society has not come to grips with this pandemic of automobile accidents. As a people apparently we are unwilling to do what needs to be done, to keep unsafe cars off the roads, to cut automatically the speed of our cars, to build into cars all the safety features that have been recommended.

Fifty or a hundred years ago society was unwilling to do much about water and sewage, but as population centers grew things were accomplished. Perhaps with the increasing congestion and hazards on our highways the time will come when we shall do some of the things that need to be done about the automotive environment. The contributions of aviation medicine have been appreciated more in the armed forces than among civilians and it is perhaps not surprising that leadership in the field of automobile accidents should be found in the same place. There is in the Armed Forces Epidemiological Board a commission on accidental trauma. This group is sponsoring very revealing studies of accidents both in military and in civilian experience.

Another broad problem that has caused concern among public health authorities is the lack of a resolute approach to the stimulating information uncovered by a study in the city of St. Paul (Bradley Buell and Associates, *Community Planning for Human Services,* Columbia University Press, 1952). This study underscored vividly a fact that should have been emphasized earlier. It was demonstrated that a small nucleus of the population, constituting 6 per cent of the families, accounted for over half of the public and private expenditures by medical, welfare, and other correctional agencies. The mobilization of the various social and professional organizations concerned is not sufficiently good to get at this hard core who contribute so materially to our community problem. Why is it that this group of families that costs us so much have so much disease, disability, delinquency and antisocial behavior? Do we need more freedom to experiment on this problem? Perhaps we need to get rid of our prejudices in our approaches to these families. Perhaps none of our insurance, medical care plans, hospital organization, public health organization, nursing organization, or any other community approach gets down to solve these problems with people.

Sometimes the people and the groups which are most vocal about these problems are also the least active. As an example of initiative in a somewhat related community problem, an interesting experiment is under way among old folks in a large metropolitan area, not in the confines of an old folks' home. The New York Hospital and Cornell Medical College, both private organizations in the fields of health and education, are cooperating with the New York City Health Department and several foundations in this study. They have taken an appropriate sample, picked by a sociologist, of all the old people in the area. They have determined what problems these old people have, and have elicited what problems the oldsters cause their families. On the basis of the problems, they are building the services that are needed to solve these problems. Although there is a medical component, it is not chiefly a medical problem. For example, the lack of financial support, with the inability or unwillingness through ignorance to use the financial props available in the community that would help the financial picture, is one important problem. The oldsters do not know about old-age insurance or they do not know how to go about getting it. They have job difficulties too. But with a little bit of prompting many will go out and get a job. Sometimes finding out, medically speaking, what kind of jobs they are still capable of doing opens up new jobs.

The Cost of Medical Care

There are not many subjects of more general interest than the cost of medical care and perhaps in no other frame of reference is cost so glibly separated from the value of what is purchased. The family that purchases a television set, whether it can afford to or not, expects to pay for it and is likely to have a genuine interest in the quality of the set purchased. Persons of moderate means are the largest purchasers of automobiles, home appliances, cosmetics, beverages, entertainment, and other features of so-called "optional consumption."

To what degree are the responsibilities for health services to be individual? To what extent does or should the government enter into the planning of health services? By contrast, to what extent does this same question apply to matters of food supply, housing, transportation, and social security?

For background material, attention might be called to the fact that the total annual charges for health services in the United States are currently in excess of ten billion dollars per year. Charges by physicians total approximately 37 per cent of this total, and those for hospitals amount to two billion dollars, nearly 20 per cent. Medicines cost 1,500 million dollars, roughly 15 per cent, and are largely patent medicines and pharmaceuticals. Other medical services consume about 13 per cent, and dental services about 1,600 million dollars or 16 per cent. The average family is spending just over two hundred dollars per year for health services. However, approximately 3,500,000 families incur charges of five hundred dollars a year or more. It is estimated that a million families spend on health services one half of their annual income, which introduces the question of catastrophic illnesses, to which insurance companies are now giving so much attention.

The over-all statistics on the cost of health services are often used indiscriminately to bludgeon the medical profession, because it is rather convenient to have a "whipping boy" who is somehow impersonal. For example, the argument that there are so many million persons or so many million families whose annual earnings are less than two thousand dollars a year, and therefore cannot afford to pay the costs of medical care, glosses over the fact that these unfortunates also cannot afford a great many other things, and ignores the fact that the medical profession traditionally renders more free service to the indigent than any other group except the clergy. Of course there are some doctors who never perform any free services and there are some who charge exorbitant fees. Curiously the public in its sometimes strange reaction often adulates the one who charges exorbitant fees believing that he is *ipso facto* an unusually good doctor. The American Medical Association, speaking through a former president of that Association, has recently and publicly taken a forthright stand against exorbitant fees even when these fees are charged to wealthy patients.

There are many other developments which are tending to level off fees for medical services. The highest fees traditionally have been charged by surgeons and are based on the practice of an earlier day when good surgery was practiced by an esoteric few. The public still attaches much more glamor to a simple appendectomy than to the far more difficult management of such non-surgical emergencies as diabetic acidosis or coronary occlusion. But within the profession it is now realized universally that one can just as easily become a surgeon as an internist, perhaps easier, and there is quite possibly an over-production of surgeons. The establishment of active grievance committees in county medical societies has helped mightily to control abuses of fee schedules. It is fair to say that the influence of outside agencies has also contributed to stabilization of fees. Insurance plans which establish limits, however arbitrary, to the amount which they will pay for specific surgical procedures have inevitably tended to level costs.

When exorbitant fees are charged, it is almost always by a practitioner in so-called solo practice. It is seldom encountered in ethical group practice. One obvious reason is that within the group propinquity and cooperation make it more than usually evident that the nonsurgical practitioners bring as much talent and effort to the enterprise as do those whose training happens to be in a surgical field. Other reasons why properly operated group practice tends to lower the costs of medical care include the following: Patients of the variety referred to as medical shoppers do not shop around from specialist to specialist in an ethically conducted group, but are seen only by such specialists as they need to see. At the same time patients who are not aware of the need for specialist attention will be referred for such care when indicated. The net result is a more economical use of the time of the various specialists.

It has been said that in the Orient the man who can afford a personal physician pays his physician only while in good health, but if the patient or patron becomes ill the physician is not paid for his ministrations. In our culture the traditional pattern has been to pay the physician on a personal fee-for-service basis when treatment is given for illness or disability. Furthermore, a few short decades ago such medical service was usually brought to the home and was often sought only when the patient had become quite ill. Nowadays home calls are made relatively infrequently. Most patients are cared for in office consultation or clinic and patients who are too ill to be ambulatory are usually hospitalized. Furthermore, although the personal fee-for-service arrangement is still predominant, it is becoming increasingly common for the physician or surgeon to be remunerated by an intermediate whether an insurance carrier, a welfare fund, or an employer on a salaried basis.

There are many interesting and controversial aspects of the developing pattern of compensation for medical and surgical care through a third party. The United Mine Workers Association Welfare and Retirement Fund has had a long and interesting experience in its effort to afford medical care to its members. This fund operated in areas where medical care was in general not very good because of lack of facilities and because of the fact that the areas, not prosperous or alluring to start with, did not attract the best trained physicians. It was necessary to endeavor to make the most economical use of the available facilities, but this was not easy. The most economical operation was through decent group clinics. Proprietary group clinics, which merely create a monopoly, are not conducive to the best interests of any except those who make up the monopoly. This experience has shown that a straight fee-for-service basis where the fees are paid by a willing and unrestricted intermediary rather than by the patient can lead to circumstances which, if not abusive, are somewhat unpalatable. For example, physicians who were relatively not very highly skilled were often able to net exceedingly high incomes by seeing an inordinate number of patients. Compensation by a fee per unit of time rather than a fee per patient seen was often indicated to be more realistic and to promise less casual medical care. In many areas the UMWA is establishing its own clinics and hospitals.

On the other hand, experience elsewhere, *e.g.* in municipal and other health services, shows that whereas payment on a fee-for-time basis may control costs somewhat, it has other limitations. In such a system it is not easy to police the quality of the professional services rendered. If long maintained without other kinds of stimuli, the payment on a time basis tends to attract and hold a good many people that the employer would be pleased not to hold so long. There is a security factor in payment on a time basis; it seems very difficult to set up standards of performance for employees paid on that basis. It is easy to confuse our objectives in moving from one economic solution to another. In solving one problem in the economic field it is possible that another problem may be created in relation to the professional quality of the services involved. No matter what system of payment may be best in a particular situation, the most important element is still the quality of medical service obtained. Low quality or cheap medical care is eventually the most expensive care, whether the fees are paid by an individual patient or by a welfare fund or by an insurance carrier. Anything which causes deterioration of quality adds to the cost.

Health Insurance

The growth of the health insurance principle is far and away the most important development in relation to the costs of medical care, important alike to the consumer and the producer of medical care. The Blue Cross movement was directed primarily at meeting the hospitalization needs of middle-class and working-class families who were able to maintain a standard of living above a subsistence level. It quickly spread to cover all social groups. The Blue Shield plans for medical and surgical expenses have had a tremendous growth. They now have over 28,000,000 subscribers. Not all plans offer the same services but practically all of them are gradually extending coverage. More than 100,000,000 individuals have some form of hospitalization insurance, and over 85,000,000 persons have some form of insurance to cover at least part of the expense of surgical operations; these figures have increased phenomenally in the past ten years. By far the largest percentage of subscribers to such insurance plans are derived from group contracts implying that the individual is enrolled as a member of an employed group. Sometimes the fees are paid in whole or in part by an employer or by a labor union treasury. Even when the employee pays the entire fee it is usually deducted from his pay and handled by the employer. The administrative advantages to the insurance carrier in such an arrangement usually result in lower premiums to the subscriber.

The advantages and indeed the necessity of such insurance coverage are so apparent that it is reasonable to assume that the number of persons insured will continue to increase rapidly until virtually all individuals are covered except the usual group of persons living at or below a subsistence level whom the gospel promises we shall always have with us. Actually it is reported by the Secretary of Health, Education, and Welfare that about a quarter of the families with annual incomes of two thousand dollars already have some form of health insurance, as does a quarter of the population over 65 years of age. Whether or not it will ever be feasible for the community to obtain health insurance for the indigent is not a medical problem. Meanwhile, at least in the larger communities, the taxpayers pay toward the hospitalization of the indigent in municipal hospitals and to a degree even in nonmunicipal hospitals. However, the degree to which the medical care of these persons is furnished free by the medical profession both in hospital wards and in clinics is commonly overlooked.

It has been asserted that in spite of the growth of prepayment and insurance plans these pay for only 15 per cent of the nation's medical bills. This is another example of how unevaluated statistics can be misleading, for the implication sometimes intended is that doctors' fees and hospital fees have risen far out of proportion to the insurance coverage. Insurance covers very much more than 15 per cent of the sickness expenses of the average American. Thus in order to reduce the percentage covered by insurance to 15 per cent there must be included in the total costs much that is not expected to be covered by insurance, such as Federal and state hospital populations. It is well known that more than half of the hospital beds in this country are in mental hospitals, largely operated by the state governments, and insurance does not cover mental illness. The Federal government takes care of huge numbers of military personnel and dependents and veterans, and this expensive medical care is paid out of tax funds and not insurance. Also it is common knowledge that many persons have insurance for certain type of accommodations but, perhaps because the insurance will pay part, desire more luxurious accommodations upon entering a hospital. There are people who do not need private nurses or certainly not around the clock, yet demand such attention. All this is included in the calculation of the total medical bill. To imply that insurance can be expected to cover only 15 per cent of the average person's medical expenses is disingenuous.

It would be surprising if anything involving as many people as does health insurance could be introduced without some abuses. There have been abuses on the part of both the purveyors and the consumers of health services and also on the part of the management of such funds. The abuses are isolated and usually exaggerated. On the part of the public, there is the subscriber who demands more X-rays than are necessary, private nursing that is unneeded, hospitalization for a checkup which could be done on an ambulatory basis. It is not easy for a physician to resist such demands, and the subscribers must be made more aware of the fact that such behavior increases the premiums for all subscribers. On the professional side there is the doctor who will perform unnecessary surgery or who will deliberately raise his fees if the patient is insured. Eventually public opinion and more directly action by the grievance committee of the appropriate medical society will control such abuses.

Management of some plans has fixed fee schedules that are arbitrarily low. For example, in one local situation a fee of thirty dollars was set for a tonsillectomy; and surgeons who continued to charge the fee of sixty dollars which they were accustomed to charge were falsely accused of doubling their fee because of the existence of the particular prepayment plan. All these abuses may be considered in the nature of growing pains and will not in any way check the lusty growth of prepayment insurance.

As indicated earlier, the insurance plans have had a leveling effect on fee schedules, and many medical leaders are coming to feel that abuses and criticisms will be avoided when fee schedules are adopted and promulgated by county medical societies. This would be on a local basis, since medical and surgical fees may be expected to vary in different areas just as every other item in the cost of living varies. Certainly doctors will have to charge higher fees if, in the community where they practice, rents, heat and utilities, salaries of their employees, and cost of food and clothing are higher than in other areas.

Failure to appreciate this simple fact underlies many fallacies in attempting to solve everything on a national level. It may be difficult to live on an annual income of two or three thousand dollars in New York City; but in many communities this would go a great deal further, for instance in Southern areas where food may be much cheaper and the need for winter clothing or for expensively heated and insulated homes is less, and real estate valuations are much lower. Problems in a coal-mining area may be far different from those in a heavily populated urban area. We complicate our problems when we try to cover too much at one time. The facilities (hospitals and clinics) are possessed locally, the professional personnel are abundant or scarce locally, the particular needs are local. A solution that may be ideal in one area may not work so well in another unless modified a great deal.

In a broader sense, when all the elements of a problem are brought into one complex, with the inference that they must be solved together, we may put off the day of solving any of them. For example, some people bring together all the elements touching upon the nation's health including economic, geographic, political, social, moral, and scientific problems. Sometimes they are inclined to stand back in awe at the monstrously complex problem they have depicted and rather hope for some gigantic genius to appear with a magic key. If the problem could be broken down to its components and these attacked on the most appropriate basis, usually local, it may be possible to solve some of our problems.

SUMMARY

America's health is the best in its history and the best in the world. In spite of this we can never permit ourselves to be satisfied and must set our goals ever higher and higher. The quality and quantity of health services are not uniform throughout the country by any means, and much remains to be accomplished. It is necessary to separate wherever possible those shortcomings which are due to economic or other social factors from those which are due to the health professions and healing arts directly.

There are forces operating within the health professions and others operating upon them from without which are steadily leading to a better distribution of medical care and to a leveling of the costs of health services. Among these are the development of group-type practice and the phenomenal growth of health insurance.

There have been a surprisingly large number of plans, programs, schemes and systems instituted in this country for the purpose of accomplishing better distribution of health services. Almost all have been appropriately and necessarily on a local basis within communities, or counties, or industries, or trade unions. Many of them are difficult to evaluate for the reason that at the outset they did not include a mechanism for evaluation or were, so to speak, not properly controlled experiments. It seems worthwhile to attempt an evaluation of these various schemes in the hope that it may be possible to identify the strongest and most productive features and perhaps to recognize and avoid those features of certain plans which may carry the seeds of failure.

It cannot be urged too forcibly that there must be freedom to experiment— by those qualified to experiment—in the more effective distribution of health services. If any physician is free to practice on a solo, fee-for-service, private-practice basis—and no one denies that freedom—it is, then, equally true that a physician must be free to sell his services for a salary whether that salary be paid by a group of physicians, a hospital, a medical school, or an agency of government.

PARTICIPANTS

DANA W. ATCHLEY, Professor of Clinical Medicine, Columbia University

GEORGE W. BACHMAN, Senior Staff Member, The Brookings Institution

GEORGE BAEHR, President and Medical Director, Health Insurance Plan of Greater New York

CHESTER I. BARNARD, Chairman, National Science Board, National Science Foundation

E. DWIGHT BARNETT, Professor of Administrative Medicine, School of Public Health, Columbia University

LOUIS H. BAUER, Secretary General, The World Medical Association

LEONA BAUMGARTNER, Commissioner of Health, City of New York

FRANK B. BERRY, Assistant Secretary of Defense for Health and Medical Affairs

DEAN A. CLARK, General Director, Massachusetts General Hospital

WARREN F. DRAPER, Executive Medical Officer, Welfare and Retirement Fund, United Mine Workers of America

ANNA FILLMORE, General Director, National League for Nursing, Inc.

ALBERT J. HAYES, International President, International Association of Machinists

MAURICE J. HICKEY, Associate Dean, School of Dental and Oral Surgery, Columbia University

JOSEPH C. HINSEY, Chairman, Executive Council, Association of American Medical Colleges

HOLGAR J. JOHNSON, President, Institute of Life Insurance

RUSSEL V. LEE, Executive Officer, Palo Alto Clinic, California

JAMES E. McCORMACK, Associate Dean of Graduate Medicine, Columbia University

WILLARD C. RAPPLEYE, Vice-president in charge of Medical Affairs and Dean of the Faculty of Medicine, Columbia University

LOWELL J. REED, President, The Johns Hopkins University

DICKINSON W. RICHARDS, JR., Lambert Professor of Medicine, Columbia University

HOWARD C. TAYLOR, JR., Professor of Obstetrics and Gynecology, Columbia University

PART FOUR

Social Services and the Free Economy

INTRODUCTION

Part Four sought to develop a concept of what social services in this country are and might be and to review issues which must be faced up to in coming years. What social services are needed? What social services can we afford? Can we provide needed services and maintain our free society?

The papers by Benjamin Youngdahl and George Davidson dealt with the scope of the field, with present needs, and with the effort to define the proper roles of governmental and private programs. Stemming from these papers attention shifted naturally to the problem of financing social services in the paper by William Haber. Limits and limitations, as these derive from social attitudes, knowledge, social setting, and problems within the profession were introduced into the picture by Gordon Allport's paper. The discussions were then summarized by Nathan Cohen.

All papers are closely interrelated and the theme of the Conference and of Part Four is developed through all of them. Lively discussion was produced among the conference participants by every paper. Reports* of the discussions, however, are not reproduced here because Nathan Cohen, who edited his paper in the light of the discussions, in effect reports them with his own comments. His effort, therefore, takes the place of a summary of discussion, and at the same time projects a synthesis with which many of the participants were in harmony. While it can hardly be called a consensus, it is certainly an expression of the basic reaction of many participants to the conference experience.

Kenneth D. Johnson
Dean, New York School of Social Work
Columbia University

* The assistance is acknowledged of Alfred J. Kahn, Associate Professor of Social Work, New York School of Social Work, who served as vice chairman of Part Four, and of the following recorders: Mrs. Alvan Martin, Mr. Irving Miller, Mr. Samuel Firestone, and Miss Carole Meyer.

Social Services: Need and Scope

Benjamin E. Youngdahl
Dean, George Warren Brown School of Social Work
Washington University

The search for security is as old as mankind. But need in the early days of our history was quite different from what it is today. The pioneers were true individualists, and most rugged indeed. Vast natural resources remained untouched and the acres of land awaited the plow. Except in periods of natural catastrophe, as long as the frontier existed the opportunities for homesteading precluded any lack of work. Our early colonists were insecure but their competition was with nature more than with man. They faced a realistic danger from the Indians, from the wild beasts of the forests, and from nature herself. The accurate rifle conquered the wild beasts, exploitation subdued the Indians, and hard work and technology conquered nature.

But new fears, new insecurities arose—of man against man; and these are more subtle and more ruthless. With wise management we no longer have to fear mass hunger or mass starvation, because we have the means to get more out of the soil and the ability to use nature more effectively. Each individual, however, has to fear whether he will get his share of the product for himself and his family; some individuals who fall by the wayside through handicapping conditions, through the compulsion of environment, or through ill fortune may have the fear of want of the basic necessities of life.

SOCIAL CHANGES CREATE NEW NEEDS

As the industrial revolution proceeded, the development of large-scale industry, mass production, corporate enterprise, and specialization brought man easier access to the necessities of life. It made his access, however, dependent upon steady employment at wages sufficient to acquire those necessities. The instability and uncertainty of continued employment raise genuine fears on his part and the increasing use of automatic machinery and the production-belt processes frequently brings problems of job interest and morale. The need

133

for leisure-time activities increases as our per-worker output increases with our growing technology.

Moreover, our society has gradually changed in character from face-to-face to secondary social groups. In this kind of development mutual aid becomes less possible and organized programs to take care of individual needs become more necessary.

With the development of industry has come urbanization, and with it the anonymity of modern living in cities. Mutual aid would not be possible now on any large scale, as the "block aid plan" of the great depression in the 1930s illustrated. Whole blocks of families were unemployed and in need—in some instances, indeed, so were whole cities. The basis of need, therefore, has widened, as social changes have taken place, from the individual to the family, to the community, to the state, and to the nation.

The late Justice Cardozo said in a famous Supreme Court opinion in 1937: "Needs that were narrow or parochial a century ago are now intertwined with the well-being of the nation."[1] Franklin Roosevelt had expressed the same concept in 1934: "Security was obtained in the earlier days through the inter-dependence of members of families upon each other and of the families within a small community upon each other. The complexities of great communities and of organized industry make less real these simple means of security. Therefore, we are compelled to employ the active interest of the nation as a whole through government in order to encourage a greater security for each individual who composes it."[2]

In addition, we have the factor of war. The increased stresses and strains resulting from war run the whole gamut of need from income maintenance to emotional adjustment. Some provision must be arranged, for example, to give help to the unwanted or neglected child resulting from a quick and unfortunate war marriage.

The decline of the large family and the deterioration of the small family also have brought increasing problems and needs. Divorce, abandonment of children, illegitimacy require some community action if only to pick up the pieces and give protection to innocent persons.

The very existence or development of health and welfare programs and the increase in medical technology have brought increasing longevity, which in itself presents a problem of income maintenance in the later years of life. Even as conservative a periodical as *Business Week* has said: "The problem of destitute old age is not new, although it has been intensified by our shift from an agricultural to an industrial economy. In approaching it, two premises must be acknowledged: (1) That few persons, no matter how industrious or thrifty, can at present save enough from their earnings to provide for a long twilight of life, even on the most modest scale, and (2) that the majority of old persons must be supported by others—whether those others are their own kin, or organized charity, or some agency of the state."[3]

The increasing number of aged who live beyond their industrially productive years in our economy presents the problem not only of income maintenance but of morale, recreation, and participation in our common life.

In addition to the natural hazards of drouth, floods, tornadoes, and earthquakes, which in themselves are an increasing problem in a congregate society, we have such catastrophes as explosions, fires, industrial accidents, etc. The community, either on a voluntary basis or through government, for its own self-protection if for no other reason, must take concern and set up programs to alleviate the results of such catastrophes.

The increasing mobility of our population, owing primarily to more effective means of transportation and communication, in itself brings about problems which require welfare services. There are people who become stranded through unforeseen contingencies, and large numbers of people may move within a short time to certain localities; thus the development of new and sometimes special social services may be required.

The very tempo of modern life, with quick changes and with the increasing emphasis in our culture on wealth accumulation and conspicuous consumption, adds to the problem of modern living for the individual. The increase in mental illness, while complex in causation, perhaps has some relationship to this rapidity of social change. Social services to meet this situation, and perhaps to prevent or reduce the incidence of mental disorders, become necessary if the social group is to exist in an orderly manner.

This is a large and varied country, geographically, industrially, and culturally. Sound planning must start with this recognition. We still have large rural areas, as well as cities, with which our planning must be concerned. Less specialization is possible in rural areas, though the variation of need from year to year is perhaps considerably greater than that in urban areas. In any case, while people in general are about the same whether they live in a rural or an urban setting, the settings and resources are different. A national public policy for welfare should consider these differences and make allowances for them. A public welfare program which will permit flexibility in administration according to local needs and which will at the same time have the necessary Federal financial aid appears to be required as a part of any total plan.

The range of needed social services in this complicated society includes not only financial, but also a large variety of nonfinancial services, as outlined below.

Here are some of the elements of need already recognized under existing services.

Needs related to income maintenance or financial dependency associated with the following situations:

1. Separation of bread winner
2. Old age
3. Sickness or disability
4. Unemployment

5. Natural catastrophe (or fire, explosion, etc.)
6. Large families with insufficient wages or incomes.

Needs involving services other than direct financial aid:

1. Child welfare services
   a. Adoptions and foster homes
   b. Protection and prevention
   c. Neglect
   d. Illegitimacy
   e. Emotional maladjustment
   f. Juvenile deliquency
2. Family casework and counseling
3. Recreation and group work services
4. Psychiatric services for adults—treatment and prevention
5. Miscellaneous services arising from need due to catastrophe
6. Organization, coordination, and development of community services
7. Research

After stating that the forces that originally created the need for welfare services are still present, John J. Corson summarizes the needs of the future as follows: "The look ahead to 1980 suggests that there will be a growing need for three types of protection we call welfare: (1) The assurance of income for millions of aged, widows, ill, and unemployed who cannot earn their living; (2) a variety of social services ranging from family counseling and child placement to recreation and psychiatric guidance; (3) the planning that welds these public and private services within the community into the integrated guarantee for the unfortunate. And the need for one of these three is as inseparable from the others as the ticks of a clock."[4]

The needs of children in our society provide a good example of required services. The publications of the Midcentury White House Conference on Children and Youth have given us some basic facts, some of the more pertinent of which are here itemized.[5]

1. The percentage of persons under 18 in the total population is increasing and will continue to do so at least for another decade; nearly four million infants were born in the United States in 1947 alone.

2. There are many children on the move. The homes of 8 million children changed in one year 1948–1949. About one million children are in families of migrant laborers.

3. The ratio of children to adults varies widely. There are 45 children under 18 per 100 adults aged 18–64 in the Northeast section of the country, whereas there are 65 such children per 100 adults in the South. There are more children per adults in the rural areas and more among nonwhites.

4. One out of five mothers with children under 18 works outside the home. Most of them do so in order to earn a living.

5. One out of eight children under 18 is not living with both parents. Two million such children are living with neither parent.

6. The average income of the nation's families in 1948 was $3,187. But it was $3,310 for white families, $1,768 for nonwhite, $3,551 for urban, $2,036 for farm, $3,272 for husband-wife families, and $2,064 for broken families headed by a woman.

7. Large families have lower incomes per person than small families. The per person income of one-child families in 1948 was $1,100 but it was only $375 in five-child families.

8. Infant and maternal mortality has declined steadily in the last quarter-century, but it is still much higher in the South than in the North.

9. Children in the five lowest states get less than half the medical care of children in the five highest states. The proportion for dental care is one-seventh.

10. One out of four counties in the nation is without a full-time public health nurse in rural areas.

11. Not a single state has adequate psychiatric clinic service for children and some states have almost none.

12. About half of the babies and children adopted in 1948 were placed for adoption by social agencies. The other half represents a potential black market.

There are a few obvious observations that can be drawn from these facts. First, in spite of the developments of the last quarter of a century, there is a vast deficit of needed services if we are to maintain a minimum uniform standard of modern requirements. Second, there is a large differential in service in the various sections of the country and the states. The child who happens to be born in a relatively wealthy state tends to get more and better service than one born in a poorer state. Some method of equalization becomes necessary if we accept the theory of what Eveline Burns calls equal access of service.[6] Third, some of the areas of nonfinancial services to children that need special attention in the next several years include psychiatric services to disturbed children, special services to migrant and mobile children, juvenile delinquency, day-care services to children of working mothers, and equalization of access to all services.

At the other end of the population spectrum we have the aged. Today about 13,600,000 persons are over 65, about 4,000,000 of whom are over 75. Of the total, 7,400,000 are females and 6,200,000 males.[7]

In 1937, a study made by Marjorie Shearon for the Social Security Board concluded that about two-thirds of those over the age of 65 are dependent and about one-third independent.[8] Since this date, Old Age and Survivors Insurance and other factors have changed the proportions substantially.

In round numbers 3,500,000 are today receiving Old Age Insurance benefits (does not include survivors' benefits), 2,500,000 are on Old Age Assistance rolls, about 1,000,000 are receiving benefits based on previous public employment (such as teachers, firemen, policemen), about 500,000 are receiving Railroad Retirement benefits, and about the same number are receiving private industrial and business pensions.[9] This makes a total of 8,000,000, which of course needs to be corrected for duplications. It is perhaps safe to generalize that more than one-half of those over 65 are receiving some kind of fairly regular financial payments from public or private insurance, assistance, or pension plans.

Old people, in general, constitute a low-income group. Despite all of the programs initiated during the last quarter of a century, the 1950 census data indicate that the median income of family groups in which the head was 65 years of age or over was $1,903, whereas the figure for the 55–64 group was $3,258.[10]

The problems of the aged and the need for new services will continue to increase. In addition to the economic aspects, problems of employment, education, health, counseling, morale, all need to be faced. Most private agencies appear to be reluctant to assume any major responsibility for case work and related services to the aged, partly due to the fear that if they go into the business seriously, it will engulf their total budgets. The problem is a large and increasing one and only government has the resources to meet the need.

In between children and the aged are many persons and families who require the services of social agencies of one kind or another. A few samples will here have to suffice.

> There are 3,800,000 alcoholics in the United States and we have hardly scratched the surface either to do the needed research to further understand the problem or to initiate required services to give individual treatment.[11]
>
> In some of our states, we are still living in medieval times as far as our efforts to do anything constructive are concerned in relation to mental ill health. Physical restraints are still the order of the day in not a few places and the lack of technical personnel to give even the known positive treatment or help is frightening. The need for the treatment and prevention of mental illness will likely continue to increase.
>
> The number of infants born outside of marriage was nearly 50 per cent greater in 1948 compared with 1938; the long-time trend of divorce continues to climb.[12]
>
> While some of our private social agencies have initiated "family life education" and similar services, the need for new techniques, for research, and for treatment services persists.

GOVERNMENT RESPONSIBILITY

If an individual is unable to care for himself and his dependents in one way or another, he may resort first to his family, or to friends and neighbors, or to voluntary organizations. If he fails to get the necessary help from those sources, then the community through government must step in to meet, as far as possible, the basic needs that exist. There are advantages in having local units of government take over certain responsibilities, but if they are either unable or unwilling to do so, the larger unit of government has the basic responsibility. In the 1930 depression, entire local communities or even whole states were inundated by unemployment and it became obvious early that only the resources of the whole nation could take care of the needs. Any need that affects a substantial group of people in the population and that is recurrent or long-continuing is an area in which government should step in with imagination and courage and do something about the problem. The *basic* responsibility belongs to government.

This does not preclude services by voluntary or private agencies and organizations; to the contrary, such services are needed just as much today as ever. The voluntary or private agencies can provide leadership in new fields, in experimentation and research, in giving support to sound public programs and in filling gaps here and there until the public is ready to accept the needed services. Moreover, they can give certain specialized services on a basis of contractual or delegated authority from some level of government. It is possible for public and private agencies to operate for the good of the whole on a coordinated basis without duplication of services, as long as the goal—the well-being of people—is a common one.

There is room for the services of private welfare agencies today and there is likely to be at all times. However, any assumption that voluntary efforts can take care of the total needs today, as widespread as they are in our complicated society, is born of sheer wish. They would get neither the required amount of money nor would they have the necessary compulsion of government to attain the agreed-upon objectives. A private agency determines the one segment of the population it is going to serve and also the particular service in which it is going to specialize. Even under the best circumstances, a system composed solely of private welfare services would leave gaps in which certain segments of the community and certain groups of the population would not be served. "Only the power of government can serve the interest of all."[13]

But there is a vocal opposition to this function of government.

During the past decade or two certain slogans and the technique of name-calling have been used frequently to prove a position. We have heard about the development of the so-called welfare state, and creeping socialism. We make a mistake when we attach negative feelings and attitudes around certain words without any rational understanding of the origin of this negative connotation.

I recall riding on a train one day in the late 1930s when a traveler who was sitting next to me began to condemn the New Deal and its program. When he was finished stating his position, I asked which of the various programs usually lumped under the term New Deal he favored, if any. First some of the less controversial ones such as FDIC and the SEC were considered and one by one he indicated his approval of each one of the programs mentioned. At least a dozen of them were discussed, and he did not oppose any of them. In other words, he was for the items of a program as he took them separately, but he was against the thing *in toto!* He was for the New Deal measures, but he was against the New Deal!

Just what is this thing that is called the welfare state? Does it mean that it is inconsistent with our democratic tradition for government to be interested in the welfare of its people? Does it mean that no matter what happens to its citizens, government should remain immobilized and let the so-called natural forces take their toll? Does it mean that government should build roads and bridges but should refuse to take steps when a region of the country is stricken by drouth and when the people in that region actually may be starving? Does it mean that government should accumulate huge stores of food products on the one hand and permit some of its own citizens to go hungry on the other? Does it mean that government should protect business enterprise but not human beings? Just what does it mean? Some writers, notably *Fortune* magazine, have called it the service state, others have called it creeping socialism. Perhaps a more correct phrase would be leadership or responsibility in government. It has been well said that we need to "analyze rather than sloganize our way through economic problems."[14]

Centralization of services *per se* is not necessarily bad in government any more than it is in industry. The crucial question is whether centralized services can be performed within the framework of democracy and with a democratic spirit. The development of mergers and large-scale industry in this country has proved to be more productive and efficient than small-scale industry, but whether that advantage will work out for the benefit of the whole depends upon other by-products, such as the control of monopoly and the prevention of unfair practices toward competitors, labor, and consumers. Centralization of welfare services perhaps can be made more efficient than segmented or balkanized local services; and whether or not a service works out for the benefit of the whole depends upon how it is administered. This is true also with local administration.

It is important that welfare services be administered with proper respect for personal dignity and sensitiveness. The *feelings* of people who need to seek help are not unimportant to their well-being. Frequently, it may cost more immediately to adopt an appropriate policy, but in the long run it pays dividends in total welfare.

The well-motivated Congressman who gives a second-hand suit of clothes to the elevator operator at Christmas time has a concern for people as individuals; but when he votes against minimum wages, social insurance, labor protection, consumer protection, he is denying the elevator man the satisfaction and independence of buying his own suit of clothes. He is denying the very free enterprise he advocates.

At least as important as bread and butter is the factor of how a person *feels* about accepting help from a relative, or from a state agency which makes the applicant feel *ashamed,* or from a community that identifies the person as a no-good or a failure. If our effort is not only to set a floor of minimum subsistence of material goods but also to maintain morale and happiness and to provide a *feeling of security,* the element of right to receive must be incorporated in any program and in its administration. We have accepted the right to receive an education and few, if any, consider this controversial any more. We assume that we have a right to be protected against certain health hazards and harm to body and property. If children have a right to such a service as education, why should they not have a right to a minimum of subsistence without which they could not live?

About a hundred years ago we said that it was not good for people to be ignorant, and so we established a compulsory school system. We say today that it is not good for people to be sick unnecessarily and so in certain areas we are establishing compulsory measures such as quarantine, minimum housing standards, and other public health measures. Is it stretching logic to say that if we think it is not good for people to be poor (not good for the people themselves or the society in which they live) we might want to consider compulsory measures of certain indirect kinds to prevent their poverty? This might sound like heresy, but actually it is not so heretical. In a sense we already prevent poverty with certain activities that have an element of compulsion. Old age and survivors insurance compels people to save for their old age; unemployment insurance compels them to save for the rainy day of joblessness; free school lunches compel the children to have at least one warm well-balanced meal a day, and so on.

Compulsion in itself is not necessarily an evil in a democracy, provided it is democratically determined, if it is used for the greatest good to the greatest number and always if it maintains or actually increases freedom of individual action *in toto*. Most of our laws carry an element of compulsion. Moreover it should be said that there is no freedom in starvation.

A Broad Program

Perhaps the best way to discuss the various needs of people is within the framework of a proposed program. Here, therefore, is a broad plan that would emphasize needs and the scope of services to meet them.

In the first place, the plan is based on the assumption that government has a responsibility for the welfare of people and that it will take a rational interest in setting up the various programs, protections, and services which are indicated. There is the necessity to plan on the broad economic front and only the Federal government, because of its size and scope, can appropriately assume this function. Such things come to mind as labor protection, illustrated by the Wagner Labor Relations Act; and consumer protection of various kinds to enable the helpless and unwitting consumer to get the quality of goods that he thinks he is getting and to protect him from adulterated and harmful materials. In a complicated society such as ours, the market place in itself is no longer a sufficient test of the worth of a product.

Moreover, government has certain broad responsibilities which have a relationship to the well-being of people. There is the necessity to keep price levels reasonably stable so that the debtor or the creditor does not get an undue advantage; there is the factor of leadership in the development of natural resources for the social good, and the development of broad recreational areas and services for the use of people. More specifically, there is the possibility of tax incentives to employers, of such things as annual wage plans, employment of older people, etc. Then there is the stabilization of the business cycle, which requires some foresighted action in areas of credit controls, installment buying, public employment, public building, etc. There are the programs of public housing for low-income groups, school lunches, and the development of broad public preventive health services through education, research, and regulation; tax systems that are geared to need and to ability to pay, regulation of commodity and stock trading, of banks and of railroads, and of other quasi-public enterprises and utilities.

These services and similar ones can be grouped together as constituting the core or the basic level of protection for individuals. They are "preventive." If we did not have such protections and regulations, the need for other more specific types of welfare programs would be vastly different and even greater. Government has a responsibility to see that large groups of people as consumers are protected from undue fraud, as industrial workers from unnecessary accidents, as investors from misrepresentations in offerings of securities, etc.

All of this means that government has an interest in people. This kind of system is not *laissez-faire* as we knew it in a simpler economy nor is it regimentation. It provides protection and some measure of equality of opportunity. If, for example, the FDIC had been in existence in the early 1930s, somewhat fewer people would have had to apply for relief; if the actions that were taken in 1933 had been taken in 1929 or 1930, the depression quite likely would not have fallen into the depths it did. If government assumes the responsibility of developing or regulating the development of our vast natural resources for the good of all the people, the conservation and proper use of these resources will be safeguarded.

These programs are preventive in nature and to the extent that we vigorously initiate and prosecute them, to that extent will there be less need for more treatment of pathologies as contrasted with preventive services.

Social Insurance and Assistance

The second part of my proposal deals with social insurance. The first part is an effort of government to provide a milieu or framework in which the individual has maximum opportunity to get along on his own and by himself. That kind of activity normally will take care of a large proportion of our citizens, but it is not sufficient to take care of the marginal groups or even the majority of the people in some of their needs.

First, in line with the current recommendations of President Eisenhower, the Old Age and Survivors Insurance program should be expanded to include all employed people, whether they are employed by others or self-employed. Such a program properly modified in relation to changing prices, etc., could substantially take care of the minimum needs in old age of those who have been employed for a required period during their lifetime, as well as of their survivors. The present program, based on employer-employee participation, appears to be sound and it seems there is no good reason why it should not be put substantially on an actuarial basis. It was established on that basis in 1935 and it was an error not to carry out the original intent with respect to changes in rates.

The unemployment insurance program is working out reasonably well and should be continued, perhaps with some modification of the duration and amounts of benefits. Short-term unemployment, being a legitimate charge against the business, should be financed by employer contributions.

If the insurance principles applying to the Old Age and Survivors Insurance program are sound, there is no good reason why risks of disability and illness should not also be covered under a social insurance program. Second, a health insurance program is needed to cover both the cost of illness and the loss of earnings due to illness based on the same principles that now underlie Old Age and Survivors Insurance. Whether such coverage should be included under the OASI program or set up as a separate entity is a matter to be decided on the basis of administrative factors.

With the major risks of old-age dependency and of survivors dependency largely covered on a minimum basis, with the risk of dependency due to ill health reduced under a health insurance program, and with the risk of unemployment dependency partially covered for a limited time, we have a basic framework for taking care of our major hazards on an orderly plan of some sort based on the concept of "right."

Even though the social insurances are expanded to include all working people and to include additional hazards, the Federal government should continue to participate in the remaining welfare services on a permanent basis. I ask this on the basis of equal access, but partly also on the basis that the larger unit of government has a leadership function in relation to standards, which is not always assumed by local or state governments. A casual comparison of the methods used in general public assistance today (the responsibility of state and local governments) and those used in the so-called categorical public assistances (old-age assistance, aid to dependent children, aid to the needy blind, and aid to the disabled) should be sufficient evidence to indicate that if we are to make much progress, the Federal government is going to have to take the leadership.

A study of general assistance made in 1946–47 shows that general assistance grants were lower than other benefits (in which the Federal government participated), had a wider variation among the states, and that the average payments had a marked positive relationship to per capita income.[15] The states with the lowest per capita incomes tended to have low average grants, whereas those with high per capita incomes tended to have high grants. The conclusions of the study are that assistance is "often denied to admittedly needy persons," "frequently inadequate in amount" (that is, is "usually not administered in accordance with principles which experience has shown to be essential to effective administration"), and that it is "extremely unevenly administered among the various states and among different localities within a given state."

In December 1952, one person in 250 in the civilian population under 65 was receiving general assistance. In Maine and Rhode Island the ratio was one to 100, whereas in Alabama, Idaho, Mississippi, and New Mexico it was less than one to 1500.[16]

Modern public assistance based on the concept of right to aid when in need, to appeals procedures, to objective rather than punitive administration, came about when the Federal government entered the so-called "relief" picture; it was not initiated to any major degree by the local units of government. In other words, it appears that if we want to have over-all progress toward more humane and decent and sound standards in public welfare, we must not be content to "throw the system back to the states." The grant-in-aid program which I am proposing would envisage a partnership concept between the Federal government and the states, which in the welfare field in general has been operating very well for more than fifteen years. The Federal government sets broad minimum standards, but the state and/or local agencies are the primary administrative units and have considerable leeway in setting up their programs and services to meet their own needs. It would be a mistake to go back to the day when we had no formal provisions for fair hearings or appeals procedures and when the test of need on the part of children was whether the parents were "deserving."

COORDINATION OF SERVICES

There are numerous situations which for one reason or another will not be covered under the social insurance programs, and there are many social services which the programs themselves are not designed to cover. For these situations I propose, therefore, one over-all public welfare program with grants-in-aid from the Federal government to the states, each state determining whether the program should be administered by a state agency or by counties or districts within the states. If the state chooses a plan other than its own administration, state supervision should be required. In any case, there will be in every county or district in every state a public welfare agency or office that would take its place as a basic function of government operating side by side with such other service units as public health and education. The public assistance aspect of this program would be covered by one single category of general assistance, thus greatly simplifying present procedures.

Such a public welfare program would have several major functions. In the first place, it would have the function of providing residual financial assistance to families or individuals who might find themselves in need and not properly covered by any of the more basic programs. There is the person who is unemployed and has run out of his unemployment benefits; there is the one who has not worked long enough to be covered under the basic Old Age and Survivors Insurance program; there are those who have suffered extraordinary catastrophe and whose needs are greater than the established minima under the basic programs; there are scores of miscellaneous types of human situations that need some kind of financial help by a social agency.

A second function of such a public welfare agency would be the care and protection of children. This would include all of the usual activities encompassed by the term child welfare services, including more attention than we usually give to prevention in relation to local needs. Bertram M. Beck of the U. S. Children's Bureau has pointed out that the current problem of juvenile delinquency is one in which public welfare agencies must assume leadership.[17] If they do not, "the vacuum will be filled, but it may be filled by those who would destroy." He emphasizes both the preventive and the individual treatment aspects.

Third, this agency should also give general social work help in troubled family situations, in developing preventive measures relating to mental illness, and in taking care of any welfare need that might happen to arise in the community. It would give individualized service, it would develop preventive programs and regulations, and it would carry on research. An illustration of the broad preventive aspects of such a program is a current situation in southeastern Missouri. A period of several years of drouth has brought some basic problems. Added to the difficulties of the drouth, there is a creeping technological unemployment brought about by the substitution of the cotton-picking machine for the older method of picking cotton by hand. Thousands of people who have lived in that section their entire lives and earned a minimum living by picking cotton are now stranded and, without some major basic action on the part of somebody, the problem will continue to become acute. The current public-assistance administration has the narrow function of determining eligibility. No agency takes responsibility.

An adequate public welfare program would include the function of stepping in regardless of the type of need and regardless of the extent or scope of the solution. An agency with broad functions could bring in other services to help in the long-time solution of a particular problem, but it would be expected to take the initiative where want and need of people are involved. The next step in the development of public welfare in this country should be a broadening of responsibility or function.

Fourth, such an agency should assume the responsibility of an informational and referral office. Life is complicated for many people and frequently they are shunted about from one agency to another and often with large-scale frustration. One office would be the repository of all kinds of information dealing with human beings as individuals and their rights and prerogatives. This one office may not have all of the information in detail about any one subject pertaining to a problem of an individual, but it would have enough to know where to refer the person, whether it be to a county superintendent of schools, a health department, a local office of the Bureau of Old Age and Survivors Insurance, a private agency, or what not. This is a type of service which England has developed very well, but which has not yet been initiated in this country to any great degree.

Such a public welfare plan would have a flexibility that would enable it to step in when any need arose. It is necessary in peace, but in war it is vital. In case of war, we would have a framework to carry out some of the activities that are made necessary by war. If women and children or whole populations need to be moved out of some of our cities, here we would have an agency that would have the skeleton know-how in advance. If a tornado or other natural catastrophe strikes, here we have an agency that could step in at once to give the appropriate kind of assistance.

There should be one grant-in-aid from the Federal government to the states for these public welfare services, leaving it up to the states to determine the distribution of the funds among the various programs. There should be a matching type of grant in which the Federal government carries at least 50 per cent of the financial responsibility as a base and with the variable grant principle applying above the minimum based on the per capita incomes of the states. If we are going to have equalization of access to certain basic services, the variable grant principle must be followed in this plan or certain low-income states will not or cannot take care of the needs. The answer to Eveline Burns' question that was raised in a recent article on this subject in the *Social Work Journal* is simple: We social workers are in favor of a policy of redistribution of income among the states.[18] If we weren't in favor of that, we could not logically propose the variable grant principle.

Actually a redistribution process is now taking place in a number of ways. The progressive income tax results in larger per capita contribution from the richer states to the Federal treasury, and even if the funds were returned to the states on an equal per capita basis, it would tend to redistribute income among the states. If we assume, in the Social Security Act and in other legislation, for example, that every child no matter where he happens to be born should have about the same rights and privileges as a child who happens to be born elsewhere, then we must accept the policy of redistribution of income. The figures published by the Department of Commerce covering the year 1952 show that the per capita income in Mississippi was $818, whereas the per capita income in New York was $2,038.[19] Assuming that per capita income measures ability to provide services, New York has about 2½ times the capacity of Mississippi. Without some extra help going to the people of Mississippi from the outside, the social and other similar services available to the people in that state would necessarily be lower than those in New York. Moreover, Mississippi has more children in relation to adults than does New York.

The striking dependence of assistance standards upon the economic level of states may be seen today in the general assistance program in which there is no equalization through Federal participation.[20] It becomes clear that if we wish to establish broad common standards for all the people of the country in all of the states, not only is a grant-in-aid system necessary, but it must be of the variable type based on differences in need and capacity to take care of that need.

I propose that these grants should be made under a system of state plans that would need the approval of the granting agency. Some protection must be provided whereby a state could not use all or an undue proportion of its funds to take care of one need while some other needs were being completely neglected. The program should be increasingly preventive as we identify causes and contributing phenomena. Other protections included in our current grant-in-aid programs should be continued.

A nationwide network of broadly conceived public welfare departments with Federal grants-in-aid would permit a minimum reasonably uniform standard of service with emphasis on prevention and rehabilitation.

QUALITY OF SERVICE

Any discussion of need that fails to consider personnel resources is incomplete.

According to a study made in 1950 there were 75,000 persons in the United States classified as social workers.[21] Of these, two thirds had college degrees and one half had some graduate work, mostly in social work. Only 16 per cent had two or more years of graduate education. Those working in mental hygiene clinics had the most, over 80 per cent having at least two years. The social work profession has set two years of graduate training as the accepted minimum for professional training.

The need for more trained personnel is evident on every hand. While the requirements of services are expanding, the professional schools of social work are graduating each year no more than about 2,000 persons, which is hardly more than enough to maintain status quo, let alone lessen the gap.[22]

The American Association of Medical Social Workers reports that 3,500 new medical social workers are needed by 1957.[23] The Women's Bureau of the U. S. Department of Labor states that "graduate schools of social work are not producing enough students with casework training to fill the continuing demand from long established family agencies and also take care of expanding services."[24] The U. S. Children's Bureau reports that "the problem of recruiting and holding a fully qualified staff will have to be solved if services are to be extended to all children in need of the kind of help child welfare workers can provide."[25] The U. S. Public Health Service, the American Association of Psychiatric Social Workers, and others report the same situation with respect to mental hospitals, child guidance clinics, and other similar agencies.

It seems clear that if we are to have enough professionally trained people to take care of needed services, the profession will have to be made more attractive through increased salaries, and more and enlarged scholarship plans be initiated to help relieve the burden of the high cost of professional education. Such scholarship plans have grown during the last several years, but any diminution in the available funds will make the problem even more critical. Funds are needed from both public and voluntary sources to meet this need. It is futile to talk about unmet needs unless we can train enough professional personnel to man the projected services.

Finally, there is a desperate need for research. We have hardly scratched the surface in the accumulation of knowledge about man and his personality, interpersonal and intergroup relationships, the development of the child from infancy, dependency, and the hundreds of other human problems about which we know little or nothing for sure. As far as the social and behavioral sciences are concerned, we are still living in the age of Galileo. It is a sad commentary upon our culture that we are willing to spend billions of dollars on the development of physical sciences and are so reluctant to spend even small sums on research in the social sciences or in human relations.

For years, the U. S. Children's Bureau unsuccessfully has sought appropriations for even a minimum research program. The Fact-Finding Report of the Midcentury White House Conference on Children and Youth has a final chapter entitled "Next Steps in Research."[26] The report concludes that there are gaps in knowledge about healthy personality development and that "areas of insufficient knowledge have been noted again and again throughout the report." There is a "high priority on the need to ascertain the influences that determine direction in human behavior, especially those that encourage the attainment of adequacy and maturity."

There are a few hopeful indications of interest. A bill currently before Congress provides, among other things, "grants to states and public and other nonprofit institutions of higher education for paying part of the cost of projects which, in the judgment of the Secretary, hold unique promise of making a substantial contribution to the solution of child health and welfare problems common to all or several States. . . ."[27] Apparently, this includes the possibility of experimentation and research.

The Social Security Act provided wisely for the accumulation of statistical data; and for the first time in our history we are beginning to develop adequate statistical series in the area of financial dependency and poverty. Some studies are being made by Federal, state, and local governments, but much more needs to be done if public policy is to be soundly based.

The job to be done is so large that no single agency can assume the entire responsibility. The universities, public and private social agencies, government, and charitable foundations all share the task ahead.

The needs of people as individuals, in an age fraught with danger, anxiety, and frustration, but charged with challenge, are essentially important in a democracy. Robert S. Lynd has significantly said: "Presumably, an important test of a good society is how much preventable real trouble it removes from the shoulders of its citizens, and, after that, how rapidly and effectively it marshals what it knows to repair the damage done by nonpreventable trouble."[28]

That summarizes our task: Prevent what hurt and problems we can and treat the individual situations we are unable to prevent. There are many important areas of public policy, but few, if any, more important than the welfare of individual people.

FOOTNOTES

1. Helvering vs. Davis, 301 U. S. 619 (1937).
2. Address to 73d Congress, June 8, 1934, *Congressional Record,* 78: (Part 10), p. 10770.
3. *Business Week,* October 22, 1938, p. 48.
4. John J. Corson, "Can We Afford Welfare?" *Community,* 29:132, March 1954.
5. See especially, *Children and Youth at the Midcentury.* A Chart Book. Midcentury White House Conference on Children and Youth, 1951.
6. Eveline Burns, "Wanted: More Thought About Grants-in-Aid." *Social Work Journal,* 35:11–14, January 1954.
7. Clark Tibbetts, "The Aging." *Social Work Yearbook,* 1954.
8. Marjorie Shearon, "Economic Status of the Aged." *Social Security Bulletin,* 1:5, March 1938.
9. Clark Tibbetts, *op. cit.,* p. 37.
10. *Loc. cit.*
11. Ernest A. Shepherd, "Alcoholism." *Social Work Yearbook,* 1954, p. 43.
12. *Children and Youth at Midcentury.* A Chart Book, Chart 14.
13. Justice Cardozo in Helvering vs. Davis, 301 U. S. 619 (1937).
14. Lewis E. Wagner, "A Road to Economic Disaster?" *Iowa Business Digest,* 25:1, January 1954.
15. Felix Gentile and Donald Howard, *General Assistance.* Pamphlet published by the American Association of Social Workers, 1949, p. 35 ff.
16. Anne Geddes and Charles Hawkins, "Public Assistance." *Social Work Yearbook,* 1954, p. 403.
17. Bertram M. Beck, "Juvenile Delinquency—A Public Welfare Responsibility." *Public Welfare,* 12:53, April 1954.
18. Eveline Burns, *loc. cit.*
19. *Survey of Current Business,* 33:13, August 1953.
20. A recent unpublished analysis by William Gordon of Washington University showed a high correlation (.71) between average general assistance grants and state per capita income. When translated into dollars, this means that recipients in states with a per capita income of $1,000 received an average of $20 per month in assistance. Recipients in states with a per capita income of $2,000 received $60 per month. While general income drops 50 per cent, the assistance standards measured by average grants drops 67 per cent. Recipients in poorer states are, therefore, both absolutely and relatively more economically deprived.
21. *Social Workers in 1950.* Prepared by Bureau of Labor Statistics. New York: American Association of Social Workers, 1952.

22. Council on Social Work Education, "Statistics on Social Work Education, November 1, 1953, and Academic Year 1952–1953."

23. "Medical Social Workers Needed for Hospital Health Work." Mimeographed Fact Sheet published by American Association of Medical Social Workers, 1954.

24. Woman's Bureau, U. S. Department of Labor, "The Outlook for Women in Social Case Work with Families." Bulletin No. 235–4.

25. U. S. Department of Health, Education and Welfare, "Personnel in Public Child Welfare Programs, 1952." Children's Bureau Statistical Series No. 16.

26. Helen Witmer and Ruth Kotinsky (Editors), *Personality in the Making.* New York: Harper Bros., 1952, pp. 434 ff.

27. H. R. 7448 introduced by Congressman Reed of New York, 1954.

28. Robert S. Lynd in preface to Earl L. Koos, *Families in Trouble.* New York: King's Crown Press, 1946, p. vii.

Responsibility to Meet Social Service Needs

George F. Davidson
Deputy Minister of National Welfare
Department of National Health and Welfare, Canada

The preceding paper has dealt with the moral and philosophical bases on which our social service programs rest. Here we consider a more work-a-day problem: the question of responsibility for the implementation of social welfare policies and the attainment of social welfare objectives.

In more specific terms, this paper endeavors to deal with four main problems:

1. The relative roles of public and voluntary social services in a free society
2. The problem of coordination in the social service field as between the public and voluntary agencies
3. The same problem as it affects the various levels of government
4. The implications of the patterns and relationships we have developed, and how they affect the impact of our social service programs on individuals and on the community at large

I will not attempt to divide my presentation into watertight compartments under these headings; but these will be the main points of reference to which we shall return from time to time as we endeavor to determine the principles and trends which underlie the allocation of responsibility for meeting social service needs.

Before seeking out the old familiar landmarks on this much-traveled trail, let us pause for a moment to take thankful note of one important fact. We cherish the knowledge that ours is the kind of society which permits a discussion of the relative roles of public and voluntary effort in the social service field. So long as we live in a free society, this problem of fitting together the jigsaw puzzle of our social service structure will continue to baffle and bewilder us, to tax our energies and ingenuity, and to provoke discussions such as we are entering upon this afternoon.

There is no such problem, likewise no such possibility of discussion, in the monolithic state. There no colorful mosaic of voluntary welfare organization exists. The gray pall of uniformity hangs heavily like a blanket over all welfare services. This state monopoly of responsibility for every human need, of every humanitarian motive, smothers healthy discussion, stifles the initiative not only of the beneficiaries of the welfare services, but also of such persons who, in a free society, are proud to serve as leaders of the community's welfare thought and action.

This monolithic concept of responsibility for all social services stands in sharp contrast to the patterns of our democratic society in the Western world. We piece together all the many patterns and corners of our welfare programs—voluntary and governmental—into an intricate mosaic of services whose infinite variety and proclivity to constant change are at once its most bewildering feature and its greatest strength.

PRINCIPLES AND TRENDS

Now to our subject for discussion: responsibility to meet social service needs. What questions does this suggestive title raise in our minds? Perhaps the first is a question that most of us in the social welfare field have disposed of in our own thinking long ago. What responsibility? Is there any responsibility whatsoever, on anyone but the individual himself, to provide for his social needs?

This question may not require extended consideration, since all but the most embattled, die-hard individualists will probably admit that in any form of society certain hazards exist of a social, health, or economic nature which lie beyond the powers of the individual to cope with, and require the collective action of the group.

In the minds of many, this collective group action to lift the burden from the shoulders of the individual should be centered so far as possible, even in 1954, on the close-knit family unit. The majority, however, recognize that today the family, the clan, the religious sect, or the work group, while able to deal with many of the social welfare problems which lie beyond the ability of the individual, are themselves too narrowly circumscribed, too limited in their resources, to cope with the major hazards of our modern industrial society. These major hazards, most people now recognize, must be dealt with on the basis of the collective action of the whole community.

Thus we can answer our first question, "What responsibility?," by saying that we find today widespread acceptance of the view that, while the individual and his family are expected in normal circumstances to provide for their own requirements, there is a responsibility resting on the shoulders of the whole community to meet those social service needs which lie beyond the more limited capabilities of the individual and his family.

So far, so good; but we have answered one question only to raise another one. What do we mean by the word *community?* Community, as used here, is capable of many definitions. It includes the action of a group on a voluntary basis. It includes, likewise, the action of the same group, large or small, through what we choose to call governmental action. At whatever level this governmental action may be undertaken—parish or ward or poor district, village or town or township, city or municipality, county or borough, state or province, Federal or national—it should always be recognized that the machinery of government is the chosen instrument for community action in the social service field just as truly as any voluntary association of the group in the form of a private philanthropic or charitable agency.

Too often this simple truth is overlooked. Too often it is our tendency to look upon government as something apart from the community—an agency or instrumentality imposing its will or program in some mysterious fashion from above. We fail to identify ourselves with that government action. We fail to recognize it as our chosen instrument for carrying out our will in a particular social service field to the same extent and to the same degree as we recognize our voluntary community welfare agencies. We talk of the government agency as "they," while in the same breath we talk of the community welfare agency as "we." Yet they are both equally the chosen instruments that we the community have established and set in motion to carry out our collective responsibilities in the social service field.

The bogey of the welfare state has done a lot in recent years, I fear, to becloud our vision on this important fact. Our social services have become the reluctant shuttlecock in the political badminton game between free-enterprise capitalists on the one side and socialistic state planners on the other. As a result, we tend too often to think of the voluntary social services as something different—inherently better or inherently worse, according to our particular point of view—from the social services operated under public auspices. We look upon the public and the private social services as largely separate and independent one from the other. We recognize, of course, the need for a *modus vivendi* and devote much effort to bridging the gap between them. We struggle to achieve a sense of teamwork and partnership, or at least a common basis for coordination and mutual cooperation; but we tend to forget that they are not two separate things, but rather separate manifestations of the same thing. Both express through separate mechanisms the community's sense of responsibility for meeting social service needs. Both endeavor through different forms of organization to fulfil the sense of mutual obligation within the group, large or small, that we have chosen to call the community.

The United Kingdom Parliamentary Committee on Charitable Trusts, in its report of December 1952, underscores this point in a passage which is worth remembering:

> The important point to notice in the context of the present discussion is that state action and voluntary action were not the antitheses of each other; rather they sprang from the same roots, were designed to meet the same needs and had the same motivating forces behind them—indeed, historically, state action is voluntary action crystallized and made universal. . . . Neither

in the historical record nor in the examination of these motives would there be discovered the making of a fundamental distinction between state action for public welfare and voluntary action for the same purpose.[1]

If we can accept this Siamese-twin concept of the relationship between the public and the voluntary social services—if we can look upon them as branches of the same tree, nourished in the same soil of our religious, charitable, and humanitarian traditions, fed by the same roots of belief in political democracy and in the basic equality and common brotherhood of man—then our problem of establishing the appropriate relationships between the public and the private agencies becomes much simpler.

We are not then obliged to try to reconcile them as two essentially hostile and opposing forces jealously dug in on the same field of action. We can set aside the arguments, though not the prejudices, of those whose attitudes to public or private social services are governed by their own particular political beliefs: the state planners who brush aside with contempt and supercilious arrogance the efforts of the private welfare agencies as though they were mere poultices on the festering sores of capitalism; and the die-hard, free-enterprise, rugged individualists who look upon all governmental action in the social service field as though it were a headlong plunge into the welfare state or socialism or something worse.

If we can thus clear away the ideological debris that clutters up clear thinking, we can then examine this question of public-private relationships in the social service field on a purely pragmatic basis—considering honestly the merits of each of these mechanisms by which the same community, comprising the same people, motivated by the same humanitarian considerations, endeavors to discharge as fairly as it can what it conceives to be its responsibilities for meeting the social service needs of its people.

How, then, on the basis of this pragmatic approach, should we, the community, determine which of our responsibilities in the social service field should be discharged through the mechanism of the private voluntary agency and which through the governmental or public authority? Surely this is a decision in which the governing principle must be that of flexibility. Miss Bessie Touzel has expressed this very concisely in the following paragraph:

> Each community, whether it be the nation, a province, or a city or town, will present a different pattern of services. The amount and organization of public services and the amount and organization of private services will reflect citizen opinions, understanding, and resources. Because of these basic differences, there will necessarily be differences also in the way in which partnerships will be worked out. Linton Swift has said: 'No single and universally applicable pattern is or can be offered for a uniform division of specific services between public and private agencies, but we can at least seek underlying principles which may guide the development of varying patterns in different communities.' Let us then maintain these two attitudes: (1) acceptance of variety in patterns of services, public and private, and of relationships between them; and (2) determination to seek underlying prin-

ciples to guide policies affecting the division of services and their relationships.[2]

The infinite variety of the pattern of public-private relationships in the social service field is, of course, but a symptom of the way in which our services have evolved by patient democratic processes down through the ages. It is an oversimplification, but basically true, to state that originally in each of our communities we started to discharge our collective responsibilities for meeting social need through voluntary, rather than through governmental action. Human need existed long before we had developed either the concept of governmental responsibility for meeting human need or the machinery by which government could act in this field.

So long as the *laissez-faire* concept of government prevailed, the private agency, religious or philanthropic, was almost the sole instrumentality by which the community sought to discharge its social service responsibilities. As *laissez-faire* began to give ground to a more positive, more dynamic concept of the role of government in society, some of the responsibilities in the social service field began to shift from the voluntary agency to the strong, but inexperienced and still none-too-willing, shoulders of the governmental authority.

This change from *laissez-faire* to a more active role for government was an uneven development, varying from nation to nation, state to state, from community to community. Obviously, therefore, this produced an infinite variety of relationships in different communities between the public and the private agencies in the social service field; and the pace of the transfer of responsibilities from private to governmental authorities in respect to social services was just as uneven as the pace of the broader movement of which it was a part.

Slowly, however, some trends or guide-lines began to emerge. These are the so-called principles to which Miss Touzel and Linton Swift and many other writers have made reference. Some of these trends, together with the underlying forces which helped to develop them, may be summarized as follows:

1. Mass services, the need for which was apparent in respect to large numbers of families in the community, soon came to be regarded as fit fields for action by the public authority. Selective services affecting limited numbers in the community were more likely to remain in the domain of private philanthropy.

2. Services catering to the needs of special minority groups (sectarian, ethnic, linguistic, etc.) continued in most instances as the special interest and responsibility of voluntary groups.

3. Services which were widely popular, which had achieved a widespread measure of public acceptance on the part of all sections of the community, shifted naturally to the side of the public authority. Those of more limited appeal, which lacked a wide measure of acceptance or were even contro-

versial, remained the responsibility in each community of the sectional groups which believed in them.

4. The public authority in the early years was slow to experiment and to pioneer. The voluntary sector of the social service field had to carry most of the early burden of pioneering, experimentation, and research.

5. Services calling for the expenditure of inordinately large sums of money tended inevitably to become the responsibility of government. Private philanthropy found it could not raise sufficient funds to finance all the services which it had demonstrated to be the proper responsibility of the community. In consequence, the community, having accepted the responsibility, had no alternative but to use its broad-based taxing authority to raise the necessary funds to support these services; and assumption of administrative responsibility in these fields followed closely on the heels of the transfer of financial responsibility.

6. Services containing a low "personal-relationship" component, with relatively simple administrative procedures capable of being organized on an assembly-line basis with push-button, adding-machine methods of operation, moved over invariably to the public side of the ledger. By contrast, services involving the exploration of intimate personal relationships, requiring a highly individualized and flexible approach not susceptible to mass production methods, remained the time-consuming responsibility of the private agencies.

7. Services involving a high component of economic maintenance shifted over to the only basis of financing which could support them—that of the tax-supported public agency. This left as the special domain of private social service those areas of need where economic maintenance was incidental and personal service or the treatment of personality defects was the main component in the program.

8. Almost by definition, the voluntary sector of the social service field retained those areas of operation where the opportunities of volunteer participation in the program or the treatment process were the greatest. By contrast, undertakings which offered little real scope for direct personal citizen-participation tended to become the bureaucratic responsibility of the public agency.

It will be recognized that the points listed are not mutually exclusive one from the other. They overlap to a considerable extent. In some instances, they are largely opposite sides of the same coin. Each one of them tries to state a general historic trend which the passage of time has at least partially crystalized into a principle; but important exceptions come to mind which seem to contradict the validity of almost every one of them.

Mass services, for example, have not always and inevitably swung over to the side of the public authority. The long history of the Friendly Societies in the United Kingdom is a case in point. The case of the cooperative and other nonprofit housing associations so common in the Scandinavian countries and especially in Denmark also comes to mind. The growing trade-union programs in the social service field and the large-scale development of voluntary hospital and health insurance on this continent might be cited to contradict the proposition that mass services come exclusively within the domain of the public authority.

Similar exceptions could be adduced to question the soundness of other trends listed. Costly services are not always shifted to the public sector. In fact, it can be argued that services which are very costly in terms of each individual case, where the component of skilled professional service is unusually high are the very services which the public authority is reluctant to take over. They remain with the private agency. Our skilled family casework services are a case in point.

Take again the recreation services. These surely include mass programs covering vast numbers of people, susceptible in part at least to assembly-line or mass production methods; yet this is the sector of the social service field in which the tendency to public agency control has emerged perhaps more slowly than elsewhere, and in which citizen participation and voluntary direction have remained most vigorous.

These are important exceptions which appear to question or even contradict the trends outlined; yet this may not really be the case. These exceptions are rather, in most cases, of a temporary nature—illustrations of the uneven pace of developments in the social service field.

Most of the illustrations given relate to services on the fringe of what we regard as the social services in the narrower sense. The Friendly Societies, the cooperatives, the nonprofit housing associations, the trade unions, the voluntary hospital and health insurance plans, the recreation services—these are in large part fringe areas lying on the border line between the social services and other fields such as education, health, labor relations, economic development, and community planning.

The more closely one limits examination to the central core of what we today regard as the social services, the more the validity of these trends will be confirmed. They are trends which have the whole of our history and our industrial urban development behind them. These trends have emerged out of the irresistible financial pressures which have developed in the course of our evolution from a rural to an urban society, from an agricultural to an industrial economy, from a laissez-faire concept of government to the newer, though in some quarters less welcome, concept of government as the "chosen instrument" for the promotion of the public welfare.

Whether these trends are good or bad is beside the point. They are part of a larger, more fundamental trend developing in our twentieth-century society; they cannot be reversed without reversing at the same time all that has led to the development of the modern industrial society that stands today as the chief characteristic of our way of life in the western world.

Let us not, therefore, waste too much time or effort trying to reverse the course of history by urging the return of a larger measure of responsibility for our social services to the control of voluntary agencies. Likewise, we should be on guard against the urgings of those who would have us force too hastily the pace of the trend which has developed to shift segments of responsibility in the social service field to the various levels of government. The first course is futile, foolish, and reactionary; the second reckless, irresponsible, and dangerous.

It will profit us nothing to resist "the realization that universal provision cannot be made by private philanthropy"; and that "the growth of humanitarianism and of scientific knowledge and the emergence of new attitudes towards poverty and the functions of the state have brought about revolutionary changes"[3] in the organizational pattern of our twentieth-century social services.

Nor will it help to deny, with a blind and stubborn doctrinaire insistence, that there are elements of strength and skill and humanitarian conviction in the voluntary sector of our social service field which cannot be matched or duplicated in their dynamic qualities by what we can find in the governmental programs. "That manifestation of the philanthropic motive which consists in the giving of personal service is the most valuable element in it. It is the true heart of voluntary action and, indeed, of democracy itself. The giving of time and effort without personal reward, the willingness even to court misunderstanding and contumely in order to promote the well-being of one's fellow men, the freedom to pioneer and the will to pay the price—these are the characteristics of the philanthropic motive at its best."[4]

These quotations from the United Kingdom Parliamentary Committee's Report on Charitable Trusts express so well the basic philosophical justification for the retention of the voluntary agency in the social service partnership with government that further quotation from this important document is fitting:

> The democratic state as we know it could hardly function effectively or teach the exercise of democracy to its members without such channels for and demands upon voluntary service. Not only does voluntary service act as a nursery school of democracy, but also as the field in which good neighbourliness may be exercised. . . . In an urban society like ours, too prone to become 'a disordered dust of individuals,' it is the informal, unorganized actions of the good neighbour which make satisfactory social relationships possible. . . . It is therefore essential that such voluntary action . . . should come to be regarded as a normal part of citizenship in the modern democratic state.[5]

This quotation places in proper perspective the true purpose of voluntary social service organization in our democratic society. We can argue until doomsday about the relative characteristics of the public and the private agency, about what functions or services or segments of responsibility one or the other should perform. It is inevitable that there should be growing pains through the years as we have endeavored to establish the relationships of public and of private agencies within this constantly changing partnership. Too often "large claims to superior performance have been made by both statutory authorities and voluntary agencies, and each has sometimes felt the other debarred by its very nature from doing a good job."[6] But as mutual respect and reciprocal recognition of integrity in performance have developed, as higher standards of professional personnel have entered the public agencies, partly through transfer from the voluntary sector, this partnership has come to work more smoothly and with a larger measure of trust.

Likewise, the role and the function of the public authority in the social service field now seems to be emerging with greater clarity. This role and function has been well stated in the report entitled "Freedom and Welfare— Social Patterns in the Northern Countries of Europe," published in August 1953, under the joint sponsorship of the Ministries of Social Welfare of Denmark, Finland, Iceland, Norway, and Sweden. Through the public authority, in the words of this report (paragraph 498), "the community has assumed main responsibility for ensuring a decent minimum standard in certain fields of vital importance to the life of every citizen, the scope of this responsibility as well as the order of priority being decided by ordinary democratic procedure."

This concept of the role and function of the public authority in the social service field establishes the basis for the modern partnership between the statutory and the voluntary agency. Surely no one in this twentieth century can deny that in our complicated society basic responsibility for meeting basic social need must be placed squarely on the shoulders of the chosen instrument of the community, state, or nation best able to bear the financial burdens inherent in this responsibility. That chosen instrument must generally be the democratically elected instrument of government—municipal, state, or Federal, as the case may be.

To place this responsibility where it belongs is no disservice to the voluntary social service agency. It frees that agency for the performance of that multiplicity of undertakings which fill out and complete the mosaic of our social service structure. That agency's function is to fill the gaps, to experiment, to pioneer; to relieve the massive monotony and uniformity of our governmentally-operated services; to educate and endow with deep conviction the successive generations of social welfare leaders whose job it is to keep the lamp of humanitarian concern for individual human need burning ever more brightly in our democratic society.

For such leaders and for such voluntary agencies which provide the framework for their urge to social action, there will always be an important function and a worth-while job to do. For, to quote the words of the British Report again, "there is no finality about human needs or the span of human desire. While a society is alive and growing, it will not make rigid choices between state action and voluntary action, but both alike will expand as the common expression of its vitality."[7]

THE PROBLEMS OF COORDINATION

The first part of this chapter has dealt with the considerations—principles and trends—affecting our concepts of the roles of public and voluntary agencies in the social service field. Let us turn now to examine the problem of coordination of the various elements in the social service picture.

This is not just a question of mechanics, of isolating certain operating principles; for here, too, we are under the influence of history. We have to consider and explore two important areas of coordination: that which involves the operational relationships of public and private agencies, and the equally important question of coordination among the three levels of government—municipal, state or provincial, and Federal. While this latter question poses special complications in federal states, like the United States and Canada, it will be recognized that similar problems of coordination exist in the unitary states, and that the differences are in large part those of degree and not of kind.

There will be general agreement that in the complex social service patterns we have developed—involving public-private agency relationships, and Federal, state, and local areas of responsibility—the task of coordination is not plagued by monotony or bedeviled by simplicity. Our varied organizational patterns make the task of coordination not only more difficult but also more important.

We have only to go back to the early years of this present century to get a picture of the disorder which was all too evident in our community social service patterns before the necessity of adequate coordination was recognized. In our largest North American cities, the separate community welfare agencies were numbered in the hundreds; each of these pursued zealously and earnestly its chosen objectives with little awareness of other organizations in the same community.

It was the disorderly profusion of these voluntary agencies and their conflicting claims upon the time and bounty of the same community leaders and supporters which led on this continent to the first serious attempt at community social service coordination—the Community-Chest and Council movements.

E pluribus unum might well have been taken from the outset as the motto of this coordinating movement; for this phrase reflects the spirit in which our Chest and Council leaders have sought to achieve the strength of unity out of the great diversity that originally characterized the voluntary social service movement.

The motive force leading to the federation of community welfare undertakings was largely at the outset that of financial pressure—the simple and understandable desire on the part of many community welfare leaders to avoid a multiplicity of separate financial appeals, with all that this meant in terms of demands upon their time and energy. From federation for financial purposes and the development of coordinating machinery that arose from the budgeting process came a recognition of the value—indeed the necessity—of coordination of policy, planning, and program through a new instrument called the Council of Social Agencies or Community Welfare Council.

Great credit must be given to community leaders in the voluntary social service field for having been the first to recognize the necessity of adequate machinery for coordination. This machinery has grown and flourished now over more than a generation in our North American communities, and its scope has expanded to cover within the community the programs not only of the voluntary, but also to a degree of the public, social service agencies.

While this machinery for coordination has contributed much to the orderly development of community social service patterns and has been reasonably effective in the voluntary sector of the community welfare field, it has not met adequately, in my judgment, the problem of coordination as between the public and the voluntary agencies at the community level. Governmental agencies have generally found it difficult to relate themselves to this machinery for the coordination of community welfare planning. This is true especially of the state (or provincial) and Federal agencies and arises from the fact that the territorial scope of their programs embraces not one community, but many. Since community welfare patterns vary from place to place and since the effort at coordination is directed principally to those services operating within and for the particular community itself, it follows that state and Federal agencies have more than ordinary difficulty in coordinating their large-scale programs with the great variety of different programs operated on a local or community basis.

What has been said with respect to the state and Federal social service programs is, of course, less true of the programs operated under municipal authority. Yet even here it has been difficult in most communities for public social service agencies, operated as part of a total civil bureaucracy and responsible to the elected heads of local government, to achieve effective methods for coordination and cooperation with the voluntary social service agencies. In some communities a greater measure of success has been achieved in this regard than in others; but, by and large, while community welfare planning and coordination as carried on through the machinery of the community welfare council is reasonably effective in relation to voluntary social service programs, it falls far short of adequacy with respect to that sector of the social service field administered by municipal, state, or Federal agencies.

One of the weaknesses in the present arrangement is that the community social service planning agency is looked upon by representatives of the public authorities as being itself (as, in fact, it is) a private, voluntary organization. The public agency representative does not in many cases feel free to discuss new policies or plans or proposals (for which he is responsible to his ultimate superiors, the elected representatives) with groups of voluntary social service representatives having no statutory or elective relationships with the whole community, and working within the framework of a voluntary, nongovernmental, coordinating agency.

From time to time, one finds communities in which the public agencies or certain officials connected with them succeed in bridging this gap in acceptance and in understanding of the function of the community welfare council; but these exceptions only serve to prove the general rule. In the majority of communities, the local coordinating agency still has a long way to go before it acquires the prestige and standing in its own community which will bring officials and elected heads of public agencies at all levels to recognize and accept wholeheartedly a full-fledged working relationship. It may be necessary, in fact, to change the form or structure of our present coordinating agencies and to give them more official status in the community as agencies that are neither public nor purely voluntary (if that is possible), but agencies whose place is formally and officially recognized by the public authority as entitling them to exercise for public and for private agencies alike the appointed function of coordination.

If these difficulties of coordination exist within the individual community as between public and voluntary agencies, the problem is even greater as between the various levels of government. Here we have done even less than at the community level or in the voluntary social service field to achieve satisfactory machinery for coordination of policy and program. There has been, of course, a degree of internal coordination at each of the separate levels of government. Each government at each level usually endeavors to ensure that there is reasonable integration of programs and full cooperation within the governmental departments or agencies dealing with social service problems. Yet even in this limited area, all of us have encountered instances of particular municipal, state, or Federal agencies operating their programs and even embarking upon new ventures in apparent ignorance or disregard of other agencies at the same level of government, responsible to the same elected authorities. But certainly at different levels of government the major problem which has not been dealt with is the building of adequate bridges to ensure orderly development and coordination of social services.

There has been, of course, consultation between different levels of government at all times and in every conceivable variety of situation. Free consultation is a vital part of the democratic process; and there may be some who will say that this is enough, or that, even if it is not enough, it is the best we can do in the circumstances. That might be true if our public social service programs were limited in scope, if they affected only a small number of people, or if they involved only limited expenditures. But this is not the case. The social-service problems we are dealing with through governmental agencies are the problems of millions of Americans and Canadians. They involve large sums of public money—hundreds of millions of dollars. And the main characteristic of our public social services at the present time is an undirected trend which has become increasingly apparent through the years, which affects not only the United States and Canada, but also all the countries of Western Europe, and, in fact, every industrial nation in the modern world. This is the trend toward centralization of our social services. This centralization affects not only the governmental services, but also the voluntary as well; for what else is federation for financial purposes or for community welfare planning but a form of centralization?

This trend toward centralization of the public social services has been motivated by the same forces which brought into being the federation movement in the voluntary field. The motivating force is once again that of financial pressure. As our community social services have become increasingly expensive to operate, requiring the raising of increasingly large sums of money, financial pressure has forced their transfer from voluntary to public auspices at the local level. Here, in turn, as the financial burden of local public welfare services has become too onerous for the local community to bear alone, pressure has developed in every local community to have the senior state or provincial government absorb an increasingly large proportion of the administrative and financial load. And this is not the end; for, as we know, within the last two decades financial pressures once again have forced the state and provincial governments to turn for help in financing and administering their public social services to the national government with its broader tax resources and its moral, if not constitutional, responsibility to ensure a measure of equity for all the citizens of the nation, whatever the city or state in which they live.

This trend toward centralization does not come about, as some would have us believe, solely because of the lust for power and authority of a few ambitious, power-hungry politicians at the center. Anyone who has witnessed through the last two decades of depression, war, and inflation the struggle of our municipal, state, and provincial authorities to maintain the services for which they have accepted responsibility knows that these pressures are generated in large part from below, from the local to the state or provincial level, and, in turn, the state or provincial to the Federal level. By and large, in Canada at least, the Federal authorities have endeavored to resist this trend. They have tried to avoid or, if you will, to back away from these responsibilities. Time and again they have argued that these are not the responsibilities of the Federal government, but of the provincial or local authority. If there are any centralizers in Canada, most of them are to be found at the local and provincial levels.

You will best be able to judge for yourselves whether the same is true or not of the United States of America. Whatever the answer, it is certain that these inexorable financial pressures have been operating in your country as in mine. They have been operating likewise in Australia and New Zealand, where the public social service structure has developed comparably with our own. The same is true of the countries of Western Europe.

This is what the representatives of the Ministries of Social Affairs in the five Scandinavian countries have to say about this question in their publication *Freedom and Welfare—Social Patterns in the Northern Countries of Europe* (page 509):

> It is probably correct to say that in the Northern countries a large majority today considers the community as the final carrier of responsibility for the broad welfare of the population. . . . A significant corollary of this widening of public responsibility has been the marked long-term trend towards centralization, the State coming to occupy an ever more dominating position as against local authorities. This trend has followed inevitably from the development of an increasing number of national schemes which entail uniform rules for the whole population and where the central government carries the main part of the financial burden.

This phenomenon is not an isolated or unusual one limited to the domestic experience of our two countries. It is shared by every country which has been building a modern system of public social services to meet the needs of twentieth-century industrial society. It is the most important single trend in the entire field of social services today. That being the case, should we leave the evolution of this trend to the natural process of drift and to the slow, but remorseless, upward thrust that is generated by financial pressures arising from our lower and local units of government? Should we not have better machinery for examining this trend, the pace at which it is moving, the direction it is taking? Should we—or should we not—have means of controlling and regulating it, of guiding and directing it, of slowing it down or speeding it up if the pace is either too fast or too slow?

Who are at present coordinating, directing, and regulating this trend? The leaders of our municipal governments goaded on by the financial pressures which press in on them from every side? The leaders of our states and provinces, already loaded down with heavy financial responsibilities and under continuing pressure from local units of government to take over more and more of the financial responsibilities for social services? The Federal government, manned, as some would have us believe, by a group of power-hungry politicians, lurking like spiders at the center of the web, drawing in unto themselves for their own devious uses all the sources of power in our federal states? The voluntary leaders in the social service field? The professional social workers, zealously trying to build a Utopian heaven here on earth? The trade unions, or the veterans organizations, or the socialists, or the leaders of some other ideological or pressure group? Who are directing, guiding, and influencing the course of this and other main trends in the development of our social service patterns in the public field? What machinery have we—or do we need—to ensure the proper evolution of these patterns?

The answer is not, of course, a clear or simple one. It could not be, given the complicated nature of our social service structure. We have only, in fact, begun within recent years to establish the basic elements of the machinery necessary to coordinate our public social services.

In Canada, prior to World War II, only three of the provinces had established ministries of social welfare to guide the development of provincial welfare policies. Seven provinces, and along with them the Federal government, were carrying out uncoordinated public welfare measures involving the expenditure of large sums of money and affecting the lives and well-being of hundreds of thousands of Canadians without the necessary machinery for the development of properly coordinated plans. Many cities and municipalities struggled through the depression without bothering to establish a properly organized local public welfare department. The record of United States cities and states may be somewhat better than it was in Canada; but, lest too much complacency result from this thought, it may be noted that it was not until 1952 that you established at the Federal level a full-fledged Cabinet Department of Health, Education, and Welfare.

This serves to illustrate how slow we have been to recognize publicly and permanently the important social service functions and responsibilities of government in our present-day society. However slowly these developments have come about, we should now be encouraged by the fact that, at long last, we have begun to establish at Federal, state, and local levels the machinery through which the processes of policy-making and coordination can be developed. We lack no longer the machinery by which Federal, provincial, and municipal governments can integrate and coordinate, each at their respective levels, their own particular machinery for administration of their social services. What we still lack is the formula for the creation of intergovernmental coordinating machinery that will be accepted at every level in the joint planning and coordination of all our governmental social services.

It should not be concluded that no effort of any kind is made at the present time to ensure intergovernmental coordination of our social service programs. Actually, the problem of coordination of intergovernmental programs breaks down into several separate problems. It is not just a question of ensuring municipal-state-Federal cooperation. There is, in addition, the problem of coordination at the municipal level among the various municipalities themselves.

We have in our countries loose federations of municipal organizations, associations, or federations of municipalities within the states and even on a nation-wide basis. Through this machinery, a limited amount of coordination of effort can be achieved; but associations of this kind are beset with so many problems in so many fields that the amount of effective coordination in the social service field which is capable of accomplishment through machinery such as this will always be at best very limited.

What has been said with respect to relationships at the municipal level of government applies equally to the states. Here we have the same internal problems of coordination within each state government in respect to its state-operated social services, and also the problems of interstate cooperation and coordination. Here again, such groupings as the Governors' Conference, the Council of State Governments, and others provide some possibilities for effective coordination of state-level social service policies. We have no comparable machinery for mutual cooperation among provincial governments or premiers in Canada. But at best again, the coordination of social service policies is for such groups as these only one of many concerns. We can look perhaps to this source for some help in coordinating our public social services; but at best this help will be of a casual, informal, and sporadic nature.

To the organizations mentioned, we should add, as we reach the level of Federal-state coordination in the social service field, the contribution made through groupings such as the American Public Welfare Association with its special Councils of State and Local Administrators, the National Social Welfare Assembly, and its Canadian prototype and counterpart, the Canadian Welfare Council. Through such channels flows a constant stream of consultation and exchange of views. They contribute much to the orderly arrangement at various levels of our social services. They undoubtedly influence at many critical points the development of our public social service patterns. They achieve on a modest, yet effective, basis much of what can be achieved through the process which might be called *coordination by consultation*. But the fact remains that, having said all this, there is still too great a temptation and opportunity for the senior levels of government to affect the trend of social service development through unilateral action based upon decisions taken from above. This achieves an *ex post facto* kind of coordination only, forcing subordinate or junior jurisdictions to make the necessary adjustments in their respective programs to take account of new changes at the national level.

It may be that we cannot escape this altogether. It may be that we cannot hope for or expect the establishment of more formal machinery to ensure consultation between the various levels of government in respect to social service matters—consultation out of which would follow by mutual consent and arrangement the necessary coordination of policy and program at all levels. It may be that to establish formal machinery for such consultation and coordination in the social service field would bring us too close to the creation of machinery for the development of a planned society, which is anathema in some quarters. Whatever our views on this, we shall have to recognize that, as matters stand at present, we lack any recognized channel in our respective countries by which we can ensure on a formal and official basis adequate consultation among the various levels of government with respect to important social service developments at any level; and by the same token, we lack machinery for the effective coordination of the social service machinery which our various governments operate.

The important measure of coordination which can be achieved—largely through the imposition of coordination from above—by the machinery of conditional grants-in-aid should be mentioned. These are an important feature of the social service relationships between our various levels of government. It might be called *coordination by supervision*. From another point of view, it involves rather the establishment of administrative standards and the maintenance of a measure of uniformity among the various subordinate jurisdictions, rather than the achievement of coordination in the proper sense of that word. For does not the very term "coordination" imply the negotiation of mutually acceptable arrangements among equals? Can we have, then, such a thing as true coordination imposed or dictated, however gently and persuasively, from above?

Let us summarize where we stand at the present time. We have indicated the problems which arise when we try to achieve an effective measure of coordination within the diverse and variegated framework of our public and private social services. We have no doubt established, with partial effectiveness, devices for coordination within the voluntary and public sectors of the social service field. These devices at best are partial and incomplete. There is need for more effective machinery for coordination in two particular areas: the area that affects the relationship of public to voluntary agencies; and the area that affects the social service relationships of the three levels of government. Until more adequate machinery can be established than those devices for cooperation and coordination by consultation and supervision which I have already mentioned, we shall have to recognize the weaknesses and the limitations of our present public-private and intergovernmental working partnerships.

IMPACTS UPON THE PEOPLE

Let us pose the following question: What are the implications of the patterns and relationships we have developed in the social service field? How do they affect the impact of our social service programs on the people whom they serve and on the community at large?

Out of the many issues that could be raised under this heading, only two appear to be of the utmost importance, because they pose the real dilemma of the social services in our society today. Along with much that is good and beneficial, the patterns and relationships which we have seen developing through the years have produced the following undesirable results:

1. Our social services are moving farther and farther away from the people.
2. The people are moving farther and farther away from our social services.

These are two separate points. The first means that out of the shift from voluntary agency to local government, from local to state, and finally to Federal government, we are witnessing a process of centralization of our social services which inevitably results in greater and greater distances, both physical and psychological, between the administration of the services and the people whom they are designed to benefit. Too often our public social services seem remote and distant and impersonal. Sheer bulk and volume require them to be mechanized, standardized, impersonalized, and oftentimes, unless we guard against it carefully, dehumanized. The miracle of mechanization makes possible large-scale administrative operations, and nation-wide social welfare programs now have taken shape which would literally have been impossible a generation ago. But there are dangers inherent in this miracle; and we have not taken all the measures possible to counteract the damage that remoteness, distance, and punch-card administration can do to the personal human component in our public social services.

This is one of the most significant implications of our present administrative structure in the social service field. It is one of the important results of the trend to centralization we have witnessed and are still witnessing. The impersonal quality of so many of our public social services constitutes a most important present threat to the continuity of that humanitarian tradition which has characterized the history of our social service effort through all the centuries of the Christian era.

It is not suggested that we can or should reverse the trend of centralization described above. But we must give increasing thought to countermeasures which will offset this serious and growing tendency for our social services to become farther and farther removed from the people whom they serve.

The other serious administrative implication of our present structure for the impact of our programs on the people is that the people are getting to be farther and farther removed from the social services. In both the voluntary and the public sectors of the social service field the element of genuine citizen participation is growing less and less. Too much of the responsibility for policy, too much of the operation and administration of our voluntary social services, is today in the hands of the professional executive and his staff. Too much of the planning and development of our public social services and of their detailed administration is left today to the administrator and the bureaucrat.

How often have we seen in our communities, states, and nations a lively upsurge of interest in a particular social problem, a genuine humanitarian crusade, citizen-led and citizen-inspired, pointed toward the attainment of a worth-while goal in social welfare legislation. That is a heartening sight indeed, because it is citizen participation at its best. But when the goal is achieved and the legislation on the statute books, what happens? Too often we have seen the interest vanish, the field left empty, the element of genuine citizen participation and interest lost. The legislation is enacted and put into effect; the program carries on; its benefits carry forward into the community. But too often citizen interest flags or shifts completely to some other area of need; and, with the objective gained, the actual operation of the program becomes part of the monotonous routine, the dry dust of civil service or private agency administration.

The special problems inherent in the maintenance of a significant element of citizen participation in our public social service programs must be recognized. We have done a little through citizen boards, advisory committees, appeal tribunals, and other similar devices to maintain a link between the citizen and the public welfare services. But, by and large, we must admit the ineffectiveness of these devices in maintaining the degree of citizen interest and participation that would make our public social service programs truly responsive to the disinterested advice of citizen leaders not carrying the burden of elective public office.

Some of the very machinery we have created and maintained to achieve co-ordination has an unfortunate effect on this maintenance of citizen interest and participation. For example, in the voluntary sector of the social service field, the federated approach to giving often tends to base its arguments on the plea that busy individuals in a community cannot easily determine for themselves those charitable causes to which they should fairly allocate their contributions. The job of determining which agencies to support—and how much to give— involves so many complications of a budgetary and policy nature that busy individuals cannot properly decide these questions for themselves. So runs the argument. If the heart of the giver is left to decide and he gives on the basis of emotional attachment, some agencies get too much money, others get too little. But instead of asking each individual to apply his mind and not his heart to the solution of this problem, we tend, through our federated giving programs, to take the responsibility off his shoulders altogether; to do his thinking for him; to ask him to give once and for all and let the coordinating machinery of the council, chest, and budget committee decide just how his giving should be allocated in the interests of the community.

This principle—unless we watch it carefully—has much the same effect on citizen interest and participation as comes from the shifting of the burden of particular social services to the tax structure and to public administration. The element of personal choice and judgment, of personal interest and citizen involvement in a particular cause, is weakened and diluted. It is true, of course, that unlike the tax levy, the voluntary contribution remains a voluntary act—an act of personal decision containing still an element of voluntary citizen participation. But does it really? How much is really left of the element of voluntary choice in the methods used today to raise the money for private social services? How strongly do we emphasize in our federated fund-raising campaigns the freedom of individuals to choose *not* to give, as well as their obligation to contribute? Have not the community social pressures, the organizational methods we have developed through the campaign machinery of the federated charities, equated very largely the business of giving to private philanthropy with that of the tax collector?

In the minds of hundreds of thousands of individuals who give through group solicitation, payroll deduction, and other devices to the support of private social services, the margin of difference between their contribution to voluntary philanthropy and their tax support of governmental social services is very slight indeed.

It surely follows from this situation that by such devices, even in the voluntary social service field, we are isolating the individual more and more from the possibility of genuine personal involvement in the social services which he supports.

This could be carried further into an analysis of the extent of citizen participation today in the formulation of our private social agency policies. Here there is still admittedly a large area of opportunity for genuine, intelligent citizen participation. But too many of our private social agencies tend to rely on the agency executive to evolve policy, subject only to the passive acquiescence and approval of the citizen board.

There is an ever-present tendency and danger in the voluntary social service structure to place the participation of our citizen leaders and supporters more and more on a formalistic and ritualistic basis. They lend their names. They give generous financial support. They participate in financial campaigns, raising money from friends, associates, and neighbors on the basis of a vague conviction, vaguely communicated, that this is a good cause, that the agencies are doing good community work. They serve somewhat vaguely, remotely, absent-mindedly on boards that purport to determine policy and to control the administration and the program of the agency. But many of these areas of citizen participation in the work of our private social services are remote from the reality of the day-to-day situation. Our citizen leaders find it increasingly difficult to get the feel of the problem they are working with.

Here, surely, is another real element of danger in our present social service pattern.

For these are the recognized leaders, the chief supporters of our private social services. These are the people who carry the responsibility for educating succeeding generations of their fellow men to the need of maintaining our complex network of private and voluntary social services. These people are the justification for our peculiar partnership in the United States and Canada between the public and the private welfare agencies.

If we are to preserve the values we believe in, if we are to safeguard the patterns we have labored to develop for many generations, if we are to maintain a vital, living partnership between our voluntary social service agencies and the governmental services which support and reinforce them, these people must not be allowed to lose contact with the realities of the causes they support and lead. We must at all costs ensure that these, the guardians of our voluntary social service traditions, handed down to us over hundreds of years, do not become too far removed from the social services of our community.

If we do not succeed in this, then surely we are abdicating our responsibilities, as citizens in a free society, for the maintenance of those social service causes and programs we believe in. If we forfeit by neglect this leadership, who else is left but the all-powerful state to take the sole responsibility for meeting social service needs?

CONCLUSION

At the beginning of this paper we tried to answer the question "What responsibility?" by showing that in our present-day society we recognize the duty of the community to meet those social service needs which lie beyond the capability of the individual and his family. A final word should be added, in conclusion, to suggest how far that responsibility extends.

We have today two differing concepts of the place of the social services in modern community life.

There are those, on the one hand, who regard the social service field as static and limited. They take the view that man has certain basic human needs which must be met, and that is the limit and extent of the social service function. For those who take this view, the encroachment of governmental services into larger and larger areas of the social service field has only one result. It diminishes the area of the voluntary agency; and as the trend to enlarge the area of the public authority continues, the role of the private agency lessens in scope and usefulness, and finally withers away completely. For those who take this static and limited view of the function of our social services, the historic trend from voluntary to public social services has elements of danger which are very real and urgent at the present time.

Not all share that static and limited point of view. There is another and a better way of looking at our social service development. It is the dynamic concept of the role of social services in our society. It is based on the simple principle which has motivated man's relations with his fellow men through all the ages. Stated simply, it is this: Man's desire and his capacity for helpful service to his fellow men is not limited, but is infinite. Man will never reach the end of his desire to render in an infinite and ever-changing variety of ways helpful human service for the good of his neighbors and the good of his community. The restless human spirit is embarked upon an endless search for the methods and means of human betterment. The horizons of human helpfulness are infinite and limitless. They extend beyond the limits of the vision of our present generation and will ever move forward and provide the beckoning, far-distant goals toward which the generations of the future will continue forever to aspire.

If we can accept this concept of our democratic society and its application to our functions in the social service field, we will always find new fields for adventurous pioneering, new experiments to undertake, new social crusades to lead, new areas of human helpfulness in which the enterprise of our voluntary and public social service agencies can make their contribution—ever changing—to the rich and full development of our community life.

FOOTNOTES

1. Report of the Committee on the Law and Practice relating to Charitable Trusts, December 1952, paragraph 39. (H.M. Stationery Office—Cmd. 8710).

2. Bessie Touzel, "Some Factors Affecting Public-Private Relationships in Social Work," *Proceedings Canadian Conference on Social Work,* 1952.

3. Report of U. K. Parliamentary Committee on Charitable Trusts, paragraphs 48, 51.

4. *Ibid.*

5. *Ibid.,* paragraph 53.

6. *Ibid.,* paragraph 49.

7. *Op. cit.,* paragraph 61.

The Problem of Financing Social Services

William Haber

Professor of Economics, University of Michigan

Frederick Lewis Allen, in his provocative review of the development of economic security in the United States, called attention to the fact that during the dark decade of the 1930s two principles gradually won general acceptance by the American people.[1]

The first of these was that the fortunes of individual Americans are inextricably interlocked, so that if any of us fall into deep trouble it has become the responsibility of the government—that is, all the rest of us—to help out. This task has come to fall not only on the family, friends, and neighbors, or even upon the local community and the state alone, but if need be upon the Federal government itself. This development represents a radical alteration in the traditional pattern of self-help and largely voluntary assistance to people in need.

The second principle which appears to have won equally wide acceptance is that it is the job of the Federal government to see that there shall not be another great depression. Most people realize that there are genuine dangers in the extension of power of the Federal government and are aware also of the effect which such an extension might have on economic liberty for ourselves as individuals. Our experience tells us, however, that in a severe economic emergency we shall have to rely on the instrument of government to avert an economic decline and thus protect us against the loss of economic security.

Taken together the combination of these two ideas has produced a phenomenal transformation in the social politics of the United States. Its most significant manifestation is the almost unanimous adoption of the Social Security Act in 1935 and the equally widespread endorsement of the extensions and liberalizations of that measure since then, including the broad liberalization in 1954, together with the supporting legislation in all of the states.

173

THE EXPANSION OF SOCIAL SERVICES

In less than two decades we have fashioned an extensive system of social insurance, public assistance, and social services for a steadily increasing proportion of our citizens at an annual cost of many billion dollars. While still developing, with obvious gaps and inadequacies, our complex program now consists of a national system of old-age and survivors' insurance, covering almost four out of five paid civilian jobs and providing monthly benefits to insured retired workers and their wives and widows and to dependent husbands, widowers, and parents aged 65 or over, to the children of retired workers and of deceased insured workers and to the mothers of these children.

All states have unemployment insurance laws covering most employees in industry and commerce; workmen's compensation laws providing cash benefits and medical care to most workers outside of agriculture who are sick or disabled as a result of occupational injury or disease, and to their survivors. Four states have temporary sickness insurance programs providing cash benefits to workers who are unable to work because of sickness. All states participate in the Social Security Act's grants-in-aid for public assistance for needy aged persons, blind persons, and dependent children; and similar grants have recently been made available to needy persons who are permanently and totally disabled. Local public assistance programs for general relief not included in these specific categories are also provided in varying degrees of adequacy in most states and localities.

In addition to this vast array of income-maintenance programs provided for the general population by social insurance and public assistance, one of the largest income-security and medical-care programs exists for veterans and the families and survivors of veterans. These public programs are supplemented by private group plans, to a considerable extent growing out of collective bargaining agreements, providing for retirement pensions to over 10 million employees and disability payments to an increasing number of wage earners.

The magnitude of this undertaking can perhaps best be appreciated by reference to the numbers who are involved in these programs for benefits and services and the amounts expended.[2] Over 7,393,000 individuals received monthly retirement and disability payments in January 1954, under the four Federal programs provided by the Social Security Act, the Railroad Retirement Act, the Federal Civil Service Commission, and the Veterans Administration. Another 3,169,800 received survivors' benefits under these programs, including a small number for whom lump-sum settlements were provided. During the same month, under the railroad legislation, the unemployment insurance, and the four states' temporary disability programs, payments were made to an average of 1,834,600 persons. To these social insurance programs should be added over 5,144,800 individuals and families who were in receipt of public assistance payments. Considering income payments alone under these legislative acts, over 17,500,000 individuals were in receipt of payments during the month of January in the rather prosperous nearly full-employment year of 1954.

There is nothing particularly stable about the number of persons in receipt of assistance or insurance payments. Changing price levels have a direct bearing on the numbers who find it necessary to apply and who qualify for public assistance. General economic conditions and changing employment levels immediately influence the numbers who become eligible for unemployment insurance benefits. These fluctuations may therefore be up or down. There is small risk, however, in predicting that an upward trend in over-all totals is almost inevitable. While the old-age assistance totals are bound to decline in time, there is universal agreement that the number of old-age and survivors' insurance beneficiaries will increase steadily over the next decade even under relatively good economic conditions. The arithmetic concerning the age distribution of our population over the next two decades compels us to contemplate income and assistance security programs for 20,000,000 persons even under conditions of relatively high-level employment.

The cost implications of such an undertaking are of tremendous significance. In the fiscal year 1951–1952 the social welfare expenditures in the United States under civilian public programs by the Federal, state, and local governments exceeded $16,196,700,000.[3] These expenditures included outlays for social insurance, public aid, health, medical, and other welfare services, and under veterans programs. If expenditures for education were included, the total for that year would exceed $24,950,000,000, equal approximately to 7.4 per cent of the gross national product. While some programs have been declining during the past fifteen years, the over-all expenditures since 1943 have been increasing steadily, even after allowances are made for changes in the purchasing power of the social-welfare dollar. There can be no question that social-welfare costs will increase in the next decade, even without any additional liberalization in unemployment insurance or retirement benefits or in increased coverage of persons or risks. Many older persons will qualify for retirement pensions as the program matures; and this prospect, including the increasing proportion of older persons in the population, will result in substantial future increases in expenditures for benefits under this program.

Income-maintenance programs, however, represent only one facet, a very important one though it is, of the expanding relationship between the government and the citizen in our free society. Social services represent another area, one in which not only the Federal, state, and local governments, but private agencies as well, have played an important part. In a progressive and growing economy, an increasing proportion of the labor force is released from the production of essentials, from providing food, clothing, and shelter, and enabled to participate in the ever-expanding area of personal services. Every decennial census confirms this occupational shift. Unless one were to assume that a slower rate of technical progress and growth in productivity is to prevail in the next generation, this shift from making things to providing services will continue for some time to come. In brief, an ever-growing proportion of our population is available for the service and professional occupations which have shown such phenomenal growth during the past forty years.

By their very nature many of these services are performed by public authority. One need cite only a few to indicate the broad and expanding area of public social services. Among these we include vocational rehabilitation and counseling, the employment services, child-welfare services, the whole array of services to veterans and their families, and large areas of research concerning the health needs of the nation. The public health services include not only the traditional functions of control of communicable diseases and sanitary engineering services at all levels of government, but also the growing support by the Federal government of research in the fields of mental health, cancer, and heart disease and other diseases affecting older people. At the local and state levels, especially in the field of public welfare "case work," services to families and children are often provided quite apart from required financial aid.

THE PROBLEMS OF FINANCING

The proper financing of such large and apparently increasing outlays for income-sustaining programs and public social services has become one of the major fiscal problems of contemporary social policy. The issues can be readily identified. They are concerned primarily with controversies about four critical problems.

The first has to do with the question how the cost of financing these payments should be distributed, whether they should be assessed in large measure against those who may become eligible to receive the benefits or the employers or the general taxpayer should be required to finance all or a portion of the cost. This question is pertinent whether applied to income-security programs for unemployment or retirement or to social service programs like health insurance. If and when general public programs for medical services are adopted in this country, we shall have to determine to what extent these services are to be financed primarily by imposing the costs upon the potential consumer of such services, or upon his employer or upon the general taxpayer.

The second problem is concerned with the issue of Federal-state relations, whether the state or the Federal government should be required to finance assistance or insurance payments or social services. This issue is, for the present, largely confined to problems growing out of the financing of income-maintenance programs, particularly unemployment insurance and public assistance. While the problem is present in the areas of public health, vocational rehabilitation, and child welfare services, the relatively small amounts involved have not created serious controversy as to the distribution of the costs between the Federal and state governments. The grant-in-aid principle appears to be firmly established in these programs, although vigorous debate exists as to the proportion to be borne by the Federal government and whether equalization grants on the basis of the financial resources of the states should be established.

The third problem touches the current debate on the pay-as-you-go method of financing in place of the reserve requirements now provided for some programs. This issue is primarily confined to the financing of the old-age and survivors' insurance program and has no immediate relevance to the financing of social services. Were we at some future time to embark upon a compulsory health-service program, the issue of reserves versus some other basis of financing such services might become important. Even in such an eventuality, however, the limitations of reserve financing are readily recognized.

Finally, the question how much social welfare the nation can afford is uppermost in the minds of all who are familiar with the present costs and future trends.

That there is no unanimity of agreement concerning the answers to these questions should not be surprising. Our social services have traditionally been provided locally and often by private social service agencies. Public social services for rehabilitation and health and child welfare are, except for the traditional function of the public health departments, of relatively recent origin. Our present social security program for insurance and assistance payments is largely an outgrowth of the depression of the 1930s. Since its adoption at that time, the Congress has evaded the establishment of a definitive policy on the central issues of financing our retirement and survivors program. In fact, the original program embodied in the 1936 Social Security Act was radically modified in 1939, but the Congress froze the contribution rate several times in order to retard the accumulation of the reserve. While substantially liberalized in its benefit provisions in 1950, 1952, and 1954, it cannot be said that the Congress is even now agreed on how this program is to be financed on a long-term basis.

While the method of financing the public assistance programs appears to be quite firmly established, the high costs and the failure of the assistance programs to decline have led to much criticism in recent years. These criticisms are concerned with the increasing share of the costs of these programs borne by the Federal government and the great variation in grants among the states. While the grant-in-aid method, which has provided the financial basis for public assistance, is not likely to be set aside in the near future, there are many proposals for its modification.

As is true of public assistance, the method of financing unemployment insurance appears to be firmly entrenched and not likely to be radically revised, although considerable criticism against experience-rating has had wide currency since 1940.

With respect to social services, there have been many proposals for their expansion and more adequate financing. The most controversial of these has been the proposal for compulsory health insurance, urged during the preceding administration, and the more modified plans suggested by the President's Commission on the Health Needs of the Nation. How to finance the nation's health services remains the most controversial issue in this area.

Specific proposals for alternative methods of financing our social welfare programs have long been urged. The Brookings Institution, in Lewis Meriam's *Relief and Social Security* published in 1946 and in *The Cost and Financing of Social Security* issued in 1950,[4] proposed a basic revision in our method of paying for social security. The Chamber of Commerce of the United States in its 1953 report on *Improving Social Security* also urged us to depart from the present financing provisions and to pull the Federal government out of the old-age assistance program altogether.[5] And Congressman Carl T. Curtis, the Chairman of the Subcommittee on Social Security of the Committee on Ways and Means of the House of Representatives, is proposing a fundamental revision of our methods of financing and other features of our old-age retirement plan.[6]

Nor are these the only critics of our present scheme of paying the social security bill. Others, friends and skeptics alike, who are seriously concerned with keeping these costs within bounds are groping for alternative financing arrangements which might reduce expenditures or shift a larger portion of the burden either to the potential beneficiaries or to other than the now participating units of government. They are disturbed by the lack of a "system" of social security in this country, its gaps, its patchwork character, and its inconsistent financial features; and they hope to introduce a more orderly system and greater consistency by simplifying its financial basis.

This is a commendable objective, although one should not be in too much of a hurry in unifying our social security system or in correcting its inner contradictions and inconsistencies. By foreign standards, our experience has been exceedingly brief. Even after a longer passage of time, however, we shall probably not achieve a fully consistent and unified pattern, such as is possible in a smaller nation with a centralized government. Americans do not espouse full-blown programs. Logical developments and consistency will have to follow many years of experimentation with specific programs designed to deal with special problems. Thus programs for children, the blind, or the aged have a special appeal and win wide public support. Over-all approaches fail to win such support even though they may be more logical and comprehensive. Nor is it without significance that most of the clamor for unifying our social security program or for radical changes in social security financing comes not from the friends of the social security movement but largely from those who have been quite critical of this approach for dealing either with the problem of income loss in our society or with the need for social services. Those who formulated the American scheme which Congress adopted and has thus far retained have opposed most of the proposed changes, particularly those which might weaken the contributory principle, provide more uniform benefits, introduce some form of income or means test, or transfer a portion of the problem to the states.[7]

THE DEVELOPING POLICIES

Both foreign and American experience, short though the latter may be, strongly suggests that the policy of not imposing the total cost of social security benefits upon those who receive them is rather firmly established. In the area of noncontributory benefits, such as public assistance, financing through general tax funds has been the traditional method. While special taxes are occasionally employed to finance public assistance programs in some states, no general proposal that these programs should be financed by sales or payroll taxes has been seriously considered. Public assistance is, after all, only a more palatable name for the traditional public welfare responsibility of the American community. Its partial absorption by the state and by the Federal government has not generally been accompanied by proposals that these activities should be financed by special taxation designed to fall on the very persons who may eventually qualify for such aid.

·When it comes to social security benefits, available as a matter of right without any test of need, the contributory principle has been widely employed. It has both financial and psychological advantages. The "premium" concept, taken over from private insurance, gives to such contributions and resulting benefits a degree of respectability and propriety quite superior to assistance payments, no matter how general the latter may be. In addition, such premiums in the form of payroll taxes provide a simple and steady source of income to the insurance fund, a strong reason for the retention of such financing once adopted. Finally, the relationship between benefits and past contributions (or wages and employment) is intended to provide in part a logical basis for differentiation of social security payments as between individuals and in part as a check upon levels of benefits. In foreign systems, where flat-rate benefits prevail, contributory payments by the insured have more limited objectives. In this country, however, the wider differentials in wage rates and earnings among the various classifications of workers represents a strong argument against a system of uniform social security payments for all wage earners. Contributory payments based on such earnings, therefore, become a simple and understandable device to justify differences in social security benefits.

Were this reasoning carried to its logical conclusion, as it is in individual private insurance, it would impose too large a burden upon many insured persons. As a result, experience has led legislative bodies to modify this principle. In some programs, the contribution is levied only upon the employer. Such is the case in the American legislation on industrial accident compensation and also in our unemployment insurance legislation. There is no clear agreement among economists as to the actual incidence of this social security tax. As a generalization, it is not possible to determine whether this tax is transferred to the insured in lower future wage rates or to the consumer in higher prices or to the employer in reduced profits. A complex number of market forces concerned primarily with the nature of the competitive process and the level of employment will influence the incidence of such a tax. It can at least be assumed that it does not always come out of wages.

Extension of this principle beyond industrial injuries or lay-offs, two risks quite directly traceable to jobs and working conditions, is more likely to be seriously questioned and resisted. Proposals for a payroll tax on employers to finance health insurance, for example, would have to be justified on different grounds, such as ability to pay or convenience rather than that of industrial responsibility. Employers do contribute to collective-bargaining health plans administered through such organizations as Blue Cross or Blue Shield for illness or disability which is not work-connected. In the case of old-age and survivors' insurance, the cost of financing is imposed on both the employer and the insured person and, perhaps eventually, in part upon the general taxpayer as well. Thus in these programs, in this country and abroad, the costs of social insurance payments have traditionally been assessed against others than the insured person alone.

In doing so it has been possible to provide either an unearned benefit to the insured worker in the form of more liberal amounts to all, or a larger sum to the low-income person than he would receive were the benefit related only to his personal contribution. Such "inequities" would hardly be tenable in any private insurance contract. They become indispensable in a social security scheme. The objective in such a plan is not necessarily to allocate costs on an equitable basis, but to provide a fixed, certain, reasonably adequate income as a protection against predetermined contingencies. How these payments are financed is less important than that they be provided and that they be available rather automatically when the contingency materializes.

These rather elementary observations appear necessary only because in the perennial debate on how best to pay for social security these questions keep recurring. Thus the problem whether old-age benefits or unemployment compensation are really insurance or something different, whether what the "insured" have is a contract or something less than that, occupied many a page in the hearings of the Curtis Committee this year. Little is to be gained in attempting to equate the social insurance program with private annuity or other insurance contracts. Social insurance is a special form of protection against income loss, developed by society and financed by whatever method is most likely to achieve its objective.

These observations are equally applicable in considering the issues whether either social security payments for insurance and assistance or appropriations for social services should be financed by the state or by the Federal government. Here also fine distinctions as to the proper distribution of public functions are not really as significant as they may appear. These matters apparently were of minor consequence in the early 1930s when the local communities pleaded for state aid and the states sought Federal appropriations. The sole criterion which guided public policy at that time was the practical problem created by the deep depression with which the localities and the states had to grapple. Somewhat similar considerations are applicable at all times. The issue is less concerned with theoretical problems of intergovernment relations than with the practical aspects of financial capacity and resources.

Several aspects of this issue are reasonably clear and not subject to serious dispute. The first is that during the past quarter-century an increasing number of economic and financial functions have tended to be assumed by larger units of government. This development did not arise by accident nor by any imperialistic inclinations of the larger governmental units. The major explanation for the trend will be found in the taxing and other financial limitations under which the smaller units operate. Primary reliance upon the property tax, constitutional and charter limits on taxing and borrowing powers, and other similar restrictions prevail quite generally in most local governmental units. Other shortcomings, though much less restrictive, often apply to the state government. As a general principle, however, the larger units have fewer restrictions and a more flexible taxing and borrowing capacity. In this respect our Federal government has distinct advantages over the smaller state and local units.[8]

In addition, there are special reasons why certain types of social security programs require wider geographical coverage and rule out local administration and financing. Unemployment insurance, for example, requires at least state-wide application, and legislation on the basis of a smaller geographical area was never considered. Old-age and survivors' insurance, on the other hand, was considered to be financially manageable only on a national basis. The varying age-distribution of our population among the states and the high degree of mobility suggested that an approach to an old-age retirement program on a state-wide basis would be impracticable from an administrative as well as from a financial point of view.

As a result, the Federal government had to undertake the financing of our old-age retirement program. In order to equalize interstate competitive costs, the Federal government in the Social Security Act undertook also to facilitate state legislation for unemployment insurance by imposing a uniform tax on all employers in all states. It is too early to determine at this stage whether unemployment insurance can, in fact, be financed on a state rather than a national basis. As of this moment, it certainly appears that such financing is practicable. On the other hand, there is already some evidence that several states are likely to be in financial difficulty, even as to solvency, should we experience recurring recessions more frequently than in the past ten years. In other words, while the unemployment insurance reserves to the credit of the forty-eight states at the moment appear to be reasonably adequate for all but a few states, it can hardly be said that our unemployment insurance programs and its accumulated reserves have really been subjected to the practical test of economic adversity.

In view of this uncertainty, specific proposals have been made from time to time for more direct Federal participation in the financing of unemployment insurance, through either grants or loans to such states whose funds are inadequate. Such reinsurance legislation was adopted by both houses of Congress in August 1954. It provides for repayable loans to states whose reserves are low. This legislation should be adequate to meet the sort of difficulties experienced by Rhode Island and Massachusetts during the postwar readjustments.

The factors which determined the role of the Federal government in financing old-age insurance and unemployment compensation apply to a lesser degree to the financing of social services and public assistance programs. In these areas the issues are largely concerned with financial capacity. There are no technical or actuarial obstacles against local financing and administration of public assistance or social service programs. However, local incapacity, or often local disinclination, does actually prevail. The states entered the field to assist communities in financing aid or service and to assure reasonably uniform standards throughout the state. The Federal government was drawn into these activities only in 1933 when the states found themselves unable to respond to the localities' demand for financial assistance.

In the Social Security Act the objective of the Federal government was "systematized" in at least two directions. First, its objective was to provide financial assistance as an inducement to the states to embark upon a public aid program. The grant-in-aid method was entirely effective to accomplish this purpose. A secondary objective was to provide for more uniform administration within and among the states and to raise standards of aid and administration. This objective also was achieved to a greater degree than many would have considered possible only 15 years ago.

Somewhat similar considerations influenced public policy in the area of social services. While some programs, such as public health, have significant national implications and call for national policy, there are not the same inherent reasons for the participation of the Federal government in other programs. For example, individual casework, standards for counseling and family service, health needs of the family and its financing, do not necessarily require state intervention and even less so that of the Federal government.

That the Federal government did enter the fields of child welfare services, vocational rehabilitation and counseling, public health, and medical research is primarily due to a recognition of the fact that financial inducements would stimulate the adoption of these services where they did not prevail and their improvement where they already existed. To a considerable degree this has also been realized. In fact, as we shall see below, it is because of the great degree of progress already achieved that many are urging an expansion of Federal financing of social services.

The grant-in-aid is not new. Only in relatively recent periods, however, has it been developed to become one of the most significant aspects of government finance and administration.[9] Its use in the field of social welfare can be traced back to 1917 when it was first employed for vocational education. Grants for maternal and child health programs were initiated in 1921. With the depression in 1930 and the adoption of the Social Security Act in 1935 the grant-in-aid principle became a significant aspect of government finance and administration.

Without the use of the grant-in-aid method our public assistance program would not have developed in its present proportions. This and other grant-aided programs increased steadily from 1935 on. Welfare grants stimulated the developmental programs for maternal and child health and personnel training for social service work. The public assistance grants were essential for the poorer states and resulted in higher standards among the wealthier states. They also reduced the "differences in the availability and level of assistance among the localities within states and among needy individuals within localities."[10] The effect of the formula according to which the Federal government matches a higher proportion of low average assistance payments than of higher payments has been to channel relatively more Federal funds to the poorer states. In addition the amounts of assistance payments have been steadily increased, standards of need liberalized, and improved administrative procedures widely adopted.

Several questions concerning the Federal grants-in-aid for public assistance currently agitate students of this problem and critics of the social security program. The first has to do with the mounting sums spent for this purpose. Old-age assistance cases and costs continue on an exceedingly high level, even after the liberalization of the old-age and survivors' insurance law. Changing price levels and increasing liberality in appropriations, with redefinition of what constitutes minimum budgets for needy persons and families, have combined to increase the amounts appropriated by Congress for this purpose. A second question grows out of the fact that the Federal government has relatively little control over the amount of the public assistance grants, since under present legislation it is bound to match state appropriations up to the maximum permitted by law. Since the Federal government pays a substantial proportion of the cost of all public assistance programs, many states are said to have taken advantage of this situation by being more liberal in such grants than they would be if the costs were not so distributed. This problem would be further complicated by the proposal that the Federal grant-in-aid should vary with the state's economic capacity. It has been vigorously urged that states with a lower per capita income should be aided on a more generous basis than states more fortunately situated.

Mounting costs, disproportionate grants to liberal states, lack of control over Federal outlays as a result of "open-end" grants—these and other criticisms have led many to urge a reappraisal of the grant-in-aid method of financing. "There is no system," writes the Council of State Governments. What we have, it says, are several grant-in-aid programs, "each developed, established, and operated without relation to the others."[11]

One proposal is that the Federal government withdraw entirely from the public assistance field. The United States Chamber of Commerce would begin this retreat by transferring to the states the full responsibility for old-age assistance. To make this palatable, it recommends that all persons over 65 who are not now eligible for old-age insurance should be covered immediately and become eligible to receive monthly annuity payments of at least the minimum benefit of $25. This proposal is fortunately receiving only scant support and the Administration's plan for revision of the law, already approved by the Congress, calls for the continuance of the present grant-in-aid features for old-age assistance.

To adopt a piecemeal revision on the theory that it might be cheaper is hardly the most sensible way to revise our legislation. However, there is no justification for assuming that it would cost less. All that can be claimed is that some of the cost now borne by the Federal government would be transferred to the states. Should the states fail to increase their appropriations, the aged would receive smaller assistance payments than are now provided. There is much more to be said for meeting the old-age program as a whole, including the responsibility of all levels of government.

A more lasting solution is to provide retirement coverage for the entire population. If that were done without delay, in time, and with the "new start," all who reach retirement age would be provided for on an insurance basis and the assistance program would soon be confined to residual aid only. This cannot be achieved by the Federal government's withdrawing from the assistance field and transferring the full responsibility for assistance to the states. The inequities which exist arise from the failure to provide full coverage. "To the extent that we delay . . . we perpetuate discrimination and inequities and thus invite increasing demands for scrapping the whole insurance idea."[12] Even more important than the insurance idea, however, is our responsibility for dealing with the assistance problem realistically. The grant-in-aid device is merely a method by which the national interest in the social welfare problem is expressed. So long as these problems exist and wherever states "are unable, reluctant, or unwilling to act alone,"[13] the grant-in-aid will be found an effective instrument for achieving a national purpose. In our form of government, the grant-in-aid idea is the most effective instrument we have yet devised which makes it possible to meet social and economic problems without centralizing administration in the Federal government.

UNMET NEEDS

Lady Rhys-Williams, writing in 1953 on financial aspects of social welfare in Great Britain, makes a significant observation which we, in our preoccupation with costs, should seriously consider. Commenting on the industrial revolution in England and on the poverty and degradation of the British working class, she writes that "the widespread ill health and incapacity among the workers, to which this poverty gave rise, has extended to the third and fourth generations, and is casting a heavy burden of maintenance and care of the sick upon the present generation."[14] Thus the increase in material riches in Great Britain during the nineteenth century was "seriously overbalanced by the high toll of death and disease due to extreme poverty and lack of adequate welfare services among the working people." This experience leads her to plead against attempts to seek major economies in the social services.

Are we closing our eyes to the price we shall have to pay in the future for our inadequacies in housing, in inadequate child welfare services, for our failure to deal more aggressively and imaginatively with juvenile delinquency, with the vocationally handicapped, with the admittedly unequal health services in rural areas, and with the lower-income family units in all our communities? The grant-in-aid principle has been effectively utilized in our social security income-maintenance programs. We have been too cautious in employing it more aggressively in our social services.

Vocational rehabilitation may be a good illustration. This is one of our "older" social service programs, established in 1920, largely as a result of our experience growing out of World War I. The grant-in-aid principle was employed to induce states to embark upon a program designed to restore the productive ability of handicapped men and women. The evidence was clear. Mary Switzer, the Director of the Office of Vocational Rehabilitation in the Department of Health, Education, and Welfare, reported that there was a close relationship between neglected disability and public dependency.[15] "Nearly one half billion dollars is spent each year through Federal and state public assistance programs because of neglected physical disability."[16]

In this light, failure to provide necessary funds for retraining the physically handicapped is far more costly in the long run. By such failure we are now creating the public dependency case load for the decades ahead. And the evidence that this is being done is quite overwhelming. For example, each year, according to reports of the Department of Health, Education, and Welfare 250,000 persons disabled by disease, accident, or congenital conditions come to need vocational rehabilitation in order to work. Yet only about 60,000 disabled persons are established in productive work each year under the state-Federal program. We have accumulated a backlog of 2,000,000 disabled who need rehabilitative services to live full and productive lives. Not all of these can be rehabilitated. Some are over 65 years of age, about 5 per cent; in some cases the disability is due to congenital conditions, about 2 per cent; some reside in institutions, about 10 per cent. A very large majority of these men and women, however, could be rehabilitated and enabled to become self-supporting.

This problem of avoiding what Dr. Rusk calls "vocational sterility" requires vigorous national leadership, a large increase in trained personnel, and in time a vast increase in appropriations. The dividends appear to be tremendous. From a purely economic point of view the evidence is quite convincing. For example, of the 64,000 disabled persons who were rehabilitated in 1953, 76 per cent were out of a job when they began to receive vocational rehabilitation services. They were all employed when the rehabilitation process was completed. The total earnings of the group was increased to $115,000,000 per year compared to $17,000,000 before the rehabilitation services were undertaken.[17] A fourfold increase in the number of handicapped persons to be restored to productive employment would in time increase the national product by many times the cost of the service, not to mention the human values associated with a successful adjustment of the individuals affected.

How to finance such an undertaking appears to me less important than that it should be done. If the only way to achieve it is a completely Federally-operated undertaking, that would not be an argument against it. However, the tools at hand have been tested and found effective. The grant-in-aid system, perhaps modified to encourage a substantial increase in trained personnel, along with larger state appropriations, can in a short time stimulate an expansion of the program to reach the goal which everyone agrees is socially and economically desirable.

The problem of financing medical care presents greater difficulties. That great progress in the growth of voluntary health insurance has been made during the past decade is generally known. The most recent study by the Health Information Foundation[18] reveals that in July 1953 over 87 million people, or 57 per cent of the population have some hospital insurance and that 74 million, or 48 per cent have some surgical or other medical insurance. What is more significant is the finding that only 4,900,000, or 3 per cent of the population have "substantially complete physicians' services."[19] Equally significant is the fact that a far smaller proportion of the lower-income families have some type of health insurance than of the families whose income is over $5,000 per year. Only 30 per cent of the families in the United States earning less than $2,000 per year have some type of health insurance, while 80 per cent of the families earning $5,000 and over have some coverage.

Perhaps the most significant item in Dr. Anderson's objective study is that "of all (medical) charges incurred by families 15 per cent are covered by insurance benefits."[20] The proportion of the family medical bill which is covered by insurance varies with the type of service, as would be expected. Thus 50 per cent of hospital services are so covered while only 38 per cent of surgery and a mere 13 per cent of all physicians' services are covered by insurance policies. Equally significant is that about 7.5 million, about 15 per cent, of all the family units are in debt for medical care to the amount of about $900 million.

Several significant observations can be derived from this statistical information concerning the medical bills of the American people. First, that 43 per cent of the population do not possess even the limited hospital insurance coverage available through the Blue Cross service or private insurance policies. This is in part due to the difficulties of coverage for self-employed and people employed in very small groups. Such insurance is not unavailable to such persons, but the acquisition costs are greater. Even if such persons could be grouped for such purposes, many would find even the small financial costs a bar to coverage.

The second fact which emerges is that only an exceedingly small proportion of the population, less than 5 million families, 3 per cent of the total, have complete medical service covered by insurance. The obstacles to a substantial increase in that number are not always financial. Even for those who may be able to afford such coverage, complete service is not available due to local medical facilities and practices.

One may note further that cash indemnity for hospital and surgical costs deals with one segment, an important one to be sure, of the medical care problem. General medical services are not included. One critic observed that in the quest for an insurable risk in the health field, according to life and fire insurance principles, "preference has been given to illnesses which require hospitalization or surgical care. Thus surgical care has been overemphasized and a host of minor surgical procedures covered, while the most important prehospital, posthospital, and nonsurgical complaints remain ignored or neglected. Cash payments are made to take care of the ingrown toenail as a surgical procedure, while heart disease and cancer are often excluded until the patient is brought to a hospital."[21]

There can be no question but that the trend is toward expansion of the insurance principle to cover *all* medical needs. Only a few years ago the application of the insurance method to medical care was strongly resisted by the medical organizations throughout the nation. That opposition has largely disappeared. A phenomenal growth of voluntary insurance has occurred. What is required now is the expansion of the health insurance method in the direction of full coverage of the population and for all medical needs. Our system will evolve in that direction, but "it must evolve visibly—at something more than a snail's pace."[22]

It is not likely to move fast enough. For one reason, the easy coverage through large industrial groups has already been accomplished. From here on the coverage of individuals or of groups in very small establishments is not likely to be as efficient and will be more costly. Secondly, numerical coverage is not enough. The next forward move must be in the direction of general physicians' services and eventually comprehensive care. That is likely to come very slowly. Snail-pace evolution in this direction will, in my opinion, increase public pressure for government intervention in financing general medical care.

COUNTING COSTS

How much can we afford to spend for social welfare payments and services? In the public mind the issue of costs is of critical importance. It arises in part from the fact that the sums involved are already high by any previous standard of comparison. Further, these high outlays have been increasing during good times when jobs were relatively plentiful. To the average citizen, this trend is not quite comprehensible. Why are these expenditures so stubborn? Why are they increasing at the very time when we might expect costs to decline? To what extent is this likely to be due to wasteful practices, to poor administration, to easy Federal grants? Are these costs putting an undue strain upon our economy, increasing our taxes and injuring incentives and economic progress? Are these programs creating dependency? Since these costs are bound to increase, public understanding of their nature and of their relative importance in our society has become more necessary than ever.

Several elementary aspects of social welfare costs should be emphasized at the outset. A rather substantial proportion of what we spend for welfare—social security, public assistance, social services—are not items about which we have much choice. These expenditures cannot readily be evaded. We must provide for the aged who are in need, for the jobless whose incomes have ceased, for the ill and the disabled, for the veterans and their families. These obligations have had a high priority in our scheme of values throughout our history. Whether we can afford such expenditures is hardly a pertinent question. We will make them in any event.

Nor are these outlays, now made primarily by local, state, and Federal public agencies, new expenditures, created by the liberal social welfare legislation of recent years. People have been cared for in some way by private charitable organizations and by relatives and friends. To a considerable extent, therefore, these large public outlays may be said to represent a method of social cost accounting and not a new and added drain upon our national income and resources.[23]

While this is true, it is necessary to recognize, however, that the assumption of public responsibility quite inevitably results in considerably more spending than prevailed for these needs before. Public administration tends to focus attention on the unmet needs, reveals the full size of the problem, and improves standards—all resulting in larger expenditures.

In so far as public social welfare costs represent transfer payments they should not be classed as new direct costs but rather as transfer of purchasing power from one group to another. This is true for most of our social insurance programs; for example, the benefits paid to our unemployed and the retirement annuities to our aged. While these payments do not represent additional demand upon our production and resources, they may, under certain circumstances, adversely affect our productivity and national income. This would

occur if such benefits were to dampen the spirit of enterprise, adversely affecting incentives to work or save. High taxes may, under certain conditions,
discourage risk taking by business and industry and thus reduce our national
product. While much has been written on this topic, there is no conclusive
evidence that our social security legislation has produced such a result, either
on worker incentives or on business growth.[24]

In national terms, our social welfare costs, while increasing at a rather
rapid rate during the past fifteen years, are huge only in terms of the absolute
sum involved at current prices. When proper allowance is made for the decreasing value of the welfare or social-security dollar and account is taken also
of the relationship between these expenditures and the growth of our national
product, the result is much less startling than one would expect. For example,
Ida Merriam's excellent study shows that in the 1950–1951 fiscal year, the
total cost of social welfare, including expenditures for education and for veterans, exceeded 23.3 billion dollars. This is a huge sum, especially when compared with only 7.7 billion dollars in the fiscal year 1936–1937. However,
when adjusted for price changes, the increase was to 12.5 billion dollars or 64
per cent higher.[25] Inflation thus creates a false picture concerning the rapid rise
in social welfare costs.

An equally sobering result follows when these outlays are related to the
gross national product. In 1936–1937 the 7.7 billion dollars paid out for welfare costs represented 9 per cent of the gross national product for that year.
This proportion began to decline with the onset of the war in 1941 and fell to
but 3.6 per cent in 1944–1945. In 1951–1952 these expenditures were 7.6
per cent of our gross national product, actually a smaller relative outlay than
in 1936.[26]

Furthermore, exploring the specific programs which make up these expenditures reveals that the most significant increases occurred in the amounts spent
for veterans' programs. As a per cent of the national product, the outlays for
veterans increased threefold, while those for social insurance were only by
one-half. Public assistance actually declined, while expenditures for education,
as a per cent of the national product, did not change materially. Expenditures
for social services, at the Federal and state levels, for vocational rehabilitation and counseling, public health and child welfare, for example, increased
sharply in this period. The total sums involved, however, represented but a
small fraction of the public welfare dollar. The mass programs are costly.

This brief statistical reference suggests that public welfare and social services have had a far less important responsibility for our government's fiscal
embarrassment than many people imagine. The most common explanation for
the growth of public spending places the responsibility on war and preparation for war and on public welfare and social security. To couple these two
items as if they were of relatively equal force is obviously unjustified. Social
welfare accounted for but 20.8 per cent of Federal government expenses for
all purposes in 1950–1951. This appears to be a relatively stable figure, in fact

declining each year since 1946–1947.[27] When veterans' programs are excluded from these calculations, social welfare costs represent less than 10 per cent of the Federal government expenses in that year. Considering local and state governments, welfare costs represent a far larger proportion of their total outlays, exceeding 54 per cent of state and local government expenditures for all purposes each year but one since 1936–1937.

What about the future? Is the trend which began in 1930 and continued without interruption, except for the war years, likely to continue? Can we bear it? There is no doubt that the upward trend in welfare outlays will continue at least for another decade or two. Important unmet needs remain in almost every major area of social welfare. In spite of serious controversy concerning how best to deal with medical care, there can be no question of a considerable expansion in public outlays in this field.[28] The same is true in the field of education, where present gaps and future needs are being increasingly recognized. In the field of social insurance, responsible opinion suggests that wider coverage, more adequate benefits, and the addition of protection for temporary and permanent disability are likely to be provided sooner than many expect. And more adequate public assistance provision is required for an appropriate residual program.

Whether these funds will be provided will depend first upon how high a value the American people are prepared to place upon these programs and services. They have had wide public support during the past quarter-century, and this support does not seem to have abated in recent years. However, whether social welfare can continue to hold a high priority depends in part upon competing claims for the public dollar and upon the continued growth of our national income. Defense and national security and international commitments have been and will for many years continue to provide the first claim upon our public funds. Social welfare must win and hold wide public understanding and support if it is to continue to receive an increasing share of public funds.

There is reason for optimism that this will take place. There is no substantial evidence which suggests that the growth in productivity that has characterized our economy during the past 50 years is likely to be reversed. On the contrary, there have been bold predictions of even greater economic progress as a result of the huge investments in industrial research and atomic energy.[29] Under such conditions of economic growth, even assuming that no larger proportion of the nation's income will be available for social service purposes, it should be possible to meet the increasing costs with no danger to our institutions and our economy.[30]

Arnold Toynbee observed that this is the "first age since the dawn of civilization in which people dared to think it practicable to make the benefits of civilization available to the whole human race." This may be the most significant revolution of all time.

In many respects, it is most unfortunate that in public discussion of social welfare there is so much preoccupation with costs. Our failure to take the long view, to recognize the role of social welfare in our society, is likely to produce serious consequences. Some of these can already be identified. There is, for example, the all too ready tendency to focus public attention on individual abuses. Public confidence in the integrity of the program or the administrators is easily shaken when generalizations applicable to the whole group are built upon individual instances of malingering. The proposal to retire the Federal government from public assistance grows out of a refusal to see the total problem and to think only of costs as between levels of government. In the same category are the suggestions that some form of means test or income test should replace the present right to benefits and that the reserve should in time be replaced by a pay-as-you-go method of financing.

Social security is a relatively new idea in the American scheme of values. Its rapid adoption and wide acceptance are in part due to a realization that our free society is more certain to remain free and democratic when all of its citizens, including those who cannot participate in the process of producing wealth and providing services, can participate in the gains of economic progress. Our society can afford it.

An Evolving Pattern

This review of some of the problems in financing social services suggests several concluding observations. The first is that there is no necessarily right or wrong way of financing these activities. The character of the financial arrangements represents an evolutionary development. It is influenced by changes in social and economic institutions, by political forms and problems and economic conditions. Thus in the United States the present magnitude of the grant-in-aid method, as was noted earlier, is largely an outgrowth of the depression of the 1930s. The Federal-state controversy both in financing and administration is a reflection of larger issues in intergovernment relations, so much in the public mind during the past twenty years. Similarly, the absence of some compulsory scheme for prepayment for health services is primarily due to unique institutional and cultural factors characteristic of our society. We must view these programs and how they are financed in the light of the complex institutional pattern of which they are a part. Thus we can explain why certain programs like workmen's compensation or unemployment insurance are financed by the employer. We can understand also why the old-age and survivors' plan is nationally administered, why the role of the private charitable society has changed since the depression, why temporary disability protection is following a pattern radically different from the pattern in other countries or in unemployment compensation in this country.

Second, it follows from the above that our program is evolving. There cannot be a static social security and social service pattern in this country. Our economy is too dynamic. Nor are plans that are found attractive and effective elsewhere necessarily applicable to our requirements. This leads to the conclusion that it is perhaps too early to create an American Beveridge Report. The absence of a "system" is not an indictment. The central test should always be whether the plan meets the needs of the people, not whether it is free of internal contradictions and inconsistencies. I am less concerned about a full-grown and simple social security structure with a unified financial base. That may come in time, the present may be too early.

Third, the problem of financing social security and social services often represents broader economic and institutional issues. Basically, financing methods are designed to bring about a proper distribution of costs over groups of people,[31] or over time, or between levels of government. The search for equity in the relationship between unemployment benefits and wages, for example, has less place in a social insurance scheme than in private insurance. There is no "right" answer to the problem of distribution of costs between levels of government. Transferring the financing of a particular program to another level of government should be countenanced only if that would be a more adequate way to deal with that problem. It is not "wrong" for the Federal government, for example, to finance old-age assistance.

Fourth, the question of how much we can afford should be restated in terms which would emphasize that we cannot afford *not* to spend the social-welfare dollar. The costs of neglect in the field of social services may have to be met in the second or third generation. Failing to deal with the problems which are the by-products of our modern urban high-tempo industrial society may weaken the very foundations of our family and institutional life.

Fifth, our preoccupation with income security, a most natural development of depression unemployment and economic insecurity, has unduly subordinated the service programs at all levels of government. There is urgent need for greater public understanding of the place of social services in our community. In terms of financial outlays the amounts involved, in contrast with income security payments, are exceedingly small. A liberal expansion of outlays for social services across the board, including health services, is essential if our human resources are to be strengthened, economic adjustment facilitated, and personal and family happiness assisted.

FOOTNOTES

1. Frederick Lewis Allen, "Economic Security: A Look Back and a Look Ahead," *Economic Security for Americans,* The American Assembly, Columbia University, 1953, p. 12.

2. *Social Security Bulletin,* Jan. 1951, pp. 22 and 27.

3. Ida C. Merriam, "Social Welfare Programs in the United States," *Social Security Bulletin,* February 1953, pp. 3–12 and October 1953, pp. 14–15.

4. By Lewis Meriam, Karl T. Schlotterbech and Mildred Maroney.

5. *Improving Social Security,* an Analysis of the present Federal Security Program for the Aged and the proposal of the Chamber of Commerce of the U. S., Washington, 1953.

6. "Analysis of the Social Security System," *Hearings* before a subcommittee of the Committee on Ways and Means, House of Representatives, 83rd Congress, First Session.

7. See, for example, testimony of Arthur J. Altmeyer and Edwin E. Witte in *Hearings*, preceding reference.

8. See "The Role of Government in Economic Security," by Eveline Burns, especially pp. 142–149, in *Economic Security for Americans, op. cit.*

9. Merriam, Ida C., *Social Security Financing*, Federal Security Agency, Social Security Administration, Division of Research and Statistics, Bureau Report, No. 17, chapter 4, pp. 84–116, 1953.

10. Same, pp. 98–99.

11. Council of State Governments, *Federal-State Relations*, 1949, p. 135, cited in Merriam, I. C., p. 109.

12. Larson, Arthur, in *Economic Security for Americans, op. cit.*, p. 59.

13. Merriam, Ida C., *Social Security Financing, op. cit.*, p. 110.

14. Rhys-Williams, J. E., *Taxation and Incentives*, Oxford University Press, 1953, p. 68.

15. Testimony of Secretary of Department of Health, Education, and Welfare, before Subcommittee of Senate Appropriations Committee, April 16, 1954, p. 9 (mimeographed).

16. Same, p. 6.

17. Same, Chart G.

18. O. W. Anderson, *National Family Survey of Medical Costs and Voluntary Health Insurance*, Health Information Foundation, New York, 1954.

19. Same, p. 11.

20. Same, p. 25.

21. Pollack, Jerome, "A Labor View of Health Security," paper read to 24th Annual Tri-State Hospital Assembly, 1954, p. 7 (mimeographed).

22. Ford, Benson, from an address before Blue Cross Plan of Wisconsin, cited by Pollack, above, p. 8.

23. Burns, Eveline, "Can Our Economy Afford Social Security?", read at Annual Meeting, Massachusetts Conference on Social Work, 1951.

24. See Joseph M. Becker, *The Problem of Abuse in Unemployment Benefits*, A Study in Limits, Columbia University Press, 1953.

25. Merriam, Ida, *Social Security Bulletin*, Feb. 1953, p. 10.

26. Merriam, Ida, *Social Security Bulletin*, Oct. 1953, p. 4.

27. Merriam, Ida, *Social Security Bulletin*, Feb. 1953, p. 11.

28. *Building America's Health*, A Report to the President, Volume I, Findings and Recommendations, Dec. 1952, 83rd Congress, First Session.

29. Colm, Gerhard, *The American Economy* in 1960, National Planning Association, 1952.

30. Harris, Seymour, "Social Welfare in an Expanding Economy," paper read at National Conference of Social Work, 1953.

31. Larson, Arthur, in *Economic Security for Americans, op. cit.*, p. 59.

The Limits of Social Service

Gordon W. Allport
Professor of Psychology, Harvard University

A century ago both Thoreau and Emerson spoke out sharply regarding the limits of social service—of philanthropy as they then called it. In *Walden,* Thoreau criticizes the tendency of the would-be benefactor to project his own ailments onto others. Because he himself suffers a stomach ache he thinks that the whole world has been eating green apples. Thoreau advises the benefactor to cure himself, to grow cheerful, to abandon his melancholy projections, and thus permit the victims of his "charitable" impulses to do the same.

Emerson points to a different shortcoming. In *Self-Reliance* he writes, "I tell thee, thou foolish philanthropist, that I grudge the dollar, the dime, the cent, I give to such men as do not belong to me and to whom I do not belong." Where no spiritual affinity exists, charity is in vain. Emerson deplores the thousandfold impersonal relief societies devoted to distributing "alms for sots."

When we think back on the unwisdom of nineteenth-century benevolence we applaud these thrusts of criticism. But we recognize the critics' error. Thoreau and Emerson were presuming to condemn all social service because they mistook momentary limitations for ultimate limits. They could not foresee the enlargement of horizons and improvement in practice that would come through the labors of Octavia Hill, Arnold Toynbee, Jane Addams, Richard Cabot, Mary Richmond, and many other thoughtful leaders. Nor could they predict the future influence of psychological science and psychiatry upon social service. They could not foretell the evolution of public policy to be guided by Bismarck in Germany, by the Fabians and the Labor Party in Britain, and by the New Deal in the United States.

We therefore take warning. It would be folly to set dogmatic and premature limits upon the sciences and arts that comprise social service. Unlike Thoreau and Emerson we know that its methods and its philosophy are still evolving. Present faults and shortcomings surely exist, but most of them, we suspect, are removable. As such they constitute *limitations* in social service but not outer *limits*. In the course of our discussion we shall hit upon boundaries beyond which neither public nor private social work may proceed. But for the most part we shall be concerned with limitations that can in principle be overcome.

EVALUATING SOCIAL SERVICE

The brightest feature of the present situation is the spirit of self-objectification, self-scrutiny, and self-criticism that marks contemporary social services. We are less inclined than formerly to mistake our good intentions for good results, or our own professional growth for growth in our clients. We have reached a stage of wholesome skepticism. Today the question is whether social service—public, private, family-centered, community-centered, person-centered, manipulative or interpretative, based on psychoanalytic theory, economic theory, religious theory, or no theory—whether the varied philosophies we hold and the assorted methods we use do in fact achieve the results we aim to achieve.

It is now thirty years since leaders of social service began to call for an evaluation of results. To some extent the impetus came from donors who rightly wondered whether society actually benefits from their financial support of social work. But chiefly, I think, the impetus for evaluation has come from ardent workers who wish to know whether their efforts are truly in the public interest or reflect merely pleasant conceits of their own. Among the early voices raised in behalf of evaluative research were those of Porter R. Lee, Dr. Haven Emerson, Dr. Richard Cabot.[1] Two of the earliest investigations were those of Miss Theis, who followed the later careers of nearly 800 foster children, and of the Gluecks who traced 500 former inmates of the Concord Reformatory.[2] The former study made us hopeful concerning the policies and practices of child-placing agencies, while the latter thrust us into a state of despair regarding the outcome of our efforts to rehabilitate delinquents. No subsequent evaluation of penal practices has in any respect restored our hope. When evaluative results turn out to be negative, we are not entitled to say, "Nothing can be done." Rather we feel goaded to restate our aims, alter our approach, and redouble our efforts. For example, we might decide to study the few cases of successful reformation, and retool our practices accordingly.

Deeply disturbed by this failure with adult delinquents, Dr. Richard Cabot, shortly before his death in 1938, established and subsidized the Cambridge-Somerville Youth Study, perhaps the most elaborate evaluative investigation yet attempted. It was action-research; that is to say, it instituted a program of long-continued treatment of predelinquent children for the express purpose of discovering whether such social service could in fact check later delinquency. Specially established action research of this type has marked advantages over the cursory evaluative investigations that are all we can expect from agencies busy with daily demands. The financial resources are more adequate, research specialists are employed, and the important condition of having a control group can be observed. The three hundred boys in treatment were matched at the outset of the study with an equal number of controls. In this way it was possible to estimate the amount of change that occurred as a result of treatment, rather than as a result of gradual maturing in the average community setting where schools, churches, and assorted social agencies are likewise engaged in the building of character.

The results of this elaborate study, as set forth by Powers and Witmer, are not as conclusive as we might wish.[3] The treatment plans were badly interrupted by the coming of the war; for at the age of 17 many of the boys entered service at the very time when the most effective casework might have been done. Speaking in general terms, the study showed that by police standards approximately the same number of treatment and control boys turned out to be delinquent. Thus, in a sense, even five to seven years of casework, commencing between the ages of six and ten, proved ineffective. This pessimistic generalization, however, masks certain subsidiary findings of potentially great importance. There was some evidence, for example, that treatment boys, though they tangled with the courts as often as control boys, did not continue into careers of serious and aggravated criminality. There was likewise evidence that the boys who benefited most from the program were boys who, like their parents, were genuinely fond of the counselor; who were relatively free from severe neurotic or pathological traits; and who seemed to need most of all guidance and example in making up for minor defects in the home. At the same time the study found that caseworkers were rarely, if ever, able to provide full and sufficient emotional anchorage for a boy whose own parents rejected him. Social service—at least of the type we are here discussing— seems unable to compensate for wretched emotional situations in the home. This example shows that evaluative research can help us determine the limits of an agency's work, and help determine the types of cases that can and cannot be rehabilitated.

It also came to light in the Cambridge-Somerville Youth Study that certain types of caseworkers seemed to have greater success than others. Specifically, the warm or friendly or informal workers, who to some critics seemed actually "unprofessional" in their approach, apparently had more success than the highly trained, diagnostic-minded, and theoretically-oriented workers. While too few cases are involved in this comparison to justify a generalization, the finding is potentially of great significance. If substantiated it will cause us to examine sharply some of our current presuppositions regarding the selection and training of personnel, and regarding our whole philosophy of the "professional approach."

While I have used for illustrative purposes a study in the field of delinquency prevention, I could point to numerous areas that have recently yielded to evaluative penetration. The advances have been impressive. In 1952, David G. French published his book, *Measuring Results in Social Work*, a survey that places the whole subject in excellent perspective. One of its merits lies in setting forth a detailed proposal for an Institute for Research in Social Work that would supply agencies and programs with expert assistance in conducting evaluative investigations. Meanwhile an avalanche of special and limited evaluative studies have been tumbling from the press.[4]

The trend toward social evaluation reaches far beyond casework. It embraces psychotherapy, health education, recreational programs; the effects of study in foreign lands, of summer camps, of programs for the reduction of ethnic prejudice; the efficiency of information services, even of general education in our colleges; and many other socially relevant policies and practices. Recently Dr. Henry W. Riecken of the Department of Sociology at the University of Minnesota prepared a comprehensive *Memorandum on Program Evaluation* that sets forth the requirements for scientifically sound procedures in assessments of this order.

In the field of social service anecdotal proof of success has given way. We can no longer say that failure to assess our efforts is in principle a major limitation. The chief obstacles now are scant funds and shortage of technical skills. Evaluation is not a job for amateurs. It requires shrewd planning, inventiveness, technical training, and great caution in interpreting results. But these barriers are not insurmountable. If progress in the next twenty-five years matches progress in the past we shall have this important instrument well under control.

THE GOALS OF SOCIAL WORK

There is one cardinal requirement for successful evaluation that forces us to pause and take stock. Every evaluator agrees that we cannot measure progress unless we know our objectives, and unless these objectives are stated in accessible (that is, operational) terms. And so we are brought face to face with the question of the goals of social service. While the question is familiar to us all, it is none the less true that only a tiny fraction of the mountainous literature on social service is concerned with its *raison d'être,* with its philosophical guidelines and moral objectives. Such formulations as we do encounter are often too general or too vague to help the evaluator.

It may well be that, in certain respects at least, we face an insoluble problem. If we accept as our goal "growth in personality" (and this is a goal upon which most of us would agree), how can we measure progress? How long after a program of treatment shall we attempt to determine growth? And what, pray tell, is our criterion for "growth in personality" or for "improvement in character," or, for that matter, for "self-reliance," "wholesomeness," "good citizenship," "happiness," or even "normality of adjustment"?

Occasionally our stated objectives are less elusive. When we say, for example, that our goal is economic rehabilitation of a client, we can set a reasonable criterion, such as holding a job steadily for a year. We can then determine what proportion of our clients reach this criterion of success. Even more general objectives, which may appear at first like clouds of vapor to a social scientist, can be, and have been, reduced to accessible operations. There comes to mind the criterion of "movement" deemed desirable in certain casework philosophies. Hunt and Kogan have captured this will-o'-the-wisp and with considerable success impounded it for reliable measurements.[5] But it remains true that our deepest concerns and highest ideals are not likely to lend themselves to exact measurement. And so we are faced here with the necessity for compromise. Measurement we surely want, but not if it tempts us to state our aims and objectives in brittle or trivial terms. Where meaningful and concrete operations are statable, let us use them in our evaluative procedures; but let us not assume that our total philosophy is reducible to criteria of this order.

Social service now proceeds under a wide variety of philosophies. While we hear a good deal about the need for a single integrative professional philosophy, the fact remains that such articulate axiology as exists—and there is not a great deal of it—is far from receiving unanimous endorsement. Scientific humanism, as represented by Bisno, asks social service to adhere to a philosophy of science that is empirical in outlook, pragmatic in method, relativistic respecting values, and negative toward all absolutes.[6] Some form of the philosophy of self-realization is more widely endorsed. For Richard Cabot, Mary Richmond, and many like-minded workers, the supreme test of social service is growth in personality.[7] Does the personality of clients change, and change in the right direction? Right direction is determined always by reference to the unique potentialities of the individual in relation to the rights and privileges of others. The emphasis of Roman Catholic social service is somewhat different. It advocates bringing man under the sway of reason, in order that this distinctive human faculty may assist man, who is made in the image of God, to "find his way back to God."[8]

Is such disagreement on basic philosophy a serious limitation? The matter can be argued both ways. On the one hand, it could be said that social service, lacking a single ethical direction, slips easily into adulation of techniques. It does so because science and technology are the idols of our society, and, lacking an explicit conscience of its own, social service unconsciously adopts the idolatry of the day. Four hundred years ago Rabelais warned us that science without conscience spells only the ruin of the soul. We have minimized the warning of Rabelais and have lived rather by the faith of Karl Pearson, who in his *Grammar of Science* prophesied that the gradual spread of scientific objectivity to the common mind will cure us of all passionate prejudices and improve our human relationships. Yet up to now science has brought only slight visible improvement in this regard. It, like social service, seems to require a doctrine of man, and a firm ethics by which to test its practices.

On the other hand, it may be argued that agreement on matters of such ultimate importance is impossible to achieve and not really desirable. Final truth we cannot know; human wisdom evolves best through diversity. A rough proximate agreement is all we need, and this we have already achieved. We know that social service aims to insure the survival and smooth functioning of the group; also that in a democracy it aims to contribute to the fullness of individual life by helping remove limitations that impede self-reliance. Sophisticated philosophers may try, if they will, to order these proximate goals under a framework of ultimates, but the harder they press their logic of values the greater will be the resulting disagreement. Their final formulations will be as diverse as positivism and Thomism, humanism and existentialism, quietism and socialism. Why worry about the matter when a rough working basis already is at hand?

What shall we say about this dispute? My own inclination is to concede that agreement on ultimates is neither possible, nor at this time desirable. Yet if we are content with only a crude working basis we may easily be trapped by the ideology of engineering, and find ourselves preoccupied with techniques and gadgets, thus embracing, without fully knowing it, a directionless and conscienceless scientism. The safeguard is to foster continuous consideration of the aims of social service and the frames of axiology into which it may fit. Students should receive nutritive doses of ethics in schools of social work and should be encouraged to debate the matter, in order to develop their own views. No one is bound to accept the final philosophy of another, but a philosophy of some kind he must have. It is a serious shortcoming of social service that it pays too little attention in its curricula of training, and in later professional years, to its goals, objectives, policies, and ethical premises, and to philosophies of life under which the daily activities of social workers may be ordered.

PUBLIC AND PRIVATE SERVICE

We all know that modern social work developed from the attempt to offset the pauperizing effects of almsgiving and indiscriminate charity. We know too that it soon became apparent that private efforts as represented in the Charity Organization movement were hopelessly inadequate to repair the ravages caused by the industrial revolution and by the long period of *laissez-faire* that accompanied it. Action by the state became imperative, and gradually throughout the western world the ideals of social insurance, social security, state and Federal assistance to the sick, the aged, and the unemployed, and to children, became accepted practices.

Now in a democracy, having a free economy and reasonable opportunities for upward mobility, as well as respect for the dignity of the individual, the ideals and aims of social service are essentially the same whether the service is governmental or private. While there is a division of functions, both forms of service wish to reduce unnecessary suffering, to preserve a basic social order, and to maximize the opportunities of individuals to develop their potentialities.

The division of function that has occurred follows essentially the arrangement predicted and approved by Sidney Webb forty years ago.[9] This author employs the metaphor of the extension ladder. Public welfare services are charged with filling the gaps that exist in the basic economic and institutional structure of society. They provide means by which individuals obtain physical care, decent housing, protection against disability and poverty in old age, even though they cannot pay for such services in a competitive market. Thus public agencies provide a standardized form of assistance to all who meet certain specifications.

It is commonly agreed that the function of private social service, on the other hand, is to assist individuals to make the most of the resources of society, including the benefits that the government provides. Relieved of many of the burdens of economic relief, private social service has turned more and more to the understanding and treatment of personality. The ideal of casework above the poverty line emerged in the First World War, when the Home Service rendered by the Red Cross to the families of men on military duty demonstrated that human needs are by no means always economic. As early as 1909 Richard Cabot had written that he could see no reason why social work should be done only with the poor.[10]

This ideal of professional service above the poverty line has spread so widely that today we find a large percentage of the services privately rendered paid for by the client. This trend seems to hold not only for casework and guidance services but likewise for recreational and group work. A decreasing proportion of the funds raised by Community Chests goes into direct relief and a larger proportion into administration, organization, and even research. The trend is made possible by the creation of what has come to be called the welfare state, where unemployment, industrial accidents, health services, child care, social security, are now recognized matters for public rather than private responsibility.

Originally Sidney Webb held that voluntary agencies are superior to public authorities in three main features: in invention and experimentation with new services and new methods; in their ability to give special and individualized care to particular cases; and in their freedom to bring religious or other moral influences to bear on clients. On the whole it has been felt that voluntary agencies maintain high standards that act as a model and monitor for public service. Today these distinctions are less sharp than formerly. Excellent casework is now done by civil service appointees. Public officials may be as imaginative and experimental as private workers. Nearly all of our personnel in public service is trained in private schools of social work where the ideals and methods of voluntary agencies prevail.

Whatever their functions may be, we note that the spread of public agencies has been continually and vigorously fought by economic and political conservatives. They profess to see in it the undermining of initiative, as well as threatening dislocations caused by excessive taxation, bureaucracy, and loss of freedom. A century ago conservatives objected to the elimination of the workhouse test for relief, and held firmly to the principle of less eligibility. Unless a pauper is stigmatized, they argued, we shall all lose our sense of shame and gladly become paupers. No battle was ever lost more decisively. Conservatives have been losing ground for decades—to such an extent in fact, that we are now obliged to ask whether there is not some validity in their position. We need not include here conservatives whose transparent motivation is the preservation of their own privilege and status.

The plain fact is that the scope of social service has expanded, and is still expanding, at a spectacular rate. Private social services in the United States currently receive and spend approximately one and a half billion dollars a year. In one cluster of 117 cities gifts to Community Chests have more than doubled since 1941.[11] Government expenditures have mounted at a still more rapid rate. Two and a half billion dollars is the annual outlay of states. The Federal government spends currently approximately 9 billion on all social services including programs for health, welfare, veterans benefits, and social security. In all the total annual expenditure is around 13 billion dollars, and ever rising.[12]

The reason for this mounting outlay is not increased destitution, but rather a change of the public's attitude toward social responsibility. Problems that received no attention a few decades, or even a few years, ago, now are accepted as legitimate and pressing obligations of society. The conservative's alarm merits fresh attention. Are we growing reckless and extravagant in our outlay? Do individuals cease to exert themselves and weakly prefer public bounty? Are we all passengers on the gravy train?

The danger does not lie in the expansion of social services, nor even in the increasing fraction of the national income invested in them. The philosophy of both public and private service, and of their interrelationships, is essentially sound. The danger is a more subtle one. We might phrase it in terms of the growing insistence upon rights and a diminishing emphasis upon duties.

For example, take the social worker's own mental attitude. His profession sensitizes him to the injustices he encounters. He is led to demand basic rights for dependent children, for victims of desertion, for the aged, for minority ethnic groups. It is proper that he should do so. But there is the reciprocal question whether in fighting for rights, social workers and American citizens generally are aware of such duties as they in turn owe to their community and their state. We greedily scramble for our share of public benefits, but pay our taxes reluctantly, and sometimes not at all. Almost half of us do not vote. Very few participate in civic affairs. Do social workers in dealing with clients try to inculcate in them an awareness of such duties as they owe, and can discharge, to their community and to their state? Or do they intensify the sense of rights that is already so prominent in the American's mind? In the Japanese culture, we are told, heavy emphasis is placed upon the sense of obligation, far less on rights. In our culture the burden of emphasis is precisely reversed.

To give another example, young people training for the profession of social service prefer, in the great majority of instances, to work for private agencies and shun opportunites for public service. This is true in spite of the large number of scholarships and other inducements offered by such public agencies as the Veterans Administration, National Mental Health Foundation, State Welfare Departments, and others.[13] The reason for this disaffection is, of course, fairly apparent. It is felt to be somehow less pleasant to be bound by public bureaucracy than by private bureaucracy. It is disagreeable to be exposed to political control and the hazards of McCarthy-like persecutions. Yet how are we to build and maintain our public services if we as citizens shun them? Approximately half of the openings in social service today occur in public agencies; but jobs in private agencies are greatly preferred. The basic philosophies of the two types do not greatly differ. What we need is a more cordial and equal relationship between them, and in particular a higher sense of obligation to public service, an area that will continue to grow by leaps and bounds.

While we deplore overemphasis upon private and proprietary conceptions of social service, let us bemoan also our national provincialism. When we view the world situation as a whole, we are forced to conclude that some of our refined distinctions and preoccupations look like fancy embroidery.

We quarrel, for example, over the hairline boundary between casework and psychotherapy, while most of the world has never heard of either. In most countries of the earth the poor survive only with the help of the poor. The professions of social work and psychiatry are totally unknown. Voluntary service is nonexistent. Most countries have no public assistance, no social security, no community resources to which the needy can be referred. Sickness, poverty, and desolate old age are so familiar that the people, submerged in despair, ignorance, and apathy, have lost feeling for them. In these countries social service for the present can mean only the launching of some vast social change that will lift the masses to the point where individual problems can be perceived and differential treatment become possible.

It is a limitation of American social service that, lacking world perspective, it cosily believes that the United States lives safely on an island, unaffected by the misery of other nations. Their revolt into communism and into other desperate experiments can easily cause a world conflagration that will wipe out the painful gains of social service in the United States. The question is whether those of us who are engaged in social service are living to some extent in a fool's paradise. It would seem to be high time for us to concern ourselves more actively with the new international ethics of mutual aid.[14]

PROFESSIONALISM

A dilemma of a different order confronts us when we consider the motivation that sustains social service. Unless there are elements of love, compassion, and a desire to share one's own life-benefits with others, the whole process of social service is likely to turn into a husk. At the same time it is fatal if these altruistic impulses are concentrated into fitful ecstasies and allowed undisciplined expression. Nor is it enough for the social worker to engage in the immediately rewarding contacts of good casework. The needed discipline requires also a long-range focus sustained by a social and personal philosophy tempered by patience, by a sense of political strategy, and by all other virtues of sturdy citizenship. Discipline requires also freedom from self-deception.

In these days of strict self-scrutiny social workers are expected to examine their own motives. They are, for example, supposed to be aware of the dangers of projection—the same pitfall that Thoreau denounced when he accused philanthropists of surrounding others with the remembrance of their own cast-off griefs and despair and mistakenly calling the process "sympathy." Most social workers today agree that their professional equipment requires, first of all, a fundamental security in themselves, and, secondly, an ability to understand that other people have different needs and ways of thought.[15]

But projection is only one form of self-deception. There is also the bias of optimism that often leads the worker to put a too rosy complexion upon his relationship with a client. Technically we speak of a parataxic dyad whenever the worker or the client (or both) seriously misperceives the attitude of the other respecting their relationship. In a study of delinquency prevention, Teuber and Powers discovered that in about a third of the cases the counselor or the boy was ignorant of the true attitude of the other. A counselor, for example, might describe a boy's attitude toward him as trusting and affectionate, while the boy really believes that the counselor is a paid detective, hired to spy on bad boys. Instead of affection and trust the boy feels fear and hostility in the relationship. In parataxis it is usually the worker who takes the rosier view of the state of rapport, and overestimates the therapeutic value of his efforts. In the Teuber-Powers study it turned out that parataxis was greater, and rapport less, in cases where the worker approached his task with rigid ideas concerning what constituted admissible and inadmissible professional practices. The dyadic relationship, in general, was much better among workers who adhered to a friendship theory of social service.[16]

The friendship theory has met strenuous objections. Its opponents argue convincingly that we do not choose clients on the same basis that we choose a friend. There are insuperable barriers of age, of contrasting educational and economic status, and life-long differences in habits of thought. Still worse, clients demand of the caseworker far more patience, objectivity, and self-control than do friends.

Here then is the dilemma. The basic motive for social service can only be charity, compassion, and tolerance—all of which are central ingredients in friendship. At the same time we are rightly warned that these virtues may lead us into sentimentality and unwisdom. Only strict objectivity and a professional view of our roles will save us. And yet professionalism may freeze the heart, lead to parataxis in our relationships, and betray us into harmful excesses of specialism.

Specialism is a peculiar hazard in any profession devoted to helping people in distress—whether medicine, the ministry, or social service. Distress defies job analysis. We know how in medicine the decline of the general practitioner has created problems for many a sick person whose real difficulties elude the succession of specialists he visits. The problem is growing acute in social work. Increasing emphasis on defining agency function can lead to a rat-race of referrals, sometimes demoralizing to the client and hence unethical. Even if referrals themselves do not damage the client, he may find at the end of his trek that for his distress there is no rubric and therefore no agency to help him. An unmarried girl in a certain town could find no help; she was seven months pregnant and the only appropriate agency had a rule that no applicant more than six months pregnant could be accepted. Good casework, the agency said, could not be done at this late stage of pregnancy. But, we ask, is good casework an end in itself? Are we wrong in assuming that social service exists to aid mortals in distress and not to sharpen skills or to gratify the professional self-image of the worker?

Another peril of excessive professionalism is overemphasis upon diagnosis. Ever since the ideal of social diagnosis was set before us in Mary Richmond's epoch-making book forty years ago, it has seemed self-evident that without knowing the nature of the problem and its roots it is folly to launch into a program of treatment. While no one wishes to retard the development of diagnostic methods, we do well to keep in mind their limits.

In the first place, a worker—whether in a public or a private agency—may be so preoccupied with diagnosis that by placing his client under a lens, he sets up a relationship dangerous to his ultimate chances of helping him. Even in medicine successful therapy may be blocked by excessive shunting of the patient from laboratory to laboratory. And the therapeutic relationship in social work is even more delicate and easily torn. A client who discovers that he is regarded as a specimen, as an exercise in diagnosis and manipulation, draws back from the friendly relation which, in most cases, is the essential condition of helping him.

In the second place, it is simply not true that successful treatment invariably presupposes accurate diagnosis. Many a client, like many a medical patient, has with friendly support and encouragement mastered his trouble without ever enjoying the luxury of a diagnosis.

Finally, diagnoses are likely to be little more than coarse classifications. Certainly the present rubrics of psychiatry and of psychology are not final. It is not particularly helpful to decide that a certain client had unfortunate conditioning, or feels rejected, or harbors resentment against authority figures. All these diagnoses may be true, but one cannot pluck out the root causes one by one. Better to view the person himself, in all his maladaptive complexity, and the immediate environment he faces, as the cause of his trouble. Best to work with him where he stands.

Let me repeat, I am not arguing against diagnosis; but am pointing to the fact that excessive emphasis upon diagnosis, as one aspect of excessive professionalism, may constitute a serious limit to the effectiveness of social service.

Another dogma of social service may prove a handicap if it is carried to extreme: the view that would limit efforts to those individuals and families that express a conscious need for help. Granted that the chances for effective work are greater with those who present a "growing edge" to the social worker, is such initiative a final measure of ability to profit from an agency's service? We have heard of the agency that rejected a dependency case because the five-year-old child in question had expressed no "felt need." Such extremes engender countermovements. We hear nowadays about "aggressive casework," first practiced on a large scale by the Cambridge-Somerville Youth Study, and about "reaching the unreached." Without presuming here to judge the merits of these new movements, I venture merely to point out the need for sensible balance in settling this matter of policy in social service.

My remarks on certain aspects of professionalism in social service may seem excessively critical. If so, I can only plead that my assignment calls for a certain acidulousness. If my criticism is in part justified, it points to a wholly understandable weakness. Social service is a young profession. In setting its standards and defining its policies it is very likely to overshoot the mark, to exalt its insight into the realm of dogma, and then, perhaps, to oscillate between extreme positions. In time we can expect a better equilibrium to be achieved, but only if we recognize dogmas and excesses for what they are.

THE FOUNDATIONS OF SOCIAL SERVICE IN THE SCIENCE OF PSYCHOLOGY

Social service is what August Comte called concrete science. That is to say, it borrows and applies theories and principles derived from the more basic abstract sciences. It is the laws and formulations of biology, sociology, and psychology that supply the foundations for the practices of social service, as they do for education, therapy, and all other skills in human relations.

I suggest that a weakness of social service lies in its faddist tendency to borrow too heavily from some theory currently fashionable in the underlying abstract sciences. Early in the present century we know there was an almost total blindness to psychological laws of motivation and learning, as well as dense disregard for psychiatric principles. It was thought that the restoration of capacity for normal living could be secured merely by obedience to one sociological law—that the *family* is the primary unit of human association, survival, and adjustment. Somewhat later the biology of tonsils became an obsession. Social workers stood their charges in line outside tonsillectoria, hoping for biological magic to restore a capacity for normal living. But these fevers were as nothing compared with the awesome regard for the human psyche that settled upon us during the 1920s.

At first William Healy, Ernest Southard, Richard Cabot, Adolf Meyer, and Mary Jarrett pushed us gently toward the psychiatric point of view. Then suddenly depth psychology descended upon us! Our watchwords became "transference" and "countertransference," "attitude therapy" and "rebirth," "clarification" and "insight development." We were supposed to "support neurotic equilibrium" and to recreate in our client "a sense of the security and emotional dependency of the childhood period." My quotations are all from the recent literature of casework.

It would be most unbecoming for a psychologist to criticize social work for giving enthusiastic if belated recognition to the basic importance of the human psyche. However, it should be pointed out that for the most part the enthusiasm has been directed toward *psychiatry* (the art of treating sick people), rather than toward *psychology* (the science of the normal mind). Psychology is a less vivid, more mundane, and more time-consuming subject for study. Like psychiatry and psychoanalysis, it is fallible. Yet it offers principles of learning, of motivation, of social interaction, of leadership, of group dynamics, of thought processes, of personality growth, of assessment and diagnosis— these ought not be overlooked in favor of easier and more dramatic formulations, even though these too have great merit.

Now if social service follows the best thinking available in psychology and psychiatry it will be subject to the limitations of this best thinking. Psychology, psychoanalysis, and psychiatry are at the present time in a stage of rapid development. It would be unreasonable to expect social service to advance more rapidly than they. But because the change is so rapid, it becomes necessary to recommend caution and balance in adopting dicta that may be more fashionable than true.

Let us take one proposition by way of illustration. Freud, seconded by Rank, Bowlby, and Melanie Klein—all of whom have had a marked influence upon social work—tells us that the essential foundations of character are established by the age of three. This proposition is startling. It may be true. But as yet it is unproved. A great many social workers accept it as if it were gospel.

Such a fatalistic and dispiriting view leaves only a few relatively mean functions for the social worker to perform. He may, to be sure, enter the family constellation and help steer its prevailing neurosis. In a self-sacrificing mood he might offer himself as a scapegoat and try to channel the mother's aggression from her long-suffering husband and children. At best a "limited therapy" might be undertaken with a client, provided there were vestiges of warmth and security in early childhood upon which to build. But for infants wholly deprived and, therefore irretrievably warped, nothing can be done in later life excepting to distract them from their errant ways with such ingenuity as the worker can muster.

Within this framework of thinking there is little merit in friendliness or in spiritual support unless there is also a suitable early soil on which to build, and unless the personality of the client can be suitably matched to the personality of the worker. By the time depth diagnosis is accomplished, and the matching of the neurosis of the client with that of the worker is completed, all human impulses to sympathy and understanding may have evaporated.

It would be wrong to deny that recent researches have indeed indicated the importance of early years in the formation of character. My point is merely that these researches are as yet of limited scope, and do not justify a sudden and complete revising of the whole philosophy of social service. While Freudian and Rankian theories undoubtedly contain valuable truths, they contain no more truth than certain opposing theories that maintain that personality is subject to constructive influences all through life, and possesses inherent resources for growth and change at every period, and that no character is conclusively set at the age of three, or thirteen, or thirty.

If we knew the full truth about the foundations of human nature we should have to include within our view the limitations that heredity sets upon our efforts. At present psychology, psychoanalysis, and social work all proceed with an environmentalistic bias (though for psychoanalysis the environment is of little consequence after the infant years). The social worker secretly knows that nature sets iron-clad limits to its labors through constitutional defects, perverse temperament, and mental inadequacy. But until we understand human genetics better than we do, we cannot say how serious these limits may be. Meanwhile it seems sensible to continue to attack human problems with an environmental bias, while waiting to have our bias corrected if and when it becomes necessary to do so.

Those who engage in social service, as well as those who are charged with the curricula in our schools of social work, would reply that no school of psychological thought today is followed blindly, but that the insights gained are synthesized and adapted to the realities of casework. Certainly the admirable effort spent on devising "an integrated program of professional education for social work "reflects a commendable breadth of view.[17] My fear is not directed primarily toward the unbalanced curricula of instruction—though certainly more varied psychology, more philosophy, ethics, and concern with public policy are needed. I am worried rather lest a given social worker, confronted by the tangled skein of a human life, will oversimplify what he learns, and gravitate toward a pet psychological formula in order to "understand" the problem presented. It takes detachment, maturity, and wide study of psychology, not to compress a given life into an easy, and probably erroneous, formula.

In no field of human endeavor is it more essential to balance science and art. On the one hand, a client is a representative of the human species to whom universal laws of health and disease, instincts and impulses, frustration and resentment, ego-defense and prejudice, reason and irreason are likely to apply. General laws of economics, cultural expectation and taboo, family structure, and the role requirements of our society are likewise relevant to understanding the concrete case. At the same time every individual is an idiom unto himself; his course of becoming is unlike any other. His problems and his assets are his alone, so too his suffering and his bid for affection.

Now the busy social worker is likely to let the particular be overwhelmed by the general. It is easier to conjure with the principles of psychoanalysis than to make a separate study of development and growth in each individual. It is easier to recall the general principles of criminology than to understand the particular malefactor. It is simpler to categorize in terms of neuroses and therapeutic roles than to comprehend and treat personal patterns of trouble. How to handle general knowledge and knowledge of the particular in the right proportion poses a harder problem for social service, I suspect, than for any other occupation.

And this problem is directly related to the issue previously mentioned: the need for balance between the professional theory and the friendship theory of social service. Friendship is precisely that human relationship wherein the particular takes precedence over the general. Yet, as we have seen, it would be too simple to say that social service should be exclusively a relation of friendship; for the relationship from the beginning imposes certain restrictions. One member of the dyad is, by definition, older or wiser or stronger or more resourceful. The other is the weaker, the suitor, suffering from adversity. Yet little can be done for the client unless some of the virtues of friendship, along with the perception of the particular and the art of individualizing, are well represented.

To sum up: It is the fate of social service to seek broad and accurate foundations for its policies and practices. It must balance its dependence upon the general with regard for the particular. It must borrow from sociology, psychology, psychiatry. It must do so allowing for the complexities of these sciences and for their unfinished state. Such a dexterous balance is more difficult to achieve than in other professions. Many of our current disputes over the "true function" of social service arise from denying its essential and unavoidable versatility. Who can say whether the social worker is an adjustment adviser, a teacher, a resource person, a big brother, or a psychotherapist? If he places the need of the client first, he will be all of these things at different times and under different circumstances. It is only when we mistakenly place agency function or one-sided theories of science first that we find ourselves quarreling over the precise role or attitude that is, or is not, appropriate to social service.

Before leaving the relationship between social service and social science I should like to point to a present one-sidedness in their communication. Why should social service do all the borrowing? Why should not the bulging files of social agencies be made to yield up their buried knowledge to help build a more comprehensive psychology of motivation, of learning, of personality growth, and of human relations? There are mountains of case records awaiting analysis and inductive handling, but our files are for the most part graveyards of knowledge. They should rather become treasure-troves for the development of new principles of human nature and of social relations.

The Limits Imposed by Social Change and Public Apathy

An atomic war might set all of us who survive to foraging for edible weeds and a cave to dwell in. One spasm of international madness could at a single sweep destroy the intricate fabric of social service and turn its fine philosophy into an absurdity. Even short of an atomic war, we rightly fear what may happen to the values of our unique democratic society as communism spreads more widely in the world. Already we see how its grim pressure is straining our historical conceptions of civil liberties, of individual rights, and of mutual trust and respect. The extension of public service—which we welcome—can conceivably turn into the crude statism of Stalin or, more likely, into the subtler but equally destructive statism of Hitler. Our demagogues are pushing hard. We feel ourselves to be on the defensive before titanic forces of social change.

The ideals and practices of social service are among the finest fruits of the orchard of democracy. Their existence depends upon maintaining the soil, the roots, and the main trunks of our way of life. It is fatal blindness if social service does not realize, and act in accordance with, this fact. Today the social worker who does not labor to preserve the foundations of democracy is like a squirrel nibbling fruits others have planted in an orchard now withering.

Here I am speaking from the structural point of view. Sociologists and historians often tell us that as individuals we are nearly helpless before the sweep of social change. It is the total frame in which we live that conditions our acts. Social service as we know it will survive only so long as it is maintained by political democracy, economic free enterprise, and by our subtly evolved sense of social responsibility based on a delicate blend of protectiveness toward, yet autonomy for, the individual person. The structural argument is harsh. It holds that this intricate framework is subject to historical changes, no matter what you and I may will to do.

The same argument takes another form, drawing not on the inevitabilities of social change but upon the now familiar creed of natural selection. It asks whether social service is viable from the point of view of Mother Nature. Evolutionists from Herbert Spencer to Raymond Pearl have warned us that arrogant interference with nature's law can bring misery, if not actual destruction, to the human race. From their point of view the protection and unnatural preservation of the inept fills the earth with misfits whom nature, left to herself, would promptly despatch. Like medicine and public health, social service conspires to negate nature.

This issue has been tiresomely debated, though it has never been definitely settled. One thing only is clear: we have decided deliberately to disregard the simple logic of natural selection. We have asserted once and for all that nature's coarse standards are not a proper measure of man's worth nor of his right to survive. In place of rugged individualism our society has decided in favor of a socialized individualism. We may be wrong, but we shall have to make the best of it. As we reap the consequences in terms of high birth rates, increasing maladies of old age, and possible overpopulation, we shall have to learn step by step to straighten out the dents and bulges that medicine and social service may have caused in our society.

In this matter we can say that social service has contracted to transcend its own limits. It hopes that by adapting to altered conditions it can continue to work out its ideals. A cataclysm, to be sure, might prove fatal; but short of it we shall endeavor to adjust to, and, when possible, guide and direct, social change. So far as the spectre of natural selection is concerned, we believe that here too the strategies of intelligence will enable us to meet and master whatever dislocations may result from abandoning the jungle theory of survival in favor of higher ethical ideals.

I do not mean to imply that these commitments are conscious and deliberate on our part. Few people think about the philosophy that underlies their support of social service. The public gives generously to private philanthropy and votes decisively for an extension of state and Federal benefits. Yet the social worker knows that he cannot count on consistency in the attitude of the public. While wanting more state and Federal services, the public is definitely antagonistic toward paying taxes. While wanting freedom for themselves, many people are ready to deny it to others. While wanting better opportunities for their children than they themselves enjoyed, people hold to resistant and stagnant ideologies of child training into which neither social workers nor educators can successfully penetrate. While deploring the contagion of delinquency in society, neither the public nor their legislative representatives will sanction the drastic types of reform we know to be needed. All in all, public attitudes are conservative, far more so as a rule than the attitudes of those who are active in social welfare. It is, therefore, a major frustration of our calling that those who are engaged in its practice will be limited and often defeated by public ignorance and apathy.

SELF-CONFIDENCE AND ITS ENEMIES

Since social service is severely restricted by social structure on the one hand and by public apathy on the other, it seems ungracious to blame it for feelings of inadequacy. Yet it is a defect in social service (the final defect of which I wish to speak) that it lacks self-confidence—a firm sense of conviction as to its own goals.[18] In part confidence is weak because social workers feel at a disadvantage in a society where competitiveness and aggressiveness reap conspicuous rewards, while the ideals of cooperation, to which social service is committed, represent a minority point of view. In part low confidence is engendered by the atmosphere of doubt in which we live, by the very same atmosphere that causes us to engage in wholesome self-scrutiny, self-evaluation, and self-criticism.

But self-assessment should take into account assets as well as liabilities. Among its assets social service can reckon its recent achievement of the status of a full-fledged profession. The two major characteristics of any profession, writes Dean Ralph Tyler, are its use of technics that are derived from general principles and its possession of a code of ethics.[19] I have already pointed to the present alertness of social work in deriving its procedures from underlying sciences. To be sure, I have criticized a certain one-sidedness in the derivations currently popular, but the trend in general is wholesome. Likewise social service is making good progress in the formulation of an explicit code of ethics.[20] Thus the advance to professional status in both public welfare work and in private social work is clear and gratifying.

Still some of us, caught in the current atmosphere of doubt, tend to lack courage. We are not as certain as we once were that our efforts will succeed. Who can be? The existentialists remind us that men may be only half-sure without at the same time being half-hearted. Accepting our doubt, and admitting every hazard, we are still free to elect and pursue our option. Living requires that we know the worst, and make the best of it. Some of us would benefit from a generous injection of this type of existentialist courage at just this time.

But we need not rest content with a philosophy of make-the-best-of-it. Deep inside each of us knows that the spirit that lies behind social service knows no limits. The finest fruit of Judeo-Christian ethics, this spirit is eternally sound. How ironical it is that the scriptural word charity as used by St. Paul has in our profession become a sign of opprobrium rather than of inspiration! The motive behind social work always has been, and will continue to be, *caritas,* and this motive is infinitely valid.

The root problem of social service is how to express the impulse of charity effectively with the technical skill and flexible intelligence that complex modern conditions require. The chief lesson we learn from the nineteenth century is that good intentions are not enough. Nowadays we know a great deal more about sound means of fostering growth in personality, about the basis of human motivation, about a proper relating of public and private effort. When we reflect on our progress in theory and in practice, we have every right to reassert our faith and stiffen our courage. While there are plenty of obstacles in our path, and many trends that need correcting, we can expect —barring global catastrophe—continued development in the right direction.

Possessing greater clarity of perspective than does politics or commerce, social service can press for the stabilizing reforms that are needed to make life rich, meaningful, and just, in a system of free initiative and individual liberty. By asserting its own convictions more loudly than it has done, social service can make itself not merely the servant, but likewise the prophet, of democracy. And today, as never before, democracy needs both servants and prophets.

Social service has both limits and limitations. It likewise has the saving virtue of self-criticism, and is daily growing in shrewdness and sense of strategy. Its foundations are eternally valid. The balance is, therefore, in its favor.

FOOTNOTES

1. Dr. Cabot's presidential address to the Fifty-eighth National Conference of Social Work in 1931 is an important historical landmark. In it he gives a review of the handful of evaluative studies available at that time, and pleads with unmatched eloquence for a continuing program of evaluation in all social agencies. Cabot, R. C., "Treatment in Social Casework and the Need of Criteria and of Tests of its Success or Failure," *Proceedings of the National Conference of Social Work,* Chicago, University of Chicago Press, 1931.

2. Theis, Sophie van S., *How Foster Children Turn Out,* State Charities Aid Association, 1924.

Glueck, S., and Glueck, Eleanor T., *Five Hundred Criminal Careers,* New York, Knopf, 1930. See also, Glueck, Eleanor T., *Evaluative Research in Social Work,* New York School of Social Work, 1936.

3. Powers, E. and Witmer, Helen, *An Experiment in the Prevention of Delinquency,* Foreword by G. W. Allport, New York, Columbia University Press, 1951.

4. Among representative evaluative studies are the following:

Allport, G. W., *The Nature of Prejudice,* Cambridge, Addison-Wesley, 1954, Chs. 29–31.

Axelrad, S., Frings, J., Herzog, Elizabeth, *A Study of Short Term Cases,* New York, Research Department, Jewish Family Service, 1951.

Borg, I. A., "Measures Before and After Therapy," *Journal of Clinical Psychology,* 1952, 8, pp. 46–50.

Blenkner, Margaret, "Obstacles to Evaluative Research in Casework," *Social Casework,* 1950, 31, pp. 54–60, 97–105.

Cannell, C. F., Wale, F. G., Withey, S. B., "Community Change: An Action Program in Puerto Rico," *Journal of Social Issues,* 1953, 9, No. 2.

Coffey, H. S., Freedman, M., Leary, T., Ossorio, A., "Community Service and Social Research—Group Psychotherapy in a Church Program," *Journal of Social Issues,* 1950. 6, No. 1.

Eysenck, H. J., "The Effects of Psychotherapy: An Evaluation," *Journal of Consulting Psychology,* 1952, 16, No. 5, pp. 319–324.

Glueck, S. and Eleanor T., *Unraveling Juvenile Delinquency,* New York, Commonwealth Fund, 1950.

Healy, W., and Bronner, Augusta F., *Treatment and What Happened Afterward,* Boston, Judge Baker Guidance Center, 1939.

Hoch, P. (Ed.), *Failures in Psychiatric Treatment,* New York, Grune and Stratton, 1948.

Hunt, J. McV., "The Problem of Measuring the Results of Psychotherapy," *The Psychological Service Center Journal,* 1949, 1, No. 4, pp. 122–135.

Kogan, L. S., "Evaluative Techniques in Social Casework," *The Social Service Review,* 1952, 26, No. 3, pp. 305–309.

Kubie, L. S., "Objective Evaluation of Psychotherapy: Roundtable," *American Journal of Orthopsychiatry,* 1949, 19, 463–491.

Miles, H. H. W., Barrabee, Edna L., Finesinger, J. E., "Evaluation of Psychotherapy with a Follow-up Study of 62 Cases of Anxiety Neurosis," *Psychosomatic Medicine,* 1951, 13, pp. 83–105.

Perl, R. E., and Simon, A. J., "Criteria of Success and Failure in Child Guidance," *American Journal of Orthopsychiatry,* 1942, 12, pp. 642–658.

Rashkis, H. A., and Shaskan, D. A., "The Effects of Group Psychotherapy on Personality Inventory Scores," *Am. Journal of Orthopsychiatry,* 1946, 16, No. 2, pp. 345–349.

Rich, G. J., "Preschool Clinical Service and Follow-up in a City Health Department," *Am. Journal of Orthopsychiatry,* 1948, 18, No. 1, pp. 134–139.

Sells, S. B., "Problems of Criteria and Validity in Diagnosis and Therapy," *Journal of Clinical Psychology,* 1952, 8, pp. 23–28.

Watson, R. I., "Research Design and Methodology in Evaluating the Results of Psychotherapy," *Journal of Clinical Psychology,* 1952, 8, pp. 29–33.

5. Hunt, J. McV., and Kogan, L. S., *Measuring Results in Social Casework: A Manual on Judging Movement,* New York, Family Service Association, 1950.

6. Bisno, H., *The Philosophy of Social Work,* Washington, Public Affairs Press, 1952, 92.

7. Cabot, R. C., *The Meaning of Right and Wrong,* New York, Macmillan, 1933.

Richmond, Mary, *What is Social Case Work?* New York, Russell Sage Foundation, 1922.

8. McCormick, Mary J., *Diagnostic Casework in the Thomistic Pattern,* New York, Columbia University Press, 1954, 13, 51.

9. Webb, S., "The Extension Ladder Theory of the Relation Between Voluntary Philanthropy and State or Municipal Action," *The Survey,* 1914, 31, pp. 703–707.

10. Cabot, R. C., *Social Service and the Art of Healing,* New York, Moffat, Yard and Co., 1909.

11. *Trends in Giving,* Community Chests and Councils of America, 345 East 46th Street, New York 17, Table 12.

12. Kurtz, R. H. (Ed.), *Social Work Year Book, 1954,* New York, American Book-Stratford Press, 1954, 221.

13. See *Social Work Fellowships and Scholarships in the United States and Canada,* Council on Social Work Education, 345 East 46th Street, New York, New York.

14. A good place to start self-education in this regard is with the valuable reports of the Economic and Social Council of the United Nations, for example, the "Proramme of Concerted Practical Action in the Social Field of the United Nations and Specialized Agencies," Report E/ CN.5/ 291, March 2, 1953.

Of significance likewise is the work of private international organizations, such as the International Conference of Social Work with its many branches, the International Federation of Social Workers, and the International Committee of Schools of Social Work.

15. Cf. Robinson, Virginia P., *A Changing Psychology in Social Casework,* Chapel Hill, University of North Carolina Press, 1930, 180.

16. Teuber, H. L., and Powers, E., "Evaluating Therapy in a Delinquency Prevention Program," Chapter 12 in *Psychiatric Treatment,* Vol. 21, *Proc. of the Assoc. for Research in Nervous and Mental Disease,* Baltimore, Williams and Wilkins, 1953.

17. Annual Meeting—1952, New York, American Association of Schools of Social Work, 1 Park Avenue, New York 16, New York.

18. L. H. Towley has made this point forcefully in his address entitled "Professional Responsibility in a Democracy," *Education for Social Work: Proceedings Annual Program Meeting,* New York, Council on Social Work Education, 1953, pp. 10–21.

19. Tyler, R. W., "Distinctive Attributes of Education for the Professions," *Social Work Journal,* April 1952, 5.

20. "A Proposed Code of Ethics for the Social Worker," *Social Work Journal,* April 1949.

An Over-all Look

Nathan E. Cohen
Professor of Social Work-Community Organization
New York School of Social Work, Columbia University

The four chapters within Part Four have dealt with the following: need and scope of social services; responsibilities to meet social services; the limits of social services; and the financing of social services. This chapter attempts an integrative and additive summary as an inventory of where social work stands today and as an indication of the major challenge which social work must face as it moves into the future. An analysis of the four chapters reveals that the following problems received major consideration: unmet needs; the changing pattern of meeting needs; the role and relationship of the public and private agencies; problems of coordination of the private and public services; the financing of social services; the development of social work as a profession; and citizen participation in the social welfare program.

UNMET NEEDS

There is general agreement among the participants of the conference that "the range of needed social services in this complicated society is wide. It includes not only financial, but also a large variety of nonfinancial services," such as casework and counseling, recreation and group work, child welfare, psychiatric treatment services, and coordination and planning.

In almost every major area of social welfare, there remain large and unmet needs. It is not possible to enumerate all of them, but the following represent some of the high lights:

Demographic Changes

There is a marked increase at both ends of the population curve, and an increase in the average size of family. Along with the growing need for expanded services for the very young and the very old is the resulting pressure on family life. Husband and wife will be faced not only with the added respon-

214

sibilities of increased size of family, but also the problems of helping their parents. Furthermore, the educational, recreational, health, housing, and economic resources of the nation are not geared to this changing pattern of family life, and until we catch up with it many social and emotional problems may result. In the case of the aged, as stated by Dean Youngdahl, their problems and the need for new services will continue to increase. "In addition to the economic aspects, the problems of employment, education, health, counseling, morale, all need to be faced."

Another significant demographic factor is the mobility of the population. The shifts from large metropolitan areas to Suburbia are marked. These shifts are creating problems for the large cities, as they still have to maintain basic services, plus transportation facilities utilized only part of the day. Furthermore, the moving population is being replaced by a lower economic group, resulting in blighted and slum areas with a need for more social services. Leadership also is being lost to the suburbs. The nonwhite population is more mobile than the white, moving into the large metropolitan areas. For example, the 1950 census showed that since 1940 the nonwhite population had more than doubled in California and Michigan, and increased more than 50 per cent in New York and Illinois.

Technological Changes

America is continuing to increase its productive capacity, and the machine is continuing to replace the human. The mass-production method, first introduced in the automobile industry, continues to set new horizons for the productive capacities of the nation. Man is more and more able to produce more in a shorter period of time, but as yet does not have a greater guarantee of his share of the increased productivity. Indeed the increased productivity without a planning concept for its consumption makes his economic position more hazardous and his personal insecurities greater in twentieth-century America.

Health Needs

The recent report of the President's Commission on the Health Needs of the Nation points up the large and important unmet needs in this area. The report recommends more than doubling the present Federal expenditures for health, and proposes, in addition, Federal expenditures of approximately one billion dollars, apart from the recommended grants to the states to make tuberculosis, mental disease, and chronic illness facilities available to the entire population without a means test.[1] The Midcentury White House Conference on Children and Youth reported that children in the five lowest states get less than half the medical care of children in the five highest states; that the proportion for dental care is one-seventh; and that one out of four counties in the nation is without a full-time public health nurse in rural areas.

Education Requirements

There is growing concern about the inadequate facilities and the shortage of properly trained teachers to meet the expanding educational needs of the nation. A recent survey of school building needs, made by the U. S. Office of Education at the request of Congress, reports that to bring present facilities up to standard and to construct the necessary new facilities would cost 10.7 billion dollars. Funds are needed also for additional teachers, and for special programs such as for handicapped children and for children of working mothers. Furthermore, if the nation is to keep pace with its need for scientists, doctors, dentists, nurses, teachers, social workers, etc., a government-subsidized program of scholarships equivalent to the amount spent on the program of education for veterans in recent years is necessary.[2]

Economic Needs

The Midcentury White House Conference on Children and Youth reported that one out of five mothers with children under 18 works outside the home, and that most of them do so in order to earn a living. About 25 per cent of the American people have personal or family incomes of less than $2,000 a year. As stated by Frederick Lewis Allen:

> These people are not the masses; they are not a proletariat. They are, rather, a great number of very widely scattered people who for one reason or another are out of luck, such as small business men whose ventures have foundered; farmers who have had a bad year or series of years; lone widows, deserted wives and children; migratory laborers; workers of marginal ability; and invalids and defectives.[3]

These groups are the least covered by insurance plans and have access to few financial resources. They represent not merely an economic but also a social problem.

Social insurance programs to maintain income are inadequate. Further consideration must be given to more complete coverage; protection in the event of temporary or permanent disability from non-work-connected causes; minimum insurance benefits for all aged persons; and an expanded use, through increased funds and personnel, of the special welfare services provided under the vocational rehabilitation program, and under the maternal and child-health and child-welfare programs.

Mental Health

One out of every eight draftees in World War II was rejected because of personality or mental difficulties. It is estimated that 8½ to 15 million people in the United States either are now suffering from some form of mental difficulty or will be at some time in their lives. There is a significant rise, among mental diseases, in psychosis associated with alcoholism. The population of mental hospitals is growing at a rate of about two per cent a year. More than

800,000 patients are treated in the country's approximately 950 mental hospitals during the course of a year. It is estimated that mental hospital facilities must be expanded eighty per cent to approach the necessary proportion of five beds for every 1,000 in the population; and that community clinics must be increased from the present number of 600 full or part-time to 1,800 full-time. Psychiatric services for schools, colleges, courts, and prisons are also woefully inadequate. In the area of personnel there are under 20,000 in the total force of psychiatrists, psychiatric nurses, clinical psychologists, and psychiatric social workers, to deal with the mental health problems affecting a minimum of 8½ million citizens. The amount of money being spent under both government and private sponsorship for research in mental health is infinitesimal compared to the sums being spent on cancer, polio, etc. Although prevention would involve work with children, not a single state has adequate psychiatric clinic service for children and some states have almost no service.

THE CHANGING PATTERN OF MEETING NEEDS

The motives, methods, and programs for helping people have changed with the changing economic, political, and social climate. Present at all times, however, has been the object of helping people who were having difficulty in coping with the conditions of stress and strain.

Generally speaking, the earliest formulation of social work was in terms of religious motivation. In its narrowest sense the giving of alms was viewed as an obligation in the striving for salvation. Emphasis was placed on the effect of giving on the soul of the giver rather than on what it did for the recipient. The attitude toward the recipient was punitive and moralistic. As religion received a broader interpretation, there emerged a distinction between alms-giving for personal salvation and helping people to change their ways.

For centuries, however, a distinction was drawn between the deserving unfortunate and the undeserving misfits. The deserving were those who had run into misfortune because of conditions beyond their control. This group included widows, orphans, disabled, and aged. The undeserving were those who had run into difficulty because of their moral weakness. This group included criminals, able-bodied unemployed, alcoholics, and unmarried mothers. The method of dealing with these two groups varied. In the case of the deserving, charity could be given without fear of destroying their moral character. In the case of the undeserving, the giving of charity without punishment and moral persuasion might encourage their moral defectiveness.

A residue of this distinction, especially in the area of public welfare, rears its head even to-day. Generally speaking, this latter type of emphasis held sway on the American scene until about the middle of the nineteenth century. During this period social welfare was undifferentiated from general voluntary efforts to help one's neighbors. The only real organized efforts were the public programs on a local community level for taking care of the poor. The main area of concern was economic need, and the personnel who dealt with the problems were volunteers.

By the latter part of the nineteenth century, with the nation beginning to feel the impact of the industrial revolution and the accompanying urbanization, the attitude toward people in economic need began to shift. Experience with mass poverty was new, and as more and more people were involved there began to emerge the realization that poverty might be socially caused rather than the fault of the individual.

Progress in this direction of thinking was aided by the following developments:

1. Increased education, both formal and through the life experience in industrial living, was making people more sensitive to the needs of others.

2. The growing advances in both the physical and the social sciences were creating an attitude of searching for causes rather than dealing only with symptoms. The work of such pioneers as Charles Booth and the Webbs helped throw light on the social causes of poverty and unemployment.

3. Advances in science, especially in the area of health, brought the realization that problems were not inevitable and could be dealt with on a preventive basis.

4. Sociological thinking shifted from the deterministic theories of Spencer and Sumner to the scientific formulation of society by Comte with its projection "that human society is not to be considered as a mechanical process determined by fate or cosmic laws incapable of control, but is rather a process which can be studied and, to some extent at least, guided."

5. Humanistic liberalism, with its emphasis on the emancipation of human nature and the placing of human rights above property rights, gained greater impact.

6. Mutual aid societies, such as trade unions and cooperatives, emerged. This represented a moving away from a narrow concept of individualism to a greater recognition of the interdependence of society.

It was during this period that the pattern of meeting social welfare needs began to shift from the confines of the informal individual, family, and neighbor conception to include the more formally organized private agency. With the introduction of the Charity Organization Societies in 1877 responsibility for charity began to assume a community approach. In the beginning the C.O.S. were primarily concerned with bringing about better organization, perhaps better business efficiency, into charity. Their more intensive study of needs, however, and their use of the friendly visitor led to a growing interest in community conditions. A body of knowledge began to emerge from this experience which might be called the early roots of modern casework.

This period is marked also by the efforts of the social reformers, some of whom were active in social work, especially in the settlement house movement. The tragic contrast in the conditions of life of the rich and the poor led to a greater sensitivity to broader social causes. It was not an attempt to change the social structure of society, but more an application of the moralistic attitude toward environmental problems. In a sense reform was looked upon as a form of prevention and as a way of changing human nature. Closely related to the social reform movement were the growing mutual aid societies such as cooperatives and trade unions. These three types of developments—the more coordinated and efficient method of dealing with the destitute and economically dependent individual, the social reform movement, and the mutual aid associations—traveled parallel roads running into each other occasionally through overlapping leadership.

Developments during this period were more extensive in the private or voluntary field than in public services. In the area of public welfare the earlier principles still held sway. These included: local autonomy; strict enforcement of the settlement law; the liability of relatives; the principle of less eligibility; and keeping government services at a minimum. Expansion and change in public services involved principally such special categories as children, the handicapped, the deaf, the blind, and the ill. Assistance to these groups did not challenge the prevailing philosophy of rugged individualism as did aid to the able-bodied. The period 1870 to 1890 saw significant changes in the attitude toward the juvenile delinquent. Reform rather than punishment became the new emphasis.

The period 1900 to World War I showed other significant changes in the pattern of meeting social welfare needs. This brief period of eighteen years might well be called the most important transitional period in social-work history. The impact of the social sciences was now being felt. Surveys of social institutions began to appear and a tie-up between social conditions and economic factors was made. Legislation as a method of attaining social welfare goals became prominent. Prevention of social problems was discussed and the need for striking at the cause of dependency emphasized. By 1910 Jane Addams was expressing social-work goals as "raising life to its highest values." Between 1904 and 1918 such major events took place as the establishment of the National Association for the Study and Prevention of T.B.; the National Child Labor Committee; the American Association for Labor Legislation; the National Committee for Mental Hygiene; the National Recreation Association; the National Federation of Settlements; the Family Service Association of America; the National Organization for Public Health Nursing; the American Social Hygiene Association; the Children's Bureau; and Survey Associates.

Other important developments which reflected the new look were the First American Conference for the Prevention of Infant Mortality; the first White House Conference on Children; and the first National Conference on Social Insurance. Workmen's compensation, the earliest form of social insurance in the United States, was first enacted in 1908. "By 1917 this modern legislative remedy had been accepted by a majority of the states, and in that year it was upheld by the Supreme Court of the United States." Workmen's compensation represented another peg in shaping a plan for meeting the economic problems of individuals. With its emphasis on the cooperative responsibility of the employee, the employer, and government it pointed the way for later attacks on problems of unemployment, health, and medical care.

In 1917 the National Conference of Charities and Corrections changed its name to the National Conference of Social Work. The Conference broadened its interest beyond that of administrative problems of public institutions. Although it did not as yet show a concern for changes in the poor-law system, it did discuss new forms of public aid and proposals for social insurance at the state level. Compulsory health insurance was also discussed.

Not only were there marked changes emerging in point of view and program, but also the beginnings of a new methodology. Of great interest to the 1917 Conference was the work of the new Division of Neuropsychiatry in the Army. The groundwork was being laid for the advances in psychiatry which were to have a deep effect on social-work methodology, and which were to add a new dimension to the concept of need.

From World War I to the depression of the 1930s, social work focused on its new-found methodology, but unfortunately did not integrate it with the earlier emphasis on social causes. There were two reasons for this new direction: the growing impact of Freud's teachings and the climate of reaction which set in after World War I. Political reaction was accompanied by fear of social experimentation. As stated by Elizabeth Wisner:

> Among social workers, social reform or social action was shoved out of the spotlight by findings of psychiatry, and psychoanalysis, the application of which resulted in an overemphasis upon personal inadequacy and individual adjustment to the "realities" of social life, "realities" which were too often conceived in static terms.[4]

During this period Mary Richmond made one of the first attempts to view social work as a whole with the basis of integration as the aim of social work, namely adjustment and development of personality. She distinguished four related methods of social work:

> Case work consists of those processes which develop personality through adjustments consciously effected, individual by individual, between men and their social environment; group work serves it by dealing with people face to face but no longer one by one; social reform serves it by effecting mass betterment through propaganda and social legislation; and social research serves personality by making original discoveries and reinterpreting known facts for the use of these other forms of social work.[5]

Although this formulation attempted to include both the individual and the environmental factors, social work was to have difficulty in escaping the emphasis of adjustment of the individual to his environment, to the gradual exclusion or lesser emphasis of changing the environment to make it more suitable to what we regard as the ends and fulfillment of human life.

Other developments during the war period which have a bearing on the changing pattern of meeting needs were the following: (1) The Red Cross, with its task of serving as a liaison between the man in the service and his family, expanded social work services beyond the economic dependent; (2) the general climate of cooperation toward the war effort gave impetus to the movement for coordination and federated financing; and (3) under the chairmanship of Judge Julian W. Mack, president of the National Conference of Charities and Corrections in 1912, the plan for the Amended War Risk Insurance Act of 1917 was drawn up. The Act was based upon the philosophy of the workmen's compensation law.

Public welfare, during this period, also began to move out of the charities and corrections stage toward more modern concepts. Public welfare still remained primarily the responsibility of the states and local communities, but progress was made in "actual reorganization, legislative and administrative development, and technical study of programs and principles. The enactment of the Illinois Administrative Code in 1917 represented the first move toward the consolidation of the numerous state commissions and boards dealing with different aspects of social welfare and toward greater administrative control. It marked a shift from Boards of Charities and Corrections to State Departments of Public Welfare. By 1930 a majority of the states had consolidated their numerous social welfare functions into a single major public welfare function. There also emerged greater coordination of state and local activities with a trend toward the use of the county as the administrative unit. Improved coordination on the state level stimulated better coordination of social welfare activities on the local level. State departments also increased their supervision over local private agencies.

On the Federal level, however, the pattern remained substantially the same. Welfare activities of a varying nature were being handled by some thirteen departments of the Federal government. Two attempts were made in the 1920s to integrate these activities through the establishment of a Federal Department of Education and Welfare. Both bills, however, were unsuccessful. The relationship of the Federal government to welfare responsibilities on the state and local levels also remained the same; the states and local communities continued to bear the heaviest proportion of the costs of ordinary public welfare activities.

The nation was entering the greatest depression in its history with a public welfare vehicle that was being overhauled administratively but which for all intent and purpose was still the same one which had been constructed to meet the needs of dependent people living in a simple economy. The power by which it was propelled still flowed from the poor or pauper statutes which had remained practically unmodified from colonial days. The growing unemployment in 1927 and the emerging problems of relief gave rise to question in some quarters as to the adequacy of the vehicle and whether replacement with a more modern model rather than further repair was the answer. Several developments which stimulated such thinking were as follows:

1. Although community chests were raising larger sums of money—297 chests raised $64,000,000 in 1927—the sums raised were insufficient to meet even minimum welfare needs in these communities.

2. Public welfare expenditures were increasing at a greater rate than private social welfare expenditures.

3. Local and state public welfare expenditures were becoming inadequate to meet the growing needs on even a minimum basis.

In searching for a new vehicle, clues were offered by several of the different types of developments during this period, among which were the following:

1. The continuing practice of transferring to public responsibility activities first undertaken by private efforts. Thus, by 1930, forty-seven states had enacted legislation providing for some form of public aid to children in their own homes. By 1930 there was also evidenced a growing concern for public aid to the aged. Thirteen states had some form of plan in operation for aid to the aged.

2. The introduction of the methods of the private agencies in public settings. This practice began to break down the stereotype that the public program could deal only with mass problems and could not operate on a high-quality level.

3. The growing experience with plans of social insurance. First Workmen's compensation on a state level, and then the amended War Risk Insurance Act of 1917 on a Federal level, pointed to a new approach by government to meet the welfare of the people.

With the advent of the depression it was necessary for the Federal government to enter the arena and to begin an ever increasing role in and responsibility toward social welfare services. As stated by Frederick Lewis Allen, two new political principles emerged in this atmosphere: First, "that the fortunes of individual Americans are inextricably interlocked; that we are all in the same boat; and that if any of us fall into deep trouble it is the job of the rest of us—not simply family and friends and neighbors, or even the local community, but the federal government itself if need be—to help them; and, secondly that it is the job of the federal government, through whatever means, to see that there shall not be another Great Depression."[6] Professor Haber, commenting on Allen's two principles, observed: "Taken together the combination of these two ideas has produced a phenomenal transformation in the social politics of the United States. Its most significant manifestation is the almost unanimous adoption of the Social Security Act in 1935 and the equally widespread endorsement of the extensions and liberalizations of that measure since then, together with the supporting legislation in all of the states." The pattern of meeting needs had changed. The *laissez-faire* philosophy with its emphasis on rugged individualism, which had prevailed before the depression, was defeated by America's democratic and humanitarian mores. Experience had shown that the philosophy and attitudes born out of a pioneer and rural period were not adequate to meet the problems growing out of a rapidly expanding industrial and urban society.

The concept of need today is being understood in broader terms than meeting the desire, wish, or drive of the individual. It includes, besides the psychological element and the recognition of the social conditions which are necessary for the optimal functioning of the individual, the social philosophy or objectives of a democracy. The three factors are interrelated and must be dealt with as such. The method and extent of fulfillment of the individuals' desires and drives is related to what a democracy needs of its citizens to continue as a democracy, and in turn to the role it plays through the individual citizens, the organized private voluntary groups, and the government in providing the essential social conditions and services for achieving its goal.

The nub of the approach is in the maturing concept of democracy. Such basic concepts in American life as individualism and humanitarianism, which determined the pattern of meeting needs for many years, had to be redefined within the framework of democracy as a way of life. Individualism could no longer be regarded in the narrow terms of the least amount of government being the best kind of government. Within a concept of democracy as a way of life which pervades the totality of our experiences—political, social, and economic—individualism has come to be regarded as a relationship of interdependence as well as independence. There is growing recognition that man does not exist apart from his social relationships, and must not only learn his rights in a democracy, but also develop a sense of responsibility to other men and their cooperative understanding. Humanitarianism, too, had to learn to find its expression through democratic channels, to enter into the main stream of democratic institutions, if it was to contribute to the democratic values and goals of American life.

There was general agreement in the conference on these changing patterns of meeting needs, on the fact that government as well as individual and private voluntary efforts were essential. The question of how much government, however, brought differences of opinion. The problems basic to these differences are dealt with in the sections which follow.

THE ROLE AND RELATIONSHIP OF THE PUBLIC AND PRIVATE AGENCIES

Historically, the major role in social work was played at first by persons interested in public institutions. They formed the Conference of Boards of Public Charities, which met under the auspices of the American Social Science Association. In 1879 it became an independent body under the name of the National Conference of Charities and Corrections. During the latter part of the nineteenth century the private agencies began to come into their own and to assume the role of leadership. This role continued unchallenged until the depression of the 1930s. Then, to the credit of organizations for social work, although deeply immersed in the individual approach and primarily focused on private agencies, they showed their flexibility and rallied to the problem. Schools of social work forgot temporarily the training program which they had outlined, and in cooperation with government agencies sponsored short-term training programs to help supply the thousands of new workers needed for emergency services.

Despite this flexibility, there is question as to whether the field understood clearly the full meaning of the changing pattern of meeting needs. Although a large number of workers had entered the field with only limited training— approximately only 10 per cent were members of the existing professional organizations—the Association of Schools of Social Work voted in 1937 to place professional education completely on a graduate level as of January 1, 1940. Social work had moved more quickly into this conception of graduate education than had such other professions as law, medicine, dentistry, and engineering. It was almost as if social work regarded the developments during the depression as an emergency that would pass rather than the beginnings of a new era in social welfare services. It was as if social work had laid aside its tools to help the nation fight a disaster, but once the disaster was under control, like the returning soldier, it tried to pick up again at the point where it had left off.

Remnants of this attitude still persist. As pointed out by Professor Allport, ". . . young people training for the profession of social service prefer, in the great majority of instances, to work for private agencies and shun opportunities for public service. . . . Approximately half of the openings in social service today occur in public agencies; but jobs in private agencies are greatly preferred. The basic philosophies of the two types do not greatly differ. What we need is a more cordial and equal relationship between them, and in particular a higher sense of obligation to public service, an area that will continue to grow by leaps and bounds."

Professor Allport has raised a key question when he refers to a "more cordial and equal relationship." There are those who see an emergency role for public services, but refuse to give them permanent status. On the other hand, there is a group who with the advent of the new public program no longer see a role for the private voluntary services. In between is the largest group who do not see the problem as involving an either/or decision but rather a relationship of both/and. For this latter group, however, there is still need of understanding the basis of the relationship.

Dean Youngdahl sees the common goals as the connecting link. He states: "There is room for the services of private welfare agencies today and there is likely to be at all times. However, any assumption that voluntary efforts can take care of total needs today, as widespread as they are in our complicated society, is born of sheer wish. . . . 'Only the power of government can serve the interest of all.' . . . It is possible for public and private agencies to operate for the good of the whole on a coordinated basis without duplication of services, as long as the goal—the well-being of people—is a common one." Professor Allport approaches the problem in a similar vein. He states: "Now in a democracy, having a free economy and reasonable opportunities for upward mobility, as well as respect for the dignity of the individual, the ideals and aims of social service are essentially the same whether the service is governmental or private. While there is a division of functions, both forms of service wish to reduce unnecessary suffering, to preserve a basic social order, and to maximize the opportunities of individuals to develop their potentialities."

Dr. Davidson goes beyond the conception of common goals and ideals binding these two types of services together. In a sense he lays to rest the possibility of a dualism by viewing them as springing from the same roots and as being not two separate developments, but rather "separate manifestations of the same thing." I use the term dualism advisedly because there are some who see the public services as catering to the body, and the private services as catering to the soul. He states: "If we can accept this Siamese-twin concept of the relationship between the public and the voluntary social services—if we can look upon them as branches of the same tree, nourished in the same soil of our religious, charitable, and humanitarian traditions, fed by the same roots of belief in political democracy and in the basic equality and common brotherhood of men—then our problem of establishing the appropriate relationships between the public and private agencies becomes much simpler."

This interesting formulation provides a workable philosophical framework for understanding the relationship of public and private efforts in a democracy. It still leaves, however, the question of the division of functions. Dean Youngdahl sees the private agencies providing "leadership in new fields, in experimentation and research, in giving support to sound public programs, in filling gaps here and there until the public is ready to accept the needed services . . . and in providing specialized services on a basis of contractual or delegated authority from some level of government." Professor Allport reminds us that the distinctions on the basis of experimentation, leadership, and quality of performance "are less sharp than formerly." Dr. Davidson emphasizes the importance of looking at the problem in dynamic rather than static terms. We are dealing not with the cutting of a given-sized pie into two slices, but rather with a constantly changing and expanding situation in which "the horizons of human helpfulness are infinite and limitless." He states that if we can accept this concept of our democratic society and its application to our functions in the social service field, we will always find new fields for adventurous pioneering, new experiments to undertake, new social crusades to lead, new areas of human helpfulness in which the enterprise of our voluntary and public service agencies can make their contribution—ever changing—to the rich and full development of our community life.

Within this monistic and dynamic conception of the relationship and role of public and private services, it becomes a question not of how much of one or the other, but rather which of a variety of patterns best meets the given set of facts. Dr. Davidson sees emerging from experience certain trends of guidelines which more and more can serve as a set of principles. Thus, on the side of public services, one tends to find at this time mass services, services which have received popular acceptance, services calling for the expenditures of large sums of money, services which lead themselves to an assembly-line approach, and services which do not demand extensive volunteer participation. On the side of private services, one tends to find selective services affecting limited numbers, services catering to the needs of special minority groups, services of more limited appeal, services involving a highly individualized approach, services where economic maintenance is minimal, and services where opportunities of volunteer participation are present. Again, these are not to be construed as static yardsticks, but rather as flexible operational guideposts which may change with the changing trends in society.

PROBLEMS OF COORDINATION OF PRIVATE AND PUBLIC SERVICES

Coordination and planning in the local and national community has reflected the different stages of man's maturing process in human relations. In the same way that man in his developmental process tries to move from self-centeredness to a level of relationship which might be termed the universal—where humanity and human values are placed above personal gain and even above personal loyalties—so, too, the social institutions developed and run by man have tried to move from an agency centeredness to a level of relationship which expresses the fullness of community coordination and planning.

Historically, the first efforts were made in the private field with the establishment of the Charity Organization Society movement in the latter part of the nineteenth century. The goal was to coordinate better the work of the numerous societies dealing with the economic dependent. Although at first the motivation involved greater efficiency in exposing the impostor and making it more difficult for the poor to "take advantage" of the charity societies, the Charity Organization Society moved along to develop the pattern of the present Council of Social Agencies. Their programs included not only coordination and exchange of information and experience, but also fact finding and social action.

The Community Chest Movement, which was first introduced in Cleveland, Ohio, in 1913, also began with the motivation of financial pressures. Its main theme was to avoid the multiplicity of drives and to protect the energies and interests of the business community. Money, however, had to be distributed as well as collected, and the experience around the budgeting process led to a greater interest in coordination and planning. Growth in this area at first was slow, but the need for coordination and planning growing out of the impetus of World War I hastened the progress. Today every community with a population of over 100,000 has some form of central fund-raising and coordinating machinery.

Although there is a relatively long history of coordination and planning in the private field we have only scratched the surface. The obstacles are numerous. One of the problems is that although the national agencies have been in a crucial position to help further this developmental process of community planning they have not always played a positive role. Too many national agencies have a tendency to regard local communities as the vehicles for their special interests. On the national level itself, the attitude toward inter-agency planning has not been as positive as in the local community. National agencies have been moving slowly toward a more mature level of relationship.

Another problem is our failure at times to realize that a community is not bounded on all sides by a community chest and a council of social agencies. Federated financing has its limitations and cannot be regarded as an end in itself. In 1951, for example, ten of the independent drives raised $164.3 million as compared to $212.9 million raised by all of the chests in the nation. Another factor which has a bearing on coordination and planning is the increase in corporation giving to chests in the past thirty years. Corporation giving now represents over 40 per cent of the total raised by chests. This trend can eventually affect not only the stability of the financing of private agencies, but also the whole area of policy making.

Councils of Social Agencies are making efforts to broaden their base and move in the direction of community councils. There is difficulty, however, in letting go of the early pattern of control by the core of private social agencies. It is again as if the developments in the public services were of a temporary nature or represented a separate group from another planet. As stated by Dr. Davidson in his discussion of the council structure:

> While this machinery for coordination has contributed much to the orderly development of community social service patterns and has been reasonably effective in the voluntary sector of the community welfare field, it has not met adequately, in my judgment, the problem of coordination as between the public and the voluntary agencies at the community level. Governmental agencies have generally found it difficult to relate themselves to this machinery for the coordination of community welfare planning.

Part of the difficulty is related to the different structure and units of operation in the public services, but much also goes back to the question of attitude. Although the increase of public as compared with private funds has been phenomenal—a study of sources of support of health and welfare services in 17 of the large communities by chests and councils showed that only 10.9 per cent came from private funds, while 56.7 per cent came from public sources—public agencies are given the same representation in the council as a small private agency with a budget of $20,000. Because of these attitudes, the public agencies tend to view the council not as a representative community structure belonging to the total community but rather as another private, voluntary agency.

In analyzing this problem, Dr. Davidson offers an interesting suggestion, namely, an agency that is both public and private, through the attitude of both the public and private agencies toward it:

> . . . to change the form or structure of our present coordinating agencies that are neither public nor purely voluntary, but agencies whose place is formally and officially recognized by the public authority as entitling them to exercise for public and for private agencies alike the appointed function of coordination.

This approach is consistent with the philosophy of the relationship between public and private services outlined by him earlier. It would also provide a channel for studying the growing pattern of public payments or subsidies to private agencies, and for the development of machinery to handle it. There was much discussion about this growing trend, with marked differences of opinion as to its meaning, value, and desirability, both for the philosophy of public services and the retaining of private-agency control and philosophy.

The problem of coordination is not limited to the private agencies and to their relationship with the public services. As pointed out by Dr. Davidson, "the problem is even greater as between the various levels of government." This includes not only relationships between the three levels of government, but also the problems of intergovernmental coordination within each, namely, the municipality, the state, and the Federal government. One of the priority problems which needs coordination and direction is the trend toward centralization of the public social services. This trend toward centralization is not limited to the public services alone but is related to the financial pressures growing out of an expanded program of social welfare services. There is need to better understand the forces which brought this trend into being and are constantly affecting it, rather than to attribute it to "the lust for power and authority of a few ambitious, power-hungry politicians at the center."

Professor Haber, commenting upon the increasing number of economic and financial functions assumed by larger units of government, states that "the major explanation for this trend will be found in the taxing and other financial limitations under which the smaller units operate. . . . As a general principle, the larger units have fewer restrictions and a more flexible borrowing capacity. In this respect our Federal government has distinct advantages over smaller state and local units." The procedures available at present for coordination are consultation, conference groups, and supervision around the grant-in-aid programs. Dr. Davidson does not regard these procedures as adequate. He states that "until more adequate machinery can be established . . . we shall have to recognize the weaknesses and the limitations of our present . . . intergovernmental partnerships."

The conference discussion indicated the need for a clearer differentiation between objectives on the one hand and policy on the other; between coordination on the policy level and coordination on the administrative level. It was pointed out that there is a sharper distinction between these in the public than in the private services.

THE FINANCING OF SOCIAL SERVICES

Professor Haber has described the extensive system of public social services fashioned in the past two decades at a cost of many billion dollars. He states that the proper financing of this program has become "one of the major fiscal problems of contemporary social policy," and identifies the following four major areas of controversy:

1. How should the cost of financing these payments be distributed?

2. Should the states or the Federal government be required to finance assistance or insurance payments?

3. Should the pay-as-you-go method of financing be substituted for the present system of reserve requirements?

4. How much social welfare can the nation afford?

In regard to the first three questions, opposition was voiced to most of the proposed changes, particularly those "which would weaken the contributory principle, provide more uniform benefits, introduce some form of an income or means test, or transfer a portion of the problem to the states." Professor Haber observed that "little is to be gained in attempting to equate the social insurance program with private annuity or other insurance contracts. Social insurance is a special form of protection against income loss, developed by society and financed by whatever method is likely to achieve its objective." In regard to Federal versus state government, it is his opinion that the "issue is less concerned with the theoretical problems of intergovernment relations than with the practical aspects of financial capacity and resources." The attack on the grant-in-aid program for public assistance by the Chamber of Commerce was not approved, and their proposed pay-as-you-go proposal was not regarded as a feasible solution. Coverage for the entire population, it was felt, represented a more lasting solution. This approach in turn made it essential that the Federal government not withdraw from its financial responsibilities.

In approaching the problem of how much social welfare can the nation afford, the trend of expenditures in the past two decades was explored. The combined expenditures for civilian public programs, such as social insurance and public assistance programs, public health and medical services, vocational rehabilitation, child welfare, and veterans' pensions and medical care, for the year 1950–51 was approximately $16.2 billion. If expenditures for education are included, the total would be approximately $23.3 billion. If compared with expenditures for the year 1936–37, which were approximately $7.7 billion, the total dollar expenditures for civilian public programs has about tripled in this period of 15 years. Adjustments must be made, however, for the change in price level and for the increase in population during this period. Adjusted for change in price level, using 1935–39 as the base, the increase is approximately 64 per cent, that is, from $7.7 billion to $12.5 billion. Adjustment for population increase in terms of the adjusted dollar shows an increase in per capita expenditure from $64 to $84. When measured in relation to the gross national product there has been a decrease from 9 per cent to 7.6 per cent.

In the private, voluntary field, figures are available only for the years 1929–1949. The increase in this 20-year period was from $1.2 billion to $4 billion. These figures are not adjusted for change in price level, and, furthermore, include giving for religious and educational purposes as well as health and welfare. A study of 180 community chests reporting continuously between 1929 and 1950 showed an increase from an index of 100 in 1929 to 191.7 in 1950. During this same period, however, national income increased from an index of 100 in 1929 to 256.1 in 1950. Because of the lack of adequate data it is difficult to determine whether the amount raised by chests is increasing, but there seems to be little question of the fact that public expenditures are providing for an increasing proportion of the total expenditures for social services. As indicated earlier, a study of 17 large communities showed that only 10.9 per cent of the funds for health and welfare services came from private funds, while 56.7 per cent came from public sources. Professor Burns, in a paper presented at the recent National Conference of Social Work, pointed out that more than 90 per cent of all welfare expenditures in the nation were for public programs.[7]

A further analysis of the growth of public expenditures in the 15-year period, however, reveals that the largest change has been in veterans' benefits, which have increased 12-fold. There has been a sharp decline in expenditures for public aid, and little change in expenditures for civilian health and medical services. The steadiest growth has occurred in the social insurance payments. As stated by Professor Eveline Burns,[8] the major part of the growth in public social service expenditures could be accounted for by veterans' programs, social insurance, and public assistance. If these areas are subtracted only 1 per cent of the national income is being devoted to all other types of public welfare, which, as she points out, is a far cry from the accusation that we are moving toward a welfare state. Professor Haber added to this type of analysis the moral issue. He stated:

> Several elementary aspects of social welfare costs should be emphasized at the outset. A rather substantial proportion of what we spend for welfare— social security, public assistance, social services—are not items about which we have choice. These expenditures cannot readily be evaded. We must provide for the aged who are in need, for the jobless whose incomes have ceased, for the ill and the disabled, for veterans and their families. These obligations have had a high priority in our scheme of values throughout our history. Whether we can afford such expenditures is hardly a pertinent question.

The question of how much social welfare the nation can afford seems to be tied up as much with our attitude toward the place of welfare services in our society as with the economic question. Most economists agree that the constant rate of growth of our national income will continue. As pointed out by Ida C. Merriam,[9] if this rate continues the gross national product will be about $425 billion by 1960, and if the present ratio of social welfare expenditures continues they will increase by $8 billion by 1960. It is her opinion, furthermore, that even with the war expenditures more funds could have been devoted to social welfare services in 1951. The task, therefore, is an educational one in which the private, voluntary agencies have as much of a stake and responsibility as the public agencies. Change in attitude toward the responsibility of government in meeting these large areas of unmet needs will also bring a better understanding of social work in general. Furthermore, it will provide a greater opportunity for the private, voluntary agencies to pioneer, to set new sights and new standards.

SOCIAL WORK AS A PROFESSION

Social work, like other professions, has moved from the early stage of exchange of experience to conceptualization, and more recently to the third stage of attempting through research to validate its concepts. As stated by Professor Allport, "the brightest feature of the present situation is the spirit of self-objectification, self-scrutiny, and self-criticism that mark contemporary social services. We are less inclined than formerly to mistake our good intentions for good results, or our own professional growth for growth in our clients. We have reached a stage of wholesome skepticism." Within this context he then proceeds to outline the following problems which need critical scrutiny:

1. As we move into the stage of measurement we must avoid the error of measurement as an end in itself. Social work is closely related to the warp and woof of the life situation in a democracy, and the approach reduced to one of techniques and gadgets without relation to goals and values can become sterile. In a sense social work can best be regarded as science at work in the interest of human values. Although it is not possible or desirable at this time to state the philosophy of social work in ultimate terms, the training program for social workers, in order to insure a concern for goals and objectives, should provide the necessary knowledge and stimulation for them to develop a philosophy.

2. Social work emphasizes self-awareness primarily around psychological factors, around needs and rights, but tends to neglect self-awareness in the area of citizenship responsibility. This pattern tends to carry over into the client relationship. Professor Allport asks: "Do social workers in dealing with clients try to inculcate in them an awareness of such duties as they owe, and can discharge, to their community and to their state? Or do they intensify the sense of 'rights' that is already so prominent in the American's mind?" In essence the question is whether social work has correlated a narrow concept of adjustment with a philosophy of democracy. In the same vein the question is raised whether we have become conceptual imperialists in our relations to

social services in other countries by projecting our emphasis on therapy without taking into account the problems, stage of development, or philosophy in these countries. Have we lost our world perspective and are we tending to become an "island within" in our approach?

3. Have we gone overboard in stressing objectivity in worker-client relationships at the expense of what Professor Allport refers to as the friendship theory, the ingredients of which are "charity, compassion, and tolerance"?

4. Have we become so specialized in our approach that there is a tendency to place the needs of our body of knowledge before those of the person in need?

5. Have we placed too much faith in and dependence on social diagnosis, without realizing that social diagnosis within the present rubrics of psychiatry and psychology is likely to lead to little more than coarse classification? In so doing are we running the danger of losing sight of the individual in relation to the total forces affecting his situation?

6. Is there too much of a tendency to limit our services only to those who express a conscious need for help? Is there enough evidence in terms of potential results to warrant our not reaching out more to the unreached?

7. Have we limited ourselves too much in borrowing primarily from psychiatry without enough attention being given to the social sciences? In this connection Professor Allport refers to psychiatry as an "art of treating sick people" as contrasted with psychology as "the science of the normal mind."

8. Because of the limited approach, is there the danger that the social worker will tend to "oversimplify what he learns, and gravitate toward a pet psychological formula" when confronted with a complicated problem?

These are challenging and important questions. Some historical perspective may help to understand them. As indicated earlier, social work had been moving through a rich period of social reform, with an emphasis on social causes, when it began to feel the impact of the newly evolving psychoanalysis. It was around this same period that Abraham Flexner, who had made a study of medical education in 1910, addressed the National Conference on the question, "Is Social Work a Profession?" He applied the same criteria which he had utilized in his study of the medical profession, and found that social work in its then stage of development could not qualify as a *bona fide* profession. Some of the areas in which it was found lacking were the following:[10]

1. Basic preparation in the social sciences
2. A body of exclusive and distinctive knowledge and a transmissible professional technique
3. Definite educational and professional qualifications tested under state supervision
4. Professional organizations
5. A code of professional practice

Bruno, commenting on the impact of Flexner's paper, made the following observations:

The effect of Flexner's paper was profound and far-reaching. The challenge was accepted at face value, and has set social workers to defining and perfecting their methods with a singleness of purpose that has all but blinded them to the fact that method is only a test. Philosophy—what is it all about, why is it undertaken; what are its ultimate goals and its relationship to other activities—is as essential to a profession as method. It is tragic that an impetus in that direction was given social work at the very inception of its professional consciousness.[11]

It is interesting to note that the search for a methodology occurred just at the time that the impact of psychoanalysis was being felt. Did social work in its haste for professional status reach out for a ready-made methodology in the "art of treating sick people," closing itself off from the influences of developments in the social sciences? In this connection it is important to keep in mind the emphasis in the social sciences during this era, and what they had to offer to an applied field. As stated by Professor Allport:

> The individualistic era was principally a time when the methods and concepts of experimental psychology were in the ascendancy and when individual mental operations, interpreted with the aid of statistical method, were held to explain adequately all social behavior. Freudianism with its highly individualistic emphasis was easily assimilated into this line of thought. Two decades ago a reaction set in when both sociologists and anthropologists spoke up vigorously concerning the importance of status, role, caste, and pattern, and of the significance of the situation, both immediate and remote, in determining present conduct.[12]

In other words, the contribution of the social sciences to an operational approach is just emerging. Social work has been sensitive to the effect of such factors on mental health as hunger, poor housing, inadequate medical care, unemployment, low wages, etc. What has been lacking, however, is not only a formulation of how the social factors affect personality adjustment, but also how this knowledge can be translated into an operational dimension which can be integrated with our psychological approach. Social work has given lip service to an integrated two-prong approach, the psychological and the social, but because of the problem described above has found itself with the tendency to lean completely on the psychological dimension alone. There is evidence, however, in the changing curricula of social work education, in the cooperative ventures with social scientists, and in the emphasis on the social sciences especially in the newly developed doctoral programs, that social work is becoming sensitive to these developments and is beginning to broaden its horizons.

On the matter of the friendship theory to which Professor Allport refers, historical perspective may again be helpful. Social work historically has utilized volunteers more than any other profession. In its attempt to move from the "heart" approach to a more professional method, it has encountered resistance from the layman. As stated by Charles Dollard:

> Of all the forms of activity in which men and women engage, social work has at once the greatest claim to be a professional activity and the greatest

difficulty in establishing its claim. . . . The difficulty which has plagued social work in its development as a profession is that the social worker's dedication is to a degree shared by all good men and women. Most human beings have a deep need to be their brothers' keepers. Hence we all resist and resent the notion that the task of the social worker requires a peculiar combination of temperament, intelligence, training, and experience. The result is that social work has had to fight a constant rearguard action against the pervasive notion that any man with love in his heart can do the job.[13]

A professional discipline has never been regarded as a substitute for love in the heart. Love in the heart and something in the head have always been viewed as the ideal combination. Because of the problem described above, however, there may be a tendency to take love in the heart for granted and make professional discipline stand out as a contrast, as an either/or proposition, rather than as both/and.

Social work as we know it today is young, we might say in its adolescence. Two world wars and a depression have forced it to run before it was ready to walk, and to become articulate before it was ready to talk. Like the adolescent who is so concerned about his own problems and seeks the security of his own group against what he regards as a hostile adult world, so too the social worker fearful of outside scrutiny and criticism may at times show the tendency to seek security within his own fashioned concepts and theories, in a sense within his own "peer" culture. Social work has built its relative feeling of security and status in a period which emphasized differences as the rationale for existence. Today we are moving rapidly toward an interdisciplinary approach with its emphasis on looking for similarities. As social work shares its approach with the social sciences it will face much criticism. The challenge is to be able to maintain a spirit of self-objectification, rather than in adolescent fashion to withdraw among its own and to utilize its body of knowledge to defend itself by analyzing the motives of the critics rather than what they say. If social work follows its historical traditions it should have no great difficulty, for one of its great strengths has been its flexibility in being able to change in helping to meet new needs growing out of the changing economic, political, and social climate.

Citizen Participation in the Social Welfare Program

Explicit in all four papers is the importance of citizen participation. Professor Haber states that "social welfare must win and hold wide public understanding and support if it is to continue to receive an increasing share of public funds." Professor Allport includes public apathy as one of the limits of social service. He states:

All in all, public attitudes are conservative, far more so as a rule than the attitudes of those who are active in social welfare. It is, therefore, a major frustration of our calling that those who are engaged in its practice will be limited and often defeated by public ignorance and apathy.

Dr. Davidson emphasizes that genuine citizenship participation in both public and private fields is growing less and less. The tendency seems to be to utilize the citizen as a source of expanding funds for social welfare programs through an appeal to his heart, but not enough appeal to his mind to help find a solution to the problems with which we are confronted. He observes that even in the private, voluntary agency, where there is a "large area of opportunity for genuine, intelligent, citizen participation," there is a growing tendency "to rely on the agency executive to evolve policy, subject only to the passive acquiescence and approval of the citizen board."

Again, with our zeal to professionalize, it is almost as if we are saying that the addition of professional staff alone will solve the complex problems of the day. If prevention is our intent, citizen volunteers must have a role that goes far beyond just fund raising. They must be encouraged to become interpreters and doers for improving the level of the total institutional structure which affects the lives of people. In order to achieve this, our training of volunteers must emphasize objectives and principles more than it does. What we need are not amateur social workers with an amateur knowledge of methods and techniques, but rather citizen volunteers who understand the place of social welfare in a democracy. Their contact with our agencies should give them the type of knowledge about social problems that makes them better informed citizens on the general welfare of the community. In this scheme of things social agencies must reverse the trend toward becoming a housing unit for a professional staff and return to a larger sense of social responsibility. From their accumulated knowledge of work with particular individuals, they should be in an excellent position to give leadership to the community in matters pertaining to the human welfare of people in general. Democratic goals can be achieved only through a real partnership between the professional and the citizen.

As we move ahead professionally, we might give heed to the following observation by William James:

> Most human institutions, by the purely technical and professional manner in which they come to be administered, end by becoming obstacles to the very purpose which their founders had in view. Notoriously the great reforms in many at least of the professions and institutions have been first advocated, or at least have been greatly aided, by laymen rather than by the official keepers of the seal. And there is reason arising from the very nature of a professional and technical institution why it should easily get out of touch with human life. For the scientific and the technical is necessarily the objective, the impersonal, the intellectual, as distinguished from the subjective, the personal, the individual, the emotional. It gives us, as Professor Royce phrases it, the world of description, not the world of appreciation.[14]

WHAT OF THE FUTURE?

An attempt has been made not only to discuss the myriad of problems as they appear in the present, but also to fill in some of the historical data which have a bearing on them; for to gaze into the future involves knowing not only where we are but also what has happened to us along the way. In the area of unmet needs it is quite evident that there is a sizable job ahead on both a quantitative and qualitative basis if the health and welfare of our nation is to be dealt with on a level befitting a democratic nation.

The pattern for meeting these needs also should be evident. Certainly, without an ever expanding role on the part of government, progress cannot be made. It may be helpful to keep in mind that the trend toward government responsibility for health and welfare is not one that suddenly emerged, but rather has been growing, at a varying rate, certainly since the days of Theodore Roosevelt. Although there is today in many quarters a more articulated abhorrence and fear of the philosophy of the welfare state, President Eisenhower's State of the Union messages do not indicate a withdrawal of the Federal government from its responsibility in meeting the health and welfare needs of the nation. The method and timing may differ, but the Federal government is still very much in the picture.

As a nation we have been able to rationalize at least the emergency concept of the Welfare State, and we tend to forget that the past decades—including as they did a major depression and two world wars—have represented 40 years of emergency living. It does not take much crystal gazing to observe that the present state of affairs, with its alternating cold and hot war climate and growing arms race, also represents a period of emergency which may well continue for several decades. In periods of this kind, government cannot default in its role of responsibility toward the total national security. This in turn calls for planning in all areas of the nation's program.

In brief, even though we seem to be backing into the conception of the Welfare State negatively, the course of events has been such, and will continue to be such, that even as we protest against it there is not much we can do to stop it, for survival depends on it. Thus we find the present Administration projecting a liberal program for improving the old-age insurance system. True it has avoided moving ahead in other related areas, such as unemployment insurance and minimum wage, but only because the economic situation is still fluid enough to permit it to gamble. The Administration knows, however, that the *laissez-faire* philosophy, with its emphasis on rugged individualism, can be carried only to a point, for vivid in their minds is the fact that such a philosophy was defeated during the depression by America's deeply rooted humanitarian and democratic mores, and can be defeated again if people's needs are not met.

It is no accident that the group who would turn the clock back to an earlier conception of meeting human needs contains the core of or is closely related to those who are gambling with the destruction of our basic human values. They know only too well that unless our deeply rooted humanitarian and democratic values are confused and destroyed, they cannot hope to win an all-out war against the social gains of the past several decades. The attack, therefore, against the personnel of those institutions which are the transmitters of basic values, such as the teachers, the clergy, and the social workers, is deliberate. The growth of the democratic pattern of meeting needs will be stopped if this particular group is successful; their success means the destruction of our democratic society. If social workers are hesitant about their role and responsibility in this present conflict, and rationalize that it does not fall within our special area of competence, let us remember that our methods and objectives are so intimately related to the system of humanitarian and democratic values that destruction of the values means death to social work.

The problems of the role and relationship of private and public agencies, and coordination of services both within and between them, are related to the issues discussed above. The dilemma in moving toward a greater acceptance of a both/and conception of public and private agencies and toward greater coordination and planning is intimately tied up with our American mores, with our deeply rooted tradition of individualism, and our corresponding fear of anything that implies a planned society. Our humanitarian motivation enables us during periods of crises such as depressions and wars to move toward a planning concept, but once the crises have passed there is a tug to return to "business as usual." Fortunately, there is a sufficient residue left from each cooperative venture to prevent a complete return to the *status quo ante*. Part of the tug toward a return to "business as usual" is tied up with our almost naive view that the interdependence of society is something temporary and belonging only to the period of crisis. We tend to disregard the fact that technological advances, including improved communications and transportation, give a permanence to the concept of interdependence. The more interdependent a society, the more organized it must be to meet its needs, if we mean by "organized" a growing perspective in all groups that the yardstick of policy must be in terms of the relation to the welfare as a whole. This is part of the equalitarian movement expressed in the writings of our founding fathers and further articulated in the social and economic advances of the past two decades.

Better coordination and planning is a priority. We must, therefore, rethink both our goals and our methods if the modern type of agency like modern man is not to become obsolescent in a rapidly moving world. We must move agencies from agency-centeredness to a better understanding of the concept of interdependence. Might not thinking interdependently include the following?

1. Reaffirmation of the principle that agencies are a means to an end and not an end in themselves—that the end sought by all agencies is the welfare of the individual.

2. Reaffirmation of the principle that the welfare of any individual is inextricably interwoven with the welfare of the whole. Therefore, all agencies must be concerned with the development of material, human, and social resources to meet all the needs of all the people, rather than the vested-interest

approach of one segment of the population, of a particular agency or a particular organized group.

3. Recognition that, although agencies may utilize different highways and byways to reach these goals and such differences can contribute to the richness of the whole, there is need for sufficient emphasis of similarities as well as differences if over-all goals are to be achieved.

4. Recognition of the local community as the macrocosm of social existence, but at the same time recognition that many of the problems affecting the local community are related to factors on the state, national, and international levels, and therefore cannot be dealt with by the local communities alone, but must rather be dealt with in relation to higher and broader forms of community planning and coordination.

5. Recognition of the national community as another form of relationship in meeting common problems rather than as different from and in competition with the local community.

The question of increased finances for social services is to a large measure dependent on how quickly the cold-war climate can be relaxed. Social services have had always to compete with other services for a fair share of the national income. Competition with national defense, which is absorbing 68 cents of every dollar the government spends, is not an easy task. Even within a budget of this type, more money can be made available for social services if the importance of the services to the objectives of the nation are properly understood. The real task, therefore, is to bring back into the open forum again the thesis that the furthering of human welfare and human rights not only in this country, but also in the total world scene, is an essential weapon in a total peace offensive. We know that throughout history man has often resorted to the force of arms when he has been faced with unsatisfied political, economic, and social needs in his life situation. A total peace offensive must help meet these needs. Strength of arms is not a total plan for any nation, and by itself is no plan at all. Unless our objectives become clearer, and the importance of health and welfare services in relation to these objectives better understood, we shall find it difficult to obtain an expanding share of the government dollar for social services both at home and abroad.

One important area where the economic impact is being felt is the continuing drop in the enrollment of students in schools of social work. There has been a drop of 9.8 per cent since 1949, or a decrease of 392 full-time students from the 1949 total of 3,625. Of this total, 2,276 were enrolled in private and 1,349 in public universities. The drop in the tax-supported schools where tuition is minimum was 2.7 per cent whereas in the private schools it was 13.5 per cent. Evidently, the cost of social-work education and the salary competition from other types of services with higher status play an important role. In view of the shortage of trained social workers in both public and private services, this trend is a serious one. Government subsidy for fellowships is essential if trained personnel are to be made available.

In essence we have been discussing the present climate and its meaning for social work. It is obvious that the economic, political, and social climate affects social services markedly; unfortunately more than social services affect the climate. This is another way of pointing up the importance of forming a partnership of social work with the people if its democratic goals are to be achieved. The tendency to move away from the citizen as we professionalize can be only self-defeating in meeting the needs and attaining the objectives which brought the profession into being.

Finally, what of social work as a profession in the future? There is no question that the demand for trained workers will grow. What, however, should be the direction in which we move? Some of the problems which need attention have been outlined earlier. They include greater critical scrutiny; broadening the body of knowledge to include more social science content; a better integration of objectives, principles, and methods; an intensification of the partnership with the citizen; and a stronger emphasis on the social responsibility of all, including the agencies.

Perhaps most important to the question of direction is how we view our objectives, how broad or narrow our perspective is, how concerned we are about prevention rather than remedy. As stated by Marie Jahoda:

> At the present cost of psychiatric treatment, and in view of the relative scarcity of psychiatrists and the magnitude of the problem, the knowledge that psychiatry can restore mental health of young people contains, unfortunately, no promise that the mental health of a generation can be improved.[15]

Prevention necessitates not only a better knowledge of how to work with the individual, but also a better understanding of and greater responsibility toward the social conditions conducive to mental health. A Dean of one of the Scandinavian Schools of Social Work pointed up the problem as follows during a recent visit with me: She stated that in her country the primary concern is to see that the social institutions function adequately. Even if they are functioning adequately, she went on to say, there are some people who need help in utilizing them. These people become the core of the social-work load. In this country, however, she observed, no one worries about social institutions. Everyone works with individuals and hopes that through some magic by working with enough individuals social institutions will be changed.

Social work must not lose its traditional concern for social conditions and social justice. Furthermore social justice and concern for democratic values cannot be fragmented into a partial methodology. For example, our concept of self-determination, our helping individuals to make their own choices, is democratic in that it frees them of an authoritative outsider telling them what to do. It is only one-half of the process, however; for freedom from authority does not mean freedom from fact. If the social conditions include such factors as hunger, poor housing, inadequate medical care, unemployment, low wages, etc., the individual really has no alternatives to choose from. In this type of situation self-determination can become a manipulative, deceptive, and *status quo* concept, unless we take the responsibility for helping to loosen the environment so that there are alternatives.

As we face the future, we must give more emphasis to the place of social work in society today. Our concern must be the furthering and development of social work and not just of the social worker. This involves a training program which educates for professional responsibilities rather than just for professional practice. Our future social worker must be not only "skillful in the diagnosis and treatment of the individual and group problems which he meets in day to day practice," but also able "to speak with knowledge and understanding of the wider social issues involved," and with "authority on possible courses of action and development for society as a whole."[16]

We cannot predict the future, for there are many unknown variables. We do know, however, that what we will be we are now becoming. The way in which we approach our responsibility toward "Man's right to knowledge, and the free use thereof" will help determine where we arrive. It is a three-dimensional task. First, we must work shoulder to shoulder with others in the struggle to maintain a democratic climate, for our continued existence as a nation of people ruled by and for the people, for only then will man have the right to knowledge and the free use thereof. Secondly, we must demonstrate the value of knowledge by making full use of it within a framework of self-objectification and constant critical scrutiny. Thirdly, we must regard knowledge, not as an end in itself, but as a means to an end, namely, a better life for all mankind.

FOOTNOTES

1. Merriam, I. C., *Social Security Bulletin,* Feb. 1953, Vol. 16, No. 2, p. 11.
2. Merriam, I. C., *op. cit.*
3. Allen, F. L., in *Economic Security for Americans,* The American Assembly, Columbia University, 1953, p. 18.
4. Wisner, Elizabeth, "War and Social Services," *Proceedings, National Conference of Social Work,* 1944.
5. Richmond, M. E., *What Is Social Case Work?,* New York, Russell Sage Foundation, 1927, pp. 98–99.
6. Allen, F. E., *op. cit.,* p. 12.
7. Burns, E., "The Role of Government in Social Welfare," paper delivered at National Conference of Social Work, May 10, 1954.
8. *Ibid.*
9. Merriam, I. C., *op. cit.,* p. 12.
10. Flexner, Abraham, "Is Social Work a Profession?" *Proceedings of the National Conference of Charities and Corrections,* 1915.
11. Bruno, Frank J., *Trends in Social Work,* Columbia University Press, New York, 1948, p. 141.
12. Allport, G. W., "The Genius of Kurt Lewin," *Journal of Social Issues,* Supplementary Series No. 1, Dec. 1948, p. 16–17.
13. Dollard, Charles, in *Bulletin of the New York School of Social Work,* Sept. 1952, p. 4.
14. Tufts, James H., *Education and Training for Social Work,* Russell Sage Foundation, New York, p. 30.

15. Jahoda, Marie, "Toward a Social Psychology of Mental Health," Research Center for Human Relations, N. Y. University, 1950, pp. 4–5.

16. Hoban, E. R., Unpublished Report on Observation of Social Work in the U.S.

PARTICIPANTS

GORDON ALLPORT, Professor of Psychology, Harvard University

MRS. ALFRED R. BACHRACH, Vice President, U. S. O.

PIERRE BEDARD, President, Parsons School of Design

ROBERT BONDY, Director, National Social Welfare Assembly

NATHAN E. COHEN, Professor of Social Work, New York School of Social Work

GEORGE DAVIDSON, Deputy Minister of National Welfare, Canada

MARGARET EMERY, Children's Bureau, Department of Health, Education, and Welfare

PERRIN C. GALPIN, Executive Director, The Grant Foundation

LESTER B. GRANGER, Executive Director, National Urban League, Inc.

WILLIAM HABER, Professor of Economics, University of Michigan

GORDON HAMILTON, Associate Dean, New York School of Social Work

JANE HOEY, Director, Division of Social Research, National Tuberculosis Association

LAURIN HYDE, Executive Director, National Travelers Aid Association

KENNETH D. JOHNSON, Dean, New York School of Social Work, Columbia University

ALFRED J. KAHN, Associate Professor of Social Work, New York School of Social Work, Columbia University

DOROTHY C. KAHN, Chief, Social Service Section, United Nations

MARION KENWORTHY, Professor of Psychiatry, New York School of Social Work

JOHN C. KIDNEIGH, Director, School of Social Work, University of Minnesota

MRS. JOSEPH P. LASH, Executive Director, Citizens Committee on Children

ERNEST NAGEL, Professor of Philosophy, Columbia University

ERNEST OSBORNE, Professor of Education, Teachers College, Columbia University

THE RIGHT REVEREND DAVID E. RICHARDS, Bishop, Diocese of Albany

ARTHUR L. SWIFT, JR., Professor of Church and Community, Union Theological Seminary

HERBERT WECHSLER, Professor of Law, Columbia University

FREDERICK WINANT, U. S. Office of Defense Mobilization

ELLEN WINSTON, Commissioner of Public Welfare, Department of Public Welfare, North Carolina

DONALD YOUNG, General Director, Russell Sage Foundation

BENJAMIN YOUNGDAHL, Dean, George Warren Brown School of Social Work, Washington University

PART FIVE
Income Security for a Free People

INTRODUCTION

The purpose of Part Five was to identify some of the major issues pertinent to the formulation of sound national policies in the field of income security, and to inquire into the contribution which a university might make to their solution or clarification. Because other parts of the conference dealt with health insurance for medical care and with government action looking toward maintenance of full employment, these topics were not covered by this Part, which focused upon income security measures in the more technical sense, (social insurance, public assistance, income-conditioned pensions and statutory cash benefits) as well as private industrial pensions and guaranteed wage plans. In view of the underlying concern of the whole conference with the problem of the apparent conflict between the values of individualism and of social collectivism, attention was paid to its specific manifestations in the public measures concerned with economic insecurity. This issue figured prominently in discussions of the question of the nature and level of income security to be assured and the methods of financing the programs.

Four papers were prepared and distributed to all participants prior to the conference. At each session, the author gave a 15-minute summary of his main points or emphasized those which he would like to see more extensively analyzed. This was followed by brief comments from one or two discussants, and thereafter the meeting was thrown open for general discussion. The major papers and the comments of the discussants are given *in extenso* in what follows, with a summary of the general discussion prepared by the Reporters.

Certain broad themes or general conclusions emerged from the series of meetings. In the first place, it was noteworthy that the group as a whole appeared to attach little importance to alleged conflicts between the assurance of minimum economic security and individual freedom, at least in societies where the spirit of individualism and democracy is vigorous. Again and again the point was made that without a minimum of economic security there can be no real freedom, and that for most people public income security systems represent an extension, rather than a limitation, of freedom. Attention was drawn to the fact, however, that some types of public assistance programs submit the applicant to certain social controls not applied to other persons and thus restrict his freedom to behave in his own manner. But this was regarded, not as an argument against all efforts to assure income security, but as a reason for rejecting some systems in favor of others.

At the same time, since in a democracy the ultimate safeguard of freedom lies in the willingness of the citizens to accept the responsibilities of self-government, concern was expressed that more attention had not been paid, with the development of comprehensive public income security programs, to the twin problems of ensuring popular understanding of the issues at stake and of enlisting the participation of the beneficiaries and/or the wider citizenry in policy-making and appropriate phases of administration.

The problem of incentive, of the effect of income security payments and of the taxes levied to finance them on the will to work and to save, received more attention. While apparently believing that this was a more realistic problem than that of the effects upon freedom (at various points it was shown that the two were often confused in popular discussion) the conference brought out that this too is not a general problem inevitable in, or even common to, all types of social security systems and affecting all the people all the time. Furthermore, it was noted that the problem is not peculiar to public security programs; it may arise also in industry, or collectively-bargained income security plans.

Some types of income security programs are better devised than others for dealing with this problem (a general preference was indicated, for example, for a wage-related benefit system in a country such as the United States). Some types and levels of taxes might have adverse effects on incentive; others would not. It was also shown that there is a variety of devices which can be embodied in the provisions of income security systems and tend to keep to a minimum adverse effects on the will to work.

It was, however, recognized that certain groups of workers with a relatively weak attachment to the labor market, namely young workers, married women, and the habitually "work-shy" or casual worker, present a problem for which appropriate solutions have not yet been devised.

One broad conclusion emerged from the discussion: the danger of making broad generalizations about income security programs as such which would be valid for all types of democratic societies, or at all times within any one country. It was clear that income security measures have assumed a great diversity of forms, and that even within any one form, such as social insurance or public assistance, differences in specific provisions of the law will have very different economic and social effects. The quality of administration was also shown to influence vitally the impact of the program.

Furthermore, throughout the discussion it emerged again and again how greatly, in a democratic society, the nature of the income security program itself, and the effects of its specific provisions, will be influenced by the characteristics of that society at any given time. Among these are economic conditions (levels and trends of national income, patterns of income distribution, differentials in wages between occupations and geographical areas); demographic characteristics (broad population trends, changing proportions in different age groups and notably the balance between those in the employable ages and those too old or too young to work); employment conditions and practices (willingness of employers to hire old or female workers, the presence or absence of seniority rules, fringe benefits, and other factors tending to attach a worker to his job, the force of collective bargaining, and the nature of the principles governing wage determination); patterns of family life (whether or not it is normal for wives to work, and the extent and nature of the burdens of rearing children); and political conditions (even in a democracy, the political system may be more or less well-designed to give proper representation to minority and majority views).

Social attitudes, too, were revealed to be equally decisive in influencing the type of income security system adopted at any given time and its specific effects. Among these are attitudes toward the desirability of economic security itself and what people mean by that term; attitudes to the family system (the nature and extent of mutual responsibility for support among members of the family); attitudes toward maintaining status and toward what it is that confers status; attitudes toward government (and in particular the extent to which people trust their government and believe that it is responsive to the will of the majority rather than to special groups); attitudes toward those who are in economic need (whether they are regarded as responsible for their own condition or as the victims of circumstances, and if the latter, how generously the community desires to make provision for them); and attitudes toward economic inequality as such.

It was clear from the discussion, too, that any democratic society aiming to assure income security has to make some difficult choices between competing values. Among these are such questions as how to draw the line between equity and adequacy, between the objective of ensuring that benefits reflect previous differences in wages or contributions and the objective of assuring a realistic minimum of security even to the lowest-paid worker; the extent to which the vast mass of self-respecting and responsible income security beneficiaries are to be penalized by provisions written into the law to protect society against the malingerer or the work-shy; the allocation of social security costs among different categories of people, when considerations of economics and of "fairness" point in different directions; and the extent to which the advantages of local self-government are to be sacrificed in order to assure a minimum of security to all citizens, wherever they may reside.

Finally, the conference revealed all too many areas in which income security policy today has to be formulated on the basis of assumptions, rather than verified knowledge. Among the areas in which research might enable a nation to ground its policies more securely on fact rather than theory are the specific role of economic, as compared with other incentives to work and save; the nature of prevailing attitudes toward security; the actual role of economic factors in fostering family stability and sense of coherence; attitudes toward retirement, toward means tests of various kinds, and toward status. Research was shown to be needed also to determine the specific consequences of particular provisions in the income security programs. Among these are the extent to which the contributory method of financing achieves its objectives; the extent to which social security payments are a burden on the economy; whether or not interstate and international competition affect or are affected by income security programs; the stabilizing effects of experience-rating programs; the actual level of living assured by various types of income security systems; the effectiveness of various controls embodied in the programs; the specific nature and extent of the problems of administering disability insurance programs; the nature and extent of abuse; and the effectiveness of different methods of enlisting public interest and participation.

It was here, the conferees believed, that the universities had a great role to play. Much of this research could not suitably be carried out by the public agencies administering income security programs, either because the investigations would be so broad as to preclude their support from funds granted for program administration, or because it would be difficult for them impartially to investigate the consequences of programs for whose policies and administration they were responsible.

By training more research workers with special skills for this type of inquiry, by paying more attention in the curriculum to this important area of social policy, and by fostering and supporting research undertakings, the university could make a major contribution to the development of income security programs compatible with the objectives of a free society.

Eveline M. Burns
Professor of Social Work
New York School of Social Work
Columbia University

Major Issues Raised by Contemporary Trends in Income Security Policies

Pierre Laroque

Honorary Director General
Social Security Administration, France

The spreading of the idea of social security is one of the major facts which have dominated social policies throughout the world during recent years. In a great number of countries social security schemes have been planned and put into execution. Governments, private institutions, employers, workers' unions, separately or in cooperation with each other, have contributed more or less to the elaboration or the enforcement of social security measures.

Achievement of income security is the main aim of these efforts. One must not underestimate the other aspects of social security policies, the importance of the health service for example, or the new trend towards psychological security sought by a better organization of family relations. But the main preoccupation of the individuals in all countries is to be sure that, in all circumstances, they will be able to provide for themselves and their dependents at an acceptable standard of life or to keep the standard of life they have attained.

Such a preoccupation might at first sight be considered as a permanent human characteristic. Why are social security policies so recent? Why has the idea itself spread so fast and with such success during the last years? To answer these questions we have to analyze first the factors influencing the need for security and its evolution. This will lead us to understand the progressive transformation of the institutions tending towards the satisfaction of that need, the actual trends of the income security policies resulting from this evolution, and the major issues raised by those trends, mainly in the relations between individuals and families on the one hand, and the collective institutions providing income security on the other.

THE NEED FOR SECURITY

The existence and the importance of the need for income security directly result from the feeling of insecurity of the mass of the people. That feeling itself is affected by a number of various factors, of an economic, demographic, psychological, ideological, and political nature.

Economic factors

It is obvious that the feeling of security or insecurity of a population largely depends on economic conditions. The determining element is not the wealth or the poverty of the country—the feeling of insecurity is often more widespread among inhabitants of a rich country than among those of a poor one—but the type of civilization of the population concerned.

In a country of *traditional rural and handicraft* civilization, the need for income security is felt to a relatively small extent. First, in such a country the conditions are stable; there is little prospect that the situation of an individual or a family may be modified by external factors. The same piece of land or the same shop is often kept by the same family for hundreds of years. Secondly, the people are generally unable to think of anything else but the status which has always been theirs and their ancestors': their education and their knowledge of the external world do not enable them to aspire to new conditions of life, as long in any case as they are not submitted to external influences. Thirdly and chiefly, in a civilization of such a type, income security is achieved, in a way by itself, through the family. The family is an economic unit as well as a social group. It identifies itself with the farm or with the handicraft undertaking. Each member of the family takes part in the productive activities of the group; he really has no personal income distinct from the income of the family, on which depends the subsistence of all. The family is generally large, including two or three, sometimes four generations, depending on the size of the farm or the shop. The common income and family solidarity provide for the security of all. Children, sick, crippled, and old people are supported by the group as a whole.

In such circumstances there is no individual insecurity but only possibly a collective insecurity threatening the whole family. But causes of insecurity of that kind have more a political or an economic character than a social one. The political risk is that the tenant may lose his farm owing to the local status of his tenure; in that sense new agrarian legislation, protecting the farmers against abusive eviction, contribute substantially to the achievement of income security among rural populations. The same could be said of the measures tending to protect the farmers against the loss of their crops or livestock. Though such measures are not generally considered as part of social security legislation, their aim is mainly income security. In any case, the achievement of income security in rural and handicraft civilizations can hardly be separated from a more general policy aiming at better conditions of rural and artisan economics.

If, in the most developed countries, rural populations often ask for the extension of social security legislation established for the urban and industrial populations, that is mainly because they consider those laws as bringing new privileges to the people who get their benefits and want not to be excluded from such privileges. And just as the rural populations try thus to follow the example of the urban ones, underdeveloped countries often try to follow the example of the more developed, without always considering if the measures they want to extend or introduce are really adapted to their own needs.

The fact is that the need for income security, such as it now exists, has its origin in the development of industrial civilization. First, industry has created new causes of insecurity: economic causes, such as unemployment, resulting from economic crises, unknown at least to such an extent in the past; technical causes, bringing industrial accidents or diseases or obliging workers to stop working at a rather early age because of the new character of industrial work.

Secondly, the new industrial civilization has resulted in a disruption of the family, henceforth unable in most cases by working as a unit to provide for the security of its members. The family is not in that sense an economic unit any more. The typical undertaking today extends beyond the scope of the family, depriving the family group of its former economic basis. The parents, often both parents, may work outside the group, spending a considerable part of their time far from each other and far from their dependents. The worker lives day by day from rather modest earnings which do not allow him in most cases to save and accumulate reserves for difficult times to come. Even if the earnings are high enough to provide a decent standard of life for the worker, his wife, and his children, they cannot cover the exceptional expenses required by a severe illness, and still less provide for the subsistence of old people, unemployed or crippled. Any cessation of work means total destitution for the whole family group.

At the same time the need for income security considerably increases owing to the economic and technical causes mentioned above and because of the longer duration of human life resulting in an enormous increase of the number of old people, and the old instrument of security (the family) is no longer in a position to carry out its mission. Insecurity is henceforth a permanent threat.

In addition, this insecurity is one of the main factors of the feeling of dependence, of the inferiority complex which characterizes the working class in many countries. And the increasing effort of that class to free itself from dependence, to react against inferiority, is largely directed towards more security, towards the suppression of the uncertainty about the future which affects all who live on the product of their work. The constant pressure of the mass of the workers, as well as the unrest which may result from their pressure, adds new force to the general trend towards income security.

But while there is a general evolution from the traditional rural and handicraft civilization towards urban and industrial civilization, the populations show actually considerable differences. The most important part of the world population still lives in civilizations of the earlier type. Among the others, the degree of industrialization is very unequal. The need for income security is quite different from one country to another, and the differences are not only of degree but even of kind. If often the same words are used, income security in fact has not the same meaning.

The level of the individual income also has an influence on the nature of the income security problem. Indeed, the people who are the most deeply attached to that security are not always, and perhaps not generally, the poorest. People who have a certain tolerable standard of life often are more zealous to keep their property and income intact than are poor people who have less at stake. The better-off are in a position to save on their normal incomes a certain amount to provide for their own security; as far as income security is attained by individual effort, they feel no need for intervention by the community. The extent of the necessary income security legislation is largely determined by the average level of individual incomes, mainly wages, and by the distribution of those incomes and wages among the populations. The fact is that the social security institutions have been specially developed in countries where the individual incomes and wages may seem rather high if compared with less developed countries, but where income security was or had been threatened by special circumstances which had led or could lead to a reduction in the average income level or to a modification in the distribution of the national income.

Demographic factors

The insecurity of a population largely depends on the demographic conditions of the country. In overpopulated areas there is generally a low average income and much permanent unemployment. The mass of the population is underfed. Most of the people live in a state close to destitution. The word security cannot have the same meaning in such conditions as it has in a rich and prosperous country with a small population relative to the national income.

In a country with a low birth rate, on the other hand, the security of the whole community may seem threatened by the possible reduction of the population. The decline of the active population may result in lower production and thus in an impoverishment of the country. This explains why a social security policy may tend toward encouraging births. Some family allowances schemes show the mark of that concern.

But in modern countries the demographic factor which most affects income security is more probably the increase of the duration of life. The proportion of old people is becoming larger and larger. For example, in most countries of Western Europe more than 14 per 100 of the population are over 60, and in France the proportion is close to 17 per 100, as compared with about 10 per 100 in the United States. A social security scheme supposes that the involuntarily inactive population is taken care of by the active population. The burden of such a scheme increases as the ratio of the inactive to the active population rises. The increase of the number of old people adds to that burden. The total risk of insecurity is greater, and greater also is the difficulty of providing for it.

What is true of a whole community is also true of an individual or a family.

The degree of security of an individual or a family varies with the number of persons included in the household. The presence of numerous dependent children results in a diminution of the standard of life and a greater difficulty of saving, thus increasing the gravity of the factors causing insecurity. Not only does the illness or the invalidity of a dependent bring a new burden to the family, but the illness, the invalidity, the unemployment, or the death of the breadwinner has much deeper consequences than in the case of a bachelor, because the whole family is threatened by the loss of the normal earnings of its head. It is always a mistake to speak of the security of individuals. Social security and income security are essentially the security of a family.

It is thus easy to understand that the need for income security and consequently the extension and the character of the social security schemes vary considerably from one country to another owing to the demographic conditions in each of them.

Psychological, ideological, and political factors

If income security essentially depends on economic and demographic factors, security itself is a psychological concept, the feeling that one is not submitted to any serious threat, that tomorrow will be like today, if not better. The need for security is part of human nature. Some people like risks, are stimulated by the uncertainty of the future; they are rare exceptions. The feeling of insecurity has always been and is still today the origin of more or less violent reactions, resulting in unrest or in revolutions. But it is only in countries with a high degree of civilization that the real nature, the causes of the feeling of insecurity, can be fully understood. In underdeveloped countries, and even among the mass of the population in many modern countries, the feeling of insecurity remains confused and the reactions it provokes are often not understood. This explains why income security policies are so recent and also why they have been built up progressively, empirically, in response to the pressure of circumstances.

The nineteenth century has been marked by the conquest of political freedom in most Western countries. Political freedom by itself means security, elimination of arbitrariness in the government, the administration, the police. Men hate arbitrariness as well as disorder; both are aspects of insecurity. Behind the occasional circumstances which explain the establishment or the removal of any political regime, the essential condition of the permanence of such a regime has to be found in the guaranties of security it offers, in the security the people expect from it. During long periods, the human aspiration for security was limited to political security. The frequent external threats and internal disorder gave to that want priority over any other consideration.

When political security is attained or considered as attained, men aspire to complete it by economic and social security. They want to be protected against the threat of possible destitution, and even against the effects of any event which could deprive them totally or partly of their means of livelihood. The aspiration toward income security is only one aspect of the human aspiration for security in general.

This aspiration reflects a certain stage in the psychological and sociological evolution of a certain group of the population. First it reflects a certain concept of justice. Income security policies are based on the admission that economic and social insecurity is unjust. Indeed, moral and religious principles have always fostered a fight against poverty, to help destitute people. But security means more than that: it means that justice requires abolition of want, and in addition the right of any individual not to be deprived of his normal standard of life because of economic and social factors which are beyond his control.

The modern aspiration for income security implies the common admission that it is possible to achieve such security, that the threats to be faced are not fatalities beyond the reach of man. To speak of an income security policy is to recognize that the human will is stronger than natural forces; moreover, that it is possible by human means to alter the normal effects of economic laws. This view would have been almost inconceivable at the time when the pure liberal doctrines (in the early nineteenth-century sense) were considered as absolute truth. Although income security is certainly not socialism, income security policies have been made possible through a psychological evolution largely due to the influence of socialist doctrines or at least antiliberal or nonliberal economic doctrines among which the socialist have been predominant.

Then, having admitted that something can or must be done to achieve income security, we face a conflict of principle which, consciously or not, has had a deep influence on recent social security schemes. Some think, in accord with the early liberal view, that achievement of security is primarily an individual responsibility. It is the individual first who must take care of his own existence and provide for the security of his income; the government need only help the efforts of these individuals by establishing adequate institutions. Others state that the community has the responsibility for the security of its members; security is a collective need, which can be satisfied only by collective means. The application of both concepts does not necessarily lead in practice to very different measures. But the spirit of the institutions and their general orientation are deeply affected by the prevailing principle.

In fact, the choice between these two concepts, as well as the impact of the ideas of social justice, depends on the social structure of the populations concerned, on the group which dominates political and social life.

In the United Kingdom, for example, where about 90 per cent of the economically active population are employees, the general attitude cannot be the same as in France where self-employed people, representing more than 35 per cent of the economically active population and including farmers, traders, artisans, individual manufacturers, and professional people, have a deep political influence. The propaganda of the various political parties as well as of the unions and associations of all sorts tends to create towards the security need a different spirit, which influences the policy enforced. Moreover, there are changes in political majorities and in the dominant group from time to time. Each one brings its own contribution to the general evolution of the collective psychology of the population and determines the orientation of the policy applied during that period.

The existence of the demand for security and the degree of security needed also bear the influence of circumstances. We have seen that in traditional rural and handicraft civilizations the problem of income security is not generally raised. The real reason for that situation is that such a civilization is essentially stable. One can hardly have a feeling of insecurity in a society which has not fundamentally changed for centuries, where every man and woman has the same conditions of life as his parents and ancestors and does not expect any change. The instability of modern civilization has been one of the main factors influencing the modern aspiration for security. In the United States the Federal Social Security Act (1935) resulted directly from the economic crisis which had started in 1929 and had upset the situation of so many people throughout the country, indeed throughout the world. The possibility of such crisis weakened the people's trust in the future and reinforced, if not created, the desire for guaranties of security.

The same could be said of the second World War, specially among the people who have severely suffered from it. Those people have come out of the war longing for security—security against war first of all, no doubt, but also against all the economic and social dangers which may threaten individual and family life. Such circumstances also contribute to make the demand for social justice more acute; differences of incomes and of standards of life are all the more resented as the impoverishment of the countries concerned often makes it impossible to provide a decent level of living to the mass of the people. Moreover, in such countries, the effort which was necessary owing to economic reconstruction involved extensive reliance on the workers; inevitably they were called upon for additional sacrifice and strain, in order that ruined equipment might be replaced and the countries restored to their former level of prosperity. To call for this effort without giving the workers certain guaranties in exchange was morally impossible; nor could the enthusiasm and the will to work, which are so essential to productive efficiency, be obtained from them unless they were at the same time relieved of the danger of poverty tomorrow—in fact, unless they were given real social security.

Another circumstance which contributes to create or to increase the desire for income security is the instability of money. The depreciation of the currency deeply modifies the economic and social equilibrium of a population. Specially, by depriving savings of a large part of their value, inflation brings a number of old people to complete destitution. That again results in a general feeling of insecurity, in an aspiration of the mass of the population for new guaranties of income security.

These examples show that the problem of income security cannot be defined in abstract and general terms. Its scope and its character vary in large measure not only with the economic and demographic conditions of each country and each social group but also with the contingent factors which determine the psychology of a given country at a given moment. If there are general trends in income security policies, they are because of the increasing interdependence of all parts of the contemporary world, because of the common characters of the economic, demographic, and ideological evolution, because of the influence exercised everywhere by the same world events.

GENERAL EVOLUTION OF THE INSTITUTIONS PROVIDING FOR INCOME SECURITY

Even though social security policies as we understand them today are recent, all countries and all regimes have known some kind of legislation or institutions contributing to the achievement of certain aspects of what we today call social security.

Assistance

Assistance has been the first and oldest method used to help people deprived of means of living. It has involved the extension to a wider group of the principles of family help. The solidarity existing within a tribe or a parish led to provision for the needs of destitute individuals or families in the same way as the family normally provided for the needs of its members. But the concept of assistance has been progressively widened, first on moral and religious grounds, secondly by the extension of the activities of government at a higher level, partly substituting for local authorities and embodying national solidarity.

Most, if not all, religions put emphasis on charity as a moral obligation of all members of a community. In addition to individual charity, a number of private or religious institutions in nearly all countries help poor and destitute people. Such methods have the advantages first of an extreme flexibility permitting an adaptation of the kind and importance of the help to all individual situations, and secondly of keeping a human touch in the manner the help is given. On the other hand, the personal relations between the assisted people and those who give assistance, expressing an inequality of social conditions, have a humiliating character. And, above all, the resources of individuals or private institutions are generally too small and inadequate to the need.

This explains the great development of *public assistance,* both at the local and at the national level. Often public assistance simply corresponds to the use by local or national authorities of the methods of private assistance. If these authorities freely decide in each case whom they want to assist and to what extent they want to give assistance, such a system gives no real feeling of security to the assisted people. Admittedly the existence of public assistance institutions, as well as of private agencies, may encourage the needy to hope that if necessary they will not remain without help; but the uncertainty of the decisions to be taken by the competent agencies may endanger any feeling of security resulting from such a hope. Therefore in a number of countries assistance has become a right, guaranteed by a judicial process: if certain conditions are fulfilled, mainly related to the level of the individual or family resources, the benefits of the assistance legislation have to be awarded without any possibility of arbitrary decision. The existence of a right to public assistance is a real and important element of security.

Even those formulas of public assistance, however, have a limited efficiency. First, they can be applied only to definite and restricted categories of people. The essential condition of any kind of such assistance lies in the means test. Assistance can aid only the most destitute people, or in any case the individuals or families having a very low income. Today the need for income security is felt by much larger groups of the population. An increasing number of individuals and families, sometimes nearly the whole population of a country, although they cannot be considered as having a specially low income, want to be protected against the eventual loss of their normal income, of their standard of life. Second, from a psychological and moral standpoint, assistance, in the sense of relief in exigency, is never a good method to rely upon. It gives to the assisted people the habit of expecting part or the whole of their resources from the outside; it deprives them of their sense of responsibility; it brings moral if not material destitution.

This does not mean that the assistance method is, or must be, abandoned. While it has ceased to be the sole way of helping people in need, no country today has been able to renounce using it. There is everywhere a group of the population, more or less important, for which assistance is necessary, as a complement to or a substitute for other social security institutions.

A special mention must be made of a kind of private assistance which has a quite peculiar character; that is, the help given by an employer to his employees. In most industrial countries, an important number of employers allow various benefits to their employees in need: sickness allowances, old-age pensions, family allowances. In Western Europe family allowances were originally established by employers. These actions have their basis either in moral preoccupations—the concept that the authority exercised by the employer must have its counterpart in an obligation of tutelage, of protection of the employees—or in principles of economic and rational management, the employees' feeling of security being a condition of good labor relations. From the standpoint of income security, the benefits thus provided appear as a complement to the security of employment: the employer guarantees that the equivalent of at least a part of his wages will be paid to the employee who becomes unable to work or retires. But the link established between the benefit and employment also marks the limit of the real security provided: the employee loses the guaranty if he loses his job. The importance of the loss of a job is increased and so also is the feeling of dependence of the employees in their relation with their employer. The situation may be different when the benefits guaranteed by the employers are provided for in collective agreements or paid through workers' unions. But in such cases one cannot speak any longer of assistance by employers; income security is then a part of a new system of labor relations, including a social security partly based on collective bargaining.

Voluntary insurance

Systems of insurance, if this word is given its widest meaning, are nearly as old as assistance. In periods and countries where individuals have no independent existence outside of the group to which they belong, the same solidarity as existed in the family group could be found in local or craft groups. The old guilds used to guarantee certain benefits to their members in return for contributions paid. Assistance by local authorities and insurance by guilds were not so different as one could think at first sight. Both were expressions of a collective solidarity in limited circles.

At a later period voluntary insurance gave birth to two main kinds of institutions. In countries with old traditions of guilds and craftsmanship, nonprofit institutions had a lively development, mainly in the form of mutual aid societies. In new and young countries, where the tradition of mutual aid was not so strong, the first place has been taken by commercial insurance companies, namely in the field of life insurance.

Both kinds of institutions call for an effort by the individual to save from his normal income a certain amount which, through a collective fund, could either be distributed among the members struck by certain events or be capitalized to be given back as a pension or a lump sum at a certain time. This means that the efficiency of such institutions is limited to people having already a rather high degree of comfort and education, to people financially and morally able to save, permanently and periodically, part of their income. This cannot be expected from people with low incomes, living day by day on limited earnings. It requires also great moral strength not to spend the whole amount of a current income, especially when the income is not very high.

Just as assistance applies to poor people, voluntary insurance applies, if not only to rich people, at least to moderately well-off and somewhat informed or educated people. Such arrangements have specially thriven in countries with old traditions of mutual aid or with a high average individual income. In such countries they may be really efficient, if not always for the whole population, at least for an important part of it.

Compulsory insurance

The success and the considerable extension of systems of compulsory social insurance during the recent period have corresponded to the increasing importance in industrial countries of a category of people for whom neither assistance nor voluntary insurance is thoroughly adapted. Such people are normally able to provide for themselves as far as their own needs are concerned; they even are in a position which allows them to make a certain effort to provide for their future. But their income is not high enough to enable them to contribute in such a way as to cover all possible risks, chiefly because of the constant increase of threats to income. Moreover they may often be morally unable to contribute permanently if they are left to themselves to do so.

Therefore it has been necessary both to make insurance compulsory and to add to the contributions of the insured person contributions of the employer, if the insured is a wage earner, and in any case contributions of the community.

The mechanisms of the systems of compulsory insurance until very recently have been directly inspired by the pre-existing systems of mutual aid societies or commercial insurance, the same technique being applied, subject only to the adaptation required by the obligation of insurance and the combination of several contributions.

The various laws have not always applied the same formula to all risks covered. As far back as the period 1883–1889, Germany had established a system of compulsory insurance against illness, old age, invalidity, and industrial accidents, at least for employees with wages under a definite ceiling and for a small number of self-employed. Denmark and Sweden have developed systems of voluntary sickness insurance covering in fact the major part of the population (nearly 90 per cent in Denmark, over 60 per cent in Sweden), and established old-age pensions financed by the State and paid to all old people residing in the country. Switzerland has various systems of voluntary insurance against sickness, involving a large part of the population and based on mutual aid societies subsidized by public authorities, and a federal system of compulsory old age insurance, covering the whole population. France, besides older schemes for miners, railroad workers, seamen, and civil servants, established in 1930 a compulsory insurance system protecting all employees with earnings below a definite ceiling, or their dependents, against the loss of income due to the worker's illness, maternity, invalidity, old age, and death, which has been generalized by the recent social security plan. The United Kingdom put successively into force schemes of compulsory insurance against the risks of sickness, unemployment, and old age, before introducing the comprehensive national insurance system. The United States established in

1935 compulsory systems of insurance against the risks of unemployment and old age, while a few states have established compulsory systems of short-period sickness insurance; and recent collective agreements tend to complete the official schemes.

Those few examples show the general character of the evolution. While the formulas applied vary in a considerable measure from one country to another, compulsory insurance for some groups has appeared in all modern countries during the last half-century in response to the prevailing economic and social conditions.

From social insurance to social security

The new essential factors of the last years are the appearance, since the second World War, of comprehensive social security plans. The Beveridge Report and the International Labor Conference at Philadelphia in 1944 mark the starting points of a remarkable succession of such plans.

Social insurance usually had taken the form of separate fractional schemes, each one restricted to certain risks and certain population groups. Even in Germany, France, or the Scandinavian countries, where comprehensive social insurance schemes were applied, several schemes coexisted, independent of each other, each one with its own scope and its own methods. The new step made during recent years tended to deal with the income security problem as a whole, with all its economic and social implications, and for the whole population of each country.

This development has led to the revision of all techniques used in pre-existing schemes. The problem is no longer how to apply assistance to certain people and insurance to others, or how to extend to the social field the insurance techniques which had long been of current use in the economic and commercial field, but rather to enforce a general policy involving numerous aspects in various fields. Admittedly one still speaks of assistance and insurance, but usually as technical means among others by which income security may be reached.

The evolution is indeed far from complete. If many countries have enthusiastically adopted and supported the new concept, others are still reluctant. Germany, for example, which has the oldest social insurance scheme existing in the world, and is deeply attached to it, hesitates to pass from it to a new social security plan. The matter is today subject to discussion in wide areas throughout the world.

PRESENT TRENDS OF SOCIAL SECURITY POLICIES

Present social security policies show considerable differences both in the scope of the legislation and in the techniques used. These differences result from the variety of the economic, demographic, and psychological conditions of the populations concerned. Even inside a given country there may exist various schemes, each one corresponding to a certain part of the population, owing to the economic, demographic, and, chiefly, psychological conditions of that social group. However, some general tendencies and trends appear in this extreme variety.

The most obvious is the proliferation of social security legislation itself. The simple fact that such laws are passed almost everywhere, in countries showing considerable differences in development and in economic and political regimes, reveals, in spite of the difference in the content of this legislation, the existence throughout the world of a strong and general current toward income security. The most socialist and the most "liberal" ones, in this field, resemble each other more closely than they differ.

Besides this main trend are other common trends concerning the link between income security policies and general economic and social policies; the tendency towards generalization of income security; the character of the benefits; the administrative and financial organization; and the internationalization of the income security problems.

Income security policies and general economic and social policies

Income security is an objective which can be attained in various ways, and in fact requires the simultaneous use of various different methods.

All these ways and methods are dominated by an essential economic factor: most people are living from the product of their work. Income security first depends on the existence and permanence of employment. Every man and woman capable of work and willing to work must be provided with a means of livelihood, with a job; unemployment must be wiped out.

This involves an organization of the economy such as will enable depressions to be avoided and full employment to be maintained; an organization of man-power such as will permit the best adjustment of labor supply and demand by coordinated policies of placing, guidance, and vocational training; a wage policy providing each worker with sufficient and stable pay.

It is striking to note that, even in countries deeply attached to the principle of free enterprise, the search for full employment has become an essential part of the mission of the government in the economic field. In the United States, the Employment Act (1946) provides the Federal government with powers specially directed to that end. And there is in fact hardly any country at the present time in which fighting unemployment and maintaining or achieving full employment are not stated as leading principles of the whole government policy. Such policy is part of the income security policy and must be considered as such.

Moreover, the other aspects of income security policy may be, and sometimes are, directed towards the achievement of the objective of full employment.

For example, the Beveridge Report underlines the link between the social insurance scheme it suggests and the maintenance of full employment as well as the prevention of mass unemployment. It states that the scheme will itself have some effect in promoting realization of that objective. Payment of unemployment benefits will maintain the purchasing power of work people, if a trade depression begins, and will thus mitigate the severity of the depression. More generally, since the income provided by the system to persons who are sick, unemployed, injured, or past work will almost invariably be spent to the full, the scheme will bring about a general increase of private outlay, favoring full employment. Lastly, since the total amount of contributions varies with the level of production, the scheme in effect taxes surplus incomes during boom periods so as to be able to make a corresponding refund in times of depression, thus helping towards the economic equilibrium typical of full employment and avoiding recurrent slumps.

In certain South American countries the link between income security policy and general economic policy appears in a different way. The existing schemes currently pay out in benefits a total amount which corresponds to only a small part of the contributions collected. The surplus is capitalized to give in the more or less remote future higher pensions and allowances. Capitalization is openly used as a means to develop investment, and thus the economic possibilities of the country and the national income, making it easier to bear the burden of the benefits when those benefits have to be paid.

There is today no country in which the economic implications of social security policy can be ignored. The enormous amount of the contributions collected or of the benefits paid has necessarily a deep influence on the whole economic life. Either the income security institutions may be used as instruments of economic policy or income security policies must at least be coordinated with economic policies and integrated into them.

What is true of the link between income security policy and economic policy is true also of the link between income security policy and other aspects of social policies. Income security implies for a worker the power to work. Workers must be able to rely on maintaining the gainful activity which is their sole source of livelihood; they must therefore be safeguarded against all risks which may involve total or partial loss of their capacity for work. Consequently it is not possible to disentangle from income security policy the whole problem of medical services, with their preventive as well as curative mission —nor the problem of preventing industrial accidents and occupational diseases and of enabling persons injured in this way to recover their working capacity. On the other hand, maintenance or restoration of ability to work means increasing the output of the persons so assisted, and therefore of earnings in the aggregate, while reducing the total alternative income required for distribution among the sick and disabled.

Economic policy aimed at full employment, medical policy of equipment and organization for the struggle against disease, including both preventive and curative action, and technical policy for the prevention of industrial accidents and occupational diseases—these are really parts of an income security policy, if understood in its widest meaning and implication, which includes, as a last resort, the distribution of alternative incomes to those who have lost their gainful activity or have to face exceptional expenses.

All countries are today more or less conscious of the wide scope and implications of the income security problem. This is something new. And the national policies are deeply affected by that new factor.

Tendency toward generalization of income security

The first private or public institutions providing for income security and the first laws passed in this field were limited to definite groups of people and definite contingencies. One of the main features, perhaps the most important feature, of the income security policies in all countries during recent years, is the general admission of the fundamental unity of social security, thus resulting in the generalization of income security legislation and institutions to the whole population and to all contingencies threatening that security.

Scope of income security policies. The need for security is no longer limited to a definite part of the population. Economic crises, world wars, depreciations of currency, have shown that anybody may be struck almost at any time by unexpected blows, that insecurity in fact is the common lot of whole populations. Moreover, all parts of the population of a country, if not of several or all countries, are interdependent; the insecurity of any part of it reacts on the security of the other parts. And, if income security is understood in its widest meaning, the very multiplicity of the economic, technical, and social factors which the new plans involve does not allow these plans to be fractional: they must apply to the whole population. No full employment policy, no health service, not even income distribution schemes, can afford to be restricted to certain groups of people. Such schemes must all—one might almost say by definition—extend to the country as a whole.

A first consequence of that trend is the tendency to abandon the means test as a condition of the protection given. There are indeed still a number of assistance schemes confined to people without means. But in most countries the scope of the main schemes, either contributory or even noncontributory, is not restricted to people with limited resources. The assistance benefits are considered as a complement to be added to the normal income security benefits or as a substitute for these benefits when they cannot be obtained. The means test is the condition of supplementary help and not a condition of coverage by the income security plan itself. This solution, which normally results from the general trend of income security policies, is also dictated by sociological considerations: it is never good to divide a population in two parts, one well off and left outside the scope of the social policies, and the other in a state of social inferiority and needing help as such. Such a division would be purely artificial and could create psychological antagonisms inside a community of which all members are interdependent and must have a feeling of solidarity.

While assistance schemes are normally limited to people without means, or at least without sufficient resources, most social insurance schemes were initially restricted to employees, and even to employees earning less than a certain amount. Contributions were required only from these employees and for them, and the benefits were given only to them. This was the case, for instance, in Germany and France. Such a formula is nothing more than a new application of the means test, but with an important difference: the formula usually takes into account not all the resources of the person or the family concerned but only the wages received. Nevertheless the basic principles are the same as in the case of the means test: above a certain level of wages or income, people are supposed to make an individual and voluntary effort to insure themselves against the risks to which they may possibly be exposed. The recent evolution has led to the extension of social insurance schemes to all employees without consideration of the level of their wages: France and Belgium, for example, have modified their legislation in this direction. However, some countries, such as the Netherlands, still keep the old system of a "ceiling" on wages above which the employees are not insured.

The same evolution normally involves the extension of income security policies to nonsalaried people (i.e., not earning wages or salaries), self-employed or not employed. In some countries the social insurance schemes did not originally make any distinction between employees and nonsalaried people: in Scandinavian countries and in New Zealand, the schemes from the first applied to all groups of the population. Generalization is not so easy when starting from schemes established for wage earners and organized with regard to that special category of people. It has been achieved, however, in the United Kingdom since 1948, subject only to the limitation to employed people of the employment injuries and unemployment benefits. But since 90 per cent of the active population are employees, the extension affected very limited groups. Elsewhere difficulties have been encountered owing first to technical factors (the necessary adaptations of existing machinery to people in a different economic and social situation), and, second and chiefly, to psychological factors. Even if the self-employed and nonemployed feel the need for income security, they are reluctant to accept inclusion in the same schemes as the wage earners or the mass of the workers. They consider themselves as having the benefit of a privileged social status, as compared to the workers; and they are not ready to give up that status, to accept what seems to them a kind of proletarization. The distinction of social classes and the class spirit have thus a deep influence on the evolution of income security policies.

The countries having a high proportion of self-employed in agriculture, trade, and liberal professions are often also those where a special importance is attached to individual responsibility in the achievement of individual or family security. The social structure of each country directly influences the evolution of social security policies and explains the differences in that evolution from one country to another.

Extension of the contingencies covered. The extension of income security policies to all possible contingencies does not encounter similar difficulties. Here again there is a general tendency towards covering everybody against all risks which may threaten income security. But the existing schemes have often been established for one definite contingency, or perhaps only a narrowly limited range. The regrouping of the various schemes in a coordinated whole requires adaptations and sometimes deep alterations in the existing laws and institutions. If we examine the various contingencies generally covered by modern income security plans, we see the importance of the transformations involved by the recent evolution.

Types of contingencies covered

Employment injuries and occupational diseases. Historically the first legislation to be passed providing for the coverage of a definite type of contingency has often concerned employment injuries. The idea has appeared early that an employer must be liable for the consequences of the injuries related to the work done in his undertaking. Sometimes it has seemed enough to determine the extent of that liability, leaving to the employer the choice of insuring himself or not, and, if he decided to, the free choice of the insurance company or institution. Later on, guaranties have been established in order to ensure that the victim of an accident always gets the benefits to which he is entitled. In some countries like Belgium, such guaranties result only from the existence of a special fund able to take the place of an insolvent employer; elsewhere the insurance has been made compulsory, the employer however being free to choose the insurance company or institution (as is the case in Spain, Sweden, Denmark, Finland, Netherlands, and a number of states of the United States). But in Germany, Switzerland, and Italy, freedom of choice does not exist; the employers must be insured with specialized institutions, administered either by employers' delegates, as in Germany, or by the State itself, as in Switzerland, Italy, and most Canadian provinces. The most recent laws go even further and give less and less importance to the concept of employer's liability, which is now tending to disappear. Employment injuries and diseases are considered as contingencies not different from the other contingencies covered by social security plans, and are to be provided against by the same methods. Their coverage is part of a whole system, and, while the benefits may sometimes be different, the general principles applied are common to them and to all other contingencies. The recent French and British social security plans are characteristic in this respect: the British plan goes so far as to require a contribution from the workers, as well as from the employers, to finance the costs of employment injuries benefits.

Sickness and maternity. Sickness and maternity threaten the individual or family income in a double sense: first, because they bring new, unexpected, and often heavy expenses; second, because when they strike the breadwinner they deprive the individual or the family of their normal livelihood. The first kind of consequence is normally provided for by the organization of health services, free of charge, either for the whole population or for people without sufficient means, and in other cases by the repayment of medical expenses by special agencies such as private and nonprofit institutions like mutual aid societies, Blue Cross, and so on, private and commercial agencies like insurance companies, or public or semipublic institutions like social insurance funds, in which the people concerned are compulsorily insured. The loss of normal earnings is compensated by daily, weekly, or monthly allowances eventually paid by institutions of the same kind.

Historically, besides the assistance institutions, the main role has first been played by mutual aid societies, freely created and providing their members both medical help and sickness allowances. In some countries, in fact very few, free mutual aid societies controlled and subsidized by the State are still the basis of the actual schemes; that is the case in Denmark, in most Swiss cantons, and, still for a few more months, in Sweden. The education, the sense of solidarity, and the saving spirit of the people in those countries have been such that this formula could be efficient. But in most modern countries it has been necessary, to reach the same target, to establish systems of compulsory insurance. Some of those systems, like the Belgian, leave room for free mutual aid societies among which the insured person may freely choose his insurance institution; but, here again, the tendency today is to consider sickness and maternity insurance as part of a whole social security scheme, without specialized agencies.

There are still important differences from one country to another owing to the unevenness of the evolution and to the peculiar social structure of each one. But throughout a large part of the world the trend is very much the same.

Old Age. During a long period, there was no other help to old people without means than the eventual entrance into almshouses or relief given by private or public assistance institutions. But, relatively early, legislation appeared providing for old-age pensions in favor of certain categories of people, mainly public servants, soldiers, and seamen. Later, mutual aid societies on the one hand, insurance companies on the other, offered to people with enough resources ways to save for their old age, each country giving priority to one or the other formula, depending on its own social structure and traditions. But in this field perhaps more than in any other compulsory insurance early appeared as the sole efficient way to achieve income security. As soon as the family is no longer in a position to cover the needs of its old people, the community is in fact obliged to take charge of them, either directly, by noncontributory pensions financed from taxes, or indirectly through systems of compulsory insurance. Both formulas are applied. In most modern countries compulsory insurance is actually preferred, the insurance institution being either semipublic funds or State administration. But in Denmark, Sweden, and New Zealand, old-age pensions are directly paid by the State, and, even when a special tax is collected to cover the corresponding expenses, it is part of the general tax system and has none of the characters of an insurance premium or contribution.

In some countries, namely in Latin America and in a way in France, several schemes are applied corresponding to different economic branches or social categories. Brazil, for instance, has separate schemes for seamen, commerce, transport workers, bank employees, public servants, and so on. In France, besides a general social security scheme including all employees not covered by special schemes, one can find autonomous regimes for public servants, railroad workers, miners, seamen, farm workers, and also for self-employed persons. The inconvenience of such a multiplicity of schemes is easily perceptible. But it has been necessary to take into account the particularism of certain groups and the psychological and social implications of the systems to be established.

However, the general tendency throughout the world is toward unification of the schemes of old-age pensions, at least as far as a basic scheme is concerned, without excluding the possibility of adding complements adapted to the peculiar situation of each group. The inclusion of old-age pensions in a comprehensive social security scheme appears more and more as an absolute necessity, owing to the considerable amount of funds required by such pensions, which necessitate coordination and control in the interest of the whole economy of the country.

Survivors' benefits generally appear as a complement of systems of old-age pensions. Their evolution has been very much the same and does not require special explanation.

Invalidity. The same may be said of invalidity benefits, as of survivors' benefits. In fact, in many countries invalidity pensions have been and are still considered as part of the old-age pensions scheme: the invalidity pension appears as a premature retirement pension. But in a number of modern schemes invalidity benefits are separated from old-age pensions and treated either as autonomous benefits or as the prolongation of sickness benefits. Experience shows that in most cases invalidity (or inability to work), when not resulting from an employment injury, does not involve a native weakness or infirmity but only long-time, chronic diseases. In accordance with the peculiar character of each national scheme, the evolution of invalidity benefits has been connected to that of either old-age or sickness benefits. The tendency towards including all aspects of income security in comprehensive schemes lessens and even suppresses the previously existing differences.

Unemployment. In spite of the essential differences existing between sickness and unemployment, the evolution of the coverage of these two contingencies has been similar. Mutual aid societies, namely those created on a professional basis, provided for unemployment benefits as well as for sickness benefits; often there was no distinction between real unemployment benefits and help given to workers on strike. Later, workers' unions sometimes tried to organize unemployment funds, either by themselves or with the help of the public authorities. In rare instances the most important part of the workers have progressively been involved in these funds: in Sweden the basic unemployment scheme is administered by the unions and covers all members of the unions, and in fact almost all workers of the country, the resources of the funds coming from contributions of the workers to the unions and from State subsidies. In some other countries, like France, unemployment benefits are directly paid by public authorities, without any contributions at all.

But here again the system which is most frequently applied is compulsory insurance. The first application has been the British one, in 1912, but the example has been followed by many countries: Italy, United States, Canada, Belgium, etc. The technical methods used vary from one country to another, and even, inside the United States, from one state to another. Here the employers alone contribute; elsewhere the employees also may have to pay a contribution. But the general principle of compulsory insurance is everywhere the same.

However the inclusion of unemployment benefits into the new comprehensive social security schemes has not been so complete and so general as that of the other benefits. Even in the United Kingdom, where the unemployment benefits are part of the National Insurance system, the administration of that part of the scheme is left to the Ministry of Labor and National Service. And in most other countries, unemployment schemes are still autonomous. The reason is the necessary link between the unemployment benefits and the employment services. The objective is less to provide the unemployed with an alternative income than to help him to find a new job. The refusal of such a job may lead to the denial of the benefit. Unemployment benefits cannot be disentangled from the application of the general employment policy. And, as far as that policy is independent from the general social security policy, unemployment schemes must be left more or less outside the income security schemes.

If, for the reasons mentioned, the general evolution is not so apparent for unemployment as for sickness or old age, for example, there is nevertheless, even in this field, a tendency to bring together, or at least to coordinate, unemployment benefits and other income security benefits. Socially, the effect of unemployment is not essentially different from that of the other contingencies. Like sickness, it temporarily deprives an individual or a family of the means of livelihood. And if unemployment benefits are limited to people able to work, the ability to work is subject to discussion. The same problem appears as far as old people are concerned. Will an old man be entitled to unemployment benefits? Could he receive both those benefits and an old-age pension? The retirement age and the rate of the old-age pensions are thus closely connected with the solutions to the problems raised by unemployment. Even unemployment appears as part of a whole comprehensive income security policy.

Family benefits. Family benefits have been developed from three different starting points.

Family allowances first appeared in France, as a supplement to wages. The Government had already developed such family supplements for its own servants. Private employers started doing so during the first World War in 1917. The success of this action came from the creation of "compensation funds" by which the employer members undertook to share between them on a rational basis the burden of family allowances, instead of each of them having to pay allowances corresponding to the number of children of his own employees. But during several years the payment of such allowances and the membership of a compensation fund resulted from a voluntary decision by each employer. The system became compulsory for all employers and all employees in 1932, but the principles were not changed. Family allowances were considered as a certain part of the wages. Belgium applied the same system, adding to it a "national compensation fund," in charge of establishing a proper equilibrium between the various funds existing in the country.

Other countries have developed a system of family allowances on a completely different basis, as a direct help from the State to the family. New Zealand, Australia, Uruguay, Brazil, and Finland have established such allowances, subject initially, and still today for the last three countries, to a means test. They were part of an assistance scheme. The abandonment of the means test in New Zealand and Australia has changed the character of the scheme, which now appears simply as a redistribution of part of the national income in favor of children. The new family allowances scheme in force in the United Kingdom is based on the same principle.

Another principle appears, more or less clearly, in the schemes established in Italy, Chile, and Spain: the concept of a compulsory insurance of the family income. Contributions are collected from employees as well as from employers and have their counterpart in allowances partly compensating the family expenses. Such systems are directly inspired by the familiar compulsory social insurance dealing with other contingencies involved in income security. The extension of the family benefits in France and Belgium to self-employed people led to the application of comparable formulas for these new groups of beneficiaries.

The recent evolution of income security policies has resulted first, in a considerable extension of the family benefits schemes; second, in bringing together the various formulas. The extension of the family benefits to the whole population implies the abandonment of any link between benefits and employment; allowances are no longer part of wages. The new schemes are based on the principles already laid down in New Zealand and Australia. The British and the French schemes, for instance, treat family benefits as a compensation for family expenses, and also as part of the whole income security plan.

It could seem at first sight that family benefits are very different from the other social security benefits. The existence and the number of children in a family cannot be considered as risks to be compared to sickness, invalidity, or unemployment. But a thorough study of the question shows that the differences are less important than the common features. If family benefits may seem remote from sickness benefits, they are very similar to old-age benefits. In both cases the problem is to ensure a livelihood to a noneconomically active part of the population—children on one hand, old people on the other. Any income security policy must determine what ought to be done for each of these two categories as well as for sick, invalid, and unemployed people. Such a problem must by necessity be taken as a whole, in order to weigh the possible efforts which can and must be made for each group, taking into account as well the proper needs of each one and the general economic, demographical, and social situation of the country.

Differences of Approach. The economic trend of recent income security policies is thus no longer to treat separately each contingency, but to envisage the problem of income security as a whole and to solve the special questions raised by each contingency on a common basis and in relation to each other.

Such common trends could have led to similar schemes in all countries having reached a comparable degree of economic and social development. In fact, it is striking that despite the common purposes, despite general agreement regarding the essential principles behind income security, the institutions existing in different countries today represent profound differences of approach.

This may be explained by the economic, demographical, and psychological conditions proper to each country, by the pre-existing institutions, and by the whole historical evolution of the legislation and agencies. Besides, each country, when establishing its new social security plan, had to face the problem in the light of its own particular "first priorities."

Thus the British plan is entirely governed by a determination to fight unemployment. Its methods, its very principles, make it first and foremost an unemployment insurance scheme enlarged. Just as full employment is this plan's basic objective, so may also the whole British legislative scheme of income security be described as an extension of unemployment insurance to cover the other contingencies, using the same methods and machinery.

France approached the problem of social security from an entirely different angle, that of its own demographic situation. The fall of the birth rate and the increasing proportion of old people in the population, as well as the effects of the depreciation of the currency, explain the outstanding importance attached to family benefits, to the problem of old age and, by way of consequence, to a major effort in the field of health organization, preventive medicine, and industrial safety, in order to increase the active part of the population and its total output, and so make up to some extent for the cost of inactive members. If unemployment was the primary concern in the United Kingdom, France's was family help, relief for the aged, and the struggle against sickness and accidents.

What is true in the comparison between the British and the French plans would be equally true if we compared other plans to these two. This does not mean of course that the same preoccupations do not appear in one way or another in all modern plans. But the way in which the problems have been approached has a deep influence, if not on the extent of the schemes, at least on the methods used and the orientation of the solutions.

Character of the benefits

In mutual aid societies or insurance companies, the benefits are based on the amount of the contributions or premiums paid. There is no definite relation between the benefits and the needs. The insured person receives not what he needs but the counterpart of what he had been able or willing to save. All modern income security schemes try to face the real needs, without establishing a necessary link between contributions and benefits.

1. This new trend involves first a rational calculation of the benefits. Most typical of that kind of effort are the Beveridge Report and the British National Insurance. The individual and family needs have been thoroughly studied and estimated. The various members of the community have been classified, taking into account their different ways of life, in six classes: employees, others gainfully occupied, housewives, others of working age, below working age, retired above working age. Eight kinds of primary needs of income security have been determined. To each class of people is attached a definite benefit which is supposed to meet the need thus estimated.

The fundamental unity of income security enforces a calculation of the benefits in relation to each other. All who lose their livelihood are in a similar position whatever the cause of the loss. Some differences may be justified owing to the permanent or occasional character of the loss of income and to its probable duration. But all rates of benefits must be established on a rational basis. Only a comprehensive income security plan can achieve such result.

There are few schemes as perfect as the British one. But everywhere the trend is towards a coordination of the nature and the rates of the benefits. Links are established between sickness, invalidity, and employment injuries benefits, between orphan pensions and family benefits, and so on. The regrouping of previously independent systems, based on different principles, each concerning a single sector, into comprehensive schemes leads to such transformations.

2. But if the rationalization of the benefits and their rates is a common trend, the solutions adopted result from two quite different and even opposite concepts.

Some laws aim to guarantee a decent minimum standard of life, but nothing more. They adopt the principle of flat rates of insurance benefits, irrespective of the amount of the earnings which have been interrupted by unemployment or disability or ended by retirement. The flat rate is intended in itself to be sufficient without further resources to provide the minimum income needed for subsistence in all normal cases. It gives room for additional voluntary provision or for supplements based on assistance. These are the principles of the British National Insurance scheme; they are also at least partly applied in New Zealand and in Scandinavian countries.

In the other schemes, on the contrary, the rates of benefits are generally proportioned to the amount of the income lost. The basic concept is here that real security implies the guaranty to keep, if not the same standard of life, at least conditions related to that standard. Most income security laws provide for benefits corresponding to a certain percentage of the previous earnings of the people concerned.

The choice between these two concepts is often linked up with the system adopted to finance the benefits paid. When resources come from general taxes or from flat-rate contributions, flat rates of benefits are preferred. On the contrary, schemes graduating the contributions by income generally provide for proportional benefits. It would often be difficult to ask for a rather important financial effort, by way of contributions, from people who cannot expect benefits to have any real significance for them, or, in any case, to give them an appreciable degree of security.

Psychological as well as social factors thus determine the choice to be made. Where individualism prevails, one is naturally inclined to an individualization of the benefits, to their adaptation to the proper situation of each individual or family, in spite of the complexity thus brought to the administration of the scheme. Where a strong feeling of solidarity and a developed civic spirit may be found, it is easier to be satisfied with flat rates of benefits.

Such flat rates also suppose the existence of voluntary insurance institutions largely developed, appealing to the mass of the population and able to add to the benefits of the compulsory insurance a supplement making the sums received close to the loss. These conditions are not always fulfilled, especially in countries where the average income does not easily allow important individual savings or where depreciations of the currency have led to a certain popular distrust of voluntary insurance institutions unable to adapt their benefits to the increase of the cost of living.

However, the gap between the two concepts is perhaps not so wide as it could seem at first sight. Even in the countries which are the most deeply attached to the system of variable benefits, an increasing number of benefits are calculated on flat rates; that is the case for all noncontributory benefits, and also sometimes for some contributory benefits, such as family allowances of which the rates never vary in any country with the family income. On the other hand, the relation between the benefit and the lost earnings is generally corrected by a ceiling: the earnings are taken into account only up to a certain amount, above which the benefit is calculated on the figure taken as the ceiling.

3. Another trend of the recent income security schemes lies in the increased importance given to the family factor in the determination of the benefits. In the past benefits were generally individual, without any consideration of the dependents of the insured person; benefits tended to replace part of the lost income and nothing more. But it appeared more and more that the security of the individual cannot be disentangled from the security of his dependents. Security is essentially familial in character. A benefit has no real

social meaning if it does not take into account the total amount of the expenses the beneficiary has to meet from it.

The appearance and the generalization of family allowances are of course the main aspect of that new tendency. But all benefits have been affected by it. Most of them include supplements for dependents, not only for children but also for wife or husband, or parents or any dependents who do not themselves receive benefits. For instance, the loss of a certain amount of earnings has not the same meaning for a bachelor or for the breadwinner of a family of several persons. The bachelor, when taken to a hospital where he is treated free of charge, does not need much money for his own subsistence; but, when there are dependents, they have to live on the benefit paid. A retired worker does not need the same amount if he has to provide only for his own subsistence as when he has a dependent wife. All these factors are today more and more taken into account in the calculation of the benefits.

Another feature of the modern income security schemes which is worth being underlined is the tendency towards an adaptation of the benefits to the variation of the cost of living. The International Labor Office Convention concerning minimum standards of social security (1952) provides that "the rates of current periodical payments in respect of old age, employment injury (except in case of incapacity for work), invalidity, and death of breadwinner, shall be reviewed following substantial changes in the general level of earnings when these result from substantial changes in the cost of living." Most countries had approved the principle of such revisions. Some of them have organized an automatic adaptation, at least of long-term benefits such as old-age pensions, to the changes in the cost of living. Some others, though accepting the principle, leave it to the legislator or to the Government to take the appropriate measures according to circumstances. But there is no serious disagreement on the necessity of such adaptation; no real security can be obtained without it.

It is obvious that such a principle can be applied only in comprehensive State schemes. A private insurance institution, or even a public scheme of a narrow scope, is not in a position to fulfill such requirements. Only schemes which are integrated into the whole national economy and whose resources vary with the evolution of that economy can do it, with financial methods determined in accordance with that objective.

Administrative and financial organization

Administration. In the administrative field there is a considerable variety of formulas from one country to another and even sometimes inside one country, depending on the security branches or the population group concerned. Assistance by local authorities or private institutions, mutual aid societies, insurance companies, employers' liability, union funds, cooperative institutions, semipublic funds, State administrations, all formulas find here or there some applications. This variety can be explained by the existing differences in the economic and psychological conditions, by the unequal evolution of the institutions, and by the hazard of the successive laws—for it is often more difficult to change an existing institution or law than to create an entirely new one.

The recent evolution shows, however, two main trends towards unity of the organization and towards public administration.

The unity of organization is far from achieved everywhere. In a number of countries various independent institutions are juxtaposed, although based on different principles and concerning different sectors; sometimes in the same sector several institutions may be found in competition with each other. But the new concept of the unity of social security could but result in a reaction against that multiplicity. Reduction of administrative costs, convenience of the insured people, efficiency of the administration, and suppression of overlappings and gaps have brought all recent legislation to adopt the principle of unity which is also imposed by the necessary unity of the policy to be applied. The multiplicity of institutions corresponds to a situation in which each individual or family was free to choose the mode of protection he thought the best with regard to his personal conditions; it is incompatible with the concept of national income security policy, based on rationalized benefits, included in a general economic policy, and based on a national solidarity of all members of the community.

The same factors led to the development of public administration in the field of income security. The degree of interference of the State is very different from one country to another and varies also according to the contingencies concerned. Old-age pension schemes, for example, have always been submitted to a State administration more largely than sickness insurance or employment injuries schemes. Sometimes the trend towards public administration results simply from the imposition of a coordinating board on multiple existing institutions. In Belgium a National Social Security Board has thus been recently established with the mission to collect one common social security contribution, the amount of which is then distributed among old-age institutes, mutual aid societies in charge of sickness insurance, family allowances funds, and unemployment funds. Elsewhere, the old institutions have been replaced by new funds forming, as in France, a coordinated hierarchy under the control of the State. In other cases, a State administration has taken charge of the whole scheme. This formula, which is found more and more frequently, is the British one as well as that of New Zealand, Australia, Ireland, and, as far as old age and unemployment are concerned, the United States.

In a few countries, special Government departments have been created, to administer social security schemes. The Ministry of National Insurance in the United Kingdom, the Social Security Administration in the United States, the Department of Social Security in New Zealand are examples of this tendency, while in numerous countries social security is still included in the jurisdiction of Ministries of Labor or Health or Social Affairs. In fact the legitimacy of an autonomous department is subject to discussion. Even where there is one such department, some part of the income security scheme is often kept outside of it. The British Ministry of National Insurance leaves the practical administration of unemployment benefits to the Ministry of Labor and National Service. The Federal government in America has no power over the state employment injuries schemes. Moreover income security problems cannot any more be disentangled from other aspects of social security such as health programs, full employment, prevention of industrial accidents and occupational diseases, and even from the more general problem of distribution of the national income. The existing links between all aspects of social security policies are themselves the basis for the increasing intervention of the Government in that field. They show that, even when for technical reasons special departments may have been established, the policy itself must often be elaborated at a higher level.

Finance. The financial aspects of the income security policies show the same tendencies as the administrative organization.

First there is a general trend towards unification of the machinery providing the resources of the schemes. The multiple contributions of the past, paid to various institutions, each corresponding to a definite contingency, are more and more being replaced by one blanket contribution covering all aspects of income security. When several contributions are maintained they have often the same basis and are collected at the same time and by the same machinery. Differences exist, as we have already stated, as regards the choice between flat-rate contributions or contributions related to earnings or income. Both formulas are applied. No definite tendency can be found in favor of one or the other.

More important is the question of financing income security by taxes or by contributions. Most countries use both methods, the resources obtained from contributions of the insured persons or their employers being supplemented by subsidies from the State—that is, from public funds, coming from taxes. But the proportions, in which each country has recourse to each method are very unequal. It was usual in the past to make a sharp distinction between the two methods: in the case of insurance, contributions were required from the insured and sometimes their employers; in the case of assistance, compensation was paid by the authorities from public funds. Seen in the light of new social security policies, the distinction loses most of its meaning.

From the moment the problem is considered as one to be solved for the whole population by a general policy and under a general scheme, it is comparatively unimportant whether the money has been obtained by means of contributions or drawn direct from public funds. In either case, the national economy taken as a whole will be bearing the expense. It is only a question of technical and psychological convenience whether the resources necessary to meet income security expenditure in the aggregate should be collected by one method rather than another. The common tendency is towards considering the financing of income security with regard to its economic implications, in the framework of a general economic policy, taking into account both the production requirements and the social impact of the distribution of the national income.

The same evolution results in the abandoning of traditional insurance methods, namely in the frequent disappearances of all connection between contributions and benefits. The financing of the scheme is one thing, the right to benefits another. In noncontributory schemes, of which the importance is increasing, there can be of course no question of basing entitlement to benefits upon contributions. But even in contributory schemes such conditions are less and less required. They lose their meaning with comprehensive income security plans covering the whole population of a country against all contingencies eventually threatening their security.

The old problem of the choice between methods of capitalization and distributive methods takes on quite a new aspect within such income security policies. All social insurance systems have in the past given an important place to the capitalization principle, providing for investments as in private insurance companies. The evolution of policy has given more and more importance to distributive methods, allowing the immediate payment of benefits, and avoiding the possible consequence of deterioration of the currency. In fact, as soon as an income security scheme involves a whole population, the total amount of the benefits is always paid from the national income of the current year, whatever the system applied.

There is real capitalization only if the total amount of contributions or taxes collected for the social security scheme exceeds the total amount of the benefits paid, and if the surplus is used in productive investments, increasing the national income for the years to come and making it easier to bear the burden of the social security expenses. We have seen that many Latin American countries openly apply such a policy. But in such a case the investments are not really part of the income security scheme; they are investments of the whole community. Outside of such a situation capitalization has no interest and no real meaning in the general framework of a comprehensive income security scheme, which cannot be disentangled from the whole financial and economic life of the country.

The practical effect of such a scheme, from the financial standpoint, is finally to achieve a redistribution of part of the national income in favor of the children, the old people, the sick, the invalids, the unemployed. The normal income of the economically active part of the population is reduced in order to provide for the needs of those who, for one reason or another, are not in a position to earn their own livelihood. The part of the national income thus redistributed may attain 12 or 13 per cent. Income security in that sense is nothing else than the expression of national solidarity organized to give real security to all the members of the community.

Internationalization of income security problems

When one speaks about income security, one generally thinks of national laws and institutions. However, and especially during recent years, the rapid progress of the concept of social security throughout the world has resulted in raising international problems in addition to the problems peculiar to each country.

The first problem is to achieve a coordination of laws and institutions of various countries in order to ensure that all individuals and families get the benefit of the national schemes, whatever their country of origin or residence.

There have been in fact two different stages in that direction. From the social standpoint, all persons should be entitled to the same protection against social risks, regardless of nationality; there is a widespread movement towards equality between aliens and nationals with regard to income security benefits under the legislation of the different countries. Substantial progress has already been made in this direction. The second stage has corresponded to the efforts made towards the maintenance of migrants' rights acquired or in process of acquisition, in order that migration does not result in loss of the protection involved in income security legislation.

Both results have been achieved, partly or totally, through ILO conventions and bilateral or multilateral agreements. Most conventions adopted since 1919 by the International Labor Conference in the field of social security provide for equality between aliens and nationals as part of the minimum standards laid down. A special ILO Convention has defined principles to be applied in case of migrations. But such conventions are often ratified by only a few countries and thus may not provide a complete guaranty. A number of bilateral and multilateral agreements, during the last years, have given force to the principles thus established. Such agreements have been concluded among most European countries. The five countries signatory of the Brussels Pact and the fifteen countries members of the Council of Europe have signed, besides bilateral treaties, multilateral agreements achieving a high degree of coordination of the application of their social security legislation as far as their respective nationals are concerned.

A second and more difficult problem is to achieve a satisfactory equilibrium of the level of the various national income security schemes, to ensure to the people of every country, if not the same level of social protection, at least a decent level of income security, to achieve a certain degree of equality with regard to social progress. An important effort is being accomplished in that way through technical assistance; that is, through an international cooperation organized to favor social progress by way of fellowships, missions of experts, or seminars.

Another aspect of that trend is seen in the adoption of international standards of social security. That has been and is still one of the main objectives of the ILO. A number of "conventions," adopted from 1919 to 1939, and concerning various branches of social insurance, sickness, unemployment, old age, and invalidity, have had a considerable influence on the development of social insurance throughout the world. Since the last World War, the ILO has taken account of the social security problem as a whole, in the framework of the general evolution of the concept. That has been the basis, first, of the recommendations adopted in 1944 by the International Labor Conference of Philadelphia, concerning a general guaranty of means of living and medical care; secondly, and chiefly, of the Convention adopted in 1952 on the minimum standards of social security. That Convention, of a quite new type, provides that the ratifying countries must commit themselves to achieve for their people a minimum level of social security. But that result can be obtained in different ways, adapted to the proper conditions of each country. In the general framework of that formula, the countries which are members of the Council of Europe are actually studying the establishment of European standards of social security, taking into account the proper economic and social conditions of those countries and implying higher standards than the minimum provided by the ILO Convention.

Another and quite different problem is to achieve an international equilibrium of the costs of income security schemes. The same law applied in different countries may lead to an extreme disparity of the costs borne by the economy of each country, for the demographical conditions, also the level and distribution of the national income, may vary enormously. The problem here is an economic one; it is to prevent inequality in income security expenses from modifying the conditions of international trade competition. Studies have been undertaken in that field. But they are at their very beginning. They meet considerable difficulties, first of a technical character, but also because of the essential nature of the problem itself. The real question is to know whether it is possible to organize a solidarity between nations as regards the maintenance of the children, the old, the sick, the unemployed, and generally the unproductive elements of the world population. It is certainly not an easy task, and we cannot expect important achievements along these lines before a long time. But the simple fact that such a problem can be raised, studied, and discussed is one of the most striking consequences of the general and recent evolution of the concept of income security.

RESPONSIBILITY IN THE NEW INCOME SECURITY POLICIES

The recent trends of income security policies are toward comprehensive schemes covering the whole population of a country against all possible contingencies through mechanisms of a more and more formal administrative character, in which the State takes a more and more important place, and which are linked up with general economic policy. Such evolution may appear to be leading to a collective organization in which individuals pay for their security by the loss of any initiative and responsibility.

On the other hand, the tendency of all modern social services throughout the world is to develop the principle of self-determination and self-help. Their objective is much less to satisfy directly individual or family needs than to help individuals and families to solve by themselves their own problems, to make them able to take their own responsibility in facing their own needs.

That fundamental tendency has also a deep influence on the contemporary evolution of income security schemes. The ways in which that influence appears vary considerably from one country to another, but it manifests itself everywhere.

Fractional character of the coverage

With perhaps a few exceptions in some Eastern countries, the coverage of the possible risks is always fractional. Benefits provided by income security schemes correspond to only a part of the lost income, either a definite percentage of that income or a flat sum allowing a minimum livelihood. The community does not assume the responsibility of maintaining, whatever the circumstances, the standard of life of all its members, but only of achieving a minimum security for everybody. Such limitation of the coverage is imposed on both technical and financial grounds (it would be in fact impossible, in most cases, to give a complete guaranty of the income) and by ethical and psychological considerations. The main objective of income security is, by relieving the human being from his most urgent worries, to give him full opportunity to expand his personality and develop all his own possibilities. This result would not be achieved if income security resulted in depriving individuals and families of all responsibility as concerns their livelihood. There is in fact no scheme which does not leave to the individual a responsibility to provide for a more or less important part of his livelihood, generally a substantially important part of it, besides of course all possible improvements in the existing standard of life.

Importance of voluntary schemes and institutions

Individual initiative and responsibility are encouraged also by voluntary schemes or institutions offering the possibility to obtain, by a personal effort, an increased security. The importance of such voluntary schemes or institutions has indeed declined with the spreading of comprehensive income security schemes. But we have seen that a few countries, mainly Scandinavian countries, still give an important place to such formulas in their basic scheme itself, for either sickness insurance or unemployment benefits. And in most countries a number of schemes or institutions exist, either purely private or subsidized and controlled by the State, either nonprofit institutions or commercial companies, which tend to complete the general and basic schemes by complementary benefits, through an individual or voluntary insurance. Mutual aid societies and insurance companies have everywhere an important place among the means to achieve individual or family security.

Contrary to what could have been expected, the development of public income security schemes has generally given a new impulse to voluntary schemes and institutions, as if the fractional security automatically guaranteed induced the people concerned to seek a fuller security by their own effort.

Sometimes complementary schemes have themselves become compulsory by way of collective agreements concluded between employers' and workers' unions, the voluntary effort being in that case no longer individual but collective. A number of such agreements have been concluded in the United States during recent years, to provide either supplementary old-age pensions to be added to the Federal Security pensions or sickness benefits, serving as substitute for absent official health insurance schemes. Some such schemes may be found also, with more or less development, in most other industrial countries.

Contributory character of the schemes

Another way to favor the individual sense of responsibility is to give income security schemes a contributory character. We have seen that, technically speaking, there is no essential difference, in a compulsory scheme, between contributions and taxes as ways of financing the payment of benefits. But the obligation to pay contributions may give to the insured persons an interest in the scheme itself, the feeling that security is at least partly the product of their own effort. And that is not a fiction. It is obvious that what is received in security benefits is taken from the national income, and, in consequence, from individual incomes, which are reduced in a corresponding proportion. The payment of contributions makes that essential fact visible. Most modern income security schemes are, at least partly, based on contributions. Even New Zealand, in which the whole scheme is financed from public funds, has established a special supplementary income tax to cover security expenses; such a tax, in spite of its name, is from a psychological standpoint very close to a contribution.

Participation in the administration of the scheme

Perhaps even more important is the part played by the interested people or their delegates in the administration of the scheme. Their is indeed a definite tendency towards unification and centralization. But a number of countries endeavor to keep or establish strong links between the institutions and the beneficiaries. Some, as Belgium or Denmark, use mutual aid societies as basic local agencies for the application of the scheme; others, as France, entrust elected bodies with the administration of the institutions created, while yet others provide for the representation of the workers' unions in the committees in charge of that administration. There is an extreme variety of formulas; but always there is the common objective of associating the individuals through their representatives in the day-to-day working of the income security institutions, to give them here again the feeling that they have the responsibility for what is done for them, that security is not a windfall from an anonymous

State administration but the fruit of institutions conducted on their behalf—the fruit in fact of their own efforts within the wider bounds of national solidarity.

Even in countries where Government departments are entirely in charge of the administration of income security schemes, consultative bodies, representative of all kinds of interested people, are generally appointed to advise the competent authorities. Preference given to administration by Government departments in a number of recent schemes does not mean that in the countries concerned less importance has been attached to the cooperation of the interested people in administration. But when a scheme covers the whole population of a country, it may seem that the representation of the people concerned is in fact obtained as perfectly as possible through the elected local or political assemblies. New representative bodies would duplicate such existing assemblies, which are in a position to control the security schemes as well as all collective services.

The different solutions adopted reflect in fact fundamental differences of conceptions as regards the relations between the individual and the State in free democracies. In some countries like Belgium, France, or the Netherlands, the administration of income security schemes by special representative bodies corresponds to the notion that individuals must be protected against the community, against the State. Government is considered as threatening the individual, who finds protection against it through these bodies. In other countries, like the United Kingdom, Australia, New Zealand, or the Scandinavian countries, emphasis is put on the fact that each individual is a member of the community; he is and must be conscious that he takes part in the collective responsibilities of the Parliament and the Government. There is thus no problem of protection of the individual against the Government, but only that of ensuring that the individuals take as large a part as possible in all public affairs, the Parliament and Government decisions expressing the common will of all.

Nothing can show better how, in countries so close to each other, the same words can hide profound differences of conceptions owing to the traditions and psychology of each people. Quite different ways may lead to the same end.

Benefits in cash or in kind

The attempts made towards maximizing individual responsibility within an income security system have another aspect, which is not usually so well known or emphasized. It concerns the types of benefits themselves. We have already underlined the increasingly familial character of the income security benefits in most new schemes. Benefits are intended to secure an appropriate standard of life not only for the individual but for the whole family group. But the beneficiaries, the family concerned, are free to utilize the amount received as they want. They have full responsibility in making the best use of it.

As obvious as it may seem at first sight, this statement raises an important problem. A number of assistance institutions give relief not in cash but in kind. It is thought better to distribute food or clothes, for example, than to give money, of which a bad use could be made. It is certain that benefits in kind are often more efficient and perhaps also more economical. Such methods may bring better social results with the same amount of expenses. Certain countries, such as the Scandinavian ones, largely apply these methods. They prefer, for instance, to help children by distributions in kind rather than to pay family allowances to the parents. But, in spite of undoubted advantages of such formulas, they all come up against the objection that benefits in kind deprive the individual of his responsibilities.

This is especially striking as far as children's education is concerned. There is no field in which personal responsibility is more important. If we do not want to weaken the family links, which are already so much imperiled by modern civilization, it is necessary to avoid as far as possible, and of course outside of desperate cases, substitution of the community for the parents. This explains why, in one recent congress, the International Union of Family Organizations emphasized the superiority of allowances in cash to family help in kind; such allowances being given not to children, nor to meet any definite need, but to contribute to the general family expenses, with freedom to use them for the best of the family interests. The considerable extension of the institution of family allowances, perhaps the most striking of all postwar developments in the social security field, may be considered, as far as it has corresponded to the decline of assistance benefits in kind, as tending to reinforce personal and family responsibility.

Such methods may of course lead to abuse when the beneficiaries make bad use of the benefits they receive. This danger may be faced both by certain controls and chiefly by social education. Most countries combine one and the other in various proportions.

Income security and social services

Income security schemes may seem insufficiently human in another respect. In the social field there are rarely general situations. Each case is an individual one. The security of each individual, or at least of each family, raises a special problem. Statutory schemes are necessarily rigid. They provide everybody with the same benefits, or at least without regard to the particular situations. The fundamental unity of the new schemes, their comprehensive and administrative character, have increased this uniformity and this rigidity.

The counterpart is the tendency to establish an even closer relation between income security schemes and other social services. The individualization of the benefits that may be noticed in some national legislation is already a step in that direction; as far as the nature and the rate of benefits may be adapted to the proper situation of an individual or a family, there is already a beginning of humanization of the scheme.

But most countries go much farther. In some of them, social security institutions themselves are in charge not only of dispensing income security benefits but also of promoting a number of other social services. Having to bear the eventual consequences of illnesses or accidents, they are allowed and encouraged to undertake preventive work in the medical field or in the field of industrial safety. Providing benefits for old people or families, they organize services of social workers, home helps, holiday camps, generally all kinds of services—making the help given as individual as possible, and giving each family the sort of security for which it particularly feels the need. They have also developed social education in order both to prevent possible risks and to induce beneficiary families to make the best use of their benefits. Such a tendency is specially marked when autonomous bodies are in charge of the administration of the scheme. The presence of representatives of the interested people in the management of these bodies makes it easier to adapt the social effort undertaken to the proper needs and situation of each group of the population.

When the administration of income security schemes belongs to Government departments, the link between those schemes and the other social services is not so visible. Different agencies are normally in charge of income security on the one hand, and of social welfare on the other. But even in such cases the development of both kinds of services is and must be parallel. Participation of social workers is always necessary to help the people draw the full profit of any income security scheme, to educate them, to teach them the new responsibilities involved in the benefits of such schemes.

Income security must never be considered as sufficient by itself. It is part of a whole social process. All elements of such a process must progress at the same pace.

CONCLUSION

Finally the main issue raised by contemporary trends in income security policies is the problem of the impact of income security on individual freedom.

Everywhere throughout the world there has been during recent decades, there is still today, a powerful current towards social security in general, and specially income security. It appears as the modern aspect of the human struggle for liberty. For undoubtedly income security in itself is liberty. Freedom from want is freedom, at least an essential form of freedom.

Considerable masses of people totally identify security with liberty. They are unable to conceive any other form of liberty. Because of their general conditions of living, political liberty, individual freedom, and freedom of thought have no meaning for them. Their permanent state of destitution excludes any other aspiration than to keep on living, at best to improve their material conditions.

Such a state of mind, the pressure of such masses, could compromise individual freedoms, reduce them, at least reduce the chance of making new progress. The risk is all the more serious as the general tendency of income security policies is towards comprehensive schemes, extension of the powers of public authorities, sometimes towards giving security in ways that reduce the individual and family sense of responsibility

This risk, however, does not justify setting up an irreconcilable conflict between income security and liberty. If it appeared that security and liberty were incompatible, that a choice was unavoidable between them, it is possible that a great majority of human kind today would choose security against liberty; an immediate and certain advantage against a word deprived for them of any concrete content. It would be a serious mistake nevertheless to oppose the general trend towards income security, which corresponds to a deep and general aspiration of all human beings.

The real problem is to promote income security policies giving the largest possible room to individual and family freedom, to individual and family responsibilities. Many examples show that this is possible. And if this is possible, it must be the goal of all free countries, for freedom by security, and income security with freedom, are the best way, if not the only way, to allow every man and woman to make the best use of his own potentialities.

COMMENTS

Fedele F. Fauri

Dean, School of Social Work, University of Michigan

Pierre Laroque presents a comprehensive review of the major issues arising from contemporary trends in income security policies. He gives an excellent summary of the various factors resulting in the spread of income security programs throughout the world. The present remarks are limited, however, to that part of the chapter relating to the tendency towards generalization of income security. Concentrating on this one aspect may be helpful in pointing up some of the lacks in the social security system in the United States which do not exist in some of the other countries referred to in the paper we are to discuss this morning.

Mr. Laroque has stated: "One of the main features, perhaps the most important feature, of the income security policies in all countries during recent years is the general admission of the fundamental unit of social security, thus resulting in the generalization of income security legislation and institutions to the whole population and to all contingencies threatening that security."

Has there been general admission of the fundamental unity of social security reflected in the social security programs in the United States? I do not want to minimize the progress that has been made in the last two decades in affording income security to the population as a whole. We have made and we will continue to make substantial advances in affording protection against the risks of unemployment, old age, and premature death. The fact remains, however, that our social security system is still fractional—both as to coverage of the population and as to the contingencies covered. There has not been general admission of the fundamental unity of social security on the part of the legislative bodies that enact the basic policies governing social security programs.

As to the coverage of the population, up to now the Congress has seen fit to exclude a substantial part of the population from the old-age and survivors' insurance system. Even the new 1954 legislation ignores the need for extending coverage to most of the migratory farm workers. Also, some domestic workers, policemen, firemen, and physicians would continue to be excluded. In many states unemployment insurance is not available to employees working for firms employing less than eight individuals, and farm labor and several other groups are excluded from the system.

Moreover, not only are there still wide gaps in the protection of large segments of the population under social insurance, but public assistance is not universal in coverage of those in need. Residence requirements preclude the granting of assistance to individuals who have not resided in a state for a specified period of time—often five years out of the last nine years for old-age assistance. In some states, noncitizens are not eligible for public assistance. General assistance—the program which is supposed to be the "catch-all" for those not having their minimum needs met by social insurance categorical assistance, or by other methods—is not available in all communities.

As to protection against all contingencies that threaten the security of individuals, the United States does not fully measure up to Mr. Laroque's conclusion that there is ". . . a general tendency toward covering everybody against all risks which may threaten income security."

Among the risks Mr. Laroque mentions, when he speaks of "covering everybody against all risks," are sickness and maternity, invalidity, and family benefits. These contingencies are not covered for the general population in the United States by public non-needs-test programs. Moreover, there is no apparent groundswell in the United States to cover everybody against all these risks.

Let us look at the developments in so far as one of these risks is concerned, that is, invalidity or extended disability, in which there has been considerable interest. Public programs on a non-needs-test basis currently limit protection to veterans, railroad workers, and individuals with a disability that is occupational in origin. The one broad public program of Federal-state aid to the permanently and totally disabled—which, incidentally, is not in effect in all states—provides payments only after individuals have become needy.

Thus far, those opposing the extension of social insurance to individuals suffering the loss of earnings from extended disability have succeeded in preventing the inclusion of this risk for the general population of the country. Allegations have been made that such a program is administratively not feasible, the costs are too high, and it would encourage malingering. Instead of providing compensation payments to disabled individuals, it is urged that all efforts should be directed toward providing rehabilitation services so as not to stifle incentive to work. Compensation payments and rehabilitation need not be incompatible, but none the less we have seen strong sentiment develop to divide the extended disability problem into these two separate parts—with rehabilitation labeled as feasible and desirable and compensation payments as not feasible and not desirable.

One question raised by Mr. Laroque's statement about the trend to increase the risks covered against income loss is why foreign experience has not been a factor in late years in influencing the broadening of the United States' social insurance programs. In the field of extended or permanent and total disability insurance, foreign experience has been cast aside as not germane for one reason or another. We should not be so willing to discard foreign experience even though the problems inherent in operating social insurance systems in the United States may be different in some respects from those encountered in other countries.

Among the many major issues, we must not overlook the role of a university. Universities should take more leadership in providing objective evaluation of foreign experience in affording income security, which may be pertinent for the use of legislative policy makers in the United States. Only our Chairman and a few other university faculty members have been actively engaged in reviewing foreign systems.

In the field of permanent and total disability insurance, for example, detailed objective study in various countries by faculty members, thinking in terms of what would be useful to those determining legislative policy in the United States, could aid our policy makers in evaluating the allegations that have been made against including loss of earnings due to permanent and total disability within our social security system.

In addition to encouraging studies on the part of faculty members or other professional personnel interested in the field of income security, we need to interest key policy makers in observing the operation of foreign systems at first hand. Members of Congress having jurisdiction over legislation in the health field have been engaged in reviewing foreign experience. The members of committees charged with legislation relating to income maintenance programs have not reviewed the actual operation of such programs in other countries. Such review, coupled with the professional studies mentioned, would bring the United States more closely in line with Mr. Laroque's statement concerning the broadening of income security programs as to risks and as to the population covered.

In conclusion, excluding medical care programs, if the United States is to keep pace with the contemporary trends in income security policies described so well by Mr. Laroque, there are six questions that should be answered in the affirmative:

1. Should Old Age and Survivors Insurance coverage be extended to include all gainfully employed and self-employed individuals?

2. Should Unemployment Insurance coverage be extended to include employees regardless of size of firm?

3. Should Unemployment Insurance coverage be extended to additional occupational groups?

4. Should social insurance protection be provided for persons unable to work because of disability, however caused?

5. Should grants-in-aid for public assistance vary in accordance with fiscal resources of states and communities?

6. Should residence and citizenship requirements for public assistance be eliminated?

REPORT OF THE RECORDER

Herman D. Stein

Lecturer in Social Work, New York School of Social Work
Columbia University

The relationship of public assistance and social insurance as methods of income maintenance was a principal focus of discussion. Dr. Goldmann stated that public assistance first came in as a supplement to private charity, then the social insurances emerged as supplements to public assistance. But the insurances have developed to cover a wide variety of risks. He suggested that public assistance should be reduced to an irreducible minimum, since it is not preventive, it is inadequate, it does not encourage self-help, and insurance is far more important.

Mr. Lewin observed that public assistance was here to stay, and that public assistance and the insurances do not exist in competition. There is nothing necessarily destructive to personality in public assistance, but there is the necessity of improving the program.

Dr. Wootton noted that in England there has been a complete revolution in the attitude towards public assistance during the last 25 years. It has been hated and resented. Now there is a much more accepting attitude, and the line has been blurred between insurance as related to right and public assistance as related to need. The distinction no longer operates clearly. There is need for more information as to the subtle influences causing these changes in attitude.

Professor Linford stated that we have not achieved the necessary balance between public assistance and the insurances in this country, nor have we achieved nondestructive administration of public assistance. Although there has been modification of the old Poor Law concepts, there are still recurrent charges of fraud, chiseling, and there has been the use of police methods in ferreting out chiselers, a revolting but growing development. Despite the fact that we have had insurance for twenty years, there are five million people still existing under this negative program. Professor Linford further observed that the English experience with public assistance suggests merely a failure to keep insurance benefits up to date with the cost of living. For a society to maintain two different systems to take care of the same people is ridiculous.

Professor Morgan believed that the changed attitude in Britain toward public assistance was due principally to the British wartime experience. Reparations for damages due to bombing were paid on the assumption that people were telling the truth, rather than under the suspicion of chiseling. This assumption, born of necessity, was found to be valid, since on a later check it was found that less than two per cent of the claims were found to be fraudulent. Professor Morgan favored the continuance of public assistance to take care of individual variation. He agreed with the general tenor of the discussion that there was the continuing problem of helping the public assistance and insurance systems to stay in balance, but he felt the initial problem was not economic, but administrative.

Professor Morgan also stressed the right of establishing judicial process, particularly in public assistance. A vast body of *administrative* law is developing. Skill is needed in correcting administrative misinterpretations or arbitrariness, and it is questionable whether the rights of the individual recipient can be truly protected without the scrutiny of the judicial process. In this area, there is need for much sociological knowledge which we at present lack.

The importance of programs in the health area was stressed by several participants. Professor Somers pointed out that social security should not be confined to income maintenance. Rehabilitation is a vital field. Further, workmen's compensation, originally conceived as a wage substitute, today compensates for anatomical loss, irrespective of wage loss, in 47 out of 48 states. He noted that workmen's compensation should not be confused with rehabilitation; it contributes little either to rehabilitation or to prevention.

Professor Blanchard observed that amounts for medical and surgical care under workmen's compensation have steadily increased, but Professor Somers held that rehabilitation should not be subsumed under medical and surgical care, for sometimes these are not rehabilitative.

Dr. Goldmann emphasized the interdependence of health care and income maintenance. There is no point in providing income to those who cannot earn if they have to use the money to pay medical and hospital bills. Conversely, there is no point in providing health care if there is no money for food or housing. Both aspects of security must operate together.

Professor Morgan took issue with Dr. Laroque's explanation of the development of family allowances after the war. M. Laroque had stressed demographic reasons in France as shaping this system, and protection against unemployment as shaping England's general social security program. Professor Morgan felt that the family allowance program, as in Canada, was also a means of redistributing income and assuring a broad basis of purchasing power—considerations of special importance to economists and social planners after the war. But, basically, the family allowance is a symptom of an industrial society. Socially the individual employee is a family breadwinner, but industrially he is simply one unit and the number of his dependents is unrelated to his industrial function. Neither considerations of demography nor of unemployment are basic, but rather the social need of strengthening the family in an industrial society, so that the family would not be submerged.

Mr. Wilbur Cohen felt that inadequate attention had been paid in M. Laroque's paper to survivors' benefits, probably the program where the United States had done its best job. Nine out of ten breadwinners have the protection of survivors' insurance, and it can be shown that such a program makes a great contribution to a productive economy. Mr. Cohen also took exception to M. Laroque's statement that "few schemes are as perfect as the British." It may reach perfection with respect to the rational relationship of the parts of the program, but not as a perfect program in and of itself. Its flat benefit system, for example, is not well adapted to a free enterprise system.

This point led to the general question of the relationship of a wage-related social security system to an economy where an upward trend in wages is assumed. Mr. Cohen pointed out the increasing proportion of beneficiaries in the U.S. who in fact received flat rates, due to the impact of arbitrary maximums. How can income security systems maintain a balance when there is increase in wages, productivity, and continued inflation?

Mr. Clague spoke to this question, observing that almost all social security systems perpetually lag behind the cost of living, only one country having included automatic adjustments to the cost of living. In the United States we started by covering in Old Age and Survivors Insurance (OASI) all wages earned below $3,000, and we are now operating on $3,600 maximum coverage. On the basis of the 1939 $3,000, the equivalent amount now, related to the cost-of-living increase, is $6,000; and, if related to the average gains in earnings, it is $9,000. Yet we remain, like most social security systems, tied to a legalism.

Professor Burns focused on this problem of keeping benefits in pace with rising prices and productivity. There are techniques for taking care of that. Sweden has not only an automatic cost-of-living increase, but a standard-of-living increase. What stops societies, and particularly the United States, from using these available techniques? This question of failure to utilize techniques developed elsewhere can be seen in other aspects of income security programs.

Professor Harris and Mr. Altmeyer commented on this, stressing the difficulties in copying programs of other countries. Professor Harris pointed out, for example, that the scope of France's social security system is related to the facts that France does not have too many high incomes and has a lower standard of living than the United States. The wage earner has to depend more on fringe benefits, such as family allowances. The most effective aid there is related to need, since there is less income than can be transferred from those with high to those with low incomes.

Mr. Altmeyer emphasized the nonimportability of social security programs from the point of view of the day-to-day administrative decisions that shape a program, sometimes basically. He illustrated with the example of OASI, where at its inception both the design and the administrative features of the program could have had authoritarian implications, but through able administration (of Mr. Corson) lasting features were built into the program (for example, through staff-training) that have given it a social and democratic character.

Throughout the discussion, participants picked up Professor Fauri's theme of the role of universities in clarifying issues in social security, particularly in studying foreign experiences. Most of the suggestions were related to research which universities could carry on.

Dr. Goldmann suggested research (1) on the impact of social security schemes on the individual—not only whether there is abuse, but the actual utilization of the schemes—present evidence being that abuse is uncommon; (2) on determining whether income maintenance programs are really a burden on the economy—his feeling being that there is no evidence to support this contention, for prices need not go up when industry supports such programs, since costs can be offset in gains in productivity, less absenteeism, and other factors; (3) on the relationship between security and freedom—not mutually exclusive, since in forty countries the present evidence is that opportunities to work, to lead personally satisfying and socially useful lives, are created to some degree by social security measures, which thus promote freedom.

Mr. Cruikshank suggested that universities should study domestic as well as foreign experiences. There is a larger program in disability insurance in the United States, for example, than in some foreign countries. There is constant criticism of disability insurance on such grounds as the danger of malingering and the corrosive effect on the medical profession, yet such criticism is not related to the actual experience with the two million people who are already covered. Studies should be made of the current operation of these systems.

Mr. Cruikshank added that the universities can do a better job in the preparation of doctors, who should be more than merely technicians trained to provide medical service (flesh mechanics). Our society suffers from the fact that many doctors are not men educated in social problems, and do not comprehend their role as citizens. The colleges should do more to correct these deficiencies.

Professor Klineberg, agreeing with M. Laroque's point that security was in part a psychological phenomenon, suggested research on what the attitudes of people actually are with respect to security; what people actually mean by the term. He contrasted absolute ("it is human nature") and relative concepts of security, the latter being based on how secure people one knows may be. What also is known about people's willingness to take chances?

Professor Morgan suggested research into what actually changed the British public's attitude toward public assistance, offering his own explanation (as indicated above) that it was related to wartime experience.

Professor Harris raised several questions: (1) Whether social security expenditures are really a drain on the economy, and if so, how and to what extent? (2) Whether international competition is really a problem in the development of social security programs in various countries? Professor Harris was not sure this was a problem. If it really meant an increase of costs for some countries, it might simply lead to a different structure of trade. (3) Whether it really made no difference whether compulsory contributions or payroll taxes was the method of financing? This did not seem true to him since there are differences in the amount of fixed charges, and differences in equity to be considered, among other factors.

Several points were raised in relation to unemployment insurance. Professor Brissenden observed that, while we have become more inclusive, we originally excluded large groups, and that one of the ways our program remains not generalized (in M. Laroque's term) is in the fact that the program is restricted to firms with a minimum number of employees. The reason is the assumption of administrative difficulties for firms with fewer employees, but he questioned whether the administrative difficulty is really so important.

Mr. Clague pointed out that the unemployment insurance systems have now reached a point where a man's wage credits can be canceled. He questioned whether this is equitable and pointed out that the multiplication of systems results in a mixture of incentives. Professor Blanchard observed that other types of attack on insecurity should be kept in mind. Along with such developments as deposit insurance, they are part of a social security system.

In his final remarks concerning the points raised during the discussion, M. Laroque indicated that he would not deal with the relationship of insurance to assistance, nor with financing, since these were subjects more appropriate to other sessions; nor would he deal with problems unique to the United States.

With reference to the increasing generalization of a program, he considered it important to be conscious of the special needs of special groups. To farmers and farm employees, for example, crop insurance is important.

M. Laroque agreed emphatically with the need for scientific studies in the field of social security. However, such studies require the cooperation of a great number of specialized disciplines, and therefore the best way to undertake such studies is to have a committee representing such disciplines inaugurate them. He agreed also with the necessity of maintaining judicial process, for without it there was no real security. The question was what kind of judicial process. Neither the *ordinary* courts, such as are used in England, nor *administrative* courts, such as are used in some other European countries, are truly adapted to the problems of social security. M. Laroque favored the establishment of special courts in the social field, with judges specially trained in social law and social problems, so that they could deal adequately with social claims.

There is a necessary link, he stressed, between income security in the form of social insurance, rehabilitation, and prevention. Income security should not be considered primarily as furnishing a substitute income, but rather as preventing its loss in the first place. Industrial safety is thus part of income security. All social security programs are interdependent.

The Nature and Level of Income Security for a Free Society

Richard A. Lester

Professor of Economics, Princeton University

This paper deals with the nature and the level of income that should be assured in a free society to persons whose earnings are sharply curtailed or interrupted by such risks as unemployment, accident, illness, or superannuation. By the "nature of assured income" is meant primarily the basis by which eligibility is determined and the important criteria that govern the sum granted; whether, for example, the weekly or monthly amount of income supplied is based on need or calculated deficiency in the family budget, or is related to previous earnings or contributions and is granted with little regard to personal needs. In other words, is it granted on a relief basis or a social insurance basis?

Our main concern will be with the level of assured income and the issues arising therefrom. The subject will be discussed in terms of social insurance benefits. Relief or assistance levels will be considered in relation to benefits under the social insurance programs, and differences between the two will be examined.

Unfortunately one cannot arrive at the determination of the proper level of social insurance benefits by mathematical means, or by scientific tests, or even by pure logic. The answer depends upon one's economic and social philosophy —the sympathy he has for human misfortune, the stress he places on preserving individual dignity, and the kind of society he envisions as desirable. The answer will vary also with the kind of economy in which the level is to apply (the general standard of living, the distribution of personal income, and the division between market determination and governmental determination of economic affairs) and with the traditions, history, and culture of the society in question. Consequently, the appropriate level of assured income under a social insurance program cannot be discussed *in vacuo* or in abstract terms. Its fitness must be judged in relation to a particular society and economy. The discussion here, therefore, will be in terms of the United States in the mid-1950s.

In an analysis of the level of security benefits for American conditions, a number of "relationship" factors must be taken into account. The level of assured income should be discussed in relation to such matters as the following: the type of economic risk (unemployment, accident, illness, superannuation); the duration or time span of benefit payments; previous contributions on behalf of the beneficiary; the size of the family unit; overlapping or supplementary provisions including private programs, public assistance, and earnings in uncovered employment; tax provisions and take-home pay; changing price levels and living standards; and the society's notions of equity and obligation. The bearing of each of those items on the proper level is considered in the first section of the chapter.

Even more important perhaps are the effects of different levels of benefits upon various aspects of the economy. The method of calculating social insurance benefits and their size may have favorable or adverse consequences for worker incentives and morale and therefore productivity; the operation of labor-market forces, including wage adjustments, labor mobility, and labor-force attachment; the income distribution and growth of the national income; seasonal and cyclical swings in employment; personal savings and investment; and also the influence of government on the individual and the division between public and private powers. Although there may be some overlap among those six items, each will be examined separately in the second section.

The third section of the chapter discusses benefit levels in the light of the objectives of the programs. Consideration is given to the political and economic factors that influence benefit levels, the extent that benefit levels differ by type of risk, the role that minimum needs of beneficiaries should play in the establishment of benefit levels, and the question whether Federal benefit standards are necessary or desirable.

The final section of the chapter offers some concluding observations and discusses the kinds of studies that would aid in answering some of the important unsettled questions with respect to the nature and level of income security in a free society.

FACETS OF THE LEVEL PROBLEM

We shall examine first the relationship factors and then the possible effects of different benefit levels.

Type of Economic Risk

The first of the six relationship factors listed above is the type of economic risk. Unemployment, illness, and nonpermanent injury are temporary risks. The worker, it is assumed, will return to gainful employment, and programs of compensation for wage loss must take account of possible effects on incentives to return to full-time work.

Unfortunately, social scientists have not made an adeqate investigation of the influence of insurance benefits on work motivation. A general belief exists that workers are more prone to malinger on public benefit than on private benefit under a company program. In some social groups, "beating" the government may not be considered dishonorable. Nevertheless, the social pressures are strong for continued gainful employment for the heads of families, although perhaps less so for youths and married women. A man's friendships, self-respect, and place in society are tied up with his participation in economic activities of the community. The desire to maintain work relationships undoubtedly is a factor in explaining the results of surveys of beneficiaries on old-age and survivors' insurance, which show that only about 5 per cent stopped work on their own accord, in good health, to enjoy a life of leisure.[1] One's job connection has considerable value in lines of business in which seniority and promotion-from-within are the practice, so that perhaps four-fifths of the community's production workers are firmly attached to their companies.[2] Under such circumstances, unnecessary work absence or other activities that reflect adversely on the worker's reputation as an employee are likely to be known in the shop and to injure his worklife prospects with the firm.

This whole matter will be discussed more fully in the section on effects. All that needs to be mentioned here is that opposition to improved benefit levels appears to be greatest in the case of unemployment compensation, which is a wholly public program and which tends to affect wage levels in lines like agriculture. Since sick or injured workers are not available for work, there does not seem to be quite the same pressure to keep ceilings on workmen's compensation benefits low as there is in the case of unemployment compensation. These remarks refer to views of the benefit level as such, entirely apart from the cost aspects of the matter.

Lifetime risks, such as retirement with superannuation or injury resulting in total and permanent disability, may separate the person from normal employment, thereby largely eliminating the question of the short-run effects of benefit levels on work incentives. The issue of long-run adjustment might still need to be met in the case of permanently disabling injuries, and is tied up with the next topic of benefit duration.

Duration of Payments

The length of continued benefit payments has a bearing on benefit levels in the case of both temporary and life-time risks. The higher the benefit level, the less financial pressure there is on the worker to adjust to a lower relative wage —to recognize that injury has reduced his value to employers or that for new employment he will have to accept, as "suitable," a job much farther down the occupational hierarchy than the one he previously had.

Duration, of course, varies with the type of risk. Retirement pay should continue throughout retirement; permanent disability benefits should be paid as long as the disability is permanent. Under state workmen's compensation acts, however, a fixed money maximum per case is often specified in the law. Even where such maximums are not rigidly established, the issue of higher level of benefits or longer duration arises whenever benefit liberalization is under discussion.

Because unemployment insurance is conceived as short-term compensation for involuntary wage loss, after which resort, if necessary, is to assistance, there may be a strong argument for a relatively high benefit as protection against forcing a worker to make too rapid a drop down the job ladder. With adequate temporary protection, he may be able to avoid having to make such a sharp step-down in occupational rank. On the other hand, where some adjustment is inevitable, as may be the case with retirement or permanent injury, the argument for a high temporary level of benefits may not be valid. Problems of adjustment and mobility are analyzed below.

Contributions

Contributions, paid by beneficiaries or their employers, that vary with workers' earnings establish a basis for differentiated benefits and promote relatively high benefits for high-wage employees. Connecting both contributions and benefits to a worker's wages helps to develop the notion of earned rights and to subordinate the element of need, which stresses uniformity of treatment and tends to disregard pre-existing differences in personal living standards. In other words, the notion of prior contribution and earned rights which are wage-connected presumes a range of benefits from a minimum to a maximum, whereas flat contributions regardless of personal earnings or assistance based on need imply a uniform minimum standard or floor of security.

Family Unit

Social insurance benefits varying with the size of family or number of the worker's dependents may seem not only to introduce but to emphasize the element of need. Additional sums for dependents are provided under the Federal Old Age and Survivors Insurance program; in eleven states with dependents' allowances under unemployment compensation; and in a number of states under workmen's compensation.[3] Extra benefits for dependents might seem to introduce "unearned" elements, and the principle of uniformity by numbers, into the benefit program. However, gearing benefits to the worker's past earnings and varying the supplementary benefits with such earnings tend to preserve the notion of earned rights and permit the payment of differentiated benefit levels according to work records.

An exception to the differentiation of supplemental or dependents' benefits occurs in unemployment compensation, where they have been a flat sum for all regardless of the person's level of prior earnings or the size of his basic benefit. Such uniformity makes possible, of course, benefits equal to or above normal earnings, especially if the uniform dependents' allowances are of any significant size. The effects of such possibilities on worker incentives are discussed later. Here it is necessary only to point out the desirability of some total limit in terms of normal earnings, such as the 80 per cent maximum under Federal Old Age and Survivors Insurance, and also the wisdom of having benefit differences for dependents under short-term risks take the form of variations in the benefit ceilings rather than simply a uniform amount for all regardless of any relationship between the resulting total benefit and normal earnings. This matter is discussed more fully later and raises questions of ethics and equity which are considered below.

Supplementary Provisions

Benefit levels under public programs have to be considered in the light of supplementary or overlapping programs, which are specified under collective agreements or have been unilaterally installed. By 1953, for instance, private pension plans covered about 12,000,000 workers, or roughly one out of every four persons covered under the Federal Old Age and Survivors Insurance program.

In this country, the administrations of Old Age and Survivors Insurance, unemployment insurance, and workmen's compensation are completely separate. One result is that it is possible for a person to be drawing concurrently from two different public programs: a widow may be receiving both state workmen's compensation and Federal survivors' insurance, or a beneficiary may perhaps be drawing both Federal old-age benefits and state unemployment compensation.

An example will illustrate the implications of duplicate benefits. In New Jersey in 1953, after the maximum benefit for widows was raised to $30 a week, a surviving wife with two children whose husband's gross weekly wage was $50 would receive $97.50 a month under workmen's compensation (figuring 4⅓ weeks per month) and $145 under Old Age and Survivors Insurance (primary benefit $72.50),[4] or total monthly benefits of $242.50, compared with a monthly wage income of $211.81 when the husband was living and adding to the family's living costs. In other words, a family of three would be receiving temporarily $30 more than when it had four members. With higher incomes the differential of benefits over normal income for a widow with two children under the New Jersey and Federal programs would have been as follows: $29 a month for gross weekly income of $60, $18.75 a month for gross weekly income of $70, and approximately $16 for gross weekly income of $80.

Supplementary private arrangements, such as company programs for pensions or sickness benefits, mean that workers on benefit (public plus private) may receive wage-loss compensation close to their normal earnings. Under some programs they may actually receive the same, or, in a few cases, more money income on benefit than when normally working. Under private programs, managements seem not to be too troubled about the incentive effects of such results in cases of retirement or of illness or injury.

Where the level of social insurance benefits is relatively low, they may need to be supplemented by assistance payments. In England, which has low, flat-rate old-age benefits plus dependents' allowances, about 25 per cent of the households receiving insured retirement pensions in 1952 needed supplementation by assistance payments on a needs-test basis.[5] In the United States, about 11 per cent of those receiving Federal Old Age and Survivors Insurance in 1953 also were in need of public assistance.[6]

Perhaps it should also be mentioned that the possibilities of earnings outside of social insurance coverage have been significantly reduced as the coverage of those programs has been extended and as the opportunities for self-employment, say in agriculture and distribution, have been contracting.

Take-home Pay

Social insurance benefits are not taxable. Therefore, it is claimed, the level of benefits should be related to actual take-home pay rather than to wages prior to tax deductions. With high personal income taxes at the Federal (and possibly the state levels) and with other deductions such as the Old Age and Survivors Insurance tax of 2 per cent on workers' wages, average take-home pay may really be only about 80 to 90 per cent of nominal pay, depending, of course, on the worker's wage level, the number of claimed dependents, etc. In addition, a worker has certain extra costs when working, such as transportation to and from the job and the added cost of lunch away from home.

On the other hand, he may have losses in addition to the wage loss when he is out of work. Mostly these are losses of various fringe benefit rights, such as hospital and sickness and accident protection, life insurance, vacation and holiday rights, possible reductions in Old Age and Survivors benefits and in unemployment compensation benefits, and so forth. With the cost of fringe items amounting to as much as 15 to 20 per cent of payroll,[7] such losses may be significant to a laid-off worker, depending of course on the length of the lay-off and whether or not the worker does return to employment with the same firm.[8]

So many factors affect individual cases, one way or the other, that it is difficult to generalize concerning the difference it would make if benefits were related to correct take-home pay with full allowance for loss of certain benefit rights and protections while on, say, unemployment compensation.[9] As a practical matter, it would probably be impossible by legislation to base benefits on such a calculated figure. Nevertheless, there is considerable validity to the contention that, in determining the proper level of benefits under social insurance, account should be taken of the level of personal income taxes and the value of fringe benefits lost by unemployed workers.

Adjustments

In a dynamic and expanding economy, benefit levels need to be adjusted to changes in living costs and in living standards, if benefits are not to become obsolete. When wage levels rise but benefits do not, society tends to be divided into a part that gains the advantages of productivity increases and another part (say those on old-age benefits) that does not share in the general improvements in real wages. In addition, the more benefit levels lag behind rising living costs, the more social insurance benefits need to be supplemented by assistance grants.

It is claimed that social insurance benefits should not increase in the same proportion as the community's general level of living. On the premise that only a basic minimum of income security should be assured under a public social insurance program, it is argued that such a basic minimum does not and should not advance in step with general living standards—say, at a rate averaging 2 or 3 per cent a year. Private arrangements are proposed as the means of meeting the growing gap between legislated benefit levels and advancing levels of living.

That contention raises at least two issues. The first is whether it is presumed to establish a principle that applies with equal force to each type of risk. Does it apply in the same way to unemployment compensation, for which private insurance is not available, as it does to old-age insurance? Is the principle of the basic minimum applicable in like manner to temporary disability and permanent total disability from industrial accident under workmen's compensation? One is a short-term and the other a life-time risk, for which benefit payments may extend over three, four, and even five decades.

The second question is the proper distribution of protection between public programs and private arrangements. That certainly is one of the basic elements in the subject of this paper. Further consideration of both issues is postponed until after the treatment of the topics of personal savings and supplementary private provision in the next section of the paper.

Equity and Obligation

Social values and thought patterns peculiarly affect notions regarding the correct levels of social insurance benefits. Development of the insurance concept of benefits as a matter of right and its application under social insurance permitted a sharp distinction to be drawn between work-connected payments and needs-test assistance. Insurance benefits have come to be considered, not public charity, but an earned right that the beneficiary, his employer, or both, have bought and paid for. The cost may be levied solely on the employer, because he is presumed to be able to reduce the risk by preventive measures, or because he should assume it as part of the regular costs of doing business. Benefits are related to previous earnings on which contributions have been paid. Such notions obviously foster differentiated benefits and influence popular conceptions of proper benefit levels.

Undoubtedly the size of the wage base on which the contributions are levied also influences value judgments about benefit levels and reinforces the idea of benefit ceilings in absolute dollar amounts. The opposition to any increase in the wage base above $3,000 a year in the case of unemployment compensation and $3,600 a year in the case of Old Age and Survivors Insurance has seemed, in part, to be an opposition to higher benefit ceilings. Indeed, the concept of a dollar ceiling on benefits under a system of only partial compensation needs much more thorough examination than it has had, and we shall return to it at a later point.

The establishment of a percentage of wage loss to be met by social insurance benefits is obviously an arbitrary matter. Social objections apparently arise when the percentage for a worker suffering from a "temporary" risk is much below 50 per cent or when it approaches 100 per cent. Nevertheless, in Illinois under workmen's compensation widows with three or more dependent children receive 97½ per cent of the normal wages of the husband at the time of the fatal accident within a ceiling of $30.60 (three children) or $34 (four or more children), and in Michigan workers with dependents who receive weekly wages up to $30 receive unemployment compensation benefits up to 90 per cent or more of their wages during employment in the base period. Such weighting in favor of low-wage workers, so that a higher percentage of their wage loss is compensated for than in the case of high-wage workers, does not seem, under social insurance programs, to raise much objection in terms of equity or earned rights. Dependents' benefits or allowances also do not seem to have given rise to a feeling of basic conflict with the principle of benefits geared to earnings.

Although value judgments concerning social insurance benefits may be unprecise and their formulation surrounded by much obscurity, it seems clear that objections to high benefit levels frequently arise from assumptions regarding their effects on work incentives and the operation of the economic system. That is a subject to which attention is now directed.

ECONOMIC AND POLITICAL EFFECTS

Social insurance benefits are generally considered a burden on the economy because they involve payments to people when they are not contributing to the stream of production. Often a question is raised as to the amount or size of social insurance benefits that the economy can stand.

In attempting to analyze the economic consequences of different benefit levels, it would be desirable to be able to build a set of models whose application and manipulation would lead to valuable inferences concerning the effects of various benefit levels. Unfortunately, the complexity of the problem seems to render such a program practically impossible, at least at this stage in the development of economic analysis, and we are forced to resort to a much less rigorous procedure.

Also, the issues involved extend far beyond the domain of economics into areas of psychology, politics, and social philosophy. That, for instance, is true of the first aspect of the subject of this section, to which we now turn; namely, the effects of benefit levels on work incentives and labor productivity.

Productivity

High benefit levels may affect the workers' incentive to produce on the job, their readiness to leave work for life on benefits, and their desire to return to work following a period of unemployment. The issue under discussion is whether or not the assurance of a benefit of 75, 85, or 100 per cent of normal pay when workers are laid off, sick, injured, or nominally retired, will serve to discourage industriousness and ambition so as to affect labor productivity adversely and encourage malingering on a benefit instead of searching for work. The issue arises particularly when the worker claims that he is unable to find work or is unable to work because of ill health.

Little statistical evidence appears to exist to support a claim that high assured benefit levels reduce the industriousness and productivity of labor while at work. General knowledge and logic also fail to lend support to such a contention. Under the American philosophy of social insurance, widely supported by management and labor spokesmen in this country, benefits are related to work records. Up to the benefit ceilings, larger earnings mean higher benefits; one improves his benefit possibilities by improving his performance and pay. The graded benefit structure partially preserves and protects earned differentials in economic status, and, to that extent, reinforces the normal economic motivation to increase one's earnings by turning out more on incentive pay and by climbing up the occupational ladder. The connection of benefit levels with prior earnings largely eliminates any conflict between security and incentive, at least so long as a differential exists between wage-loss compensation and established earnings after taxes.

Although the benefit structure may embody an incentive "carrot," it may be claimed that social insurance benefits weaken the "stick" or the penalties for poor performance. That claim is not so appropriate for injury, illness, or even old age as it is for unemployment. With respect to unemployment, however, one may question whether workers worried about wage loss from job insecurity would have a frame of mind conducive to high level output. Moreover, with seniority governing the order of lay-off, even in many nonunion plants, the use of discriminatory lay-off as a threat to induce better work performance is largely eliminated. Disqualifying provisions in the law, which deny benefits where the unemployment is not deemed involuntary, also serve to reduce any threat to workers' initiative or enterprise that benefits might seem to contain.

Much more difficult to answer is the question whether benefits may cause workers to prefer, at least temporarily, idleness on benefit to work for pay, and whether one can draw up some kind of schedule of propensity for benefits in relation to the size of the differential between benefit and normal pay. Such a "relationship" would mean that, as the differential diminished or disappeared, the propensity, and hence the number of workers preferring a benefit status, would increase.

In considering this question, distinctions should be drawn between different types of risk and between different elements in the work force. The propensity to retire may rise as a worker's combined retirement benefits approach normal pay; nevertheless, as already indicated, studies show a surprising reluctance among older workers to retire even when they are eligible for fairly high benefits. In the temporary risks, the existence or nonexistence of ill health may be difficult to prove, and the willingness of an unemployed worker to accept "suitable work" may be troublesome to determine.

Within the nation's work force, certain groups seem more prone to accept or seek benefit status than to work, if the differential in terms of take-home income is small or negligible. The propensity for benefit status appears to be highest among the less settled workers whose attachment to the work force is loose, such as casual and short-service workers, secondary family workers like working wives and children, and young single workers.

Such mobile and unstable groups are responsible for most of the threat of abuse under a social insurance program. In his book on *The Problem of Abuse in Unemployment Benefits,* Joseph Becker states that claimants violating the law tend to be more numerous among female workers, lower-income workers, employees in seasonal industries, longshoremen, and workers habitually shifting between industry and agriculture.[10] On the other hand, workers with dependents, he concludes, are less likely than others to prefer benefits to a job.[11]

Experience with temporary sickness insurance in Rhode Island seems to have confirmed the view that female workers, because the strength of their labor-force connection varies over a period of time, are more prone to abuse the law by staying away from work. The Cash Sickness Act passed in Rhode Island in 1943 was, however, particularly open to abuse. It was, for example, possible for a sick worker to collect benefits from both workmen's compensation and the cash sickness program. In the early years, about 8 per cent of total benefit payments under cash sickness compensation were to people who were collecting simultaneously under both programs, a quarter of whom by such duplication received a total amount which exceeded the full-time weekly wage that they would have earned if they had been working.[12] In addition, some employers had private arrangements for sick benefits or wage-continuation plans, on top of which benefits were payable under the state plan. Moreover, pregnancy was included as a compensable illness and the medical administration in the early years was wholly inadequate. The result undoubtedly was some malingering, but no thorough study was made of the matter before a limit of 90 per cent of normal pay was placed on combined workmen's compensation and cash sickness benefits in 1948 (reduced to 85 per cent in 1949), employers with continuation-wage schemes began to deduct the state sickness benefit from the wage payment, benefits for sickness resulting from pregnancy were limited to fifteen weeks, and an improved system of medical checks was instituted. This experience did demonstrate the connection between benefit levels and good administration, which is the point that employers have emphasized in continuing to pay 100 per cent of wages under private sickness programs.

In discussions of wage-earner motivation, insufficient stress has been placed on the fact, already mentioned, that normally perhaps four-fifths of the manufacturing employees have sufficient seniority to be fairly well attached to the company and concerned about their future with that firm. Seniority, in-plant promotion, and on-the-job training have emphasized investment in company attachment. Malingering under a social insurance program or preference for benefits over employment would adversely affect the worker's record and prospects with the company. Consequently, a well-attached employee is not likely to compare real income on employment and real income on a benefit status over very short periods of time with a view to shifting between them temporarily. Little evidence exists, for example, to indicate that the main breadwinner of a family, who has a few years of seniority at a plant, would be motivated by a preference for lay-off rather than work if benefit levels reached 75, 80, or even 85 per cent of normal pay under unemployment compensation.

Studies reveal that most manual workers place a high priority on job security despite the existence of unemployment compensation,[13] even with relatively high rates of compensation such as have obtained, for instance, in Mississippi. Wage-earners, especially heads of families, need work for social as well as economic reasons, which also helps to explain why the likelihood of abuse under unemployment compensation is greatest among the loosely attached and short-service elements in the work force. Myers and Shultz, for example, found that most of the people drawing benefits and not looking for work following a partial shutdown of a textile mill were married women who wished to attend to their family responsibilities.[14] The requirement of a fairly long record of work attachment in order to qualify for benefits helps to screen out those who frequently move into and out of the community's labor force. There is thus a connection between the height of benefit levels and the length of employment necessary to be eligible for benefits.

This discussion of the effects of benefit levels on work incentives has indicated the kinds of qualifications that any answer should contain. The results may be influenced by such conditions as eligibility requirements, good administration to check on possible abuse, and the length of the waiting period. Workers satisfied with their employer are not likely to leave work for benefits under unemployment compensation or even to stay away from work an excessively long time in connection with a sickness. If their employment connection is severed, they may, of course, seek to draw sickness benefits to supplement any rights to unemployment compensation. A relatively high level of benefits may encourage a worker to continue on benefits once he has been laid off or has lost a job, and the same may be true for sickness benefits.

Careful examination, however, indicates the practical impossibility of drawing up a schedule of quantity of malingering in relation to benefit levels and, from such a schedule, seeking to determine the best percentage figure to use for calculating the weekly or monthly benefit. Undoubtedly, the larger the differential between normal weekly pay and the weekly benefit, the more the avoidance of work to receive benefits is discouraged. But how much malingering is discouraged or encouraged by different benefit levels is difficult to determine, if for no other reason than that the picture is complicated by so many other variables, including other provisions of the law, the administration of the program, and the cultural environment. Much may depend upon how stable the work force and the hours of work have been and what job horizon and earnings prospects the workers have. Another difficulty with any schedule concept is that a significant volume of malingering tends to stimulate more, by affecting general attitudes toward the whole program. On the other hand, low benefit levels may serve to defeat the chief purposes of the program.

It should be pointed out, however, that under state unemployment compensation laws, low-wage workers generally receive benefits amounting to the largest percentage of their weekly earnings. In Michigan, workers with four or more dependents and with weekly earnings of $20 to $30 may receive benefits amounting to 90 to 95 per cent of take-home pay after Federal tax deductions. From the point of view of malingering, that is the reverse of the desirable relationship, for the low-wage workers are generally more prone to malinger because by and large they have the loosest attachments to particular firms and to the labor market.

Labor-market Forces

The level of benefits may affect the operation of labor-market forces by influencing a worker's willingness to shift from benefit to new employment or an employer's willingness to hire him. High benefit levels permit workers to maintain, temporarily, high reservation prices for their services, whereas with low benefits they might be financially pressed to accept low-paying work.

Undoubtedly benefit levels do influence the willingness of unemployed workers on benefit to accept a new job which is low-paying, unattractive work of a short-term character and offers little prospect of promotion, such as seasonal work in processing farm products or harvesting on the farm. This may be especially true if a worker is only on lay-off from a company with which he has accumulated seniority and to which he expects to be recalled before his benefit rights are exhausted. Unemployed workers drawing good benefits, who lack such a company connection, are more prone to accept a new job at low wages in another concern if its pattern of employment is hiring in at the bottom of the firm's wage and occupational hierarchy with promotion from within into the higher-paying jobs. That, by the way, seems to be the typical pattern for manufacturing firms with two hundred or more employees.[15] In such firms, new employees have to, and are willing to, sacrifice during the first few weeks or months of employment in order to gain seniority rights and promotion opportunities.

Managements may refuse to hire workers on lay-off from other concerns who have accumulated a few years of seniority there, for the reason that such workers are likely to return to that firm when recalled. However, in case of an employer's refusal to hire such laid-off employees, their benefit levels as such may have no bearing. Employers may also not use the public employment offices for recruitment purposes, or do so only as a last resort, or look with a critical eye at all referrals therefrom; but all that has no direct connection with benefit levels. Benefit levels would presumably be a consideration in an employer's hiring program only if they were sufficiently high so that doubt might arise whether a worker with such benefit rights would remain on a new, low-paying job long enough to get promoted into higher-paying work. Because labor turnover is expensive, managements seek to screen out applicants who are not likely to stay attached to the firm.

For unemployment compensation, then, the answer seems to be that relatively high benefit levels may permit and encourage beneficiaries to avoid taking new employment that is unattractive from a short- and long-run viewpoint. The issue of disqualification for refusal to accept "suitable work" is involved in the question how soon workers on benefit should be forced to accept new employment in, say, blind-alley jobs or in lines of work that have little appeal to the beneficiary and are ill suited to his background and training. This issue is concerned more with the level of his previous earnings than with the percentage of past wages used to calculate benefits. The influence of the benefit level would be through the degree of financial necessity or pressure on the worker to accept unattractive employment.

To the extent that benefit levels encourage workers to maintain either a higher reservation price or a more restricted classification of acceptable jobs, the supply of labor available for certain kinds of work may be curtailed. Much, of course, depends on the severity with which the agency interprets and applies the "suitable work" provision. In so far as the benefit level does restrict the available labor supply for low-paying or low-grade work, it is a force exerting pressure for improvement in the wages, work conditions, or promotion prospects on such jobs. Here again, distinctions need to be drawn between different elements in the labor force (that is, females, young males, and heads of families), and between types of employment (that is, between a temporary job devoid of promotion possibilities and a starting job in a well-established firm that offers real security and promotion possibilities).

From a social viewpoint, a good argument can be made for pressure to improve the long-run attractiveness of jobs, where that possibility exists. Of course, for workers only temporarily in the labor market, a temporary type of work may be suitable. Even so, one may be able to make a valid case for mild upward pressure on the wage rates of the lowest-paying jobs in manufacturing on the same economic grounds as are used to support a legal minimum wage that directly affects only a small fraction of the work force.[16]

Benefit levels may influence not only wages but also labor-force attachment and labor mobility. As indicated previously, high benefit levels may affect the propensity of workers to remain out of the labor market on benefit, following lay-off, retirement, or a period of sickness. Partly the problem may be one of defining eligibility, especially for unemployment compensation, so that benefits are not paid to workers whose attachment to the labor market is loose (that is, those who work only in peak seasons of the industry). Questions of labor-force attachment or labor mobility normally do not arise under temporary sickness or accident benefits, since the employee presumably will return to his or her regular job.

In cases of old-age retirement and of total and permanent disability, the question arises whether it is desirable for the recipients to remain completely out of the labor market. Their willingness to do so undoubtedly can be influenced in some degree by benefit levels. Whether, from a social viewpoint, it is desirable for them to withdraw completely from gainful employment is a question to which no categorical answer is possible. Much depends on the personal circumstances, business conditions, and kinds of available employment. The question is far too broad for adequate treatment here.

Levels of benefits under public programs seem to have had little influence upon inter-firm, inter-industry, or interstate movement of labor. As already mentioned, relatively high benefits could possibly cause low-wage employers to hesitate to hire such workers for fear that they might soon seek to leave the job to return to a benefit status. No evidence has been uncovered in field investigations, however, to indicate that such discrimination against high-benefit workers has actually occurred for that reason. On the other hand, large accumulated old-age benefit rights might reduce an employer's resistance to hiring workers over, say, fifty years of age. That possibility has been frequently mentioned, but again good evidence is lacking. Also, there seems to be no convincing evidence that marked differences in the levels of unemployment compensation or workmen's compensation between neighboring states have served to attract or repel workers, or that programs of temporary disability benefits in four states have influenced workers in the selection of jobs. Studies of the effectiveness of company benefit programs in attracting and holding employees reveal that new applicants seldom inquire about them before accepting a job, although such programs may be effective in helping to retain employees once they have enjoyed benefit rights under them, which would be lost by transfer.[17] In short, any connection between mobility within the labor market and benefit levels under public programs seems to have been so tenuous that it is difficult to discover.

Income Distribution

The level of benefits under social insurance programs has some effects upon income distribution and the growth of the national income. Cash benefits generally represent a transfer of income from producers to nonproducers, from higher-income to lower-income groups. That is so because the income of beneficiaries whose benefits are a percentage of wages is generally below that of employed workers, and because benefit formulas tend to favor lower-wage workers. Rough estimates made in 1946 indicate, however, that the redistributive effect under the then existing programs of unemployment compensation and Old Age and Survivors Insurance would not be large. Assuming 10 per cent unemployment in a year in the early 1950s, the combined effect of the two programs would have been to increase the income of those receiving under $1,000 a year by about 4 per cent and to decrease the income of those receiving $3,000 to $5,000 and those receiving over $5,000 by from 1 to 2 per cent.[18] Pensions promise to be the most costly element in the social security program; yet a study by the National Planning Association shows that the total cost of Old Age and Survivors Insurance by 1975, assuming its benefits are constantly liberalized to keep up with a rising level of living and its coverage is extended to groups not under a government plan, would be only 2.3 per cent of the estimated national income at that time.[19]

Such statistics indicate that, viewed broadly, the redistributive consequences of benefit levels 50 per cent above those now prevailing would not be as large as might generally be assumed. This is not to minimize the marginal effects, say on consumption and savings, of transfers of income in such proportions between income classes.

The significance of benefit levels for the growth of national income has been partly covered in the preceding discussions of the effects on work incentives and on propensities to remain in or withdraw from the labor market. Undoubtedly, benefits under Old Age and Survivors Insurance have encouraged some workers to retire from employment; nevertheless, the number of nonworkers per active worker in this country has been decreasing from 152 nonproducers per 100 workers in 1930 to 140 in 1940, 137 in 1950, and 135 in 1952.[20] With the large number of births since 1945, a slight reversal may occur in the increase in active workers to nonproducers during the next decade, but over the long range a continuation of the moderate decline in the proportion of nonproducers seems probable. If so, growth of the national income is not likely to suffer curtailment from a net decline in labor-force participation. The evidence so far does not seem to indicate that relatively high benefit levels would represent a significant threat to the national product on that score.

The taxes levied to finance social insurances may, under some circumstances, tend to retard growth of the national income, in which case the larger taxes necessitated by higher benefit levels would magnify the retarding effect. With no governmental contributions, presumably only employer tax contributions are involved in this question. The incidence and economic consequences of employer payroll taxes are unsettled issues. High payroll taxes may discourage employment and encourage capital investment. The net consequences to output and employment over the long run are obscure, and any attempt to work out an answer would require an elaborate set of assumptions that would be open to serious objection. Of course, one obvious conclusion is that the smaller the proportion of wages in total production costs, the less significant would be the economic consequences.

Undoubtedly the existence of relatively high benefits under unemployment compensation helps to reduce workers' resistance to dynamic changes in the economy, such as the introduction of labor-saving devices. The existence of cash sickness benefits may help to improve the health of the working population. Retirement of superannuated workers may keep the work force more dynamic and adaptable. It is, however, impossible at this juncture to attempt to make any estimate of the influence of such factors on national real income.

Fluctuations in Business

Benefit levels may also influence the functioning of the economy by their effects on seasonal and cyclical fluctuations in business. Benefit levels that would cover a larger percentage of the wage loss under unemployment compensation, it is claimed, would give employers a greater incentive to regularize their employment throughout the year because their tax savings under experience rating would be greater. In other words, higher benefit levels provide employers with greater incentive to iron out seasonal swings in employment. The opposite side of the coin is, of course, that they would increase the financial penalty for laying off employees and, to that extent, tend to discourage employment expansion.[21]

Cyclical swings in business may be mitigated by increasing the percentage of wage loss covered by benefits, especially under unemployment compensation. Higher unemployment compensation benefits would, of course, help to maintain consumer spending during a business decline. In addition, social insurance programs have a large outgo relative to income during slumps and the reverse during upswings; this is true not only of unemployment compensation but also old-age benefits. Clearly the higher the benefit levels relative to wages, the greater would be the difference between the program's income and outgo on the upswings and downswings of the cycle.

These comments obviously raise questions concerning the aims of unemployment compensation and other social insurances—whether they are intended primarily to meet elemental needs or the stress should be placed on their influence upon the operation of the economy as a whole. That issue is discussed later on.

Private Savings

Another unsettled issue is whether high benefit levels under the social insurances discourage or encourage private savings. On the one hand, it is claimed that, with high benefits under unemployment compensation, sickness and accident compensation, and old-age insurance, workers would feel less need to set aside savings to cover the risk of unemployment, illness, or accident, or to provide for retirement income. On the other hand, the guarantee of benefits provides protection to private savings, since savings do not need to be consumed to meet needs covered by benefits. That, of course, is a decided encouragement to the accumulation of savings. In addition, public programs in some lines like old-age insurance have stimulated private programs for supplementing the benefits under social insurance.

Certainly, despite a rising price level during the past two decades since enactment of the Social Security Act, the volume of private savings has been relatively high, amounting to over 7 per cent of disposable income for the country as a whole during the past three years. In view of recent economic developments, including private programs under collective bargaining, an argument against high-level benefits on the ground that they would be injurious to the volume of savings is not likely to be convincing, unless or until it is supported by more satisfactory evidence.

Influence of Government

High benefit levels have political aspects. With as many as 30 to 50 million workers covered under social insurance programs in this country, their political implications are fairly obvious. The collection of billions of dollars by taxes and their disbursement under benefit formulas is, of course, a collective decision, even though the spending of the benefits is a matter of individual preference and personal decision. The direct payment of large sums of money by the government to millions of persons does raise the possibility of the use of such funds for political advantage and punishment, for buying allegiance and influencing behavior.

The threat is not so much in terms of the height of benefit levels but promised changes in them and discrimination between beneficiaries, as Hitler demonstrated under the German pension system. True the higher the level, the more significance the benefits have for the recipients—the more they are dependent on public rather than private sources of income. A countervailing factor, however, is the firm establishment of objective criteria for benefit determination and the tying of benefits to previous contributions or wage credits in a way that eliminates discrimination and forces consideration of contributions whenever benefit increases are under discussion.

We have considered above the various ways in which benefit levels might affect the nation's economy. Although no attempt will be made to summarize the discussion, a few of the conclusions can be restated as follows: Relatively high benefit levels that approach normal take-home pay would probably have little, if any, adverse effects on the labor productivity of employed workers, labor mobility between firms, the total volume of savings, or the growth of the national income. Such high benefit levels are likely to exert some pressure for the improvement of wages and other job attributes in unattractive work— a pressure which, under some circumstances and in moderate measure, could have beneficial consequences. The greatest possibility of undesirable effects would seem to be in terms of malingering under "temporary" risks so as to bring discredit to the program. Since the threat of malingering under employment and sickness compensation is greatest among less settled workers who have a loose attachment to the labor market, it can be reduced by the requirement of a fairly long work record for benefit eligibility and by good administration that tests availability for and willingness to accept "suitable work."

OBJECTIVES AND BENEFIT LEVELS

In this country, the objectives of social insurance vary somewhat with the risk. Prevention has been stressed in workmen's compensation and unemployment compensation, with employer contributions varying under experience rating. Dependents' benefits have played a large role in life-time risks, such as old age and in death cases under workmen's compensation. The maintenance of consumer income as a countercyclical measure has been stressed in connection with unemployment compensation.

Social insurance programs generally represent some sort of compromise between such separate aims as compensation for wage loss, maintenance of consumer purchasing power, prevention of dependency, elimination of want, and incentives to reduce risks. Experience, research, and pressures on the legislatures reshape and reinterpret those aims and develop new compromise positions in legislation.

In this section, the purposes of social insurance benefits and the relationships between objectives and benefit levels will be considered under the following topics: the forces influencing benefit levels, benefit differentiation by type of risk, the element of need in social insurance benefits, including the relation of benefits to relief and supplementary private programs, and Federal benefit standards to achieve national objectives.

Forces Influencing Benefit Levels

The benefit provisions of social insurance legislation in this country have been influenced by political pressures exerted by employers, organized labor, the aged, and interested community groups. However, economic factors seem to have had considerable responsibility for the differences between our benefit structures and levels and those prevailing abroad, especially in Europe.

Benefits in this country are relatively high and have such a wide range of differentiation largely because our thinking was influenced by the practice under earlier private plans, because we have had relatively wide differentials in wages among occupations and localities, and because our standard of living has been high and increasing rather steadily. In addition, organized labor in this country has had much greater economic strength than it has had political strength, so that, particularly since the 1930s, it has been able to make more gains at the bargaining table than in the legislative halls. Therefore bargaining demands and the results of bargaining have influenced benefit provisions in the laws. That has particularly been the case with old-age benefits and, more recently and to a lesser extent, with unemployment benefits.

Other economic factors, however, have tended to keep benefit levels relatively low compared with industrial wages. One factor has been the low level of farm wages and some farm incomes, which is of special legislative significance in view of the overrepresentation and political influence of the population of rural areas. Another has been the rapidly rising wage levels with inflation during the past two decades. Benefits specified in legislation have lagged behind the wage level, and, although generally they have been adjusted after years of delay, some have not. The lag is particularly true under workmen's compensation; private carriers are paying to widows and to permanently and totally disabled workers benefits fixed on the basis of wages being earned by the injured or killed worker two or three decades ago when the accident occurred.

Probably the most important economic factor in holding down benefit levels under state programs is interstate competition. This is especially the case in view of the fact that state programs of workmen's compensation and unemployment compensation, under the influence of notions concerning prevention, are financed entirely by employer contributions. Thus employers have a direct financial interest in resisting increased benefits, and can use the argument that their competitors in some other states would have a competitive advantage with a lower contribution rate.

Benefit Differentiation

Because in this country each social insurance program (workmen's compensation, unemployment compensation, Old Age and Survivors Insurance, and cash sickness compensation) has developed under different circumstances (legal background, objectives, level of government, and extent of contracting out), benefit provisions and levels are remarkably dissimilar. The lack of uniformity is particularly noteworthy in the case of such state programs as unemployment compensation and workmen's compensation.

In the 48 states, wide discrepancies exist between formulas used for calculating the weekly benefits to compensate for wage loss due to unemployment and formulas used for temporary total disability (or for permanent total disability[22]) under workmen's compensation, and also between the maximum weekly benefits possible under each of those programs. For example, in the 35 states for which direct comparisons can be made of the percentage of wage loss replaced,[23] workmen's compensation in 1952 replaced for temporary disability a higher percentage of wage loss than did unemployment compensation in 28 states, the same percentage in 4 states, and a lower percentage in 6 states. In a number of states, the percentage formula for workmen's compensation was 66⅔, whereas for unemployment it was 50 or 52 per cent. With respect to maximum weekly benefits the situation was similar. In about three-fourths of the states, the workmen's compensation maximums for temporary disability were higher by $2 to $15 a week; the maximums were the same under both programs in half a dozen states, and were higher by $1 to $4 a week under unemployment compensation in perhaps half a dozen other states.[24]

How can one explain such differences in benefit levels under the two state programs? Undoubtedly it would be difficult to do so simply on ethical or economic grounds. Apparently the subject has not been carefully studied. Undoubtedly, the higher levels of workmen's compensation benefits in most states are to be explained in part by the way the two programs were started, the length of experience under them, methods of administration (particularly the role of private carriers in workmen's compensation), the smaller likelihood of malingering under workmen's compensation, and the greater effect that unemployment compensation may have on the acceptance of jobs less attractive in terms of wages and working conditions. The two programs cost the average covered employer about the same dollar amounts,[25] but temporary disability and permanent total disability generally account for less than one-tenth of the total cost of workmen's compensation. The big cost item is permanent partial disability, which generally accounts for over four-fifths of total compensation costs, with fatal accidents representing about as large a total of compensation payments as temporary and permanent disability combined. To employers, therefore, an improvement in benefits for temporary and permanent total disability alone would be only about one-tenth as costly as would a corresponding improvement in unemployment benefits.

The benefit level under Old Age and Survivors Insurance is lower for single persons than under unemployment and workmen's compensation, but much more generous for dependents. Benefits under OASI are calculated as 55 per cent of the first $100 of average monthly wages and 15 per cent of the next $200 up to a maximum of $300 average monthly wages. The state formulas for unemployment compensation and workmen's compensation average around 57 and 63 per cent of wages respectively. The maximum benefits under OASI are $85 a month for a single person and $168.75 for a family, with an additional over-all limit of 80 per cent of the insured worker's average monthly wage. The average state maximum without dependents' benefits would, on a monthly basis, be approximately $125 for temporary or permanent disability under workmen's compensation and $110 under unemployment compensation.

Dependents' benefits under OASI are especially liberal, indicating that need has more influence on benefit provisions under that program than under workmen's compensation or unemployment compensation. A widow's, parent's, or first child's benefit under OASI is three-quarters of the primary benefit, while a wife's or an additional child's benefit is one half of the primary benefit, so that a retired man with a wife and one child or a surviving wife and two children would be likely to find their total benefits restricted by the limit of 80 per cent of the primary worker's average monthly wage. In death cases in the

30 states with dependency provisions under workmen's compensation, a child dependent of the widow increases her benefit only about 10 per cent on the average, with the over-all limit being 55 to 66⅔ per cent of base wages in all except a few states. Under unemployment compensation, dependents' allowances are provided in only 11 state laws, and generally amount to $2 weekly per dependent, with the average extra allowance for workers with dependents amounting to about $4 a week or an increase of 18 per cent in benefits.

In lifetime risks like retirement and death, dependents' allowances do not present the same problems of malingering and adverse effects on the willingness to work that they do under temporary risks like unemployment and sickness. In the former case, the beneficiary is not expected to return to normal full-time employment for a considerable period of time, if ever, so that tests of ability or willingness to work are not included in the law.

Social Insurance Benefits

Benefits under social insurance should be sharply distinguished from public relief payments, and the level of such benefits should not be geared to relief standards. Relief presumably is based on the extent to which a family is unable to provide from its income for the family's minimum essential needs. Such a budget-deficit concept based on lack of means is, however, foreign to the American philosophy of social insurance, and goes counter to some of the purposes that social insurances are designed to achieve. Our social insurance programs have aimed at compensation for wage loss in such a way as to preserve self-respect and incentive. Benefits are fixed in the legislation and granted as a matter of right, with direct relationships between the recipient's past earnings and the size of his benefit payments. An additional objective, especially of unemployment compensation, is to help sustain consumption during an economic downswing, when incentives to invest may be weakened.

What role then, if any, should need play in determining the level of social insurance benefits? Should, as some have contended, public programs merely assure an income that will cover only a basic minimum of essential needs, leaving the rest to personal savings and private programs? To do so would be to favor ungraded benefits plus dependents' allowances, and to have weekly benefits correspond closely with public relief standards.

Any such concept of benefits would, of course, involve abandonment of the principle of compensation for wage loss and protection of earned differentials in living standards. Not only would such a benefit standard blur distinctions between statutory benefits and means-test relief, but would result also in forcing a considerable proportion of beneficiaries under social insurance programs to apply for supplementary public relief. One test of the adequacy of benefit levels is the percentage of recipients who are also concurrently on relief.

Presumably a somewhat higher benefit level would result if the objective were to cover, for most beneficiaries, that portion of their past wages that is required for "non-deferrable" living expenses.[26] "Most beneficiaries" can be assumed to mean at least three-quarters of them. An operating definition of the volume of consumption that constitutes "non-deferrable" living expenses would be difficult to develop, but presumably it would include, for the whole family, a calculated sum for food, housing cost, household operating expenses, and clothing if the benefit period exceeded, say, six months. Undoubtedly such a standard would be somewhat more flexible and liberal than the relief standard. Certainly one of its chief purposes would be to ensure that no more than a small fraction of the beneficiaries under social insurance programs would be in need of any public relief while drawing benefits.

A significantly different benefit standard would prevail if emphasis were placed on the principle of compensation, in large part, for wage loss resulting from the risk or contingency. The proportion of wage loss covered by benefits could, of course, vary with the type of risk and with the stress put on the additional objective of maintaining consumption expenditures in order to combat an economic slump. Application of the wage-loss principle without modification for dependents might be more justified for temporary risks than for lifetime risks.

As already explained, an obstacle to high benefit levels for temporary risks is the encouragement they may give to recipients to malinger rather than to return to gainful employment. The threat of malingering arises particularly if the worker is not expected to return to his old job, but has to seek new employment. In such cases, workers who are marginally in the labor force, especially women, may actually not seek gainful employment, yet may make every effort to draw all their benefits while out of the labor force. The limited groups in which high benefits might provide additional encouragement to malinger have been discussed, and some of the necessary safeguards in terms of eligibility requirements were mentioned.

Undoubtedly the aim of minimizing the incentive to malinger conflicts to some extent with the aim of compensation for wage loss, which is designed to prevent for a few months any sharp reduction in living levels in the case of short-term risks and thus to avoid forcing workers to accept new employment in unattractive jobs (discussed above) during a short-period separation from a payroll. Any percentage compensation of wage loss is some sort of compromise between those two aims. Assuming that, by and large, take-home pay (taxes deducted) averages 85 per cent of wages, a 75-per-cent compensation for wage loss would mean benefits 12 per cent less than take-home pay.[27] That, of course, makes no allowance for the already-discussed losses of job rights or "fringes" that beneficiaries might suffer while out of work. Whether such a 12-per-cent differential is a good compromise for "temporary" risks would depend upon current labor conditions and the stress placed on different objectives.

Emphasis upon such a narrow differential between benefit levels and take-home pay would leave little opportunity for weighing the benefit formula in favor of low-income groups or for providing significant dependents' allowances in the case of temporary risks. Low-income groups, for reasons already discussed, are likely to have a relatively high proportion of persons loosely connected with the labor market, who have a propensity to malinger. Moreover, dependents' allowances are more difficult to justify for short-term risks than for long-term risks unless levels of benefit are low or the allowance per dependent is only a token amount.

The question of malingering, as previously explained, is not so relevant for lifetime risks, like superannuation and permanent and total disability, nor for survivorship where the survivor is over 65 or has dependent children. Such beneficiaries generally are not expected to engage in regular full-time employment. Also, where a long interval of time is involved, rigid adherence to the principle of wage-loss compensation may be less appropriate. Over long periods, the wage base on which benefits are calculated recedes farther and farther into the past and may seem to have less and less significance. On those grounds one may justify, for such risks, a benefit formula giving much more weight to low income, and also fairly large dependents' benefits that would bring total benefits to 80, 90, or even 100 per cent of past wages in cases where the breadwinner is incapacitated.

Benefit ceilings in dollar amounts, in addition to limitations in terms of percentage of wages, have not been founded on a well developed philosophy systematically applied. The argument for such ceilings has been to conserve the available funds. Conserve them for what purpose? Presumably so that a larger proportion may be used for benefits to low-wage beneficiaries. Any such contention, however, raises questions concerning the necessary volume of reserves and the size of contributions.

Another argument for such ceilings is that public opinion will be unfavorable to the payment of a weekly or monthly benefit that is at or near the average earnings of employed workers. This, however, seems to be largely supposition, unsupported by objective investigations.

It is sometimes assumed that, if more than a certain fraction of benefit payments are at the ceiling figure, the ceiling is too low. But what is the proper standard—10 per cent, 15 per cent, 25 per cent, 35 per cent, or 50 per cent? No accepted rule has been developed. Much will depend, of course, on the purpose that the program is intended to achieve. Those who favor confining the public social insurances to a basic minimum will not be disturbed if a high proportion, even a majority, of all benefit payments are at the weekly or monthly maximum specified in the law. Personally, it is my opinion that, under a program such as unemployment compensation, no more than 15 to 20 per cent of all benefits should be cut off by the dollar ceiling. That, however, is only one man's view, based largely on what I conceive to be the purpose of unemployment compensation.

Any ceiling figures should be buttressed by a much more elaborate analysis than has heretofore been developed. Unfortunately, we lack the basic material, including field studies, for an adequate analysis. The practical significance of this issue is indicated by the fact that in 1952 a total of 55 per cent of all weeks of total unemployment were compensated at the basic maximum weekly benefit amount.[28] To that extent, unemployment compensation in this country was a flat-benefit program. With dollar ceilings cutting off a significant percentage of all benefits, a good case can be made for ceilings that vary with the number of dependents—rising, say, three or four dollars a week for each dependent up to a maximum of four or five dependents. Such a provision would not affect the benefit formula but would lighten ceilings somewhat for families in the higher-wage groups, whose benefits under present laws may only amount to one-third or less of normal earnings.

An additional argument for benefit ceilings is to reserve a sufficient area for private programs to supplement the public program. Private insurance companies have been particularly interested in supplementary programs in the area of old-age and survivors' insurance. In the fields of workmen's compensation and cash sickness benefits it is primarily a question of either public or private arrangements, with supplementation not too practical. In the case of unemployment, private insurance carriers have not sought that business, so that supplementary arrangements presumably will take mainly the form of "guaranteed annual wage" plans under collective bargaining.

Private supplementation of Old Age and Survivors Insurance raises a question as to the proper level of the combined benefits and also as to the effects of private programs on labor mobility. Under the Federal program, a long-service worker earning $250 a month would receive a retirement benefit amounting to 31 per cent of his previous wages if he is single, and 47 per cent if he is married. Supplementation by private plans would generally raise the percentage to between 40 and 60 per cent of previous wages for a single man and 55 to 75 per cent for a married man.[29] For higher-wage workers, the Federal program provides lower percentages of previous wages (for the $400-a-month worker, 21 per cent if single and 32 per cent for a couple), and so the combined percentages would be smaller. Whether the loss of pension rights on transfer serves to bind workers to particular companies in ways that are detrimental to the dynamic functioning of the economy is difficult to determine. From the point of view of the best allocation of labor resources, it may generally be desirable to have employees with many years of seniority remain with their present employers. Seniority and other job perquisites based on length of service also serve to attach the employee to a particular company, so that it may be difficult to isolate the restrictive effects of private pension plans per se. It is doubtful that they will cause undesirable restrictions on labor mobility to any significant extent if the Federal program continues to provide, say, benefits of 40 to 50 per cent of wages for long-service married workers whose earnings are equal to the current average in manufacturing.

Federal Benefit Standards

Although an extended discussion of Federal benefit standards in unemployment compensation would be out of place here, brief treatment of the subject can hardly be avoided in a paper dealing with benefit levels under social insurance in this country. Interstate competition in tax reduction in order to make states attractive for business has been a significant factor influencing the benefit provisions of state unemployment compensation laws and also the benefit provisions in state workmen's compensation legislation.

Under unemployment compensation, employer contribution rates have been sharply reduced, yet benefit levels have lagged behind the rise in wage levels. From 2.7 per cent of total payroll in the 1930s, employer contribution rates declined to an average of 1.4 per cent on the first $3,000 of wages during the period of the last eight years, or a drop of about two-thirds in actual tax burden. On the other hand, average weekly benefits for total unemployment declined from 41 per cent of average weekly taxable wages in the states in 1939 to 33 per cent of such average wages in 1952, and state benefit ceilings decreased from an average of 67 per cent of taxable wages in 1939 to an average of 44 per cent[30] in December 1953. Consequently, the percentage of weeks of total unemployment compensated at benefit ceilings rose from 25 per cent in 1939 to 55 per cent in 1952.

Some states have been particularly prone to reduce employer contribution rates at the expense of adequate benefit levels. For example, Texas, Florida, Virginia, and the District of Columbia have had benefit ceilings of $20 or $22 under unemployment compensation, and their employer contribution rate for the past six years has averaged .6 to .9 per cent of payrolls; whereas near-by states[31] with benefit ceilings from $26 to $38 have had employer contribution rates averaging 1.0 to 1.7 per cent for the past six years. Such data indicate what happens when benefit levels are subject to the influences of interstate competition to reduce employer taxes under state social insurance programs.

The Federal government has a vital interest in the volume of unemployment and the levels of unemployment compensation, as is evidenced by a series of legislative acts during the past two decades, including the Employment Act of 1946. The economy of the nation is affected by such levels of benefit payment. Unemployment compensation is designed to assure laid-off workers willing to work a certain level of income for a short duration in order, among other purposes, to help maintain consumption and to restrain any tendency for a cumulative downward movement to develop with reduced consumption reacting adversely on investment planning. In enacting the tax-offset provisions of the Social Security Act, the Federal government attempted to enlist state support for that compensation objective. As long as competitive reductions in state tax contributions are encouraged by experience rating under the Act, it seems necessary to include in the Act some minimum benefit standards that state laws should meet. Apparently that step is required if state benefit levels are to be adjusted to general wage-level increases, especially during an inflationary period.

CONCLUDING OBSERVATIONS AND RESEARCH NEEDS

From the foregoing discussion, it is obvious that conclusions concerning the proper benefit levels in different social insurances cannot be drawn with confidence that they can be supported by convincing proofs. The problem is complicated by too many considerations and too many imponderables. In the absence of adequate research studies, one is forced to put on the hat of a social philosopher and pose as a wise man.

With respect to benefit levels, however, a wise man can make serious errors if he fails to allow for the social, economic, and political milieu in which the program will operate. A society's mores have deep and complex roots. But views regarding the level of benefits under social insurance do change over time. Undoubtedly, the development of programs of "guaranteed annual wage" on any significant scale could, for example, change the accepted percentage of wage-loss compensation from 50 or 66⅔ per cent to 75, 80, or even 85 per cent under unemployment compensation.

Benefit objectives do vary somewhat among the different social insurance programs. Some persons would differentiate benefits even more sharply by type of risk; others desire greater integration and uniformity in benefits for temporary risks and also in those for lifetime risks. Sharper distinctions in benefit objectives are sought, for example, by economists who would gear unemployment benefits more closely to countercyclical aims. It has even been proposed that benefit levels vary with labor market conditions, being lowered in prosperity and raised in downswings, in order to help maintain consumption and thus prevent an accelerated reaction on investment. Such cyclical variation in benefit levels under unemployment compensation would, however, severely conflict with prevailing notions of equity and earned rights, both of which lend support to uniformity in benefits among the various social insurances.

Considerations of equity and earned rights to benefits based on wages also reinforce a demand that benefit levels, and particularly benefit ceilings, be automatically adjusted to changes in wage levels. The arbitrary and unreasoned character of many benefit ceilings, particularly for temporary risks, has been discussed. Certainly the subject of ceilings needs thorough examination, especially in terms of the objectives of the programs and the ability to adjust to inflationary or deflationary developments. When benefit levels and ceilings were first established in the 1930s, emphasis was placed on the need to husband funds in the expectation of continued swings in the business cycle of considerable severity. Since the mid-1930s, we have had a long period of prosperity and a rising 50 per cent in per capita disposable income in terms of real purchasing power.

Experience has revealed a tendency, particularly under state programs, to use favorable experience to lower contribution rates rather than to adjust benefit ceilings for changes in wage levels. It would be interesting and instructive to find out how political processes brought about that result and the influence exerted by such factors as interstate competition, high tax burdens in general, allegations of extensive malingering, and complaints that benefits permit the jobless to be too choosy.

Malingering and preservation of job status present some of the most serious issues in any consideration of benefit levels, especially for temporary risks. Widespread belief, whether well founded or not, that a significant amount of malingering is currently occurring could serve to discredit the whole program. If the propensity to malinger does rise sharply with an increase in the benefit level, say, from 66⅔ to 85 per cent of regular wages before taxes, then strong grounds would exist for questioning the desirability of such a move. That would be true also if, as seems less likely, a particular increase in benefit ceilings had the same effect. To the extent that high benefit levels help beneficiaries to preserve temporarily their relative job status, opposition will be encountered, especially from low-paying firms and farmers. On grounds of the best allocation and use of available human resources, a good case can be made for benefits geared to previous earnings in such a way as to permit workers to maintain, for a few months, a reservation price or job standards not far below past wages and employment. But it may be difficult to gain general acceptance for that concept without more study of the matter.

In the area of social insurance benefits, much can be accomplished through research and education. Research is not, of course, a substitute for judgment. It can, however, serve to clarify issues and correct unfounded conclusions. Education can direct attention to the national interest and stress the need to consider various factors and the long-run development of human resources and the economy.

Research concerning the consequences of benefit levels involves study of the motives of workers. It must, of necessity, rely heavily upon new interview and polling techniques. Psychological as well as statistical studies are needed in order to discover the effects of different benefit levels upon incentives to work or to withdraw from the labor market, upon worker resistance to economic change, or upon the reservation prices and job standards of beneficiaries. The effects of dependents' allowances on work incentives likewise should be investigated.[32]

Good case studies of legislative experience could also contribute valuable information. It would be helpful to know, for instance, why benefits differ under the various programs in the states, where benefit improvements tend to develop first, and what forces are responsible for benefit changes. Also, we need much more knowledge of the factors that determine whether favorable experience will result in lower contribution rates or higher benefits, including the role of interstate competition in such decisions.

Furthermore, the economic effects of different benefit levels need to be more thoroughly explored. How would various benefit levels affect income distribution? What would be their effects on consumption and investment expenditures during different phases of the business cycle? How would they influence seasonal fluctuations in employment and the mobility of labor?

Unfortunately, the research resources devoted to such questions have been insufficient to provide satisfactory answers. Labor economists and psychologists have been too preoccupied with other areas of study. University research on social insurance problems has, in recent years, been on the meagre side. Yet the sums of money involved in such insurance programs are huge, and their impact on our lives, industry, and society is great and growing.

Social insurance in this country is still in the experimental stage. As our economy and institutions grow and change, our social insurance programs need to be reexamined in the light of new perspectives and altered objectives. Much remains to be learned; some precepts may have to be unlearned. No aspect of social insurance needs such rethinking more than the whole area of benefit levels.

In considering benefit levels, one must bear in mind that a free society rests on independent, self-reliant citizens. Families affected by either temporary or life-time risks ought not to be set apart from the rest of American society to exist on a special minimum living standard. They should continue to be integrated into the community through benefit structures that protect hard-earned differentials. That is the real significance and the social contribution of a benefit program based on the concept of insurance against wage loss. Other countries may stress different benefit principles, but a social insurance program that, in good part, reflects the wage structure of the community seems the most appropriate for the American high-productivity economy and fluid, almost classless type of society.

FOOTNOTES

1. See Margaret L. Stecker, "Beneficiaries Prefer to Work," *Social Security Bulletin,* January 1951, pp. 15–16.

2. This is based on a study of the Trenton labor market during 1951 through 1953 that the author has been making and on confirming data in studies like Lloyd Reynolds, *The Structure of Labor Markets,* 1951.

3. Additional benefit amounts are provided in 19 states in the case of widows, 10 states in cases of total and permanent disability, 10 states in cases of temporary disability, and 8 states in cases of permanent partial disability.

4. Computed on the basis of the "new start" provisions under Old Age and Survivors Insurance; no allowance is made for periods of part-time employment or unemployment or for extra earnings, and $4.85 a month for employee contributions to OASI, unemployment compensation, and state temporary disability benefits.

5. Arthur Larson, "The American Social Insurance System: Structure, Coverage, and Current Problems" in *Economic Security for Americans,* The American Assembly, Graduate School of Business, Columbia University, November 1953, p. 43.

6. Ruth White, "Concurrent Receipt of Old Age and Survivors Insurance and Public Assistance," *Social Security Bulletin,* XVI (July 1953), pp. 12–13.

7. See, for example, *Fringe Benefits, 1951: The Nonwage Labor Costs of Doing Business,* Economic Research Department, Chamber of Commerce of the U. S., Washington, October 1952.

8. Employers' payments on various insurance programs generally cease when the worker is laid off or shortly thereafter.

9. The UAW estimates the typical weekly value of certain fringe benefits lost by an unemployed worker averaging $88 in weekly wages at $9.56 or about 11 per cent. If the worker has two or more children it is estimated that the loss of fringes exceeds the combined Federal withholding and Social Security taxes. See *Facts on Pending Unemployment Compensation Legislation in Michigan,* UAW (CIO), Detroit, 1954, pp. 15–16.

10. Joseph M. Becker, *The Problem of Abuse in Unemployment Benefits, A Study in Limits,* 1953, p. 308. See also pp. 255–66.

11. *Ibid.,* p. 313.

12. Data on experience with cash sickness in Rhode Island have been taken largely from Nathan Sinai, *Disability Compensation for the Disabled Sick,* Bureau of Public Health Economics, University of Michigan, Ann Arbor, 1949, pp. 17–45. See also Mortimer W. Newton, "Cash Sickness Benefits in Rhode Island," *Social Security in America,* National Conference on Social Security, Chamber of Commerce of the U.S., January 1944, pp. 93–95.

13. See, for example, Richard Centers, "Motivational Aspects of Occupational Stratification," *Journal of Social Psychology,* XXVIII (November 1948), pp. 187–218; and Charles A. Myers and George P. Shultz, *The Dynamics of a Labor Market,* New York, Prentice-Hall, 1951, Chapter 6, pp. 101–134.

14. See Myers and Shultz, pp. 88–92.

15. This is brought out clearly in a study by the author of the hiring practices of 82 firms in the Trenton, New Jersey, area soon to be published by the Industrial Relations Section of Princeton University.

16. For such an economic justification for legal minimum wages see R. A. Lester, *Labor and Industrial Relations,* New York, Macmillan, 1951, pp. 362–69. Of course, the necessary qualifications for differences in circumstances should be added. Note also that these remarks apply to manufacturing; the same arguments cannot be used for extractive industries or businesses providing services directly to consumers like laundries.

17. This statement is based on the Trenton study referred to in preceding footnote 15.

18. See Ida C. Merriam, *Social Security Financing,* Division of Research and Statistics, Social Security Administration, Bureau Report No. 17, November 1952, pp. 139–40.

19. *Pensions in the United States,* A Study Prepared for the Joint Committee on the Economic Report by the National Planning Association, Joint Committee Print, Government Printing Office, Washington, 1952, p. 43.

20. See *ibid.,* p. 40. From 1930 to 1952 the retired older workers and their wives rose from one-twentieth to one-tenth of all those who were not gainfully employed.

21. For a discussion of the merits and drawbacks of experience rating as it operates in practice, see Charles A. Myers, "Experience Rating in Unemployment Compensation," *American Economic Review,* XXXV (June 1945), pp. 337–54.

22. With one or two exceptions, the same percentages and maximums applied in each state under both types of disability. Many states, however, have total dollar amount limitations on payments under permanent total disability.

23. Comparison is difficult in the seven states with annual wage formulas and weighted schedules under unemployment compensation; that is also true where a varying percentage applies under one or both programs and the percentage under one program is within the range of variation of the other.

24. For a few states, comparison is difficult because of differing dependents' allowances under both programs or dependents' allowances only under one program.

25. See Herman and Anne Somers, "Workmen's Compensation—Unfilled Promise," *Industrial and Labor Relations Review,* VII (October 1953), pp. 38–39.

26. Reference is made to this benefit standard in *Adequacy of Benefits under Unemployment Insurance,* A Staff Report Prepared for the Committee on Benefit Adequacy

of the Federal Advisory Council, Bureau of Employment Security, U. S. Department of Labor, Washington, D. C., September 1952, p. 9.

27. Or take-home pay 13⅓ per cent higher than benefits.

28. Excluding dependents' allowances in the eleven states providing for them.

29. See *Pensions in the United States, op. cit.,* p. 13.

30. Including the maximum allowance for dependents in nine states, but excluding Massachusetts which has no upper limit.

31. Mississippi, Georgia, Kentucky, and Maryland.

32. This could readily be done in Massachusetts where there is no over-all limit to the number and amount of dependents' benefits per family under unemployment compensation.

COMMENTS

Harry Becker

Director, Social Security Department, United Automobile Workers, CIO

Professor Richard A. Lester carefully surveys the various elements of the problem of nature and level of income security. In an objective manner he has outlined the essential considerations. To study his chapter is once again to be impressed with the complexity of the task of formulating concepts about the nature and level of income security—a task which seems to grow in complexity with the facets to be evaluated multiplying each year.

Professor Lester shows that today, in many respects, we have much less agreement on many of the fundamental public policy issues than we had when we, bravely and with conviction, fought for the basic state and Federal legislation that now constitutes the legal basis for much of our social security programs.

There is one observation, or reflection, that seems to override all others. It is that after almost two decades of experience with major parts of our social security program, and even a longer period of experience with other parts, there is too little agreement on philosophy and objectives and on administrative procedures and on methods of financing. It is difficult, if not impossible, to do more than set forth the considerations that affect the level of our income security when we lack agreement on such matters as philosophy and objective. Before many of the questions on income security levels can be discussed we must reach common agreement on what it is we are really trying to do and what philosophy is going to govern how we do it.

Professor Lester has dissected the facets of the problem of eligibility and benefit levels. He has presented the questions that need to be answered. But, for the most part, he has not suggested the answers. Many times he frankly, and with honesty, states that the research data are lacking on which to base an answer, on which to formulate a public policy decision. It is a sad commentary that this is true. And especially so when it is a gap that could so easily be filled.

But even more important than the lack of research data needed to resolve many questions is the fact that we have not fully used what experience and data are available to us. Gaps in our knowledge are not sufficient reason for our failure to build an informed public understanding of the philosophy of social security, the risks to which we are exposed, the social and economic problems involved, and the methods by which these risks can be minimized. The public is well informed on many things far less important to personal and national well-being than the social and economic effectiveness of prevailing public and private social security provisions. However, it is not until unemployment confronts us or we suddenly find ourselves forced to retire for reasons of age or disability, that we as individuals come to know the adequacy or inadequacy of today's income security levels. And then we know our society's level of income security only in so far as it affects us as individuals seeking security.

In a democracy there must be an informed public, a knowledgeable public, if public social insurance programs are to have the underpinning which is necessary for growth and eventual maturity.

We as technicians must find a way to bring more order to our ideas and convictions about social security benefit levels and related matters. Until we do this we cannot expect to have an informed public that will, through the legislative process, seek the action that is needed to correct the weaknesses in our social insurances and protect their strengths. The students of social security must lead the way. They must reach general agreement on issues and then submit their thinking to the give-and-take of public debate. In this way, and only in this way, can we as a body politic crystallize our thinking and know that our social security benefit levels reflect the will of the people.

Can we accept, as an aim of our social insurance programs, the provision of compensation for wage loss in such a manner as to preserve self-respect and incentive? If we do, it follows that benefits are fixed in legislation and granted as a matter of right, with a direct relationship between past earnings and the size of benefits. But do we really accept this concept when we speak of social security benefits as a "floor of protection" and impose maximum benefit ceilings which negate, for a major portion of all beneficiaries, the relationship between past wages and present benefits? These two concepts—benefits related to past earnings and a floor of protection—are incompatible. If one is right, the other is wrong!

The public must be informed on these kinds of issues so that it can make decisions on the aims of our social insurance programs. Until these decisions are made our programs cannot have the solid base of public support which they will need in the years ahead to meet the requirements of a changing society and to protect past gains from those who might wish to destroy them for momentary advantage.

Again, are the wide disparities between states in the amount of benefits to compensate for wage loss due to unemployment or to compensable disability, and similarly within the states, consistent with the social and economic purpose and objectives of these programs? Obviously not, in view of the degrees of disparity which exist today. Why then do they exist? Largely because the public has not been sufficiently informed on the risks to which we are exposed and on the level of income security required for a reasonable standard of protection. We cannot consider income security levels without giving attention to the why of existing disparities and existing benefit gaps.

An informed public is a *requisite* to a firm public policy decision on what shall constitute a satisfactory standard of social insurance benefits. All around us it is evident that gaps in benefit and administration provisions exist because we have not, in more than two decades, given sufficient attention to public education. The nature and level of our income security are more political in origin than economic or social. What does this sentence say, if anything? Public education is the determining influence affecting political action.

Today a very significant proportion of all employed persons have entered the labor force since workmen's and unemployment compensation programs were, for example, a matter of public debate. Many of our workers under forty years of age do not know the social and economic problems which gave rise to our social insurance provisions for old-age and survivors' protection. We are increasingly more illiterate on social security matters.

Not only must we look to the country's universities and colleges to assume leadership in setting forth and evaluating the issues in such social security matters as benefit levels, but we must look to these institutions to carry forward an intensive program of public education. Our government agencies, our voluntary organizations and trade and professional associations with specialized viewpoints, have an important role in public education. In the final analysis, however, we must look to our universities and colleges to evaluate the facts, to weigh all points of view and considerations, and to give the public the analysis that is needed for policy-making. Universities and colleges have been negligent in not assuming this responsibility to the extent indicated. Partly, perhaps, this negligence has stemmed from a fear that identification with social insurance might bring the academic group into an area of political controversy. If this fear did exist, it surely need not exist today.

Before academic institutions can give leadership to building an enlightened public thinking on social security matters there must be conferences such as this one to clarify ideas and to sift out the unimportant. Many more such conferences, held with frequent regularity, should be held under academic sponsorship. It is only out of such conferences that can come the "sense of direction" needed by the experts who must follow through in their respective states and communities in fact-finding and interpretation.

In the field of social security we have depended almost entirely on governmental agencies for evaluation of data and for interpretation of social security needs. To some extent special-interest groups have supplemented what governmental agencies have done, by accumulating information and interpreting their findings. But only to a very limited extent have the universities and colleges given the problems of social security the attention they should receive.

Although few things affect our daily social and economic lives more than do our society's provisions for income security, only few state universities have given particular attention to such problems as the nature and level of income security in their states for unemployed persons, for disabled persons, or for persons handicapped because of accident or disease resulting from their employment situation. Many universities are even now failing to recognize problems of social security in a free society as a special concern.

The questions that Professor Lester poses must be resolved by students of social security—students who, in an atmosphere of intellectual freedom, are free to work without bias in their conclusions due to the source of funds from which their salary is paid. Such students must initiate the research and the analysis which is needed for objective thinking and for programs of public education. They must also help supply the materials for training.

One is made aware by Professor Lester's presentation of the many unanswered questions with respect to what superficially seem to be simple problems. Laws are passed, administrative policies are made, without in many instances the use of factual data which could very easily and quickly be made available by university-sponsored research projects. Legislation fails to be enacted because of failure to know from experimental or pilot programs what has proven workable and what has not. In the decade ahead public and private schools will conduct the research and do the interpretation that will answer many of the questions raised by Professor Lester. Many of the questions cannot be answered today on a factual basis, but they can be answered when our schools, in cooperation with governmental, industrial, labor, and other interested organizations in their areas, develop the research projects and use the other tools for collecting and evaluating information.

Mention should be made also of the very great and urgent need for organized training programs to prepare persons for work in the field of social security. In the twenties and early thirties universities gave considerable thought to the training of students for work in the field of income security programs. Since the war, interest in training persons for work on social security problems has not kept pace with public interest and activity in the field of income security. There is a great scarcity of trained persons for work in governmental and nongovernmental programs. The unavailability of trained people is a major reason why research in this field has lagged behind research in other fields of social and economic activity.

Mention should be made, though briefly, about the whole problem of private versus governmental income security programs. Experience has already shown that private income security programs established under labor-management contracts cannot, and will not, substitute for basic governmental programs providing income maintenance for the aged, the unemployed, and other groups without wage income. However advantageous for specific groups of workers, income security provisions established in collective bargaining are at best only a supplement to governmental provisions. In an expanding and flexible economy, such as we have, where labor-force shifts from old to new industries are commonplace and illustrative occurrences, final reliance for minimum levels of income security must be on government provisions.

One of the more significant functions of the private income-maintenance programs, particularly those in industry, is to provide a research laboratory for experimentation. What is proven to be unsound can more easily be discarded than could a similar provision enacted by Congress on a nation-wide scale. The private plans offer opportunity for exploring administrative techniques and cost considerations, and in other ways to test the validity of a given type of security or a given level of benefits. In some instances these private programs may demonstrate what would be feasible in a local, state, or Federal public program. In other instances they will demonstrate what is not feasible.

We need a vast amount of research on all aspects of the income security problem. Where have we a better laboratory than in the thousands of industrial plans providing an endless variety and type of benefits? This source of information has hardly been tapped. We can find in almost any given geographical area operating experience for answering most, if not all, of Professor Lester's questions. We need not speculate about the effect of benefit levels and malingering or about benefit standards in relation to needs of various classes of beneficiaries, for experience which will reveal the data needed is available; its analysis requires only the imagination of the research worker.

Professor Lester has given us what we need to think with in considering the nature and level of income security for a free society. But, after all the data are available and analyzed, we must trust our good judgment and our hearts to help us make the right decisions. The needs of people must in the final analysis be our focus and our concern. Given the facts, the public, through the democratic process, will make the right decision on benefit levels. Our task today is to gather, evaluate, and interpret the facts that will help us to make the public policy decisions which are confronting us. This is a task which our universities and colleges, in the future, are going to assume to an increasing extent.

COMMENTS

R. A. Hohaus

Vice-President and Chief Actuary, Metropolitan Life Insurance Company

This institution we have come to know as Social Security reaches out into almost every area of life—social, economic, political, scientific, psychological, and even moral and religious. It derives its being and inspiration from many different disciplines, and calls on the talents of many professions. The intricate network of relationships with which we are concerned involves not only various technical aspects, but also broader social and economic questions. These general questions are such that there will always be room for differences of opinion as to the degree of emphasis to be placed on one or another of the numerous factors they embrace. Yet analysis may naturally develop certain broad concepts, which in turn lend themselves to the formulation of a basis of policy.

Professor Lester considers some of the interdependent social and economic questions involved in the benefit-level phases of our social insurance plans, with emphasis on the interplay between them. He provocatively discusses a subject that has many facets. It covers with brevity and clarity many of the questions which suggest themselves—consciously or unconsciously—to a diligent student of social insurance.

Especially stimulating is the way in which he stresses, and documents this excellent statement:

> Unfortunately one cannot arrive at the determination of the proper level of social insurance benefits by mathematical means, or by scientific tests, or even by pure logic. The answer depends upon one's economic and social philosophy—the sympathy he has for human misfortune, the stress he places on preserving individual dignity, and the kind of society he envisions as desirable. The answer will also vary with the kind of economy in which the level is to apply (the general standard of living, the distribution of personal income, and the division between market and governmental determination of economic affairs) and with the traditions, history, and culture of the society in question. Consequently, the appropriate level of assured income under a social insurance program cannot be discussed *in vacuo* or in abstract terms. Its fitness must be judged in relation to a particular society and economy.

The following considerations, which are particularly pertinent to the United States scene, might be added:

1. The appropriate roles of local, state, and Federal governments in a nation's political organization. Related thereto, of course, is the extent to which a nation's structure is homogeneous or heterogeneous.

2. The nature and degree of interest which various major segments of a nation's society take in the nation's social insurance programs and the influence they exercise. Related to this is the nation's religious atmosphere and the concern various church organizations have as to social insurance matters.

As an aside, whether the author intended it or not, his analysis strengthens my feeling that the activities of the International Labor Office in the social insurance field should be reappraised. Instead of aiming at international conventions embodying specific detailed proposals for eligibility, benefit levels, and the like, that body should content itself with furnishing an international channel for exchange of ideas and experience. The object would be to make clear to nations contemplating adoption of social insurance plans, or reconstruction of existing plans, that there is a variety of social instruments and approaches available, from which measures appropriate to their particular economies and social structures can be developed.

A major point in Professor Lester's analysis is the distinction made between "temporary" risks, such as unemployment, and "lifetime" risks such as old-age retirement. He brings out clearly how various considerations apply differently in these fields, and how important it is that these two kinds of risk be studied separately. Conclusions which may be reasonable for one area may be quite inappropriate in the other. The discussion also suggests to this reader added reasons for continuing our present setup under which our different types of social insurance are handled through separate programs and by different agencies and levels of government.

Among the points which Professor Lester's paper raises, and which we might profitably discuss, are the following:

1. Benefit levels are part of a trinity consisting of benefits, coverage, and financing. No one of these can be considered independently of the others.

2. There are disadvantages in our national government providing benefits, directly or indirectly, on a means test basis.

3. "Lifetime" risks involve a special problem because of the implied long-range commitments.

4. Coverage of self-employed under OASI also raises special problems.

5. Separate administration of OASI, U.I., and W.C. programs need not rule out a provision that a person will not be entitled to draw benefits concurrently from more than one program.

6. Should social insurance benefits be taxable?

7. Malingering is a problem under private, as well as public programs. Under sickness benefit plans managements are often troubled about adverse effects of wage-loss compensation close to normal earnings.

8. Economic conditions have an important effect on the questions of (a) malingering, through the relation of benefit to normal pay, and (b) attitudes on a compulsory retirement policy.

9. Financial experience with eligibility requirements, waiting period, and quality of administration under both public and private plans requires careful study.

10. A controlling factor in setting the level of benefits is, or should be, the productive capacity of the nation. While there can be work without income security, we cannot have income security without work.

In his concluding section, Professor Lester comments that "in the absence of adequate research studies, one is forced to put on the hat of a social philosopher and pose as a wise man." In that spirit, I should like to outline my philosophy regarding old-age benefits under the Federal program, the objectives of which have been stated as inclusion of all workers, employed and self-employed; payment of benefits related to prior earnings and as matter of right without a needs test; and financing on a contributory basis. I am in full agreement with these objectives.

For us the individual by his very nature is a free man, and the democratic form of society is a community of free people banded together in the spirit of mutual respect and self-discipline. We have faith in the ability of the common man, together with his fellow-citizens, to direct and mold the future of his country. But we know—the impacts of war and defense have brought it home to us even more clearly than before—that with freedom and power goes responsibility, and much is expected of the individual if he is to be worthy of the rights with which he is born.

We recognize that definite obligations rest on the individual in at least three directions: to himself and his family; to those for whom and with whom he works; and to society as represented by his fellow-citizens and himself, and by the agencies they have set up for their common good.

We know that in the forefront of these obligations is the provision of a measure of protection against loss of earnings due to death, old age, disability, and unemployment. As a people we have accepted the challenge in each of the foregoing three directions by the development over the years of three different classes of insurance.

The first class of insurance, in order of time, is *individual insurance*—protection the individual secures for himself and his family; the second, a variety of employee benefit plans, of which group insurance is an outstanding American contribution; and the third, social insurance—designed for the well-being of our fellow-citizens in times of adversity. Each has a special function to perform and need not, and should not, compete with or overlap the others. When soundly conceived, each class of insurance should in fact derive mutual support from the others and perform its role better because of their existence. Properly integrated, they may be pictured as a three-legged stool affording firm and well-rounded support for the citizen.

In thus focusing attention on insurance I recognize, of course, that there are other approaches to loss of income protection and I do not belittle them. However, America perhaps more than any other nation has come to appreciate the special merits of the insurance approach.

The success of democratic processes depends largely on the extent to which the individual assumes his responsibilities as a citizen and as a family man. Among the responsibilities he naturally feels most keenly are such as concern the security and welfare of those dependent upon him. He will wish to set his own level of protection, and *individual insurance* programs give him the opportunity to do so. Indeed, individual insurance is an institution essential to and characteristic of that innate spirit of self-reliance which is and must continue to be traditionally American. The very large volume in force expresses more eloquently than words the real value of this insurance to our people.

Group insurance is historically a much later development than individual insurance. The idea may be traced to the more or less natural feeling of responsibility on the part of the employees in an organization and their employer for the welfare of the individual worker and his family in times of stress.

Various types of employee benefit plans, aiming to give a more definite measure of protection in a manner suited to preserve the beneficiaries' self-respect and dignity, were therefore developed. In some cases those plans were initiated and operated solely by the employer, in others by the employees, and in still others by joint action of employer and employees, who shared the cost between them.

Recent years have seen a great expansion of soundly conceived and operated plans. They have expanded both in the scope of benefits provided and in the number of employees covered, and we may expect this to continue. By providing a measure of security on a basis designed to preserve or bolster the dignity of the individual employee, such plans have indeed become an important element in maintaining not only good industrial relations, but also that faith and confidence in the existing order on which the democratic spirit relies and thrives.

In this country *social insurance* is the newest but by no means the least of the three branches of insurance to which we have referred. Without proper preventive or protective safeguards against loss of income, the individual is naturally exposed to certain economic risks which may take such large tolls in terms of human and financial values as to warrant their description as social hazards. For a social hazard that lends itself to this form of treatment, social insurance generally aims to fulfill in a more orderly and systematic manner—better adapted to the existing social and economic environment—a responsibility society had to a large extent assumed in the past through other channels.

Though differing in important respects from individual and group insurances, social insurance has borrowed the name "insurance" from them because of certain important broad resemblances. It provides benefits specifically determined by formula, payable upon the fulfillment of specified conditions, which do not, however, include subjection to a test of means. This permits the beneficiary to accept them without any sense of incurring the stigma of charity, especially if a "consideration" in the form of contributions or ear-marked taxation has been required of him.

Important, however, as the contributory principle may be, its limitations should be clearly understood. It should not mislead a contributor into misapprehending the social nature of the plan and the financial realities behind it. It should not, for example, lead him into feeling that he has paid in full for a protection to which actually his contribution has been only nominal, or into thinking that because funds are on hand, the nature and purpose of which he does not comprehend, therefore larger benefits are in order.

The fundamental objective of social insurance, it may be said, is to serve society and its constituent individuals. By providing for as large a proportion of its citizens as is practicable a measure of economic security on a self-respecting basis, the state may be relieved of a potentially serious burden of dependency. For benefit levels to be socially adequate for this purpose, a major factor in determining them would be the probable minimum requirements to keep the family from becoming public charges. This in turn suggests that consideration be given to variation in the amount of benefits by the number of dependents of the insured. However, while that basis has wide acceptance for lifetime risks, its appropriateness for temporary risks is very much of a controversial issue.

Under such a philosophy the level of protection and the formula for arriving at it are usually quite different from what is appropriate to either individual or group insurance. By reason of its social adequacy objective and its compulsory character, social insurance cannot and need not pursue individual equity in the sense of a mathematical adjustment between the benefit and the risk as measured by an appropriate premium—an adjustment which, in voluntary insurance, must on the average effect a long-range equivalence between costs and charges, if insolvency is to be avoided.

This does not imply, however, that all considerations of equity should be excluded from a social insurance plan. Rather the point is that, of the two principles, adequacy takes first place. Entirely aside from the question of introducing a degree of equity for its own sake are other reasons that have been advanced for admitting it in some form. Among these are that it acts as an incentive for the proper payment of the prescribed contributions; that it automatically provides some measure of individualistic treatment on the basis of earnings, and that it causes the benefits to reflect automatically (though to a limited extent only) some of the differences in costs and standards of living between geographic regions and other groupings of people.

Just exactly what is meant by equity in social old-age insurance, however, is not a clear-cut matter. The precise construction adopted in private insurance conceives of the individual's benefit as the annuity produced by the accumulation, at interest and with appropriate allowance for mortality gains during any period in which that factor is involved, of specified contributions previously made by him or in his behalf. This construction is, of course, quite incompatible with the fundamental purposes of social insurance, since it completely precludes the role of adequacy in the initial stages of the operation of a plan. Quite different in its effect on the range of benefits is the concept that the amount of benefit should bear merely a limited relationship to some base (such as average earnings) reflecting the individual's economic status. Whatever equity is injected into a social insurance benefit formula, therefore, should be based on this concept.

Having concluded that both social adequacy and equity should be reflected in the old-age insurance benefit formula, the next question is how to blend the two elements. Here the analogy of the best formula for a dry martini is helpful. While it seems to be generally agreed that much more gin (adequacy) should be used than vermouth (equity), there are decided differences of opinion as to what the ratio of adequacy to equity should be. Also a given person's ideas as to the blend and even the kinds of adequacy and equity may be quite different for lifetime than for temporary risks.

This question cannot be divorced from the scope of coverage and the financing of the plan. The closer coverage is to being universal, the less weight need be given to equity, although some equity should always be included under a plan which is financed in part by contributions of potential beneficiaries. A review of the developments over the last twenty years in our Federal old-age plan indicates clearly that it would be unrealistic to consider benefits (conditions of eligibility as well as level of payment) apart from coverage, or from financing. Furthermore, a good case can be made that this applies to the "temporary" as well as the "lifetime" risks.

Without passing judgment on either the present or proposed numerical factors in the benefit formula for OASI, the type of formula now in effect is a simple and effective one for blending adequacy and equity. It permits ready adjustment in the amounts of benefits when this is desired because of changed conditions.

However, it does introduce anomalies and abuses as long as the plan does not cover substantially all employed and self-employed persons. For that and other reasons Congress should enact the proposals recommended by the President for extension of coverage and the recommendations it has received for inclusion of the Federal Civil Service employees and armed forces under OASI.

In conclusion, I should like to refer to an area in which research and study are greatly needed. I have long been deeply concerned by developments over the years whereby the Federal Treasury absorbs more and more of the costs of old-age assistance.

Public assistance and social insurance represent entirely different approaches which, like oil and water, do not naturally mix. That, however, does not mean that conflict or even competition must necessarily result between them. After all, they have a common purpose as defenses against want, and there is no reason why they could not function harmoniously in achieving that end. But, if this is to happen, it is necessary that each be assigned its proper place and keep to that place without encroaching on the preserves of the other.

Hence the first step is to define these proper places. When that has been determined, it is the task of the legislators to devise a working plan in the light of what is possible and desirable within the framework of the definition, and of the administrators to see that neither the assistance nor the insurance concept oversteps its proper bounds.

It is my conviction—and I judge it to have also been the philosophy of those who planned our original Federal Social Security legislation of 1935— that old-age assistance should play a definitely subordinate role. It was clearly the intent of the President's Committee on Economic Security, and of the legislators who followed the main outlines of their blueprint, that public assistance, though necessarily large at first, should decline as social old-age insurance grew stronger, and should eventually retain no more than a residual function.

When the OASI benefits were liberalized in 1950 and 1952, one might have expected the Congress to amend the Old Age Assistance provisions so as to reverse the trend of more and more Federal grants. Instead, over the years, Congress greatly liberalized the formula for the Federal government's share of the assistance grants. The present outlook is that OASI benefits will again be liberalized substantially this year, but with no retrenchment in the assistance field.

The issue of the Federal government's withdrawal from the old-age assistance field and various proposals for accomplishing that, in whole or in part, have been the subject of extensive debate for well over a year. This debate generated so much heat that it probably deferred rather than advanced the day when the issue may be resolved on a sound basis.

There is in my opinion no other issue as important as this in the old-age field. It calls for an early solution mutually satisfactory to all concerned. While complicated and controversial questions are involved, I am confident that a study of them by a representative group of individuals determined to explore them as objectively as possible will result in proposals which will be generally acceptable and will call a halt to the race between social insurance and assistance. I do hope that through the sponsorship of a public or private agency or group such a study project will be undertaken in the very near future. Unless the great weaknesses of the present old-age assistance arrangements are removed by one method or another, we cannot consider that the Federal government's role in old-age security is on a sound basis.

REPORT OF THE RECORDER

Elizabeth G. Meier

Associate Professor of Social Work, New York School of Social Work, Columbia University

Discussants addressed themselves to three questions raised by Professor Lester: What is the level of assured income toward which social insurance benefits should aim, and how is this level to be adjusted to changes in the standard of living and the cost of living? How do the objectives of the various social insurance programs differ from each other? What effects do the social insurance programs have upon individual incentive and national productivity?

Professor Pierre Laroque contended that the concept of social security has extended beyond those social insurance programs described by Professor Lester. He pointed out that plans for family allowances and the annual wage, neither of which was considered in the paper, must also be regarded as forms of social security which raise the level of assured income. The system of social security cannot be transplanted in its entirety from one country to another.

Nevertheless, the widespread adoption of family allowance schemes, not only in Europe but in Canada, Australia, New Zealand, and some South American countries as well, has been one of the most spectacular developments in social security in the last few decades. Professor Laroque cited Dr. Barbara Wootton to the effect that it is quixotic to provide special benefits for children in times of emergencies, as some unemployment insurance (or compensation) and workmen's compensation laws do, and yet ignore the fact that the family's standard of living at all times is affected by the existence of dependent children.

Mrs. Ida Merriam deplored the fact that our anxiety, lest incentive and productivity be stifled by high benefits, sometimes blunted our perception of the dangers involved in levels of benefits which are too low either to provide the individual with a sense of security or to support the consuming power of the nation. The standard of living of large numbers of persons, who in their productive years were in the middle-income group, is not adequately protected either by the public or the private insurance programs. Greater understanding is needed that only the broad public programs can and must be responsive to changing wage and price levels, and thus protect the living standards of beneficiaries.

Dr. Burns outlined the dilemma which is created by the continuous and conflicting pressures upon the social security system. On the one hand, there is a constant thrust toward adequacy of benefits; and on the other there is the insistence that the system continue to provide benefits which are differentiated according to the previous earnings of the beneficiaries. If adequacy is to mean that most beneficiaries be able to maintain themselves without supplementation from other sources, then a fairly high level of minimum benefits must be set. Yet, if the same system is to maintain differential benefits, then the necessity for increased contributions arises. This provokes the question, "How large a proportion of the working population is willing to set aside how much to insure their future benefits?" It has been assumed, Dr. Burns pointed out, that our philosophy insists that the worker's equity in his benefits be sizable, and that there is a strong feeling for differential benefits. Since recent years have witnessed marked departures from these ideas, further information is needed as to the reality of the assumptions.

Mr. Arthur Altmeyer agreed that the dilemma posed by Dr. Burns existed, but he questioned whether experts are needed to evaluate attitudes of the public in regard to adequacy of benefits and differentials. The national Congress and state legislatures, he averred, were sensitive barometers of public opinion in these matters. Also, adequacy is a term about whose meanings experts are likely to disagree, since the concept involves values that are intangible as well as tangible, and since ours is a high-level economy wherein wide variations in standards of living are found.

Professor Paul Brissenden advised further probing to determine which level of government can best accomplish the objectives of programs. He asked whether data available from accumulated experience are sufficiently conclusive at this time to decide whether programs should continue to be administered by the levels of government now responsible, or that a readjustment is warranted. Professor Frank de Vyver commented that insufficient attention is paid to the role which practical politics plays in determining what kinds of standards for social security can be set on a national level, and what governmental unit shall be responsible for administration.

Dr. Franz Goldmann characterized common attitudes toward government as highly tinged with emotion. Government is regarded as either a Santa Claus, a "suspicious character," or a "last resort in time of crises." A more rational attitude toward government's role in social security is developing and can be further encouraged by education of the public and by governmentally operated programs which are demonstrably good.

The nature of the hazards covered, the level of benefits, and the costs of the program—Congress must constantly keep these three interrelated aspects in balance, Mr. Wilbur Cohen suggested. Up to this year, premium costs had been regarded as the fixed and constant element, with 6 per cent of payroll seen as the level which could not be exceeded in projected tax rates. This was the fixed figure to which estimates of benefit levels needed to be scaled. Mr. Cohen regarded it as especially significant that this year Congressional thinking seemed to change. In a recently reported bill, the 6 per cent payroll tax was no longer regarded as the constant around which the level of benefit payments needed to accommodate itself. Rather a $7\frac{1}{3}$ per cent payroll tax is envisaged in order to support the greater long-run costs of increased coverage and of more adequate benefits.

Changes in the nature of the programs, he said, also affect the balance of the three elements. There is some sentiment that the retirement-age test should be eliminated, as has been done in European programs, but increased costs would require an additional one per cent of payroll. Lowering the retirement age, similarly, would result either in an increase in over-all costs or in reduced benefit levels. Extension of coverage through such means poses the problem whether the subsequently reduced benefits would be sufficiently high to maintain most of the beneficiaries who are dependent upon them for their needs, without their needing to have supplementary public assistance. "What are the social priorities?" Mr. Cohen asked. Perhaps greater social values might be realized by expanding the Federal social insurance system to include disability as a covered risk, than by lowering the retirement age or dropping the retirement test.

The propitiousness of unforeseen events, not scientific inquiry, sometimes disposes the course of social legislation, Mr. Altmeyer contended. There was no public clamor that survivor's benefits be added to Federal old-age insurance legislation in 1939, he recalled, but an enormous reserve fund was being built up and so Survivors Insurance was added to Old Age Insurance. Mr. Altmeyer, then administrator of the program, conceded that the possibility of such expansion had not been altogether remote from the thinking of those persons who were close to the program's development.

Are we too ready to assume, Mr. Robert Goodwin asked, that the American social security system should follow the paths taken by European plans? Given our high wage levels, and the psychological values we attach to insurance principles, it may be neither necessary nor desirable to extend the American system to cover other kinds of social contingencies, such as those provided by European systems in family allowances and health insurance.

Sometimes the social aims within a program contradict each other, Dr. Goldmann pointed out. A high benefit level is regarded as desirable, yet, if such is to be maintained, it has been assumed that persons over 65 must be willing to stay out of the labor market. This collides with another social objective—good health—for "enforced inactivity," Dr. Goldmann asserted, "is the major cause of physical and mental breakdown in older people." Mr. Hohaus disputed the assertion in his closing remarks, commenting that such breakdowns were less likely to occur if the older person's economic well-being was secure.

Referring to problems of interstate competition described by Professor Lester, Dr. Goldmann maintained that it might be highly desirable for the Federal government to designate the floor below which adequacy of benefits must not fall, but he warned against the imposition of ceilings, since this might inhibit economically favored states from developing high level programs which they were capable of sustaining.

Father Joseph Becker agreed that interstate competition might depress the level of benefits, but held that in some instances it serves to increase them. Satisfactory experience with liberal legislation in one state encourages similar developments elsewhere. Also, factors other than economic competition, such as the political complexions of state legislatures, influence legislation. It is difficult to liberalize social insurance measures in states where rural representation in the legislature is heavy.

Father Becker cautioned against the approach to problems of social security becoming too generalized. He doubted whether it is possible to think in terms of the whole population and all social contingencies. He agreed with Professor Lester that research focused upon specific problems was necessary. In his experience, Father Becker stated, interdisciplinary efforts are frequently wasteful, serving only to highlight the need for students to engage in further research within their own specific areas of competence.

Father Becker contrasted workmen's compensation with unemployment insurance. Acknowledging that further improvements are needed in workmen's compensation, this program, nevertheless, is more acceptable to employers and liberalization is more readily secured. They are wary on the other hand, about liberalizing unemployment insurance benefits. This difference in attitude can be accounted for partly because the likelihood of malingering is less in workmen's compensation. Also, wage levels are less related to problems of malingering in this program than in unemployment insurance. Whereas industry and labor have frequently been able to present legislatures with "agreed bills" in workmen's compensation, such agreement is exceedingly rare in unemployment insurance measures. Employers' interests and workers' interests are difficult to reconcile in unemployment insurance legislation, particularly as they are affected by regulations which qualify or disqualify an individual for benefits.

Professor Herman Somers challenged the validity of Father Becker's assumption that workmen's compensation benefits had increased. Research in this area is badly needed, but research is dependent not only upon qualified personnel, but also upon administrative structures wherein research is possible. While it is loosely stated that states administer workmen's compensation, in actuality it is administered by insurance companies who may report their activities to units within the states' governments. In fact, states do not always know how many persons receive compensation, nor the amounts that are granted. This, Professor Somers asserted, leads to erroneous notions about the program. He described the varieties of limitations and ceilings affecting benefit levels—limits in regard to conditions covered, and the type of injury sustained, and maximums in regard to previous earnings, weekly amounts, total amounts, and length of benefit periods. Disputing Professor Lester's figures, Professor Somers maintained that only in a few states do workmen's compensation benefits exceed 30 per cent of the beneficiary's previous earnings. Permanent total disability and fatality benefits are 15 per cent and 10 per cent respectively, on an average, of earnings which might have been anticipated had injury not intervened.

Illusions about the generosity of workmen's compensation facilitate agreed bills, Professor Somers contended. Except for medical provisions, benefit levels in terms of purchasing power are lower than in 1911. Furthermore, it is not the benign attitude of industry toward workmen's compensation which produces agreement; rather, it is that industry fears that the common law rights of the injured workman may be resorted to, and in this era its protection tends to be more generous than the benefits provided by legislative enactment. Workmen's compensation laws have "taken full advantage of their right to deteriorate." In spite of the greater rationality of a unified system of social insurance to replace our individual programs, Professor Somers concluded that pluralism is valuable. It can protect against the danger that the decay of one system will affect all persons for all risks. Furthermore, pressures can sometimes be more effective if they are directed toward improvements in a specific program.

Professor Seymour Harris denied the claim that social security programs were causing an excessive tax burden. Economic security measures must be seen in relation to the total economy. At the present time, expenditures on those programs have not risen in proportion to the rise in national income. Furthermore, experience in England has shown that when expansion of welfare measures substantially increases their costs, the burden of taxes tends to revert back to those who benefit from the services. Professor Harris suggested that Professor Lester had underestimated the significance of transfer payments. In the decade between 1940 and 1950, there were marked changes in the distribution of income. The $23 billion spent for various social security and welfare measures substantially influenced this change. Receipt of benefits accounted for increased incomes in the lower-income levels, and thereby provided a stabilizing factor in the national economy.

Do we want more or less savings? This question, Professor Harris believed, was not clearly considered in Professor Lester's analysis. Wide variations in savings in two consecutive postwar years during which social security contributions and benefits remained fairly constant suggest that factors other than social security measures influence trends in savings.

We are extraordinarily unempirical when discussing the question of incentives, Dr. Barbara Wootton chided. She called attention to the tendency to see only two extremes when we speak of work habits—steady employment or complete idleness. In reality this is not the true issue. Rather, there is a real problem in helping turn the young unsteady worker into a steady employee. The concept of incentive is complex, and the individual in whom we examine this trait is subject to social, psychological, and cultural pressures, as well as economic need.

Mr. Arthur Altmeyer maintained that insecurity, not security, is a deterrent to incentive. Steady work and decent jobs, adequate housing, rehabilitation of the injured, and the cure of those who are diseased—these are social aims toward whose accomplishment much energy is needed. These are the conditions which provide freedom and which stimulate man's urge to achieve.

In his concluding remarks, Professor Lester agreed that the question of how to combine a high minimum benefit with acceptable differentials was a crucial issue. He also felt that with state-administered programs interstate competition was a significant factor. Mr. Hohaus reiterated that "adequacy" was not a matter to be determined by a slide rule; what is regarded as adequate has changed in the past and will change in the future. He emphasized the close interrelationship between the three components of all social security measures: benefits, coverage, and methods of financing. In answer to a question, he stated that the availability of OASI benefits had not adversely affected the sale of life insurance.

Mr. Becker thought it was inevitable that in a democracy there should be difference of opinion and continuous struggle about the appropriate level of benefits. Yet the ranges of difference could be materially narrowed if more facts were available. He emphasized again the need for research, especially by the universities, as he believed governments could not do the kind of research needed because the findings would too closely affect policy and decision-making. He urged the universities to train more people equipped to undertake such research and to serve as social security administrators.

Current Issues in Financing Income Security

Marion B. Folsom
Under Secretary of the Treasury of the United States

Income security, the theme of this conference, may be interpreted in various ways. In a broad sense it encompasses all the economic factors involved in maintaining a high level of income and those devices that contribute to a maximum of productive employment and the full utilization of resources. In real terms it is the total production of a nation that constitutes the prime measure of its capacity to assure economic security for its people. Less broadly, the term may be confined to whatever contributes to an individual's or a family's means of livelihood when the customary income is cut off from whatever cause, whether temporarily or permanently.

Important and interesting as it would be to explore the subjects of productive capacity, employment, and other factors that make for a high per capita volume of goods and services, our immediate interest centers on those means which help individuals sustain themselves when they cannot do so by their own current productive efforts. These mechanisms are many and varied, and in considering some of the basic issues involved in financing income security, we shall direct attention to the highly diverse nature of these efforts, and the current problems being faced in each field.

We may perhaps deal with them most conveniently if we classify them according to the person or agency that is the prime mover behind them: the individual himself, the employer or the employment relationship, and the government. The value of the protection we have developed in this country lies in no small measure in the wide scope and diversity of this three-pronged attack on potential economic adversities. We are not dependent for income security on the success of any one kind of program or activity.

INDIVIDUAL EFFORTS TOWARD ECONOMIC SECURITY

It is one of our strongest traditions that the individual shall rely first of all on his own efforts to acquire the protection necessary for those periods when

339

income may be interrupted or terminated. In all of our plans, both in government and in industry, we proceed on the assumption that such efforts on the part of the individual will be continued, if not intensified. For example, our social security program has been consciously formulated with a view toward providing no more than a basic minimum of protection so that it will stimulate additional, supplementary efforts by the individual. By providing this minimum protection, old-age and survivors' insurance was designed to encourage additional efforts to achieve a comfortable retirement.

Various indicators suggest that, on the whole, individuals have acquired a greater measure of protection against the loss of earnings than ever before. That protection takes various forms, including cash and bank deposits, home ownership, investment in securities (both privately issued and governmental), and the ownership of insurance and various property, including productive business enterprises.

At the end of 1953 liquid assets in the hands of individuals in the form of currency, bank deposits, deposits in savings and loan associations, and U. S. Government bonds amounted to about $230 billion. This was equivalent to an average of over $4,500 for each of the approximately 51 million families and unattached individuals.

An increasing proportion of American families own their own homes. It is estimated that at the beginning of 1953, 54 per cent of all nonfarm families owned their homes compared with 41 per cent before World War II. Among families headed by individuals aged 55 and above, the proportion is even higher—66 per cent in 1953 compared with 59 per cent in 1940.

Investment in equity securities of American industry is another form of individual savings that is becoming increasingly more important in the total picture. It is estimated that there are 8,500,000 persons who own stock directly and there are many millions more who own equities indirectly through investment trusts, insurance companies, and trust funds. Nor is such ownership restricted to high-income families.

Satisfactory statistics are not available regarding the ownership of stocks by income groups, but the wide diffusion is well illustrated by an analysis recently made of the more than 200,000 share owners of the U. S. Steel Corporation. This survey showed that 74 per cent of their shareholders had income of less than $10,000 and that they owned 53 per cent of the stock; that 56 per cent had income of less than $5,000 and they owned 37 per cent of the stock.

By partially relieving existing double taxation of dividend income, the pending tax revision bill before Congress would stimulate further investment in equity securities. It would give full relief to the first $100 of dividend income ($50 in the first year) in the hands of individuals, and a credit of 10 per cent (5 per cent in the first year) on dividends above this amount. An individual and his wife investing up to $4,000 in common stock at an assumed yield of 5 per cent would be completely relieved of the double tax. [The bill referred to was adopted, Public Law 591, 83rd Congress.]

Life insurance constitutes a major form of voluntarily achieved individual protection in this country. At the end of 1953 we had $225 billion of ordinary and industrial life insurance in force. If we add $80 billion of group life insurance, made possible largely through the employment connection, we have a grand total of $305 billion of life insurance in force, representing protection for more than 90 million policyholders. Virtually four out of five families now have some life insurance on one or more of their members. It is worth noting that life insurance in force at the end of 1953 was more than double that at the end of World War II. In addition, there were about 4.5 million annuities in force—current and deferred—representing an aggregate annual income of some $1.6 billion, of which group annuities represented about half.

EMPLOYER-SPONSORED PLANS

In addition to the individual's accomplishments on his own account, there have developed over the years employer-sponsored plans aimed at providing additional protection. These plans are often financed by joint contributions by employer and employees, and advantage can be obtained from the lower costs due to group rates. Even before the adoption of social security, but especially in recent years, industry has been active in endeavoring to fill the gap between individual resources and the amounts necessary for proper maintenance in periods of income loss. As a result, many different types of plans have developed: thrift and savings plans, profit-sharing plans, industrial pensions, group life insurance, and health and welfare plans.

Though it is far less significant than some of the other employer-sponsored plans, the thrift and savings type of plan is receiving increasing attention. These plans are designed to encourage thrift on the part of employees, to assist them in purchasing homes or in acquiring more adequate income on retirement, and to provide protection against emergencies. They generally call for the employee to set aside a regular sum out of his earnings. This may range from one to ten per cent of wages, with a specified dollar maximum; it is then supplemented by an employer contribution, such as one-half the employee savings. In some cases the combined amounts are used to purchase government bonds, company stock, or shares in investment trusts in the name of the employee. In some, only the employer contribution may be used to purchase company stock. Under most savings plans, the employee's right to the employer contribution becomes vested in a relatively short time, while the employee always retains the right to his own contribution. While these savings plans have not been in operation long enough to permit an adequate evaluation, there are indications that they enjoy a high degree of popularity among employees. In a recent study of such plans it was found that on the average 86 per cent of employees eligible participated.

Another type of plan often sponsored by employers, with the object, among others, of providing the workers with greater economic security, is the profit-sharing plan. A wide variety of such plans have been devised. Under one popular form, a specified percentage of the profits is set aside. Under another type, employees receive a wage dividend based upon the dividend paid to stockholders. The proceeds of a profit-sharing plan may be distributed on either a current or a deferred basis. Under the current distribution type, profits are paid in cash, as earned, at intervals of one year or less. Under the deferred distribution type, they are deposited in a fund, usually an irrevocable one; but, while credited to the accounts of the employees as earned, these deposits are not distributed until some future occasion such as retirement or the occurrence of disability. Such funds can and often do take the place of the regular type of pension plan.

Although the full extent of their development is not known, industrial pension plans are by far the most important, financially, of the employer-sponsored plans. In 1940, it was estimated that there were about 2,000 private pension plans covering some 3.7 million persons. At the end of 1953, it was estimated that there were 17,000 pension plans covering some 11 million persons. At the present time, the Internal Revenue Service is receiving applications at the rate of about 3,600 a year for the approval of pension, profit-sharing, and stock bonus plans for the favorable tax treatment accorded plans that do not discriminate in favor of stockholders and key employees.

As in the case of other types of employer-sponsored plans which supplement individual provision against income loss, there are a number of business motives behind the establishment of an industrial pension plan. It helps to attract capable employees and reduces employee turnover. The firm's position in the community is enhanced. Efficiency is increased by making it feasible to retire older employees without exposing them to economic hardship, and by making it possible to promote younger employees to their jobs. The retirement of one highly placed executive may open up better jobs to several younger employees, thereby improving the organization and its morale.

The establishment of a sound pension plan involves a number of complex issues. Pension costs are apt to increase over a long period of time. This comes about as a result of the natural growth of an enterprise. If a firm has enjoyed a normal rate of growth, the number of its employees who reach retirement age will increase as the life of the firm increases. Moreover, as a pension plan gets under way, more people are added to the rolls each year than are taken off through death. Increasing longevity also may tend to increase annual pension costs. As a result of these factors, provision must be made to accumulate funds representing the liability created by the pension plan if a large annual addition to payroll costs is to be avoided.

One way of handling this problem is to "fund" a pension plan. This involves the preparation of careful estimates of cost covering an extended period of time. The liabilities arising by virtue of past employment as well as the liabilities arising out of current employment must both be taken into account. Through the funding device, the burden of pension costs can be spread out over an extended period.

What are the principal problems now being faced in this field of company pension plans? It has been estimated that approximately $2½ billion a year are now being contributed to pension plans. The reserves of such plans have already reached $20 billion and may reach the magnitude of $35 to $40 billion within a decade. The investment of these funds, together with accumulations in various government pension programs, will require increasing attention. However, the rate of accumulation in government programs may decline significantly within the next few years, thus offsetting in part the increasing reserves of private pension funds.

Another problem associated with industrial pension schemes relates to the vesting of employees' rights in the pension fund. One of the objectives of a pension plan is to make continued employment with a firm more attractive to the employee. Accordingly, there is a tendency to require a relatively long period of service with a firm before an employee's rights in a pension fund are vested. One study of pension plans that were put into effect during the years 1950 to 1952 indicated that in more than half of the plans where only the period of service determined vesting rights employment for 15 years or more was required.

From the point of view of the economy as a whole, a shortening of the service requirement as a condition of vesting would be desirable. This would facilitate the movement of employees between companies, industries, and regions, in accordance with changing economic requirements. From the point of view of the employee, vesting after a shorter period of service is very desirable since it would increase the likelihood that he would obtain a supplementary private pension. One of the problems, therefore, which must be faced in the future is how to reconcile these two seemingly conflicting objectives so that the interests of the employer will be secured at the same time that the employee's interests will be safeguarded. The logical solution would be a gradual lowering of the vesting period.

Provisions as to the vesting of pensions may be affected by whether or not the employee participates in financing a pension plan. Where the employee does participate, the service period prior to vesting tends to be shorter than in other cases. In this connection it is of interest to note that a special study of pension data submitted by employers with their 1951 tax returns indicated, with respect to about 3.7 million employees designated as being covered by either a contributory or a noncontributory plan, that about one-third were included under contributory pension plans.

Another problem which confronts industrial pension plans is their integration with the OASI program. By providing a basic layer of protection and so reducing the supplementary task to be accomplished by a private plan, social security benefits facilitate the establishment of such plans. The enactment of the Social Security Act in 1953 greatly stimulated the adoption of pension plans, and this stimulation has continued to be a strong factor in recent years.

The revenue revision bill now pending in the Senate contains several provisions designed to clarify and simplify the rules to qualify pension plans for tax deduction, especially in regard to their integration with OASI. At the same time, safeguards are maintained against the qualification of discriminatory plans. These provisions, if adopted, should make it easier, especially for smaller companies, to inaugurate plans.

Changes in social security in response to changes in wages and price levels may disturb the pattern previously established between private pension plans and OASI. Many companies made no changes in their supplementary plans as a result of the 1951 increase in benefits under OASI, because they felt that their pensions plus the prior level of OASI benefits had become inadequate in relation to increased living costs. Other companies made some adjustments. The problem will arise again if the bill now pending in Congress is enacted; both the benefits and the wage base will be increased. This again would enable individual employers to continue their pension plans as before without adjustment if they consider the present package of OASI benefits and pension payments inadequate. [The bill referred to became Public Law 761, 83rd Congress.]

A relatively new form of industry effort designed to promote income maintenance is the conscious application of managerial techniques to stabilize employment. A business enterprise may not be able to cope with large swings in the business cycle. However, during ordinary times of prosperity there are relatively short-run fluctuations in production which can be mitigated if an attempt is made to organize production in the light of the sales pattern prevailing in the industry. There are advantages to all concerned from steadier operations of a business and from the steadier jobs that flow from it. It means better utilization of plant, lower overhead costs, and reduced unemployment compensation taxes. It means a more permanent work force with higher employee morale and greater security.

There is now available carefully analyzed information regarding specific plans now in use by widely diversified companies. A successful plan requires a thorough survey of fluctuations in employment, sales, and production, exploration of techniques for stabilizing sales through changes in merchandising procedures, market diversification and product diversification, improved sales forecasting, revised purchasing policies, and community and inter-company action. The possibility of increasing employment stability by the widespread adoption of plans of this type offers a real challenge to management of American industry.

Group life insurance plans are a very popular form of employer-sponsored security plans. At the end of 1953, 27,000,000 employees were covered by

$74 billion of group life insurance out of the total of $80 billion in force. Because of the employer contribution and low administrative expenses on a group basis, term insurance can be obtained at a cost to the employee well below the ordinary individual premium. The cost to the employee in the con- tributory plan probably averages around $6 per year per $1,000. There has been a strong tendency in recent years to increase the amount of protection, now quite often amounting to two years' salary. More and more plans are also providing for coverage on a more liberal basis after retirement with the entire cost borne by the employer. This is naturally expensive, but by providing for a gradual reduction over a period of years to a specified minimum, the costs can be held within reasonable limits.

GOVERNMENTAL PROGRAMS

In view of the traditional reliance on individual initiative in the United States to make provision against various risks of income loss, and in view of the variety and magnitude of the plans developed through employer-employee relationships directed to the same end, it has been possible to keep govern- mental action directed toward the problem of income security on a far more limited scale than prevails in many other countries.

In some countries the volume of socially provided income has reached a point where it constitutes a large proportion of the current income of workers. Payroll taxes have approached 25 and 30 per cent of wages, and the level of benefits under government plans sometimes appears to evoke greater interest than wage rates. Political pressure is exerted to obtain increases in benefits or governmental supplements of one kind or another. In such cases the economic forces normally at work in industry are to a large extent replaced by political forces, and industry has been saddled with rigid cost structures which seri- ously impede competition and the adaptation of industry to changing economic conditions. Such practice also greatly reduces the incentive of both the worker and the employer to increase production. So far in this country the levels of payroll taxes and benefits under governmental plans have been kept within the limits which were originally envisaged of a minimum basic protection.

The governmental programs established in the United States deal with four major causes of income loss: industrial accidents, old age, death of the family provider, and unemployment. The first of the programs to reach more or less full development was workmen's compensation. Each of the states now has in effect workmen's compensation laws which seek to assure the prompt payment of statutory benefits to persons injured on the job. Various methods are used to achieve this objective, including compulsory and voluntary insurance. While various points are at issue in this field, methods of financing give rise to rela- tively little controversy. In the case of the other social security programs, how- ever, problems of financing are very much in the foreground and are the sub- ject of extended debate.

SOCIAL SECURITY FOR THE AGED

In the United States governmental income maintenance for the aged is handled through a compulsory contributory plan and a public assistance program. The Old Age and Survivors Insurance program (OASI) provides benefits to qualified aged persons as a matter of right. The benefit amounts are explicitly stated in the law and are not subject to any discretionary authority. Public assistance, on the other hand, is paid to those who meet a means test, and the amount varies with the real or presumed need of the recipient. The insurance scheme is financed from the proceeds of an earmarked payroll tax, while the public assistance costs incurred by the Federal government are financed from general revenues.

Although the initial tax rate imposed to finance the OASI program was 1 per cent each on employees and employers and although this rate was retained until 1950, a reserve fund has been accumulated of approximately $19 billion. If the schedule of tax rates originally enacted had been permitted to go into effect, a 3-per-cent tax rate would have been reached by 1949, and the reserve accumulated would have been substantially larger than it now is. The retention of the 1-per-cent rate for as long as 14 years reflected widespread uncertainty about the desirability of the method of financing which was initially adopted. This uncertainty has revolved about the question whether the program should be financed on a full-reserve basis, on a pay-as-you-go basis, or on some intermediate plan such as a contingency reserve.

Reserve fund versus pay-as-you-go financing

In many forms of voluntary private insurance where the acquisition of new memberships and the continuity of premium income cannot be assured, an accumulation of reserve funds is essential to insure the discharge of all assumed obligations. Legislation regulating insurance companies is directed largely toward assuring the adequacy of such reserves.

Under a national compulsory governmental plan, on the other hand, the situation is entirely different. Because of the taxing power of the government and its authority to require membership in a plan, actuarial reserves are not needed to assure the payment of benefits to individuals. Consequently, justification for large reserves has been based on other grounds.

To some extent the accumulation of a reserve fund has been unavoidable. Since the program was predicated on contributions by all benefit recipients, thus excluding those persons already retired or close to retirement from the program, benefit costs were initially very small. If contributions had been kept to a level merely sufficient to pay for current benefits, they would have been only token amounts in the early years.

One consideration on which support for a large reserve fund is generally based is that the earnings of this fund in future years can help to finance benefit costs. The significance of this argument lies in the fact that while benefit costs at the beginning of the program were only a small percentage of payrolls they are expected to rise to a level of 8 or 10 per cent. Earnings of a reserve fund would make it unnecessary to impose tax rates of this magnitude.

It has also been argued that a reserve fund would tend to guarantee the payment of statutory benefits. Congress, it is said, would be less likely to reduce benefit payments in accordance with current political considerations. It has also been held, however, that the existence of a reserve fund tends to produce excessive liberalism in benefits, and to encourage governmental expenditures for other purposes.

Another purpose of a reserve is to make it possible to keep payroll tax rates from fluctuating in accordance with changes in benefit costs or economic conditions. It meets the purpose of a contingency fund, out of which temporary excesses of benefits over receipts could be met without disturbing prevailing tax rates.

It was originally anticipated that a reserve fund would reach a magnitude of nearly $50 billion. There was serious concern about the manner in which funds of such a magnitude could be invested. Many changes occurred after the adoption of the social security program which quickly made the original estimates obsolete; but the current program also may produce very large accumulations in the trust fund and pose serious investment problems. The transfer of a substantial part of the present publicly held Federal debt to the OASI trust fund would require shifts in the investment policies of those now holding Federal bonds. The magnitude of this problem may be gauged from the fact that under high-employment assumptions an intermediate cost estimate indicates that the reserve could reach $63 billion by 1980. This assumes no change in the present benefit structure or in the contemplated tax rates.

The maintenance of a reserve fund is dependent upon forecasts of benefits and receipts over an extended period of time. Experience thus far has revealed that such forecasts cannot be made with any great amount of confidence. There are many variables which affect prospective receipts and expenditures. Some of these may change rapidly and exert an important influence on actual receipts and expenditures. Thus a rise in the general level of wages would have an immediate impact on tax collections, but the effect on benefits would be less pronounced since they are related to the average wages of an individual over an extended period. A rise in the average age of retirement might significantly reduce benefit costs.

The building up of a reserve fund may have significant economic consequences. Payroll taxes have reached a substantial magnitude, and from an economic point of view it would be desirable that they be broadly coordinated with over-all fiscal policy.

As already noted, a reserve fund has already been accumulated of considerable proportions. The issue of the reserve fund versus pay-as-you-go financing is therefore one which relates to the system henceforth, and not to the system over its entire life. And even with respect to the immediate future, the question of pay-as-you-go is rather academic, since for at least several years tax collections (at the current 4 per cent rate) will exceed benefit costs, even if the current benefit changes under consideration by the Congress should be adopted. The excess collections will, however, gradually decline. In the meantime, in accordance with the law, the trustees of the fund will report each year as to the estimated receipts and expenditures for the succeeding five years, so that any unusual trend can be readily observed. It is also advisable to have a new unbiased survey of the system made about once every five years, similar to those made in 1938 and 1948.

If we should adopt a pay-as-you-go policy at some time in the future, the reserve fund already accumulated would be available as a contingency reserve to avoid abrupt changes in tax rates; it could be drawn upon in a period of reduced employment and high benefits to be replenished when general economic conditions improve. This would raise a question as to the timing of tax-rate changes. One approach which some have suggested and which may be worth exploring would be the adoption of a formula by which the tax rate would be increased according to the relationship between the reserve fund and taxable payrolls.

Trust fund investments

Existing law requires that the amounts in the OASI trust fund which are unnecessary to pay for the current costs of operating the program shall be invested in Federal government securities. This practice has created doubt in the minds of some people whether there is in fact a reserve fund. The argument is made that this form of investment simply means that the government uses the payroll tax collections to finance ordinary government expenditures, and that the funds are not available for social security benefits. The bonds are said to be government IOUs having no substance behind them.

The validity of this argument can perhaps best be tested by comparing the investment features of the OASI program with those of a private insurance company. A private company uses part of its current receipts to meet current operating costs and invests the excess in income-producing assets. The types of investment are limited by law so that policyholders will be assured that their claims against the company will be satisfied when they become due; government bonds represent a considerable part of these investments. The purpose behind the investment is of course to obtain earnings which will help meet the future costs of the company and reduce the premiums that policyholders would otherwise have to pay for the insurance.

Excess social security contributions are handled in much the same way. However, the Secretary of the Treasury, who is the managing trustee of the OASI fund, is limited by law to only one type of investment; that is, bonds issued by the Federal government. There are two principal reasons for such a restriction. One is similar in nature to that which motivates legislation dealing with the investments of private insurance companies. It is designed to insure the safety of the fund. Government securities constitute the preferred form of riskless investment. The second reason is that the government is precluded from entering into the money market to compete with private institutions for investment outlets. In some countries it is, indeed, common for a public insurance program to invest reserve funds in various ventures. However, this would seem to be completely out of harmony with our conception of the proper scope of governmental activity.

The question of double taxation

One of the persistent criticisms leveled against the present method of financing the Old Age and Survivors Insurance program is that it involves double taxation. The precise form of the argument is not always made clear, but it seems to run along the following lines: Sometime in the future, interest earned by the OASI trust fund will be used to help finance benefit payments. When that time comes, the interest will have to be raised by the government from general tax revenues. But an amount equivalent to such interest could be allocated from general revenues for use in the same way without the accumulation of a trust fund. Hence the imposition of heavier social security taxes than are required to pay current benefits and the accumulation of a trust fund, it is argued, mean that taxes have been imposed twice for the same purpose.

This argument tends to ignore some of the major consequences of the present financing arrangements. Suppose that the trust fund had not been built up in past years and that the tax rates had been kept at a level just high enough to pay for current benefits. During the years when the government was financing World War II, postwar aid, and defense expenditures in connection with Korea, it would not have been able to borrow from the trust fund the nearly $19 billion which it has borrowed. Instead, it would have had to increase its borrowings from the general public by that amount. The debt would have come into existence in any case. At an interest rate of 2½ per cent, the interest charges on this $19 billion would be $475 million annually. Consequently, the government would now have to raise from the general taxpayer not only the $475 million necessary to help pay social security benefits now provided by the interest on the debt held by the trust fund, but an equivalent amount to meet the interest on the $19 billion of debt held by the public. A total of $950 million would have to be raised from general taxation to meet all obligations.

In one special situation, however, the accumulation of a reserve fund would result in additional taxation. If the existence of the fund should in any way lead to an increase in general governmental expenditures and make them higher than they would otherwise be, the total amount of government debt would be increased. Bonds in the trust fund would represent an increase in debt rather than a substitute for publicly held debt. In such a case, taxes would have to be imposed to service the enlarged debt.

The contributory system and blanketing-in

Partly as a result of the concern over reserve fund financing and partly as a result of other factors, there has developed sentiment in some quarters for extending the OASI program to pay benefits to all the present aged irrespective of whether they have hitherto been covered by the plan and paid contributions under it.

Contributory social security has acquired widespread support in the United States. In the minds of most it is associated with a program which provides benefits as a matter of right without any means test. The contributory requirement makes recipients feel that they have helped earn their retirement benefits.

The contributory feature has also been considered essential in a program that provides variable benefits, which in turn are regarded necessary because of the range of income, and because of the variations in wage levels and living costs in urban and rural areas and in different parts of the country. A flat benefit which may be adequate from the point of view of one group may be too small for another or excessive for a third. Only a contributory system and one in which contributions are variable, it is argued, can justify differential benefits.

A contributory system, it is also felt, is likely to be more enduring and less subject to change as a consequence of variations in the political climate. Finally, a contributory system provides an important source of revenue which could probably not be tapped except for purposes of a social security program.

It was recognized from the beginning that a contributory system would exclude in the early years those persons who had already reached retirement age, or who were so close to retirement age they would not be able to meet the eligibility requirements. It was expected that administrative problems which delayed the inclusion of some groups would be solved and that the OASI program would then apply to substantially the entire working population. Until such time as most of the aged would qualify for OASI benefits, provision was made for an old-age assistance program, administered by the states, with the Federal government sharing in the costs. The assistance program was viewed as a transitional device which would become less important as OASI benefits became payable to an increasing number of persons. However, the expansion of the OASI program did not take place as rapidly as many had anticipated, and there still remains a large segment of the working population that is not covered by the program, although this may be remedied shortly by legislation. [Coverage was extended in Public Law 761, mentioned above.]

As a result of the slow expansion of the OASI program, old-age assistance has not declined in accordance with expectations. The number of old-age assistance recipients reached a postwar peak in 1950. There has since been a steady decline; nevertheless in January 1954 there were about 2.6 million recipients of old-age assistance compared with 2 million in June 1940. The continued high level of old-age assistance expenditures has given impetus to the proposal that the present aged should be "blanketed-in" under OASI.

The cost of "blanketing-in" would depend on the details of a particular plan but it would be substantial under any of those that have been suggested. With a minimum monthly benefit of $35 under "blanketing-in," it has been estimated that the initial additional annual cost would be $2 billion. This compares with current annual OASI expenditures for old-age beneficiaries and their dependents of about $2.4 billion.

Despite the large increase in OASI costs which would be involved, "blanketing-in" would not eliminate the need for a public assistance program. The average old-age payment is about $51.50 a month, and many public assistance recipients receive considerably more than this amount, as is inevitable in a program based on need. In December 1952, 40 per cent of the old-age recipients received $55 a month or more. "Blanketing-in" might make it feasible for the Federal government to withdraw financial support from public assistance, but it seems evident that a substantial public assistance program would have to be continued. "Blanketing-in" would also change the method of financing the costs borne by the Federal government with respect to the needy aged. The amounts now paid out as grants to the states come from general revenues. Under OASI the amounts spent on the needy aged would come from payroll taxes.

Another argument used in support of blanketing-in is that it would mature the insurance program, and tend to put that program on a pay-as-you-go basis. As already indicated, however, it is not essential to take this step in order to achieve a pay-as-you-go system of OASI financing. With the various changes now under consideration, including benefit increases, the OASI program may approach a pay-as-you-go basis within the next few years. Thus, if pay-as-you-go is considered desirable, it could be achieved without blanketing-in.

Perhaps the most serious aspect of blanketing-in is the transformation it would make in the character of the OASI program. By paying flat benefits to a large number of persons on a noncontributory basis, it would depart from the major characteristics of the present system, to which the 1948 Advisory Council on Social Security (Senate Document 208, 80th Congress, Second Session) gave its endorsement in the following terms:

> The Council favors as the foundation of the social-security system the method of contributory social insurance with benefits related to prior earnings and awarded without a needs test. Differential benefits based on a work record are a reward for productive effort and are consistent with general economic incentives, while the knowledge that benefits will be paid—irrespective of whether the individual is in need—supports and stimulates his drive to add his personal savings to the basic security he has acquired

through the insurance system. Under such a social insurance system, the individual earns a right to a benefit that is related to his contribution to production. This earned right is his best guaranty that he will receive the benefits promised and that they will not be conditioned on his accepting either scrutiny of his personal affairs or restrictions from which others are free.

Supplementary protection for the self-employed

Attention has been directed to the various ways in which individuals have built up out of their own resources protection against loss of income, and to the variety of plans which industry has developed that supplement such individual efforts. A special problem exists with respect to the self-employed. They have been subject to high individual income tax rates over a long period of time, but they have not been able to qualify under the pension-plan provisions of our tax laws which permit the deferral of tax on amounts accumulated by employers over a period of time for distribution to employees after retirement, until such time as distributed to the employees.

Accordingly proposals have been made to grant self-employed persons the privilege of tax-deferral on amounts set aside through an insurance company or otherwise, up to a specified proportion of their current income, which would become available after they reached retirement age. One plan would permit the accumulation of 5 per cent of earned income up to a specified maximum. An additional ½ of 1 per cent would be allowed for each year that a person is over the age of, say, 55. This would take account of past years when the individual was not permitted to make such an accumulation on a tax-deferred basis. The proposal would also allow a one-year carry-over of this privilege in order to take account of years in which an individual had no income or in which it was unusually low.

Difficulties would be experienced in defining eligibility. For instance, should the privilege be extended to the employees who are not covered under pension plans or to those who do not have vested rights in a plan?

The British also have been concerned with this problem, and a special committee appointed by the Chancellor of the Exchequer to look into the matter recently made a proposal with respect to the tax treatment of retirement income which is very similar to the plan just noted.

Self-employed persons and others with retirement income, particularly those not receiving OASI benefits, would be aided by the tax bill now pending in the Senate. At present OASI benefits are exempt from income tax, but other retirement income is taxable. To correct such differentiation, a credit would be allowed persons aged 65 equal to the tax, at the first bracket rate, on retirement income up to $1,200 a year. An adjustment would be made to take account of pensions already excluded from gross income. The retirement income credit would be in addition to the present special exemption for the aged and would be conditioned on substantially the same test of retirement as is used for OASI. [Some adjustments were made by the 83d Congress.]

PUBLIC ASSISTANCE FOR THE AGED

The Social Security Act created a program of old-age assistance in which the states were left free to establish their own standards of need and to determine the amount of assistance payments, while the Federal government shared the cost. Total old-age assistance payments for the fiscal year 1937 amounted to $244 million, while in fiscal 1953 they amounted to $1.6 billion. This increase in expenditures was not merely a reflection of the increased cost of maintaining aged persons due to inflation or to a changing standard of adequacy. The number of recipients more than doubled in the same interval. At the end of fiscal 1937, there were 1.3 million old-age assistance recipients and at the end of 1953 there were 2.6 million. This is a reflection in part of the aging of our population. In 1930 there were about 6.6 million persons aged 65 and over; in 1953 it is estimated that there were about 13.4 million persons in that age group. In 1930, persons aged 65 and over represented 5.4 per cent of the total population; today, they represent nearly 8½ per cent of the total population.

In addition to these factors, however, Federal expenditures for assistance to the aged have been affected by revisions in the sharing formula. When the Social Security Act was first adopted, the Federal government shared on a fifty-fifty basis the cost of assistance payments up to $30 per month to the recipient. That formula has since been altered several times, until today the Federal share of public assistance payments amounts to 80 per cent of the first $25 of average public assistance payments and 50 per cent of the balance, up to $55 a month, paid to any individual. The increasing proportion of assistance payments borne by the Federal government, it has been argued, has tended to expand the benefit rolls unduly and to make the old-age assistance program a noncontributory pension plan.

There is considerable diversity among the states concerning the proportion of aged persons who are on the assistance rolls. As of June 1953, it is estimated that for the country as a whole about 19 per cent of those 65 and over were receiving old-age assistance payments, but the range among the states was from 5 per cent to nearly 60 per cent. Several factors may account for such variation in the percentages, also in the old-age assistance rates, among the states. Definitions of need are established independently and differ from state to state. There are variations in the legal responsibility of relatives for the maintenance of aged persons. The so-called "lien laws" differ among the states. In some instances aged persons are required to assign all their property as a condition for eligibility for public assistance, and this tends to reduce the number of aged persons seeking public assistance. In other states there are no such conditions.

One important factor in determining assistance rates appears to be the extent to which aged persons in a state qualify for benefits under the Old Age and Survivors Insurance program. In general, the public assistance rate is high in those states where a relatively small percentage of aged persons qualify for OASI benefits. In those states where OASI coverage is small, old-age assistance rates tend to be high. But this is not uniformly the case. There is variation among the more industralized states where OASI beneficiaries are concentrated, as well as among the less industrialized states.

It is generally conceded that some type of old-age assistance must be maintained, although not necessarily with Federal participation. Since OASI is designed to provide only a portion of what is necessary for adequate maintenance, individuals must build supplementary income sources. But there are always likely to be some individuals who will not have done so. This may occur because of illness or accident, the lack of economic opportunity, unwillingness to save, or investment losses. Moreover, there have been long delays in extending the OASI program so that large numbers of people have not acquired protection.

The number of old-age assistance recipients, though it is now twice as large as it was in 1937, has been declining gradually but steadily in the last few years, paralleled by a more or less similar reduction in total old-age assistance costs. With the expansion of OASI coverage and increased benefits, this trend should be accelerated. Nevertheless, proposals have been made for revision of the present structure of assistance grants, which would give added impetus in this direction.

One proposal that has been made for altering the present Federal old-age assistance grants is to vary them on the basis of the relative economic capacity of the states. Legislation has been proposed to provide for a basic Federal grant of 65 per cent of the state's total old-age assistance expenditures. This percentage would be adjusted, however, according to the relationship between the state's per capita income and the national per capita income. A state with per capita income the same as for the country as a whole would receive the basic 65 per cent from the Federal government and pay 35 per cent from its own revenues. If a state had a per capita income 10 per cent higher than the national average, its share of the old-age assistance costs would be 10 per cent higher than the basic 35 per cent, or 38.5 per cent. The Federal grant would be 61.5 instead of 65 per cent.

The same bill includes another modification in the Federal grant, to vary it inversely with the number of aged persons in a state receiving OASI benefits. For every 5 per cent of the aged in a state receiving OASI benefits, the Federal share in public assistance would be reduced by 1 percentage point. Suppose, for example, that on the basis of the general formula, a state would be receiving 65 per cent of its public assistance costs from the Federal government. If 25 per cent of the aged in the state were receiving OASI benefits, the Federal share would be reduced by 5 percentage points to 60 per cent.

Another modification that has been proposed is to have an annual appropriation of a specified amount to be allocated among the states according to some index of need and of economic capacity. From time to time the annual appropriation would be scaled downward, and ultimately the Federal government would move out of the public assistance program as was anticipated when the Social Security Act was first established.

The Commission on Intergovernmental Relations has as one of its many subjects for review the system of Federal grants for public assistance. The outcome of its work in this area cannot be forecast, but its recommendations will be awaited with great interest.

UNEMPLOYMENT COMPENSATION

The third major program in our social security system, unemployment compensation, is primarily the responsibility of the individual states. The Federal government levies a tax of 3 per cent of payrolls on employers of eight or more employees, but allows a credit for 90 per cent of this tax (2.7 per cent of payrolls) for contributions paid under an approved state unemployment compensation law. To be approved, a state law must meet certain requirements, but these do not involve the amount or duration of benefits.

The full tax credit of 2.7 per cent is allowed even though an employer may actually pay less than that to a state under its experience rating provisions. In most of the postwar years, the average employer tax for the country as a whole was 1.5 per cent of wages or less. However, the range of rates ran from no tax at all for some employers to rates as high as 4.0 per cent.

The only source of revenue for financing the state unemployment compensation programs is the tax on employers, except that in two states a tax is also imposed on employees. (In past years there were nine states that imposed taxes on employees.) This is in sharp contrast to the financing policies pursued abroad, where the cost is often shared among employers and employees and where frequently the government makes a contribution from general revenues.

The dependence in the United States upon employer contributions to finance unemployment compensation reflects the historical development and underlying philosophy of the unemployment compensation program. It is based on the assumptions, first, that the cost of unemployment compensation is a proper charge against industry and, second, that employers can help to stabilize employment. An employer tax varying with the volume of unemployment is intended, as in the case of workmen's compensation, to offer the incentive to achieve maximum stability.

Present benefits are generally lower in relation to current wages than they were originally. In 1953, unemployment compensation payments represented about one-third of weekly wages. The average payment was $23.58 a week for the country as a whole, but it ranged from $16.38 in one state to $27.57 in another. In only nine states was the maximum benefit payable under the law equal to one-half the average weekly wage earned in the state. Another indicator of relatively low unemployment benefits is the fact that in many states a large majority of those claiming unemployment compensation were eligible for the maximum payable under the state law. Even if benefits are related to take-home pay instead of earnings they tend to be low.

The President has suggested that the states raise the present maximum benefit amounts so that benefits to the majority of beneficiaries will equal at least half their regular earnings. He also suggested that the potential duration of benefits for all persons with a specified amount of covered employment or earnings be increased to 26 weeks by all states. At present, only 24 of the states have such a maximum duration and in only four states does it apply to all unemployed persons who qualify for benefits.

Experience rating

Every state has adopted experience rating as a part of its unemployment compensation program. Employers are subject to a basic tax rate, generally 2.7 per cent of wages, which is subject to adjustment in accordance with some measure of unemployment experienced by their employees. Ordinarily the adjustment is downward, but in some states there may be an upward adjustment of rates as well.

Various measures are used to determine employer experience. Commonly they depend upon the relationship between net contributions (taxes paid by an employer less benefits to his employees) and payrolls, or on the relationship between benefits paid and payrolls, with some modifications to take account of the over-all size of the state's reserve or of fluctuations in aggregate payrolls. Different types of plans produce different variations in tax and employers with identical experience might be subject to substantially different tax rates if they operated in different states. In 1952, the average employer tax in six states using one type of plan was 0.91 per cent of wages, and in five other states using a second type of plan it was twice as high.

In virtually all states the movement of employer tax rates under experience rating is apt to be one that accentuates economic change. If employment conditions deteriorate and benefit payments increase, reserve funds will tend to decline. Under these conditions an increase in tax rates may occur, making more difficult the problem of economic readjustment. As business conditions improve, experience rating provisions tend to produce a reduction in employer tax rates. It has frequently been suggested, therefore, that experience rating be revised so that reserve funds will be built up through higher tax rates during periods of full employment and depleted through benefit payments and rate reductions when employment drops. As yet there has been no generally accepted formula developed which would provide this result in a satisfactory fashion. This is an important problem which requires study.

This is not the occasion to enter into a detailed analysis of various state laws as they bear on experience rating. However, attention might be called to recent revisions one or two states have made that may be moving in a desirable direction. Under the New York State experience rating formula, employer contributions depend upon the size of the state fund in relation to payrolls and upon individual employer experience. The formula has been constructed so that (1) it tends to produce higher contribution rates when payrolls are increasing in size; (2) a differential in tax rates among employers is guaranteed at all times, irrespective of the size of the fund; and (3) it prevents sharp changes in contribution rates from year to year for most employers. Wisconsin has adopted a scheme which tends to produce a lower schedule of tax rates when payrolls are declining.

New employers

Another problem associated with experience rating is the impact that it has on new employers. Under the Federal law, a state's experience rating provisions must provide that an employer shall have at least three years of employment experience before qualifying for a reduced tax rate. The result is to place new enterprises, or newly covered firms, at a competitive disadvantage compared with older firms. A new employer is obliged to pay a full 3-per-cent tax on his payroll (Federal and state taxes combined) while others may, over the years, have been able to reduce their contribution rates to 1 per cent or less. This differential in cost would be particularly troublesome if the Federal Unemployment Tax Act were extended to employers of one or more employees, as has been proposed. To deal with this problem, it has been suggested that the minimum experience requirement be reduced from three years to one year.

Small employers

It has frequently been urged that the Federal law be extended to cover employers of one or more instead of eight or more. Several states cover employees of these small establishments and the administration problems have been satisfactorily solved. The system would be improved by extending protection generally to these workers.

Federal grants for administration

The amounts collected by the Federal government from the payroll tax of 0.3 per cent (after allowing for the credit for state taxes) were intended to finance Federal grants to the states to administer their employment security programs. The Federal grant permits equalization of facilities among the states. In some states administrative costs are high in relation to payrolls because industry is diffused over a broad geographic area and the volume of industrial employment is relatively low. In other states opposite conditions prevail and administrative costs are relatively low in relation to payrolls. However, the system of appropriations by the Federal government and uniform administrative standards involve many rigidities.

There are some who urge that the Federal government should cease to collect any payroll taxes and that the states should be completely independent in administering their unemployment compensation laws. Others propose that part of the Federal tax collections in excess of administrative grants be made available to the states for administrative purposes. Such a supplement to Congressional appropriations would make the Federal appropriation procedure almost meaningless. Appropriations are presumably based on an appraisal of the amounts necessary to do a proper job; and, if such decisions are sound, supplementary payments to the states for the same purpose would seem wasteful. On the other hand, if the present appropriation procedure is unsound, then that would seem to be the appropriate place to take corrective steps.

Reinsurance of unemployment costs

The exposure of state unemployment funds to the risk of depletion varies considerably. In some states the accumulated funds are large enough so that only the most prolonged depression would reduce the fund to a vanishing point. In other states, however, the solvency of their reserve is precarious. At the end of 1952, some states had reserves of 12 to 14 per cent of payrolls, while others had reserves of 4 to 6 per cent of payrolls.

The Federal tax collections of 0.3 per cent of payrolls have in the past been substantially in excess of the administrative grants made to the states, and it has been proposed that future excess collections be used to assist those state funds which get into difficulty. There has been some question whether the assistance should be in the form of a grant or a loan. In support of the loan approach is the view that the states would then have to keep their financial houses in order. If tax collections are inadequate to finance benefit schedules, the states would have to increase taxes or revise their benefit schedules. Proponents of the grant approach take the position that a state would be powerless to make such adjustments without imposing a competitive disadvantage on its employers or cutting benefits excessively. They point out that in most cases a state that required aid would have reached a point where all employers were paying a tax of 2.7 per cent.

Legislation now before the Congress provides for loans to states that require assistance. Federal tax collections in excess of the amounts necessary to finance administration would be set aside in a loan fund until it reaches $200 million. Any further excess collections would be distributed among the states in accordance with their respective payrolls for use in the payment of benefits (and possibly for administrative costs).

The loan fund would be used to make loans to the states when the amount in a state fund falls below the cost of benefits paid in the preceding year, and the amount of the loan would be equivalent to the highest quarterly benefit payments during the preceding year. Provision is made for automatic repayment of the loan, in case it is outstanding for more than one calendar year, by a reduction of the credit allowed employers under the Federal law. Instead of a credit equal to 90 per cent of the 3-per-cent Federal tax (or 2.7 per cent of wages), it would be 85 per cent. The proportion of the Federal tax allowed as a credit would be reduced each year that the loan remained unpaid by an additional 5 per cent.

It has also been proposed that the states organize an independent reinsurance fund. The states would contribute a part of their tax collections to the fund; and, if the unemployment benefit costs of a state should exceed some "normal" figure, the reinsurance fund would bear a part of the excess cost. The development of such a plan probably requires a good deal more experience than we have yet had in dealing with the problem of unemployment. It would be difficult to develop an adequate basis on which to calculate a state's "normal" unemployment benefit costs. Moreover, adequate incentives must be established for the states to enter into such a reinsurance plan. It seems doubtful that an incentive can be created for those states where funds have been accumulated to the point where they exceed any likely demand upon them.

PROGRESS IN SOCIAL SECURITY

Good progress has been made in meeting many of the problems faced in the administration of the social security program in this country.

The multiplicity of financing problems associated with our public programs for the assurance of income maintenance should not obscure the fact that we have a program that has thus far functioned remarkably well. That is due in part to the resiliency of our economy. It is due also to the fact that our social security program has been designed to stimulate individual thrift and initiative and not to replace them. The future achievement of the program will be measured by its continued stimulus to these ancient virtues.

The problem areas associated with the financing of income security involve issues that are varied and complex. The resolution of these issues requires imagination, hard thinking, and a willingness to cope with them. It is essentially a tripartite job, requiring the efforts of the individual, industry, and government. Discussions of the type we are having in this conference should be very helpful in pointing the way to meet current problems and to improve all three approaches.

COMMENTS

Seymour E. Harris

Professor of Economics, Harvard University

As Secretary Folsom points out, income security programs are both private and public and hence both private and public finance are relevant. In order to discuss this problem adequately, we have to consider the size of the national income, the major sources of financing, its distribution, the availability of savings out of past income and their distribution, the availability of revenues to government and especially the distribution of revenues and responsibilities for income maintenance programs between the Federal government on the one hand and state and local governments on the other. Finally, it is necessary to consider also the kind of taxes used to finance these programs, in turn related to the dependence upon Federal as against other governments, and also upon the degree to which recourse is had to pay-as-you-go versus reserve financing.

Secretary Folsom has discussed many of these problems in his admirable contribution; but his major emphasis has been on the availability of private resources and in particular liquid savings, securities, and private insurance, on the serious problems raised by reserve financing, and on the great progress made in social security. He did not say that of all businessmen over a period of more than twenty years he has made the greatest contribution to income-maintaining programs of this country.

This commentary is in part an expression of agreement with Mr. Folsom's views on reserve financing and the growth of liquid assets and private insurance; but in large part it is devoted to several major issues not treated or inadequately treated by Secretary Folsom; and a major dissent is expressed concerning his views on the adequacy of liquid assets and his failure to deal properly with their distribution.

BROAD RELEVANT FACTORS

Income security, by which we mean the maintenance of family or individual income at an accustomed or reasonably close to the accustomed level, depends on many factors. (More broadly, we would include services offered by the government such as medicine and education as maintenance programs.) The higher the national income, the more easily the minimum needs of food, clothing, shelter, etc. are met and hence the greater the security. At higher average incomes, not only is financing income security programs easier, but more relative dependence upon private financing is possible. From this viewpoint the rise of *real* gross national product (GNP) of 189 per cent in twenty years or of per capita GNP of 178 per cent or 102 per cent in real per capita disposable income is, of course, very important. This rise of real income is explained by the increase of man-hour output, which seems to average about 2½ per cent per year; and by the large gains of employment.

In the thirties, total employment inclusive of the military averaged 43 millions; in the years 1940–1953, the average was 60 millions. This gain of about 40 per cent accounts for a large part of the rise of income in recent years, and is compounded of a large drop in unemployment and an abnormal increase in the numbers on the labor market, a response to extraordinary demands.

Past savings also are available to help stabilize spending and standards of living, and thus finance income security programs. From this viewpoint the accumulation of more than $230 billion of liquid assets, the rise being considerably in excess of 200 per cent since 1939, is significant. But we should note also that debts have increased greatly as well as prices and population. In fact, from 1945 on the real value of liquid savings has actually declined.[1] Furthermore, a large part of the increase in cash and bank deposits since 1939 has been required for a smoothly functioning economy.

Savings are, of course, important. But also of much significance is the manner in which these savings are allocated. For example, the table below gives the breakdown of savings from 1939 to 1952. It will be noted that the total of liquid savings by individuals from 1939 to 1952 was $220 billion. Roughly 45 per cent went into cash and bank deposits; 40 per cent into insurance and pensions; 33 per cent into securities; 7 per cent into savings and loan associations; and 25 per cent into increased debt (about two-thirds into mortgages). The last is, of course, a dissaving (125–25 = 100).

Is this the optimum distribution of savings for the maintenance of income? It is not easy to say. Per dollar of savings, insurance probably contributes more towards income maintenance than a dollar of other kinds of savings. This follows because upon the occurrence of a contingency—for example, unemployment, illness—the insured who suffers from the occurrence of the contingency is financed in part by the contribution of others, who are frequently not in need. (The advantage of putting savings into securities or cash is that they are available for all kinds of contingencies.) Even a dollar saved for old-age insurance is more productive in contributing towards income security than a dollar of ordinary saving, the explanation being the contribution of the employer, the concentration of payments to those who survive after 65 and later years, and the special treatment of the present old.

Individual Personal Savings, 1939–52
($ billion)

All	220
Currency and bank deposits	101
Insurance and pension reserves	88
Securities	70
Savings and Loan Associations	15
Liquidation of debt	—55
(38 billion = mortgages)	

SOURCE: *Economic Report of the President*, January 1954, p. 179.

A broader category of savings is gross savings. These include personal savings, undistributed corporation profits, business depreciation charges. In 1952, the total was $54.7 billion, of which personal savings were $16.9 billion; undistributed corporate profits, $9.5 billion; business depreciation charges, $22.3 billion; and capital outlay charged to current expense, $4.0 billion. The last three items are not available for income security though ultimately they contribute towards higher incomes. From 1930 to 1940 inclusive, gross private savings amounted to $76 billion; from 1940 to 1952 inclusive, the total was $505 billion. (Gross savings include, of course, savings to cover depreciation required to keep plant up to date.)

Government deficits contribute towards income and maintenance in that they absorb savings in the economy and hence contribute towards total spending, demand, and employment. All government deficits amounted to $16 billion from 1930 to 1940 and $133 billion from 1940 through 1952. (These totals include deficits only on product and income transactions.) In periods of high demand the effect of a government deficit may, of course, be largely inflation rather than a contribution to employment and real income maintenance. Surely a discussion of income security requires a consideration of the relevance of government deficits.

But at this point what is especially worth noting is the contribution of insurance under government versus insurance under private auspices. Over the years 1939–52 savings under private insurance and pensions reserves were $46 billion and under government insurance were $42 billion. In 1952 the total was $9.1 billion, with savings under private insurance and pension reserves $4.8 billion and under government insurance $4.3 billion.[2]

This large expansion of reserves resultant from insurance savings raises serious problems, as Secretary Folsom is well aware. Obviously, in so far as programs of income security, whether private or public, are financed in a manner to reduce total income (for example, through excessive accumulation of reserves), they not only increase the difficulties of financing income security programs because they cut national income, but they put a greater strain on these programs because average income is reduced. There are many advantages of government insurance over private insurance, not the least of which is that the need for accumulating reserves is not so pressing as under private insurance. The diversion of savings to insurance reserves has a continued deflationary effect. In the deflationary thirties, the results were unfortunate indeed; in the inflationary forties and early fifties, the results were on the whole beneficial (though the stepping up of rates in 1954 in the midst of a recession might be interpreted as aggravating a cyclical downturn).

Savings under government insurance have important advantages. First, it is possible to *require* contributions by employers, which to some extent are passed on to consumers or backward to wage earners. (This does not imply the unimportance of voluntary employer contributions under private insurance.) Second, it is possible to adjust payments on the basis of the requirements of the economic situation. (In practice, the government's record is only fair on this score. In the thirties, rates on old-age insurance were not raised; but in the forties, when they should have been, they were not.) Under government insurance, the pay-as-you-go principle can be more nearly achieved than under private insurance, and hence deflationary effects may be contained. Third, contributions can be adjusted to income and benefits to needs, and (related) to inflationary trends. Hence for every dollar contributed, the welfare gains are likely to be larger than under private insurance. This result is clearly attained under Old Age and Survivors Insurance (OASI), when the low-income groups and the present old receive generous benefits relative to what they pay in. Potential gains could be achieved here also under a national health insurance scheme. In private insurance grading of charges according to income, with benefits not closely related to contributions, is not workable in any large sense.

One other aspect of government insurance should be noted. In this country the trend has been to use the payroll tax to finance government insurance. But it is also possible to have recourse to general revenues. In later years this may be necessary to some extent under OASI. In many countries (for example, New Zealand and Canada), the financing of the social security program is largely concentrated on the income tax. In this manner, the burden of insurance can be transferred to some extent to the higher-income groups, though it might be unwise to depart too far from a contributory system. The payroll tax might be implemented by recourse to general revenues. Professor Eveline Burns has suggested that under OASI the burden of paying the old and their survivors the excess of benefits over contributions in the early years of the program might well be put upon general revenues.

REDISTRIBUTION

Let us come now to the problem of the redistribution of income or rather improved income distribution. Since income security is a more serious problem the lower the income, its financing is eased by an improved distribution of income. In the United States, income distribution has become much less skewed than before the late war. The explanation of this improvement lies in part in the rise of employment and the decline of unemployment; in the greater gains of low-income groups (unskilled workers and farmers) in a period of high demand; in the increased importance of transfer incomes, which favors the low-income groups; and in the increased progressivity of the tax system (though this last is relevant in a comparison with 1929 rather than with 1939). It is interesting that in the United Kingdom a similar change in the distribution of income has occurred; but in the United Kingdom the main explanation is held to be the elimination of unemployment. It is even shown that the increased subsidies for low-income groups since before the war were more than offset by the rise of taxation paid by this group.

In the United States, the change in income distribution is evidenced by the following table. It will be noted that the lowest (in income levels) quintile of households increased their *purchasing power* by 42 per cent (after personal income taxes), whereas the highest quintile increased their purchasing power by only eight per cent and the top five per cent suffered a decline of two per cent.[3]

Average Family Personal Income after Federal Individual Income Tax Liability, for Quintiles and Top 5 Per Cent of Consumer Units Ranked by Size of After-Tax Income, 1941 and 1950

	1941		1950	Per Cent Increase in
	1941 dollars	1950 dollars		Purchasing Power from 1941 to 1950
Lowest	450	750	1,060	42
Second	1,040	1,730	2,360	37
Third	1,680	2,790	3,440	24
Fourth	2,430	4,030	4,690	16
Highest	4,940	8,190	8,880	8
Top 5 per cent	9,070	15,040	14,740	−2
All incomes combined	2,110	3,500	4,090	17

In the British case it will be noted that, whereas the consumption of the working classes rose by an estimated 22 per cent, that of the middle and wealthy classes declined by 18 and 42 per cent, respectively.[4]

Indicated Division of Consumption Goods and Services between Different Classes in Great Britain

	1938		1949		Percentage
	Amount (£ million)	Per Cent of Total	Amount (£ million)	Per Cent of Total	Increase from 1938 to 1948
Working class	2,364	63.4	2,891	73.2	22
Middle class	1,131	30.4	924	23.4	−18
Wealthy	230	6.2	134	3.4	−42
Total	3,725	100.0	3,950	100.0	6

A somewhat different attack on the problem is to be found in an able paper by Alfred H. Conrad.[5] Conrad takes into account transfers resulting not only from taxes but also from public expenditures. The results are necessarily rough and do not consider secondary effects:[6]

The share of the lowest group increased from 1.43 per cent of the original to 3.9 per cent of the final sum: money transfers produced half the increase (1.4 per cent) for this group, and for many units provided the major or sole source of income. The highest group, which received 26.28 per cent of the first variant, was reduced to a share of 19.4 per cent in the final; the effective tax rate of 42.4 per cent on these incomes withdrew 39.5 per cent of the total revenue bill from them, which may be compared to the allocation of 15.7 per cent of total benefits to this bracket. The lowest three groups experienced substantial gains from the fiscal system after paying taxes, and most of the gain was made at the expense of the top income class.

TOTAL OUTLAYS FOR INCOME SECURITY

Income security depends in part upon the expenditures of government for income security: in part these expenditures may be in services (*e.g.,* education and medicine), for insurance programs, and for public aid. (Folsom's definition is narrower.) Outlays of this type have increased greatly. For example, total outlays rose from $7.8 billion in 1936–37 (the beginnings of our social security program) to $23.4 billion in 1950–51. These totals include income maintenance narrowly defined and real income provided by government. As a percentage of national income, however, there was a decline from 11 to 9 per cent. (But the Budget Bureau, which excludes veterans' benefits and government insurance programs from its calculations here, finds that, whereas social security, welfare, and health accounted for 43.8 per cent of the *Federal* budget in 1939, the total was but 3.4 per cent in 1953 (fiscal years).[7]

These results might be compared with the British experience where the percentage devoted to social services rose from 9.2 per cent in 1938–39 to 14.1 per cent in 1950–51. The British, with a per capita income of but 40 per cent that of this country, were spending about 50 per cent more relatively on social services.[8] According to one study, income maintenance programs, narrowly defined, cost 3.9 per cent of United States income and 5.09, 5.53, 6.07, and 9.23 per cent of the incomes of Australia, Canada, United Kingdom, and New Zealand respectively. The figures for all social security expenditures were 5.52 per cent for the United States and 7.30, 7.99, 11.87, and 13.18, respectively, for the others.[9]

In this connection, it should be noted that the allocation of responsibilities among different levels of government, in large part based on historical accidents, determines both the total amount spent, and the distribution of spending among services and programs. In this connection, the following table clarifies the situation:

Social Welfare Expenditures, Total All Levels of Government and Per Cent by U. S. Federal Government, 1950–51

	$ Million	% Federal Contribution
All	23,367	41
Education	7,627	2
Veterans' programs	5,506	94
Social insurance	4,642	58
Public aid	2,583	46
Health and medical	2,512	13

SOURCE: *Social Security Bulletin,* February 1953, p. 8. (My calculations.)

The small responsibility assumed by the Federal government for education and health and medicine accounts for inadequate outlays on these services and is a serious threat to income maintenance in important areas of spending.[10] It is important that along with responsibility should go financial capacity. It is no answer to the crisis in education or the problems of medicine to insist that these are local responsibilities when at the same time the Federal government arrogates to itself the most productive revenues. It is well here also to stress the point that the government outlays are not all additional: they in part represent insurance payments by the insured and in part substitutes for private medical outlays.

The peculiar financial organization of the United States, with heavy revenues for financing social security required of state and local governments (44 per cent in the United States and an average of 17 per cent for four other English-speaking countries) explains in part the unusual distribution of our income maintenance outlays. Whereas this country spends 26.5 per cent of these outlays on veterans (financed primarily by Federal government), the other four English-speaking countries spend only 15 per cent (the British 13 per cent). Our outlays are far below the others on family allowances (zero) and disabilities.[11]

In times like these there is a tendency to emphasize the need of concentrating on the cold war—especially in view of the heavy burden of taxes and the large debt. Yet social service expenditures also increase income. Consider the anticyclical effects of income and outgo of these programs, the rise of income associated with improved medicine and education, and the maintenance of spending related to income redistribution involved in many of these programs.

It is significant that in 1954 those who stress the need of containing welfare programs also support a tax remission program in 1954 which may well cost the Treasury $13 billion per year, once the full effects are felt and inclusive of revenue effects of a fall of national income of five per cent. Is there not a case for allocating $1–2 billion of these resources to income maintenance programs—subsidies for comprehensive prepayment health insurance, for school education, for hospital construction, for reinsurance or partial Federal financing of state unemployment programs?

INCREASED ASSETS HELD

Now, having dwelt on some aspects of the problem rather neglected by Secretary Folsom, let us turn more directly to aspects to which he has devoted most attention. His emphasis is quite rightly on the vast advances in private savings and insurance, inclusive of pension programs, the growth of liquid assets, the spread of home ownership. This survey of advances along the non-governmental front is valuable, and the emphasis on the importance of large personal contributions to programs for income security is well placed. Here, however, are some reservations:

First, the Secretary notes the $230 billion of liquid assets (cash, bank deposits, and government securities), or $4,500 per family. But he says nothing about their distribution. According to the Federal Reserve Board, 26 per cent of all spending units had no liquid assets early in 1954; 15 per cent, from $1 to $199; 24 per cent, from $200 to $999 (so 65 per cent had less than $1,000); and 24 per cent had from $1,000 to $4,999. The heavy concentration is suggested by the fact that, though the average was $4,500, only 5 per cent held $5,000 to $9,999 and 4 per cent held $10,000 and over.[12]

Nor am I impressed by the Secretary's statement about the wide holdings of U. S. Steel Corporation stock: 74 per cent of the shareholders with incomes of less than $10,000 owning 53 per cent of the stock. But according to his own Treasury Release, which he does not quote (No. H-266, October 8, 1953), less than 4 per cent of shareholding taxpayers with incomes in excess of $10,000 receive more than 75 per cent of dividends paid out. In other words, concentrating on taxpayers and not on shareholders and on all dividends not on U. S. Steel statistics (could we have the documentation for the Steel estimate?), we find that taxpayers with incomes above $10,000, on the average, had about 75 times as large a stake in dividend incomes per taxpayer as taxpayers with less than $10,000 a year. (In relation to all households, not merely taxpayers, the discrepancy would still be greater.) According to this same report, persons earning $25,000 or more received more than one half of all dividend income, though they were only eight-tenths of one per cent of all taxpayers. Apparently, 92 per cent of American families own no stock whatever. Of the remaining eight per cent, six-tenths of one per cent own eighty per cent of all publicly held stock.[13]

Finally on housing, the Secretary notes that, whereas only 41 per cent of American families owned their own houses in 1941, the percentage was 53 per cent in 1953. This gain suggests a large improvement. But one reservation should be noted. Mortgage debts have risen greatly. Thus, from 1939 to the end of 1953, mortgage debt on 1–4 family houses rose from $16.3 to $65.0 billion; and mortgage debts of individuals rose by $38 billion.[14] It is not clear that income security has been increased as a result of the rise of home ownership, though, as Mr. Ball of the FSA pointed out, this may be of great importance for the old. This is aside from a rise of consumer credit from $7 billion in 1939 to $29 billion late in 1953—a problem not treated by Secretary Folsom.

THE PROBLEM OF OLD AGE INSURANCE AND RESERVES

In the area of government insurance, Secretary Folsom makes many penetrating observations. I agree heartily with what he says about reserves vs. pay-as-you-go financing; on the wisdom of not depending excessively on reserves; on the able attack on those who see in the reserves a myth and see reserve financing as double taxation; on the wisdom of adhering to some form of contribution principle and tethering benefits to past payrolls to some extent. (Hence, also, he is wise to repudiate the "blanketing-in" program, which in fact is an attempt to use up OASI reserves by putting *all* under a most inadequate program and thus to cut expenditures currently, giving an impression of an improved financial position, to abandon the contributory principle, and generally to reduce the benefit schedule for the old.)

But I do not fully support the Secretary's proposal to reduce the tax burden on employers not subject to OASI, and even alleviate it to make up for failure to benefit from OASI in the past. The exemption of income paid into pension funds might be granted for a minimum amount (say, up to 5 per cent of incomes up to $10,000). The Secretary's suggestions seem to me to go too far and to extend the income-security principle far beyond what is required.

UNEMPLOYMENT INSURANCE

Secretary Folsom's recommendations on unemployment insurance do not seem adequate. He still stresses too much the contribution of the individual businessman towards the stabilization of unemployment. Experience or merit rating (adjusting payroll taxes to the unemployment record) is intrinsically bad, because it is based on the theory that American businessmen can stabilize employment (even Secretary Folsom's examples may mean merely that one businessman's unemployment is passed on to another). Economic fluctuations depend on forces not controllable by businessmen; and the increased role of government further stresses the significance of this point. A case might be made out for rewarding employers who, say, stabilize operations so that the worker is in the factory forty hours every week rather than thirty in one week or fifty in another. But merit rating is not primarily oriented towards achieving this result. To get rid of merit rating would be a courageous and wise policy, though vested interests are powerful. Without merit rating we would have had much larger unemployment insurance reserves, or lower rates and better distribution of burdens, or somewhat lower rates and an improved benefit structure. With it, we have encouraged cut-throat interstate competition to reduce benefits and taxes; we have put heavy taxes on states, regions, and industries in a vulnerable position; we have encouraged incessant struggles between employers anxious to show a good employment record and the unemployed demanding their benefits.

Not alone in merit rating, but also in other aspects of unemployment insurance, the Secretary moves too cautiously. A program which would require the Federal government to sponsor a minimum tax of 1.5 per cent for all states and to set Federal minimum standards would be helpful. (A recommendation of this kind was made by the Stettinius Advisory Council to the Senate Finance Committee.) To this extent, unhealthy competition would be moderated and the scope of merit rating reduced. Along with this, we should have a reinsurance program, possibly by pooling the resources obtained from the 1½-percent tax. (This proposal would also help correct the perverse cyclical effects of merit rating; for at present, as Folsom notes, taxes rise with depression and fall in prosperity.) It is not enough for the President to ask the states to increase benefits to one half of wages and extend duration for 26 weeks. As long as merit rating is on the statute books, the pressure will be to compete in benefits.

The President's proposals might be more effective if the Federal government should provide supplementary resources required to finance the extended benefits or somehow obtain a pooling arrangement. Allocation of general revenues for financing a more extended unemployment compensation program as against concentrating on tax reduction would also help. Finally, the Federal government should make available the $500–$1,000 million of payroll taxes collected for unemployment administration and disbursed for other purposes. Here again the Secretary does not go nearly far enough.

OTHER SIGNIFICANT OMISSIONS

Secretary Folsom has concentrated on the large rise of savings, liquid assets, corporate securities, and insurance; and on what manner public insurance programs may be improved. But it is important to stress significant omissions.

Income security depends on employment, productivity, and income; on distribution of income; not only on the total of savings but also on their distribution and the assets in which they are embodied; for example, on the proportion going into cash, securities, private insurance, public insurance. In this connection, we stress again the point that a dollar of savings put into insurance may be much more effective as a contribution toward income security than a dollar of savings going into other channels; in part because the beneficiary receives contributions from the insured who are not confronted with the insured contingency. Government insurance may be an especially cheap mechanism for achieving income security, because here employers may be forced to contribute, contributions may be based in part upon incomes and benefits, and contributions need not be closely associated with benefits.

We are not told by the Secretary how much the economy can afford for income maintenance, for either future use or for current transfers. We are not told, for example, what proportion of the expected *rise* of GNP (30 per cent or $110 billion) in 10 years should be put aside for income security. At the current ratio of outlays for welfare, the amount might well be $10 billion.

How much we can afford depends, among other things, upon the distribution of the burden among Federal and state and local governments. Clearly, we can afford much more, the more that is put upon the governments with productive tax sources: the Federal government as compared with state and local; state as compared with local. In this connection, a recent budget revealed that the Federal government was to raise 80 per cent of its tax revenue through direct taxes on income and profits; but state and local governments depended on these taxes for only 7 per cent of their revenues. A shift of financial responsibility to Federal government would not only yield larger revenue and services but would increase income security because the tax burden would be imposed more nearly in accordance with ability to pay. It is well to remember that our tax system is regressive (higher tax burden, as a percentage of income, at low incomes than at high incomes) and becomes progressive only at the $7,500 level and higher. For a recent year, effective tax rates for receivers of income under $1,000 were estimated at 20.2 per cent; for $2,000–$3,000, at 18.8 per cent; for $5,000–$7,500, at 21.4 per cent; for $5,000 and over, at 35.1 per cent; and for all, at 24 per cent.[15]

The Secretary seems to be critical of the foreign practice of depending so heavily on fringe benefits financed largely through government channels. The result is, he tells us, heavy fixed charges on industry. Indeed, with our higher average incomes, the need for these fringes is less. But it should be noted that our heavy reliance on payroll taxes and on state and local governments, with their emphasis on general property taxes, means a heavy fixed charge, which might be alleviated if greater recourse were had to Federal taxes and especially taxes on income.

In discussing these problems, we should never lose sight of the gains to the economy in large programs for maintaining incomes. First, the antidepression effects are substantial, both through transfers at any one time and in transfers of payments over time. Second, against the costs of these programs is to be put the favorable effects on income—e.g., of more and better education and health. We should observe also that government outlays are often substitutes for, not additions to, private outlays. This is true, for example, in part in the government medical outlays and old-age insurance (a substitute for private savings). Incidentally, insurance frequently means economies in government spending: health insurance might cut outlays on government medicine.

In summary, Secretary Folsom's paper demonstrates the large gains that have been made in furthering income maintenance; and his analysis of the OASI program seems to me to be beyond criticism. I wish that he had presented a more frontal attack on merit rating and generally on the inadequacies of our unemployment (and incidentally illness) insurance. And his discussion should have treated the relevance of total income and employment, of fiscal policy, of distribution of income, to the financing of these programs; and the relative importance of insurance vs. noninsurance savings, of private versus public savings, and of the secondary beneficial effects of these programs.

FOOTNOTES

1. See Joint Congressional Committee on Economic Report Hearings, *January 1954 Report of the President*, 1954, p. 874.
2. Figures in the last few paragraphs calculated from *The Economic Report of the President*, January 1954, and *Survey of Current Business, National Income* numbers.

3. Goldsmith, Jaszi, Kaitz, and Liebenberg, "Size Distribution of Income Since the Mid-Thirties," *Review of Economics and Statistics*, February 1954, p. 26.

4. F. Weaver, "Taxation and Redistribution in the United Kingdom," *Review of Economics and Statistics*, August 1950, p. 212.

5. "Redistribution Through Government Budgets in the United States, 1950" in *Income Redistribution and Social Policy*, edited by A. T. Peacock, 1954.

6. *Ibid.*, p. 259.

7. House Subcommittee on Ways and Means, *Analysis of the Social Security System*, Part 2, 1954, p. 195.

8. *Social Security Bulletin*, February 1954, p. 11.

9. Canadian Department of National Health and Welfare, *Social Security Expenditures. . . . 1949–52: A Comparative Study*, 1954, p. 10.

10. Medical expenditures for veterans are included under veterans' programs.

11. Canadian Department of National Health and Welfare, *op. cit.*, pp. 6, 14.

12. Hearings, Joint Committee on *January 1954 Economic Report of the President*, 1954, p. 894.

13. See Joint Congressional Committee on *January 1954 Economic Report of the President*, February 1954, p. 27; *Internal Revenue Code of 1954*, Report of Committee on Ways and Means, 1954, pp. B7–8.

14. *Federal Reserve Bulletin*, February 1954, p. 188; and *Economic Report of the President*, 1954, p. 179.

15. R. A. Musgrave and others, "Distribution of Tax Payments by Income Groups," *National Tax Journal*, March 1951, p. 47.

COMMENTS

Mabel Newcomer

Professor of Economics, Vassar College

Mr. Folsom has made clear both the growth in provisions for social security and the remaining needs.

He has emphasized particularly the soundness of the three-fold development of individual savings, employer-employee savings and pension plans, and the government's social security program. This approach to economic insecurity is a healthy development. Yet we may doubt that it has reduced materially the public obligation to provide an acceptable minimum of income for individuals and families without jobs or other sources of income. The indications are, rather, that the private programs are primarily useful to provide incomes after retirement, or for any nonearning period, substantially better than anything that a public program can or should be expected to provide.

Beginning with the growth of individual savings, Mr. Folsom notes that liquid assets per family averaged $4,500 at the end of 1953. And that two-thirds of the heads of families over 55 years of age own their own homes. In addition the great majority of individuals own life insurance, and a large number own corporation stocks. All this is true, but it is also true that much the largest part of these assets belong to the higher-income groups.

Life insurance is the commonest form of private savings. More than three-fourths of all families in the United States have some life insurance, not including government life insurance held by veterans and service men. The average amount of such insurance, for insured families, is greater than one year's average family income. The proportion of families with insurance among the low-income groups is somewhat smaller. But even among families with incomes under $2,000 in 1951, more than half have some insurance. No data have been found to indicate how many of these have the equivalent of one year's income, but it is probably relatively small. The average amount per policy or certificate for industrial and group insurance—the forms most prevalent among low-income groups—is about $700. For industrial policies, which constitute half of all policies, the average is only $328.

Turning to home ownership, while more than half of all nonfarm families own their own homes, nearly half (47 per cent) were mortgaged in 1953 and one-fifth were subject to mortgages in excess of $5,000.

Most of the smaller savings are invested in life insurance and in homes and other durable consumer goods. Only for those whose net worth exceeded $25,000 did business, investment, and liquid assets exceed the value of consumer capital goods in 1952. Two-thirds of the families had holdings of liquid assets of less than $1,000. One-fourth had none at all. And, according to the Brookings Institution study of *Share Ownership in the United States* (1952) less than 5 per cent of the families with incomes below $5,000 in 1951 had any holdings in corporation stocks. Finally, 11 per cent of all families have debts that exceed their assets, other than life insurance, and the net worth of those having any net assets is less than $3,000 for an additional third of the population. Those of all income classes whose net worth (including homes and cars, but not life insurance) exceeds one year's income are approximately half of the total population, and of wage-earners less than two-fifths.

This is not to minimize the important contribution that individual savings are making to living standards. These comparisons should be sufficient to demonstrate that savings of all kinds provide important additions to income, and for many families they are sufficient to tide them over short periods of unemployment and other emergencies. But they offer little security for that half of the population in the lower-income groups.

The second development in the private sector of the economy is that of the employer-sponsored plans for pensions and other savings. The variety and form of these plans have been adequately described by Mr. Folsom. He points out that the private pension plans covered some 11 million persons at the end of 1953 and that there is every indication that they will continue to expand rapidly in the immediate future, as they have in the past. Reserves for the funded plans amounted to $17 billion at the end of 1953, and it is estimated that they will exceed $19 billion by the end of 1954—or nearly the same amount as the reserves for OASI.

Since these pension plans necessarily cover the same individuals that are covered by the OASI program, they do not ordinarily provide pensions for individuals not receiving benefits under the government social security program. The most important exception is that some of them provide for disability benefits. The number of these is, however, small. Their principal importance lies in the fact that they supplement the government program, so that the group of workers covered will enjoy an income after retirement more nearly comparable to the earned income they are accustomed to than OASI provides. In fact, a number of these plans provide for retirement incomes which, combined with OASI benefits, amount to two-thirds or more of pre-retirement earned incomes.

Another advantage of the private plans is that it is possible to invest the funds, at least in part, in equity securities which, in the long run, earn more than bonds and adjust better to inflation. The public program can, of course, achieve equal or greater flexibility by the simple device of increasing benefits from time to time as changing costs of living demand, and meeting the cost through increased payroll taxes or contributions from the general revenues.

These important advantages of the private pension plans are in some measure offset by their limitations. One of the reasons for establishing such programs has been to attract and hold the best workers. Since the funds set aside by the corporation for this purpose are not taxable either to the corporation or to the worker, the dollars thus invested go farther toward the workers' protection than equivalent dollars paid in wages. The other side of this is, however, that most workers covered can enjoy the full amount of these benefits only if they remain with the same employer for long periods of time. If they shift jobs they will lose most, and perhaps all, of their accumulated benefits. As Mr. Folsom has noted, the majority of the plans require employment with a particular firm for ten or fifteen years before an employee gets any vesting rights. And only one worker in ten of those covered gets any vesting rights at all in less than ten years. Even then he will probably lose some of his accumulated benefits by changing employment. Eight out of ten have no vested rights. And while workers shift jobs less in the later years of their working life than in the early years, it is clear that a very large part of the 11,000,000 employees covered by such plans today will never benefit from them or will benefit only by forgoing the advancement that a job with another corporation might offer. Moreover, the corporations offering such plans are increasingly unwilling to employ workers over forty years of age. These are serious limitations.

These disadvantages can be mitigated in some measure by lowering the vesting period, as Mr. Folsom suggests, or by extending the coverage beyond a single firm, in order to permit some shifts in employment without loss of rights. Some of the union-negotiated plans cover several employers in the area, and a few cover most of the members of the union, regardless of their employer. If in the future these employer-employee-negotiated pension plans can be extended to a larger number of employers, and the vesting period is reduced, the limitations noted above will be greatly diminished. And if they include benefits in case of long-term disability they will reach a group that thus far is inadequately protected by the OASI or any of the existing public programs.

Turning to the public programs, Mr. Folsom has discussed the problems of financing so fully that I have little to add. The principal virtues of the reserve fund, which he has mentioned, are (1) that it equalizes the cost of the system over long periods of time, and (2) that contributions both to the OASI and to unemployment insurance are at their peak when employment is highest, and drop with rising unemployment—thus providing a built-in contracyclical factor in government budgets. None of the dangers of such funds that some critics prophesied when they were first established have materialized. And even if, as Mr. Folsom notes, the reserves for the OASI reach $63 billion by 1980, it seems probable that this will not be a large enough proportion of the total federal debt to create any disturbance in the banking system or the general investment markets.

It seems more probable that benefits will be extended more than taxes, so that reserve funds will tend to decline. The probability of exhausting unemployment funds appears to be greater than that of exhausting old-age funds, partly because the former have not been pooled for the entire United States, and partly because any substantial and prolonged unemployment will constitute a heavier drain on these funds than any predictable drain on old-age funds. In the long run this drain would necessitate contributions from the general tax revenues, or, temporarily, from government loans. There is ample precedent for this action in the experience of other countries with their social security programs.

In short, in view of all the uncertainties, both in the fluctuations of the economy and in future Congressional legislation, there is no certainty that the reserve funds will be adequate. But the financial powers of the government should be sufficient to make the necessary adjustments as need arises. It is important that there should be reserve funds, so that taxes need not be increased in periods of recession, but it is not important that they be sufficient to cover any and every contingency.

The use of payroll taxes as practically the sole source of support has also proved satisfactory. It justifies the use of graded benefits, as support from the general revenues would not. Moreover, the demands of the Federal budget on our tax system have increased so greatly that a wide tax base is inevitable. Without subscribing to the older theories of diffusion and elision, it has to be admitted that no tax achieves complete equity, and it may be safest to distribute the inequities over a large variety of taxes. In any case, once taxes have been imposed, the economy adjusts to them, so that changes may only create new disturbances.

With regard to the proposal for blanketing the old-age assistance pensioners into the OASI, Mr. Folsom's criticism is well taken. There are many shortcomings in the current state provisions for old-age assistance, but there are other ways of remedying these. And the extended coverage of OASI—both that of 1950 and that contemplated by the current proposals for including 10,000,000 self-employed and others not now included—will greatly reduce the importance of the old-age assistance program. In other words the real answer to this problem appears to be the extension of the OASI program in the direction planned in the Administration program. But it will be necessary to extend it beyond the present contemplated program, at least to include those under sixty-five who are unemployable because of disability.

This of course raises questions as to costs. Can the desirable minimum reasonably be financed from payroll levies? The answer is yes. But substantial contributions from the general revenues offer a reasonable alternative as long as the payroll taxes form the major source of financing.

With regard to the tax-exemption proposals, Mr. Folsom notes the inequity resulting from the fact that the self-employed are subject to income taxes without any exemption for income saved for retirement, and discusses some of the proposals for dealing with this inequity. The proposed allowance in the current tax bill is a reasonable and adequate provision. I am not completely happy about the introduction of further tax exemptions, although this one has more merit than some already available. Sooner or later we are going to have to face the fact that even the progressive personal income tax will achieve only rough justice at best, and that, sometimes in the interest of equity and sometimes to grant unwarranted relief to favored groups, we have been undermining the base of both our personal and corporate income taxes to a serious degree. Even equitable exemptions may open the way to unwarranted and unintended evasion and avoidance.

However, it is out of the question to change the tax law the other way— taking away the exemptions now available for income applied by corporations to their private pension programs. Consequently, an answer is to extend such exemptions to the self-employed, putting them on as nearly the same footing as possible with the corporation employees in respect to retirement funds. But it is also urgent to extend the public system enough to diminish the importance of such provisions. We can afford to do it, even if it necessitates some subsidy from the general revenues. The government is already meeting approximately half of the cost of the private pension schemes, inasmuch as the money thus invested would otherwise be subject to heavy corporation income taxes. Surely the public system, which gives basic coverage to practically everyone, rather than providing comfortable additions to a few, has prior claim on the government tax revenues.

REPORT OF THE RECORDER

Herman D. Stein

*Lecturer in Social Work, New York School of Social Work,
Columbia University*

Professor Morgan opened the general discussion with a reminder of the importance of the needs of people, over such considerations as the strategy of allocating manpower, in considering social security objectives. He further challenged the tendency of economists to accept unsound sociological assumptions, such as Professor Lester's assumption of a classless society in the United States; or the tenet of desirability of stable employment, as if a person who moves around in jobs is morally wrong, while he who stays in one job is morally good—an assumption which is not necessarily valid, since mobility may be healthy for the economy and reflect well on the individual; the proposition that thrift is a virtue—which can properly be questioned—and if thrift is not a virtue in itself, then the place of savings is not so important. If the individual has no confidence in the future value of his money, he feels no security in savings. Another questionable assumption is that money is the principal incentive. There are many other incentives, social and psychological, and a much more sensitive analysis of incentives is required.

Father Becker doubted whether greater mobility can be considered a sign of greater maturity. The practice of skilled workers moving from job to job has been recognized as bad, and the development of seniority and private pension plans has served to keep the skilled worker, particularly, more attached to his job. However, Father Becker felt there is too much emphasis on retirement, and perhaps the middle-aged worker who wishes to change jobs for "the last stretch" should be encouraged to do so, and not penalized.

Professor Wootton warned against the use of the word mobility as a blanket term. Unsteady work is not a matter of enterprise or maturity. To have ten to twenty jobs in six months is simply instability. The whole subject of mobility might be studied in universities, with respect to variations by skill levels, geographical area, age groups, and the like.

Professor Lester agreed that much movement between jobs is wasteful, also taking issue with Professor Morgan. There may be some learning, but not the accumulation of valuable experience. Further, advancement in many firms is possible only by starting at the bottom, and seniority is important. Thrift, moreover, should not be depreciated; if all reacted by discounting savings, the price level would be very unstable. Finally, perhaps economists have overemphasized monetary incentives, but they are concerned with the distribution of money incomes, and must therefore watch incentive effects. Professor Lester also commented that his reference in his paper was to a tendency towards a classless society in the United States, not to its existence.

Dr. Goldmann raised the question of financing income maintenance in periods of temporary disability, which accounts for an annual loss of $15 billion a year.

The discussion then turned to the general area of unemployment insurance, considered by several to present the most difficult problem in financing. Mr. Goodwin pointed out that the incidence of unemployment varies among the states. Rhode Island, for example, has a high incidence of unemployment and therefore has a high tax, although benefits are lower there. It is not possible for some states to finance unemployment insurance within the original cost of

2.7 per cent of payroll. Rhode Island will have either to raise the rates above 2.7 per cent or to use some other financing device. The solvency situation is almost equally critical in Alaska, and there is a potential problem in other states.

Professor Brown asked whether the Federal-state arrangement in unemployment insurance was not a mistake. It has created many problems a national program might have averted: labor markets have been cut up; the financial problem of adequate use of effective funds has been intensified; problems of certain areas, like Rhode Island, have been aggravated, leading to a vicious cycle of higher benefits, higher rates, less favorable conditions for new industry, and less effective use of local manpower.

Mr. Altmeyer, speaking of early developments in the history of unemployment insurance, referred to the Business Advisory Council of 1934, on which Mr. Folsom served ("by all odds the single employer who has had the greatest influence on the development of social security in this country"). The Business Advisory Council in 1934 stated it was uncertain whether Federal unemployment insurance was not really the best plan and at first recommended a system of 100 per cent Federal grants to the states, in part because it would be easier to change to a Federal system later on if desirable. However, it was felt an intermediate Federal-state arrangement was best for "an experimental period." Now this "experimental period" has become frozen into our economy.

Mr. Altmeyer did not think the President's suggestion to the states to improve their unemployment insurance laws will have appreciable effect, on the basis of past experience. Three states have acted thus far, but the changes may actually have made their systems less liberal. A bill, however, has been introduced to provide for more effective Federal action.

Mr. Altmeyer felt that in order to induce the states to improve their unemployment insurance programs, the taxing provisions should be changed, and it might be feasible for the Federal government to pay to the states fifty per cent of benefits. He questioned whether minimum Federal standards were necessarily good. Sometimes they can be based on the lowest possible denominator (avoiding change in many states) and can thus actually serve as a deterrent to improved standards.

Mr. Cruikshank observed that the level of compensation in unemployment insurance was not just a fiscal problem but related to political problems. Unemployment is not a state problem, and the refrain that the state is "nearer to the problem" is meaningless today. The closeness of the worker to the program has nothing to do with his geographical proximity to the state legislative seat, but only to his democratic representation there, which is often sparse indeed. No railroad worker wants to transfer his unemployment insurance program to his state capitol. Rural areas are proportionally overrepresented in state legislatures. Workers in California and Connecticut cities feel closer to Washington, D. C., from the point of view of representation, than to their state capitals. A Los Angeles worker has more representation in Washington than in Sacramento, where because of overrepresentation of some areas three per cent of the population are in a position to veto any legislation. The appropriate level of government can be seen only with reference to the adequacy of representation in the democratic process.

Mr. Cruikshank also noted, with reference to Professor Harris' comments on employer experience rating, that the basic evil here is that such rating is based on the false asssumption that employers can control the level of employment. More money in rebates and forgiveness of taxes has gone to employers for "stabilizing employment" than has been paid out in benefits. Instead of acting as an incentive to stabilize employment, experience rating seems to be an incentive for employers to nullify the program by removing employees from the eligibility rolls.

Professor Brissenden approved Secretary Folsom's stress on individual and employer efforts in employment stabilization. He asked about the use of government funds to aid employers in the direction of such stabilization—for example, in the provision of an annual wage.

Mr. Ball referred to the relationship of public programs to other efforts in income-security financing. Studies of the aged (some five million now receive monthly benefits) reveal that, except relatively few, they have practically nothing in the way of cash income, but two-thirds of the aged couples own their own homes and eighty per cent of these own them free of mortgage. The greatest threat to their security is the threat of expenses for medical care. By and large, they get by financially through various means, but their small savings are vulnerable to the first major illness. Home ownership has thus far been underrated in importance for this group, cash savings overrated. Public programs will always lag behind what can be done by some companies, and combination plans are needed. The issue is not public vs. private plans, but how they should supplement each other. Mr. Ball further pointed out that the technical minimum for OASI affects a very small proportion of recipients, those with a slight attachment to the labor market. Men who are now coming in are nearer to the maximum benefit level; it is important to keep in mind actual payments, not theoretical minimums.

Professor Burns commented on Secretary Folsom's and Professor Newcomer's support of the contributory principle in OASI financing. Recognizing the arguments concerning the desirability of having differential contributions if there are differential benefits and the possible importance of the contributory principle in emphasizing to beneficiaries the relationship between benefits and costs, Professor Burns pointed out that this was nevertheless a regressive method of financing and the tax on employees had many undesirable economic consequences. As the costs rise higher and higher, wage and payroll taxes rise. Yet almost one-third of the OASI cost is for unearned benefits; the possibility of contributions from the general revenue to meet this cost should be considered, for unearned benefits can properly be regarded as society's burden. Such financing from general revenues is not only a matter of justice, but would leave the payroll tax more available for other social security programs. Can one not contemplate charging at least these unearned costs to the general taxpayer, even if in principle the on-going system is to be financed solely by wage and payroll taxes?

In her concluding comments, Professor Newcomer referred to Professor Burns' question and pointed out that payroll taxes have thus far been adequate, but the time may come when financing will have to come from general revenues. Professor Harris observed that, because of our commitments for unearned benefits, our national debt is higher than we think it is.

Mr. Folsom made a number of points in connection with the discussion by Professor Harris and Professor Newcomer, and the various questions raised during the general discussion:

1. Referring to unemployment insurance, he stated he was still an advocate of experience rating, for it does have an effect on stabilizing employment. The majority of the Advisory Council in 1934 had recommended a Federal grant-in-aid program, but the Administration put in a Federal-state (tax-offset) system rather than Federal grant-in-aid, because of constitutional issues.

2. With respect to Professor Harris' observations re stock ownership, Mr. Folsom pointed out that he did not say that stock was extensively owned by lower-income groups, but referred rather to the tendency toward wider ownership of common stock. Studies have shown that 37 per cent of the U. S. Steel stock is owned by individuals with under $5,000 income.

3. It is a mistaken notion, he said, that private insurance plans pay after retirement a high percentage of the individual's earnings when working. Few pay more than fifty per cent. The basic problem is to increase productivity; the incentives are different for different population groups, but all will benefit from greater productivity. Pension plans provide incentives for many, which results in greater productivity.

4. The new tax bill, he believed, will take care of many inequities.

5. He agreed with Professor Lester's position on the importance of thrift.

6. He believed too much attention has been given to general and comprehensive health insurance plans. The big problem is provision for catastrophic illness, where group sharing can result in low costs. This type of protection is as important as Blue Cross or Blue Shield.

7. He does not approve loans to employers to stabilize employment. He does not favor a guaranteed annual wage. Only a small number would be affected, and they are the people who don't need it. The emphasis should be on stabilization, not on a guaranteed wage.

8. With respect to the financing of OASI, he noted that the 1948 Senate Advisory Finance Council had suggested the possible use of general revenues when the receipts from a 2½ per cent tax rate proved to be inadequate; at that time the cost of old-age assistance to the Federal Treasury should be substantially less. It would certainly be a mistake to tap general revenues any time in the near future with the existing high level of income taxes. This is a ques-

tion of fiscal policy, but it is an academic one for many years. In any case, there seems to have been little objection to the present two per cent payroll tax which will finance the system for several years.

9. Employee stabilization does not mean to him that the worker should stay in the same job all his life. Many workers will do better in staying with one company for a long period than in moving, and companies are encouraging this through promotions from within. The advantage of stabilization is in providing steady work throughout the year.

The Impact of Income Security upon Individual Freedom

Barbara Wootton
Nuffield Research Fellow
Bedford College, University of London

In the next twenty-five years some half-dozen major questions affecting social security will have to be answered one way or another: the main purpose here is simply to codify these questions, to present the issues. The answers that are favored will both affect and reflect the standards, the social valuations, the way of life, of each community concerned. Neither the questions nor the answers will be the same in any two countries; always they will be conditioned by the shape of particular local history. Nevertheless, common elements will be present everywhere; and national frontiers will not arrest the spread across the world of subtle changes in the mental climate in which decisions on these issues will be made.

A few comments on that climate may therefore be appropriate by way of introduction. Conspicuously ours is a security-minded age. Social security has become an entirely respectable expression; as a goal it is not felt to be in conflict even with the virtues of American free enterprise. This attitude stands in remarkable contrast with the early phases of industrialism, which showed much less squeamishness about letting the devil take the hindmost. Perhaps, however, the essential change is not so much in the value set upon security as in the choice of who shall be secure. The more prosperous sections of the community have always protected (and still do protect) themselves against the hazards of industrial life on a scale quite beyond the dreams of the ordinary wage-earner; and many of those who have taken large risks have done so against a background of security which guaranteed something to fall back upon in the event of disaster. Even today the salary-earner enjoys on the whole a longer period of notice, better sick pay and vacations, and a more generous pension than his wage-earning colleagues. Just for these reasons, little was heard of security so long as it remained the privilege of the few; that

381

which is taken for granted is never the subject of discussion. Perhaps, indeed, the apparent security-mindedness of the time represents not so much the rise of a new idea as the extension of an old one to new circles. It is part of the process of democratization. Increasing sensitivity to privilege, rather than any decay of the spirit of adventure, has been the operative factor in its growth.

A MAJOR REVOLUTION

The change of climate itself, however, amounts beyond doubt to a major revolution; and a very quick one, too. Let me illustrate the measure of the change by a few quotations from a volume of papers, most of which appeared in the London *Spectator*.

> It may be necessary—it no doubt is necessary in certain cases—to support men and women out of public funds, but it is useless to pretend that in doing so we are not injuring the human material with which we deal.
> If it [the Poor Law] could be entirely swept away . . . the poor would be thrown upon their own resources . . . and those (the comparatively few in number) whose indigence had not been produced by their own fault would be cared for, and again started on a career of independence by private benevolence.
> The citadel of manliness and individual responsibility is being attacked and undermined."[1]

These passages echo strangely in a world in which social security has become a household word, and in which measures for income-maintenance are written into legislation across the world from India to the United States, from Chile to Greece. But at the time that these sentiments were published, the author of the present paper was already ten years old.

Notwithstanding this revolution, the fear of conflict between income-maintenance projects on the one hand and personal freedom or initiative on the other is still never far away. It appears indeed to be lurking as a concealed major premise in the choice of a title for these discussions; for this title assumes the existence of at least some connection between income maintenance and freedom. The validity of that assumption remains, however, a matter of guesswork: little, even today, is known of the actual effect of income security upon initiative, enterprise, or freedom. Common sense suggests that the questions involved are quantitative: the larger the income to be had without working, and the less rigid the restriction of income-maintenance schemes to persons physically excluded by age or infirmity from the labor market, the greater no doubt the risks. Greater, also, one must suppose is the chance that industrial development will be strangled or distorted, if a highly complicated system, rather than one that is simple and flexible, is imposed. But where, in given conditions, does the danger line run? Nobody knows. Nor can it safely be assumed that all the factors involved weight the scales on the same side. Social security may be defended as being good business as well as good humanity. The hungry are not free; neither are they efficient.

If we stick to the facts of experience (in a field which is rich with prejudice) the few generalizations that can be hazarded at least give little ground for alarm.

The period which has seen the rapid maturation of social security systems has been also the period of an unprecedented growth of productivity. In the United States output has touched levels never reached before; and in Britain the establishment of one of the most comprehensive social security systems in the world has been accompanied by an expansion of industrial activity equally unparalleled.

Again, a long run of near-full employment has shown that few are really unemployable, and that the number of those who are both willing and able to live on social security benefit (at the levels so far prevailing) in preference to their own earnings is insignificant. In Britain at least it is not the chronic wasters so much as the unstable frequent job-changers who have made difficulties for the authorities concerned with income maintenance; and even the disturbance that they create hardly amounts to more than a ripple on the surface of a generally smooth-running stream. Nor do the elderly appear to be tempted into premature retirement; many old people continue in employment after they have reached the age at which pensions are payable. In the United States, at least until 1952, something like a third of those eligible for old-age and survivors' benefits were not drawing what was due to them.[2] In Britain, the Ministry of National Insurance has in hand at the moment a special inquiry into the factors affecting retirement; but we know already that of the men who reached pensionable age at mid-1949 about one-third were still at work three and a half years later, the corresponding figure for women being approximately one-quarter.[3] The will to work, or the need to work, seems to die hard on both sides of the Atlantic.

At the same time it may be salutary to remind ourselves that this new security is not altogether secure; and that social security policies, as ordinarily understood, can claim only modest credit for what has been accomplished. A run of fifteen years without a major recession has done more to transform the industrial climate than even the most generous measures of social security. In Britain a generation has grown up which has simply ceased to think of unemployment as a primary hazard of their lives: the harrowing tales of the nineteen-thirties have become for them no more than a slice of (rather tedious) history.

The realities of the situation were vividly brought home to us by inquiries conducted by Messrs. Rowntree and Lavers into conditions in the city of York, England, in 1950, as contrasted with those prevailing at the date of Mr. Rowntree's earlier investigation in 1936. The percentage of the working-class population (exclusive of those living in institutions) who were found in 1950 to be living below a very low poverty line was only 2.77 per cent as compared with 31.1 per cent in 1936. Nearly one-third of the poverty in 1936, however, was due to low earnings, as against 1 per cent in 1950; while unemployment accounted for 28.6 per cent of the 1936 cases and none of those of 1950. It is true that welfare legislation as a whole (including family allowances and food subsidies as well as income-maintenance measures in the narrower sense) had made a significant mark; if the welfare legislation of 1950 had been the same as it was fourteen years earlier, the proportion in poverty would have risen, it was estimated, from 2.77 per cent to 22.18 per cent; but it was nevertheless clear that the whole improvement would be extremely vulnerable to any fresh outbreak of serious unemployment.

As the authors of this study noted, the rates of insurance benefit payable under the National Insurance Acts "are not alone sufficient to maintain a family above the poverty line even if the other welfare measures are taken into account. It follows that large-scale unemployment, such as occurred in the 1930s, could result in widespread poverty which would be alleviated, but not prevented, by the welfare legislation at present on the Statute Book."[4] It would seem that it is to the late Lord Keynes rather than to Lord Beveridge that we in Britain owe such alleviation of the burdens of poverty as we have lately enjoyed. And American experience is broadly similar.

Times have changed; but the philosophy of an earlier epoch and the natural fear that income maintenance may resolve itself into income disappearance have left many marks (or should one say scars?) on the structure of contemporary social security. It is indeed the effort to reconcile what is valid in the old with what is valuable in the new which is chiefly responsible for the critical issues of today. To a review of those issues we may now proceed.

MAINTENANCE OF INCOME—FOR AND BY WHOM?

First comes the question: *Do we, in fact, want to maintain income?* No public scheme of social security ever has done so; or even come near to doing so, except for the very lowest income groups of all. "Less eligibility"—the principle that every public beneficiary must be kept to a lower standard of living than the lowest-paid independent worker—is today seldom explicitly applauded; but every social security scheme in the world pays it practical respect. In Britain the actual scales of assistance, which are the last line of defense for those who are unable to maintain themselves, are appreciably higher than the current rates of insurance benefits. Yet even these scales are set so low that the rule that they must be reduced whenever they exceed normal earnings needs to be invoked only in a handful of cases. True, ignorance may play some part here; since information as to the actual, not to speak of the hypothetical, earnings of individuals is notoriously hard to come by; but there can be no question but that public provision, in any shape or form, suffices to maintain only a fraction, and generally a small fraction, of normal income. And the British scheme ranks among the more lavish of those with flat-rate benefits and allowances.

Where benefits are proportional to earnings, the principle of less eligibility, in the old-fashioned sense, is less conspicuous: beneficiaries with normally large incomes may receive benefits higher than the customary earnings of less highly-paid workers. But proportional schemes themselves are habitually subject to a rule as to maximum payments; and even apart from this, proportionality, of course, by definition ensures that the condition of the individual recipient should always be less eligible when he is on benefit than when he is at work.

The unanimous answer thus appears to be that we do *not* want to maintain income. In fact, social security schemes commonly include provisions designed to guarantee that in no circumstances will they maintain incomes. And the hardly less unanimous response of the public is that what statutory systems of social security leave undone, ordinary people will try to do for themselves. Private pension plans, together with extensive systems of fringe benefits in the form of sick pay or medical care, spring up all over the place. The Americans led the way here; but the rest of us are not slow to follow. Professor Titmuss has estimated in a recent article[5] that "something like one thousand" separate pension schemes have been established in the British public services, while a similar "situation of confusion appears to be developing at an astonishing speed in the field of private employers' pension schemes."

Private schemes of income maintenance tend, moreover, to be much more generous than public social security; they do not seem to be haunted, to anything like the same degree as their public counterparts, by the fear of encouraging idleness or of discouraging thrift. Some of the schemes for professional personnel are really very generous indeed, especially in the matter of sick pay; my own university is prepared to pay its permanent staffs full salary during at least six months' absence on sick leave, subject only to deduction of the modest insurance benefit to which practically all British employees are entitled. The fear of encouraging the malingerer, so prominent in general discussions on sick pay, seems to have been successfully kept at bay in these arrangements—which are, it should be added, in no way exceptional. The social implications of this confidence in the trustworthiness of the higher-paid employee are striking—and a remarkable contrast to the elaborate safeguards applied lower down. May not this confidence also, like other assumptions about human behavior, be destined in time to spread beyond the upper reaches of the social scale?

Evidently there are still felt needs unsatisfied by any public provision. In principle, no doubt, the determination of the public to provide for themselves, or to extract from their employers, that which official systems of income maintenance fear to supply is just what the architects of social security would wish to encourage; everyone hopes that we shall continue, and continue vigorously, to help ourselves.

The consequences of this initiative can, however, prove embarrassing. The multiplicity of private pension plans can become a serious obstacle to industrial mobility. Individual cases constantly come to the notice of anyone concerned with appointments, especially at an executive or administrative level, in which the difficulty of transferring pension rights acts as a real discouragement to changes of employment which may be desirable from the angle both of the community and of the individual concerned. The difficulties that have arisen in the United States in transitions from covered to uncovered employments and vice versa hardly need to be emphasized here.

Moreover, problems of equity also arise—especially where public or semi-public services offer benefits much superior to those available to the population as a whole. The relatively favorable position of railway employees in comparison with other workers in the United States is a comparatively mild example. Where (as in Britain) doctors, medical auxiliaries, social workers, and university staffs, as well as teachers, civil servants, and municipal employees, are all largely supported from public funds, acute conflicts of equity are involved in the practice of taxing the public at large in order to provide these groups with retirement incomes on much better terms than those applied to the working community in general.

All this means, perhaps, that our first question ought to be rephrased. The issue is not so much whether we wish to maintain income, as what should be the respective shares of public and of private activity in income maintenance? And within the private sphere, how far should protection against industrial and other hazards be linked to particular employments? The growth of fringe benefits—a kind of modern version of payment in kind—has been due to many forces, among which considered social policy ranks as one of the *least* influential; in some countries, at least, the desire to circumvent heavy taxation has played a much more conspicuous part. In the next decade or so we shall have to decide whether still further proliferation of individual job-linked security schemes is to be encouraged or discouraged; and in this decision weight must be given to the claims both of industrial mobility and of equity. Considerations of cost, on the other hand, cannot be the decisive factor in the allocation of the burden between private and public funds. The social cost of income maintenance to the community depends upon the share in the national output consumed by those unable to earn, without regard to where that share comes from; and the economical intentions of the most parsimonious social security scheme will be frustrated if the gap which they leave is promptly filled from other sources.

THE ROLE OF SOCIAL INSURANCE

Next comes the question: *What is to be the future of insurance and of the "contributory principle?"* Here the sheet is far from clean; and one may guess that if it were we should be most unlikely to reproduce the writing now inscribed upon it. If social insurance had not been imported from nineteenth-century Germany it would probably not have been invented in twentieth-century England or America. As things are, everybody now recognizes an increasing element of fiction in current insurance schemes. As Americans have cause to realize, the coverage of income-maintenance schemes tends almost irresistibly to expand. But as these schemes become more generalized, their insurance basis becomes more and more illusory; until in cases where, as in Britain, virtually universal coverage has been attained, fiction ousts fact altogether.

At this point, the simple facts of the situation are that benefits on a prescribed scale have been promised, and that funds must be provided to meet them; that is all. In these circumstances, the allocation of precise fractions of contributors' payments to cover particular risks becomes an academic, rather than a genuinely actuarial, exercise. The performance of this exercise in the sacred name of insurance demands, however, elaborate and expensive systems of recording the experience of millions of beneficiaries. These monumental systems are indeed a tribute to the skill and accuracy of the administrators who devise them, and to the ingenuity of the mechanical devices employed in their operation; but are they really necessary, and have they, indeed, any meaning? Is it, in fact, worth maintaining what has become no more than a façade?

Lord Beveridge told us in 1942 that it was worth maintaining; and the reason offered was the "established popularity of compulsory insurance," and the alleged preference (at least of the British people) for benefit in return for contributions rather than free allowances from the state. The virtue of insurance is presumed in fact to lie in its association with the "contributory principle."

This doctrine that the public *wishes* to pay contributions is often confidently asserted; but it has not anywhere been objectively tested. It may be true on one or both sides of the Atlantic. But it is not as simple as it looks. It is, for instance, generally accepted that it does not apply to employers' contributions. Beneficiaries are said to like paying contributions; but not so their employers. Indeed the justifications offered for employer contributions have been consistently uneasy; and they seem to wear thinner and thinner as the individual employer's control over the hazards of industrial life becomes demonstrably more and more tenuous; significantly, today you in America speak of "experience" rather than of "merit" rating.

The supposed preference of beneficiaries for contributory schemes is generally ascribed (as in the Beveridge Report) to a presumed dislike of means tests. The strands in the argument here, however, seem to have become somewhat tangled; for contributory insurance is not, of course, the only possible alternative to a means test. Noncontributory schemes in which the categories of beneficiaries are clearly defined can also be (and are) used to establish title to benefit irrespective of the claimant's personal circumstances. Again, it is disconcerting for those who put their faith in the public's preference for contributory systems to find that, in some countries at any rate, contributors have the most confused and erroneous ideas as to what they are paying for. In Britain, for example, it is widely believed, in direct contradiction to the facts, that the national health service is substantially financed from insurance contributions.

Indeed, the evidence in support of any clear preference for contributory systems is altogether so thin that one may be tempted to dismiss it as little more than a convenient rationalization for the moral judgment that no one ought to get something for nothing. That judgment, perhaps, is the best justification for the contributory principle. But even here, the argument cuts both ways. For if this principle embodies the rule that we ought not to get something for nothing, it may equally evoke a determination to get something for something. Payment of contributions, in short, may protect our self-respect; but it does not necessarily encourage a public-spirited attitude towards the services provided.

Among all those uncertainties, one thing, however, is clear. Respect for the principle of contributory insurance can lead to radical departure from methods of taxation that are otherwise generally respected. Under flat-rate schemes this principle is indeed responsible for acceptance of what amounts to a highly regressive poll tax, such as it would never have been politically possible to introduce under, so to speak, its own name. Contributions do not have to conform to the standards expected of taxes.

MEANS TESTS

After insurance, the question of means tests falls next to be considered. *Where and when, we have to ask, should such tests be used?* Here generalizations are particularly rash. Perhaps we can say with confidence only that, since every means test involves exposure of intimate personal matters, public reaction is important. But the quality of public reaction is remarkably varied; no such thing as a general attitude to means tests exists. What happens in New Zealand is clearly different from what happens in the United States, and again different there from what happens in Britain.

Indeed the British reaction has not been at all consistent at different times. Twenty years ago the Assistance Board's test provoked continual explosions. Today, the Board applies a standard, comparatively simple test to over one and a half million beneficiaries (exclusive of their dependents). If there are complaints, hardly a ripple reaches the surface in publicity. For this change of attitude, a revision of the method of assessing family responsibilities is commonly held responsible. But is that the whole story? The question has never been put to objective test. And all the time other tests, for school meals, for educational assistance, for subsidized milk, have been in continuous use, again apparently without friction. In 1939 it was estimated that at least 19 separate means tests were in operation in Britain;[6] and some of these were applied at quite high levels of income. Clearly in this matter much weight must be ascribed to such intangibles as smarting memories from a recent past, the manners of officials, or the legacy of a Poor Law tradition.

The use of means tests, in the narrower sense, may be regarded as only one aspect of a much wider process of adjusting benefit to individual circumstances. Here we touch on one of the most persistent conflicts in the whole social security field: the clash between the demands of realism on the one side and of administrative simplicity on the other. Individual needs vary so greatly that no scale can be devised which will fit every case exactly. Accurate adjustment of payments to needs requires, therefore, either that scales should be dispensed with altogether or that, if they are used at all, they should be multiple and complex.

In the post-Beveridge British system with its universal coverage, standardized flat-rate insurance benefits, and national scales of assistance, it may be said that simplicity has won a fine victory over realism. But even here there are concessions to the opposite principle: insurance benefits are not completely standardized (note, for example, the higher rate paid during the early months of widowhood); assistance scales are exclusive of rent, the actual rent (subject to certain rules as to maxima) being paid in each case; and there are special rates of assistance for blind and tuberculous persons.

By contrast, the American system with its still incomplete insurance coverage, its graduated scales of benefit, and its elaborate three-tier structure of insurance, special assistance, and general assistance, presents a picture of astonishing complexity. To some degree these complications are, no doubt, to be explained as the product of a Federal constitution operating in a large and highly diversified country; but is that the whole explanation? To an outsider, at any rate, it would seem that the American structure, though conscious of the pressure for simplification, cherishes its complexities as evidence of a determination *not* to pretend that everybody can be treated alike. Certainly whichever side one favors—simplicity or realism—one is all too conscious of the attractions of the opposite course; nor is it surprising that the simpler security systems appear to be getting more complicated, while the more complicated become simpler.

SOCIAL SECURITY AND FAMILY PATTERNS

Next comes the question of the relation between social security and family patterns. *What are, or should be, the interactions between public systems of income maintenance and the structure of mutual obligations within the family? Where in fact is the line to be drawn between the family's responsibility for those unable to earn, and that of the community?*

The answers to these questions will have to take account of the realities of family life. In a sense it could be said that the traditional attitude of our society to the family is one of light-hearted disregard. The currently accepted family stereotype consists of a "breadwinning" male, responsible for the support of a dependent wife and children. Later, the dependent roles are reversed, and children must maintain their parents. No definite provision is, however, at any time made for dependents: the same wage is paid to a single man as to the father of ten. As the late Miss Eleanor Rathbone has forcibly put it,

> . . . wives and children appeal only occasionally, together with butchers' meat and alcohol and tobacco, as part of the "comforts and decencies" which make up the British workman's standard of life and enable him to stand out against the lowering of his wage. I do not think it would be an exaggeration to say that, if the population of Great Britain consisted entirely of adult self-propagating bachelors and spinsters, nearly the whole output of writers on economic theory during the past fifty years might remain as it was written, except for a paragraph or phrase here and there, and those unessential to the main argument.[7]

This type of dependent family, as Miss Rathbone was concerned to point out, is not part of the immutable order of nature. It was, in the first instance, the product of a rising industrialism which, in its early stages at least, deprived wives and families of their accustomed opportunities of contributing to a joint family income. It has, however, proved to be an extremely clumsy instrument for meeting vital social needs; indeed it almost amounts to a pretense that those needs do not exist. During the past two centuries this model of family life has been subject to strains and stresses from more quarters than one. The story is familiar enough, though we seem unable, in our social arrangements, to keep up with the consequences.

First comes the steady prolongation of the period of child dependency. Communities which until recently made (and some of which still make) no provision, except in emergency, for the maintenance of their children continually postpone the age at which these children are permitted to support themselves; and parents whose sons and daughters hope to acquire professional skills find that the duration of training grows ever longer and longer. It is one thing for a breadwinner to support his family up to the age of seven or eight, but a different matter to have them on his hands up to a minimum of sixteen or seventeen, and in some cases well into the middle twenties.

Meanwhile, at the other end of life, the burden of maintaining the aged becomes increasingly heavy. Growing longevity plays its part in this, though the *increase* in the expectation of life of the elderly (according to the British life tables, under two years for men and just over three years for women at age 60 as compared with the first decade of this century) is less than is sometimes represented. Not less significant is the decline in family size which spreads the costs—both financial and physical—of caring for aged parents over only one, two, or three, instead of any number from a half-dozen to a dozen descendants. This change is felt, of course, particularly by women, and most of all by the unmarried, many of whom carry grievous burdens in their dual role as daughters and as employees.

In other ways, too, the changing social and economic position of women has helped to loosen the bonds of nineteenth-century domestic dependency. As women emerge from a condition of social inferiority, economic dependency becomes increasingly irksome; no one likes to have to ask for every carfare even from husband or father. Women in general, and married women in particular, have, therefore, seized with both hands any opportunities of employment outside the home; and in the brisk state of the labor market these opportunities have been abundant. Today the number of married women in employment (many of them mothers of young children) appears to be far greater than before the war, perhaps than ever before; while, thanks to the smaller family, those who do yield for a time to the claims of domesticity find themselves free to offer many years of active work to the labor market after only a short interlude of child-bearing and child-rearing. Contemporary women workers, moreover, demanding as they do (though not always successfully) wages equal to those of their male colleagues, are no longer content to work for mere pin-money; and a new incentive to seek employment is added by the difficulty of maintaining accustomed standards of living in a period of continually rising costs.

Many British wives do not know what their husbands earn; and it is said (though I know of no comprehensive inquiry to substantiate this) that postwar increases in earnings (particularly where, as under systems of payment by results, these fluctuate from week to week) are often secretly retained by the wage-earner for his personal spending, without any proportionate advance being made in his wife's housekeeping money. This indeed may be only a local peculiarity, due to atavistic British customs in regard to the management of family income; but, for whatever reasons, everywhere wives are going out to work, and dependent wifehood is ceasing to be the norm.

Social and economic relationships within the family are changing fast; the architects of social security must move in step with the evolution (or should one say the passing?) of the dependent family. Here and there legislation has already recognized a narrowing of the circle of mutual responsibility. In Britain, under the Poor Law, fathers, mothers, grandmothers and grandfathers, husbands and children, stepfathers, and wives with property of their own were required to contribute to the support of poor relations who might be unable to work; only grandchildren were omitted on the ground that "natural affection descends more strongly than it ascends."[8] Today all such specific obligation has been done away; and, in the assessment of means by the National Assistance Board, household income is no longer pooled. Natural affection, it seems, can no longer be relied upon to ascend even the length of one generation upwards. There remains only the duty of husbands and wives to maintain each other, and jointly to provide for their children up to the age of 16; and it is in keeping with the spirit of the time that this obligation is now laid on each spouse in exactly identical terms.

Social security laws have, however, done more than make occasional concessions to autonomous changes in family patterns. More significant is the countermovement originating from that side. Social security benefits have always been more realistic than wage payments. Even the Poor Law had to use some standard of subsistence; and to recognize both that personal needs vary from one case to another and that subsistence for one person is not the same as subsistence for several people. Schemes of assistance or of "categorical" aid, which are the Poor Law's lineal descendants, followed suit; and finally insurance schemes, though many began by providing purely individual payments, were soon forced to recognize that more than one person may have to live off a single income, and the pressure for dependents' benefit quickly proved irresistible. In consequence, modest though scales of income-maintenance may be, they represent a conception of the nature and functions of income itself radically different from that of the wage system. Indeed, the very term "income maintenance," which describes a wage-earner's own security benefits fairly enough, makes no sense as applied to his dependents, since in the ordinary course of events they have no income to be maintained.

The paradox created by these contrasting concepts is too blatant to endure. Children do not spring into existence when their father falls sick or out of work and vanish when he returns to work; to provide for them in emergencies is only to call attention to the absurdity of ignoring their existence at other times. Besides, if security payments are, and wages are not, adjusted to meet family needs, the risk that benefits will run close to, or even sometimes pass, normal earnings is much enhanced; and the only logical answer is to provide for children's needs irrespective of the employment status of their parents. To the force of that logic the rapid spread of child allowances, payable without regard to parental circumstances, is a remarkable tribute.

By high-lighting the contradictions of a system under which incomes are paid on one principle and maintained upon another, income-maintenance schemes are compelling us to look at the traditional assumptions of the whole wage structure. New standards of social security and changing family patterns thus act and react upon one another. Income-maintenance plans under which those with large families find themselves better off out of work than in, force us to recognize the irrational features of established systems of wage payment; child allowance measures follow; and the conflict raised by income maintenance is partially resolved.

From one angle, the critical issue may be seen as a matter of determining the right distribution of income through life. Today, with income unadjusted to the varying expenses which they have to meet, the most severe economic hardships are borne by the very young or the very old. In the modern world, it has been said, the five ages of man proceed from an impecunious childhood to a brief period of affluence in adolescence and early manhood, until parenthood inaugurates a second phase of impoverishment, only to be followed again by a long golden afternoon when the children are self-supporting and the parents still at work (often at a higher level of income than at any other time), until this in turn fades into the chilly economies demanded by the drop of income on retirement. The reality of that sequence has been statistically demonstrated more than once;[9] but to a greater or less degree the human struggle and tragedy which it figures begins to be mitigated by social security measures.

THE NORMAL WORKING LIFE

Clearly the distribution of income through life cannot be considered apart from the distribution of work and leisure. *What then is to be the length of the normal working life? And how far should security schemes encourage or discourage early retirement?* In the past, the unfortunate authors of these schemes have been repeatedly tossed to and fro by vacillations of social policy on this issue, as first one and then the other of two contradictory economic theories has come into vogue. First, the doctrines of scarcity economics (which have the merit of being agreeable to common sense) teach that thrift and work are the keys to prosperity: the longer and the harder everyone works, the better will it be for all. Then, with the swing to economics of depression, common sense is abandoned in favor of the paradox that it is not saving but spending, not working but withdrawal from work, which conduces to economic health. In the course of a history which has hardly anywhere yet lasted for more than half a century, the major social security schemes of the world have had a hard task to accommodate themselves to the alternating validity of these rival assumptions, and to the dizzy leaps made by the economists from one to the other. In the later nineteen-twenties and thirties, in deference to depression theories, pension schemes had to be designed to lure workers out of an overstocked labor market. Ten years later every inducement had to be contrived to encourage late retirement. Security measures enacted in the first period could hardly be appropriate to the second.

Faced with the mounting cost of pensions in aging populations, the social security planner naturally has his own angle on the economics of this problem. Already in Britain the national insurance fund is running into the red for the first time since the comprehensive legislation of the nineteen-forties came into force; and, unless there is a material change of policy, the deficit is due to get larger and larger for many years to come. It is indeed, as Lord Beveridge has put it, "the first red shoot of a tree that will grow to overshadow the lives of all Chancellors of our Exchequer for decades to come."[10]

The prospect is even more alarming than it appears at first sight since a high proportion of pensioners are women. Women not only live longer than men; they frequently drop out of the labor market before they reach pensionable age, and so, as a group, are relatively insensitive to inducements to postpone retirement. In the United States in April 1952, 41.8 per cent of men over 65 were still in the labor force, as against only 8.2 per cent of women.[11] Where, as in a number of countries, women also qualify for pension at an earlier age than men, their share of the whole pensions bill is formidable indeed. Today two-thirds of British pensioners are women; and though there are those who hold that the American practice of fixing the same retiring age for both sexes is more reasonable, differentiation, once made, would not be easy to abolish.

Nor can questions of cost—or even of economic policy in its wider aspects —be treated as in themselves decisive. To the aging individual the right age for retirement depends upon his health, the expectations of his social milieu, and the balance of his work and leisure interests, as well as upon his prospective pension. Everyday experience shows that to some persons retirement appears, to quote Professor Titmuss again, as a "functionless interregnum" separating "work and death";[12] to others, as a long-awaited opportunity; while to others again financial considerations overshadow everything else. But nothing can be said as to the numbers in each category or as to their distribution by sex, social class, or occupation. Nor are we much better informed on the facts of present behavior. The physical capacity of the elderly to continue working; the degree to which their present decisions to retire or not to retire are influenced by the level of available pensions; the frequency with which, or the occupations in which, those who are pensioned from one post promptly look for another; and the measure in which these post-retirement jobs involve loss of status (as when a skilled operative accepts a post as office boy on retirement)—all these are still unknowns.

WAGE-DETERMINATION VERSUS SOCIAL SECURITY

My last question relates to the link—or rather to the absence of link— between income-maintenance schemes and the methods determining the incomes to be maintained. *How far is it possible to provide effective security in a community in which wages and salaries are fixed by unions and employers, by statutory authorities or by arbitrators, for all of whose policies that community disowns all responsibility?*

This question can be answered only if account is taken of the profound revolution in the accepted methods of wage and salary determination which has accompanied the rise of social security schemes in the past half-century. Reduced to the briefest possible terms, the essence of that revolution lies in the fact that collective bargaining has become respectable; wage rates are no longer dictated either by employers, or as the result of smash-and-grab raids by outlawed unions. Though strikes still occur on both sides of the Atlantic, formal discussions in an atmosphere of diplomatic negotiations are the rule. Indeed this procedure may be required by law, and, if the parties fail to agree, reference to arbitration, or to public inquiry, is increasingly often used; while in many occupations statutory authorities are required to fix legally binding rates of wages. Nor is collective bargaining today any longer the monopoly of the lower-paid wage-earner, or indeed of the wage-earning, as distinct from the salaried community. High salaries as well as low wages are now fixed by similar techniques of negotiation.

The many consequences of these developments include a profound, if subtle, change in the whole public attitude to wage and salary questions. Today (for the first time since at least the Middle Ages) the determination of earned incomes is recognized to be a matter of public concern. By an irresistible process of psychology representative discussions become responsible discussions; the parties to wage negotiations cannot avoid consciousness that they are in some sense accountable to a wider public for their actions. Bargains may be struck behind closed doors, but once made they become subject to widespread criticism in terms of their effect upon the general welfare; and, as is to be expected, arbitrators and statutory wage authorities are at all times deeply conscious of their public responsibilities. The formalization of the process of wage and salary fixing creates, in fact, if not the desire to do right, at least the wish to put an appearance of rightness on what is done. No union admits that it is out for all it can get; only for what is "fair."

The desire to act or to appear to act fairly implies, however, the recognition of some accepted standard of fairness. Yet no such standard exists. Its place is taken, as Professor A. M. Ross[13] has admirably shown, by conventions. Such conventions vary from one country to another; and the forms in which they are expressed vary still more. In the United States you speak openly of "wage leaders"; in Britain we prefer in this matter to follow our leaders without explicitly acknowledging their leadership. Everywhere, however, the broad lines of the pattern that emerges are the same. Wage and salary claims are justified in terms of established standards of living, or of traditional comparisons based on historical (and sometimes quite remote) precedent. The whole structure of relative wages and salaries thus tends to become increasingly rigid; if relativities are disturbed, "justice" demands their restoration.

Two aspects of this process deserve special attention in the present context. First, modern methods of wage determination are not only inflationary; what is more important, they provide a new justification for inflationary behavior. So long as justice or fairness means the maintenance of existing standards and relativities nearly all the way up and down the entire wage and salary scale, it is obvious that any increase anywhere is bound to stimulate corresponding increases nearly everywhere else. But inflation does not merely happen; *it happens in the name of equity*. In the postwar years this process has become too familiar to need any elaboration.

Income-maintenance plans are not blessed with a similar alibi. Whether rates are laid down by statute, fixed by independent national or local authorities, or left more or less to the discretion of investigating officers, the machinery for revising them is seldom comparable to that which keeps wage rates on the move. It is generally slow and cumbrous; only a few countries have been bold enough to allow their social security payments to be automatically adjusted to changes in a cost-of-living index. From time immemorial the pensioner has provided the classic case of the fixed income, the value of which is filched away by every inflation. Today the conflict of interest between the beneficiaries of security measures and the employed wage-earners has become exceptionally acute, as wage- and salary-earners at all levels have taken advantage of a favorable social climate and conditions of easy employment to improve the machinery for their own protection. As between the parties to this conflict, however, no appeal lies to any concepts of justice or fairness at all. On both sides of the Atlantic, the tradition that collective bargaining must be untrammeled, that every industry, as Lord Beveridge puts it, must be free "to fix its wages for itself without considering the effect on other industries,"[14] is still too strong.

It is indeed the tragedy of more than one insurance scheme that the high hopes of its authors have melted away before the continued decline in the value of money. The promised freedom from want has failed to materialize. In Britain it has been estimated that in 1951 the *individual* payments to adult workers for sickness and unemployment (that is, benefits other than those payable for dependents) were worth less in purchasing power than before the second World War. "Indeed, the amount of the weekly sickness benefit for an individual worker in 1911 represented a much higher proportion of the average wage; it was worth more in purchasing power and, taken by itself, was altogether more generous than the amount paid to-day."[15] And in their York investigation in 1950, Messrs. Rowntree and Lavers found that two-thirds of those living below the poverty line were elderly people whose pensions were inadequate.[16]

Benefit rates have been increased since 1950; but so also has the cost of living. We have no up-to-date over-all assessment of the combined result; but we do know that the proportion of retirement pensioners who have to supplement their pensions with assistance has been steadily increasing. One moral at least is obvious, and it does not concern Britain alone. Without either effective control of inflation, or automatic machinery to keep security benefits in step with cost of living changes, it is futile to decide, in principle, to eliminate means tests. Indeed the preceding discussion on this topic becomes irrelevant, since the decision is taken out of our hands: as the value of fixed insurance benefits shrinks, wider and wider supplementation on proof of need becomes inevitable, and the means tests come back of themselves.

The second significant aspect of modern methods of wage determination concerns not so much the immediate problems of social security as the whole question of the relation of security and progress in the modern world. It could be argued that the heart of this conflict lies right outside any formal security plan. Social security as ordinarily understood—the public provision of low minimum incomes to those unable for good reason to maintain themselves by their own labor—is a trivial factor amongst the forces which expedite or impede the rate of economic progress; it is too feeble to count for much.

The real dangers lie elsewhere; and among these, contemporary methods of wage determination, and in particular the steady infiltration into wage bargains of conceptions of equity or of fair relativity must be reckoned as formidable items. For the effect of these concepts is to nullify the effectiveness of wage changes as a mechanism for distributing labor between different occupations.

According to the traditional economic theory, movements in wage rates are the main instrument for regulating the flow of labor in harmony with changes in demand. Experience has not perhaps entirely justified the claims of theory in this respect. The deterrent effect of unemployment—inability to find a job at all—has been, throughout most of the life of industrial society, at least as potent and often more potent as a stimulus to industrial mobility than the attractive power exercised by the prospect of better pay. But without doubt in periods of full employment, when this incentive no longer operates, appropriate variations in wage rates are the *only* mechanism known to capitalist society (apart from occasional wartime emergencies) for directing workers into the jobs where there is, and out of those where there is not, a demand for their services. And it needs no argument to show that, once existing relativities acquire a mantle of justice and their disturbance becomes a source of legitimate grievance, then the efficient functioning of this mechanism is imperiled.

Any adequate analysis of the issues here would take us far beyond the limits of a discussion that is primarily concerned with measures of income maintenance. But these issues have to be raised, if only to put the role of social security projects into perspective. These projects represent a concession—but still only a small one—to the craving for security which is today everywhere found among the citizens of our dynamic modern communities. Meanwhile a far more vigorous battle for security is being fought in wage and salary negotiations than in campaigns for security legislation; and here it is a battle for security of status as much as for the actual money upon which that status depends. For the maintenance of status, inherently a relative concept, is necessarily contingent upon, as well as the strongest argument for, the sanctity of "customary differentials." It is, in short, in status maintenance, rather than in income maintenance, that the chief danger of economic stagnation is to be found.

Status is a social as well as an economic concept. Whichever way we look, therefore, the social and economic strands in the picture are seen to be interwoven.

In the industrial field the major conflict between security and flexibility turns on just this social question of status; while social considerations obtrude themselves no less persistently in the problems of income maintenance which are peripheral to this central conflict. Certainly of the six issues here raised—the level at which income should be maintained, the role of insurance, the future of means tests, the division of responsibility for income-maintenance between family and community, the length of working life, and the relation between wage determination and income-security measures—not one can be resolved in economic terms alone.

FOOTNOTES

1. Strachey, J. St. Loe, and others, *The Manufacture of Paupers,* London, Murray, 1907, pp. 6, 42–43.
2. U. S. Department of Health, Education, & Welfare; Social Security Administration, *Social Security Bulletin,* November 1953, p. 18.
3. Great Britain, Ministry of National Insurance, *Report,* 1952, p. 14.
4. Rowntree, B. Seebohm, & Lavers, G. R., *Poverty and the Welfare State,* London, Longmans, Green, 1951, pp. 30–31, 35, 39, 45.
5. The *Times,* December 30, 1953.
6. Ford, P., *Incomes, Means Tests and Personal Responsibility,* London, King, 1939, pp. 14–15.
7. Rathbone, Eleanor F., *The Disinherited Family,* London, Arnold, 1924, pp. 12–13.
8. Quoted from the 1776 edition of Burns' *Justice of the Peace* by Ford, *op. cit.,* p. 10.
9. E.g., by the British *Royal Commission on Population.* Memoranda Volume V, 1950, pp. 6–9, and by Woytinsky, W. S., *Earnings and Social Security in the United States,* Washington, Social Science Research Council, 1943, Ch. 14.
10. The *Sunday Times,* February 21, 1954.
11. U. S. Department of Labor, Bureau of Labor Statistics, *Bulletin* No. 1092, May 1952, p. 18.
12. The *Times,* December 29, 1953.
13. Ross, A. M., *Trade Union Wage Policy,* University of California Press, 1948.
14. *Manchester Guardian,* October 23, 1953.
15. Titmuss, Professor R. M., "Social Administration in a Changing Society," *British Journal of Sociology,* September 1951, pp. 190–1.
16. Rowntree & Lavers, *op. cit.,* p. 35.

COMMENTS

Seymour Martin Lipset

Associate Professor of Sociology, Columbia University

As Professor Wootton indicates, it is difficult to relate income security to individual freedom in a significant way. Clearly if we are primarily concerned with the problem of individual freedom, we would discuss many other institutions before touching on social security. Yet there is a relationship between freedom and state provisions to guarantee income security. On one hand, any increase in the power of the central state is potentially a menace to freedom, while, on the other, any measure which reduces the economic insecurity of individuals constitutes an increase in their freedom. The basic problem of political life in the twentieth century is how can we assure freedom from want without endangering the more traditional civil liberties of the right of opposition.

My own convictions lie in the direction of using state power to guarantee economic freedom, but, for that very reason, it is all the more necessary to be vigilant about the threat to civil liberties that may occur from centralizing power in the hands of the state. Those academics who are sympathetic with liberal and collectivist economic objectives have for some time been aware of the challenge to their beliefs presented by the fact that the large private universities, presumably much more under the direct influence of big business than state universities, have been the best defenders of academic freedom. Fascism, Communism, and McCarthyism have in different ways undermined the simple beliefs which many reformers held in the past, that increase in state economic power is necessarily democratic, since it involves a reduction in the amount of undemocratic private power over the economic life of the workers and farmers.

This discussion may seem far removed from income security, for obviously the social security system is one of the least important powers of government which may affect civil liberties. Yet even here we must be vigilant. The recent uproar about Alger Hiss' pension rights indicates that many if not most Americans do not understand the universalistic norms which are the fundamental basis of any legal system. I have heard of one case in which a man who was discharged from a private company at the request of a military security agency was subsequently denied unemployment insurance benefits. Presumably the argument on which the state insurance agency based its position was that the man was discharged because of personal malfeasance and thus was not entitled to unemployment insurance payments. While denial of unemployment insurance or pension rights will probably not become an important problem in this country, one can conceive of situations in which the aged or unemployed may be inhibited from joining protest organizations which are labeled as Communist by their opponents, because of fear of losing pension or insurance benefits.

NATURAL HISTORY OF AN ISSUE

Barbara Wootton has pointed up the major change in our thinking about income security which has occurred in less than one lifetime. In the United States, the revolution in thought and action of which she speaks has occurred even more recently than in Britain. The emergence and acceptance of social security as well as other economic reforms illustrate a pattern which has occurred repeatedly in democratic politics. A small group of reformers, often considered crackpots, call attention to the need for a basic institutional change. In the United States, this has been the role of single-issue reform groups, or more generally of "third" leftist parties such as the Populists or the Socialists. If the proposal appeals to the need of some major deprived group and obtains support, it then gets incorporated in the program of one of the major parties, usually the Democratic, and becomes a bone of contention between the parties. Following a change in administration, usually coming on the heels of an economic decline, the reform is secured. A significant aspect of democratic politics is that reforms which are first advocated and enacted by the more left-wing party are subsequently accepted by the more conservative group. The recent vote in Congress for the extension of social security coverage is an illustration of this pattern. The continued sharp cleavage between the Democrats and Republicans on other issues has made many of us forget the extent to which the Republicans accept premises today which leaders of both parties regarded as socialist 25 years ago.

The fact that the conservatives accept the basic assumptions of the reformers should not lead us to believe that the issue then disappears. If we omit foreign policy issues, the basic conflict between conservatives and liberals is between those who would redistribute income and those who oppose or fear the consequences of such change. This struggle is a never-ending one and takes on new forms, even when the specific principle involved seems to have been accepted by all sides. For example, the battle of the income tax continues through attempts to modify the interpretation of clauses of the law. Business has found many methods to partially circumvent the intent of progressive taxation, through expense accounts, stock bonuses which result in capital gains, new depreciation formulas, and other devices. Professor Somers pointed out the way in which labor has lost the battle of workmen's compensation, which presumably was accepted before World War I. His findings suggest that workers who are not covered by workmen's compensation and who must go to court to recover damages are better off than those who are covered.[1] The efforts to place many government controls and benefits under state rather than Federal authority are often struggles to place jurisdiction with those governmental agencies which are more likely to reflect the desires of business lobbies. State legislatures, in which rural and small-town voters are overrepresented, are almost invariably more conservative than Congress.

Similarly the battle of social security continues between those who would redistribute income and those who prefer the *status quo*. One weapon built into our economy which favors the latter group is secular inflation. As the value of the dollar declines, there must be a continued struggle simply to maintain the existing level of benefits, and the attempt to increase real benefits becomes proportionately more difficult.

In this connection it is interesting to note an observation of Joseph Schumpeter that there is a difference between the period when a society is psychologically and politically receptive to proposals for social reform and the time when it is economically in a position to support these reforms.[2] During periods of great prosperity, societies can afford to extend social welfare measures, but such periods are usually characterized by political conservatism and resistance to economic innovation. On the other hand, during depressions, the electorate is ready to adopt reform measures, but the reduced tax revenues and the demands for short-term depression-born expenditures lead to resistance against further burdening the taxpayer or the economy. Thus while social security was enacted to provide a low level of income support in the depression, there has been much opposition to efforts to raise this low level during subsequent prosperity, although doing so would probably help avert another depression.

A second related problem which is raised by Professor Wootton is whether social security should be paid for by progressive taxation, or by the present system of an "insurance" tax. This is a basic question of social policy. Should old-age and survivors' or unemployment benefits be paid for by a regressive tax, or through a transfer payment which comes disproportionately from those who have more? The emphasis on the presumed insurance character of such payments serves the positive function of eliminating the charity aura from state support, and of helping to remove pressure for a means test, but it also serves the function of giving a politic label to a system of regressive taxation. I do not know which function is more beneficial socially.

One may question the evidence which underlies statements, such as have been made at this conference, that people prefer to pay for their old-age payments. This may be so, but has anyone actually made a study to discover what workers receiving under $3,500 a year actually think about paying an extra thirty-five or seventy dollars a year? Maybe workers prefer to pay the cost of their pensions, but we should find out whether they do, not simply assume it. Personally, I do not know why workers should prefer to pay for their pensions, while at the same time they do not want to pay directly for their children's education. There may be an important psychological difference in the popular view between support of pensions and support of education, but let's find out if there is. It was not too long ago that free education and later state-supported universities were denounced as examples of socialism, and as interference with the freedom of the family.

PRIVATE SYSTEMS OF INCOME SECURITY

The growing drive to build private pension plans is another example of a socially desirable tendency which may have dysfunctional consequences. These plans, which are usually secured by the best organized and thus politically most powerful section of the workers, reduce the effectiveness of the demand that society as a whole pay for these greater social benefits. One may argue that private plans are preferable, for they reduce the potential control of the state. However, do the dangers involved in a larger state system outweigh the social dysfunctions of private systems? I shall cite only a few of these.

The creation of private welfare funds has opened the door to a new source of corruption within the labor movement. The present stabilized labor movement is increasingly led by a career bureaucracy, which in many cases retains little of the idealism which built the unions. The private plans are relatively unpoliced, since many employers are uninterested in how the union runs its fund, and most trade unions do not have a democratic opposition group to check on the actions of the leadership. This permits legal graft through the payment of commissions on insurance premiums or welfare fund investments to union leaders, their relatives or friends, and gives greater patronage to union leaders in the form of jobs administering these plans. This point is attested to even by leaders in labor.[3]

The private plans also reduce the extent to which the labor movement is interested in using its political strength to gain increased state social security or health insurance. As union leaders get control of these benefits, they become opposed to seeing an area socialized which they control.

One example of this phenomenon was the reluctance of California unions to support Earl Warren's attempt to liberalize the sickness benefits in California. The California system permits companies to insure either with the state or with private insurance companies which paid more benefits. The state fund, which clearly obtained the worst risks, has been accumulating considerable surpluses under the existing schedule of benefits. Warren, while Governor, proposed extending the benefit schedules considerably. This could be done without changing the tax or insurance payment. To the surprise of many persons interested in extending benefits, the bulk of the California union movement refused active support of Warren's proposals. The union leaders, AFL, CIO, and Communist alike preferred to keep control of increased benefits as part of union contracts, so that they could claim credit with their members for any gains. Some union officials also wanted to keep insurance in the hands of private companies because they could then obtain commissions from them. If minimum benefits were extensively liberalized, private insurance companies would lose interest in handling the insurance.

The private plans also serve to increase the discrepancy in benefits between the union and nonunion sectors of the working class. Thus the groups which are probably most in need of pension rights, and of health insurance, are least likely to obtain them.

An area about which we know very little is the effect of private pension plans or labor mobility. Are workers less likely to change jobs or move from one city to another because they have paid into a private plan? While seniority systems are probably more effective in restricting mobility than pension plans, my guess is that the latter plans also have some effect.

Pension plans under the control of trade unions also restrict the freedom of choice of union representation which workers have. Recently, when a large minority faction in the Textile Workers of America (CIO) seceded to join the AFL union, many locals found that they could not secede without losing their pension funds, which were controlled by the international union. This fact, in large measure, destroyed the secession effort.

This discussion of private pension plans and their possible effect on the extension of income security and the problem of individual freedom is obviously far from complete. I have introduced a few problems to highlight some of the rarely discussed social complexities involved in the simple effort to establish a private pension plan. The emphasis on the labor movement in this section is not a result of any belief that it is a special sinner, but rather flows from my belief that the trade unions are the most powerful force in American society for social reform. Any factor which serves to reduce their contribution to social change is, therefore, of importance to those outside of the labor movement as well as to those within it.

CLASS STRUCTURE AND MOBILITY

One of the basic principles or values in American life is equalitarianism. This is presumably what Professor Lester means when he writes of the United States as a "classless type of society." This value, of course, does not mean that we believe that all people are equal, or that there should be no differences in status or reward. Rather, it assumes that a democratic society should recognize no inherent differences among men on account of their family background *per se*. All men should have the opportunity to reach that station in life for which they are best fitted. Discussion of the reality of this assumption or value necessarily leads us into a discussion of the facts concerning social mobility. And various studies in this area indicate that one's ultimate occupational and social status is often determined by that of the father, although considerable upward mobility occurs.[4]

If we are to maximize opportunity, we must make it possible for men to receive the training and education which they have the ability to use. And in our society, this means the opportunity to secure higher education. The relationship of educational opportunities to American values was recognized by the President's Commission on Education when it suggested plans to double and even triple our present college population. Yet is the expansion of educational plant sufficient to secure a more equitable distribution of opportunity? I would suggest that an income sufficient to permit the children of the lower socio-economic strata to attend school is also required.

In a survey study of social mobility in the San Francisco Bay area we found, as all such studies do, a minority who were downward-mobile. A large proportion of this group was individuals who had received less education than one would expect from their reports of their fathers' occupations. Unfortunately, we did not focus on this problem, but we did ask the question, "Why did you leave school at the time that you did?" Many of the downward-mobile individuals reported that their fathers had died or that their family had broken up before they could complete the amount of education they had planned for. It is clear that many of the downward-mobile, as well as many of those whose families were always poor, dropped out of school because of lack of support.

In considering plans for support of families without a male breadwinner, we have concentrated on supporting and keeping the family together until the children are finished with high school. Recently Congress recognized that college education is a basic part of American life by granting income-tax allowances for older children still attending university. Should our aid to dependent children system ignore the fact that university education is a necessary prerequisite for many positions?

Another and more general solution to the problem of support for financially impoverished prospective college students has been adopted in Sweden and

Great Britain. In Sweden, all young people who meet the academic standards for attending the university receive a maintenance bursary from the state. This bursary is given to all who qualify for the university and have the financial need, not simply to the brightest. In Britain, similarly, the state provides a tuition scholarship and maintenance to qualified students. If the poorer Swedish and British economies can support needy university students, should the much more wealthy United States remain far behind?

There can be little doubt that this problem is related to the question of income security and freedom. Without the freedom to complete one's educational plans, one does not have the freedom to choose one's career.

FOOTNOTES

1. Herman and Anne Somers, "Workmen's Compensation: Unfulfilled Promise," *Industrial and Labor Relations Review,* October 1953, pp. 32, 42.

2. Joseph A. Schumpeter, *Essays,* Cambridge, Addison-Wesley Press, 1951, p. 115.

3. See, for example, David Dubinsky, "Safeguarding Union Welfare Funds," *The American Federationist,* July 1954, pp. 10–13. Also A. H. Raskin, "Unions and the Public Interest," *Commentary,* February 1954, pp. 104–105; and Daniel Bell, "The Scandal in Union Welfare Funds," *Fortune,* April 1954, pp. 140–142, 196–206.

4. See Natalie Rogoff, *Recent Trends in Occupational Mobility,* Glencoe, The Free Press, 1953; Richard Centers, "Occupational Mobility of Urban Occupation Strata," *American Sociological Review,* April 1948, pp. 197–203; and "Jobs and Occupation: A Popular Evaluation," *Opinion News,* September 1, 1947, pp. 3–13.

REPORT OF THE RECORDER

Elizabeth G. Meier

Associate Professor of Social Work
New York School of Social Work, Columbia University

Professor Barbara Wootton raised the question, "What should be the respective shares of public and of private activity in income maintenance?" Certain problems derive from this question. To what extent do public and private pension plans threaten individual freedom and thwart incentive? Does participation in a pension plan tend to keep the worker stabilized in a job, to the detriment of his making use of his capacities to move on to a better job with a different firm?

Professor Richard Lester pointed out that a pension plan is but one factor in the variety of influences which determine a worker's attachment to a firm. Seniority, on-the-job training, tenure, and opportunities for advancement within the plant are other factors. He quoted employers as believing that medical and hospitalization programs are more potent than private pension plans in holding workers to employment. Professor Ralph Blanchard suggested that vesting plans which do not interfere with employment changes can be worked out, citing the example of Columbia University's pension plan, which does not interfere with the individual's freedom of mobility.

The contributory principle in insurance plans was defended by Mr. Robert Ball. The contribution is symbolic of the desire of the American people not to be helped but to support themselves as far as possible, either through their work record or through their direct contributions. Old Age and Survivors Insurance in this country not only serves the function of substituting for old-age assistance, but benefits are also received by many persons who would not need assistance, even if they did not receive benefits. Professor J. Douglas Brown endorsed this interpretation of American psychology. Because of its contributory aspects, old-age and survivors' insurance creates an entirely different attitude than does unemployment insurance. The setting aside of specific amounts each pay day makes use of the natural instinct of thrift. Mr. Robert Goodwin also identified himself with the above views and suggested further that unemployment insurance, for want of a contributory principle, engendered a feeling that these benefits were "relief" rather than insurance. Introduction of a contributory basis into this program was urged as a means of making it more compatible with the national psychology.

As a discussant, Dr. Otto Klineberg recommended scientific study of community attitudes. He deplored the tendency toward loose generalizations regarding how an undifferentiated "people" thought and felt. In his closing remarks, Dr. Klineberg quoted some of the phrases which participants had used to apotheosize the American psychology and to endow human beings with the "natural instinct of thrift," and he ruefully concluded that his argument had not caused any diminution of the tendency toward generalization.

Dr. Franz Goldmann questioned whether endorsements of the contributory principle were based on scientific findings, or reflected emotional attitudes. Within these questions concerning the effect of insurance programs on individual freedom, he saw a larger issue. Does the impact of income security upon individual freedom depend upon the source of funds? There may be a proneness to assume that programs sponsored by government carry a greater threat within them.

Mr. Reinhard A. Hohaus likewise pleaded for additional research; nor should research be confined to academic halls and legislative chambers, but it should permeate industry itself. Mr. Hohaus commented that major research is needed in *how to do research* in these areas. Frequently the questions being studied have hidden within them assumptions and attitudes upon which solutions are predicated, regardless of findings. He pointed out that some plans for blanketing persons into a pension scheme, extending coverage and liberalizing vesting rights, are posited on the belief that employees want these advantages, but actually they frequently do not. "A democracy," Mr. Hohaus reminded, "gives the individual the right to do something foolish."

Professor Wootton pointed out that in England public reaction to the means test has changed markedly in the last twenty years; a simple means test is now applied for a variety of social benefits, with little public reaction against it. Dr. Alton Linford denied that any comparable relaxations in public attitude had taken place in this country. While the threat of social security to freedom is overestimated in regard to some forms of benefits, the impact of the threat remains in public assistance. Admittedly, whatever their form, income-maintenance aids expand the individual's freedom in that he is relieved of the burden of economic want, has the freedom to secure an education, to attend church, to take part in the community's social activities. Nevertheless, the person accepting public assistance is liable to certain social controls not applied to other persons, and thus his freedom to behave in his own manner of choice is curtailed. For example, parents requesting aid to dependent children are still, in some localities, subjected to rigid inquiry whether their home is suitable. In other forms of public assistance, the recipient's freedom to move to other localities is restricted by settlement laws. Sometimes citizenship is an eligibility requirement.

Mr. Wilbur Cohen similarly pointed out that the injection of moral issues into eligibility requirements impinges upon the freedom of the assistance recipient. The Federal requirement that the applicant for Aid to Dependent Children must be willing to have desertion of the breadwinner reported to a law enforcement agency exemplifies one of the threats to freedom in this program. Some deserted wives, out of fear, guilt, hope of reconciliation, or other complicated psychological motivations, prefer to withdraw their applications rather than to submit to this requirement.

Mr. Cohen stressed the danger of lumping all assistance programs together in our thinking. He referred to Mr. Folsom's presentation wherein the return of total responsibility for assistance programs to the states was discussed. Mr. Cohen indicated that the children for whose benefit ADC is granted pose a different type of problem than do the aged. The majority of these children have estranged parents. This breakdown in family relationships is a risk not covered by social insurance nor can the problems be expected to diminish. Rather, the increased birth rate since the war years makes it likely that the number of children needing such help will increase. Therefore, it would be most unfortunate to place responsibility for the ADC program upon the states in the erroneous assumption that expanded coverage of Old Age and Survivors Insurance will reduce assistance needs and make it possible for the states to carry full responsibility.

Professor Wootton pointed out that the community takes responsibility for setting the levels of income security provided through social insurance measures; it does not assume similar responsibility for setting wage levels. This raises the question whether effective security on a wage-related basis can be provided for those persons dependent upon the social security measures, since the variability of wage levels produces constant shifting in the value of benefits. Furthermore, in flat benefit systems the problem of maintaining any desired relationship between benefits and wages is greatly complicated. She expressed the view that social security as ordinarily understood is "a trivial factor" among the forces which affect the rate of economic progress, as compared with others, and notably with contemporary methods of wage determination which tend to nullify the effectiveness of wage changes for distributing labor between different occupations.

Mr. Ball averred that benefits can be adjusted to changing economic conditions. Old Age and Survivors Insurance has adjusted to changing price levels, and long-range cost estimates for the program assume that benefits will continue to be adjusted to changing price levels. Mr. Ball believed that changes through legislation are preferable to automatic price-index adjustments, since legislation permits a more thorough examination of the whole program with opportunity for the introduction of other appropriate changes, in addition to changes in benefit levels.

Professor Harris regretted that only the detrimental aspects of inflation are usually presented. He urged that a reasonable degree of inflation, say about two per cent a year, is beneficial, resulting in increased production, increased output, and full employment. The percentage of national income involved in income security measures is very small. Nevertheless, these measures have a healthy effect upon the economy, for funds for these purposes are taken out of the income stream during inflationary periods and are expended in potentially depressed periods, thus placing a brake upon downward trends in economic activity.

Social security may expand freedom as well as possibly contract it, Dr. Burns reminded the group. She questioned the alleged effect on freedom of various requirements in social security measures, such as the retirement test. For many persons in an earlier era, the choice between retirement or a pension did not exist. They had no choice other than continuing to work or starving. In this respect, their freedom is now enhanced. The more important problem concerns the effect on initiative, not on freedom.

Dr. Pierre Laroque indicated that income security measures must be analyzed from two points of view—their *contribution* to freedom and their *threat* to freedom. Freedom from want is a cornerstone of liberty and thus the contribution of security measures is indisputable. However, we must also be aware of their potential threat. First, from a psychological point of view, the protection of too much security may stifle the spirit of adventure and the feeling of freedom. Secondly, and more practically, a limitation to freedom is experienced by those workers who do not wish to leave employment in one place to seek it elsewhere because they would lose their union rights or their vesting rights in pension plans. Thirdly, administrative procedures may constitute a threat to freedom. Registration cards and records could conceivably provide a bureaucratic government with tools for the control of the population. This danger is not insoluble; good administration will keep in mind the needs of the individual and its responsibility to the people.

Dr. Laroque advocated social education to help people realize that security is the "fruit of a common effort," achieved by methods which are freely chosen by the population. Such awareness would contribute to a sense of social solidarity and an appreciation that security for one's neighbor is security for oneself. This sense of solidarity, it was conceded, is difficult to create in a heterogeneous and widespread community.

Dr. Burns emphasized the problem of how to interest the mass of the population in a program and its administration. She suggested that the present American device of advisory committees and groups was not very effective, because the membership was not truly representative of all groups of the population, but tended to be composed of members of the great bureaucracies of organized labor and business.

In her concluding remarks, Professor Wootton reiterated the need for economists to develop a more realistic approach to problems of social security. For the solution of these problems, economists must draw upon knowledge in the fields of politics and administration. New knowledge from the discipline of psychology is particularly needed to deepen our understanding of human needs, motivations, behavior, and aspirations. Professor Wootton concluded that the wording of the topic, "The Impact of Income Security on Individual Freedom," had within it the concealed major premise that security threatens freedom. Discussion has brought this premise out into the open and has revealed it to be "a spectre that has departed out of the window."

PARTICIPANTS

ARTHUR J. ALTMEYER, Former U. S. Commissioner of Social Security

ROBERT BALL, Deputy Director, Bureau of Old Age and Survivors Insurance, U. S. Department of Health, Education, and Welfare

HARRY BECKER, Director, Social Security Department, United Automobile Workers, CIO, formerly Associate Director, Commission on Financing Hospital Care

FATHER JOSEPH BECKER, Institute of Social Order, St. Louis University

RALPH H. BLANCHARD, Professor of Insurance, Columbia University

PAUL F. BRISSENDEN, Professor of Economics, Columbia University

J. DOUGLAS BROWN, Dean of the Faculty, Princeton University

EVELINE M. BURNS, Professor of Social Work, New York School of Social Work, Columbia University

EWAN CLAGUE, Commissioner of Labor Statistics, U. S. Department of Labor

WILBUR COHEN, Director, Division of Research and Statistics, Social Security Administration, U. S. Department of Health, Education, and Welfare

JOHN J. CORSON, McKinsey and Company, Washington, D.C.

NELSON H. CRUIKSHANK, Director, Social Insurance Activities, American Federation of Labor

FRANK DE VYVER, Professor of Economics, Duke University

FEDELE F. FAURI, Dean of Social Work, University of Michigan

MARION B. FOLSOM, Under Secretary of the Treasury

MARION H. GILLIM, Associate Professor of Economics, Barnard College

FRANZ GOLDMANN, Associate Professor of Medical Care, School of Public Health, Harvard University

ROBERT C. GOODWIN, Director, Bureau of Employment Security, U. S. Department of Labor, Executive Director, Defense Manpower Administration

SEYMOUR E. HARRIS, Professor of Economics, Harvard University

REINHARD A. HOHAUS, Vice President and Chief Actuary, Metropolitan Life Insurance Company

OTTO KLINEBERG, Professor of Psychology, Columbia University

PIERRE LAROQUE, President of the National Social Security Fund in France, Conseiller d'Etat

RICHARD A. LESTER, Professor of Economics, Princeton University

T. F. LEWIN, Assistant Professor of Social Work, New York School of Social Work, Columbia University

ALTON A. LINFORD, Professor of Social Service Administration, University of Chicago

SEYMOUR MARTIN LIPSET, Assistant Professor of Sociology, Columbia University

CLARENCE D. LONG, Council of Economic Advisers, Washington, D. C.

ELIZABETH G. MEIER, Associate Professor of Social Work, New York School of Social Work, Columbia University

IDA MERRIAM, Assistant Director, Division of Research and Statistics, Social Security Administration, U. S. Department of Health, Education, and Welfare

JOHN MORGAN, Professor of Social Work, University of Toronto

MABEL NEWCOMER, Professor of Economics, Vassar College

HERMAN SOMERS, Professor of Economics and Political Science, Haverford College

HERMAN D. STEIN, Lecturer in Social Work, New York School of Social Work, Columbia University

LEO WOLMAN, Professor of Economics, Columbia University

BARBARA WOOTTON, Nuffield Research Fellow, Bedford College, University of London, formerly Professor of Social Studies, University of London

PART SIX

Religion in Education

INTRODUCTION

The material in Part Six is noteworthy because of its scope and incisiveness and the wide range of competence and experience represented by the contributors. They addressed themselves to one of the most difficult problems of general education in our time: how schools and colleges—especially those which are tax-supported—can make adequate recognition of the role of religion in our culture and in the life of man, and at the same time maintain due respect for constitutional limitations and avoid objectionable forms of indoctrination. With insight and patience and an impressive degree of mutual respect and understanding the members of the group explored the many angles of this problem.

The discussion was in no sense conclusive, as the reader will readily see. The complexity of the problem precluded arrival at precise findings. Moreover, the exploration made clear the important fact that American education has no fixed patterns or norms but is in process of gradual development, marked by continual adjustment to regional and local differences. It is hoped, therefore, that the record of our discussion may furnish a map, so to speak, of a vast problem area, illuminated by the insights of scholarship and the lessons of experience.

On the one hand, the thinking of the group reflected a deep concern for the preservation of the spiritual heritage of our culture. On the other hand, there was profound respect for that freedom of the mind which has been the theme of the Bicentennial: "Man's Right to Knowledge and the Free Use Thereof."

Henry P. Van Dusen
President, Union Theological Seminary

412

Religion in American Life

Ralph H. Gabriel
Professor of History, Yale University

In our time America, born of Western Europe and now risen to power such as no nation ever before possessed, stands as the final bastion of the free world. Our civilization, harnessing the energy of the stars, moves forward like the progress of the whirlwind. Yet anxiety fills our thought. An attempt to scan the future ends only in frustration. Faced with a powerful, determined, and implacable enemy who challenges our nation, our values, and our religion, we suffer from a sense of insecurity.

Frustration and insecurity are, relatively speaking, novelties in our history. For brief times in our early national history we looked abroad with apprehension. But from 1815 to 1914 a sense of national security and security for our values and our religion provided the background for our thinking. World War I was a shock. The depression of the 1930s raised up apprehensions that led to vigorous constructive actions within the domestic scene. The fall of France in the summer of 1940 brought to Americans the sudden realization that an old and familiar world had disappeared and that the rising flood of a new war had washed away old defenses. Since the summer of Dunkirk Americans have felt insecure. Power and insecurity, the paradox of the mid-twentieth century, have gone together. Perhaps Americans, at long last, are learning to face the facts of life, namely that the essence of life is hazard.

The rise of interest in religion stands out as one of the most conspicuous aspects of an age of anxiety. Evidence for this interest appears on every hand; the lists of best-selling books, the station coverage of religious television programs, the Sunday congregations in synagogues and churches. A conference on religion and education reflects the felt needs of the times.

A Heritage of Cultural Change

American civilization stems from the Middle Ages, the Reformation and the Renaissance. American religious tradition began in the seventeenth century in that spiritual anxiety produced, in the words of Paul Tillich, "by the basic social conflict of the disintegrating Middle Ages." Out of this anxiety came some of our oldest and most important symbols: the Pilgrims, refugees for conscience' sake; William Penn, architect of a frontier settlement where men might be free to hear and to heed the inner voice; Roger Williams, wilderness prophet of religious freedom; the *Ark* and the *Dove,* bringing the men who established the Medieval Church on the shores of the Chesapeake. America came out of an age in which the struggle among the variant forms of religion evidenced the importance of religion itself for the men of those times.

But seventeenth-century England saw, along with the King James translation of the Scriptures and the triumph of Cromwell, the culmination of what Herbert Butterfield has called the scientific revolution. As the first Americans enlarged their clearings and built their houses between the sea and the forest, Boyle brought forth chemistry out of alchemy; Harvey discovered the circulation of the blood; Newton, looking out into the heavens, mastered the mechanics of the solar system and discovered the laws of motion; and Locke, friend of Newton, grappled with the problems of the human understanding. In the following century, while colonial cities in America grew and the fringe of settlement moved westward, Enlightenment philosophy, a rationalism and humanism born of the triumphs of science and the philosophy of Locke, stirred Western thought including that of the English provinces in North America.

In 1803, as the nineteenth century opened, a Presbyterian clergyman in New York City, Samuel Miller, pointed out to his countrymen what he conceived to be the significance of seventeenth-century philosophy and science:

> At the close of the seventeenth century, the stupendous mind of Newton, and the penetrating genius of Locke, had laid their systems of matter and of mind before the world. Like pioneers in an arduous siege, they had many formidable obstacles to remove—many labyrinths to explore—and the power of numberless enemies to overcome. But they accomplished the mighty enterprise. With cautious, but firm and dauntless steps, they made their way to the entrenchments of fortified error; they scaled her walls; forced her confident and blustering champions to retreat; and planted the standard of truth, where the banner of ignorance and falsehood had so long waved.

Miller's phrases suggest the bright colors of what the eighteenth-century "Philosophes" regarded as the Enlightenment dawn. But his words remind us of a basic fact in our tradition. The history of our people in what is now the United States began in the age when modern science took form, and that history has moved forward in time, pacing evenly with the annals of creative scholarship in Western civilization.

Religion, however, rather than science, is the concern of this chapter. In 1947 in England a group of fourteen Anglicans of the "Catholic" school of thought, selected by the Archbishop of Canterbury "to examine the causes of the deadlock which occurs in discussion between Catholics and Protestants and to consider whether any synthesis between Catholicism and Protestantism is possible," reported to His Grace. Though some may quarrel with details of their analysis it may have uses for our present discussion. "The loss of 'wholeness' [the primitive unity of the early church]," the fourteen asserted, "became notorious and palpable with the schisms of the sixteenth century. . . . This separated Western tradition [which had long since moved away from the Eastern tradition] has in its turn broken down into three main types of Christianity with which the modern world is familiar: orthodox Protestantism, Liberalism, and post-Tridentine Catholicism. These three types are all represented in the Church of England [in the twentieth century]." Liberalism is a word whose edge is blunted with too much using. The fourteen defined Liberalism roughly as the spirit and tradition of the Renaissance. The post-Tridentine Roman Catholicism was based on the declarations of the Council of Trent (1564).

All three types exist in the religious faith of Americans in our day. But two of these, orthodox Protestantism and the Liberalism affected by the Renaissance impulse, provide the substance of the American religious tradition as it took form in our first two and a half centuries. The third, Roman Catholicism, though Lord Baltimore brought it to the Maryland colony in the early seventeenth century, was carried in the main to the United States after the close of the Napoleonic Wars as part of the mental baggage of migrating Europeans from many lands.

The fragmentation of the Christian tradition was a product of the energy and force of Western civilization, a culture already moving outward in the fifteenth century as Da Gama rounded the Cape of Good Hope and Columbus looked upon the strange men of the New World he had found. The horizons of Europeans had already begun to expand when, in 1517, Luther posted his theses on the door of the Wittenberg church. Two years after that event Magellan initiated the greatest maritime exploit in history, the circumnavigation of the globe.

American Adaptations

Energy and force characterized the American variant of Western culture from the seventeenth-century beginnings of the English colonies. The necessities of life on a remote frontier fostered activism. The circumstances of settlement that expressed the mind of capitalism more than of feudalism brought the individual into focus. Protestantism emphasized the relation of the individual to God. In the communities, strung like beads along the coast, men going about the tasks of daily living began to consider the relation of the individual to society.

Gradually American colonials evolved a new conception of the relation of the individual to society. It was foreign to the Europe which was only beginning to move away from feudalism. The life story of Benjamin Franklin was only one among a multitude of American biographies that demonstrated the fact that in the evolving and maturing colonies the status and acceptance of the individual was not determined by his birth or place in a fixed class structure but rather by his personal qualities and achievements. This New World pattern, not duplicated in either New France or New Spain, represents what still remains the greatest American contribution to the social thought of the West.

To this achievement both the Reformation and the Renaissance contributed. Protestantism insisted that the individual, though he be the heir of corruption, must stand alone before his God. The fourteen Anglicans have defined the Renaissance impulse as it is used in this discussion:

> While the Reformation was proclaiming the helplessness of man, the "bond-age of the will," the doctrine of Justification by Faith alone, the Renaissance was asserting its own idea of the dignity of man, and pointing toward the ideal of human freedom, and the idea of history as a steady progress of man toward happiness and enlightenment. Possessing roots both in ancient classi-cal humanism and in the culture of the Western Church, the Renaissance had among its fruits many that could be called authentically Christian. The devotion to truth for its own sake, whether in the study of the Bible or in the discoveries of natural science, and the reverence for Man as created in the image of God—these insights are as necessary as is the Reformation insistence upon the priority of God's grace, or the Catholic insistence upon the visible Church.

The contributions of the Reformation and the Renaissance to the American philosophy of the relation of the individual to society sum up the most im-portant contributions of religion to American life in the century and three-quarters of our colonial history.

The Puritan doctrine of determinism and of election, dividing men irrev-ocably into classes in terms of their destiny, ran athwart American social trends. It came out of a society in which a hierarchy of classes gave to every man his place. Seventeenth-century migrants to the colonies brought with them ideas of a hierarchy of classes to which life in England had conditioned them. But virtually none of the hereditary aristocracy crossed the sea, and the feudal arrangements that supported the gentry and nobility in the Old World gained only a small foothold in the American forest. Activism, required at first as a condition for survival and later continuing and developing as New England settlements achieved stability and prosperity, caused individuals to fall into natural divisions in accord with their merits. Colonial creativeness in building a civilization in a wilderness did not fit with the rigid determinism of the Cal-vinistic system or even with the covenant theology of Massachusetts Bay leaders. Perry Miller has described the intricate and sometimes tortuous rea-soning by which late seventeenth-century New England theologians adapted a tough-minded theology to the movement of life along Massachusetts Bay and in the Connecticut valley. But the prudential ethics of the Puritans, which called upon men to be diligent and to deny themselves, suited perfectly a social scene in which the tasks were measured by the extent of the forest to be felled and where the hands to perform them were pitifully few.

The ideas of the Society of Friends accorded more closely with the movement of American life. Centering in Pennsylvania, the Friends spread from Rhode Island to Carolina. The Quakers emphasized liberty and established freedom of worship. They believed that God's voice may be heard in the hearts of the great and of the lowly, the learned and the unlettered. Out of this faith came a doctrine of man. The fact that the All Highest is willing to speak to and through the humble person gives him dignity and suggests the worth of a man. Quite logically the Quaker ascribed dignity and worth to the stone-age Indian and to the laboring Negro slave. Men were needed in the colonies and were judged by their contributions to their communities. Colonials used only infrequently the harshest punishments of the Old World. The villages and the isolated clearings needed men so much that they could not bring themselves to execute thieves or to mutilate men guilty of crimes of violence. Though seventeenth-century Americans generally believed in witchcraft, its punishment, save for the tragedy at Salem, was light at a time when witch-burning had not yet disappeared from the Old World. Quaker doctrine reinforced and sanctified these attitudes growing up on the frontier.

The growing company that came after Roger Williams also developed articles of faith and a form of government both for church and state that supported in the eighteenth century the emerging American theory of the relation of the individual to society.

In the eighteenth century the Renaissance impulse made itself felt as interest in science appeared in the faculties of colleges founded to train young men for service "in church and civil state," in particular at Harvard and Yale. Outside collegiate institutions a Quaker, John Bartram, in Pennsylvania achieved a reputation for his work in botany that extended to England. Oxford gave Franklin an honorary degree for his work in electricity. Along with science the Enlightenment emphasized liberty and humanism, teaching that the Author of Nature had endowed man with reason to the end that he might discover the laws laid down by the Author of the Universe and by so doing make progress through the generations toward the ultimate goal of perfection. Thomas Jefferson, using the language of the Enlightenment, wrote the American theory of the relation of the individual to society into the Declaration of Independence. This document proclaimed the inalienable right of every man to life, liberty, and the pursuit of happiness, the last a Jeffersonian phrase that meant the right of every man to make of himself what he can and to be accepted for what he is. If the Reformation and the Renaissance both contributed to this philosophy, it should be added that two resolute Catholics from the Chesapeake country by setting their signatures to the Declaration risked their lives in a struggle of uncertain outcome.

The Declaration of Independence, with the doctrine of natural rights as its core, has become the conscience of America. Today, wherever discrimination appears and equality of opportunity is denied, the Declaration of Independence pricks lethargic and sometimes reluctant men toward humaneness and justice.

DEMOCRACY AND RELIGION

Winthrop S. Hudson, writing in 1953, has declared that a carefully defined equilibrium of church and state has been the great tradition of American religious and political life.

This great tradition, for such it is, should be viewed against its setting. In the final quarter of the eighteenth century Americans made decisions and spelled out accomplishments destined to bring a major turn to the course of history. They separated from the British Empire, thereby exorcising the institution of monarchy from their culture. Bristling language in the Constitution forbade an official aristocracy. The same Constitution created a political structure new to history, a federal republic resting on a popular foundation.

In this republic by the First Amendment they forbade any national religious establishment. In a relatively short time thereafter such preferential position as organized religion had in particular states disappeared. Freedom of religion, a pioneering American achievement, prevailed throughout the nation. In a day when, besides the family, the church and the state were the most important institutions in society, Americans made each the separate responsibility of the people. The event carried with it the implied affirmation that the state is not coterminous with society, as Burke, following the social contract theory, had affirmed. The generation of the Founding Fathers declared by their actions the conviction that life values are not subsumed wholly within either church or state but are divided between them. Americans at the turn of the nineteenth century made both political and ecclesiastical institutions dependent upon a free people.

Mr. Hudson has argued that pre-independence religious ideas and practices contributed much to the decision. Religious freedom existed in Rhode Island and wherever the Quakers extended their influence they urged it. The natural rights theory, accepted by eighteenth-century Puritanism, implied it. The humanism and tolerance of the Enlightenment, emphasizing the pursuit of truth for its own sake, supported it. The multiplicity of religious organizations at the time required it. In America both the Reformation and the Renaissance contributed to what has become its great tradition. The building of the federal republic and the establishment of the principle of pluralism, as between church and state, together represent a peculiarly American creative achievement, building on the earlier formulation of a new relation between the individual and society.

In the crowded decades of the first half of the new century the American version of expanding Western civilization produced a further achievement. Americans had required the years between 1607 and 1775, a period of more than a century and a half, to expand their settlements from the edge of the Atlantic to the Appalachians. In the following seventy-five years they pushed west to the Pacific coast. The speed and magnitude of this conquest of the wilderness brought major problems to a growing people.

The leaders of the generation that founded the Republic understood two inevitable implications of making the state the responsibility of the people: the necessity to maintain morals and the necessity that voters be literate and informed. Protestantism took up the former challenge. The rationalism of the Enlightenment fell into disrepute among Americans in the final decade of the eighteenth century as news of the bloody excesses of the French Revolution crossed the Atlantic. The Enlightenment had centered in France and had provided the background for the revolution. Tom Paine, who had once commanded a great audience, died early in the new century, after times and attitudes had changed, neglected and virtually ostracized. Timothy Dwight, president of Yale, looking across the ocean to the tumbrils of Paris, emphasized religion as the support of morals. Religion, said Dwight, exalts moral values and reminds the people of the moral law that comes from God. This grandson of Jonathan Edwards argued powerfully that because religion is the defender of morals it is the support of civilization, particularly in a self-governing republic where the people choose their rulers. If the people are lost in immorality, the state is lost and civilization is lost. "Where religion prevails . . . ," thundered Dwight in 1798, "a French Directory cannot govern, a nation cannot be made slaves, nor villains, nor atheists, nor beasts."

In spite of the fact that the churches had always to contend with religious indifference on the part of many, Dwight's affirmation concerning religion expressed an axiom of nineteenth-century social thought. The sanctuary with its steeple pointing skyward provided in every community a material symbol for a fundamental conviction. Though in the nineteenth century Protestantism divided into multiplying denominations differing in ritual, organization, or creed, it preserved a remarkable unity in the matter of ethics. Puritanism and Quakerism had brought a prudential ethics, a worldly asceticism, to seventeenth-century America. Benjamin Franklin, though he did not accept the Puritan creed, had spread over the colonies, through the character of Poor Richard, the substance of Puritan prudential ethics. In the early nineteenth century the variously active Protestant sects carried to the expanding communities of the frontier the austere code that emphasized work, sobriety, self-restraint, and the renouncing of frivolity. In an age when westward-moving Americans improvised governments in territory after territory Orthodox Protestantism gave to new communities the moral discipline that made self-government possible. In frontier communities disfigured by the chicane of the land speculator, by the brawls of the saloon, and by the violence of thieves and bandits, the churches, often planted as missions by the men of the East, provided centers to which pioneer families who valued decency and decorum could rally.

In both East and West in the first half of the nineteenth century, moreover, Protestantism ignited spirits such as those of Dorothea Dix, Lyman Beecher, and Theodore Weld. Humanitarian movements—the betterment of the lot of the mentally ill, the provision of opportunities for education for deaf children, the battle against alcoholism—attacked the evils of the day and sought to ameliorate the suffering and enlarge the opportunities of the unfortunate and the oppressed. This story, whose climax was the antislavery crusade, needs no retelling. The humanitarian urge did not, however, stem wholly from the Reformation. The humanism of the Renaissance also contributed. Religious liberals—William Ellery Channing, Theodore Parker, Ralph Waldo Emerson, Henry David Thoreau—attacked the evils of emerging industrialism and warred against chattel slavery. Abraham Lincoln, intellectual descendant of the Enlightenment, became the emancipator of the slave.

But religion had its failures in the first half of the nineteenth century along with its successes. Emerson drove over from Concord to Cambridge one day in 1837 to address the assembled members of the Harvard Phi Beta Kappa society. He spoke frankly, almost sharply, to the young men. "He who would be a man," said Emerson, "must be a non-conformist." James Fenimore Cooper had anticipated Concord's first citizen. The creator of Leatherstocking had told his fellow countrymen in an unpopular book in the 1830s that the arrogant assertion of majority opinion in the United States threatened American individualism. Let the majority be content, said Cooper in effect, when it has enacted its will into law. Americans should permit unpopular ideas and causes to have a chance. Cooper pointed to the easy resort to violence that characterized the period in both East and West. Turbulence marred the 1830s and 1840s. Mobs recruited from the Protestant majority attacked the Catholics, whose immigration increased after 1815. In the 1830s, when Garrisonian abolition of slavery was a dangerous radicalism, a mob dragged Garrison through Boston streets with a rope about his body and another mob in Illinois shot the abolitionist Lovejoy to death. One paid a price for nonconformity.

On June 10, 1844, a crowd gathered in the village of Carthage in Illinois and moved through the main street to the stone jail. Forcing their way in, they shot and killed two brothers. One of the two was called by his followers a prophet. These followers had already been harried from place to place by hostile communities about them. Now in Nauvoo on the Mississippi they gathered, after the lynching, what possessions they could salvage and began the long trek across the plains. In Utah an unflagging faith and the discipline of an authoritarian church enabled these latter-day refugees for conscience' sake to subdue and civilize a desert. Now in the twentieth century a million believers revere the memory of the martyred prophet. They still read in their sacred writings words they believe he had from God: "Fear not, little flock. The kingdom is yours until I come. Behold, I come quickly." The nineteenth-century persecutions of the Catholics and the Mormons are also part of American religious tradition.

The events of the age demonstrated that to make religion the responsibility of the people was to subject its practice to such hazards inherent in democracy as the tyranny of the majority illustrated above. The warnings of Emerson and Cooper, both in the liberal religious tradition, against the forces making in the 1830s for conformity provide a background for similar problems arising a little more than a century later.

The men of the 1830s and 1840s, however, did not despair of democracy. Rather, they moved decisively to develop it. In these decades they completed the process of the elimination of property qualifications from voting and in nearly all the states extended the suffrage to all white male citizens. In America the age of the common man began in Jackson's time.

An American democratic faith took form. Three doctrines of this faith made a kind of triad. (1) The age affirmed a fundamental law underlying society and making it possible, a law including the idea of natural rights and the religious moral code expressed in the ten commandments of the Old Testament and in the New Testament double-love commandment. Emerson insisted that morality is the very heart of the universe, for morality is the very essence of the immanent and all-pervading Over-Soul. (2) To this general idea of a fundamental law men added the doctrine of the free individual, responsible for his conduct before the law and equal with his fellows in the rights and obligations arising from it. (3) Finally the times fostered a doctrine of mission, the mission of America, born of a struggle for liberty, to stand before the world as a witness that common men can rule themselves without the aid of hereditary aristocrats or princes.

From the Reformation came the moral overtones of this democratic faith; from the Renaissance its emphasis on liberty and on the ability of man. Confidence in progress, the advance to better things, gave a certain *élan* to this faith of the early nineteenth century. Americans assumed that, one day, life-giving democracy would spread over the world. But they assumed also that it would go in partnership with Christianity. The American democratic faith matured in a period when American Christians, particularly in the older states, turned their thoughts outward and established missions on distant and little-known continents. An oration delivered in Kentucky on July 4, 1843, suggests the blending of Christian and democratic hope characteristic of the time. "Christianity, rational philosophy, and constitutional liberty," said George Robertson of the Kentucky bench, "like an ocean of light are rolling their resistless tide over the earth."

EDUCATION FOSTERED BY CHURCH AND STATE

At home, meanwhile, Americans came to grips with another problem that must be solved if free government was to endure. James Madison had once warned that, if popular government were not to be the prelude to a farce or a tragedy, it must rest on an educated citizenry. The citizens of the Republic, responsible in the Great Tradition for both church and state, gave thought to education.

The tradition of higher education ran back to Harvard in the early seventeenth century. The religious drive of the Reformation had called the first American colleges into being. But, as has already been noted, the attitudes and the goals of the Renaissance made their impress soon after the eighteenth century opened. At the end of that century Timothy Dwight, president of Yale, sent a young man, Benjamin Silliman, to Britain to master the natural science of the time and to return to establish it at New Haven.

In the nineteenth century, though universities founded by the states appeared, Americans used organized religion to scatter colleges over the West and South. Too often the creation of these institutions reflected the urge of demoninational rivalry. But the higher motive was to bring the light of knowledge to the expanding communities of a simple agricultural-commercial civilization, in the conviction that the treasures of learning ennoble life as does the inspiration of faith. In these independent colleges the chapel bell called faculty and students to prayers before they turned to Euclid or to Livy. Williams College in western Massachusetts reflected the common primacy of religion in the partnership. "What is education," wrote President Mark Hopkins to one of his trustees in 1851, "if it does not lead the mind to its true good? How much better to be a ploughboy and a Christian, than to be a vicious, sensual, conceited collegian!"

At the same time the generation that used organized religion for the founding of most of the institutions of higher learning chose the political state as the instrument for the establishment of the public school. In an age when in the Old World social class determined the nature and even the possibility of education for the individual, Americans, guided by their democratic faith, formulated the goal of education for all. They made education the instrument for giving reality to the ideal of equality of opportunity. Taking account of the magnitude of the problem of providing schooling for the children of a people spreading swiftly over a country as large as Europe, they concluded that their voluntary religious associations were inadequate to the task. The basic assumptions of the Judeo-Christian tradition embedded in the democratic faith of the time provided the background for the multiplying schools. The moral precepts in the ubiquitous schoolbooks of Noah Webster and McGuffey carried to the desks of the pupils the spirit and outlook of the age.

Three men associated with the tragedy of the Civil War suggest in their lives that spirit and that outlook. On July 4, 1861, the Congress assembled at the call of President Lincoln. The day marked the eighty-fifth anniversary of the Declaration of Independence. Sumter had fallen and war had blazed in the border states. The President addressed to the Congress a message setting forth his policy for the preservation of the Union. "And having chosen our course without guile and with pure purpose," concluded Lincoln, "let us renew our trust in God, and go forward without fear, and with manly hearts."

Across the battle lines two men, bound together in close association, emerged to personify the Confederate will to independence. Robert E. Lee, burdened with heavy responsibility, prayed frankly for victory and did not permit failure to shake his faith. "I had taken every precaution," he remarked of an operation in Virginia, "to ensure success and had counted on it. But the Ruler of the Universe willed it otherwise and sent a storm to disconcert a well-laid plan and to destroy my hopes." Dependence upon a Power greater than man gave Lee the poise that enabled him to remain the leader of his people after his army and his nation had crumbled into dust. Stonewall Jackson, Lee's great lieutenant, held fast to the stern faith of the Puritans. He made duty his religion. On an active campaign and in independent command, Jackson made his way one evening to the bivouac of his old brigade to attend a prayer meeting. His youngest staff officer went with him and later left a record of the scene. "The camp was there. Bowed heads, bent knees, hats off, silence! Stonewall Jackson was kneeling to the Lord of Hosts in prayer for his people. Not a sound disturbed his voice as it ascended to heaven in their behalf. . . . When he left, a line of soldiers followed him in escort to the edge of the camp."

The Second Inaugural—"With malice toward none, with charity for all, with firmness in the right as God gives us to see the right"—one of the finest expressions of religious faith and purpose in our literature, stood out in the waning conflict and marked the end of an age. Whatever else may be said about the old religion—and its shortcomings were many—pride was not its besetting sin. Jackson, Lee, and Lincoln looked up humbly toward their God.

THE ACCELERATION OF CULTURAL CHANGE

I have dealt with origins. In our day when an American colossus musters vast power, Thoreau's building a hut on Walden Pond seems long ago, as does the simple life of most Americans of that time—though not simple enough for him. We had vigor then as a people. Our present power did not just happen. It was developing with each generation. It represents the creativeness of Western civilization. Two major wars slowed and hampered the creativeness of Europe. The United States, spared the invader's trail of wreckage, carried on with accelerating speed.

No less than five revolutions have intervened between Lincoln's day and our own. (1) Economic enterprise has created a mechanized industrial civilization of surpassing productive capacity. (2) Between the Civil War and World War I a river of immigrants, principally from Europe, modified the ethnic character of our people. (3) Industrialization brought urbanization and immigrants swelled the population of the metropolitan centers. (4) Faced with the insecurities for the individual rising from a complex and highly mechanized economy, Americans were driven to action by the disaster of the depression, magnified the political state, and learned to use big government for purposes of social engineering. (5) Meanwhile out of the college of Mark Hopkins' day Americans had created the modern university, the best examples of which have taken their places beside those ancient centers of learning that have given Western civilization much of its quality and character.

New Learning

Of the five great cultural changes since Appomattox the emergence of the university and the laboratory was basic. Civilization rests on a body of knowledge. The prime reason for the differences between the New England of Jonathan Edwards and that of our own day may be found in the differences in the sum of knowledge available for men to draw on to meet the needs of life. The growth of the natural sciences in Europe and in the United States made possible the evolving technology that released the energy and created the machines of a mechanized age.

As Americans in 1865 turned away from their four years' preoccupation with fratricidal war, they found themselves facing a new and strange cosmos. The natural philosophy of Benjamin Silliman's day had supplemented rather than conflicted with religious ideas, though geology had stirred apprehensions among those who interpreted the Scriptures literally. Darwin, coming into American consciousness principally after the Civil War, had proposed a revolutionary alteration in the accepted concept of the origin of man. For many Americans the old vision of a friendly universe presided over by a deity who had created man a little lower than the angels and was mindful of the fall of the sparrow in the field began to dissolve. Mark Twain, casting off the Calvinism with which his childhood had been burdened, tried to reconcile his natural generosity and humanity with a dour philosophy that man comes out of nature and that a remorseless chain of cause and effect drives nature on—no one knows whither or why. He failed to make the reconciliation, but the philosophy seized and held him, bringing black pessimism to his later years. Thousands of Twain's contemporaries, sensing the threat of the new, developing science to old intellectual securities, held fast desperately to familiar certitudes. In America in the second half of the nineteenth century the Renaissance and the Reformation clashed. The story of the beginning of Cornell University illuminates the meaning of what was happening.

In 1867 Ezra Cornell and Andrew D. White founded the university that overlooks Lake Cayuga. "Our purpose," said White later, "was to establish an institution for advanced instruction and research, in which science, pure and applied, should have an equal place with literature. . . . We had specially determined that the institution should be under the control of no political party and of no single religious sect. . . . It certainly never entered into the mind of either of us that we were doing anything irreligious or unChristian. . . . As I look back across the intervening years, I know not whether to be more astonished or amused at our simplicity. Opposition began at once. In the Legislature it confronted us at every turn, and it was soon in full blaze throughout the State—from the good Protestant bishop who proclaimed that all professors should be in holy orders, since the Church alone was given the command, 'Go teach all nations,' to the zealous priest who published the charge that Goldwin Smith—a profoundly Christian scholar—had come to Cornell (from England) to inculcate infidelity . . ." White fought back. In an address at Cooper Institute a little later he fired the first gun of a long campaign. "In all history," declared the Cornell president, "interference with science in the name of religion, no matter how conscientious such interference may have been, has resulted in the direst evils both to religion and science . . . and all untrammeled scientific investigation, no matter how dangerous to religion some of its stages have seemed to be, has invariably resulted in the highest good for both religion and science."

Long before Cornell was founded, the state university had appeared, a development that gained new impetus with the passage of the Morrill Land Grant Act in 1862. New universities established after the middle of the nineteenth century on foundations that were independent of the state were, for the most part, free from ecclesiastical control. Church-connected older universities that had not already done so tended to move toward a similar freedom. Many of the smaller liberal arts colleges that grew out of the religious drives of the nineteenth century, however, held fast to old and basic ties.

If orthodox Protestantism had its ethical code, so also did scholarship. White embarked upon a crusade to make the citizens of New York State understand the meaning and significance of the principles that govern scholarship. The scholar's code follows: To break out from the confines of ignorance into the light of new knowledge, the investigator must be free to follow the trail toward enlightenment wherever it may lead. He must be honest and sometimes courageous in recording and reporting what he finds while on his search. If he falsifies, if he warps his report to creed or party line, he makes no addition to knowledge; he only wastes his time. He must make use of the clues and knowledge gleaned by other men who took the trail before him. He must trust them and must, in turn, be worthy of the trust of his contemporaries and successors for the conquest of new knowledge is a cooperative undertaking. In order to save the truth he comes to comprehend and to profit by it the investigator must give it away, following the example of those who have gone before him.

This code, the expression of the Renaissance impulse, is absolute. The totalitarian chieftain may press his men of science into the service of the state; but, if he would have them add to the sum of knowledge, he must mark out and protect an area in which they may be intellectually free. The code is the fundamental law of creative intellectual life. It undergirds the technological civilization in which we live. It became ideal and guide to the companies of scholars comprised by the rising universities. No element in the code denied the ethics or the faith of religion. Scholars labored in a particular and limited field in the quest for truth. But within that field they insisted upon the primacy of the principles upon which they founded their work.

New Theology

After Appomattox one wing of Protestantism held fast to traditional positions as conflicts arose out of science and out of historical investigation; another attempted to understand the significance, for the faith, of the emerging body of knowledge. These latter men in the final decades of the nineteenth century, accepting the insights of the Renaissance, tried to bring them into the service of the Reformation. They attempted the formulation of a "new theology." Their ideal was essentially the same as that announced in 1953 by an American Catholic scholar, discussing possible standards and guides for action for his church. "Another standard for Catholic life and education," wrote Julian Pleasants, "is the revelation of God, not only Revelation with a capital 'R' but revelation with a small 'r': the revelation of the Artist which we find in His Art, the revelation of the Lawmaker which we find in His laws, the revelation of the Planner's intentions which we find in the way He has made things."

The Protestant creators of the New Theology fell short of greatness. They were sometimes bewildered, as were their contemporaries, including the growing company of scholars in the universities, by the surge and drive of American life as our people hurried into the unfamiliar age of power and technology. Those who shaped and those who accepted the New Theology have been charged with accepting the world. They did, if Lyman Abbott's forceful affirmation that religion must not interfere with the freedom of the investigator is called surrender to the world. They have been called complacent acceptors of the *status quo*. Yet in their day the social gospel, successor to the humanitarianism of antebellum days, took form to stir the consciences of Christians to the end that sufferers from the evils of unregulated capitalism and a burgeoning urbanism be given aid and protection. If Washington Gladden and Walter Rauschenbusch stood first among the Protestants who faced and sought to deal with the hard facts of their time, they led a considerable muster.

The men of the New Theology (to become liberal Protestantism or Modernism) shared the mind and outlook of their age. The generation that saw the century turn took progress for granted. The conquest of "yellow jack" in Cuba and the escape of earth-bound man into the air at Kitty Hawk stretched the imaginations of those who looked to the future. Historians call the period the Progressive Era because "progress" became its key word. Looking backward the men of the time saw that from its beginning America had moved forward. Evils had been imported or had arisen, with chattel slavery the blackest of all. Americans had struck slavery down. They would strike down the evils of a new day. The social criticisms in the social gospel did not conflict with the belief that the nation marched toward better things. Criticism implemented progress. Protestant men and women shared in the élan of a swiftly moving time. The Student Volunteer Movement, originating on the

eve of the Progressive Era, announced a hope and goal that could only have
been accepted in such a time of hope and confidence, namely "the evangeliza-
tion of the world of this generation." Christian doctors and teachers as well
as preachers set out in significant numbers to make the vision a reality.

Granted that, when judged by the wisdom of hindsight, the Americans
of the period, both those who prized religion and those who were indifferent,
were naïve. At least, when judged by the light they possessed, they achieved
pertinent criticism, initiated significant reforms, and cultivated a generous
sympathy. There existed a relationship, not yet fully explored, between the
concern of the social gospel and the reform or "progressive movement" in
political life. If the era ended in disaster, tragedy came because Europe col-
lapsed into war. The true twentieth century, the century of violence and
revolution, began with a shot fired at Sarajevo. Three years later Americans
in 1917, still not comprehending, still generous, believed the phrases of
President Wilson to be genuine possibilities for the future: make the world
safe for democracy, the war to end war. American Protestantism, like other
churches, because their people were Americans conditioned by their age, supported the Great Crusade.

Americans were closer to Europe in 1914 than they had been in Emerson's
day, though that fact had little to do with their entry into the war. Immigrants had completed the ethnic revolution that had begun with the close of
the Napoleonic Wars. New men and women spoke strange languages in
American streets and brought with them memories of peasant villages or
of crowded cities from places as far away as Sicily, Greece, Armenia, and
the Ukraine. They brought with them Old World religions: Roman Catholicism, holding fast to the essential doctrines of the Medieval Church; the Eastern Orthodox communion; Judaism, looking to Abraham and to Moses for
inspiration. Different religions provided consolation and a cultural focus for
different groups of impoverished and confused strangers trying to find their
places in a hustling civilization.

Because Irishmen came early and in large numbers they assumed leadership among the Roman Catholics. But, where in time Poles, Italians, and
French Canadians concentrated in sufficient numbers, the priest who spoke
their tongue and the sanctuary where they worshipped helped them to find
their own identity as a group of similar people and by so doing eased for
them the hard transition from Old World living to the strange ways of the
New. The rabbi and the synagogue, the Roman Catholic priest and his church,
and the sanctuaries of the Orthodox church performed similar services for
their congregations. Immigration brought the newer minorities into being
and these newer Americans found, with relatively few exceptions, fundamental
life values in religion. An older minority, the Negro who had been in
America since 1619, now freed from chattel slavery, found in his own
Protestant churches places of refuge where his spirit could be free and where
his prayers and songs could express without restraint his sentiments, his long-

ings, and his faith: "Nobody Knows the Trouble I've Seen," "Were You There When They Crucified My Lord?," "Little Boy, How Old Are You?" Outside their churches, in the phrase of Paul Lawrence Dunbar, they wore the mask.

RELIGION IN MODERN CULTURE

"Religion is not in a robust state of health in modern civilization," declared Reinhold Niebuhr in 1927. "Vast multitudes, particularly in industrial and urban centers, live without seeking its sanctions for their actions and die without claiming its comforts in their extremities. The sickness of faith in our day may be the senility which precedes death; on the other hand, it may be a specific malady which thought and time can cure. If history is slow to destroy that which has become useless, it may be as patient and persistent in reviving what is useful but seems dead."

Niebuhr was not alone in his pessimism. Hornell Hart wrote the report on Attitudes in *Recent Social Trends,* a study initiated by President Hoover and published in 1933. Some headings in the report indicate the nature of the material that Hart's investigation turned up: "Decline in the Proportion of Books on Religion," "Decline in the Proportion of Articles on Religion," "The Bible Receives Less than Half the Attention It Had Twenty-Five Years Ago," "Declining Approval of Organized Christianity." The report, however, was not wholly negative. "While traditional Christianity," said Hart, "has been sinking to a new low point in public interest and esteem . . . certain religious topics and concepts have in recent years reached new high levels of attention. . . . In general it may be said that the topics which have shown smallest losses of attention, or which have shown net gains, have been related to aspects not in direct conflict with science and not enmeshed in ecclesiasticism, but based on personal experience and involving applications of the 'social gospel' to economic problems."

Certain trends in the times provide a background for the religious situation reported. Disillusionment came to Americans in the 1920s. The peace did not make the world safe for democracy. The war to end war seemed to have done little more than reorient the old power struggle among the nations. The fine idealism of 1917–18 seemed in retrospect romantic dreaming. Churchmen who in 1917 had thought of themselves as participating in and sanctifying a great crusade began to suspect that they had been dupes. In company with Harry Emerson Fosdick many Protestant ministers determined that never again would they support the devilish institution of war. Among the educated public idealism in many circles fell into disrepute, interesting primarily as reflecting the mental stature of well-intentioned but soft-headed "do-gooders."

At the same time, the upsurge of Fundamentalism with its militant anti-intellectualism astounded the educated citizenry that thought the questions raised by Darwin three-quarters of a century before had largely been settled. Moreover, in its efforts to meet the Fundamentalist attack, Modernism seemed to lack assurance and power. The year of the Dayton trial extravaganza saw the Ku Klux Klan reach its peak. Two years later the execution of Sacco and Vanzetti climaxed a postwar chapter of fear and of hostility toward the radical foreigner who threatened the basic institutions of our country. The 1920s was the decade of isolationism. It was the decade of Lewis, Fitzgerald, Dreiser, Mencken, and the emerging Hemingway. It was the decade of revolutions brought about by the mass acceptance of the motor car and the radio.

The fourteen Anglicans who reported to the Archbishop of Canterbury in 1947 offered a comment that has pertinence to the American scene in the 1920s: "But these Renaissance insights [the devotion to truth for its own sake, whether in the study of the Bible or in the discoveries of science, and the reverence for man as created in the image of God] have, through their isolation from other insights into man's relation to God, led the way to some of the tragedies of modern secularism and godlessness. . . . The belief that man is created in God's image can turn into a belief in man as man. . . . The belief that there is a real connection between the Christian faith on the one hand, and culture, education, social betterment, and human emancipation on the other, can degenerate into the belief that God's kingdom is wholly within history, and may be identified with human progress."

The naturalism that Mark Twain had accepted flourished in the literature and the literary criticism of the 1920s and 1930s. Robert Frost, with a wry smile, commented on the age:

> Our worship, humor, conscientiousness
> Went long since to the dogs under the table.
> And served us right for having instituted
> Downward comparisons. As long on earth
> As downward comparisons were stoutly upward
> With gods and angels, we were men at least,
> But little lower than the gods and angels.
> But once comparisons were yielded downward,
> Once we began to see our images
> Reflected in the mud and even dust,
> 'Twas disillusion upon disillusion.
> We were lost piecemeal to the animals,
> Like people thrown out to delay the wolves.
> Nothing but fallibility was left us . . .

The poet from north of Boston was a little hard on the age. Naturalism in America in the 1920s and again in the 1930s, as it expressed itself in literature and in legal and political theory, never lost sight of the worth of man or the importance of striving for a better life. The swiftly growing social sciences, resting on naturalist assumptions, sought to add to the sum of knowledge concerning man and society to the end that man might meet more intelligently the conditions of life. With few exceptions naturalism in the United States was associated with meliorism. In America no party leader or head of state arose, as in Germany, to propose and attempt a literal and ruthless application of the concept of the survival of the fittest through the mass extermination of unwanted populations. In America the life of reason had developed a world view with a humanistic core, a view and outlook that occupied a place beside conventional religion and that generated aspiration and stimulated loyalty to human values.

Niebuhr in 1927 concluded his estimate of the plight of religion in the United States as of that year: "A psychology of defeat," he commented, "of which both fundamentalism and modernism are symptoms has gripped the forces of religion. . . . To retreat from untenable positions is no doubt a necessary step in preparation for new advances; but this necessary strategy has not been accompanied by the kind of spiritual vigor which would promise ultimate victory. The general tendencies toward secularization of life have been consistent enough to prompt its foes to predict religion's ultimate extinction as a major interest of mankind and to tempt even friendly observers to regard its future with grave apprehension."

But the century of revolution and violence that began with World War I came to a climax in what has been called an "Age of Anxiety." Anxiety transformed the place of religion in American culture. The tumultuous events of the 1940s provided cumulative illustration of the old truism that knowledge is power. It was power indeed when it created the atom bomb. But there were other manifestations. "Science," remarked Lawrence Dennis in 1940, "has given the experts more skill, knowledge, and instruments for manipulating the masses than the medicine men and witch doctors of old ever commanded." Twentieth-century men faced the paradox that, if addition to the sum of knowledge can be achieved only through obedience to an absolute ethical code, the knowledge thus won and the power it gives are neutral and may be used for good or evil ends. The paradox was compounded, moreover, by the fact that power bred fear; fear required secrecy as a divided world moved into an armaments race; and secrecy, compelled by the needs of national survival, set barriers across that free interchange of discoveries that is the lifeblood of science. Perhaps the pursuit of knowledge had by its very triumphs planted the seeds of decay in the heart of scientific civilization.

Power won by reason had, moreover, created a situation that compelled mid-twentieth-century man, the American included, to face the possibility of either suffering or inflicting mass destruction. Looking back on their recent history, Americans, while they recognized the purpose and the result of saving lives of thousands of American soldiers set for the landing on the mainland of Japan in 1945, noted that it is part of the record of history that the greatest democracy in the world pioneered in the creation and the use of the most terrible weapon known to man. In 1950, after the President had announced the decision to push ahead with the creation of an H-bomb, twelve nuclear physicists including Hans A. Bethe, formerly Director of Theoretical Physics at the Los Alamos Laboratories, proposed that the United States make a solemn pledge not to be the first to use the prospective weapon. "We believe," said the twelve, "that no nation has the right to use such a bomb, no matter how righteous its cause. This bomb is no longer a weapon of war but a means of extermination of whole populations. Its use would be a betrayal of all standards of morality and of Christian civilization itself."

Americans in the midcentury have found themselves caught in a cruel dilemma. They faced an implacable foe, armed also with the absolute weapon, who challenged not only their nation but their democratic and religious faith. To meet his threat necessity compelled them to contemplate the possible use of a weapon of horror beyond the capacity of the imagination to encompass. To curb and discipline power, therefore, became the first need of the age. Faced with this need, Americans, as never before in their history, turned to explore the realm of the spirit for help and hope. Perhaps the need to hold power in check was merely a corollary to another need. Some thought so.

"The perils that confront man today," remarked Edmund Sinnott, biologist, in 1953, "come from the fundamental difference between his spiritual insight and his rational power in the deep problems he has to face. This difference is dramatized by the divergent attitudes of those two great disciplines, science and religion, with which he tries to comprehend the universe. . . . We should not regret these differences between the discipline of reason and of spirit but rather rejoice in them. They are two halves that make man whole. From tension between them character is born. Perhaps in us is being fought a skirmish in the great battle of the universe. Man, half ape and half angel, half matter and half spirit, has a place within each world. Herein lies his glory, his tragedy, and the possibility for him of tremendous things."

Religion and General Education

F. Ernest Johnson
Professor Emeritus of Education
Teachers College, Columbia University

This statement deals only with questions of educational policy regarding religion that arise out of cultural and political factors in our national life. It does not treat questions of educational or religious philosophy or questions of educational method which do not involve issues of general policy, although many such questions may well come within the range of our discussion.

Our chief task in this conference is to wrestle with a dilemma that arises out of the cultural and political history of the United States. That is to say, we are "a religious people" and religion is too much a part of our national life to be ignored in general education—which in this country is mainly a public function; yet we are citizens of a state that is devoted to the principle of religious liberty and to the policy of separation of church and state, as defined by the United States Supreme Court. A sound educational policy, it seems clear, must take account of both these aspects of the national situation. This defines our central problem.

The two basic statements prepared for this conference deal, respectively, with these two factors, which may be more briefly expressed thus: religion as part of the cultural heritage, and separation of church and state—again, as judicially defined—as a matter of basic public policy. From the two we may reasonably draw the inference that religion in America—quite apart from particular ecclesiastical pressures, from whatever sources—is continually seeking expression through social and political as well as personal channels, and that the courts are continually, but inconclusively, trying to set a proper and durable boundary between the spheres of religion and government.

The inconclusiveness just referred to is evidenced by the sharp contrast between recent decisions of the United States Supreme Court bearing on this subject, and also by the wide differences between the relevant laws, court decisions, and authorized practices in the several states. It is possible that policies in this controversial area will be determined in future less by courts and legislatures than by efforts on the part of such persons as are gathered here to work out viable solutions of the problem in democratic fashion with due regard to regional differences and distinctive community patterns with respect to religion. In that event the role of the courts in relation to this subject may be less prescriptive and more corrective—that is, concerned less with policy making and more specifically directed to the redress of substantive violations of religious liberty.

The problem as stated above in terms of public policy comes to sharpest focus at the secondary education level, and is least serious at the college level. For it is in the secondary school that students, when relatively immature, first encounter the higher intellectual disciplines and are confronted by controversial issues in contemporary society, of which religion affords many. The question is insistently raised whether it is proper in a secular school to expose students to the cross-currents of religious opinion and belief, with attendant possibilities of religious indoctrination.

At the college level, on the other hand, students are assumed to be more mature. Moreover, college students are for the most part temporarily removed from the influence of home and the home church; consequently even a state institution of higher education finds itself obliged to have regard to religious care and counseling, even apart from the requirements of a fully rounded educational program. Thus in public higher education the line between church and state tends to be blurred. Specifically, it does not appear that public higher education ever took as applicable to itself the sweeping ban imposed by the U. S. Supreme Court in *Everson* and again in *McCollum* against aid by the state to "all religions." (The ban against aid to *one* religion had been previously recognized; what was novel in the definition was the prohibition of aid even though given to *all* religions.) The many departments of religion in state universities and the extensive cooperation between their administrations and the various churches represented on the campus constitute invaluable "aid" to religious bodies of an indirect sort. Whether or not the Supreme Court intended in those now famous words to lay down a rule of unlimited application, the bearing of its ruling on higher education seems to have aroused little more than academic interest.

At the elementary level the issues arising in the public school in connection with our topic have to do chiefly with religious exercises and observances rather than with religious instruction. Relatively little attention has been given to this phase of the matter in the literature of the subject, which is concerned more with instructional matters. In fact, however, some very vexing problems have arisen over participation by young children in religious exercises, particularly those associated with religious festivals whose significance and validity a portion of the community did not recognize.

There follow in bare outline the major positions currently defended as possible solutions of the central problem of educational policy that confronts us.

1. Many persons hold that the American people, overwhelmingly theistic in belief, should see to it that their schools inculcate in children and youth belief in God and should encourage the practice of religion. They consider that the Federal and state constitutions inhibit only "sectarian" teaching and observances, and they are disposed to regard as nonsectarian whatever a vast majority of the community accepts. Probably most of those who take this view of the matter would not advocate rigid religious indoctrination in the public schools, but they would set the educational stage, so to speak, very definitely to secure a religious outcome.

2. At the opposite end of the opinion scale are those who take the figure of the "wall of separation" with virtual literalness. They regard all religious teaching—which they may or may not approve in home and church—as *sectarian* in that an appreciable part of the community does not accept it. (This position is often called "secularist," but that term is so variously used that it has led to confusion. If it may be legitimately applied in this context it must be differentiated from all terms signifying atheism, agnosticism, naturalism, since it denotes not a negation of religion, nor any particular philosophy, but the *separation* of religion from education under public auspices. That is to say, it holds that religion has no essential relevance to public education. It is true, however, that this view is held by many who deny the relevance of religion to practical affairs in general. This view, which makes the secular realm self-sufficient and independent of religious sanctions—which are thus left with an exclusively other-worldly reference, if any—is probably the commonest form of secularism in our time. It is often found within the churches.) For the most part, probably, those who take this position are not hostile to religion, and some of them are religious leaders.

It should be said that among those who take a rigidly negative position on this subject are many who regret the exclusion of all religious subject matter from the school curriculum but who fear an "entering wedge" of sectarianism.

3. In between the two positions sketched above—and probably held by not a few persons who are ordinarily thought of as falling into one of those categories—is the advocacy of the "objective" but respectful and sympathetic study of religion in connection with the various disciplines in which religious subject matter normally appears—literature, the arts, the social studies, and so on. Those who support this proposal feel that a program of general education which neglects religion as a part of the culture is seriously deficient. (This position has been taken by the Educational Policies Commission in *Moral and Spiritual Values in the Public Schools,* and by the Committee on Religion and Education of the American Council on Education in *The Relation of Religion to Public Education—the Basic Principles.*) The crux of this proposal seems to be the matter of adequacy of teacher preparation, which is the responsibility of the teachers colleges and the colleges of liberal arts. A question of educational theory is sometimes raised on the ground that such objective study, or "teaching about," is not real education; that participation is

indispensable to learning. This raises, of course, a question concerning a large part of the secondary school curriculum where "participation" in what is studied is impossible and often undesirable but where knowledge and understanding are essential.

4. A fourth position calls for a return to religious day schools, parochial or other. Some church bodies, as is well known, regard secular education as intrinsically defective. Renewed interest in religious schools is part of the contemporary educational scene. Probably many Protestants, though by no means all, who take this view of the matter would feel differently about it if the goal envisaged under the third position discussed above could be successfully achieved. It should be noted that many who believe strongly in the public schools would stoutly oppose any restriction upon parochial or other religious schools, not only on the ground of religious liberty, but also because of distrust of a state monopoly of education.

5. The released-time movement is in reality an attempt to solve our problem by supplementing and extending, with school cooperation, the religious educational efforts of the churches that are carried on outside school hours, chiefly on Sunday. Released-time, or "weekday," religious education presupposes the secular school and undertakes to compensate its limitations. Approval or disapproval of the program does not affect the validity of arguments for changes in the program of the school itself, though adoption of released time has perhaps reduced the urgency of such proposals.

6. There remains a rather ill-defined view of public education which exalts the values of democracy and the virtues of community to the level of what may be called a secular faith. In its extreme form this is of course in striking opposition to all traditional religion. On the other hand, there probably are members of all faiths who see in democracy and in community a spiritual quality that may rise to the level of what is sometimes called "high religion." A question arises whether between a secular faith that repudiates classical Christianity and Judaism, on the one hand, and, on the other, a rigid orthodoxy that finds no religious values in secular life there is a tenable position that makes secular education itself one aspect of an inclusive experience of religious education.

In conclusion, we should note that cutting across these categories are issues that press for solution, issues that can perhaps be best presented in question form:

1. How can we reconcile the principle of local, democratic control of public education, at all levels, with religious liberty as it has been interpreted by the courts? Many of our citizens complain that freedom from what individuals here and there regard as an invasion of their liberties actually restricts the freedom of the community as a whole. In a relatively homogeneous, strongly religious community how can this conflict be resolved?

2. Granted that religious indoctrination should be excluded from tax-supported schools, is a strongly religious community justified in demanding

that some symbols of its faith be given a place in the school program—in the form of prayers, hymns, pageantry, or other ritualistic expression? To put it differently, at what point does a group ritual, participation in which is never coerced, become illegitimate pressure upon the members of any minority group?

3. If we assume with the Educational Policies Commission (*Moral and Spiritual Values in the Public Schools*) that religious sanctions may not be authoritatively invoked in the public school, what limit should be imposed, in this connection, upon the counseling process where every effort is made to enter intimately and sympathetically into the experience of the pupil, and where religious sanctions are indigenous in his family life? (A Roman Catholic public school teacher told me that in counseling a Lutheran child she would without hesitation appeal to the religious sanctions recognized in his family. Is this a valid position?)

Constitutions, Churches, and Schools

Arthur E. Sutherland
Professor of Law, Harvard University

The desire for public education interacting with the widespread religious impulse in the United States presents one of the many contradictions of policy in our government and law. We wish to think that we have a federal government of limited powers; but we also wish to require our central authority to repress whatever practices in a minority of states conflict with the desires of the majority of the forty-eight. We wish to have the police restricted within limits of decency in their treatment of citizens; but we wish to have criminals swiftly detected and punished. We wish to have untrammeled expression, but we do not wish to be offended by objectionable books. In a similar way, we like to assure ourselves that we are devoted to the separation of church and state, while at the same time large numbers of people among us feel that religion is fundamental in life, and that some religious expression in school is wholesome.

Bible reading and prayer to start the school day; the observance in school of such festivals as Christmas and Thanksgiving; the practice of "released time" for religious education—all occur in many public schools, and demonstrate that, in the nation rather generally, the public school pupil and religious manifestations are in frequent contact. Add tax exemption of church schools, public transportation for the students of religious as well as public schools; public provision of school lunches for parochial and public students alike; free text-books for parochial students with others; supervision of curricula by public school authorities in non-public and public institutions alike; compulsion by the truant officer of attendance at school which can be satisfied by attending a religiously maintained institution. The chaplains at West Point and Annapolis have long been a feature of those institutions. Various reform schools to which young people are sent whether they like it or not are provided with clergy of various faiths.

In all of these examples, and others which may be found in a quick run through statute books, it is apparent that in practice dissociation of public educational functions and religious observances is far from complete, and that public education and religious instruction are in some degree intermingled. Long custom has made many such minor subventions unnoticeable. The pervasiveness of this commingling, its persistence from generation to generation, suggest approval by large segments of the public.

Nevertheless our Federal and state constitutions contain provisions requiring, by one formula or another, the separation of church and state. The relevant provisions of the Federal Constitution appear in parts of the First and Fourteenth Amendments.

Amendment I: Congress shall make no law respecting an establishment of religion, or prohibiting the free exercise thereof; . . .

Amendment XIV: . . . No State shall make or enforce any law which shall abridge the privileges or immunities of citizens of the United States; nor shall any State deprive any person of life, liberty, or property, without due process of law; nor deny to any person within its jurisdiction the equal protection of the laws.

State constitutional clauses concerning the separation of church and state are multiform.[1] Common provisions guarantee free exercise of religion; forbid compulsory support, appropriation of public funds or preference for any sect; and prohibit religious tests for holding public office.

The early enactment and continuous maintenance of such state constitutional inhibitions, along with some small measure of religious admixture in the public school systems, indicate that both policies have wide approval. The preambles of most state constitutions give thanks to God. Either we wish, with complacent inconsistency, to permit governmental practice to depart from constitutional principle, or else we suppose that the theory of dissociated church and state does not conflict with comparatively minor instances of public cooperation in religious observances.

When considering religion in the schools it is always necessary to remember that "separation of church and state" is not a severance of two abstractions. Like other constitutional and legal questions it involves human beings with conflicting aspirations and prejudices. Although the fury of sectarian controversy seems to have cooled since the seventeenth century, religious loyalties and rivalries still retain surprising force. When these combine with affection for children and with the natural desire to have them follow in their parents' faith and footsteps, intervention of church in school can develop intense feeling.

DIFFICULTIES IN JUDICIAL INTERVENTION

Courts, Federal and state, are the ultimate arbiters of the bitterest of such differences. To evaluate the judicial role, one must keep in mind various characteristics of judicial behavior and limitations on judges' intervention.

Constitutional Wrongs without Judicial Remedies

Constitutional wrong and the availability of a judicial remedy do not always coincide. A full-scale discussion of the philosophical question whether without a remedy any right exists is not appropriate here. In 1922 Mr. Justice Holmes, in a famous opinion, spoke of such remediless rights as "ghosts that are seen in the law, but are elusive to the grasp."[2] However this may be, there are limits to the willingness of the judiciary of state and nation to intervene in human affairs, including disputes over religious activities in the schools. Our courts do not undertake to decide questions of abstract principle; their task is settlement of controversies between men. A justiciable controversy exists only when someone is hurt. It arises not simply because a man disagrees with some public policy, but because public action does him damage substantial enough to move a court to consider its redress. Thus a citizen may feel that, in our country, between church and state rises a constitutional wall of separation breached (in vivid and familiar metaphor) by any manifestation of religion in public education. But the courts have demonstrated that they will listen to his complaint of such a breach only when it does him some specific hurt.

In cases involving religion and the schools this requirement of jurisdictional hurt has been satisfied in two ways. Where a school child is offended in his religious belief by the application of public school authority, his parents, speaking on his behalf, have been allowed to assert that his liberty has been infringed. This is a familiar function of our judiciary; a number of varieties of intellectual, political, and religious activity are judicially shielded from undue restriction by nation or state.

A difficulty arises when the question at issue is not the restriction of some person's religious expression or observance, but the existence of some governmentally-sponsored religious manifestation, which by its presence offends a person of different religious affiliation without restricting him in the free exercise of his faith. Where the United States pays a Congressional Chaplain, or where a state, with public funds, remodels classrooms for a religious college, some one who differs with the policy involved may feel prompted to ask a judge to forbid the expenditure on the ground that it provides, in some measure, for an "establishment of religion." Procedural complexities appear at once. The offense to sectarian loyalty that one may feel at seeing governmental favor for a rival sect is not, without more, sufficient hurt to set a court in motion.

But certain states, by their law, permit a taxpayer to call upon judges to forbid the expenditure of public funds for an illegal or unconstitutional purpose; such a taxpayer's grievance is the second of the two types of justiciable wrong mentioned above. Inevitably in a federal nation, laws governing such "taxpayers' actions" vary from state to state. Thus in one of the states of the union a taxpayer may have available in the state courts a means of applying for judicial prohibition of the expenditure of state funds for religious activities in schools, while in another state a taxpayer may lack the same opportunity.[3] The courts of the United States decline to recognize the standing in court of a Federal taxpayer to object to the expenditures of Federal funds, and on this ground the maintenance of chaplains in the armed forces and the Congress has been held exempt from attack as "establishment of religion."[4]

A further complication arises when the Supreme Court of the United States is asked to review a state judgment which denied that the state has violated the Fourteenth Amendment by making an expenditure from tax-produced funds for a religious purpose. The Supreme Court of the United States does not feel itself bound by the concepts of state courts as to the extent of a tax-payer's interest which will justify judicial attention and may refuse to pass on the merits of the case, one way or another, even though the state court has been willing to hear and decide it.[5] There are divers other reasons why review of state judgments may not be obtainable in the Supreme Court. Here, then, is a source of variation from state to state in the part religion may play in public school activities. The highest courts in the several states may apply different standards; and, lacking a remedy in the United States Supreme Court, there may be no way of rendering these uniform. In short, the availability of judicial remedies is of cardinal importance in determining constitutional rights and wrongs in religious as in other matters.

What Courts Decide and What Courts Say

Another important judicial trait which bears on the jurisprudence of church and state is the difference between the controversies our courts actually decide and the observations made in judicial opinions. These two often differ markedly in scope. Traditionally our judges not only award judgment to one of the contenders before them; they often write out their reasons. This practice of writing opinions, though a wholesome and desirable one, is not inevitable in the nature of things. Judges do sometimes simply hand down decisions, leaving their reasons to be guessed at. But the custom of writing an opinion, an essay on the law of the decided case, is widespread, and these statements serve as guides for lawyers and subjects of study for those who pursue political science.

Judicial opinions often range rather far afield. Precedent, history, sociology, policy, all are apt to be discussed in such essays in political theory written as *piéces justificatives* for the award of a decision to Smith or to Jones. But the effect of the determination as precedent depends, at least in theory, upon what is actually decided on the facts of the case. In a case concerning religious education, a court's opinion may state as a rule some proposition far broader than is required for decision of the controversy. In appraising the effect of a judicial precedent, the lawyer accepts with caution *obiter dicta* of the courts, more sweeping than anything actually decided.

Difference between what courts say and what they decide is one of the most puzzling features of the law, not only to the novice, but to the adept. It is a judicial trait peculiarly important in controversies involving church and state, for historical and sociological elements in such cases always tempt the judicial writer, and sweeping irrelevancies abound.

Vague Words in Constitutions

Another difficulty in judicial adjustment of relations between religious activity and public education derives from the terse and epigrammatic character of constitutional provisions. They do not explain themselves. The First Amendment to the Federal Constitution provides that "Congress shall make no law respecting an establishment of religion, or prohibiting the free exercise thereof; . . ." but the reader is uncertain from the words themselves whether they either inhibit the maintenance of a chapel at West Point or forbid a chaplain in a Federal prison. Nor do the clauses of the Fourteenth Amendment make clear any requirement that the United States prevent one of the states of the union from intermingling its public education with religious observances.

To ascribe a more specific meaning to such general phrases, a judge may undertake a psychological study of the persons who sponsored and drafted the Fourteenth Amendment, to attempt to see what they expected its words would accomplish. A practical difficulty in such research is the requirement that any constitutional amendment have the approval of a large number of Federal legislators and state functionaries.[6] Must a judge read the minds of all of them? The data on any intention respecting schools on the part of the proponents of the First Amendment religious clauses are scanty to say the least. Evidence of the intentions of the sponsors of the Fourteenth Amendment is equally sparse. The introduction and passage by the House, seven years after the Fourteenth Amendment took effect, of a proposed amendment forbidding state establishments of religion and prohibiting appropriation of public school money to sectarian schools is perhaps a somewhat persuasive contemporary indication that many legislators supposed that the Fourteenth Amendment did not include such prohibitions.[7]

Instead of investigating the state of mind of the persons adopting an amendment, judges sometimes look to what is called the "practical construction" of a constitutional clause through a number of generations, to see how the people whom it governs have understood and applied it. Have religious elements existed for a long time in our public schools? Courts are reluctant to upset a long-established habit of governmental action by pointing out that it has been unconstitutional all along.

A criterion of practicability is another means of making constitutional provisions more precise. What will be the effect on our schools of a given religious observance? Will it engender bitterness and strife? Will it make the public schools divisive rather than a force for union among our people? And if it be said that these considerations are legislative and not judicial, that policy is solely for the legislatures, the answer is made that in certain matters of profound importance the state and Federal constitutions, by their mandates expressed in general terms, have left to the courts the ultimate application of policy considerations. Mr. Justice Jackson wrote in a leading church-and-school case:

> It is idle to pretend that this task is one for which we can find in the Constitution one word to help us as judges to decide where the secular ends and the sectarian begins in education. Nor can we find guidance in any other legal source. It is a matter on which we can find no law but our own prepossessions.[8]

Here, then, are three difficulties in the way of one who would gain from judicial opinions an idea of the practical effect of constitutional limitations. The unavailability of judicial remedies in certain areas; the judicial custom of extending discussions in opinions considerably beyond the range of the controversy decided; and the variation in the criteria by which judges determine the specific application of sweeping constitutional standards—these three complicate a study of the Constitution, the Church, and the Public School.

Decisions of the Supreme Court of the United States

The Supreme Court of the United States, in its long history, has handed down only eight decisions concerning religion in education. Perhaps two more should be added: *Quick Bear* v. *Leupp,* 210 US 50 (1908) involving the use of Indian treaty funds for reservation schools, and *Hamilton* v. *Regents,* 293 US 245 (1934) concerning conscientious objection to the Reserve Officers' training program at the University of California. The issue of religion in the public schools frequently appears in the reported opinions of state courts; but state constitutional provisions vary somewhat markedly from state to state, and those provisions are often the determinative grounds of state decisions.

The most conspicuous, dramatic, and perhaps most important judicial interventions have been the small number coming from the Supreme Court of the United States, when it has been asked to prohibit the people of a state from effectuating some arrangement which they wish, or which they tolerate in a local majority, but which a litigant considers forbidden by the terms of the Fourteenth Amendment to the Federal constitution. "State" activity, as this term is used in discussions of the Fourteenth Amendment, means activity of the principal state government through its executive, its judges, or its legislature; and equally any such activity of any subordinate element of the state— a city, a township, a school district, or any other. The Fourteenth Amendment governs them all.

In the first of the eight Supreme Court cases mentioned, *Pierce* v. *Society of Sisters,* 268 US 510 (1925), that Court held unconstitutional an Oregon statute requiring parents to send their children to public schools only. In *Cochran* v. *Louisiana State Board of Education,* 281 US 370 (1930), the

Supreme Court upheld a state statute providing for free textbooks in parochial and public schools alike. In *West Virginia State Board of Education* v. *Barnette,* 319 US 624 (1943), the Supreme Court declared unconstitutional a school-board requirement that, despite religious scruples, public school pupils salute the flag, overruling *Minersville* v. *Gobitis,* 310 US 586 (1940), which had held the opposite.

Seven years ago the Court, in *Everson* v. *Board of Education,* 330 US 1 (1947), upheld the payment by a New Jersey school board to the parents of students in parochial schools of the same bus-fare as that of students going to public schools. The following year, in *McCollum* v. *Board of Education,* 333 US 203 (1948), the Court struck down as unconstitutional an arrangement of the school authorities of Champaign, Illinois, permitting the use of public school buildings for short periods in the week for instruction given by religious teachers having no connection with the school system. This practice required at least one pupil, who did not wish to undergo religious instruction, to obtain the available permission to go to some other place in the school building to pursue secular studies.

The last two of the eight cases were decided in 1952. In March of that year the Court held in *Doremus* v. *Board of Education,* 342 US 429, that when New Jersey required by statute Bible reading in the first few minutes of the daily school session in the public schools, neither a person whose child had once been a pupil but had graduated, nor a taxpayer who failed to show monetary cost arising from the readings, had standing to test in the Supreme Court of the United States the question whether the New Jersey observance violated the First Amendment requirements of a separate church and state—and this although the New Jersey courts had been willing to decide on the merits. (Of course one must remember that the First Amendment has no direct application to state action. The argument was that the Fourteenth "incorporates" the First.)

The following month, in *Zorach* v. *Clauson,* 343 US 306, the Court upheld a plan in effect in New York City by which public school pupils were excused from attendance for short periods provided they went for religious instruction to points specified by their respective church organizations outside of the public school premises.

The reasoning of the justices deserves additional discussion. In the *Everson* case in 1947, upholding public transportation to parochial schools, the majority concurred in an opinion by Mr. Justice Black. The opinion discussed in rather sweeping terms issues much wider than those in the case then at bar. After reviewing the history of controversies between church and state in the early United States, particularly those in Virginia, he wrote:

> The "establishment of religion" clause of the First Amendment means at least this: Neither a state nor the Federal Government can set up a church. Neither can pass laws which aid one religion, aid all religions, or prefer one religion over another. Neither can force nor influence a person to go to or

to remain away from church against his will or force him to profess a belief or disbelief in any religion. No person can be punished for entertaining or professing religious beliefs or disbeliefs, for church attendance or non-attendance. No tax in any amount, large or small, can be levied to support any religious activities or institutions, whatever they may be called, or whatever form they may adopt to teach or practice religion. Neither a state nor the Federal Government, can, openly or secretly, participate in the affairs of any religious organizations or groups and *vice versa*. In the words of Jefferson, the clause against establishment of religion by law was intended to erect "a wall of separation between Church and State."[9]

However, as to the bus-fares in question, he concluded that the New Jersey

> . . . legislation, as applied, does no more than provide a general program to help parents get their children, regardless of their religion, safely and expeditiously to and from accredited schools.
> The First Amendment has created a wall between church and state. That wall must be kept high and impregnable. We could not approve the slightest breach. New Jersey has not breached it here.[10]

In *Everson* then, the Supreme Court indicated that some state governmental aid, extended to public and parochial school pupils alike, was consistent with the Federal constitution. On the other hand, the Supreme Court did decide the case on the merits. It deemed the interest of the complaining taxpayer sufficient to permit him to litigate the constitutionality of the payments in question, trifling though they were. And the judges all joined in various statements to the general effect that the states, restricted by the Fourteenth Amendment, must therefore comply with the same limits as those restricting the Federal government under the First.

Mr. Justice Black also wrote the Court's opinion in the *McCollum* case in 1948[11] which held unconstitutional religious instruction given on public school premises, by outside instructors, during school hours, though pupils who wished were excused from the exercise. He repeated, from his *Everson* opinion, his statement that a high and impregnable wall was erected between Church and State by the First Amendment; but here, speaking for the Court in favor of the plaintiff, Mrs. McCollum, he found the wall breached and the practice unconstitutional.

Mr. Justice Frankfurter observed in a concurring opinion:

> This case, in the light of the Everson decision, demonstrates anew that the mere formulation of a relevant Constitutional principle is the beginning of the solution of a problem, not its answer . . . agreement, in the abstract, that the First Amendment was designed to erect a "wall of separation between Church and State," does not preclude a clash of views as to what the wall separates.[12]

That Mr. Justice Frankfurter considered the Supreme Court's intervention in *McCollum* to be based on "free exercise" of religion, not on "establishment," appears from his dissent in *Adler* v. *Board of Education,* 342 US 485, 503 (1952). He wrote of *McCollum:*

. . . a parent did present an individualized claim of his own that was direct and palpable. There the parent alleged that Illinois imposed restrictions on the child's free exercise of faith and thereby on the parent's. The basis of jurisdiction in the McCollum Case was not at all a parental right to challenge in the courts—or at least in this Court—educational provisions in general. The closely defined encroachment of the particular arrangement on a constitutionally protected right of the child, and of the parent's right in the child, furnished the basis for our review.

Mr. Justice Jackson, while concurring in *McCollum,* pointed out that there was a very doubtful showing of any substantial property injury to Mrs. McCollum. A court, he wrote, could interfere with school authorities only when they invaded either a property right or a personal liberty. The cost here to the taxpayers was "incalculable and negligible."

It can be argued, perhaps, that religious classes add some wear and tear on public buildings and that they should be charged with some expense for heat and light, even though the sessions devoted to religious instruction do not add to the length of the school day. But the cost is neither substantial nor measurable, and no one seriously can say that the complainant's tax bill has been proved to be increased because of this plan.[13]

Speaking of the magnitude, intricacy, and delicacy of the task of separating the secular from the religious in education, and the lack of definite criteria in the words of the Constitution, Justice Jackson concluded:[14]

If with no surer legal guidance we are to take up and decide every variation of this controversy, raised by persons not subject to penalty or tax but who are dissatisfied with the way schools are dealing with the problem, we are likely to have much business of the sort. And, more importantly, we are likely to make the legal "wall of separation between church and state" as winding as the famous serpentine wall designed by Mr. Jefferson for the University he founded.[15]

In *Zorach,* in 1952, a New York City plan of cooperation between the public schools and various organized churches for the religious education of children came before the Supreme Court of the United States[16] at the suit of parents of school children.

The Court described the plan in its opinion:

New York City has a program which permits its public schools to release students during the school day so that they may leave the school buildings and school grounds and go to religious centers for religious instruction or devotional exercises. A student is released on written request of his parents. Those not released stay in the classrooms. The churches make weekly reports to the schools, sending a list of children who have been released from public school but who have not reported for religious instruction.

Mr. Justice Douglas, writing for a majority of six, upheld the constitutionality of the New York program. He distinguished *McCollum* on the ground that in Illinois, unlike New York, public school premises had been used for religious instruction. He wrote:

We are a religious people whose institutions presuppose a Supreme Being. We guarantee the freedom to worship as one chooses. We make room for as wide a variety of beliefs and creeds as the spiritual needs of man deem necessary. We sponsor an attitude on the part of government that shows no partiality to any one group and that lets each flourish according to the zeal of its adherents and the appeal of its dogma. When the state encourages religious instructions or cooperates with religious authorities by adjusting the schedule of public events to sectarian needs, it follows the best of our traditions. For it then respects the religious nature of our people and accommodates the public service to their spiritual needs. To hold that it may not would be to find in the Constitution a requirement that the government show a callous indifference to religious groups. That would be preferring those who believe in no religion over those who do believe.

. . . The problem, like many problems in constitutional law, is one of degree . . .

In the McCollum Case the classrooms were used for religious instruction and the force of the public school was used to promote that instruction. Here, as we have said, the public schools do not more than accommodate their schedules to a program of outside religious instruction. We follow the McCollum Case.

But we cannot expand it to cover the present released time program unless separation of Church and State means that public institutions can make no adjustments of their schedules to accommodate the religious needs of the people. We cannot read into the Bill of Rights such a philosophy of hostility to religion.[17]

Justices Black, Frankfurter, and Jackson each wrote dissenting opinions, each finding no substantial difference between *McCollum* and *Zorach*. Said Mr. Justice Jackson:

The distinction attempted between that case and this is trivial, almost to the point of cynicism, magnifying its non-essential details and disparaging compulsion which was the underlying reason for invalidity.[18]

At another point in his opinion he said:

The greater effectiveness of this system over voluntary attendance after school hours is due to the truant officer who, if the youngster fails to go to the Church school, dogs him back to the public schoolroom. Here schooling is more or less suspended during the "released time" so the nonreligious attendants will not forge ahead of the churchgoing absentees. But it serves as a temporary jail for a pupil who will not go to Church. It takes more subtlety of mind than I possess to deny that this is governmental constraint in support of religion.[19]

A summary of the cases decided by the Supreme Court of the United States concerning religious observances in schools can briefly be made. Compulsion upon the child in a public school to engage in ritual antipathetic to his religious beliefs, even where this ritual is patriotic in its nature, violates his constitutional right to liberty under the Fourteenth Amendment.

Conduct of religious instruction in the public grade-schools, by volunteer clergymen of various faiths from outside the ordinary teaching staff, unconstitutionally interferes with the liberty of a dissenting school child who is made to feel conspicuous by the difference. In the entire history of the Federal Constitution, only in these two instances, the flag salute case of 1943 and the decision of 1948 involving the Champaign plan for religious education, do we find the Supreme Court prohibiting state school activity on the ground of impaired freedom of religion. The *Pierce* case in 1925 (268 US 510) holding unconstitutional a statute which in effect eliminated non-public grade schools did not turn on religious grounds; the *Hill Military Academy* case, decided in the same opinion, has no sectarian aspect. The United States Supreme Court has never decided that any state school activity was unconstitutional as a "law respecting an establishment of religion."

The difference between the facts of the *McCollum* case in Champaign, Illinois, in 1948 and those of the *Zorach* case in New York City in 1952 seems minimal. In 1949, commenting on *McCollum,* then still a fresh case, one observer wrote:

> A phenomenon fairly common in the law is the announcement of a notable
> and drastic judgment, phrased in sweeping terms, followed after a little time
> by a series of qualifying opinions in later cases which shrink the original
> precedent to a much smaller size than its language would at first have indi-
> cated. A close examination of the McCollum case suggests that this process
> could perhaps again occur.[20]

This process has in fact now occurred. The New York case has in effect legitimated the substance of the Champaign plan, provided only that instruction is carried on in the parish house instead of the schoolroom. What instruction in religious matters the Federal Constitution permits in the schoolroom as parts of literature, history, or social studies; what devotional observances such as opening prayer or Bible reading may be conducted by the public-school teacher; what differences may exist between what the Fourteenth Amendment permits in grade school, high school, and state university—all these remain to be decided. One can only make guesses on the basis of the eight cases described.

A third of a century ago Mr. Justice Holmes deprecated

> . . . the use of the Fourteenth Amendment beyond the absolute compulsion
> of its words to prevent the making of social experiments that an important
> part of the community desires, in the insulated chambers afforded by the
> several states, even though the experiments may seem futile or even noxious
> to me and to those whose judgment I most respect.[21]

Since *McCollum,* the United States Supreme Court seems to have gone some distance to make possible at least a little experimenting in religious education.

SCHOOLS AND RELIGION IN THE STATE COURTS

In many instances a state court has the last word on state matters. The Supreme Court of the United States will not ordinarily review a state court decision which turns on a question of state law. Where no questions under the

Federal Constitution need be answered to dispose of a case, a state decision thus becomes final. Furthermore in a number of cases the Supreme Court has an option either to review state decisions or not, in its discretion. Where it elects not to review, the state decision becomes final. Because of diverse clauses in different state constitutions, local differences in religious affiliation, and varied practices in public schools, there are available many more final state than Federal decisions in the field of religion and education. State decisions are not unimportant. To those affected, final defeat in a church-school case in a state court is as significant as if judgment had been handed down by the Supreme Court of the United States. And much school law-in-action is made, not by state legislators or judges, but by administrative officials such as Attorneys-General and Superintendents of Education.[22]

State cases affect multitudes of people. Their study is essential to anyone who wishes to explore recent trends in the area of church-state relations in education. Many of the questions so raised have never been passed on by the United States Supreme Court. Comparatively recent examples involve members of religious orders teaching in religious costume in public schools,[23] Bible readings,[24] distribution of Gideons' Bibles,[25] compulsory attendance at secular school when religion required attendance at a nonaccredited religious school,[26] religious instruction on a state university campus,[27] and other questions of the same general nature. To attempt to analyze all such decisions would require a book-length discussion.[28] This paper will confine itself to analysis of two recent problems: the employment of members of religious orders as public-school teachers, illustrated by cases decided in New Mexico in 1951[29] and in Missouri in 1953;[30] and the distribution of religious literature (Presbyterian pamphlets) in public school buildings in New Mexico, discussed in a case decided in 1952[31] and Gideons' Bibles in New Jersey passed on by courts of that state in 1953.[32] These cases, together with the state cases reviewed by the Supreme Court and discussed in a previous section, fairly illustrate contemporary state litigation in this field.

Members of Religious Orders as Public-School Teachers

In a number of states, local school boards have at various periods employed as teachers members of religious bodies who wear the characteristic costumes of their orders. In past years, this practice has been repeatedly challenged on various state constitutional grounds; it has more than once been sustained. In 1894, the Supreme Court of Pennsylvania, when asked to declare it unconstitutional under a provision of the state constitution forbidding sectarian teaching, wrote:

> In the sixty years of existence at our present school system, this is the first time this court has been asked to decide, as a matter of law, that it is sectarian teaching for a devout woman to appear in a schoolroom in a dress peculiar to a religious organization of a Christian church. We decline to do so.[33]

It is worth noting that, in the year after this decision, the Pennsylvania legislature passed a statute forbidding the wearing of any religious dress by a public school teacher while performing duties; this statute was upheld by the Supreme Court of Pennsylvania in *Commonwealth* v. *Herr,* 229 Pa 132 (1910).

In 1936, the Supreme Court of North Dakota, construing a provision of the state constitution prohibiting the use of public school moneys "for the support of any sectarian school," declined to enjoin, at the suit of electors and taxpayers, the employment by a public school district, as teachers, of members of a religious order who contributed to the order a large part of their earnings, and who during school hours wore their particular religious garb.[34]

On the other hand, in other states, opposite results had been reached. In Iowa, in 1918, the state Supreme Court, citing state constitutional provisions which, among other things, forbade all taxation for ecclesiastical support, and appropriations for public funds to any institution or school under ecclesiastical or sectarian management or control, enjoined the maintenance of what in form was a public school, arranged by renting space in a parochial school building and employing as teachers Catholic sisters wearing religious costume.[35]

With this judicial background, the Supreme Court of New Mexico in September 1951, took up an action brought by certain persons as "citizens, taxpayers, and parents of school children" against members of the New Mexico State Board of Education and others, to bar sectarian teachers from teaching in the public schools and to have the expenditure of public funds in aid of parochial schools declared illegal. The action was based not only on the First and Fourteenth Amendments of the United States Constitution, but also on provisions of the constitution of New Mexico, which among other matters, provided that the public schools should be "free from sectarian control," and on a state statute which provided that any teacher using sectarian or denominational books or teaching sectarian doctrine should be discharged, that his certificate to teach school should be revoked, and that he should thereafter be forever barred from receiving school moneys and from employment in the public schools in the state.

In a large number of New Mexico public schools, teaching members of religious orders were dressed in their distinctive religious costume, and school-bus schedules were adjusted so that pupils might arrive in time for religious training. While non-Catholic children were nominally not compelled to attend services, as a practical matter in inclement weather their attendance at Catholic ceremonies was inescapable.

At the trial, 2200 pages of testimony were taken concerning the degree of activity of the Catholic church in supervising the schools and in controlling the teachers. The final action of the Supreme Court of New Mexico was to enjoin permanently from teaching a large number of Catholic "religions," but to decline to enjoin those who had not taught religion in the public schools as forbidden in the state constitution and statute.[36] The state Supreme Court further provided that if the same should again be employed as teachers in the New

Mexico public schools, they must not dress in religious garb or wear religious emblems while in discharge of their duties. They were further required to refrain from teaching "sectarian religion and doctrines," and from the dissemination of religious literature during school periods. Furthermore, they were required thereafter to be under the actual control and supervision of responsible school authorities rather than authorities of the church. "A church cannot be permitted to operate a school system within our public school system."[37]

The most significant feature of this conspicuous New Mexico case was the stress by the court on questions of detail and degree. There was no sweeping proscription of any appearance whatever of religious activity in the schools, but rather an appraisal of the extent to which schools were actually under the control of religious authorities while being publicly supported.

In June 1953 the Supreme Court of Missouri, in *Berghorn* v. *Reorganized School District,* 260 SW 2d 563, affirmed a lower court judgment enjoining the maintenance of a similar merger of parochial-public school elements.

Distribution of Religious Literature in Public Schools

Distribution of religious literature in public schools appears unsensational when compared to the New Mexico and Missouri integration of parochial schools in the public systems. However the Supreme Court of New Mexico, in a decision handed down in May 1952, *Miller* v. *Cooper,* 56 NM 355, enjoined the maintenance, by public school teachers, of Presbyterian religious pamphlets in the schoolrooms where pupils could get them. At the same time the Court refused to bar the responsible teachers permanently from teaching in the schools, and refused to forbid the holding of Baccalaureate services in a Baptist church and the holding of Commencement exercises in a Presbyterian church, where no other suitable auditorium was available.

In December 1953, the Supreme Court of New Jersey decided in *Tudor* v. *Board of Education,* 14 NJ 31, that distribution of copies of a volume containing the New Testament, Psalms, and Proverbs under the auspices of the Gideons International, in a public school building, to those school children whose parents had signed requests, was unconstitutional. The action was brought by the parent of a Jewish child and the parent of a Catholic child in the public school. Each was a taxpayer of the municipality maintaining the school, though the Catholic parent withdrew his child while the action was pending.

The Supreme Court of the state, in an opinion by Chief Justice Vanderbilt, stated that the Board of Education by permitting the distribution of the King James version of the New Testament violated the First and Fourteenth Amendments, and also a provision of the New Jersey constitution forbidding the "establishment of one religious sect in preference to another." The opinion appears to rest upon two grounds: that the distribution interfered with religious freedom of children of sects to whom the King James New Testament was unacceptable; and also that the distribution of the New Testament amounted to a preference of the Christian religion over the Hebrew faith, in violation of the quoted clause of the state constitution.

Like the Supreme Court of New Mexico, however, the New Jersey court did not undertake to eliminate from the public schools of New Jersey all traces of religious recognition. The Court in *Tudor*, did not purport to overrule *Doremus* decided by it in 1950.[38] In *Tudor* the New Jersey Supreme Court repeated a statement in *Doremus* that the Old Testament and the Lord's Prayer pronounced without comment are not sectarian, and hence that repetition of the latter, and reading of the former, provided by statute in New Jersey, did not constitute sectarian instruction or sectarian worship.

As the Lord's Prayer is part of the New Testament, one may find it difficult to understand why saying the Lord's Prayer in a New Jersey public school is constitutional, if, as *Tudor* holds, permitting distribution of the New Testament by the Gideons is repugnant to state and Federal constitutions. But such differences are continually plaguing the lawyer. In 1924 the Supreme Court of California held that provisions of the state constitution, including one prohibiting "sectarian or denominational" instruction in the public schools, did not preclude public school trustees from purchasing twelve copies of the King James Bible for a high school library. See *Evans* v. *Selma Union H.S. Dist.*, 193 Cal 54. The substantial difference between this and the New Jersey case is not easy to identify. Is it a difference in constitutional text, in geographical location, in date of decision, or between the loan and the gift of a book?

However, the *Tudor* case is here interesting at least in three respects. In the first place, it presents a state supreme court prohibiting a specific intermixture of religion and public school activity: the distribution, by outsiders on school premises, of a King James New Testament with other portions of the Bible. In the second place, the careful limitation on this opinion, by which other religious practices in New Jersey schools retain approval, shows New Jersey, like New Mexico, unwilling to take steps to expunge every slight trace of religion from its public schools. The third feature of this case is the presence of an apparently adequate state constitutional ground to produce the result, regardless of Federal constitutional provisions. As this is written, an application for review of *Tudor*, made to the Supreme Court of the United States by the Gideons and the Board of Education of Rutherford, is pending and undecided. The case thus illustrates the fact that under the various jurisdictional rules of the United States Supreme Court much diversity of state constitutional regulation may persist depending on the availability of review.

One hesitates to be confident that recent state court adjudications demonstrate any definite change of direction in the constitutional law of church and school. It is apparent that a number of state supreme courts will construe their state constitutions to forbid public maintenance of actually private religious schools, even when the legal forms of public organization are maintained. One might perhaps also perceive a tendency to forbid the distribution of religious reading-matter in the schools; and indeed if hostile sects may compete for favor by proffer of rival literatures in public classrooms, undesirable stridency may develop. But one also sees a distinct unwillingness to bar every religious manifestation from the public schoolroom. The doctrines of Justice Black expressed in *Everson* are not yet literally applied by state courts:

> Neither [state nor federal government] can pass laws which aid one religion, aid all religions, or prefer one religion over another . . . No tax in any amount, large or small, can be levied to support any religious activities or institutions, whatever they may be called, or whatever form they may adopt to teach or practice religion.

A SUMMARY ESTIMATE OF THE CONSTITUTIONAL SITUATION TODAY

The people of the United States all have some religious traditions, and in a multitude of ways the governments of nation and states reflect this background. The Federal Constitution prescribes some limit on both Federal and state religious activity; and this limitation is ultimately applied through the Supreme Court. State constitutions, too, put further and often more precise and varied restrictions on the state governments' religious activities, and the extent of these state restrictions can be measured by the judgments of state courts. What recent trends can be seen in such of these judicial decisions, both Federal and state, as concern the relation of religious activity and the public schools?

The United States Supreme Court has shown that in this area it interferes cautiously. Only twice in its history—in the 1943 flag-salute and the Champaign cases—has it declared state school activity unconstitutional on church-state grounds. Opinions of that Court have several times stated that the Fourteenth Amendment "incorporates" the First, and thus that the states, forbidden to deprive any person of due process or equal protection of the laws, are by inference also forbidden to "pass any law respecting an establishment of religion." But no decision of that Court (as contrasted to the judges' language) has clearly so ruled on a state "establishment."[39] Judicial statements, even if *obiter dicta,* can not, of course, be ignored in prediction of the future. A taxpayer may some day succeed in enjoining some state expenditure on the ground that it is a fractional establishment of religion more striking than the *Everson* bus-fares. However, unless *Everson* should be overruled, not every state expenditure furnishing some joint support to schools and religious observance will be enjoined. Minor subventions by the states will escape Federal policing. The point where small becomes too great remains for the Supreme Court to indicate.

There is much play in the joints of the Federal Constitution, even respecting churches and schools. The Supreme Court has not yet without qualification gone so far as to

> . . . decree a uniform, rigid and . . . unchanging standard for countless school boards representing and serving highly localized groups which not only differ from each other but which themselves from time to time change attitudes . . .[40]

Much local variation in church-school relationships remains possible—one aspect of a federal nation which may exasperate good and zealous men who aspire to uniformity. In some states reading the King James Bible is barred from school as "sectarian"; in some it is not so held.[41] Garbed nuns could teach in North Dakota in 1936, but not in New Mexico in 1952 or Missouri in 1953. One can only explain the legal existence of such variations by the theory of federalism itself—the theory that the purpose of entrusting the United States with only limited central powers was precisely to permit local divergences of government and law where uniformity was not necessary for the well-being of the whole nation.

State supreme courts continue to permit some religious expression. In *Cochran, Everson, McCollum, Doremus,* and *Zorach*[42] the state courts had upheld the local practice before the cases reached the United States Supreme Court. If wording may be taken at face value, the 1953 New Jersey opinion on Bible distribution[43] scarcely indicates a trend against any chemical trace of religion in public schools.

One should, in any event, be skeptical of the permanence of any such apparent trend, where constitutional prohibitions are lacking in specificity, and are unavoidably subject to interpretation according to the prepossessions of the judge who passes on them. Climates of religious opinion vary not only in space but in time. The judicial premises of today neither are, nor should, necessarily be those of generations yet to come.

FOOTNOTES

1. See for examples: *"Constitutions of the States and the United States,"* N.Y. Constitutional Convention Committee (1938). To be sure of any late amendment, one must consult an up-to-date version of the state constitution in question.

2. The Western Maid, 257 U.S. 419, 433 (1922).

3. An example of a taxpayer held without standing to complain of a state expenditure to provide classrooms and other facilities in a religious college, appears in Stichman v. Bull, 298 N.Y. 516 (1948).

4. Elliott v. White, 23 F. 2d. 997 (D.C. Cir. 1928).

5. See Doremus v. Board of Education, 342 U.S. 429 (1952).

6. Article V. "The Congress, whenever two thirds of both Houses shall deem it necessary, shall propose Amendments to this Constitution, or, on the Application of the Legislatures of two thirds of the several states, shall call a Convention for proposing Amendments, which, in either Case, shall be valid to all Intents and Purposes, as Part of this Constitution, when ratified by the Legislatures of three fourths of the several states, or by Conventions in three fourths thereof, as the one or the other Mode of Ratification may be proposed by the Congress; . . ."

7. The "Blaine Amendment." Ames, "The Proposed Amendments to the Constitution of the United States During the First Century of Its History," H. Doc. No. 353, Pt. 2, 54th Cong. 2d Sess., pp. 277, 278; printed in *Annual Report of the American Historical Association,* Vol. II (1896). And see A. W. Meyer, "The Blaine Amendment and the Bill of Rights," 64 *Harvard Law Review,* 939 (1951).

8. See McCollum v. Board of Education, 333 U.S. 203, 237 (1948).

9. Everson v. Board of Education, 330 U.S. 1, at 15, 16 (1947). Mr. Justice Jackson wrote a dissenting opinion, in which Mr. Justice Frankfurter joined. Mr. Justice Rutledge

wrote another dissent; Justices Frankfurter, Jackson, and Burton expressed agreement with him.

10. Everson, *supra.*

11. McCollum v. Board of Education.

12. McCollum v. Board of Education, 333 U.S. 203, 212, 213 (1948).

13. *Ibid.*

14. *Ibid.*

15. *Ibid.* 256.

16. Zorach v. Clauson, 343 U.S. 306 (1952).

17. *Ibid.* at 313–315.

18. *Ibid.* at 325.

19. *Ibid.* at 324.

20. A. E. Sutherland, "Due Process and Disestablishment," 62 *Harvard Law Review,* 1306, 1343 (1949).

21. Dissent in Truax v. Corrigan, 257 U.S. 312 at 344 (1921).

22. See the discussion by Chief Justice Wilson, dissenting in Kaplan v. Independent School District, 171 Minn. 142 at 157 (1927).

23. See Zellers v. Huff, 55 N.M. 501 (1951); Berghorn v. Reorg. Dist., 260 S.W. 2d 573 (S. Ct. Mo. Div. ⚹1, June 8, 1953).

24. Kaplan v. Independent School District, constitutionality of readings from King James Old Testament upheld.

25. Tudor v. Board of Education, 14 N.J. 31 (Dec 7, 1953).

26. People ex rel Shapiro v. Dorin, 199 Misc. (N.Y.) 643; affirmed without opinion 278 App. Div. 750; affirmed without opinion 302 N.Y. 857 (1951); appeal dismissed for want of a substantial federal question 342 U.S. 884 (1952). While this appeal was dismissed *in limine* and thus the case was never argued in the United States Supreme Court, Justices Black and Douglas recorded themselves in favor of noting jurisdiction, and thus hearing the case argued.

27. State ex rel Sholes v. University of Minnesota, 236 Minn. 452 (1952); judicial intervention refused for procedural reasons.

28. See for analysis of a large number of such cases of various types, Leo Pfeffer, *Church, State and Freedom,* (1953), Chapters 9 to 13, inclusive. The author has been counsel in a number of prominent cases opposing state connection with religious activity. Convenient older digests can be found in an annotation entitled "Sectarianism in Schools," 5 *American Law Reports, Annotated,* 866 (1920), brought up to 1942 in 141 A.L.R. 1144. The Winter 1949 issue of *Law and Contemporary Problems,* pages 1–169, contains articles by a number of noted authorities, treating problems of religion and public schools from different points of view. See also "Released Time Reconsidered: The New York Plan Is Tested," 61 *Yale Law Journal,* 405 (1952).

29. Zellers v. Huff, 55 N.M. 501 (1951).

30. Berghorn v. Reorganized School District No. 8, 260 S.W. 2d. 573.

31. Miller v. Cooper, 56 N.M. 355 (1952).

32. Tudor v. Board of Education, 14 N.J. 31 (Dec. 7, 1953).

33. Hysong v. School District, 164 Pa. 629 (1894).

34. Gerhardt v. Heid, 66 N.D. 444 (1936). In 1945, the Supreme Court of Errors of Connecticut, in a somewhat different type of case, involving a claim by the City of New Haven against the Town of Torrington for the education of Torrington children, held that a school, maintained in a portion of a Catholic orphanage, with two lay women and eight nuns as a teaching staff, and with the nuns teaching in religious apparel, was a "public" and not a "parochial" school. Hence, the court held, New Haven was entitled to obtain reimbursement for educating Torrington children, when apparently the opposite result would have obtained if the school were "parochial" and not "public."

35. Knowlton v. Baumhover, 182 Ia. 691 (1918). A somewhat similar result was reached by the Supreme Court of Missouri (Div. ⚹1) in Harfst v. Hoegen, 349 Mo. 808 (1941).

36. Zellers v. Huff, 55 N.M. 501 (1951).

37. *Ibid.,* at page 525.

38. Doremus v. Board of Education, 5 N.J. 435 (1950), appeal dismissed 342 U.S.

429 (1952). The refusal by the Supreme Court to pass on the merits of Doremus left the Doremus state court decision in force.

39. The Supreme Court has never held any Federal school activity unconstitutional as an establishment or on any other religious ground. In Quick Bear v. Leupp, 210 U.S. 50 (1908), the Supreme Court in a suit by Sioux Indians refused to enjoin payment of funds by Federal officials to the Bureau of Catholic Indian Missions for the education of Sioux Indian pupils at St. Francis Mission Boarding School on the Rosebud Reservation. The Court states that the funds belonged by right to the Indians and were thus in a different class from ordinary appropriations.

It may be clarifying to remind the wearied reader that Everson v. Board, 330 U.S. 1 (1947), was decided *in favor* of the school board. The taxpayer who claimed the state, by transporting parochial pupils, was enforcing an unconstitutional law "respecting an establishment of religion," lost his case. This fact tends to disappear under the eloquent statement of Mr. Justice Black that neither nation nor state "can pass laws which aid one religion, aid all religions, or prefer one religion over another."

40. The phrase is from the concurring opinion of Mr. Justice Jackson in McCollum, 333 U.S. 203, 237 (1948).

41. *Ibid.* at 237.

42. These five cases are summarized above.

43. Tudor v. Board of Education, 14 N.J. 31 (Dec. 7, 1953).

Report of the Recorder

Philip H. Phenix
Associate Professor of Education
Teachers College, Columbia University

The following is a summary of some of the main lines of discussion by the section participants. This does not include everything that was said, nor do the summarized remarks attributed to the several speakers necessarily repeat *verbatim* everything they actually said. In most cases, however, it has been possible to phrase the summary substantially in the speaker's own words. While the actual discussions were considerably fuller than the record below, it is hoped that the main points have been faithfully set forth.

FIRST SESSION

The discussions were initiated by a summary by Ralph Gabriel of his paper on "Religion in American Life."

Blau: What does Professor Gabriel mean by secularism?

Gabriel: A primary interest in man and the here and now; interest in the world in which we live as contrasted with preoccupation with a spiritual world.

Van Dusen: There are two different meanings here of the word secularism. It can be used in contrast to the ecclesiastical or it can be used in contrast to the religious.

Blau: We ought to leave the word secular out completely. I see not just two meanings but a whole cluster of them. The word religion has a similar ambiguity.

Van Dusen: Perhaps we should use the word humanism.

Thayer: There are many meanings in this word too. In our development we have seen a change from concern with theological, doctrinaire religion to the nontheological kind of religion. We finally arrive at secularism which involves a concern with common human values. It is this kind of concern with a method of creating common agreements despite a variety of disagreements which constitutes the genius of secularism.

Calhoun: Professor Gabriel's use of the word "secularism" includes a good deal more than the word "humanism" would imply. One of the forms of secularism that we have to deal with is not concerned with human beings, but with things, to the neglect of persons. It is concerned with things that start out to be tools but finally become prisons for the human spirit.

Berkson: Secularism, for me, carries a derogatory implication. As a philosophy of life, it involves a belief that this-worldly interests are all-sufficient. There is a tremendous difference between a secularist and a humanist. I am a humanist and am glad to be called that, but I am not a secularist.

F. E. Johnson: It is important to distinguish the word secular from the word secularism. The word secular, as I understand it, simply means something which is not under ecclesiastical control. For example, the secular school is a school which is not under the control of a religious institution or group. We therefore do need the word secular as a purely descriptive term. But we will have trouble with the word secularism because it has so many different meanings.

Childs: I would not regard the word secular as a word of criticism. I have great satisfaction in affirming that I am a secularist and have much less satisfaction in affirming that I am a humanist, although I am. Secularism has been that which has enabled people of divergent convictions to work together politically. Secularism is the pattern which includes us all. We have a secular school. We have to all intents and purposes a secular state. Yet this is no criticism of either the school or the state. Perhaps this is not entirely a semantic question. There may be conflicting elements in the culture itself. In our national government we do not have any religious tests for the holding of office. In this sense, we are a secular state. Now there are those who believe that religious affiliation is relevant to public office. This is one example of the conflict.

R. L. Hunt: Is it true that there is no religious test? There are elections which are determined in part by the religion of the candidate.

Van Dusen: But in a formal sense, there is no religious test for holding office. The writers of all three of our papers have made the statement, "We are a religious people." Wouldn't it be well for us to discuss in what sense this statement is true?

Gabriel: When this nation was established, a pluralistic attitude was adopted. It was assumed that the state is not coterminous with society. The government is one institution in society, the church is another, and there is no necessary opposition between them.

Wornom: Doesn't the taking of the oath imply a religious tradition? Historically it is true that the Federal constitution kept out of the religious question but the state constitutions often included religious references. There were even cases of a religious test for office in the early part of the nineteenth century. It was taken for granted that there should be religious services every Sunday in Congress, and, apart from the Jeffersonian years, there was no departure from this practice for several decades. Also in the period when religion was taken out of the public schools there was no antireligious intent; it was simply a question of fair play as between the various sects. The nineteenth-century changes therefore were not antireligious but antisectarian. In the twentieth century the issue shifted to the question whether there should be religion or no religion. Yet in the *Zorach* case it is explicitly stated that the American people are a religious people. So, even though there has been a shift between the nineteenth and twentieth centuries, it still does appear that the Supreme Court contends that we are a religious people; and it would seem to follow that religion should be a part of education.

Calhoun: We are a religious people, at least in the sense that the electorate must be a moral electorate. To be sure, the character of the morality required for citizenship is not clearly defined.

Childs: It is in terms of this morality that we are trying to educate in the common school. But now there are pressures on us to add religious sanctions for morality.

Calhoun: Would you say that the morality taught in the public schools is regarded as a function of the mores of the community rather than of some basic character of the cosmos? The transcendent reference which is taught by the churches has tended to be obscured in favor of a kind of generalization from what we customarily do. Isn't there a basic incompatibility here?

Thayer: The courts have interpreted the absence of religion in terms of doctrine. We are a religious people in the sense that there are ideals and attitudes of a spiritual nature. We are not a religious people in terms of specific doctrinal content.

Van Dusen: Historically the statement that we are a religious people meant that we are favorable to religion but that we are neutral with respect to particular sectarian creeds and institutions. It was not simply a question of devotion to ideals or values but had some references to Deity. This was the attitude of the American people at the time of the founding of the Republic.

Blau: What evidence do we have that there was a favorable attitude toward religion by the founding fathers?

Sutherland: The Declaration of Independence mentions God.

Blau: If you are talking about Deism, of course that is true of the Constitutional period.

Berkson: The use of the word *God* in the Declaration of Independence turned out to be a boomerang. A Deist in the early period was looked upon as an antireligious person. There is in the American tradition an antireligious —in the sense of an anticlerical—trend and this has been a creative element in our culture.

Van Dusen: Even today the President of the United States makes reference to the Deity in public proclamations.

Blau: But is this formal use of the word *God* to be taken as equivalent to having a religious sense? Is the person that swears by the Deity necessarily a religious person?

Van Dusen: We are not really concerned with the question of the subjective attitude of individual Americans, but with the prevailing attitude of the American mind.

Chipkin: While it is true that in the American tradition there is a favorable attitude toward religion, there has also been a favorable attitude toward people who did not profess a religion. The rights of people who did not accept a religion were equally protected with those who did.

Van Dusen: Wouldn't it be better to say *sympathetic* rather than *favorable?* Perhaps being a religious people means being sympathetic regarding the rights and privileges of irreligious people. Are we not also sympathetic towards people who are not religious in the traditional sense?

F. E. Johnson: Perhaps the word *tolerant* would be better in this context than the word *sympathetic.*

Van Dusen: Can one say that the people were tolerant toward *all* views? Certainly originally the American people were not equally tolerant of believers and nonbelievers.

Greene: What, historically, has been the American attitude toward religious minorities?

Gabriel: For a hundred years down to World War II there has been a history of opposition to minorities by the Protestant majority; for example, to the Mormons and to the Catholics. Since World War I the Supreme Court has pioneered in an extraordinary degree in assisting religious minorities, such as Jehovah's Witnesses, to gain equality of status before the law and a guarantee of full religious freedom. That has been accepted by our people. The opposition to the Mormons has been modified a great deal, and there has also been considerable cooperation between Protestants and Catholics, without, of course, complete success.

Greene: In recent times, has there not been a tendency on the part of a secular majority to override the wishes of a religious minority to have religious instruction in the schools? Haven't the tables been turned?

Niebuhr: Professor Gabriel, how would you characterize the differences between the religious attitude toward nonconformity and the secular viewpoint toward nonconformity?

Gabriel: My impression is that the nonreligious person does not take the issues raised by conformity and nonconformity very seriously. On the other hand, some religious groups (for example, the Jehovah's Witnesses) take it very seriously.

Niebuhr: The secularist at least has a tolerance which avoids the self-righteous kind of idolatry of the fanatics. A transcendent religion ought to lead both to loyalty to the transcendent object and to humility in the contemplation of that transcendent object. Unfortunately, this humility is singularly lacking in many people who have ecclesiastical loyalties.

F. E. Johnson: Doesn't all the trouble we have had in the courts over the question of religion indicate that we are a religious people; i.e., that we are concerned about religion. The *Zorach* decision bears witness to our religious tradition, even though religious instruction is not permissible in tax-supported schools.

Chipkin: Would a secularist be included in your definition of a religious person?

F. E. Johnson: Not in the context of the *Zorach* decision. It was concerned with religion in a more traditional sense, which includes belief in a Supreme Being.

Krumm: Although we may be a religious people, we are not a theological people. "Sectarian" is a bad word in the American consciousness. There has been for the most part in our times a great suspicion of sectarian differences and an assumption that there is really very little importance in theological distinctions. In recent years, however, there has arisen a greater interest in theological questions.

Thayer: Why do we raise the question, "Are we a religious people?" How inclusively are we going to use the word "people"? Is there some kind of official doctrine that we want people to accept? Is that back of this question? Is there an official content, a common core, which is to be imposed on everyone?

Childs: Behind this question, "Are we a religious people?", lies the assumption that some particular religion is to be dominant. I am concerned with finding the roots of unity which permit the diversity we have traditionally enjoyed.

McIntosh: Doesn't the significance of the question lie in the consciousness that we have become a completely different kind of nation? As our country has become more technologically advanced, it has developed a large group of people who are no longer interested in religious values, but who are taking part in a competitive society in which they want a better life in terms of their own comfort and various material values. We are asking this question because in our present social situation we find that it is absolutely essential to return to these basic concepts. We are becoming aware of the fact that what children need to live by in our society is the kind of foundation that was originally part of our religious tradition. We have taken out the vitamins from the bread and have to find some way of restoring them.

Blau: I find some difficulty with Mrs. McIntosh's point. If we think in terms of church membership in the eighteenth century, a remarkably small percentage of the people were members. At the present day, on the other hand, a large percentage, perhaps sixty per cent, are church members. How then can we say that the late eighteenth century was a period of overwhelming concern with religion and that today religion is at a low ebb? Are we to understand that where church membership is low, religion is high, and where church membership is high, religion is low?

Dillenberger: We have to distinguish between church religion and religion in general. A good many people these days are trying to put religion-in-general into the educational system. I am in favor of getting into school systems something which has to do with an understanding of the great historic religions, but oppose church control. We can be thankful that in the American tradition there has not been control by any one denomination. The tension amongst the various denominations has been a saving factor in our history. I would hope that our history in this respect can continue very much as it has in the past.

Smith: We can argue to the end of our sessions whether we are a religious people or not. This much we do know: that a belief in a relationship to a transcendent Being has been part of our culture. We should not attempt to put the teaching of a particular religious belief into education, but we should be interested in securing a balanced presentation of the kind of nation and people we are.

C. Johnson: Our concern for religion is not only a question of theological belief but much more importantly a question of the application of religion to our daily life—competition versus cooperation.

R. Hunt: Are we at the point where we can talk about a national policy with regard to religion, or is this a matter for the states and local communities?

Van Dusen: The original state provisions in regard to religion have in general been eliminated.

Friess: Our nation has had a tremendous problem in achieving cooperation among various groups. This gives us a clue to the importance of the secular emphasis on achieving a broad unity with many diverse elements. The real question today is whether we are going to conceive of cultural unity as the goal of the spiritual life or will seek for a principle of cooperation which leaves room for diversity. This is a problem not only for the present and the future but also for the interpretation of the past.

Berkson: Couldn't we say that diversity is an essential characteristic of religion in America? Anything that would minimize the diversity of religious points of view would not be desirable. What unifies the American people is what we call democracy. I would not call this secular because democracy is rooted in the Christian tradition. One of the sources of our democratic values is Christianity. There are also a Hellenic source and a scientific source.

Childs: These same values have been reached in other civilizations. The Christian tradition is not the only basis for them.

Berkson: But did not the interplay between the Hellenic and the Christian civilization produce something rather unique and then did not the interplay between this compound and the scientific development further produce something extremely significant? If we do not remember the tap roots in Judea, in Greece, and in Rome, we have cut ourselves off from the sources of vitality in our great cultural tradition.

Greene: Do we not need to rephrase our question? Is not the basic question whether we are a people who have earned freedom? The value of creativity and diversity, the weakness of watered-down common denominators, the desirability of allowing each individual to develop his maximum potentialities—this is the genius of our democratic government and way of life.

Childs: Would you then have a common school or not?

Greene: If our government is to move toward a continuance of flexibility, if it is to provide a framework for continuing experiments in creativity, the school could be operated the same way, not cutting any tap roots, but giving flexibility on all sides with mutual respect for honest diversity.

Seaver: In spite of all the things which we do not like about our society, is there not today a greater sense of social responsibility among the American people than ever before in our history? Aren't the spiritual values coming to be more and more respected even though they may not be called by that name?

Van Dusen: We may get quite different and mutually contradictory replies to that question. Perhaps there has been progress in some areas and regression in others.

Niebuhr: Haven't the much maligned secularists done a good deal to aid in the development of these spiritual values? Some time ago, a survey was made which showed that there is very little correlation between religious affiliation and ethical conduct. It showed that a good many people had success or peace-of-mind motives with no religious affiliation.

Washburne: If one takes the whole sweep of our history, our social concern has obviously increased. This is not merely a matter of opinion, it is simply a question of the number of people who have been working toward the well-being of their fellow men. We recognize the far greater degree of our interdependence—unparalleled in history.

Van Dusen: What about the world behind the Iron Curtain? What about the hydrogen bomb?

Washburne: We are recognizing to a far greater degree the interdependence of men and nations the world over.

SECOND SESSION

The discussions at this session were to deal with religion in higher education, both public and private, and in private and independent schools at the elementary and secondary levels. The session began with a preliminary informal statement by Professor Greene.

Greene: In discussing religion in education we must first consider what is included in the term religion. Ordinarily religion is taken to mean a traditional body of faith and practice. On the other hand it may be defined in terms of ultimate concern or commitment. According to this latter definition, a full-bodied, militant humanism, such as one gets in Lewis Mumford, would be religious. If we take religion in this richer and more inclusive sense, there are many variations: theistic, pantheistic, and atheistic. The teaching of religion would then mean teaching ultimate faiths which people take seriously. If we take the whole world into account, we have to include a great variety of faiths.

But we ought to focus our attention on those faiths which are dominant in our society; namely, Judaism, Catholicism, Protestantism, and secularism or humanism.

We must next consider the meaning of the word liberal. What is the essence of the spirit of liberalism in the school and the college? It seems to me that it is first and foremost a dedication to knowledge, not just in certain areas, but *all* knowledge. Liberal education and scholarship are broad and inclusive. A second characteristic of liberalism is the attitude of humility. An arrogant liberal is a contradiction in terms. A liberal is one who has a profound sense of his own limitations and a profound respect for the mind and integrity of others.

What, then, is the place of religion in liberal education? The first question is: Why have any religious education at all?

Some would say that religion is a great illusion and should be rated as most of us would rate witchcraft. I don't take an answer like that seriously. Granting that we are in an area of faith where final proof is not possible, the history of the religions of mankind is such as to merit open-mindedness regarding religion on the part of even the most skeptical.

A more serious argument against religious education is that religion by its very nature must be dogmatic. Is it possible to believe anything with religious fervor and at the same time to avoid dogmatism and the inevitable accompanying divisiveness? Historically, dogmatism and fervor have tended to go together, but I am convinced that there is no necessity for such a connection. It seems to me that the only attitude consistent with the liberal tradition is one of reflective and critical commitment.

A third objection to active concern for religion in education is that, however important it may be, it is the concern of the churches and should be left entirely to them with whatever assistance the family may be able to give. In answer we may note, first, that the churches cannot undertake the task of religious education alone; they cannot do it as well as it should be done. Religious instruction is much more likely to be divisive and dogmatic in the churches than it is on a liberal campus. The churches need desperately what the liberal campus has to offer. Similarly, the campus desperately needs what the churches have to offer. Secondly, putting the case in a fairly moderate form, what would we think of a total pattern of liberal education that wholly ignored art, or politics, or science, or language study? It would be a very unbalanced liberal arts program. Now, for better or for worse, religion has played and still does play a very important role in our society and in our culture; it has a rich and diverse history. It is literally true that you can't adequately understand literature, or history, or any of the significant movements of mankind in complete ignorance of religion. Some of us who are not teaching religion directly are greatly embarrassed by our students' abysmal ignorance of religion. For example, I have heard teachers of art, literature, and history complain bitterly along these lines.

Assuming that we are going to take religion seriously on the campus, the next questions are How? In what area? There are those who say: "Yes, bring it onto the campus but keep it in the status of extracurricular activities. Leave it to the student religious associations or leave it to the churches. Perhaps add noncredit courses to be given by local padres, or perhaps add credit courses if they are of scholarly competence. Have a general religious service if it is feasible, either compulsory if your population is very homogenous and the tradition supports it, otherwise voluntary, and then have your sectarian services on or near the campus."

I believe that all of these activities are important if one is interested in introducing our students to the full meaning of religion, but I for one cannot possibly stop at that point, because that condemns us to the very thing some of us are unhappy about—a kind of sentimentality and an inevitable parochialism in regard to religion. The only possible hope for an intellectually responsible religion is to move it right into the heart of the curriculum and to deal with it with all of the historical, philosophical, and scientific competence with which we try to deal with the other subjects in the curriculum.

The next question is: Should there be a department of religion? There are many who argue that the way to introduce religion into the liberal arts curriculum is through the nonreligious departments. They say: "Let religion be discussed philosophically by the philosopher, psychologically by the psychologist, historically by the historian." But suppose one applied the same argument, say to the study of history. Suppose we left it to the philosophers to deal with the history of philosophy, the teachers of art to teach the history of art, the economists to teach economic history? I think any of us with a serious concern for the understanding of history would realize that only the most fragmentary historical understanding would emerge from that kind of teaching. It takes a balanced department of historians to give the student the three-dimensionality of history as a rich and vital study in the liberal arts program. The same holds for religion.

Supposing that we do have a department of religion. What should it emphasize? Some say: "Let's start right off with comparative religions. If you are going to be liberal, with a global perspective, don't start on a predominantly Protestant campus with Protestant Christianity or on a Catholic campus with Catholicism. Start far away with Buddhism, Mohammedanism, and Zoroastrianism, and then work back to our own religions."

There is something to be said for this approach, but in practice it becomes very artificial. It is like starting a student of literature with far-away literature instead of the literature of his own native tongue. Of course, there are literatures which are precious and rich in other lands and cultures, but we do well to start at home and work out from there. Is it not equally natural to start at home with our own religions?

What about the historical approach as a safeguard against the dangers of dogmatism and indoctrination? Why not make the study of religion on a liberal arts campus a purely historical study? The historical approach is certainly invaluable; without it we can't get anywhere. But the merely historical approach does violence to the spontaneous interest of the student in the truth or falsity of religious belief. Sooner or later he is going to ask: "What should I believe, and why?" The historical must be supplemented by the systematic. What is really needed is a multifaceted departmental staff, including experts in the history of religion, the philosophy of religion, the social implications of religion, etc.

But someone may object that this is a purely intellectual approach, that religion is a matter of the heart, and that one is distorting religion by dealing with it merely as a theoretical study. Scientists would be exceedingly loath to teach science without the benefit of the laboratory. The artist requires the use of a studio. Social projects are being adopted by social scientists to bring home to students the social impact of the problems that surround us. Yet we can't designate specific hours every afternoon for everyone taking religion to have empirical practice in religion. It is at this point that the extracurricular activities can come in in an extraordinarily vital way. There is a place for both the intellectual side and the experiential side of religion, supplementing one another.

Finally, we need on our faculties men who believe strongly in radically different positions and who teach them openly and enthusiastically. If I did not have some faculty colleagues who were belligerently opposed to the positions I affirm, my own enthusiasms and affirmations in teaching would suffer. If ever I have a student who is afraid to write a paper attacking me and my views, I shall feel that I have not done my job as a teacher. It is important for the teacher to speak his mind, but it is equally important to bring home to the student his prior obligation to stand on his own feet and make up his own mind. What do we need in our society today more than anything else? The ability to believe things with all our hearts and still to respect those who believe differently. A university, a college, or a school that pretends to be liberal must attack this problem head-on and think of it not as a controversial nuisance but as an exciting challenge. Only thus can it function as a liberal institution in our on-going experimental society.

Smith: What do you think of the relative importance of furthering religion through the department of religion, as compared with the indirect concern of other departments in the university?

Greene: Speaking first with reference to my own field of specialization—if I had to choose between a college in which there was no department of philosophy but in which all of the other faculty members were philosophically oriented and a college in which nobody paid any attention to philosophy at all save those who were in the department of philosophy, I think I would favor the former. Religion will not get very far on a college campus unless there are deeply religious people in various departments who do not drag in religion but who also do not wince in the presence of religious factors; people who recognize religious content in literature, history, and psychology, when in fact it is present. The teaching of religion must, to be really effective, be a cooperative enterprise. I do not mean to imply that our faculties should be composed exclusively of Protestant Christians who are also good scholars. I think it is important that there be secularists on the faculty—not the sneering kind of secularists (I have as little use for a sneering religious dogmatist). Different points of view should be welcomed in this area of ultimate belief just as in the more technical area of philosophy. In our department at Yale we have worked very hard to get men on our staff with whom we knew from the start that we would disagree.

Thayer: What would be involved in the laboratory experience in religion to which Professor Greene referred?

Greene: In science, laboratory experience is the student's firsthand contact with those observations and experiments upon which our scientific understanding is based. In the case of religion, the laboratory experience would, on the one hand, be devotional, through the chapel and through smaller denominational groups coming together for worship. These can be deeply moving, illuminating experiences for many students. The other type of experience would fall under the category of good works. Any well set-up YMCA or YWCA group would have a program of social service.

Thayer: This is very valuable, but your analogy with scientific procedure may be invalid. In the laboratory one emancipates himself from the narrow point of view to a wider point of view in quite a different sense from what you do in religion. In religion you are affirming something which you already believe rather than expanding and disciplining your perception and ideas.

Greene: Not as I conceive of it. One of the nice things about Dwight Hall at Yale is that it is the one effective meeting place for persons of different religious groups, including Roman Catholics. A definite place is also made for the sincere, humanely minded secularist. This can have the effect of less parochialism, wider comprehension, and less intolerance.

Baldwin: Our experience at Andover supplements this. In addition to the courses in Bible, we have chapel services in which we try to make the experience of worship real. The social service work is also related to their religious understanding and increases tolerance for those with different points of view.

Thayer: Why do you call some of these things religious experiences? Are we going to identify religion and the religious with the moral and social? These same experiences, these new visions of life's meaning, can be found among youngsters who have gone to work camps. Without any so-called religious orientation the young people have given themselves to meeting social needs with wholehearted dedication. If you are going to call *that* laboratory experience in religion, then you mean something different from what I mean by religion. In a highly differentiated society there may be a danger in calling this religious.

Jackson: There is the same kind of feeling for social service and cooperation amongst the young Fascists and Communists. This raises a serious problem as to the basis for these actions.

Wornom: It is true that there are work camps and other means of training students in social services, but there are differences between work camps and other similar efforts. There have been work camps in which students have been pushed up squarely against the nature of man and shown clearly that mere "do-goodism" is not enough. It seems to me at this point that religion has a laboratory in which the nature of man and redemptive forces may be examined in the light of religious possibilities.

Baldwin: This is exactly what I meant also. If activity among students stops at the level of "do-goodism" it definitely has not reached the level of religious meaning.

Van Dusen: Did not the work camp movement actually originate among the church groups, as did most other types of social service?

Niebuhr: Perhaps we have a false schism here between religion as an intellectual endeavor and religion as a warm, emotional interest. In science and in art there is not this split between the work of the class and the work of the laboratory or studio.

Dillenberger: The whole laboratory analogy is questionable. Perhaps the so-called religious laboratory works best when it is not tied up too closely with the classroom work.

Greene: Aren't we confronted with a situation where a good many students are subjected to some fairly meaningless intellectual disciplines in class and then leave the classroom and plunge into their vital extracurricular activities? Isn't one of our jobs as teachers to bring home to students the meaning, the value, and joy of their studies and to let them experience the existential significance of their studies?

Van Dusen: Isn't the analogy closer in the field of art? In art you obviously have to have the experimental participation of the students; for example, in the hearing of music.

Smith: Not all students are going to develop an interest in religion by means of the classroom. Many students will develop their religious interests through experiences that are ouside the classroom. This suggests another function for the cocurricular activities in religion.

Antz: In connection with this word laboratory, there are very few of the students in science courses who really develop a scientific attitude. Most of the students' laboratory experiences simply tell them what now is but do not give them a true insight into the ongoing processes of science. In the field of religion, we have a course at New York University taught by a Protestant minister, in which students actually try to experience what the various kinds of praying are.

Childs: I want to ask how to overcome the tension between proclaiming truth and searching for it. Most students think that those who assume a religious orientation do tend to restrict inquiry.

Greene: The danger of this can scarcely be overestimated. I think we are going to be driven to a recognition of the profound difference between religious dogmatism and religious dogma, by which I mean a widely accepted major premise. In the university community we have certain dogmas and certain working premises which we accept as members of the working community. But in a liberal university there is no dogma which does not invite critical re-examination. We can deal with the curse of religious dogmatism if we believe that religion is a human response to the ultimate truth. This requires a prophetic spirit, a continuous re-examination of our finite understanding of all truth, including religious truth.

Childs: Wouldn't your position be quite in line with that of the secularists and the humanists? As I read contemporary Protestant theology, I detect quite a different movement from that which you describe as the standpoint of liberal religion.

Greene: I am speaking for a minority group.

Childs: Another question: The second part of what you said in your introductory remarks was less satisfying than the first part, because you fell too easily back into the classical liberal position. This position requires some further definition at the present time. Are we clear on what is this common body of loyalties which the university uses as its ultimate test?

Greene: We should be respectful of the intolerant person but be very intolerant of his intolerance.

Childs: There are of course great problems here in connection with Communism on our faculties.

Chipkin: Would Professor Greene's liberal spirit be accepted by all adherents of a religious position, and would that acceptance make it possible for us to translate this into religion in education in the common school? How many religionists would be willing to subject the dogmas of religion to laboratory test? How many would be willing to put this into the area of personal experience?

F. E. Johnson: There may be types of religion that are so authoritarian and rigid that they cannot be brought within this type of liberal approach. Yet I do not think that we ought to be too precipitate in our judgments. For example, I have been much impressed by the reaction of the Catholic Church to the controversy over Father Feeney.

Krumm: What about the question of the religious commitment of the teacher of religion? Is there any valid sense in which we ought to inquire about the religious practices of someone who is coming into the teaching situation, at least to the extent that he is concerned enough to do something which he identifies as religious. The analogy with art is illuminating here. To teach music and still to refuse to practice it openly would seem to indicate a complete lack of understanding of a particular discipline, and yet we are sometimes urged in the university to believe that one is not truly objective if he is really committed to a particular religious group.

Friess: Students in today's world are entitled to two things. First, they are entitled to the experience of those who are deeply committed and profoundly thoughtful. They are entitled in a university to see the significance of a subject or an area of life in relation to its many impacts upon different phases of life. So the thing we are after is not located solely in the sphere of the departments of religion or in the faculty members who are sympathetic to them in other departments. There is room also for teachers who will bring students face to face with the limiting or negative aspects of religion in culture. This is the only way in which the vitality of the subject can be secured at the university level. Hence it follows that it isn't only those who are in favor of religion that are entitled to present it. One could defend the proposition that those who are opposed to religion also have an obligation to present it. The other thing that students are entitled to is more encouragement than we usually give to active participation as citizens. For students to relate themselves to the many current developments in our world, we must think not only of what the school can do within its walls but of the whole picture. Of course this is a tremendously complicated project. We must not put our problem into too narrow a set of terms. We must encourage our students to participate in a variety of ways in the life of society.

Van Dusen: Let me attempt a summary statement to see whether we would agree substantially with it as a basis for further discussion. In the field which we have been considering this afternoon, in view of the important role which religion has had for good or for ill in human culture in general and in American culture in particular, there should be some provision for instruction respecting religion. That instruction should embrace not only historical material on the role of religion in human society and in American society in particular but also a consideration of the role of religion and the principal expressions of religion in contemporary American life. It should therefore provide for a sympathetic but critical and as far as achievable objective presentation of at least the three major faiths in American life, Protestantism, Catholicism, and Judaism, and the faith of the so-called secularists. We have also suggested consideration, as far as feasible, of religions in other cultures. There is also value in opportunities for experiencing the realities of religion in somewhat the same way as there would be in an art studio for experimentation in art, in an art gallery for appreciation of art, and in exhibitions of living music through performance and the opportunity for performance.

Dillenberger: Does this treatment of religion differ at all from the way good teaching goes on in any field? Does religion need a special formula? Perhaps there is not as much dogmatism in religion as in some other spheres.

Blau: Where in the academic sphere is there dogmatism in fields other than religion?

Jackson: What about a mathematical logician faced with the data of extra-sensory perception?

F. E. Johnson: What about the discussion between the advocates of progressive and the advocates of neoclassical educational theory?

Blau: I do not think one finds dogmatism in academic life, in the sense of an assertion that a particular position is the only position and one must believe it if he is to be right.

Berkson: In the teaching of history one could teach about the feudal system but be definitely opposed to that concept as an economic system. But suppose someone should make a similar criticism with reference to St. Thomas Aquinas. One might say that the basis on which St. Thomas reconciled faith and reason can no longer be maintained and be very critical about that particular interpretation. If we dealt with the question of religion honestly, we would agree that there have been historically as many errors in religion, or more, as in other aspects of culture and that some religions are really not defensible. Moreover, I don't see how you can teach religion as a part of culture without indicating the tremendous harm that religion and religious organizations have done at times, as well as the good they have contributed.

Van Dusen: Would anyone want religion taught in any other way than Dr. Berkson suggests? Would anyone want religion taught without regard for the truth, including the negative aspects of religion? It is a fact that in dozens of colleges religion is being taught in an objective and well-founded fashion.

E. Hunt: What is to be done about students who do not elect religion courses? Also, what about the place of religion in other courses, in history or literature, or in the sciences? In the private secondary schools has there not been a serious neglect of religious instruction?

Van Dusen: There has been a considerable increase in the number of schools where religious instruction is provided.

Baldwin: Over the past 20 years, there has been a dramatic change in this respect. Also a good many teachers in other subjects than religion have become interested in learning more about the functions of religion.

Smith: This is quite true and I would supplement this at the college level. The courses referred to as general education are one of the important means in the colleges for introducing the consideration of religion in culture.

Jackson: Students are looking for a more definite kind of religion because they meet with such dogmatism in other parts of the world, for instance in Communism and in Fascism. I detect a slight antidogmatic trend here and it is only fair to remember that we are confronted in our age with some tremendous dogmatic systems. People have come back to a sense of the need for definition.

Van Dusen: I have the impression that students these days are not as afraid of dogma as teachers are. Students want strong teaching. They are not interested in highest common denominators.

Berkson: Students want positive ideas, which does not mean that they will agree with them. They may disagree, but in order to disagree, there has to be something they can attack. This is especially true in teacher education.

Baldwin: Are we not using the word dogmatic with two different meanings? One meaning is belief in a certain set of ideas, convictions that have been tested; the other meaning refers to an inflexible method or approach.

Thayer: Have we reversed ourselves since this morning? Is the world full of materialistic, grasping people or is it full of people who are seeking for faith? We are living in an age where there is a great urge for conformity, and people who are fearful and hysterical are looking for this definiteness, but they are also anxious to impose their convictions on other people. Back of the movement to introduce religion into the schools is the intent to have teachers go into the schools with strong religious orientations which they will impose on other people.

Berkson: It is not a movement toward conformity, but it is a movement toward definition. Definition and formulation are essential in this period.

McIntosh: We would make a mistake if we tried to put the young people of this generation into categories. Each young person comes to college with a different background and different needs. The schools would make a mistake if they tried to impose on young people a series of fixed, dogmatic religious experiences. Our parents were too dogmatic and too fixed. That is one reason our generation has become unsettled and our young people are now searching for some new kind of settlement of their own. One of the chief functions of a department of religion is to call to the attention of teachers in other departments the significance of religion. The department of religion is in a sense a conscience for the university community.

F. E. Johnson: What is needed is exposure of students to the conflicting points of view of people who are thoroughly convinced of the correctness of their respective positions. There is no institutional dogmatism or authoritarianism involved in that. It is a tremendously real confrontation of students with different, seriously held points of view.

Smith: It is a matter of fact that much of the college teaching of religion is being done now on a responsible, objective basis. The responsibility of the college in the field of religion is to state what is, and this is by and large being done very well. There is a difference of function as between a college and a church.

Wornom: Professor Smith has given only one side of the picture. There are church colleges which believe that there is a body of church dogma to be taught and they so teach it.

Niebuhr: There are many colleges that do not teach religion in an objective sort of way.

Van Dusen: The important point for us is that the trend is toward the objective teaching of religion and not toward the dogmatic teaching of religion.

THIRD SESSION

The discussions on this day were devoted to the subject of religion in public education. The morning session was initiated by a summary by Ernest Johnson of his paper printed in full earlier in the record (pp. 432–36).

Childs: The issue is whether the advocacy of a secular position in public education is necessarily incompatible with a theistic faith. Charles Donohue, a Roman Catholic scholar at Fordham University, has tried to develop the conception that the loyalty to the secular which is involved in the common public school is a religious loyalty. This fits in with a total pattern of ecclesiastical strategy which is of far-reaching importance. If that be established, then it becomes a question of adjusting the claims of various groups; and this standpoint would greatly aid that part of the Roman Catholic group who want to see the parochial school system made a part of the public school system of the United States and who want to use public tax funds for the support of the parochial school system. Therefore, loyalty to the American community ought not be identified as a particular religious solution, because it is something that the other major religious groups mentioned yesterday all share. If this is religion, it is a kind of civic religion which we all share. We are striking at something very fundamental if we construe the secular to be a particular commitment of a particular group.

F. E. Johnson: There are people who would like to make the public school in a sense the temple of man. We must take account of this. Most of us would say that when democracy is made an ultimate it becomes a religion, and certainly we can speak of Communism as a religion. Wherever you find your ultimates you are in the realm of religion.

Wornom: I think Professor Childs misinterprets the intent of Professor Donohue's articles. They were directed not at the separation of Catholic schools and the securing of funds for Catholic parochial schools but were directly intended to point up how religion could be an integral part of a public school system. Donohue's views are important because high officials of the Catholic Education Association are in general and almost complete agreement with them—and that goes for some members of the hierarchy also. Donohue does not favor a common core or a secular type of approach, but he does point out that the secularist's position is one of many faiths in America and should be included along with other faiths in dealing with religion in the public school system. He points out that because this secularist position has tended to become the common view of the public school, to the exclusion of other faiths, and is then implicitly taken to be the faith of the public school system, we do not face up to a truly pluralistic situation unless we designate this secularist view as itself a faith. He would have all of these faiths, including the secularist, recognized equally in the public school system. That is pointing to a new development in the point of view of the Roman Catholic Church which it seems to me is very important for us to take into account.

Greene: We ought to welcome with open arms what Professor Childs has stated as the secular outlook. He is drawing a line around an area of common concern—political, social, moral, etc. We differ in this country as to our ultimate interpretation of these outlooks, both historically and systematically. You do not accept a theistic outlook; I do. But I have great enthusiasm for democracy, just as you do. This is a real advance in our discussion. We have a common interest in this large, diverse area of common concern. We recognize the divergencies of interpretation, and this raises the question of how to protect the majority against the minority and the minority against the majority. To sharpen that point, I should like to ask Professor Childs what, in large outline, he thinks would be the most effective program designed to promote real respect in any community on the part of the local majority for the local minorities, whether the majority be religious and the minority humanistic in some sense or *vice versa,* because both situations arise. The noisy, tyrannical religious minority is a problem for the quiet, constructive humanistic majority; and in the same way a noisy humanistic minority can make trouble for a quiet, theistic majority.

Childs: The first step in that program is a clear analysis of what the problems are. I once wrote something on "who owns the child?" I like to think that he owns himself, but the question is, "Who is going to direct his education?" We say that the community as well as the parents have joint responsibility in doing this. But there is something imperialistic in the position that the majority has the right to impose its belief on the minority.

Van Dusen: There is also something imperialistic in the other way—that a minority can enforce its views upon the majority.

Childs: Here is the difficulty. I am opposed to coercion in these matters.

Sutherland: We should renew our strength by touching the earth from time to time, by considering how things are rather than only how they ought to be. We need to remember two things: one is that millions of people in the United States think about these things in an entirely different way than we do in the universities. We live in a very artificial and encapsulated world. We don't know how people think in the market places and country towns. The second thing is that most people do not distinguish nearly so clearly as we do between what the private schools can do and what the public schools can do. Most citizens feel that the public school system which they pay for through their taxes is their own, just as much their own as the private school is regarded by the parents who send their children there. We must not forget that we are negating what a lot of human beings want when we try to say that government will come in and prevent some school program which the local people have determined. The essence of the debate today is whether we should allow people to do as they wish in a concern which they regard as essentially their own. My feeling is that we should let the people of a community do substantially as they please unless there is some compelling reason for a larger unit of government to stop them. Autonomy of the local community is important to democratic government.

Thayer: We have a problem of education here as well as a legal problem. We do lean toward granting the greatest possible amount of local autonomy, but no one would say that a local community which is convinced that it should promote the doctrines of Nazism should be permitted to do so.

Van Dusen: Today presumably a community would not be permitted to teach Communism in its schools. Are you saying that some system of thought would be prohibited only if it was contrary to national policy? Are you also challenging the right of the local community to determine its own system of religious instruction?

Thayer: Local autonomy in such matters is not good school law.

Childs: The Supreme Court decision on segregation is to the point in this discussion.

Thayer: As far as the school law is concerned, the local community is not free of the state. Local boards represent the state within the local community. We allow the greatest possible local autonomy. The state government sets up criteria and regulations which control the manifestations of local autonomy. In the same way the United States Supreme Court may rule that there are certain national considerations that operate. There are such considerations with respect to religion in education because we are a divided people in that regard since religion is such an area of doubt and dispute.

Seaver: We must remember that especially in recent years there has been a large increase in the support of local school systems by the state financially. This makes a tremendous difference in the authority of the state as far as education in the local community is concerned.

Sutherland: In no wise did I intend to differ from what my friends here have said. I did say that the local community ought to have its way unless there is a strong reason for preventing it. In cases raising such issues, our judges have to say what constitutes a strong reason. Provisions in Federal and state constitutions affecting public schools are fairly vague. It is impossible to write in clear terms constitutional prescriptions for all the manifold activities of human society. Hence arises the necessity for judicial evaluation of the comparative importance of this or that local policy complained of as objectionable by some person affected. Inevitably such evaluation becomes in some measure a subjective process.

E. Hunt: If the community is homogeneous, there can be religious exercises in the schools; but if the community is not homogeneous, religious education has to disappear from the school program. In mixed communities religion in the public schools comes in almost exclusively in the teaching of world history and here it is done on a strictly objective basis. In the treatment of American history there is almost no attention to religion, apart from the settlement of the original colonies. Most school textbooks in this subject have no chapters which deal specifically with religion. If the community is mixed in its religious loyalties, religion just doesn't get discussed. I would add that most teachers are simply not equipped to deal with this subject. Of course as the teachers colleges give more attention to this field, the situation will improve. The point I am making is that the community does not determine what goes on in the classroom except indirectly and here the minorities are very important. Only in the very homogeneous communities can there be what we call the teaching of religion.

Carman: Would you add that where there is a centralized school you are likely to have less homogeneity? In the State of New York we formerly had mostly district schools; increasingly, as we become urbanized and as these district schools are disappearing, the homogeneity tends to disappear.

E. Hunt: I would accept that, and would illustrate it further by references to the situation in Vermont and New Hampshire. As the schools there have been centralized, the religious exercises have been virtually eliminated.

Wornom: I checked a number of books in the California system and I did find sections on religion. In Los Angeles there was a syllabus on the teaching of religion. More recently the Pittsburgh school system has issued a syllabus for teachers pointing out at every age level subject matter with religious and other moral and spiritual values. The same is true of the school system of Cincinnati, and this is spreading. Undoubtedly there are other states where this is not the case.

Berkson: Every system of autonomy is a range of freedom of action within a broad system of law. But we have left out the major consideration: Should the public school be a reflection of the local community or a reflection of the American community? Are we preparing for local citizenship or for American citizenship? Where the sense of local citizenship conflicts with American citizenship, we have a right to say, whether it represents a majority or a minority, that it cannot take precedence. Professor Sutherland did seem to give the impression that a person or a community has a right to do whatever it pleases. That word "please" with reference to a moral system seems to be quite out of place. There is a conflict between the idea of allowing a local community to teach its religion in the public schools and the general American conception of what the public school is for, because the public school is preparing for a community in which there are diverse religious views and if a local community prepares its members for a particular religious community only, it is really developing sectarianism and intolerance. Our local communities, as we know, are not infrequently unenlightened centers of prejudice. The policy indicated by Professor Sutherland, giving the local community a prior claim on the educational system, seems to be opposed to anything that we would call high religion, or civilization, or enlightenment.

Van Dusen: Is not the constitutional position that the primary responsibility for the education of youth lies in the local school boards? The national government does not have a system of education. The policy of the national government is to interfere with the local educational system only where the national interest is imperiled or where the national constitution is explicitly or implicitly violated.

Sutherland: The Federal government has no affirmative responsibility for providing education save in Alaska and the District of Columbia. There are a number of negatives which emanate from Washington for the schools, but there are no positives.

Berkson: The responsibility for the conduct of educational systems rests with the state, not with the local community or with the Federal government. We have certainly given a great deal of consideration to local opinion, but, from a constitutional and legal point of view, it is each individual state that has the competence to make final decisions with reference to education. Is this right?

Sutherland: Yes. If the State of New York wished to say, for example, that no Christmas celebration should be held in any public schools and they wished to undertake the responsibility of enforcement, the state could probably oblige each district to comply.

Jackson: Where do the parents come in? It is so basic to our system in England that this spectacle of the vanishing parent interests me. What place do the parents have?

Berkson: A parent has the right to send his child either to a public school or to a private school, and that is a basic right that has been defended by the courts. We may therefore conclude that a parent who sends his child to a public school has at least accepted the philosophy of the public school as one to which he is not entirely opposed. We feel that the schools have a moral and spiritual responsibility to educate for the American community. There are two sides to this: one is the sharing of a common point of view in certain respects, and the other is helping each individual person to develop his talents to the fullest degree.

Van Dusen: The parents also have an influence on their local educational system through their vote.

Thayer: There is another contrast between American and British education. In this country we have in effect a constitutional prohibition against the teaching of religion within the public schools. In England, on the other hand, you have religious instruction under the auspices of the state, with the parent having the privilege of withdrawing the child. Here it is the opposite. If a school is engaged in the positive indoctrination of a religious point of view, then that is declared illegal. We therefore have here the mingling of two important principles. One is the legal principle which puts the handling of religion in a special category in which there is no prohibition against the study of religion but there is a prohibition against indoctrination. Then there is the second principle that every effort be made in controversial subjects to secure a sympathetic but objective presentation of the various points of view.

Childs: It is very wrong to hold the secular school responsible for the failure to deal with religion. This is a misplaced diagnosis. The reason we do not treat religion as we do other subject matters is because the religious parties would not tolerate it. Therefore, I have never been able to take this program of trying to put the study of religion into the school program at face value at all. I know of a student—a graduate of a theological seminary—who was dismissed from a school system for treating the Virgin Birth from an objective historical standpoint. The religious groups will not permit these matters to be treated in the same way as other matters are treated. As I see it, the whole movement some of you are advocating for religion in education is based on a fundamentally incorrect analysis.

Seaver: Here is another illustration. Two well-written textbooks on European history have been widely used in the high schools. The authors happen to be Roman Catholics. Because the heads of certain denominations in one southern state protested against a treatment of the Reformation which they thought was somewhat slanted it was necessary to go to great lengths to produce a special edition of the book for that state in order that it could be adopted for the schools there. The same sort of situation prevails in the treatment of democracy. There are some people who say that we have a republic and not a democracy and who therefore think we should avoid references to democracy. We cannot expect to have a common treatment of religion that will be acceptable in every state of the nation.

Van Dusen: How far in dealing with this question of religion are we dealing with the only subject on which there is risk of indoctrination? Anything which has significance involves partiality and slanting and yet it may properly exist within the school system.

E. Hunt: Religion is certainly not the only area where this problem of indoctrination arises. In the study of political systems, of labor-management relations, of sex and family life problems, there are many groups in the nation who are opposed to realistic teaching.

McIntosh: I cannot believe that there is no such thing as a common core of religious belief. Call it watered-down religion, if you will. What we are really saying here is that since we cannot agree on religion, we will have no religion taught at all. Referring to the example of teaching about the Virgin Birth, it seems to me that no teacher should attempt to teach such a very controversial subject. I am certain from my own experience that one can isolate those things which are common to our experience and avoid the seriously controversial issues. Why isn't it possible to present a common core of beliefs in the various religions without controversy and without higher criticism?

F. E. Johnson: But what about the humanists or secularists who are not at home in any one of the three historical faiths in this country? Suppose the humanist says, "I object to that because I do not accept the concept of God as an ultimate truth"?

McIntosh: Then leave God out; I am not afraid of an irreducible minimum. I think we have been too afraid or too biased to find this irreducible minimum.

Blau: Mrs. McIntosh's irreducible minimum would turn out not to be religious but ethical.

Smith: This seems to me the basic problem. We can get agreement on some of the ethical principles, but the question of the tap roots of these ethical principles is really the problem. Suppose we can agree upon the ethical principles. The question is what are the bases of these things?

Greene: Granting the danger of religious dogmatism, is there not a corresponding danger of humanistic dogmatism and imperialism? What is the best way to combat *all* dogmatism? My answer, which brings in the tap roots, is that we should not suppress them but bring them to the fore in open discussion.

Let all the dominant positions be openly expressed so that young people will learn to grow up in a controversial atmosphere, and then let tolerance and mutual respect grow from these experiences.

Baldwin: The best protection of the majority against the minority or *vice versa* is not the evasion of some of these issues. It is not to say we don't dare face them. It is in helping to develop ability to make value judgments intelligently. We should not start with the most controversial issues, of course. But if we deal intelligently with some of these questions we can help students to develop a belief in the right to differ, a respect for honest differences, and a recognition that perhaps difference is advantageous to us because it presents a challenge to us to rethink our position.

Jackson: We all seem to be agreed on this importance of clash of opinion, but don't we also need to give attention as to how and when the clashes arise? Our discussion is relevant to the university level, but not perhaps to the earlier ones. The mind is going to be indoctrinated at some point. At what point do we begin to create a mind? One can't simply bring up children on clashes. We have spent a lot more time on divergence than on the preconditions of such divergence.

Greene: The explanation for the terrible trouble the whole world is in is indoctrination. We need to address ourselves to the question of how to train, from early youth onward, world citizens who can live with one another despite all racial, religious, economic, or other divergences.

Van Dusen: Aren't you calling the development of tolerance the highest good?

Greene: In a sense, yes. It may not be harmful when parents differ quite considerably, provided it is done in an atmosphere of love and tolerance. Isn't this the perfect training in long-range, mature tolerance? Tolerance is not indifference; it does not exclude having convictions. But conviction does not arise from mere narrow, one-sided indoctrination.

Carman: Perhaps the community can agree upon certain things (along the lines of Mrs. McIntosh's "common core") that children right from the first grade on ought to begin to learn—by indoctrination if you wish—and then when they are along far enough in the adolescent period I would go all the way with what Theodore Greene has said: that the different positions be presented, be discussed, and then in the last analysis the individual will have to come to his own conclusion. He may have started out as a Presbyterian and end up being a humanist or a secularist, or *vice versa,* but I see no way to avoid this.

Van Dusen: Dr. Carman has here made a compromise suggestion, recognizing that at the most elementary level the student should be introduced to a common core. Dr. Blau is probably right that Mrs. McIntosh's common core would be a study of ethical ideals not essentially different from an American interpretation of the meaning of democracy. Then, when the child goes on to the higher level, he ought to be introduced not only to a study of the particular brand of religious belief and practice that his parents have exposed him to, but to the major religious faiths in America, including humanism. There would always be the risk that the child would change his faith; and, if the parents are not prepared to face that, then of course they will be opposed to this proposal. It would have the value of producing intelligent, critical, and tolerant citizens.

Herriott: There must be something in the young child's experience which involves commitment. The question is: Where will that happen, in the home, or the church, or the public schools? Here in New York City we have been trying to work out some agreement on a common core, a common understanding of what might be taught in the public schools of the city. A group of religious leaders representing the three faiths was asked by the Superintendent of Schools to come together to work this out. The difficulty has been that disputes and disagreements always arise with respect to doctrines and their various interpretations.

Washburne: I take exception to Dr. Carman's view that children should be indoctrinated. If by indoctrination we mean giving a one-sided picture of controversial issues, we have no right to do it.

Carman: I didn't mean it in that sense.

C. Hunt: I do not believe in indoctrination even at the elementary school level. Education is a continuum and all the things that you hope for have their end in the beginnings, in the elementary levels. Indoctrination should not be present at the beginning. I think the individual has some rights in this matter, the chief being religious expression. To whom must the individual go for redress, because he has been indoctrinated in such a way that he cannot achieve for himself free expression of his own best religion? I would regret any instruction which did not allow a student to go back in terms of his later experience and examine his earlier instruction and reform his judgment in terms of his own experience.

Washburne: When we talk about religion in the schools we have to distinguish between the different elements in it. Such things, for example, as study of the history of religions, the effects of religion in cultural history, and the role of religion in contemporary American life are clearly within the scope of the schools. They do not involve indoctrination. They involve discussion and insight. Some of them can begin in the lowest grades. Others must start with high school or college.

There is another group of things which obviously do not belong within the schools: ritual and liturgy, dogma and creed, the attitude toward revelation, the sacred character of Scripture, attempts to proselytize for any particular sect, the deliberately biased teaching of history in favor of a particular religion or denomination and the teaching of morals that are based upon a specific creed or doctrine, for example regarding divorce, contraception, diet, or church attendance. These things are quite obviously outside the realm of the public school because inevitably in such matters there is a wide difference among the various denominations and religions.

Then there is a third aspect, which seems to me the most important of all; namely, the attitude toward worship and meditation and the opportunity for reverence and ultimately for the sense of oneness with God. These are obviously not things that can be taught in the school. They are not things that can be taught at all. They are things for which it is possible only to get a favorable atmosphere. We should at least see to it that in the school there will be among our teachers some who have that deep religious sense. The contagion of a reverent attitude can set the stage for the pupil's own religious experience. Many are going to get this deeper religious sense out of literature, music, art, nature, church, or temple.

There is a fourth group of things which do not need much discussion: religious customs, including the celebration of holidays, festivities, pictorial representations, etc. Many of these are a natural part of the culture in which the school exists and are commonly included in the schools with very little resulting criticism, as long as they are merely expressions of the culture and are free from denominational interpretation and religious indoctrination.

We need to be clear about which aspects of religion can be brought into the public schools, and to recognize equally frankly the many things essential to religion which cannot be introduced.

Jackson: We do not hesitate to pass on to our children our deepest convictions. We do not say that some people believe in putting people to death in gas chambers and others do not, and now you make up your own mind. No, we take a very definite stand on this with our children. There is this aspect of forming commitment which is not completely met by educating the child into tolerance.

Thayer: The question is not one of intellectualization or verbalization completely. We don't say that it is not the function of education to indoctrinate, but we take a great deal of care in how we indoctrinate. No one argues that it is not the function of the public school to recognize certain common values. Don't we have to go back to a whole way of life within the nursery school and the kindergarten?

Van Dusen: There is no indoctrination in anything that is significant which is not also controversial.

Niebuhr: Suppose your child growing up in a home where there is belief in God goes to nursery school and meets a child whose parents do not believe in God. When that child comes home do you take the attitude that the other child is a bad child or that his home is a wrong home? No. We have to get back to the basic meaning of the experience of God in terms of integrity and so on, with respect to which you would probably agree with the basic standards of those who do not believe in God.

Jackson: Perhaps the traditional idea of "natural law" discoverable by reason is what we need to recognize. I prefer such a concept to the "irreducible minimum" that was mentioned earlier.

Dillenberger: My own experience with my children in living on a street where there are Catholic, Protestant, and Jewish children in about equal numbers has shown that it is possible to deal with these differences in religion in a positive way. We don't need to go into the details of the differences to a large extent. We simply start with an acceptance of the differences, as facts of existence.

Jackson: Isn't this interest in getting religion into the public schools at least partly a reflection of the breakdown of the other institutions of the home and the church?

Gans: Formerly the function of the family included the assumption that the children would be reared within a religious heritage. We have tended to move away from this basic concept of the family. The school has taken over a good many of the functions formerly assumed by the family. Perhaps we will be forced to look at the family function from two points of view. What does the taking over of these functions do to the family itself? And then what has the development of personality got to do with this problem?

Van Dusen: Hasn't the new interest really been a question of the widespread recognition that we are deficient in the moral and the spiritual values? The weakening of home and church is only a part of the picture.

Smith: Plus the feeling that while the schools have done many things they have not done all they could do in this area.

Van Dusen: Perhaps we have substantial consensus on these points: First, in a negative vein, we recognize that the problem which makes any reference to religion in education so difficult, namely that it is a controversial subject on which there is a variety of opinions and sharp feelings, is not a problem which is confined to religion. The school system also has to face the problem of political differences, differences in economic theory, and all the rest. Wherever there are human values at stake, there are diversities of viewpoint and diversities of loyalty. Therefore, the possibility of teaching in a way that will satisfy everyone is always problematical.

In the second place, we seem to recognize that there are important differences in the responsibilities of the school system with regard to religion at the different age levels, and that at the elementary age level it is altogether appropriate—in fact, most would say it is mandatory upon the school system—to try to introduce children to the finest common elements in the American tradition, including moral and spiritual values, in which we would include the values of democracy as a system of thought and of government.

But in regard to the high school level—now we may not be agreed on this —if a child is to be an intelligent citizen, either in the sense of being familiar with the major formative forces in the cultural life or in the sense of understanding the problems of his fellow citizens, he ought to be introduced to the major religious points of view as they are held within the American community, of which there would be at least four easily distinguishable, and the fact that these four are not exhaustive should certainly be pointed out. Furthermore, the presentation of these faiths should be made sympathetically, without any purpose of inculcating any of those views, but only of exposing the child with as sympathetic interpretations as possible to the main alternative religious attitudes which prevail within the American community.

It is another question whether that should be done simply as the material emerges in the literature, art, and social studies courses, or whether it should be recognized, as I think it ought to be, that religion is an independent interest and attitude in human life apart from its history, literature, and its social significance. Religion provides a subject matter which is just as autonomous, intellectually considered, as music or the graphic arts. Therefore it should be presented by those who are themselves well trained, especially in the history and beliefs of religion, just as one who teaches the history of the Middle Ages is supposed to have done study in medieval history or a person who teaches art is supposed to know about art.

My query with regard to the third of the six positions outlined in Professor Johnson's paper—a proposal which many of us would find very attractive—is whether it does deal in a really scholarly, realistic fashion with religion. Perhaps there is some trend toward a consensus which would embody, of the six positions, the sixth as the one that should have priority at the early levels of public school education, and something that stands midway between the first and the third at the higher levels—the third because of its insistence upon objectivity and against propaganda—the first as recognizing the autonomous reality of religion as a subject matter more than seems to be implicit in the third.

Let us move now to a consideration of Professor Sutherland's paper.

Sutherland: Whether we like it or not, there will be religion in the public schools in some way. In most instances people do not go to law about what troubles them in the public schools. It makes them too conspicuous. Most people are willing to accept what they feel are not important disadvantages, and make the best of them. This is the first point that I make in my paper: that all over the country, at the school district or city school level, there are found a multitude of petty subventions of religion by public authorities, some of which inevitably irritate part of the people affected, but most of which are nevertheless cheerfully accepted without protest. Whether it be a school Christmas pageant, or daily Bible reading, or opening prayer, or provision of bus service alike to children of public and parochial schools, the presence of some such activity is a widespread phenomenon.

The second point that I make was driven home by some of our friends this morning when they said that the control of religious activity in school has its first constitutional screening within the states. This is true. And within the states, it must be remembered, there are three levels of law, three levels of governmental activity concerning religion in schools, that must be taken into account. In volume, by far the greatest activity is at the school district or city school board level. State education departmental control reviews and changes some of this local activity. Only a small amount of such local activity finally comes up against a state constitutional ceiling, administered by the Supreme Court of the state in question.

There are in all state constitutions provisions affecting religion in education. There are two or perhaps three common types of such clauses; and of course, in state statutes, as distinguished from state constitutions, there appear relevant provisions in wide variety. Of three common forms of state constitutional provisions, one in general terms guarantees freedom of religion. Another provides that no public money shall be used for "sectarian" purposes. In the third place, state constitutions often provide that there shall be a system of free public schools. There have recently arisen a number of cases of church schools used and supported by the local authorities; in such a situation, one question may be whether the schools are in fact "public" as directed by the state constitution.

After controversies have been fought out with the local school board, and then with the senior state authorities, they may finally reach the Supreme Court of the United States on questions arising under the Federal constitution. State bodies, at lower levels, have actually had a great deal more to do with the legality of religion in the public schools than the Supreme Court; that court, however, has received a major portion of the applause and criticism.

There really have been only three cases where the Supreme Court of the United States has declared unconstitutional state provisions affecting religious education in schools. These three decisions came in 1925, in 1943, and in 1948. In the first of these, the Supreme Court declared it to be constitutionally impossible for a state to confine education to public schools. In the second case the Supreme Court said that a state, acting through its local authorities, could not compel a child to salute the flag when the child's conscience forbade it. The third was the McCollum decision.

The McCollum case involved a situation where the people of Champaign, Illinois, wished to set aside a short period each week, when representatives of three denominations—a Rabbi, a Catholic priest, and Protestant lay missionary—could come into public school classrooms and give religious instruction to children whose parents desired it. Children who did not wish to have the religious instruction were permitted to go to another room. The Supreme Court held that this imposed an undue hardship on Terry McCollum, a boy who did not wish to receive religious instruction, for it made him feel conspicuous in the eyes of his schoolmates. The court decided that this was so hard on the boy that he should not be obliged to submit to it, and therefore that the Federal government should come down and prevent the people of Champaign from having in their schools the instruction I describe. This is the law as it stands today.

Something very interesting has recently happened in New Jersey. The Gideons and the School Board of the Borough of Rutherford, New Jersey, have joined in a petition to take up to the Supreme Court of the United States for review the decision of the Supreme Court of New Jersey handed down by

Chief Justice Vanderbilt holding that it was unconstitutional both under the Fourteenth Amendment and under the constitution of New Jersey for the Gideons to distribute Bibles in the public schools.

I do not think that such a review is in order. I do not think the Gideons can persuade the Supreme Court that the Fourteenth Amendment compels New Jersey to permit the gift of Gideon Bibles to children in its schoolrooms. If the New Jersey people, speaking through their courts, wish to exclude Bible-distribution from their classrooms, this is within their power.

One feature of the Supreme Court's decisions, often overlooked, is the notable fact that there has never been a clear holding by that court that a state is forbidden to put into effect any measure amounting to an "establishment" of religion. So far as I know, the Supreme Court of the United States has never actually decided that the "establishment" clause of the First Amendment, approved in 1791, which says that *Congress* shall make no law respecting an establishment of religion, is now so incorporated in the Fourteenth Amendment of 1868 as to forbid any *state legislature* to make any law respecting an establishment of religion. Some day a taxpayer may successfully renew the contention that some arrangement for religious instruction in a school district amounts to an establishment of religion in his state, and the Supreme Court of the United States may then hold that the Fourteenth Amendment forbids that state to do what it wants in this respect. But such a pure "establishment" decision (as distinguished from a case of undue pressure on an individual like Terry McCollum) has never yet been handed down.

On May 17, 1954, the Supreme Court delivered great moral judgments in the school segregation cases. The unanimity of feeling in the court on this immense moral issue helped make those decisions so forceful. It seems to me that, in contrast, we should hesitate to ask the Supreme Court of the United States to interfere in every little controversy that arises locally. The moral power of its judgments, needed in such great issues as that involved in the Negro segregation cases, can be frittered away if we expect the Supreme Court to prevent every trifling inconvenience to some school children or their parents caused by something a local majority wants. Living in a government of majorities involves a certain amount of spiritual hardihood. Is this perhaps another lesson that our school children could well learn?

Berkson: The problem is how we are going to maintain the public schools free of destructive and divisive influences. What some of us fear about the movement to introduce a religious element into the public schools is that it will work against the fundamental agreements in American life. Of course we want to give a rounded concept of culture as against a one-sided concept of culture, but that need not mean introducing *religion;* it is simply giving a broader concept of *culture.* Any introduction of the term "religion" into the curriculum of the public schools must be avoided, perhaps as much to protect the interests of religion as to protect the public schools.

In the education of the person there must be full emphasis on the religious element, but that is the work of the home and the church. And just because we want to keep the schools free of any denominational or sectarian influence, we must permit those who ground their whole life-view in religion to send their children to parochial schools without making them feel in any way that they are upsetting the basic American school system. So, although I agree with Professor Childs that the American public school must be preserved in its unity, I do not have any antagonism toward the parochial schools.

One further point: The present system of having the child in school all day makes it very difficult to care for the religious education of the child. The church and the home have been put in a difficult position by the preemption of the whole day by the public school. Therefore, I go along with the suggestion of a released-time or a dismissed-time system. Any move that will give the home and the church a greater amount of time for religious instruction is compatible with a democratic point of view.

Smith: I am interested in the interpretation of the phrase "prohibiting the free exercise of religion." Would this clause in the Constitution permit the asking of redress in those cases where the school or college does not seem to make adequate provision for religion? For example, various religious groups may request the use of the school or college property for their meetings and this permission may be refused. Could a suit be brought in such a case to require the granting of such permission? Or suppose a teacher was barred from teaching in the public schools because of her religious position? This would be a constitutional question in which the teacher could well claim that she was being prohibited from the free exercise of her religion.

Chipkin: I am not competent to speak on law, but I was conscious of Professor Sutherland's comment to the effect that one should not go to the Supreme Court about small matters. Would we have an American democracy if we did not have recourse to the processes of law by which we define our changing conditions and conceptions of life? What would happen to America if the rights of minorities should be overlooked?

Van Dusen: We haven't talked about one important development which is taking place in the teachers colleges. Dr. Hunt, can you tell us about the new program for religion in teacher education?

C. Hunt: The teachers colleges for some time have been approaching this question in a very tentative fashion. The American Association of Colleges for Teacher Education has recently received a grant from the Danforth Foundation of St. Louis, and has organized a program which will deal experimentally with this question. There is an excellent coordinator and there are fifteen cooperating institutions which are seeking to discover relationships between religion and the academic disciplines and ways to teach them. The institutions are widely distributed through the country and are of different types. There are no commitments as to outcomes. It is a decentralized program; each institution is free to do what it wishes. This is entirely a question of curricular study to try to teach teachers how to be aware of the conditions which exist for the children in their classrooms, and to feel more intelligent in regard to dealing with religion in local situations. We are not assuming religious literacy as one of our objectives. We would be taking in too much territory in attempting an organized study of religion, except as it related incidentally to the study of other disciplines.

Antz: At our meeting on the project last February we did feel that complete religious literacy was too large an expectation, but that some partial literacy was in order as a goal. We have to recognize that a great majority of the graduates of teachers colleges are extremely illiterate in regard to religion. That leads us to another thing which we emphasize: namely that in a day when teachers' participation in the community is made so very much of, the community leadership angle is very important; that is, teachers coming into the community have to recognize what the different religious points of view are so that they can deal with them intelligently as members of the community.

Van Dusen: We must distinguish between teaching religion and teaching about religion. We have been talking here constantly about teaching about religion, not teaching religion. Surely there is no one here who would recommend the teaching of religion in the public schools.

E. Hunt: The line is not easy to draw. There are two kinds of things that enter into teaching. One, first-hand experience; and, second, vicarious experience. I don't quite see how you are going to bar the first-hand experience of children in religion in the understanding of religion in the public schools. The pupil is bound to inject religion into the teaching about religion in the schools. As we go farther up in the educational scale we increase the amount of vicarious material and the amount of controversial material. I would be in favor of introducing a unit on religion in America on the secondary school level. In college a good deal more of the narrative and descriptive material needs to be included.

Herriott: We can be very clear that we in this conference represent a point of view much less aggressive than that represented by many religious groups in the country. It is right that those of us within the religious fellowship should recognize the legitimate place of the study of religion within public education. But the whole problem has been confused by the fact that so many religious leaders seem to be saying that they want religion taught, precepts inculcated, in the formal theological sense. This has moved many people to resist what many of us are concerned about. They are moved to resistance because they feel that we have departed from the factual study of religion to indoctrination. There is also the serious practical difficulty that in many places people have not been willing to trust the teachers to interpret religion.

Van Dusen: As we look back over the history of religion in the college curricula and think of the suspicions we had 20 years ago, the main ground was that it could not be taught either with the academic competence expected in the other disciplines, or with fairness and objectivity. But in the college field we have had an existential refutation of those misgivings. Scholarly competence and objectivity have been demonstrated. This still remains to be demonstrated in the public schools.

Herriott: There are two aspects here. First, in the preparation of teachers we have to encourage an attitude of objectivity without lessening personal conviction, and, second, we need to develop the understanding of personal relationships so that, for example, teachers will not thoughtlessly embark upon controversial questions in a community which is not quite ready for them.

E. Hunt: There are similar problems in the area of secular ethics. We are getting programs in guidance, personal adjustment, group relations, and citizenship education. Teachers are getting into related areas in which they are not well grounded, but they are doing something which is just about as difficult to do as this field of religious education. Some of these secular issues are actually more controversial than the religious issue.

F. E. Johnson: Are we all ready to recognize that the situation in which we find ourselves is essentially ambiguous and complicated? The main thing which I had hoped would come out of this conference was a clarification of different points of view that are recognized as opposed to each other and yet not entirely mutually exclusive; that fit into a pattern that is characterized by tension, which is bound to be true in a dynamic society. Of course I look for some consensus, and one thing I hope for is that we will see as a result of this discussion that there is no such thing as an objective norm of practice in this country. The notion that there is an "American way" has led to all sorts of confusion, and it seems to me that we ought to be able to agree that all our theoretical formulations are really more descriptive of tensions than they are prescriptive of normal procedure. They indicate that we are operating in a tension between polar extremes. It is a dialectic process; a rough justice is the maximum we can achieve. You can't govern a society, you can't carry on public education and achieve complete justice to everyone. We have to bring the opposing views into a dialectical relationship. So we make progress in a discussion like this if we try to reformulate our principles in the light of the differing points of view that are brought out.

Summing Up

Barbara Ward Jackson
Assistant Editor, The Economist, London

RELIGION IN EDUCATION

In the free world, particularly in our own Western European and American tradition, the starting point in this great field of religion in education must be respect for the human person and his right to free choice. Since, however, in this case we are dealing with very small creatures who haven't perhaps reached the stage of knowing how to choose, it does come back very largely to the freedom and the right of the parent to choose the education of their children.

Certainly in the debate which was carried on in England in 1944, at the time of the new Education Act, the ground that was common to all elements in this controversy was the belief that in a free society you could not, except within limits which we will discuss, infringe too greatly on this free choice by parents. The underlying reason is, of course, that in a society of persons families are of immense importance, and in our own day, when the institutions of the state and of organized society have grown so strong, we have special and perhaps tender responsibility towards the smallest of all human societies, which is the family, and in which the first choices for the growing democratic citizen are made.

Having said that, one leads to the next point, that, while this may be true, the community itself certainly has some rights as well. The first of these rights in our own free society has perhaps evolved rather more clearly in the last fifteen or twenty years—since we have come to be faced with the troublesome problem of doctrines which actually deny freedom. I would imagine that one of the limiting factors the community would now place upon parents' right to free choice in education would be derived from the dictum of John Stuart Mill, "the liberty of each only limited by the like liberty of all." We would not consider it part of a parent's right of choice to decide that the child should be taught the denial of freedom, either in its fascist or in its communist form. We would regard the establishment of safeguards against an education which denied freedom as one of the essential rights of a free community. Nor do such safeguards impinge upon freedom, because obviously we have to defend free-dom against those who do not believe in it. The principle put into practice, however, can raise some ambiguous and difficult questions of interpretation.

The next point, on which there is fairly general agreement, is that there is some code or standard of conduct in which society is interested. We used a definition which to me is rather an unattractive phrase, "the irreducible mini-mum." I don't see how the imagination of the future can possibly be fired by the need of "the irreducible minimum." Some phrase which is in keeping with our great tradition would have been preferable, and I suggest the Natural Law. This is the idea that there is a moral ordering of society which is accessible to human reason. It is, perhaps, no more than the widest interpretation of the Kantian phrase, "Do what you would have done to you." But it is the general belief of civilized mankind that there is a natural order of *pietas* and of moral-ity which holds communities together and from which parents would not have the right to deviate. In other words, we obviously wouldn't want a lot of little children educated in the way Charles Addams educates his little monstrosities. The lady handing the cup of strychnine at the door would be a doubtful mother in democratic society.

This may seem obvious, but it can raise great and difficult controversies. In our own European tradition we have the tragic conflict of the Albigenses. The Albigensian heresy, although it was concerned with a lot of political issues as well, also raised a very grave issue of sexual morality. In the view of the time, it undermined Christian marriage, it undermined the family, and it made for sexual perversion. Had the parents, then, the right to bring up their children as little Albigensians? It was a very grave problem, and it was solved, as you know, by force; and that brought, or helped to bring, the very dubious instru-ment of the Inquisition into our Western society. But because we may be agonized by the means that were taken to solve this particular issue, I do not feel we can say it was an unimportant issue or that the preservation of this natural order of morality is not both essential and a very difficult part of the duty of society.

But now we come to another point. It is whether there is a relationship be-tween transcendental religion and moral and ethical values in society. Anyone looking back over history will see that in the case of some people this connec-tion has been what you might call vestigial or coincidental. Nevertheless, philosophically, a great many people would be prepared to argue that belief in a transcendent order, the idea that there is a standard of values which is out-side and beyond the control of the social community—even if it is no more defined than the "Way of Heaven" of Confucian thought—has been one of the great traditions not only in Western Society, but in all the great cultural systems of the world. Naturalism, which argues, and indeed must argue, that values are produced merely by the social process itself, is, on this point, in stark contrast to the religious tradition of the West, and the cultural traditions of every other great civilization. Nevertheless, as it was quite clear from our own group, this idea that ethical values and truths are generated by the social process itself and can be understood within the naturalistic explanation of reality is a view which people hold with the dedication and commitment which other people would give to a transcendental faith. To that extent, it can be called a commitment to final values and hence, to some extent a religious approach. And for that reason, when we were discussing the question of the differences in approach to religion in contemporary American society, we divided them into four: the three main religious traditions of the West, Catholicism, Protestantism, and Judaism, and then this other approach. There was a good deal of semanticist dispute about the right phrase for it, but it did finally come out as "humanism," a tradition of values, ethics, morality, and social order which excludes transcendental values or sanctions.

Now those four are obviously present in the American community, and any one trying to make a universal orthodoxy of any one of them would in fact be obviously defeating one of the fundamental principles of free society, which is —within the limits already mentioned—uncoerced agreement. The gap between the four approaches is clearly very wide.

On the one hand is the Catholic position, which may be best exemplified by the superb statement of Cardinal Newman at the end of the *Apologia*. Here he argues that if there is a Creator, and if He saw what extraordinary risks are inherent in the frailty of human reason and in human freedom to err, there is nothing contrary to reason in the idea that He would have given not only a revelation to mankind but have left an institution behind Him which would remain as a landmark and as a guide. This is, if you like, the extreme institutional position—one which perhaps the Jewish faith would approach more closely than does the Protestant tradition because of the close connection between Jewry, as a social community, and its religious faith.

At the other extreme, that of secularist humanism, the belief is held that the institutional expression of values is unnecessary because they are expressed, by and large, through the processes of society—society, in this sense, being understood as something separate, of course, from the state. Given this breadth of disagreement, we cannot say that there is any possible orthodoxy which could be taught generally in education in America which would not at the same time violate the uncoerced choice of values which is part of the democratic system.

There is still another attitude to be taken into account. In part it is the position of Catholics and of many Jews that their idea of education includes far more religious training than could ever be put into a secular system, and therefore they want religious education. But in part it is a new and growing feeling that a democratic society does, after all, depend upon some transcendental values, that the Founding Fathers formed their beliefs "under God," and that this recognition, too, has a part in the educational system of a free society. There is therefore coming up in your own community a demand for religion in the public schools which creates a new problem, which our group has tried to face.

We did not come to any conclusions about it, nor could we, because you can't come to conclusions if there is no agreement. And there wasn't. One of the plain facts about the American situation, and indeed about the English or the Continental position, is that there is no agreement in this field. There is agreement on the natural right of parents, within the limits described, to choose the education of their children; but there is no agreement that there is an inherent natural right to receive part of the taxpayers' money in order to give children the education of the parents' choice. One day, such a natural right may exist. At present, this is not the case. In other words, we may say that parents have a right to choose the type of education, but if they choose in such a way as does not fit in with the majority choice, then they have to pay for it themselves. This appears to be the general position, but in fact it is being steadily modified by experience and practice. It is obviously one on which we, all of us in the West, will have to do a good deal of clarification of our thought, because it has come upon us like so many things in our eclectic system, by practice rather than by theory, and maybe we haven't fully worked out the implications.

Now, within the limits, on the one hand, of the natural right of the parent to choose, and on the other, the very far from established right to have a certain share in the taxpayers' money, we have in the Western world, as you might imagine, many different ways of solving the problem of how to deal with religious education in a free society. In some states, the parochial schools receive no assistance. This is true of America, though, as you know, some church schools profit by certain ancillary services in this country. It is also still true in France, though there some attempt is being made by way of family allowances to assist the impoverished parent who wishes to choose a school for which they have to pay.

In Britain in different parts of the country we have solved the problem in different ways. In the English school system there is a considerable help to the parochial schools from the taxpayers' money, but not total support; and a very large sum, particularly for building, has to be found by the religious body itself. At the same time, there is a limited general religious instruction included in the curriculum of the state schools. In Scotland, on the other hand, where the system very much resembles the one prevailing in French Canada, it is assumed, apparently with the full support of the people, that all parents want definite, dogmatic religious instruction. Therefore the public schools are in part controlled either by the Protestant Church Assembly or by the Catholic Church. In other words, you have a public school system which is also "sectarian" according to the religious communion. So within British society there are two different ways of solving this problem, which is a reminder of the extent to which this is a matter still of pragmatic decision from community to community, and one on which it would be difficult at this stage of our endless democratic debate to be dogmatic.

I think that it also points to a further issue—where perhaps the question of religion in education goes into a rather wider field and touches the general topic of your Bicentennial. This issue is the degree to which these various local arrangements in various countries reflect a concrete historical development and an historical outlook, and the extent to which it is not possible to assess them unless one has some idea of the long historical process which has led to their adoption.

RELIGION AND THE STATE

It is a fact that, compared with geological time, the experiment of civilized living has been going on a very, very short time. Compared with the amoeba and the cockroach, man is a very new experiment, and his efforts in civilization are so brief as hardly to be in the span of history at all. Nevertheless, according to Toynbee, he has made about twenty-one efforts at civilization— all of them faulty—and he has made at least four attempts to achieve cultural unity in a broad sense, upon the basis of world religion. Now, it must be significant that in this six thousand years of civilized history, which is about all we have to consider, there is only one civilization in which freedom has ceased to be merely an aspiration and has become a practical method of organizing man's life in this world. And if you ask the distinguishing mark of Western society, you would have to say that it is freedom; because everything else, even things such as science and technology, has sprung, very largely, from the achievement of freedom, and not *vice versa*. And this element which has come up in our civilization alone is what gives us significance in the world and may point to whatever role or whatever destiny we may have to work out under Providence in our own time.

If you go back to the Middle Ages, it is quite clear that some of the roots of our freedom were established at that time, in at least three very important ways.

The first was in the respect for persons. Note the difference between the Maundy Service, at which the King took off his crown to wash the feet of the beggar, and the caste system in which the Brahmin puts away his food because it has been touched by the shadow of an Untouchable. Between those two approaches to the human person there is a gulf which will show itself in all manner of social institutions, even though all the implications of that gulf may not be worked out at any one time.

The second feature was the immense feeling for the rule of law, which led in Europe to the establishment of an autonomous legal system, to such independent institutions as the English Inns of Court, and to a great judiciary claiming a wide measure of independence from the state. Remember the words of Bracton, the great medieval jurist, that "the king is under God and the law."

And I believe it is true that in the first effort to set up a kingdom under entirely Christian auspices, in Spain about 600 A.D., the clerics decided that the king must be elected; in other words, that the kingly power itself had to be under legal institutions.

So there are two points. A third follows from them—the separation of powers. Only in our Greco-Judaic tradition, developing into our Christian Middle Ages and on into our own post-Christian society, do you have a genuine and continuous attempt to define the separation of powers. In most other societies, and as far as we know in archaic society, church and state tended to be one and the state swallowed the functions of the church, and Caesar tended to be confused with God. There was the tendency always to the centralization of all authority in the state; whereas in the Christian tradition the words were spoken, "Render to Caesar the things that are Caesar's, to God the things that are God's." This is a very difficult and ambiguous dictum to work out at any one time; nevertheless it suggests a trend of separation which, in my own belief at least, is the condition of freedom.

Just in parenthesis at this point, one would have to say something about the problem or the challenge of institutions. At times, institutions almost seem to be the consequence of sin; if we weren't fallible and weren't mortal, we wouldn't need them, and we'd be very much better off. Any man in his heart of hearts is every now and then an anarchist and would prefer those marginal and intimate and personal groupings which would be delicious if they were enough to carry on the business of living. But, owing to the actual fact and stuff of our mortal life, institutions are necessary and are divinely ordained. We have therefore to confront the fact that some institutions have an inherent tendency to acquire strength by their own momentum, and of these institutions undoubtedly the state is the greatest.

In the Middle Ages, where there was the struggle of two masterful institutions, the Church and the State, for primacy, there was—and I am convinced that this is the root of a great deal of the autonomy and of the plurality of Western society—the opportunity for the growth of a great many intermediate organizations, such as cities, universities, trades, guilds, corporations of all kinds. They had their chance to develop because of this struggle between divided authority, between Pope and Emperor, at the very apex of society.

There is not time for a close historical treatment of the theme, but you can find that this central division of power was the secret of constitutional development in the Middle Ages. Not that at that time they had formulated the division in the terms that we would use now; but they did see that it is possible in human society to have divided allegiances. And in their day the tendency of an institution to gather to itself total authority and total loyalty was checked by the inherent belief in the two orders of reality—divine and human—and the two loyalties—to Church and State.

One of the aspects of the Renaissance, however, was the destruction, for a time, of the essential and fruitful division of Church and State. This dialogue between Church and State, out of which our liberties sprang, was silenced in the sixteenth century. In its place came a union of Church and State which, in all communions, has tended to be the recipe of despotism. None of us can claim to have avoided the trap. The Orthodox church has known nothing but Byzantine and Muscovite autocracy. The Catholic church was involved in the Latin "union of Altar and Throne." Lutherans were passive citizens in Germany. In our own day, secular humanists have seen naturalism—in its Marxist form—made into the state religion of Communist states. Each belief has thus contributed something to the centralization of the power of Caesar and to the swallowing up in the power of Caesar of the rights of God.

Particularly in the sixteenth-century plunge into despotism, we have the seed of so much of the still current prejudice against religion—honest prejudice, which is one of the big issues underlying the question of education in state schools. Many people look back with fear and foreboding to the union of altar and throne and the use of religion by such monarchs as the King of Spain, or the Elector of Brandenburg, or, for a time, the King of England, as one more method to achieve uniformity within national frontiers. In other words, the use of religion as a method of reinforcing national unity is still remembered and feared. If we are going to understand historically the attitude of many honest minds to state-provided religious education, we must look back to the great hesitation aroused in liberal spirits by this crushing of freedom which occurred with the union of altar and throne in the Renaissance period.

Nor is it any coincidence that the thread of freedom, the development of freedom, which goes on, haltingly perhaps, but is still with us in our own day, survived precisely where the constitutional forms of the Middle Ages were not wholly lost—in England—and where the idea of limited monarchy was preserved while all Europe seemed lost in the winter of despotism. It was not always a very glorious survival. As President Griswold has reminded us, there were some pretty dubious features about the restoration of the monarchy in England after 1660. Nevertheless in the seventeenth- and eighteenth-century attempt to reassert the primacy of law, to revive many of the constitutional patterns of the Middle Ages, and to combine them with such new liberal rights as those to speech, assembly, and association, there was a continuity in the idea of a fruitful division of power which survived in our British system from the despotism of the Tudors and which became the basis of the separation of powers achieved in your own Republic.

Now many liberals in the past, in their distrust of the use of the church as an instrument of tyranny, have overlooked the extent to which, throughout the period of the Renaissance and the Enlightenment, the state as such was gathering strength, and the degree to which, under the union of altar and throne, it was not the throne that lost influence. On the contrary, in the sense of the state's national sovereignty, it gained a steady increase in authority. The partner in the dialogue of freedom really to lose power was, in fact, the institutions of Christianity. Particularly after such ghastly and disgraceful struggles as the Thirty Years War, the loss to religion was incalculable. These wars were fought in the name of religious dogmatism, but in fact they were really concerned with quite different dogmatisms; for example, the dogmatism which apparently still prevails in our own day, that one Frenchman is worth ten Germans or *vice versa*. But, nonetheless, it was religion that suffered. The wars did not inherently weaken the state; they merely weakened the church which had been the essential partner in the dialogue of freedom.

Now in our day, this fact is coming back to our consciousness with the advent of totalitarian dictatorship. In our own century, we have the religion of Caesar completely swallowing up that separation of powers and that division of allegiance out of which our European freedom and the freedom of our Western society grew. And it seems to me that one of the reasons why, today, people are once again asking for more religion in education, or asking for more dogmatic statements of religious belief, is because, faced with the power of the modern Caesar, they are not certain that the ethical preoccupations of unorganized groups are sufficient to counter the overwhelming pretensions of the state in our day. The extent to which totalitarian dictatorship (which has arrived, in our epoch, from both the Right and the Left) destroys all competing institutions, to absorb all authority into its own arrogant self, prompts many people to ask once again whether the overwhelming institution of the state does not require the counter of strong religious institutions if the tension and balance of freedom are to be preserved.

One can find again and again in discussions of religion in education an awareness that we are now faced with a quite new kind of Caesar, a streamlined Caesar using all the modern techniques of mass communication and of scientific organization and of mass manipulation and propaganda. There is a growing sense that, against a state of such immense institutional power, we may need religious organizations with some strong institutional framework of their own, in order to safeguard values which, we believe, go beyond the claims and authority of the state.

By way of parenthesis, it seems to me a great irony that Communism, which claims to be the very last thing in political organization, and to represent an entirely new chapter in mankind's history, appears, at least in its political aspects, to go back to what is the most archaic form of organization known to human society—which is the subordination of all values to the social process and the domination of all existence by the state. If you trace the Soviet system back from Soviet tyranny to Czarist absolutism, to the Tartar war bands, to Byzantine autocracy, to the Persian despots, and back to the archaic kingdoms of Sumer and Akkad, you must realize that the heredity of despotism in Russia is desperately old, desperately incrusted, and will be with us for a long time.

In this confrontation which we now make with the state, people are far more aware of religious values not only because they believe that they want their children to be decent citizens. Behind it lies another preoccupation. They ask whether you can, in a society which recognizes no values outside society, find the *pou sto,* the place to stand in your opposition to the total claims of the state. Can you without organized institutions which are separate from the state confront an institution of such overwhelming power as that of the modern Caesar?

Naturally these preoccupations would be very much stronger in Europe, which has been nearer to Nazism and to Communism than has the United States. Nevertheless, it is obviously a preoccupation of free men everywhere to find within our own society, and within our own institutions, reserves and defenses in depth against modern totalitarianism. That is a movement which is not confined to Europe but is now indeed a world-wide movement, taking different forms and different national complexities, but nevertheless uniform enough to be called, alas, the typical political form of the twentieth century; whereas democracy is now a traditional faith.

RELIGION AND FREEDOM

Perhaps some people may say that in this attempt to relate the question of religious faith with the great issue of freedom in the Western world, one is in some danger of making freedom itself into a sort of god, just as some people fear that there might be some danger of democracy being made into a state religion, ceasing to be a method whereby people of diverse views and attitudes can work together for social purposes, but becoming something enforced, a new species of conformity. Some people have expressed this view in relation to attempts to define Americanism, or, perhaps even more important, attempts to define unAmericanism. Many fear that there may be a reaching out within democratic society for a new form of secular uniformity which would be, lightly disguised, if not a state religion, at least a state orthodoxy.

One of the great debates that is going on among the younger members of the Socialist Party in England is whether Socialism is a view of society so total in its allegiance that it is in fact a secular religion, or is merely a method of ordering certain economic and social institutions in such a way that they work better for the democratic community. This is argument of passionate interest to many younger men, some of whose elders did in fact see Socialism as a sort of secular religion. Could one go farther and say that there was danger of making not only democracy but freedom itself into a sort of orthodoxy?

At this point, however, I would like to make my own confession of faith. I believe that there is one value that you cannot make "orthodox" in the sense of rigidly enforced. It is the value of freedom. Freedom is essentially the reaching out of the responsible human mind towards truth. In fact it is only in the light of freedom that minds can grasp anything worth calling true. I am at one with Lord Acton in believing that the essential value in human society is freedom itself. And I think I believe this on fundamentally religious grounds.

It is, as Job discovered, impossible to question finally the purposes of the

Creator. In the long run His reasons are not our reasons. When questioned by Job why the wicked should flourish like a green bay tree, His answer, roughly, was: "Well, Job, did you think up Leviathan?"—which at first glance may seem an inconclusive answer. Nevertheless, it has in it the root of this truth, that it would be almost inconceivable for any of us to have thought up this universe if we had been starting *a priori*. And it is very difficult, therefore, for us to say what sort of universe a Divine Providence ought to have created. It is a constant tendency on the part of human beings to decide what sort of universe ought to have been made, and now in many cases to liquidate any class of people who doubt whether that is the exact pattern. The attitude is not confined to political orthodoxy; in the past it has been also the shame of religious orthodoxy. But if you take the point of view that, in making this universe, the Creator took the risk of human freedom, then you can see that freedom is the supreme value for mankind, not only from the social point of view, but from the religious point of view as well.

We could probably agree that two of the highest values in human society are, on the one hand, disinterested love, and on the other, creativity. And both these presuppose freedom in a very special sense. I do not believe we would ever, as finite creatures, achieve disinterested love if every time we did something good the cupboard door opened and we had a sweet popped in our mouth. Therefore, the thought that the wicked flourish like the green bay tree seems to me to be a precondition of moral character, because if only the good flourished, then I doubt that we would be able to achieve a distinterested morality. It would be something so easy, so obviously self-interested, that the highest value, which we do conceive to be distinterested love and distinterested morality, would be inconceivable.

Therefore, as a great nineteenth century Liberal, Walter Bagehot (a former editor of my paper, *The Economist,* incidentally), said, "We could not be what we ought to be, if we lived in the sort of universe we should expect. . . . A latent Providence, a confused life, an odd material world, our existence broken short in the midst are not real difficulties, but real helps. . . . They, or something like them, are essential conditions of a moral life in a subordinate being." This very confusion and this very lack of easy moral choice in our world are the preconditions of that grace and stature which we achieve by disinterested love, by a selfless love of the good for its own sake.

And now, let us consider the second value, creativity. What is the precondition of creativity in any sphere, in art, in science, in living itself? Once again it is clear, surely, that it is freedom. In other words, if we had the kind of fixed perfect world so many of us would perhaps expect a beneficent Providence to have provided us with, we might not be in any way significant, creative, or morally responsible individuals. It is not only in material evolution that we observe the struggle of form to emerge from chaos. We experience it in our own life as we try to batter some form of moral character in ourselves out of the inchoate stuff of temperament and existence. This formlessness, this space for growth in our exterior and interior universe, is an essential condition of creativity. In other words, freedom—the possibility of error, of mistake, of evil —is equally the possibility of growth and creation and is the way in which we can achieve a significant human stature.

This precondition of freedom is the risk the Creator took in making this whole very peculiar experiment. It is a significant risk in that, quite clearly, parents and educators are asked to take the same kind of risk in the creation of the educational standards of their children. They do have to choose between love and the rod. And it looks, in our universe, as though the Lord had eschewed the rod and had chosen the way of freedom: enough light for us to grow but not enough light to make growth unnecessary.

Now, if this is the case, then clearly freedom is the supreme religious value, as well as the supreme political value, because you can have no growth in the things of the spirit without this underlying freedom. As with every other form of freedom, we have to experience it socially and historically before we know its full dimensions. In the last four hundred years the Christian communions have learned the two lessons which the Medieval period made clear: One is, that no spiritual vitality can in the long run be forwarded by force; in other words, an Inquisition, of any kind, is an unusable method for the preservation of truth. And the second is, that the churches must not lean upon the state if they are to fulfill their full vocation as the guardians of the transcendental values of society. For if they do that, they will not gain; Caesar will gain. This is the lesson of the last four hundred years that underlines not only the vital importance of the church as a guardian of freedom but also the need for the church to be separate from the state in fulfilling that role. In any relationship of dependence, it is the church that suffers, not Caesar. Caesar will be found drawing all the advantages he can from the position, and in the long run the religion of the state will tend to drive out the religion of the living God.

If you protest, "Well, isn't that risky? Aren't we leaving too much to the free play of truth, too much to the risk of freedom?," then I think I could only fall back on one of the great and abiding beliefs of our society, and say that "great is the truth and will prevail."

PARTICIPANTS

LOUISE ANTZ, Professor of Education, New York University

A. GRAHAM BALDWIN, School Minister, Phillips Academy, Andover, Massachusetts

ISAAC B. BERKSON, Professor of Education, College of the City of New York

JOSEPH L. BLAU, Professor of Philosophy, Columbia University

ROBERT L. CALHOUN, Professor of Theology, Yale University

HARRY J. CARMAN, Dean Emeritus of Columbia College, Columbia University

JOHN L. CHILDS, Professor of Education, Teachers College, Columbia University

ISRAEL S. CHIPKIN, Vice President for Research and Experimentation of the Jewish Education Center, New York

JOHN DILLENBERGER, Professor of Religion, Columbia University

HORACE L. FRIESS, Professor of Philosophy, Columbia University

RALPH GABRIEL, Professor of History, Yale University

ROMA GANS, Professor of Education, Teachers College, Columbia University

THEODORE M. GREENE, Professor of Philosophy, Yale University

FRANK W. HERRIOTT, Director of Summer Courses, Union Theological Seminary

CHARLES W. HUNT, American Association of Colleges of Teacher Education, Oneonta, New York

ERLING HUNT, Professor of History, Teachers College, Columbia University

ROLFE LANIER HUNT, National Council of Churches

BARBARA WARD JACKSON, Assistant Editor, *The Economist* (London)

CHARLES S. JOHNSON, President, Fisk University

F. ERNEST JOHNSON, Professor Emeritus of Education, Teachers College, Columbia University

JOHN M. KRUMM, Chaplain, Columbia University

MILLICENT MCINTOSH, President of Barnard College, Columbia University

URSULA NIEBUHR, Associate Professor of Religion, Barnard College, Columbia University

PHILIP H. PHENIX, Associate Professor of Education, Teachers College, Columbia University

CHARLES H. SEAVER, Editor

SEYMOUR A. SMITH, Professor of Religion in Higher Education, Yale University

ARTHUR E. SUTHERLAND, Professor of Law, Harvard University

VIVIAN T. THAYER, Visiting Professor, University of Virginia

HENRY P. VAN DUSEN, President, Union Theological Seminary

CARLETON W. WASHBURNE, Director of Graduate Studies, Brooklyn College

HERMAN E. WORNOM, General Secretary, The Religious Education Association of the United States and Canada

PART SEVEN

Academic Freedom

INTRODUCTION

The university has a special interest in the preservation of intellectual freedom, for without it it cannot function at all; it has a special responsibility for the preservation of intellectual freedom, for it is the only institution in our society at once independent, disinterested, permanent, and universal, and without prior commitments except to truth. It is entirely natural, then, that as part of the celebration of its Bicentenary Columbia University should have invited scholars and public figures to join in a discussion of one of the most urgent of all contemporary problems—the problem of academic freedom. That such an issue should need to be discussed at all is a measure of the crisis of anti-intellectualism that confronts our generation.

The men and women who engaged in the discussions so briefly summarized in these pages differed in analyses but not in principles. They differed in estimates of the seriousness of the challenge to academic freedom, but not in the fact that a challenge existed; differed in notions of how it should be met, but not in the conclusion that if it were not met and repudiated our society would suffer irreparable harm. Through the haze of discussion it is possible to discern the outlines of agreement, and these can be stated summarily. Academic freedom is in serious danger from pressure groups who wish to direct or control, in one way or another, both teaching and scholarship. These pressures are born of fear of ideas generally and of academic ideas particularly; and they are, not unnaturally, transferred from the ideas to the persons, the books, the institutions, that discover and proclaim them. The attack upon academic freedom is not merely overt; it is also negative and insidious. It consists not only in hostility to ideas and individuals, in the malpractices of censorship or persecution, but equally in a refusal to entertain and encourage new ideas and those who proclaim them. The struggle for the vindication of academic freedom is no narrow or selfish thing, no mere academic self-indulgence, but rather a defense of the validity of ideas themselves. It is something that concerns not only the university, the library, the laboratory, but the whole of society. Bound up with it is not only the welfare of universities and of scholarship but the welfare of freedom and of truth. The academic community, however, has taken its position too much for granted, and has failed to make clear to the public, to governments, to the press and the radio, to even its own guardians—trustees and regents—the relation of academic

502

to all other freedoms. Universities, and with them all institutions concerned with the discovery and application of truth, will be better able to perform their beneficent function when they have enlisted society in the great enterprise.

The discussions here summarized centered on four aspects of the problem of academic freedom: How can we defend Academic Freedom against pressure groups? How can we educate the public on the values of intellectual freedom? How should we deal with the alleged communist danger on the campus and in the public schools? Should there be any limits to freedom of investigation?

No special papers were prepared in advance of the conference for the reason that the forthcoming publications of the American Academic Freedom Project were available to serve that purpose. Selected pertinent chapters of Robert M. MacIver's *Academic Freedom in Our Time* (New York, Columbia University Press, 1955) were reproduced and circulated prior to publication. A series of questions was then propounded to help guide the discussions. The Report of the Recorder details the questions and the nature of the discussions.

Henry Steele Commager
Professor of History
Columbia University

Report of the Recorder

Julian H. Franklin
Instructor in Government, Columbia University

Each session of the conference was opened by a designated leader who addressed himself to a series of questions propounded in advance as a guide to discussion. In the reports that follow the guide questions are supplied, together with brief summaries of the participants' comments.

FIRST SESSION

How Can We Defend Academic Freedom against Pressure Groups?

What can be done in defense against the following forms of pressure?

The pressure exercised through congressional committees and also non-political groups to have faculty members dismissed for refusing to answer questions, without further inquiry or reference to the judgment of their colleagues or their institutions themselves.

The pressure to oust, to discipline, or to silence faculty members on charges of radicalism, unorthodoxy, membership in alleged subversive organizations, and so forth, emanating from local groups, Legion posts, patriotic societies, and fomented by such organs as *The Freeman, The Educational Reviewer,* and various journals.

The pressure of a similar sort, addressed to university, school, or college authorities and initiated by some alumni, an occasional disgruntled student, or a dissatisfied donor.

The pressure put on governing boards or school authorities to ban texts or readings alleged to be subversive; and the similar pressure put on public libraries to purge their shelves.

The pressure, accompanied by threats of the loss of their tax exemption, put on foundations because of their support of certain organizations, groups, or subjects of inquiry or on the ground that they employ or have employed radicals or subversives.

What consideration can we give to the following forms of defense?

The need for more effective intra-institution cooperation when attacks are made on any faculty member or department.

The need for inter-institutional and inter-faculty action when a particular institution is under fire, and the weakness of existing academic organizations to assume a common responsibility.

The need for a better understanding of the issues at stake, even among academic representatives, and the need for a closer relationship for this end between board, administration, and faculty—a *rapport* notably existing in some institutions, but lamentably absent in others.

Dean Erwin Griswold of the Harvard University Law School introduced the topic by asserting that the danger had been exaggerated. The pressure groups, he argued, had little support in the community and in proof of this he cited his experience at Harvard. He had made honest and patient reply to every serious complaint, and he had found in almost every case that the public had either endorsed his position or at least acknowledged his integrity. Applications for admission to the Law School and receipts from alumni had increased, and donations were often accompanied by letters of support. It was his opinion that the controversy over academic freedom had activated community support which would have otherwise remained inert, and that it provided an opportunity for the academic profession to state its case courageously. He suggested, therefore, that the course of academic freedom might even have been strengthened by attacks.

The next speaker thought he could agree with Dean Griswold that the effect of pressure groups on the universities themselves was negligible, but he suspected a more subtle influence. He was the director of an academic project in which public cooperation was essential, and although a yellow journal had repeatedly attacked it he had noticed no withdrawal of support. He wondered, however, whether or not he had become just a bit more cautious in his policies out of a desire to avoid unpleasantness.

The group was then concerned with the strategy of answering attacks. There were some who felt that the time and energy consumed in controversy interfered with academic work. This, said one speaker, had been notoriously true at the University of California, where the protracted struggle over the loyalty oaths had brought research almost to a standstill. He thought, therefore, that most attacks should be ignored. It was also pointed out that a university could not publicly disclaim the opinions of some members of its faculty without endorsing those of all of the others. But this assumption of responsibility, it was held, was inconsistent with academic freedom.

Others argued that, although public relations was a wearisome and time-consuming burden, in the long run it was worth the effort, since public support was indispensable to meet the attacks of pressure groups. It was suggested also that the most effective public relations would be proof that the university stood ready to police itself. The University of Colorado, for example, had conducted its own investigation into charges of subversive influences. The speaker thought that the University had thereby avoided intervention by the legislature, where the influence of pressure groups might be great, and that it had maintained the integrity of academic processes. The speaker added that he had seen little evidence of organized pressures. The initiative came from individuals, he thought, and it is correct to answer their complaints.

Others thought that there might be some middle ground between aloofness and complete accountability. The choice of tactics, it was held, must be related to the nature of the assailant and to the position of the university in the community. From whom, then, should complaints be taken seriously? On what subjects should complaints be held legitimate? At what point is an answer to be given, and to whom and in what form should it be addressed? The speaker thought that careful considerations of such distinctions might produce a more effective policy.

Another group was unwilling to accept the premise that the danger had been overestimated. The pressure groups, one speaker pointed out, were always lurking in the background, and when the soil was congenial their propanganda cropped up in individuals and "respectable" community organizations which were often unconscious of the source. Under these conditions, he had observed, the school and the public became estranged. And the danger then was not so much direct attacks upon the schools, but a paralyzing atmosphere of fear. Administrators, anxious for support, might seek to curry favor with the pressure groups; teachers, uncertain of the future, might avoid controversial topics; librarians might purge their shelves in order to forestall attacks; and publishers might drop objectionable materials or refuse to publish controversial textbooks on the grounds that the market might be poor. It was also pointed out that the elementary and public high schools, as well as the small college and the state university, were especially vulnerable to pressures since they depended directly on community support. The speaker felt, therefore, that one ought not to generalize too freely from the experience of secure institutions like Harvard or Columbia.

There was strong feeling, moreover, that the problem of academic freedom could not be discussed in isolation. The freedoms to read, to speak, to publish were held to be parts of an organic whole from which academic freedom was inseparable. Public attitudes—variously described as irrational, hysterical, and even psychopathic—were shown to be hostile to the mind as such. It was therefore argued that the academic profession could not afford to remain politically aloof. It must try to educate the public to the meaning of freedom as a whole, perhaps through an organized campaign on radio and television. It was felt, moreover, that in any campaign of education the university administrators had a special obligation, for they were the spokesmen of the profession to the public.

SECOND SESSION

How Can We Educate the Public on the Values of Intellectual Freedom?

Can we show the intrinsic value of intellectual freedom as such—the moral and spiritual significance of the attitude that puts its trust in reason and is not afraid to follow where it leads, believing that the only wise way to refute error is through the enlightenment that comes with knowledge?

Will the public recognize the other intrinsic values that are bound up and in an important measure depend on the possession of intellectual freedom—its primary relation to the freedoms guaranteed by the First Amendment and to the free play of public opinion, the prime condition of existence of a democracy?

How will we demonstrate the role of intellectual freedom in the advancement alike of the general welfare and of the entire civilization—the necessity of open-minded inquiry and the free investigation of unorthodox doctrines in the process of making new discoveries and the serious consequences to society where authoritative rules in this field are not subjected to question?

How can the appeals to prejudice and the misrepresentations of the opposing forces be best met?

How can university heads, administrations, and educational authorities most effectively show what academic freedom means, first for their own institutions and then for the public welfare?

What kinds of public appeal have been most influential under present conditions in combatting assaults on intellectual freedom?

How can more people of distinction or public prominence be enlisted actively in the cause?

Should special materials be prepared respectively for such organizations as churches, business clubs, trade unions?

Should efforts be made to enlist the services of well-disposed journalists and other popular writers for the presentation of the case to a larger public?

What are the chief weaknesses in the present defenses of intellectual freedom?

What are the roots of anti-intellectualism in this country?

In his introductory remarks Professor Robert M. MacIver of Columbia University dissented from the almost exclusively utilitarian emphasis in the defense of intellectual freedom. The argument that intellectual freedom advanced the public business by supplying useful knowledge was not inaccurate, he said, but he thought that it left something out. As moral and spiritual education, intellectual freedom is also a value in itself, an end and not only a means. This justification, he argued, was not only more far-reaching but in the long run more persuasive. Utilitarian arguments could cut both ways, depending on the ends one wished to posit, whereas the intrinsic and universal values of intellectual enlightenment could be the basis of a principled defense. He was aware, however, that opinion on these points had not yet crystallized, and he hoped that the session would investigate them, since he did not think that we could effectively educate the public unless we were certain of our grounds.

One of the speakers, returning to a point which he had raised in the previous session, suggested that we must educate the public to the pleasures of intellectual activity. Mass society had exposed the average man to ideas, but it had not yet taught him to appreciate the fun of them. And this, he felt, was the source of anti-intellectualism seen as a cultural phenomenon. The unsophisticated individual felt threatened by novel propositions because he took ideas too solemnly. He suggested, therefore, that we must teach him that ideas are not realities but only imagined possibilities, that they do not change the world, and that their potency ought not to be exaggerated. We must show him, rather, that it is as a self-liberating form of play that ideas are most important. The free exercise of mental faculties, he concluded, is a vital source of psychic satisfaction, and once the public understands this it will welcome intellectual activity.

The following speaker wished to note the ambivalence of public attitudes towards the intellectual. It was his impression that the advancement of knowledge was generally accepted as a good. But he had also observed that the public had little sympathy for the liberally educated man for whom intellectual culture was a way of life. The public, it was also pointed out, was inclined to blame the intellectual for ideas he did not really hold. This speaker was a professional librarian, and he was familiar with attacks upon librarians for harboring "subversive" books as though their contents had thereby been approved. The public seemed not to understand that a library need not endorse its books, nor a university the opinions of its staff, nor a professor all of the ideas he presents. He felt that a great many popular suspicions could be traced to misplaced responsibility.

At this point the chairman suggested an historical dimension. It seemed to him that in the nineteenth century Americans had been relatively open-minded, but now he noticed a growth of anti-intellectualism, and he wondered how the change could be explained. Among those who responded to the query, some thought that universal education and the democratization of culture in general had made possible ideological fanaticism. They were not quite sure as to the basic cause, but they wished to emphasize the fact that the circulation of ideas was no longer confined to a relatively secure élite which could tolerate the luxury of criticism. Others felt, however, that anti-intellectualism had always existed in America, and that the themes alone had changed.

This last point suggested the opinion that some misunderstanding by the public must be expected as inevitable. The speaker felt that not only the public at large, but even university students and teachers, did not fully appreciate the nature of scientific method and the way in which freedom was essential to it. But he believed also that if this gap between the public and the scientist had grown to dangerous proportions the universities themselves must share the blame. The social scientists, he noted, denied that man was rational, and many of them increasingly rejected rational discussion as the best means to influence the public. Their advice to leaders of opinion was, "Don't explain, indoctrinate!," as though values were merely to be inculcated. This trend, he thought, marked a loss of faith in reason which undercut the grounds on which we stood. He did not think that we could defend intellectual freedom if we did not believe in truth and yet he noted that the very term was increasingly unfashionable. He wished to cite, in concluding, an American social scientist who had frankly admitted the antagonism between the behavioristic approach to social life and the traditional ideals of Western civilization. This, the speaker thought, might help to explain our estrangement from the public.

The following speaker, however, could not agree that we were irrevocably estranged from the public. Broad areas of sympathy existed, he asserted, and the only problem was to activate them. He suggested that we must show the community what concretely is at stake in the fight for intellectual freedom, and that we must find the leadership which will be able to communicate our message most effectively.

It was suggested also that the universities themselves had drawn apart from the community and were now paying the price for their aloofness. The speaker recommended that they take the public into confidence, so that school and community together might revivify their common faith. Another speaker, a superintendent of public schools, cited his own program of community relations in support of the previous opinion. His policy was to seek out "opinion leaders" and to exchange ideas with them on programs relating to the schools. He had found that they were always glad to be consulted, and that in almost every case they were willing to cooperate. He thought also that one could work with the American Legion, the Kiwanis, the Rotary Clubs, and other conservative organizations, and particularly with their state and national divisions whose policies will at times be entirely reasonable. The chairman added that labor unions, some churches, and social workers could almost always be relied on for support.

On the university level, it was held, the nonteaching members of the academic governing bodies, who were often community leaders, could be especially effective allies. This was held especially true of top administrative officers, such as deans and college presidents, since their opinions had an aura of authority. The speaker felt, however, that they could render even greater service if their speeches were less uniformly platitudinous. Specific and outspoken statements were better calculated to impress the public.

It was sharply objected, however, that the academic profession would do better to take leadership itself. The speaker, whose experience was mainly with the press, had seen no evidence that the leaders of the community in general—businessmen, editors, and even university trustees—were especially sensitive to intellectual freedom. She had come to this assembly, therefore, hoping to be inspired by its academic members. Among them, she would have thought, the desire for action would be strong. She was disheartened, however, by their seeming willingness to abjure responsibility for leadership. Another speaker, also connected with the press, thought that the need for academic leadership transcended university affairs. He recalled with gratitude Dean Griswold's recent speech on the function of the Fifth Amendment. These remarks, in clear and simple language, had been generally reported in the press and his own paper had quoted them *verbatim*. He thought that they had helped to clarify the thinking of the public on the meaning of a basic privilege. This example, in his opinion, showed how academic leaders might contribute to community opinion. He wished, therefore, to emphasize the need for academic leadership in the defense of freedom as a whole.

The academic community, it was further pointed out, had been far too timid in asserting its prerogatives. If it wished to exercise its freedom, there was nothing in the law to stop it. Pressures, to be sure, existed, and the speaker did not wish to minimize them. The nonconformist teacher might encounter social disapproval; the independent institution might lose financial backing from governmental agencies or private donors. But a truly honest scholar and a truly dedicated university must be willing to accept these sacrifices. He believed, moreover, that if the academic profession had the courage to resist, if it acted with a sense of freedom, it would ultimately enlist the community's support.

At this point the chairman observed that it was not always a relatively simple matter of resistance to some overt attack—the dismissal of a suspect professor, the censorship of a book or a magazine, the requirement of excessive or discriminatory evidences of loyalty. These things the academic community could be counted upon to resist. But what was to be done in the face of negative action? What happens when a board of trustees refuses to appoint a teacher, when a librarian decides it is better policy not to subscribe to some magazines, when organizations all over the country conclude to avoid controversial subjects or controversial speakers, when the government simply withholds funds from certain colleges or certain projects? You cannot make a dramatic issue out of this. No one has a right to be appointed to a post, or to be invited to speak, or to have his books in a library, or to receive fellowships or subsidies. Yet freedom can be destroyed by this erosion as surely as it can be destroyed by open attack. As President Hutchins had observed, it is not necessary to burn books; just see that they are not read for a generation.

Another speaker, however, criticized the academic profession for demanding special privileges. If the academicians assumed the role of experts, offering specialized advice, they might be able to justify their claim. But on this point he thought them irresponsible. He had gone to many campuses to investigate threats to academic processes, and it was his opinion that the profession had often defended its incompetents in the name of academic freedom. This, he thought, might account for its estrangement from the public.

There was doubt, however, whether a claim to *expertise* would be appropriate, since an academic community could neither be unanimous nor neutral. The speaker felt, moreover, that its opinions counted little with the public, especially in the realm of social policy. He would further comment that the academic profession was no more privileged than any other group. It was to be regretted, of course, that incompetents occasionally hung on. But this was not a major problem, nor was there very much which could be done about it.

At this point, the discussion turned again to the causes of anti-intellectualism. Was it belated revenge for the New Deal, with which the intellectuals had been associated, at least in the thinking of conservatives? Was it that the American national character contained a streak of unreflecting activism? Or had the ideological character of recent international conflicts produced fear of ideological involvements? Such questions were raised but not discussed, for the session was almost at a close.

THIRD SESSION

How Should We Deal with the Alleged Communist Danger in Education?

Broad charges of communist infiltration into schools and institutions of higher learning, while they are untenable and wholly misrepresentative, constitute nevertheless the most effective strategy of the anti-intellectualist forces. Their regular device is to brand all deviation from their own economic and nationalistic orthodoxy as "subversive," "pink," half-communist," "anti-anti-communist," and so forth. A large part of our problem is the way in which, taking advantage of the cleavage and strain existing between the West and the Soviet areas, the anti-intellectualists have employed these charges to arouse apprehensions and alarms and thus advance their own objectives.

A major part of the damage to institutional morale is due to the investigations and threats of investigation for which these charges prepare the way. This fact raises a number of questions:

1. What steps should these institutions take when faced with the likelihood or threat of outside investigation concerning "subversives" on the faculty?

2. What should the institutions do to protect faculty members against whom charges are brought, so that these members will be defended against unfair treatment or unjust loss of reputation?

3. What should be the institutional attitude and procedure when a faculty member makes appeal to the Fifth Amendment?

4. Since under the laws of certain states and the regulations of certain

governing boards faculty members are automatically dismissed for the type of nonresponsiveness referred to under (3) above, and since in some instances there is good reason to believe that nonresponsive witnesses are animated by honorable motives, should there be some understanding or scheme of cooperation between institutions that disapprove of such rulings for the purpose of helping to reinstate those educators whom on adequate information they believe to have been unfairly or excessively penalized?

5. It is sometimes alleged that institutions bring on themselves the intrusion of political committees because their faculties are unwilling to "police" themselves. Has this allegation any validity? In any event, is there any ground, need, or advantage making it desirable that an institution should conduct any kind of self-investigation on the "loyalty" issue?

Since the evidence appears conclusive that the alleged communist danger to our schools and our institutions of higher learning is falsely raised and at the very least grossly misleading, would it be possible to formulate such a strong public pronouncement as the leading organizations of educators throughout the country would be willing to back?

It is sometimes maintained that academic defenses against attack and misrepresentation are lacking in strong leadership. Is this view justifiable? And if so, what is the reason and what can be done about it?

Does the situation in our elementary and secondary schools call for a different approach or different strategy from that appropriate to institutions of higher learning?

Dean Ernest O. Melby of the New York University School of Education stated that in his opinion the internal menace of Communism had been exaggerated, and that the real threat was primarily external. Communist teachers, he thought, were but a handful, and their absence from the campus was less vital for effective education than the presence of dedicated democrats who constituted the vast majority of teachers and whose morale had been impaired by irresponsible attacks. Such attacks, he thought, had imposed a quest for orthodoxy in a period when creativity was urgently required. He noted that his own students at New York University, many of them teachers or prospective teachers, seemed to shy away from controversial issues and to avoid political involvement out of concern for their professional careers. The result in the secondary schools, he thought, was the most vacuous education in the social sciences which has been given since two generations. He suspected that this was true of almost every field of education since creativity could not be divided.

How, then, he asked, should we go about eliminating communists from the campus? He thought that once they were identified, no university would hire or retain them. But he added that they must be properly identified; for unless honest dissenters were distinguished and protected, academic morale would be depressed. The solution, he thought, was for the universities to forestall irresponsible investigations from outside by moving to police themselves, preferably through committees of their faculties. This technique had been employed successfully at New York University, he reported.

It was then asked what specific dangers there might be in a communist's teaching or speaking on the campus. One response was that the fear of them was ludicrous and that the so-called communist menace on the campus was the result of diseased imaginations.

Another remarked that it would be strange, indeed, if there were no communists in universities, given the individualism of the academic profession, and that the danger from such people had been irrationally exaggerated. The policy of the speaker, a college president, was to oppose *any* propaganda in the classroom, and she would discipline any teacher who misused his position to promote a viewpoint. But this applied, she thought, to any individual or viewpoint, and she could see no reason to single out the communist.

Another college president, however, felt that even this was too restrictive. An effective teacher, he thought, will always have a viewpoint and he must have freedom to express it. The problem only is what constitutes fair activity on the part of a teacher with a viewpoint. At his own institution he knew of no case in which a teacher had made unfair use of his position to exploit or propagandize students.

It was objected, however, that there was a vital issue of scholarship involved in the claim of communists to teach. Their choice and presentation of opinions, said the speaker, was dictated by their party's discipline. In the 1930s he had been connected with an institution where the communist teachers had formed a conscious plan of infiltration involving concerted propaganda, the control of student clubs, the vilification of colleagues, and the manipulation of curricula. It seemed obvious to him that this type of party commitment was antagonistic to the principles of scholarship. He asked, therefore, whether communists could be considered fit to teach.

The chairman at this point invited a British professor to say something of the practice in England. His colleagues, he replied, did not share the jitters of Americans. It was naturally assumed at English universities that everyone would press a point of view, and English professors felt perfectly secure that they could answer communists' opinions. Nor did they feel that it was particularly important to expose or label subversive teachers. The idea of rigid categories to delimit how "left" a man might be they would find ridiculous and useless. It was his personal opinion that communists were not a danger, at least at British universities, where they were few in number and where they were regarded as somewhat peculiar by their students and colleagues, who did not take them very seriously. Indeed, he even thought their presence might be useful. They were convenient foils for those who disagreed with them. And it was often convenient to refer to them for information on points of party doctrine.

At least two Americans, however, did not think we ought to emulate this attitude. One felt that communists here were not the lovable old fuddy-duddies that they were in England, that our brand was more violent and insidious. Another argued that tolerance was all very well when the communists acted in the open, but he thought that when a communist went underground and hid his identity more vigorous defenses were required.

But to this opinion there were several strong objections. One speaker argued that the communist could never be a menace. If he promotes his doctrine systematically, he will only bore and lose his audience. And if he tries to promote it subtly he will soon discover, as the speaker had, that students were notoriously insensitive to subtle implications. Another asserted that if a teacher forms underground cells, and engages in the slander of his colleagues, he could and should be penalized. An effective administration would enforce its discipline on everyone, and if this were done there would be no need to treat communists distinctively. It was further argued that in the case of avowed communists, the students were mature enough to form their own opinions. We should rely, the speaker said, on the strength of our own traditions and the effectiveness of democratic teachers to answer false opinions.

This discussion of the danger of the communist was not pursued to a conclusion. The group was now concerned with the way in which demands for their elimination should be handled. Various procedures were suggested, most prominent among them the idea of self-policing. There was some concern, however, lest preoccupation with charges of subversion should undermine faculty morale. It seemed to one speaker that the profession was afraid to speak, that there was a growing self-censorship which was a more immediate danger than outside restraints. He thought, indeed, that the timidity of American intellectuals was all too reminiscent of pre-Hitler Germany and he noted that the Germans were now quick to point this out. Another added that concessions and compromises by university officials were a major cause of the sense of insecurity. He cited a case where an outstanding university, acting with what seemed to be the best intentions, had fired members of its staff for having invoked the Fifth Amendment. Was not this the sort of thing, he asked, which promotes the fears we now deplore?

The following speaker pointed out that his institution had successfully fought back against attacks, but that even so morale had been impaired. The attenuated struggle had disrupted academic life and sapped the institution's energies. Many teachers, who had been summoned to Congressional hearings, had been psychologically depressed by their experience. It seemed to make no difference, he added, whether the teacher had been directly accused or not, or whether the sessions had been closed or open. The teacher felt that he had been treated as a suspect, and he came away with a sense of insecurity which often worked unconsciously. In general, he thought, morale had been subtly impaired by the feeling of estrangement from the community. The spontaneity of class discussion, of research pursuits, of the interest in controversial issues, all of these had suffered, he observed, from a continuing feeling of uneasiness. He soberly noted that three years after the event the scars had not yet disappeared.

This reaction, said the following speaker, was even greater in the public schools. The people of Scarsdale, he recalled, had defended their schools against attack, but it had proved in part to be a hollow victory. The Parent-Teachers Association, for example, was more cautious in its choice of speakers; and, rather than provoke a controversy, teachers preferred to play it safe. The fear that attacks would be renewed, he noted, hung over the schools like a Damoclean sword.

One of the members, who had been greatly heartened by the success of Sarah Lawrence College in its defense of academic freedom, wondered if its president could tell the group what tactics he had found to be effective. The most important weapon, he replied, was the support of the trustees and of the students. He said that at Sarah Lawrence there had been a strong tradition of academic freedom, that policies had already been established which had been widely disseminated and discussed, and which almost everyone accepted. When the attacks began, therefore, the trustees and the rest of the community had already been committed to resistance. The campus as a whole had presented a united front, and the common struggle, he observed, had been an educational experience for the college community on the meaning of academic freedom. But, he warned, such support could not be manufactured overnight, and that if one entered a crisis unprepared the college community would split and then resistance would be futile. He would add, finally, that he had made no attempt to bargain with Congressional investigators or to buy off reactionary pressure groups. The main thing, he had discovered, was not to compromise one's principles. If one took a clear-cut stand, and stuck to it, the community would ultimately respond.

Others supported this opinion. Several speakers pointed out that the schools had been thrown into a fight and they must be willing to wage it to the end. They thought it was particularly important for the universities to win the support of their trustees.

There was some feeling, however, that the universities could go too far in asserting their prerogatives, that there was a need for social responsibility which the group had neglected to discuss. The public also, said the speaker, was legitimately concerned with education. He personally thought that communists on the campus were not a menace, but he noted that the public seemed to think so, and he thought the universities must respond to its complaints. If they did not like outside interference, they must show the community that they are able to police themselves.

To this it was objected that the universities were not obliged to take their color from community opinion. Their function was to lead and to criticize opinion, said the speaker, and he thought that the idea of social responsibility was too often a pretext for conformism. Another speaker pointed out that the universities already policed themselves. They had regular procedures for hiring and firing, as well as other devices to enforce their policies. He thought that the real problem was what should be policed. It is only if we assume, he said, that communists must be eliminated that new arrangements will be needed. And still another speaker felt that the whole concept of policing was too negative. The solution, he thought, lay in good administration and morale, in a positive affirmation of democracy rather than the repression of opinions.

FOURTH SESSION

Should There Be Any Limits to Freedom of Investigation?

What kinds of limits are proposed, and by whom?

Are there subjects that must not be investigated? What subjects are so sacrosanct?

Are there impermissible methods of investigating?

If certain subjects or methods are closed to the investigator, what reason have we to expect growth of knowledge in those subjects or methods? Who is so wise as to know what areas can with impunity be closed? Who has either the right or the responsibility to close any area to academic investigation?

Given the scale of governmental underwriting of research, how can the academic investigator be kept free from governmental interference or control?

What responsibilities rest especially on those who exercise freedom of investigation? Have they special obligations not shared with others?

Professor Richard Hofstadter of Columbia University, who introduced the discussion, thought that the first question above could be answered with a simple No. He did not agree that one could admit any limits as to the subject matter of research, since the basis of scientific method was the assumption that nothing was taboo. On the same principle, he did not agree that any person should be barred from research activities on the grounds of his opinions or beliefs. In certain cases, of course, there might be considerations of security, but he would not discuss this problem since it seemed to lie outside our topic. His third point was that acts committed in the course of scientific inquiry were subject to the usual legal and ethical proprieties. These, he pointed out, did not limit the freedom of inquiry and did not constitute a problem.

Professor Hofstadter wished to add, however, that the enormous research activity sponsored by the foundations and the government might be taken as a special problem. They had often been accused of distorting the forms of research and he thought there was a real danger to independent and humanistic scholarship in the tendency toward large budget projects devoted almost exclusively to the physical and behavioristic sciences.

The next speaker pointed out that the physical sciences were peculiarly dependent on non-university support due to the expensiveness of research and that the dangers here were very real. The government, he noted, had been very liberal with grants and did not dictate the subjects for research, but it had extended the doctrine of security unreasonably. He knew of outstanding scientists to whom funds had been denied on the basis of "derogatory information," although these projects were open and unclassified. He also criticized the foundations for having increasingly withdrawn support from the physical sciences, leaving external support entirely to the government and more especially to the military services. He suspected that the foundations' thinking could be summarized as follows: "The physical sciences now have had enough, for they are doing very well. Let's pump some life into the social sciences." He would describe this as a kind of "spigot" notion of research, involving a presumption of omniscience and omnipotence.

Another speaker pointed out that there were new areas of research in the social sciences where also the costs were extremely high, and that these had become inordinately fashionable due to the pull exerted by foundations. The foundations, he noted, preferred pretentious "team" researches, devoted to behavioristic projects, utilizing the most elaborate equipment. They gave little or no support to the individual scholar with humanistic interests using the traditional methods of research. He speculated that the bitterness between positivists and humanists could be traced in part to the discrimination against the latter by foundations.

There was some feeling, however, that these problems were not included in the topic. One speaker remarked that any decision, even the selection of academic personnel, must affect the focus of research; and so also the decisions of foundations. These decisions, he thought, might be criticized on grounds of policy, but not as restrictions on the freedom of inquiry. The foundations and the government, added another speaker, had a right to spend their money as they chose and the academic profession was equally free to turn it down. He could therefore see no issue of academic freedom.

It was objected, however, that the real threat to freedom took the shape of the carrot, not the stick; that the enormous concentration of financial influence amounted to the power of dictatorship. The speaker was much concerned with the disappearance of "free enterprise" in scholarship. He held that a multiplicity of competing viewpoints, and full scope for individual initiative, were essential to scientfic progress. And he feared that the pattern encouraged by foundations—the centralized direction of research and the collective "team" project—might stifle scientific imagination. It was therefore suggested that the only solution to the problem of this influence was the scholar's willingness to resist temptation. This speaker said that he knew of nothing he would care to work on which he thought a foundation would support, and he felt that this would be true of humanists in general. The danger, he thought, was that too many individuals were willing to compromise their standards in order to qualify for grants. The individual scholar, it was argued, must insist on working independently even if this entailed financial loss.

It was also remarked that the spread of outside grants, conjoined to the pressure for "security," might produce a direct threat to academic freedom. In this, the speaker felt, the government was particularly to blame. And he cited a case in which the Department of Health, Education, and Welfare had withdrawn funds for unclassified medical research from thirty institutions, alleging that individuals employed on their projects could not have obtained security clearances if such clearances had been required! Here, said another speaker, was yet another case of the universities' timidity. Any other group would have vigorously protested against such mistreatment. There would have been strikes or boycotts, or some other form of public protest available to groups in a democracy. But he noted that the academic community did not howl when it was hurt and that it therefore ought not to be surprised if public officials treated it contemptuously. The academic community, he thought, must learn the value of concerted protest.

This opinion encouraged various suggestions as to how the academic community might increase its political support. The profession, it was suggested, might join organizations like the American Legion to represent the academic viewpoint; it might sponsor a radio and television series on the importance of intellectual freedom; it might work out permanent forms of liaison with leaders of community opinion; it might commission books on academic issues to be available in public libraries; it might make its lobby in Washington more effective. In any case, it was argued, the academic profession possessed a vast reservoir of political leadership which it had not yet begun to tap.

It was objected, however, that the scholar could not and should not enter politics even to defend his cause. His job was intellectual research and he should not have to become a ward-heeler in order to pursue it. A congenial political climate, said the speaker, was required for scholarly activity in the same manner as were good sanitation or policing—they were things which the scholar took for granted. It was only on the basis of his special commitment, and within the limits it imposed, that the scholar could put his case before the public.

The following speaker, more or less agreeing with this opinion, undertook to qualify it briefly. The American public, he pointed out, had never accepted academic leadership. He had already remarked that the American teacher, unlike his European colleagues, was not supposed to harbor strong opinions but was expected "to present both sides impartially." And he added that the teacher had even been barred from positions of ultimate authority within the university itself. These limitations, he concluded, were regrettable but they would have to be recognized as facts. The teacher might set a good example, give advice, or offer criticism—but it was hopeless to expect him to take leadership.

This discussion could not be pursued because time was running out. In his summary the chairman pointed out that the issues were exceedingly complex and that it would have been folly to expect solutions. The purpose of this conference was not, in any event, to answer questions but rather to ask them, not to solve problems but rather to indicate their nature and character and enlist interest in their agitation and solution. All were agreed upon the importance of preserving academic freedom from the ravages of pressure groups; disagreement on the stress of those pressures, and on the methods of resisting them and eventually dissipating them, was not only natural but healthy.

PARTICIPANTS

JACQUES BARZUN, Professor of History, Columbia University
JAMES P. BAXTER, III, President, Williams College
DAVID K. BERNINGHAUSEN, Director of Library School, University of Minnesota
JULIUS SEELYE BIXLER, President, Colby College
SARAH GIBSON BLANDING, President, Vassar College
ALAN W. BROWN, President, Hobart and William Smith Colleges
WILLIAM S. CARLSON, President, State University of New York
ROBERT K. CARR, Professor of Government, Dartmouth College
CHARLES W. COLE, President, Amherst College
HENRY STEELE COMMAGER, Professor of History, Columbia University
IRVING DILLIARD, Editor, St. Louis Post Dispatch
MARTIN W. ESSEX, Superintendent of Schools, Lakewood, Ohio
JULIAN H. FRANKLIN, Instructor in Government, Columbia University
LON L. FULLER, Carter Professor of General Jurisprudence, Harvard University
BUELL G. GALLAGHER, President, College of the City of New York
WALTER GELLHORN, Professor of Law, Columbia University
ERWIN GRISWOLD, Dean, School of Law, Harvard University
LOUIS M. HACKER, Dean, School of General Studies, Columbia University
FRED M. HECHINGER, Education Editor, New York Herald Tribune
RICHARD HOFSTADTER, Professor of History, Columbia University
PAUL HUTCHINSON, Editor, Christian Century
OTTO F. KRAUSHAAR, President, Goucher College
ERNEST O. MELBY, Dean, School of Education, New York University
MRS. EUGENE MEYER, Trustee of Barnard College
I. I. RABI, Higgins Professor of Physics, Columbia University
LOUIS MEYER RABINOWITZ, Founder of the Academic Freedom Project
IRVING SALOMON, Fund for the Advancement of Education, Ford Foundation
ROBERT L. STEARNS, Boettcher Foundation
HAROLD TAYLOR, President, Sarah Lawrence College
THEODORE WALLER, Editorial Vice President, The New American Library of World Literature
CARL WHITE, Dean, School of Library Service, Columbia University

PART EIGHT
Finding a Reconciliation

INTRODUCTION

It has become fashionable, to our misfortune, to point out how effectively the partisans of a free society can disagree with each other. The political currents of our days tend to exaggerate differences between parties and factions; economic life magnifies divergences of interests between employees and employers, between farmer and laborer, between consumer and producer; social inequalities receive increasing attention. And all this goes on in a nation where there is less class division, less disagreement, less real disunity than any of us would admit prevails elsewhere. It may be true that Americans tolerate in political life an expression of deep tensions. It is equally true that American political life exists because of, and operates within, a fundamental agreement about basic objectives—an agreement so deep and so pervasive that we frequently fail to recognize its existence.

The fourth Bicentennial Conference opened its deliberations by recalling some of the current disagreements, especially those related to social or welfare policy of government. At its close the Conference reminded itself that these disagreements, while evident on the surface of events, are temporary or chimerical at the root. The essential elements of freedom are generally accepted among Americans, as both Mr. MacIver and Mr. Stevenson remind us.

James E. Russell

Government and Social Welfare

Robert M. MacIver
Professor Emeritus of Political Philosophy and Sociology
Columbia University

Our fourth Bicentennial Conference has been concerned with national policies in the areas of education, health, and social security, extending over to a subject that comes close to the key-theme of the whole Bicentennial, the subject of academic freedom. I cannot know how much of its collective wisdom, how many of its various insights, how much of the meeting of minds and sometimes of the crossing of intellectual swords escaped my attention. My concern is with the common problem that lies back of all the converging topics to which the conference has devoted itself, the role of government in the promotion of social welfare.

AN ANCIENT CONTROVERSY

Over this problem controversy has always raged and will always continue to rage. Should government feed the hungry, or protect the debtor, or find work for the unemployed or land for the landless man, or provide medical care for the poor or security against the various hazards of life? Why or why not? How much or how little? Under what conditions? With what effects on personal responsibility, on individual initiative, on essential freedoms, on the spirit of progress? Where do we need more government, and where less?

This has always been a major question, wherever men have been free enough to ask it. Today it rises again, as it rose in the Jerusalem of the days when the Jews wanted to exchange their judges for kings, or in the Athens of the great legislator Solon, or in the Rome of Caius Gracchus, or in the guild cities of medieval times, or in the transition from the feudal to the territorial state, or in the great ferment of seventeenth-century England, or in the rise of modern nationalism, or in the nineteenth-century conflicts over the factory acts, or in the United States since the foundations of the Republic to the present hour. It is the problem of thus far and no further, the problem of the proper limits to governmental powers and to their exercise.

It is an eternal question eternally restated in every time of change, which means in *every* time. Is it then merely or purely controversial, holding no solution, because it is simply a matter of opinion inspired by interest, and opinions must always clash so long as interests do? I shall put to you the thesis that it is not, need not, should not, be so; that while opinion alone will determine the precise limits of governmental action and still more the question of particular ways and means, increasing knowledge offers adequate guidance concerning the major direction of policy. Some of this knowledge is already at hand, and much more can be learned from experience and from the endless experiments conducted by many different governments under many different conditions. It is indeed this conclusion that makes the theme of our present conference so eminently proper as part of a celebration dedicated to the free use of knowledge. And the papers and the discussions the conference has generated add new strength to this conclusion.

A FALSE ANTITHESIS

In the first place, it is clear to every student of the subject that the issue is falsely stated by those who confront us with stark alternatives. We must choose order or freedom, said Thomas Hobbes, you can't mix them; they are like oil and water. We must choose between social security or individual liberty, they still tell us today. Or at least between more social security and less individual liberty. If we want security, we must invoke government with its intrusive compulsive power, and every intrusion of government narrows the realm of freedom.

Either—or? Liberty *or* governmental intervention? Liberty *or* servitude? Liberty without governmental interference, *or* loss of liberty when government in any way enters into our economic affairs, into our health programs, into our philanthropic activities. The intransigence of this *either/or* bedevils the solution of many problems. It is so unrealistic, so wholly unrelated to the evidence.

Law increases or diminishes the realm of liberty according to its kind. Government must lay down the rules of the game or it cannot be played at all. Who would dream of a game without any rules or without an umpire? A game in which every player made and interpreted the rules for himself? Who would dream up such a nightmare game and reach the extraordinary conclusion that it was the only kind to assure freedom and fair play for all?

Too often in the arena of action the banners of *either/or* are held aloft by the opposing sides. Too often it is still freedom *or* social security, more freedom *or* more social services, group welfare *or* individual welfare. The assumptions of the stark alternatives are not analyzed. The lessons to be derived from experience, from the available evidences, are not sought. It was otherwise in the conference now ended. The appeal was not to slogans, but to evidences. The criterion was not the assumption, but the result. Knowledge was invoked as the ground of conclusions. Knowledge came first and judgment followed, though with clear recognition that the knowledge was insufficient and also that, however sufficient it might be or become, judgment is still necessary and never final.

The trouble is that our doctrines and our policies are seldom in accord. We do not read into our doctrines the lessons of experience. Our policies at length reflect the urgency of conditions and the pressure of needs, but our doctrines long remain undisciplined. So the adaptations we make to our needs are grudging and inadequately enlightened. The world of power loves to flaunt the banner of the unyielding absolute, and even when it yields to conditions the outmoded banner still flies. Recent history offers most flagrant illustrations. Look, for example, at how most peace treaties are made.

Sometimes, indeed, one is tempted to conclude that the men of action are less realistic than the men who are reputed to live in the ivory tower—but then one thinks of some academicians who have migrated to the political arena, and the generalization loses some of its glitter.

Let us compromise and call it a temptation of human nature, this setting up of false alternatives, opposing absolutes. In our own day it besets us again in an aggravated form. The world is divided into two, and there is great danger that the absolutism that grips one half of it will generate a counter-absolutism in the other. Half the world is pinned down to a dogma that misnames itself communism; but what of the other half, our half? Against the irrationality of an absolute that suppresses and imprisons human nature, our democracy has a wonderful opportunity to stand for a flexible working liberalism that adjusts itself to the needs of men. The counter-appeal of such a doctrine, clearly delivered, could be immense.

But in what mode do we, the inheritors of democracy and now its prime defenders, combat the doctrinal march of the communist absolute? Some of the powerful among us present us as the exponents of the opposite and equally unrealistic absolute, the absolute of *laissez-faire*. So we lose allies, and we exchange real wounds in a fight over phantom causes,

> Swept with confused alarms of struggle and flight
> Where ignorant armies clash by night.

These preliminary reflections have to do with the broad theme of this conference, the role of government in the advancement of social wellbeing. And I say here with strong emphasis that our national interest and the causes we stand for would be greatly advanced if only we could carry into our public controversies the same spirit of inquiry that has prevailed throughout these sessions—the same concern to see the facts as they are, to examine problems in the light of conditions, and to test programs by resort to the evidence.

The conference has been dealing with highly controversial themes, but dealing with them not with the partisan drive to win a verdict, but in the spirit of open-minded inquiry, seeking a happy balance of diverse elements. There is at present no hope that this sprit, as it applies to the role of government, can come to life in the world behind the Iron Curtain. But can we not cherish the hope that it may prevail in the half that prides itself on its freedom—and not least among ourselves?

VALUES AND MEANS

Let us get closer to the actual topics of the conference. We have proper fears lest the increase of governmental controls should be hurtful to values we uphold, to freedoms we enjoy. The danger will differ according to the area of control. Any governmental control whatever over intellectual freedom is perilous, as was brought out in the conference discussions concerning academic freedom. But some governmental controls over some economic conditions may be salutary or even necessary. Social security measures do not interfere with any major business activities or with the exercise of business initiative in its more important respects; but people express concern over the effect on the attitude of the worker. Governmental subventions to higher education do not interfere in any sense with the conduct of business; but we may be concerned that they will undermine the autonomy of the educational authorities, by the giving or the withholding of funds according as the programs conform or do not conform to governmental ideas. And we always have reason to fear the common disease of organizations that grow very big and powerful, the hardening of the arteries called bureaucracy.

We are all pretty well agreed on the values we want to defend. Who doubts that initiative is a good thing? Who does not believe in the spirit of enterprise? The vast majority of us agree also that education should be available in the widest range to all who are capable of profiting by it, for the enrichment of their own lives and for the service of society. We are mostly agreed that more needs to be done to safeguard and advance the health of the people, to make available, particularly to the less well-to-do, the benefits of advancing medical knowledge. But we are in doubt about the means for achieving these desirable things. We fear, or profess to fear, their effect on other things we value.

The trouble so often is that we lay down as postulates not only our values but also the means to our values. But the means should always be open to inquiry, experiment, and constant testing. As the conditions change, the means must be subject to reconsideration and revision. To assume unchanging means for the attainment of our values in a changing world is the essence of all reactionary movements. Individual initiative and freedom of enterprise are eminently desirable things; but for centuries certain groups and interests have handcuffed these values to an adamant negative. "Want is its own best cure," "Economic depressions are self-correcting," and so forth. Their only prescription has been, "Keep government out." Keep factory acts out, they used to say; keep workmen's compensation out, keep social security out, keep out Federal aid to higher education, keep international organizations out—and keep out or throw out of the colleges and universities the people who favor any such things.

By locking the value, enterprise, to the means, *laissez-faire*, they had deliberately to reject another value, the value of social security. They knew this, but they did not know that they were endangering also the value they sought. They could not in the longer run prevent the coming of factory acts and workmen's compensation and social security measures; but by their opposition to such measures they alienated a large part of the working classes and thus made them more responsive to doctrines that sought to destroy free enterprise altogether.

The way of reason is the way of victory. This is the lesson of our industrial history, and in a time when anti-intellectual forces have become again peculiarly threatening, it is well that this position should be stoutly maintained, especially at the celebration of a great university.

The intelligent way is to take our accepted values and relate them pragmatically to the conditions and to the available means. Free enterprise is a value, but the maintenance of our values has also its necessary costs. Free enterprise is a virtue; very well, let us inquire honestly whether social security diminishes or extends its range. Initiative is a virtue; very well, let us inquire how we can preserve it. Let us ask, to begin with, whether there is less scope for initiative because we have public tax-supported education. Education is also a high value; let us consider how its development can best be made compatible with any needful governmental aid. The presence of incentives to every form of worth-while endeavor is eminently to be desired. Very well, let us examine realistically what forces balk the liberation of incentive and what forces advance it. Do lack of protection against a destitute old age and the fear of it increase initiative or have the opposite effect? Are people beset by anxiety more likely to be enterprising than people buoyed by hope?

In passing, it may be suggested that these are questions of the kind to which our social sciences might well address themselves more seriously and on a greater scale, if they want to vindicate their place in the sun. They are controversial questions, but the controversy is intensified by our prejudice and by our ignorance. They are challenging questions because there is much to be found out, and advancing knowledge can contribute much-needed guidance.

There is much experience to be tapped. The reports of this conference itself are illuminating. We learn better, for example, why our industrial civilization has, in spite of the rise in the standards of living, engendered among large numbers an increasing sense of economic insecurity. We learn how modern conditions enhance feelings of hazard and dependence. We learn how, when men have once attained some degree of political security, they inevitably aspire to economic security. We learn why the detached modern man cannot rely on self-help of patriarchal support for that security, amid the chances and changes of a mobile society. As we learn more of these things we realize the false simplicity of nineteenth-century individualism. When the devil can take the hindmost, we hand over too much of the free enterprise to the devil.

FREEDOM AND SECURITY

May not confidence, rather than rankling fear, be the spur to enterprise? May not insecurity be the comrade of subjection and not of freedom? The great apostles of early nineteenth century *laissez-faire* preached free enterprise. But free enterprise for whom? Not for the men and women and children in the mines and the cotton mills, without education, without opportunity, without any recourse. But free enterprise can never be safe so long as it is the sole prerogative of the few. If free enterprise is to be safe the range of opportunity has to be widened. Only with some opportunity for the many, only with some security for them, can the breath of free enterprise pervade the whole being of society.

This is the lesson of the conference. This is the moral that has sounded through its sessions, the background note of its deliverances.

Too often we assume contradiction where a more realistic investigation would find only the need for balance and adjustment. The first-sight view is often mistaken, especially when it is supported by our prejudices or interests. There are still survivors of the old school that roundly declares governmental aid to those in need of it will sap their initiative and create a spirit of dependence. This is a branch of the larger school that views all social welfare activities of government as interfering with the beneficent laws of nature. They say so with the same blithe assurance that has led the Marxist to discover his own immutable laws. They do not honestly inquire into the evidences for the laws they postulate. They make their own privilege or their status or their sense of power the premise of their laws, without knowing it, without reckoning the consequences, even the consequences to themselves. Take the simple fact stated by Barbara Wootton:

> The more prosperous sections of the community have always protected (and still do protect) themselves against the hazards of industrial life on a scale quite beyond the dreams of the ordinary wage-earner; and many of those who have taken larger risks have done so against a background of security which guaranteed something to fall back on in the event of disaster.

The irony of history waits near by when the otherwise secure contend that the genuinely insecure must not, for their own sake, be aided by government in attaining a minimum of security.

The service the scholar can render to society is to inquire into these things, find and read the evidences, and discover the true relations, as far as it lies in his power, in the complex skein of changing conditions and changing needs. It is a task demanding both courage and discipline, and the scholar, like other men, has to struggle with his own biases and scarcely knows when he is yielding to them. Imperfect sympathies combine to skew our very imperfect knowledge. But all experience, as well as the history of past errors, warns us that we cannot discover the relations of liberty and security, of liberty and government, *in the abstract,* and that our comfortable assumptions of simple laws of cause and effect are invariably wrong. The more we learn of the living texture of society, the more we must pass from the sheer conflict of irreconcilable opposites to the realistic equilibrium of diverse elements— law *and* liberty, social security *and* free enterprise, self-aid *and* community aid *and* state aid, authority *and* responsibility—an equilibrium controlled by experience and realistically responsive to changing conditions. The eternal advantage of democracy over all other forms of government is that it makes possible, through endless trial and not infrequent error, the attainment of this flexible equilibrium; but democracy will bring this happy result only if the lessons of experience are not overridden by narrow dogmas and narrow interests.

By the constant test of experience we must discover the place of voluntary social service and state social service in a changeful economy, the roles that different kinds of organizations are best fitted to perform, the insufficiencies and the abuses to which each kind is subject, the limits that common sense aided by knowledge should assign to each. It is a process demanding patience and discipline, but the strength and health and unity of our democracy demand it.

GOVERNMENT AND EDUCATION

Another aspect of the same lesson was brought out by the discussions in the sections dealing with national policies for education. For reasons that are in our day completely obvious school education has nearly everywhere become a function of the state, though there are a few countries where the church still retains some element of its former dominance. The system of control varies very greatly, particularly as to the respective roles of local and central governments and as to the autonomy of the educational authorities under the general supervision of the state.

The limits of governmental control remains a question that still arouses continuous controversy. But in every well-established democracy the tradition is strong that the political authorities shall not dictate the content and the actual processes of the educational curriculum. In our own country a large autonomy for local educational boards has become a guiding principle, but there have always been tendencies to encroachment on it, and in some parts of the country the principle has been less fully recognized than in others. The picture is a complicated one. Here too there is a proper place and function for each of a series of authorities, from the educators themselves up to the Federal government, if the needful provision of educational opportunity is not to be achieved at the price of the quality, the freedom, and the flexibility of the vast and endless educational enterprise.

There is, for example, much controversy over the question whether the Federal government should take on, or perhaps resume, more responsibility by way of sharing, with the states and localities, the costs of education. Now, it was generally agreed, the wrong way of dealing with this question is to say to the Federal government, "Hands off! That way lies bureaucratic control over our educational freedom."

In the first place, the Federal government has a distinctly better record, where it has supported educational projects and institutions, than have a number of state governments. In the second place, this kind of hard-and-fast demarcation, based not on constitutional limitations but only on broad assumptions about consequences, is rarely tenable and is frequently violated by other policies of its advocates. Some of the strongest supporters of this hands-off doctrine, indeed, have shown themselves enthusiastic supporters of another and a much more perilous intervention by Federal agencies in the field of education, by the way they approve the present activities of certain congressional committees. (Just as some of the most ardent supporters of the cry, "Let government keep its hands off free enterprise," are at the same time advocates of high tariff barriers.)

In the third place, the primary consideration is: how and how far can we make use of a particular agency or instrument in the service of a worth-while objective without endangering the objective itself? Federal control of educational policies, we nearly all agree, is wholly undesirable, while Federal aid without such control might now be very serviceable. Well then, if we really want the service without the control, should we not, can we not, see to it that our legislators pass the kind of measures that will assure the aid without the control? Are we not enough of a democracy to keep vigilant watch against controls to which we are opposed? If we cannot trust government, can we not, must we not, trust ourselves?

ACADEMIC FREEDOM

Now let us turn to another side of the educational picture, the question of academic freedom. There is one kind of political control over education that does not sufficiently win the attention of the people and that has nothing to do with the support or the advancement of education. State legislatures and sometimes municipal governments are making a new kind of encroachment on the proper prerogatives of the educational authorities. It is no longer simply the exercise of power to withhold funds or reduce educational budgets where the policies of these authorities are not pleasing to the politicians. Now governments are legislating more direct controls extending beyond the schools and beyond the public institutions of higher learning, to private colleges and universities.

They do this by passing certain types of loyalty acts that make conditions concerning the qualifications of educators. They do it by conducting investigations of schools and colleges, ostensibly checking on subversive tendencies, but

actually creating an atmosphere of constraint and apprehension. And sometimes they sponsor legislative proposals that would put the stamp of law on
the spirit of conformism. Our major speaker this morning could very well illustrate this last point by reference to the ten bills sponsored by the Illinois
Seditious Activities Investigation Commission, eight of which failed to receive
sufficient support in the Illinois legislature, while another, the major Senate
bill of the Commission, was vetoed by Governor Stevenson.

No more splendid watchword could be proclaimed by any institution of
learning than our own: *Man's right to knowledge and the free use thereof.*

As we explore the subject, however, we find there are also other obstacles
than those set up when interest and prejudice and bias and passion are armed
with power to prevent the free expansion of knowledge. We find, along with
these, two obstacles of another kind. One is the inertia, the disregard, the positive dislike and fear of inquiry and the inquiring mind, the deliberate know-
nothingism that for some unexplained reason has manifested itself again and
again in our country. This anti-intellectualism, this obscurantist suspicion of
the scholar, the egg-head, has, in spite of all our educating, a considerable
appeal to certain groups at the present time—even, we must admit, to some
academic groups. The other obstacle, which indeed may be only a variety of
the first, is the strong conviction of many that they already know the truth,
that it is conveyed to them by their intuitions or their indoctrinations, and that,
especially in matters that concern the ordering of society or even the ordering
of the universe, any attempt of scholars to use their intelligence in the search
for evidences, or to go to the sources from which these people claim to derive
their convictions, is a vexatious activity of mischief-making minds.

These attitudes breed a shallowness of viewpoint, a readiness to accept first-
view solutions of great and challenging issues, a superficial acceptance of noble
traditions without any perception of their power or their depth, so that the
generous impulses that move our people find no worthy expression, and so that
in times like ours we are too susceptible to the fatally simple panaceas of those
who seek to win their way thereby to greater power.

WHAT IS IT TO BE PRACTICAL?

These tendencies are indirectly aided by the remarkable expansion of American technology, since it has engendered a too exclusive devotion of our energies to the immediately utilitarian aspects of knowledge, the knowledge of
mechanism. Other forms of knowledge, the knowledge of the ends of living as
against the knowledge of the means, the knowledge of the enduring cultural
legacy of the ages, are too often regarded as impractical, merely academic. We
do not commonly recognize that this other knowledge, extending through literature and the fine arts to philosophical and religious contemplation, is not
only distinguished by being good in itself, good for its own sake, but prepares us the better to meet the greatest and most important of all practical

questions, the questions that concern our relations to one another, in our own country, and our relations to other peoples. For here we are least adept. We are more skilled in dealing with machines than in dealing with social and political situations. Our failure to enlist the peoples of the East in our struggle against communist aggression is one of the most unhappy revelations of this weakness.

Americans pride themselves on being practical. Let us urge then that Americans become *more* practical, more practical in those areas where it matters most. Let us encourage the method followed in our conference discussion, so that the relations of government to social welfare will not be decided by slogans and preconceived notions and ancient shibboleths; so that we get down instead to the evidence, the needs and the reactions of human beings; so that we seek to understand their situations and their problems and discover by experience what the consequences may be if we pursue this course or pursue that other; so that we find by wise experiment what differences it makes if people are treated this way or that; so that we seek to understand the ways of people, at least as forethoughtfully as we try to understand the ways of the machine. Then our national policies in the fields of education and health and social service will approach a decent balance of the values at stake, preserving freedom without sacrificing welfare. Then the controversies that will still arise will be more constructive, for they will be more concerned with the limits and the quality of service, as were the discussions of this conference. In the moving balance of realistic well-planned experimentation lies the only solution.

I venture to go one step further. It is only by following the same realistic approach in our relations with other peoples that we can recover that place of leadership in the world for which fate has marked us out and which may otherwise slip from our grasp beyond recall.

Hooray for America and Look Out, America!

Adlai E. Stevenson

We celebrate an institution that has had a continuous existence and tradition for 200 years—an existence that goes back to the time when there was no United States, an existence that thus connects itself with the English and the European university tradition. We celebrate the great community of scholarship, of science, of art and letters, that gives continuity to the life of man and transcends national boundaries and contemporary time.

I am a great believer in national humility, modesty, self-examination, and self-criticism, and have preached those virtues vigorously, although, of course, I have not practiced them. But of late I have been disturbed by what seems to me the chorus at home and abroad of irrational criticism, abuse, and mistrust of America, its conduct, its motives, and its people. I don't mean just the voices that have been raised, thank God, in protest against our current deficiencies—the attacks on academic freedom, the pressure for conformity, our failures in the field of foreign affairs, or the present wretched manifestations in Washington of our national neurosis. Nor do I mean the wholesome and continuous debate and examination that should and must go on among us and among our allies; the candid controversy that makes good neighbors and good friends. Rather I am talking about malice, distemper, and the new fashion of being cynical, sarcastic, and skeptical about America, or about fellow Americans in large groups and therefore about America.

There are rising voices that forget that though America occasionally gags on a gnat, it also has some talent for swallowing tigers whole; voices that tell us that our national energy is spent, that our old values have decayed, that it is futile to try to restore them. There are voices that say that at best we are as Rome; that once our bridges, skyscrapers, factories, weapons fall before the iron law of decay, no trace will be left, no great ideas, no great cause, to mark our path in universal history. And there are voices that seem to say we are as Carthage; that our vital principle is commerce. Our ethics, our politics, our

533

imaginative faculties, they say, are all bent and twisted to serve our sovereign —commerce. But let commerce dry up, and America like Carthage will leave behind as reminders only additions to the world of commerce. Other voices are crying havoc, crying in fear that America is unequal to the task. Communism, for them, is the irresistible wave of the future, just as Fascism once was. Raise the walls, they say, lock the doors, pull down the shades, and let us exert all our strength to standing still, lest a bold sally on the field of greatness end us up in an ambush set by the communists to whom history has entrusted the future.

Even novelists and poets seem to have been infected. In the new humorlessness, which passes for realism, the very excitement in a time of change and testing is itself suspect. If a Kipling arose among us to say a grand word about the American abroad in the world, I wonder if he wouldn't be shouted down as a sleep walker. Or if a Melville rose among us to portray the American in all his heroic, sometimes tragic, rebelliousness, he might be dismissed as an incurable Horatio Alger addict or a subversive.

I haven't begun to report all the abusive things I've heard from Americans and about Americans! Now some of this talk may reflect a wholesome American self-criticism—in a slightly fevered form. Some of it may even mark the reaction to the easy optimism of the nineteenth century. I don't know; but I do know that if we doubt ourselves, we will persuade no one; if we doubt our mission in the world, we will do nothing further to advance it; if we are craven before the slanders that fill our ears, we will secede from each other. To view our present and our future with sickly anxiety is to ignore the lessons and achievements of our past.

For the plain truth is that we, here in America, have written the greatest success story in human history. The plain truth is that by the record of performance we here in America have in a few years made socialism obsolete, and shown communism to be a noisome stagnant pool of reaction, a breeding ground for all the diseases of violence, slavery, and spiritual suffocation that man has spent millennia trying to escape.

And it was not merely in 1776, when King's College was a stripling, that America left its footprints on eternity. For in our lifetime, we, the seventh generation of free and independent Americans, have given a tidal force to the forward roll of what was set in motion by the first generation. If we lift our heads for a moment above the storm of criticism, doubt, and "un-American activities" and survey the past 50 years, I think you will say with me—Hooray for America!

The first and most obvious thing we have to cheer about is our unbelievable material progress. The miracle of American mass production is commonplace. And under our capitalist system we have increased our wealth to an extent almost unimaginable in 1900.

Now this increase in our wealth has greatly changed the appearance of our country. But change for the sake of change—as I tried with a notable lack of success to persuade my countrymen two years ago—is not worthy of applause. What matters is not that we have changed but how we have changed.

Our national income is distributed far more equitably today than it was at the turn of the century. In 1900 the average annual earning of an American worker was something like $500, and the income of one leading capitalist that year was $23 million—with no income tax to pay!

Even in 1935–36 there were only about a million American families and unattached individuals with incomes of $5,000 or more, and there were 17 million with incomes of less than $1,000. Fifteen years later, in 1950, these proportions were just about reversed. Even after allowing for inflation the change is still dramatic.

But it is not in terms of money and products that we can see most clearly the change that America has undergone. Rather, it is in the attitude of the people and in the role of their government. For we have succeeded not only in making our society prosperous but in keeping it fluid. And while this was easy enough in the days of the frontier, it seemed all but an idle dream by 1900. The frontier was closed, the homestead land was gone, women and children labored in dingy sweatshops, the robber barons plundered at will, and miners in company towns and immigrants compressed into filthy tenements were fast becoming a miserable proletariat.

How could the roads of opportunity be kept open? How, short of revolution, could we adjust modern capitalism to democratic ends? To many it seemed hopeless. Yet see what has happened: the gap between rich and poor has been greatly narrowed without revolution, without socialism, and without robbing A to give to B—although there may be some dissent to that downtown! Our wealth has been mightily increased and distributed better. The rising tide has lifted all the boats.

How has our transformation been accomplished? By increasing productivity and by putting government to the service of the people. Woodrow Wilson, Theodore Roosevelt, and Robert LaFollette led a revolt of the American conscience which, followed by the reforms under Franklin Roosevelt, have altered the face of America. Wilson said in his first inaugural: "We have studied as perhaps no other nation has the most effective means of production, but we have not . . . studied and perfected the means by which government may be put at the service of humanity." It is to the task of putting government at the service of humanity that we have been dedicated in our time, and in great measure we have succeeded.

The child labor laws, wage-and-hour laws, the antitrust acts, banking legislation, rural electrification, soil conservation, social security and unemployment compensation, the graduated income tax, inheritance taxes—it may be too much to say that all this and more amounts to a bloodless revolution, but it certainly amounts to transformation of our economic and social life.

Now why was all this done? Why did America adopt the concept of man's responsibility for his fellow man? Our decision that the well-being of the least of us is the responsibility of all of us was, of course, not merely an economic or political decision; it was, at bottom, a moral decision. And it was not, as some are now saying, all a sinister conspiracy of the great philanthropic foundations. It rested upon the conviction that it is the duty of the government to keep open to all the people the avenues of opportunity that stretched so broad and far before us in the days of our frontier. It rested upon the conviction that the government must safeguard the people against catastrophe not of their making.

But this great decision has brought us face to face with vexing problems which have engaged your attention this week: the problems of the conflict between freedom and security, between the individual and his social safeguards. There is something gallant about man's fight to become the master rather than the slave of the forces of nature, but there is something rather tragic about his struggle to keep himself free from the impositions of his own social creations.

It would be fatuous indeed to claim that we are anywhere near solving this conflict, just as it would be fatuous to say that because our material well-being increases year by year all must be well with America. Too many of our people still dwell in wretched slums or on worn-out land. Once again our top soil, our national skin, is blowing away out on the plains. Our schools and hospitals are overcrowded; so are our mental institutions and our prisons. Too many of our cities are wasting away in neglect. And how can we boast of our high estate when more than one of every ten of our citizens still do not enjoy fully equal opportunities among us?

Nonetheless our progress has been astonishing—more Americans are living better than ever before. The middle class, whose disappearance Marx so confidently predicted, has expanded as never before in the history of any other nation. And while the communist conspirators fulminate about the cruel capitalists, the lackeys of Wall Street, and the down-trodden masses, we have created a free society that promotes the general welfare of all of the people far more successfully than it has ever been promoted by any other system of social organization.

Briefly, I think America's record is terrific—if I may borrow a word from the younger generation. And it is my view that its performance abroad is even more spectacular.

Since the turn of the century we have successively and emphatically renounced, first, imperialism; then isolation; and finally our historical neutrality. We have transformed our foreign policy as completely as our domestic policy. Twice America has decisively tipped the scales for freedom in a mighty global exertion. Instead of isolation, our policy is total involvement; instead of noncooperation we have been the prime mover in the United Nations; instead of neutrality we have organized the greatest defensive coalition in history. And in Korea we fought and bled almost alone for the U.N. and for collective security.

But this is not all. In the process America has fathered three unprecedented ideas: Lend-lease for Hitler's intended victims in war, the Marshall Plan for

Stalin's intended victims in peace, and Point 4 to help undeveloped areas. And to pay for it all Americans have borne a tax load, I mean a collected tax load, that is without counterpart save in Britain. That is something which few beyond our borders appreciate.

What have we asked in return? Why have we done all this? Some will say self-interest; and there is truth in that, because we oppose communism and it follows the geography of human misery. Some will say magnanimity; and there is truth in that, for it would have been easy to go home as we did after the first war, or go it alone as some of our leaders have proposed. Call it what you will; the point is that to help others help themselves, to help to make independence and democracy work, to share the burdens of the less fortunate, to raise the tide a little all around the world, lifting all the boats with it, just as we have done here at home, was bold and imaginative—wise and responsible; it was good for them and good for us. As Edmund Burke said: "Magnanimity is not seldom the truest wisdom."

Now I have touched lightly, I know, on a vast subject; and, while I emphatically approve and loudly cheer America's purposes abroad, past and present, I do not mean to imply for a moment that I approve any more than you do all of our foreign policies, past or present—especially present! My purpose has been just to suggest the main outlines of a success story in which we can all take pride. As we look back to 1900 and look around us today, the infinite evidence of our creative impulses and vast achievements ought to be heralded, not mocked. We have heard the "least of these." We have enlarged our vision, opened our heart, and we have disciplined our strength. We have turned it into a servant of justice—justice not alone for ourselves, but justice for the worldwide commonwealth of free men and free institutions.

Here, indeed, is a case where mankind has a right to knowledge and to the use thereof—the knowledge of what America has done, how America has spread out the decision-making process within the parts of the private economic community; between the economic community and the political order; between the various arms of the political order—central, state, and local; and between our nation and the community of nations. It is the knowledge of how we have committed 160 million people to vast social projects, not by coercion, but by persuasion and consent, and by a balancing of the rights of the few with the needs of the many.

I say it is a grand and glorious story. On the basis of the record we have out-performed any rival proponents of communism or of fascism; and America has nobly accepted her responsibility and proudly met her time for greatness in a troubled age.

Why then all this abuse and criticism? Why then have we of late grown afraid of ourselves? Why have we of late acted as though the whole of this nation is a security risk? Why have we given in to the bleatings of those who insist that it is dangerous for a man to have an idea in his head? Why do we talk of saving ourselves by committing suicide—in the land of Jefferson?

So having said: "Three cheers for America—you've done a great job of work," we have to add: "But look out, America, your work has just begun; though you've nobly grasped the present you could meanly lose the future."

What's the matter with us anyhow? The usual diagnosis is ignorance and fear. Ignorance leads many to confuse ends with means, to act as though material progress were an end in itself rather than a means to great and noble ends. This, I suggest, is the peril in our hard-headed, pragmatic attitude that has helped us achieve our social and economic transformation, for if we ever succumb to materialism the meaning will have gone out of America. And ignorance begets fear—the most subversive force of all. If America ever loses confidence in herself, she will retain the confidence of no one, and she will even lose her chance to be free, because the fearful are never free.

But I wonder if all these alarming concerns are not America's surface symptoms of something deeper; of a moral and human crisis in the Western world which might even be compared to the fifth- and sixth-century crisis when the Roman Empire was transformed into feudalism and early Christianity into the structure of the Catholic Church, or the crisis a thousand years later when the feudal world exploded and the individual emerged with a new relationship to God, nature, and society.

And now in our time, in spite of our devotion to the ideas of religious and secular humanism, I wonder if we are in danger of falling into a spirit of materialism in which the aim of life is a never ending increase of material comfort, and the result a moral and religious vacuum. Is this leading, as lack of faith always must, to a deep sense of insecurity and a deterioration of reason? And I wonder, too, if today mass manipulation is not a greater danger than economic exploitation; if we are not in greater danger of becoming robots than slaves.

Since man cannot live by bread alone, is not the underlying crisis whether he is going to be inspired and motivated again by the ideas of the humanistic tradition of the Western culture, or instead he falls for the new pagan religions, the worship of the state and a leader, as millions of believers in the Fascist or Soviet systems have already done? That we are not invulnerable, that there is a moral and human vacuum within us, is, I think, demonstrated by many symptoms, of which McCarthyism, which has succeeded in frightening so many, is only one.

But it is even more certain that there are millions who see or at least dimly sense the danger, and who want to make life in its truly human meaning the main business of living; who want to express the humanistic tradition of reason and human solidarity—who want to understand the truth and not be drawn into the mass manipulative influence of sentimentality and rationalization.

I venture to say that there is in the world a deep, intense longing for a vision of a better life not in a material, but in a spiritual sense; for love, for human solidarity. There is a hunger to hear a word of truth, a longing for an ideal, and a readiness for sacrifice. Churchill's famous speech at the beginning of the war is an illustration; the totalitarians' appeal to emotional forces more than to material interest is another. But the conventional appeal is so often to the better life in material terms. I wonder if people are not eager to hear about the better life in human terms. And I think that deep down the ideas of independence, of individuality, of free initiative, represent the strongest appeals to Americans who want to think for themselves, who don't want to be the creatures of mass suggestion, who don't want to be robots.

The question is, I suppose, whether the human and rational emotions can be aroused instead of the animal and irrational to which the totalitarians appeal. But fill the moral, rational vacuum we must; reconvert a population soaked in the spirit of materialism to the spirit of humanism we must, or bit by bit we too will take on the visage of our enemy, the neo-heathens.

I have said to you that in my judgment America has accomplished miracles at home and abroad, but that despite all this wisdom, exertion, and goodness the horror of our time in history is that things are worse than ever before. There is no peace; we are beseiged, and we are rattled. Perhaps we are even passing through one of the great crises of history when man must make another mighty choice.

Beset by all these doubts and difficulties in which direction do we look?

We look to ourselves—and we are not ashamed. We are proud of what freedom has wrought—the freedom to experiment, to inquire, to change, and to invent. And we shall have to look in exactly the same directions to solve our problems now—to individual Americans, to their institutions, to their churches, to their governments, to their multifarious associations—to all the free participants in the free life of a free people.

And we look, finally, to the free university whose function is the search for truth and its communication to succeeding generations. Only as that function is performed steadfastly, conscientiously, and without interference does a university keep faith with the great humanist tradition of which it is a part.

We must see to it that no one, for whatever reason or in the service of whatever interest, diverts the university from its basic objective. For the university is the archive of the Western mind, it is the keeper of the Western culture; and the foundation of Western culture is freedom. Men may be born free: they cannot be born wise; and it is the duty of the university to make free men wise. The university is the guardian of our heritage, the teacher of our teachers, the dwelling place of the free mind.

More than 100 years ago William Ellery Channing defined the free mind this way: "I call that mind free which jealously guards its intellectual rights and powers, which calls no man master, which does not content itself with a passive or hereditary faith, which opens itself to light whencesoever it may come, and which receives new truth as an angel from heaven." I wonder, my friends, how many of us fulfill Channing's definition. Could that be part of our trouble today?

Index

Addams, Jane, quoted, 219
Adler v. Bd. of Ed., 444
Advisory Council on Social Security, quoted, 351
Aged, xxxvi, 120–21, 123, 134–35, 136
  dependency, 134, 137–38, 230, 389–94
  employment, 123, 394
  expectancy, 120, 134, 252, 390
  increasing number, 134, 342, 390
  pensions, xxxvi, 137–38, 143, 266–67, 341–45
  public assistance, 138, 143, 174, 266
  security: *see* Insurance, social; Old Age and Survivors Insurance
Allen, Frederick L., cited, 173; quoted, 216, 222
Allowances, family, 257, 269–70, 281–82, 288, 297, 366, 389–93, 491
  under OASI, 312, 316
  under other U.S. soc. ins., 315, 316
Allport, Gordon W., xxi, 194–213, 224; cited, 212n; quoted, 231–32, 233, 234
Altmeyer, Arthur, 289–90, 334, 335, 338, 377; cited, 179
American Association of Medical Social Workers, cited, 147
American Association of Psychiatric Social Workers, cited, 148
American Association of School Administrators, 50
American Association of Schools of Social Work, cited, 224; quoted, 207n
American Association of Social Workers, 147n
American Council on Education, cited 30, 434, 436; quoted, 11, 24, 87
American Medical Association, cited, 124
Anderson, O. W., quoted, 186
Anglican Catholics, quoted, 415, 416, 429
Antioch College, 80
Antz, Louise, 467, 486
Aquinas, Thomas, cited, 470
Aristotle, 51
Assistance, public, xxxvi, 143–44, 145–47, 174, 175, 177, 179, 182–84, 245, 256–

58, 264, 266, 287–88, 298, 353–55, 374, 384
Association of American Universities, cited, 81
Australia, 163, 269, 274, 281, 365–66

Bagehot, Walter, quoted, 497
Baldwin, A. Graham, 466, 467, 470, 478
Ball, Robert, 378, 405, 407
Bargaining, collective: *see* Unions, labor
Barnard, Henry, 6
Barrabee, Edna L., cited, 213n
Beck, Bertram, quoted, 145
Becker, Harry, 322–26, 338
Becker, Joseph M., 336; cited, 189n, 302
Belgium, 264, 268, 274, 280, 281
Bell, Daniel, cited, 401n
Berghorn v. Reorganized Sch. Dist. (Mo.), 448, 449n, 450
Berkson, Isaac B., 457, 458, 461, 470, 471, 475, 476, 484
Bethe, Hans A., quoted, 431
Beveridge, William, 260, 261, 271, 384, 387, 393, 396
Beveridge Report, 260, 261, 271, 387
Bible, cited, 421; quoted, 397, 493
  use in public schools, 437, 447, 448, 450, 451, 453, 478, 482
  See also Religion
Bisno, H., cited, 198
Black, Hugo L., cited, 448n; quoted, 443–44, 452
Blanchard, Ralph H., 288, 291, 404
Blau, Joseph L., 456, 458, 460, 469, 470, 477
Blenkner, Margaret, cited, 212n
Booth, Charles, cited, 218
Borg, I. A., cited, 212n
Borrowman, Merle L. (Recorder), 99–105
Brissenden, Paul F., 334, 378
Bronner, Augusta F., 212n
Brookings Institution, cited, 178, 372
Brown, J. Douglas, 377, 405
Bruno, Frank J., quoted, 232–33
Bryson, Lyman, xvi, 76

541